D1525296

NUCLEAR WEAPONS AND THE THREAT OF NUCLEAR WAR

NUCLEAR WEAPONS AND THE THREAT OF NUCLEAR WAR

EDITED BY

JOHN B. HARRIS
Georgia State University

ERIC MARKUSEN
Old Dominion University

Harcourt Brace Jovanovich, Publishers

San Diego   New York   Chicago   Atlanta   Washington, D.C.
London   Sydney   Toronto

TO RANDI, MARIA, AND GERI

ISBN: 0-15-566740-8

Library of Congress Catalog Card Number: 85-80871

Printed in the United States of America

PREFACE

This book is designed for use in the growing number of courses that focus specifically on nuclear weapons and nuclear war. It is the product of our own experiences in teaching more than a dozen courses on nuclear weapons issues at the University of Minnesota between 1980 and 1985, as well as our review of relevant course syllabi from several dozen other institutions.

Four basic objectives have guided the organization of the book and the selection of articles. We have endeavored to

- Provide students with a basic understanding of key facts and issues concerning nuclear weapons and nuclear war.
- Provide students with information needed to follow current issues and debates involving nuclear weapons and to evaluate policies espoused by political leaders.
- Examine these issues in a balanced, objective manner and expose students to a range of perspectives.
- Provide resources for further study.

Although there has been a proliferation of books on nuclear weapons issues in recent years, very few have been specifically designed for classroom teaching. Many of the recent books focus on single topics or issues, such as the effects of nuclear war or the principles of arms control. Others reflect a particular political perspective, whether liberal or conservative, "dovish" or "hawkish." Some are forthright polemics, arguing for or against a given weapon or policy. Such books certainly have their places in a democratic society, but they have limited value as core texts in the types of courses that are being developed.

This book is deliberately designed for classroom use. It is intended to serve as the core text for classes in which students from a broad range of academic disciplines, and with little or no previous exposure to these issues, examine a variety of topics involving nuclear weapons. It should also be useful in courses on U.S. national security policy, arms control, foreign policy, international relations, and other related areas, when instructors wish to incorporate facets of the nuclear weapons debate.

Chapter 1 recalls the atomic bombings of Hiroshima and Nagasaki and relates them to our current predicament. Chapters 2 and 3 present basic information about the physics, effects, and present characteristics of nuclear weapons systems, and the likely consequences of nuclear war. Then follow six chapters that address central policy issues: U.S. and Soviet nuclear weapons policies, the nuclear dilemma in Europe, the strategic balance, "paths" to nuclear war, and U.S.–Soviet arms control efforts. Chapters 10 and 11 address arguments about the causes and costs of the U.S.–Soviet nuclear arms competition, and explore, from several different perspectives, a topic that has not received extensive treatment in most books on nuclear war issues—the psychological and social dimensions of the nuclear threat. Chapter 12 concludes the book with a discussion of current proposals and future prospects for curtailing the risk of nuclear war. Due to limitations on space, certain topics, like nuclear weapons proliferation and the history of U.S.–Soviet arms control, receive less coverage than we would have preferred. We have tried to recommend useful resources on such topics in the bibliography that follows each chapter.

Our introductions to each chapter discuss the significance of the issues to be examined and highlight key points from each of the selections. Within each chapter, we have tried to provide a range of opinion on critical issues. Where appropriate and feasible, we have selected articles which capture a diversity of competing perspectives. These will enable students to evaluate the premises and logic in divergent arguments, and decide for themselves which is the most persuasive. We have thus included pieces by such diverse and influential writers as Frank Barnaby, Robert Jay Lifton, Carl Sagan, Desmond Ball, Wolfgang K. H. Panofsky, Colin S. Gray, Richard Pipes, Marshall D. Shulman, McGeorge Bundy, Robert S. McNamara, Edward N. Luttwak, Jonathan Schell, and Caspar W. Weinberger, to name only a few. (All authors are briefly identified in headnotes at the beginning of each article.) Where it did not prove possible to include contrasting interpretations of an important issue, we refer, in the chapter introductions and in the "For Further Reading" sections, to perspectives that contrast with those presented in this book.

We realize that selecting a text is only one of the challenges involved in developing a new course on a complex, controversial, and relatively uncharted topic like nuclear war. Fortunately, there are valuable resources available to provide advice and ideas on audio-visual materials, suggested course outlines, interdisciplinary teaching teams, gaining the approval of administrators, and so on. Perhaps the single most useful place to begin is the December 1984 issue of the *Bulletin of the Atomic Scientists,* which may be found in most college and university libraries. This issue features a 32-page supplement, "Nuclear War: A Teaching Guide," with short articles by administrators and faculty from many disciplines who have taught nuclear weapons issues, and an extensive resource guide. Copies of the Special Supplement can be obtained for 50 cents each from: *Bulletin of the Atomic Scientists,* 5801 South Kenwood, Chicago, IL 60637; phone: (312) 363-5225. Also, inexpensive synopses of dozens of courses on nuclear war may be obtained from United Campuses to Prevent Nuclear War, 1346 Connecticut Avenue N.W., Washington, D.C. 20036; phone: (202) 223-6206.

Until quite recently, academic curricula have tended to ignore the problems posed by nuclear weapons. (Students, ironically, have been carefully trained for professional careers but have not been provided with opportunities or incentives to learn about a threat that could well render those careers quite irrelevant.) However, as we have written elsewhere, colleges and universities—indeed, *all* educational institutions and *all* educators—have the potential to make crucial contributions to efforts to reduce the threat of nuclear war.*

Fortunately, the prevailing academic neglect of the nuclear threat has, in the past few years, begun to change. On campuses across the country, faculty (and often students) are initiating new courses on nuclear weapons issues, and this encouraging trend shows no signs of abating.

Acknowledgments

Numerous individuals and organizations assisted us at various points in the conception and production of this book. From 1981 through 1983, we served as co-chairpersons of the Nuclear War Education Project, sponsored by the Federation of American Scientists in Washington, D.C. In that capacity, we were fortunate to have the opportunity of working with Jeremy J. Stone and Barry M. Casper, both of whom helped us clarify important issues and conceptually organize the text. Financial assistance in the form of a World Order Studies Teaching Fellowship from the World Policy Institute in New York City helped support us during the prolonged search for appropriate articles and resources. At the University of Minnesota, the Department of Sociology, the Department of Political Science, and the Institute of International Studies provided indispensible support, ranging from sponsorship of our courses to secretarial and administrative assistance. Our graduate advisors at the University of Minnesota, Professors Robert Fulton, P. Terrence Hopman, and Brian Job, provided abundant encouragement and useful advice.

This project would never have come to fruition had it not been for Drake Bush, acquisitions editor at Harcourt Brace Jovanovich, who saw the value of our proposal and helped us revise and trim our original manuscript. Manuscript editor Bill Teague and production editor Tracy White made numerous suggestions which have improved the finished product. Eleanor Garner, per-

*E. Markusen and J. Harris, "The Role of Education in Preventing Nuclear War," *Harvard Educational Review* 54:3 (August 1984), and "Social Sciences," in "Nuclear War: A Teaching Guide," *Bulletin of the Atomic Scientists* (December 1984), pp. 11S–13S.

missions editor, helped smooth and expedite the formidable task of soliciting and confirming permission requests. We are grateful to Diane Pella, designer, and Kim Turner, production manager, for their contribution to the physical appearance of our book.

While the above-mentioned individuals provided important help to us, we alone bear responsibility for any weaknesses of the final version of this book.

Finally, we are indebted to those closest to us—Randi and Maria Markusen and Geri Harris—whose love and support constantly reminded us of both the joys of living and the urgent need to confront the risk of nuclear holocaust.

John B. Harris
Eric Markusen

CONTENTS

1

Is Hiroshima Our Text?

On August 6, 1945, the United States dropped the first atomic bomb on the Japanese city of Hiroshima, and three days later a second atomic bomb was dropped on Nagasaki. As had been hoped by U.S. officials, the unprecedented destruction wrought by the new weapons did contribute to the willingness of the Japanese leaders to surrender, and within a few days of the bombings the most destructive war in history was ended.

But the ending of World War II inaugurated the beginning of a new age—the nuclear age—in which, for more than forty years, the shadow of the mushroom cloud has grown to the point where it now covers the entire planet with its ghastly warning of possible nuclear holocaust. More than half of all the people alive on this planet today have been born since the first atomic bombs were dropped. They have entered an era unlike any that has ever existed, an era in which human inventions and human decisions have the potential to extinguish the human species.

In this chapter we briefly examine the circumstances that led to the development of the first atomic bombs and the consequences of their military use against Hiroshima and Nagasaki. This examination will serve as a prelude to the analysis of contemporary issues involving nuclear weapons and nuclear war in subsequent chapters.

In his book on the U.S. decisions to build and then drop the atomic bombs, Robert Batchelder notes the tragic irony that while Adolf Hitler rose to dictatorial power in Germany, revolutionary breakthroughs in nuclear physics were being made. He states that

> The years from 1932 to 1939 witnessed the scaling of one of the highest pinnacles of human intellectual achievement in the discovery of the key for releasing the unlimited energy hitherto locked within the nucleus of the atom. The same years witnessed the swift rise of Hitler to military dominance, the fall of Austria and Czechoslovakia, and the rising tension that brought Europe to the brink of war.[1]

Unfortunately, the nation that was to drag the world into a war that consumed as many as 60 million human lives was also the home of some

---

[1] Robert C. Batchelder, *The Irreversible Decision, 1939–1950* (Boston: Houghton Mifflin Co., 1961), p. 11.

of the world's most important nuclear physicists. These scientists were engaged in pioneering research on atomic fission—research that had the potential of being applied to the construction of a new "atomic" weapon of unprecedented destructive power. Had such a weapon become available to Hitler, there is little doubt that he would have used it ruthlessly against his enemies.

The United States decided to undertake its own atomic bomb research (which became known as the Manhattan Project) after being warned by eminent scientists, including recent refugees from Germany like Albert Einstein, that the Germans were making alarming progress in their research. As it turned out, the German scientists were never close to converting their theoretical knowledge into an actual weapon—a fact that U.S. policymakers were aware of well before the end of the war in Europe. By that time, however, the massive U.S. investments of manpower and other resources in the bomb project were showing results, and an organizational and psychological momentum pushed the project through to an actual test of an atomic weapon.[2]

At the same time, the war against Japan continued to drag on, with the American casualties mounting steadily as fanatical Japanese soldiers refused to surrender against even hopeless odds. Moreover, despite the fact that the United States Air Force held control of the air over Japan and was engaged in a vast incendiary bombing campaign that engulfed city after city in huge firestorms, the Japanese government appeared as firmly committed as ever to continuing the war.

Thus, the original rationale for the U.S. atomic bomb—preventing Nazi Germany from having a monopoly on this awesome new weapon—was replaced by the new one of bringing the war against Japan to a rapid conclusion. Some of the very scientists who had advocated the U.S. effort to develop the bomb before Germany, and who had contributed to the American success in doing so, raised moral and political questions about this new rationale. They argued that the use of such a weapon of mass destruction against civilians was beneath the moral dignity of the United States and warned that the price to be paid for any short-term benefits of such an action would be the initiation of a dangerous atomic arms race with the Soviet Union after the war. Some of them suggested that an atomic bomb be detonated over an uninhabited island, where Japanese leaders could witness it, as a demonstration of its unprecedented destructive power. However, their advice was rejected and the decision was made to use the bomb in a surprise attack against Japanese cities.

The U.S. decision to drop the atomic bombs on Japanese cities has generated considerable controversy. One of the much-debated issues involves the question of why the bombs were used the way they were. Policymakers, including President Harry S Truman, later explained that the attacks were necessary in order to end the war as quickly as possible and avoid the millions of American (and Japanese) casualties that would have been incurred if a massive invasion of the Japanese home islands

---

[2] Alice Kimball Smith, "Manhattan Project: The Atomic Bomb," in *The Nuclear Almanac: Confronting the Atom in War and Peace,* Jack Dennis et al., eds. (Reading, Mass.: Addison-Wesley Publishing Co., 1984), pp. 21–42.

had been attempted instead. Some historians have pointed out, however, that an additional motive may have been involved—namely, the desire to use America's sole possession of this revolutionary new weapon to induce the Soviet Union to adopt a more conciliatory and cooperative attitude toward the Allies in the negotiations to determine the postwar future of Europe. For example, Stanford University historian Barton Bernstein has identified three schools of historical thought that have reached quite different conclusions on this issue: the "orthodox" (which accepts the official position that the bombs were used purely and simply for the purpose of hastening the end of the war); the "realist" (which regards the use of the bomb as unnecessary, immoral, and dangerously short-sighted); and the "revisionist" (which argues that "dealing with the Russians" was an important consideration in the decision to drop the bombs).[3]

Another issue concerns how the decision was made. The entire atomic bomb project was shrouded in the deepest wartime secrecy, with the key decisions being made by a relatively few men. Indeed, so secret was the Manhattan Project that even Truman, while serving as the vice-president to the ailing chief executive, was kept ignorant of it and had to be briefed by Secretary of War Henry Stimson shortly after Roosevelt's death. (A similar concentration of crucial decision-making power and governmental secrecy characterizes U.S. and Soviet nuclear weapons policymaking today. And, as we suggest in Chapter 9, this condition inhibits public scrutiny of current policies.)

Although more than four decades have elapsed since the first use of atomic bombs against human beings, Hiroshima and Nagasaki continue to have profound relevance for our efforts to understand current issues involving nuclear weapons and the threat of nuclear war. The articles selected for this chapter convey an aspect of the atomic bombings that is indispensable to any serious consideration of nuclear weapons issues: In many respects, the atomic bombings of Hiroshima and Nagasaki give us a unique, if limited, glimpse into the realities of nuclear war.[4]

Brief but powerful eyewitness accounts of the atomic bombings are provided in the articles by Kataoka Osamu, a survivor of Hiroshima, and Michito Ichimaru, a survivor of Nagasaki. Both convey the instant and pervasive nature of the destruction, as well as the terrible burns that afflicted so many of the victims. Ichimaru also recalls the delayed effects of radiation exposure that caused lingering, agonizing deaths days and weeks after the attacks.

Additional details of both the prompt and delayed effects of the atomic bombs are provided by Frank Barnaby in "The Continuing Body

---

[3] Barton J. Bernstein, "Introduction," in *The Atomic Bomb: The Critical Issues,* Barton J. Bernstein, ed. (Boston: Little, Brown, and Co., 1976), pp. *vii–xix.*

[4] According to Japanese authorities, atomic bomb damage is characterized by at least three special features: the sheer scale of the destructiveness; the instantaneous and indiscriminate nature of the destruction; and the prolonged after-effects of burns and radiation exposure. *See* The Committee for the Compilation of Materials on Damage Caused by the Atomic Bombs in Hiroshima and Nagasaki, "Special Features of A-Bomb Damage," in *Hiroshima and Nagasaki: The Physical, Medical, and Social Effects of the Atomic Bombings* (New York: Basic Books/Harper Colophon Books, 1981), pp. 335–83.

Count at Hiroshima and Nagasaki." Contending that the official estimates of the death tolls are far too low, Barnaby concludes from his own review of the available data that the total number killed "probably greatly exceeds a quarter of a million, a death rate of over 40 percent." His discussion of the efforts by the United States to keep information about the effects of the bombings secret is also noteworthy. Not only did the U.S. authorities confiscate the medical data that the Japanese physicians had compiled, but also all films or photographs of the aftermath of the bombing. Much of this footage was locked away from public access for more than 20 years. Presumably, such governmental secrecy was justified as being in the interests of United States' national security. However, while it is debatable whether such secrecy about the effects of atomic weapons had a substantial delaying effect on the Soviet attempts to build its own bomb, there can be little doubt that it did prevent the American public from gaining a realistic appreciation of just how devastating the new weapons were.

In the final article, Robert Jay Lifton asks the question, "Is Hiroshima Our Text?" To answer it, he reviews the results of his pioneering study of the psychological and social effects of the atomic bombings. In this study, conducted in 1962, Lifton interviewed more than sixty survivors. After discussing several features of the Hiroshima and Nagasaki experience, he concludes that Hiroshima does hold out important truths for the nuclear age, among which is that the lethal influence of the bomb never ends, so delayed are the effects of radiation exposure. Moreover, he also stresses that the atomic bombings provide a unique sense of "nuclear actuality," a physical basis for extending our imaginations to comprehend what would otherwise be even less comprehensible.

However, Lifton also emphasizes that there are important truths in the *contrasts* between Hiroshima and the present situation. For example, after the atomic bombings in Japan, the outside world could respond to the needs of the survivors with infusions of medical aid, food, and other necessities. After a nuclear war, in which thousands of weapons are likely to destroy many hundreds of cities, there is likely to be no "outside world" to come to the aid of the survivors.

"FRIENDS, PLEASE FORGIVE US"
Kataoka Osamu

Kataoka Osamu is a survivor of the August 6, 1945 atomic bomb attack on Hiroshima.

I looked out of the window at the branch of a willow tree. Just at the moment I turned my eyes back into the old and dark classroom, there was a flash. It was indescribable. It was as if a monstrous piece of celluloid had flared

Source: Kataoka Osamu, " 'Friends, please forgive us,' " *Bulletin of the Atomic Scientists* 33:1 (December 1977), p. 44. Reprinted by permission of the *Bulletin of the Atomic Scientists,* a magazine of science and world affairs. Copyright © 1977 by the Educational Foundation for Nuclear Science, Chicago, IL 60637.

up all at once. Even as my eyes were being pierced by the sharp vermillion flash, the school building was already crumbling. I felt plaster and roof tiles and lumber come crashing down on my head, shoulders, and back. The dusty smell of plaster and other strange smells mixed up with it penetrated my nostrils.

I wonder how much time passed. It had gradually become harder and harder for me to breathe. The smell had become intense. It was the smell that made it so hard to breathe.

I was trapped under the wreckage of the school building. . . . I finally managed to get out from under the wreckage and stepped out into the schoolyard. It was just as dark outside as it had been under the wreckage and the sharp odor was everywhere. I took my handkerchief, wet it, and covered my mouth with it.

Four of my classmates came crawling out from beneath the wreckage just as I had done. In a daze we gathered around the willow tree, which was now leaning over. Then we began singing the school song. Our voices were low and raspy, with a tone of deep sadness. But our singing was drowned out by the roar of the swirling smoke and dust and the sound of the crumbling buildings.

We went to the swimming pool, helping a classmate whose leg had been injured and who had lost his eyesight. You cannot imagine what I saw there. One of our classmates had fallen into the pool; he was already dead, his entire body burned and tattered. Another was trying to extinguish the flames rising from his friend's clothes with the blood which spurted out of his own wounds. Some jumped into the swimming pool to extinguish their burning clothes, only to drown because their terribly burned limbs had become useless. There were others with burns all over their bodies whose faces were swollen to two or three times their normal size so they were no longer recognizable. I cannot forget the sight of those who could not move at all, who simply looked up at the sky, saying over and over, "Damn you! Damn you!"

Our gym teacher had come to the swimming pool too. Though he was moving about energetically, the sight of his burned and swollen body and his tattered clothes made everyone's heart sink. We all began to cry. But he gave us directions and encouraged us in a firm voice, urging us to gather together our friends who had lost their sight or were badly injured and to leave the burning school building behind.

There were others who could not move at all and there were probably many who were still trapped beneath the burning wreckage of the school. Were we to run away and leave them behind without caring at all? No . . . But there was nothing we could do. Friends, please forgive us.

Nagasaki, August 9, 1945: A Personal Account

Michito Ichimaru, M.D.

Michito Ichimaru is a survivor of the August 9, 1945 atomic bomb attack on Nagasaki, Japan.

In August 1945, I was a freshman at Nagasaki Medical College. The ninth of August was a clear, hot, beautiful summer day. I left my lodging house, which was one and one-half miles from the hypocenter, at eight in the morning, as usual, to catch a tram car. When I got to the train stop, I found that it had been derailed in an accident. I decided to return home. I was lucky. I never made it to school that day.

At 11 AM, I was sitting in my room with a fellow student when I heard the sound of a B-29 passing overhead. A few minutes later, the air flashed a brilliant yellow and there was a huge blast of wind.

We were terrified and ran downstairs to the toilet to hide. Later, when I came to my senses, I noticed a hole had been blown in the roof, all the glass had been shattered, and that the glass had cut my shoulder and I was bleeding. When I went outside, the sky had turned from blue to black and the black rain started to fall. The stone walls between the houses were reduced to rubble.

After a short time, I tried to go to my medical school in Urakami, which was 1500 feet from the hypocenter. The air dose of radiation was more than 7000 rads* at this distance. I could not complete my journey because there were fires everywhere. I met many people coming back from Urakami. Their clothes were in rags, and shreds of skin hung from their bodies. They looked like ghosts with vacant stares. I cannot get rid of the sounds of crying women in the destroyed fields.

The next day I was able to enter Urakami on foot, and all that I knew had disappeared. Only the concrete and iron skeletons of the buildings remained. There were dead bodies everywhere. On each street corner we had tubs of water used for putting out fires after the air raids. In one of these small tubs, scarcely large enough for one person, was the body of a desperate man who had sought cool water. There was foam coming from his mouth, but he was not alive.

Source: Michito Ichimaru, "August 9, 1945: A Personal Account," New York Times, March 28, 1981. Copyright © 1981 by The New York Times Company. Reprinted by permission.

*Editors' Note: A rad is a unit of measurement of how much radiation has been absorbed by a human. See the following article by Frank Barnaby for a discussion of the effects of radiation.

As I got nearer to school, there were black charred bodies, with the white edges of bones showing in the arms and legs. A dead horse with a bloated belly lay by the side of the road. Only the skeleton of the medical hospital remained standing. Because the school building was wood, it was completely destroyed. My classmates' were in that building, attending their physiology lecture. When I arrived, some were still alive. They were unable to move their bodies. The strongest were so weak that they were slumped over on the ground. I talked with them and they thought they would be OK, but all of them would die within weeks. I cannot forget the way their eyes looked at me and their voices spoke to me, forever.

I went up to the small hill behind the medical school, where all of the leaves of the trees were lost. The green mountain had changed to a bald mountain. There were many medical students, doctors, nurses, and some patients who escaped from the school and hospital. They were very weak and wanted water badly, crying out, "Give me water, please." Their clothes were in rags, bloody and dirty. Their condition was very bad. I carried down several friends of mine on my back from this hill. I brought them to their houses, using a cart hitched to my bicycle. All of them died in the next few days. Some friends died with high fever, talking deliriously. Some friends complained of general malaise and bloody diarrhea, caused by necrosis of the bowel mucous membrane by severe radiation.

One of my jobs was to contact the families of the survivors. In all the public schools I visited, there were many many survivors brought there by the healthy people. It is impossible to describe the horrors I saw. I heard many voices in pain, crying out, and there was a terrible stench. I remember it as an inferno. All these people also died within several weeks.

One of my friends who was living in the same lodging house cycled back from medical school by himself that day. He was a strong man who did judo. That night he gradually became weak, but he went back to his home in the country by himself the next day. I heard he died a few weeks later. I lost many friends. So many people died that disposing of the bodies was difficult. We burned the bodies of my friends in a pile of wood which we gathered, in a small open place. I clearly remember the movement of the bowels in the fire.

On August 15, 1945, I left Nagasaki by train to return to my home in the country. There were many survivors in the same car. Even now, I think of the grief of the parents of my friends who died. I cannot capture the magnitude of the misery and horror I saw. Never again should these terrible nuclear weapons be used, no matter what happens. Only when mankind renounces the use of these nuclear weapons will the souls of my friends rest in peace.

THE CONTINUING BODY COUNT AT HIROSHIMA AND NAGASAKI

Frank Barnaby

Frank Barnaby is presently a Visiting Senior Fellow in the Harold E. Stassen Project for World Peace at the Hubert H. Humphrey Institute of Public Affairs at the University of Minnesota. Previously he served as Director of the Stockholm International Peace Research Institute. His many publications include *Arms Uncontrolled*, with Ronald Huisken, and *The Nuclear Arms Race: Control or Catastrophe?*, with G. P. Thomas.

8:15 am—atomic bomb released
43 seconds later, a flash
Shock wave, craft careens
Huge atomic cloud
9:00 am—cloud in sight
Altitude more than 12,000 meters

So reads part of the flight diary of the B-29, the "Enola Gay," which dropped the atomic bomb—with the innocent-sounding nickname Little Boy—which obliterated Hiroshima on August 6, 1945.

The bomb, which exploded about 580 meters above the center of the city, is thought to have had the explosive power of about 12.5 kilotons of TNT. About 700 grams of uranium-235 were fissioned to produce this explosion, out of the 60 kilograms or so of uranium-235 in the bomb.

Little Boy was a large device—10 feet long, 28 inches wide, and weighing 9,000 pounds. It was also crude. A modern designer could use, say, 20 kilograms of uranium-235 to produce an atomic bomb with a yield of a hundred kilotons and more. And if he used it to trigger nuclear fission reactions he could produce an explosion a thousand times more powerful.

The next atomic bomb, euphemistically called Fat Man, exploded about 500 meters over Nagasaki at 11:02 am three days later. It is thought to have had a yield of some 22 kilotons. Plutonium-239 was the fissile material this time. About 1.3 kilograms were fissioned out of some 20 kilograms in the bomb. Fat Man, 10 feet, 8 inches long and 5 feet wide, weighed 10,000 pounds. . . .

Recognizing the importance of the topic, the International Peace Bu-

Source: Frank Barnaby, "The Continuing Body Count at Hiroshima and Nagasaki," *Bulletin of the Atomic Scientists* 33:10 (December 1977), pp. 43–51. Reprinted by permission of the *Bulletin of the Atomic Scientists*, a magazine of science and world affairs. Copyright © 1977 by the Educational Foundation for Nuclear Science, Chicago, IL 60637.

reau,* encouraged by many other non-governmental organizations, set up an international team of experts to study the damage done by and the after-effects of the bombings. Forty-four scientists from 14 countries (east, west, and Third World) met . . . July 21 to August 3 [1976] in Hiroshima to examine data made specially available to them by Japanese specialists. They also visited hospitals and research institutes in Hiroshima and Nagasaki, and interviewed doctors, social workers and A-bomb survivors.

The reports prepared by these natural and social scientists contain new information, perhaps surprisingly 32 years after the events. They also show up considerable gaps in existing knowledge and in research. In fact, unless much money and scientific resources are soon made available and new research techniques are used to speed up the collection and analysis of data, our knowledge of the long-term effects of the atomic bomb is likely to remain very incomplete. Most work needs to be done on the social and psychological effects. But much biological, genetic and medical data are still missing. . . .

The data initially collected in Hiroshima and Nagasaki were classified top secret by the occupation authorities. The Atomic Bomb Casualty Commission was set up to assemble the data. An advanced team of the commission arrived at the two cities in early September 1945 (the war ended on August 15) to check on radiation levels. Full-scale research began in October.

A Japanese research team carried on independent studies in Hiroshima and Nagasaki but all its findings and material were requisitioned by the occupation forces. On September 19, 1945, a so-called Press Code was issued by the occupation forces which effectively censored all articles about the A-bombs.

Several Japanese medical scientists risked severe penalties to hide pathological specimens and autopsy reports, but apparently not very successfully. Most of the data were discovered and shipped to the United States with all the other material collected. The United States was anxious to keep details of the effects of the atomic bombs secret mainly because of the rapid deterioration of postwar relations with the Soviet Union. Another reason may have been to clarify these effects in case the United States should be attacked in the future by foreign nuclear weapons.

Data Returned

Japanese research was restricted right up to 1952 when the San Francisco peace treaty with Japan was signed. But (surprisingly) strong demands by Japanese scientists for the return of the material from the United States were not made until the late 1960s. In February 1972, the Japanese government was per-

---

* The Geneva-based International Peace Bureau is a non-governmental organization dealing mainly with peace problems, currently with special emphasis on human rights and disarmament. The Bureau (awarded the Nobel Peace Prize in 1910) has over 20 million affiliated members worldwide.

suaded to formally request its return and, finally, in May 1973 the material was actually sent back.

About 20,000 items—pathological specimens, dissection records and photographs—were returned. This massive quantity of material had been excellently preserved for 28 years by the U.S. Armed Forces Institute of Pathology. It is now scattered among a number of Japanese institutes and many are anxious about its future safety.

Strong suspicion remains that some requisitioned material has not been returned. Some evidence exists to support this. But no lists of the material were made and so it is impossible to discover whether or not it has all been returned.

The pathological specimens are particularly useful for detailed studies of acute radiation diseases, and of the effects of radiation on the human body. So important is this work that the natural science group of experts meeting in 1977 recommended that

> all the relevant information obtained by organized bodies and individuals during the first few years after the atomic bombings be collected and made available to all research workers in this field as soon as possible.

About 2,000 photographs of the physical and medical effects of the bombings are among the returned material. These may be of little direct use to academic researchers, but they are invaluable to workers in Hiroshima and Nagasaki who are constructing detailed maps of the areas destroyed by the bombs. This painstaking study is to discover how many people were there at the time of the explosions, precisely where they were, and what happened to them. It should also make it possible to estimate more accurately the radiation dose to which survivors were exposed.

The need for further effort to establish the number of people "who died during the first few years after the bombings, and the causes and times of their deaths" was emphasized by the international experts. And so was the need for more information about radiation doses to extend "the number of survivors available for quantitative analysis."

Number Killed

Hiroshima is built on a flat delta, with mountains to the north and west and sea to the south. The city was damaged similarly in all directions. The damage to Nagasaki, built on mountainous terrain, varied considerably according to direction. But, according to information given to the international experts by Japanese scientists, the death rate at various distances from the hypocenter (the point on the ground directly below the center of the explosion) was about the same in both cities.

About 97 percent of all those within 500 meters of the hypocenters when the bombs exploded died by the end of 1945. About 60 percent of those within 2 kilometers died: about 75 percent of them in the first 24 hours, and nearly 90 percent within ten days. And about 3 percent of those between 2 and 5 kilometers of the hypocenters died by the end of 1945.

The number of people in Hiroshima at the time of the bomb is not precisely known. About 40,000 troops were there, for example, but the exact number is very uncertain. Also uncertain is the number of Korean forced laborers in the city. But the best estimate is that about 350,000 people were involved.

Substantial differences exist between the various estimates of the number killed and injured. A 1967 U.N. estimate, for example, of 78,000 dead in Hiroshima is a gross underestimation. The international experts concluded that the most likely figure for the number of deaths up to the end of 1945 is 140,000, give or take 10,000. But this is probably also an underestimate. Many thousands of people were reported missing in the 1950 National Census. The number that initially survived but died in the next few years is unknown. And so is the fate of the 37,000 or so people who came into Hiroshima within the first week of the bombing.

About 280,000 people are thought to have been in Nagasaki when the bomb exploded. According to the best estimate, some 74,000 died by the end of 1945. There were many Koreans in Nagasaki too. Perhaps about 10,000 of them were killed by the bomb; the exact figure is not known. There is, therefore, a large element of uncertainty in this estimate of the number killed in Nagasaki. But the official U.N. figure of 27,000 dead is certainly wrong. The number of Nagasaki A-bomb victims who died after the end of 1945 is not known. It may never be.

The number of people killed by Little Boy and Fat Man probably greatly exceeds a quarter of a million, a death rate of over 40 percent.

Scorched Land

Those killed immediately were mainly either crushed or burned to death. The combined effect of thermal radiation and blast was particularly lethal. Many of those burned to death in collapsed buildings would have escaped with only injuries had there been no fires. But as it happened, an area of 13 square kilometers in Hiroshima and 6.7 square kilometers in Nagasaki was reduced to rubble by blast and then to ashes by fire. The difference in area was due mainly to the different terrain.

About one-half of the energy generated by the atomic bombs was given off as blast. The front of the blast moved as a shock wave—a wall of high-pressure air, spreading outward at a speed equal to or greater than that of sound. It traveled nearly 4 kilometers in 10 seconds after the explosion, and about 11 kilometers in 30 seconds. Even then it still retained some destructive power. It was followed by a hurricane-force wind. But as the shock wave spread outward, the pressure behind it fell below atmospheric pressure and eventually the air flowed in the inward direction. Thus, a supersonic shock wave was followed by an exceedingly powerful wind and then, after an eerie instant of stillness, a very strong wind blew in the opposite direction.

At Hiroshima the maximum blast pressure at a distance of two kilometers from the hypocenter was about 3 tons per square meter and the maximum blast velocity was about 70 meters per second. All buildings within this distance were damaged beyond repair. Casualties due to blast were particularly severe within about 1.3 kilometers of the hypocenter. At this distance the blast reached a pressure of 7 tons per square meter and a velocity of about 20 meters per second.

About one-third of the total energy generated by the bombs was given off as thermal energy. The fireballs produced by the atomic explosions instantly reached temperatures of several million degrees Centigrade. After one ten-thousandth of a second their diameters had grown to about 28 meters and they had temperatures of about 300,000°C. They reached their maximum diameters of about 280 meters in about one second, when the surface temperatures were about 5,000°C. Two seconds later the temperatures were 1,700°C; thereafter they fell more gradually. At a distance of 500 meters from the hypocenter in Hiroshima nearly 60 calories per square centimeter of thermal radiation were emitted in the first three seconds. Even at a distance of 3 kilometers from the hypocenter, the thermal radiation emitted in the first three seconds amounted to about 2.6 calories per square centimeter, about 40 times more than that from the Sun. The thermal radiation in Nagasaki was nearly twice as intense as that at Hiroshima.

The intensity of the thermal radiation was sufficient to burn exposed human skin at distances of even 3.5 kilometers from the hypocenter in Hiroshima and 4 kilometers in Nagasaki. At these distances, fabrics and wood were charred. Many people caught in the open within about 1.2 kilometers from the hypocenters were burned to death.

Firestorms raged in Hiroshima and Nagasaki. The one in Hiroshima was particularly severe, lasting for six hours and completely burning every combustible object within a radius of two kilometers from the hypocenter.

Moisture condensed around rising ash particles as they came into contact with cold air. The rain that consequently fell on the two cities was highly radioactive and oily, known to this day as "black rain."

Hiroshima had about 76,000 buildings before the bomb was dropped. About 63 percent of them were destroyed by fire, 5 percent were destroyed by blast and 24 percent were very seriously damaged. About 25 percent of Nagasaki's 51,000 buildings were destroyed and another 11 percent seriously damaged. In the midst of such extensive damage, effective fire-fighting was impossible.

Ionizing Radiation

About 15 percent of the energy generated by the bombs was given off as ionizing radiation. About a third of this was emitted within one minute of the explosion. This is called initial radiation. The remainder, called residual radiation, was emitted by fission products and by radioactivity induced in the soil, the walls of buildings, and so on.

The initial radiation dose (air dose) at the hypocenter in Hiroshima is believed to have been about 24,000 rads (10,000 from gamma rays and 14,000 from neutrons). In Nagasaki the dose at this distance was probably about 29,000 rads (25,000 from gamma rays and 4,000 from neutrons).

It is generally thought that one-half of a large number of people receiving a whole-body radiation dose of 400 rads (air dose) will die, and that virtually all of those exposed to whole-body radiation of 700 rads or more will die in a short time. Exposed people within about one kilometer of the Hiroshima bomb and 1.2 kilometers of the Nagasaki bomb are thought to have received doses of about 400 rads.

Only rough estimates of the doses of residual radiation received are available. The maximum possible dose is thought to be about 150 rads in both Hiroshima and Nagasaki. The need to obtain much more information on

> the dosimetry of the people who were exposed only to the residual radiation

is stressed in the report of the international experts. Also recommended is that:

> A study be made of the plutonium content of the people in the fallout areas, to establish their internal dosimetry.

Many of those exposed to large doses of radiation rapidly became incapacitated, and suffered from nausea and vomiting, the first symptoms of radiation sickness. They later typically vomited blood, developed a high fever, had severe diarrhea and much bleeding from the bowels. They usually died within about 10 days.

Smaller doses of radiation produced a wide variety of symptoms including nausea, vomiting, diarrhea, bleeding from the bowels, gums, nose and genitals, and menstrual abnormalities. There was often a total loss of hair, fever and a feeling of great weakness. Resistance to infection was markedly decreased. And septicemia was a frequent cause of death.

Late Effects

Most of the survivors still alive at the end of 1945 appeared to be reasonably healthy. But later a variety of illnesses—including eye diseases, blood disorders, malignant tumors and psychoneurological disturbances—began to appear.

Leukemia among survivors increased fast for about a decade, when the mortality rate reached a level about 30 times higher than that of non-exposed Japanese. It still has not fallen to the national average.

The incidence of other malignant tumors—thyroid, breast, lung, salivary, gland, bone, prostate and so on—has been, and still is, higher among survivors than among the non-exposed. There is, the experts stressed, an urgent need for a careful study of the incidence of leukemia and other malignancies among those who were exposed to low doses of radiation, say, below 100 rads.

Children born to women pregnant when the bombs exploded show an increase in some congenital malformation, particularly microcephaly (abnormally small size of the head) resulting in mental retardation. But, surprisingly, no increase has been reported in the incidence of leukemia among such children. Also surprising is the apparent absence of genetic damage in survivors exposed to radiation.

A number of reasons were suggested for this absence. Among them are:

- the number of survivors involved, and the radiation doses received by them, are such that too few of the children examined showed genetic effects (even though these may have been present) to be statistically significant;
- the research methods used to search for effects are insufficiently sensitive;
- the mutations induced, being predominantly recessive ones, will show up only in second, or even later, generations;
- many of the irradiated persons may have died from other effects;
- and there may have been a large number of spontaneous abortions.

The experts strongly recommended that

> the reasons for the reported absence of certain *in utero* and genetic effects in the survivors

be investigated. In particular, more biochemical studies were suggested.

Social Effects

The social and psychological effects of the atomic bombings were extremely severe. The communities disintegrated. The social services collapsed. Many people went mad or committed suicide. Thousands of children became orphans.

Some of the effects of the bombs are still apparent. There is a disproportionate number of aged among the survivors. Fear of malformed offspring often prevents marriages, and unusual susceptibility to disease and fatigue often threatens employment.

The ratio of sick and injured among the survivors is almost twice the national average. Disease and poverty among the survivors are continuously aggravated by aging and failing health.

Thirty-two years have passed since the atomic bombings, yet we are still unable to grasp the totality of the disaster. The destruction produced by nuclear weapons may simply be incomprehensible.

Is Hiroshima Our Text?

Robert Jay Lifton

Robert Jay Lifton is Distinguished Professor of Psychiatry and Psychology at the City University of New York at John Jay College. Previously he held the Foundations' Fund Research Professorship in Psychiatry at the Yale University School of Medicine. Lifton won the National Book Award in the Sciences in 1969 for his study of the survivors of Hiroshima, *Death in Life*. His other works include *The Broken Connection: On Death and the Continuity of Life* and, with Richard Falk, *Indefensible Weapons: The Political and Psychological Case Against Nuclearism*.

I arrived in Hiroshima in the early spring of 1962. I intended no more than a brief visit. But very quickly I made a discovery that I found almost incomprehensible. It had been seventeen years since the dropping of the first atomic weapon on an inhabited city—surely one of the tragic turning points in human history—and no one had studied the impact of that event. There had of course been research on the physical aftereffects of the bomb, and there had been brief commentaries here and there on behavior of some of the survivors at the time of the bomb and afterward. But there had been no systematic examination of what had taken place in people's lives, of the psychological and social consequences of the bomb.

I came to a terrible, but I believe essentially accurate, rule of thumb: the more significant an event, the less likely it is to be studied. Again there are reasons. One reason, certainly relevant to Hiroshima, has to do with the fear and pain the event arouses—the unacceptable images to which one must, as an investigator, expose oneself. To this anxiety and pain I can certainly attest.

But another source of avoidance is the threat posed to our traditional assumptions and conventional ways of going about our studies. We would rather

Source: Robert Jay Lifton, "Is Hiroshima Our Text?" in *Indefensible Weapons: The Political and Psychological Case Against Nuclearism*, by Robert Jay Lifton and Richard Falk (New York: Basic Books, 1982). Copyright © 1982 by Basic Books, Inc., Publishers, of New York. Reprinted by permission of the publisher.

avoid looking at events that, by their very nature, must change us and our relation to the world. We prefer to hold on to our presuppositions and habits of personal and professional function. And we may well sense that seriously studying such an event means being haunted by it from then on, taking on a lifelong burden of responsibility to it.

I was able to stay in Hiroshima and conduct interview research with people there over a six-month period. The best way I know to describe a few of my findings that might be of use to us now is to look at the Hiroshima experience as taking place in four stages.

The first stage was the immersion in the sea of dead and near-dead at the time the bomb fell. This was the beginning of what I have called a permanent encounter with death. But it was not just death; it was grotesque and absurd death, which had no relationship to the life cycle as such. There was a sudden and absolute shift from normal existence to this overwhelming immersion in death.

Survivors recalled not only feeling that they themselves would soon die but experiencing the sense that *the whole world was dying.* For instance, a science professor who had been covered by falling debris and temporarily blinded remembered: "My body seemed all black. Everything seemed dark, dark all over. Then I thought, 'The world is ending.'" And a Protestant minister, responding to scenes of mutilation and destruction he saw everywhere, told me: "The feeling I had was that everyone was dead. The whole city was destroyed. . . . I thought all of my family must be dead. It doesn't matter if I die. . . . I thought this was the end of Hiroshima, of Japan, of humankind." And a writer later recorded her impressions:

> I just could not understand why our surroundings change so greatly in one instant. . . . I thought it must have been something which had nothing to do with the war, the collapse of the earth, which was said to take place at the end of the world, which I had read about as a child. . . . There was a fearful silence, which made me feel that all people . . . were dead.

As psychiatrists, we are accustomed to look upon imagery of the end of the world as a symptom of mental illness, usually paranoid psychosis. But here it may be said that this imagery is a more or less appropriate response to an extraordinary external event.

In referring to themselves and others at the time, survivors used such terms as "walking ghosts," "people who walk in the realm of dreams," or as one man said of himself: "I was not really alive." People were literally uncertain about whether they were dead or alive, which was why I came to call my study of the event *Death in Life.*

Indicative of the nature of the event is the extraordinary disparity in estimates of the number killed by the bomb. These vary from less than 70,000 to more than 250,000, with the City of Hiroshima estimating 200,000. These estimates depend on who one counts and how one goes about counting, and can be subject at either end to various ideological and emotional influences. But the simple truth is that nobody really knows how many people have been killed by the Hiroshima bomb, and such was the confusion at the time that nobody will ever know.

The second stage was associated with what I call "invisible contamination." Within hours or days or weeks after the bomb fell, people—even some who had appeared to be untouched by the bomb—began to experience grotesque symptoms: severe diarrhea and weakness, ulceration of the mouth and gums with bleeding, bleeding from all of the bodily orifices and into the skin, high fever; extremely low white blood cell counts when these could be taken; and later, loss of scalp and bodily hair—the condition often following a progressive course until death. These were symptoms of acute radiation effects. People did not know that at the time, of course, and even surviving doctors thought it was some kind of strange epidemic. Ordinary people spoke of a mysterious "poison."

But the kind of terror experienced by survivors can be understood from the rumors that quickly spread among them. One rumor simply held that everyone in Hiroshima would be dead within a few months or a few years. The symbolic message here was: None can escape the poison; the epidemic is total—all shall die. But there was a second rumor, reported to me even more frequently and with greater emotion: the belief that trees, grass, and flowers would never again grow in Hiroshima; that from that day on the city would be unable to sustain vegetation of any kind. The meaning here was that nature was drying up altogether. Life was being extinguished at its source—an ultimate form of desolation that not only encompassed human death but went beyond it.

These early symptoms were the first large-scale manifestation of the invisible contamination stemming from the atomic particles. The symptoms also gave rise to a special image in the minds of the people of Hiroshima—an image of a force that not only kills and destroys on a colossal scale but also leaves behind in the bodies of those exposed to it deadly influences that may emerge at any time and strike down their victims. That image has also made its way to the rest of us, however we have resisted it.

The third stage of Hiroshima survivors' encounter with death occurred not weeks or months but years after the bomb fell, with the discovery (beginning in 1948 and 1949) that various forms of leukemia were increasing in incidence among survivors sufficiently exposed to irradiation. That fatal malignancy of the blood-forming organs became the model for the relatively loose but highly significant term "A-bomb disease." Then, over decades, there have been increases in various forms of cancer—first thyroid cancer, and then cancer of the breast, lung, stomach, bone marrow, and other areas. Since the latent period for radiation-induced cancer can be quite long, and since for many forms it is still not known, the results are by no means in. Researchers are still learning about increases in different cancers, and the truth is that the incidence of virtually *any* form of cancer can be increased by exposure to radiation.

An additional array of harmful bodily influences have been either demonstrated, or are suspected, to be caused by radiation exposure—including impaired growth and development, premature aging, various blood diseases, endocrine and skin disorders, damage to the central nervous system, and a vague but persistently reported borderline condition of general weakness and debilitation. Again the returns are not in. But on a chronic level of bodily concern, survivors have the feeling that the bomb can do anything, and that anything it does is likely to be fatal. Moreover, there are endless situations in which neither survivors themselves nor the most astute physicians can say with any certainty where physical radiation effects end and psychological manifestations begin. There is always a "nagging doubt." For instance, I retain a vivid memory of a talk I had in Hiroshima with a distinguished physician who, despite injuries and radiation effects of his own, had at the time of the bomb courageously attempted to care for patients around him. He spoke in philosophical terms of the problem of radiation effects as one that "man cannot solve," but when I asked him about general anxieties he smiled uneasily and spoke in a way that gave me the strong sense that a raw nerve had been exposed:

> Yes, of course, people are anxious. Take my own case. If I am shaving in the morning and I should happen to cut myself very slightly, I dab the blood with a piece of paper—and then, when I notice that it has stopped flowing, I think to myself, "Well, I guess I am all right."

Nor does the matter end with one's own body or life. There is the fear that this invisible contamination will manifest itself in the next generation, because it is scientifically known that such abnormalities *can* be caused by radiation. There is medical controversy here about whether genetic abnormalities have occurred: They have not been convincingly demonstrated in studies on comparative populations, but abnormalities in the chromosomes of exposed survivors have been demonstrated. People of course retain profound anxiety about the possibility of transmitting this deadly taint to subsequent generations. For instance, when I revisited Hiroshima in 1980, people said to me: "Well, maybe the next generation is okay after all, but what about the third generation? The fact is that, scientifically speaking, no one can assure them with certainty that subsequent generations will not be affected. Again, nobody knows. So there is no end-point for possible damage, and for anxiety.

No wonder, then, that a number of survivors told me that they considered the dropping of the bomb to be a "big experiment" by the United States. It was a new weapon; its effects were unknown; American authorities wanted to see what those effects would be. Unfortunately, there is more than a kernel of truth in that claim, at least in its suggestion of one among several motivations. More important for us now is the idea that any use of nuclear warheads would still be in a related sense "experimental."

The fourth stage of the Hiroshima experience is its culmination in a life-long identification with the dead—so extreme in many cases as to cause survivors to feel "as-if-dead" and to take on what I spoke of as an "identity of the dead." Hiroshima and Nagasaki survivors became, in their own eyes as well as those of others, a tainted group, one whose collective identity was formed around precisely the continuous death immersion and the invisible contamination we have been discussing. The identity can include what we may think of as paradoxical guilt—the tendency of survivors to berate themselves inwardly for having remained alive while others died, and for not having been able to do more to save others or combat the general evil at the time of the bomb. In connection with the latter, the sense of "failed enactment" can have little to do with what was possible at the time or with what one actually did or did not do.

More than that, survivors underwent what can be called a second victimization in the form of significant discrimination in two fundamental areas of life: marriage and work. The "logic" of the discrimination was the awareness of potential marriage partners (or families and go-betweens involved in making marriage arrangements) and prospective employers that survivors are susceptible to aftereffects of the bomb, making them poor bets for marriage (and healthy children) and employment. But the deeper, often unconscious feeling about atomic bomb survivors was that they were death-tainted, that they were reminders of a fearful event people did not want to be reminded of, that they were "carriers," so to speak, of the dreaded "A-bomb disease."

At the end of my study of these events, I spoke of Hiroshima, together with Nagasaki, as a last chance, a nuclear catastrophe from which one could still learn. The bombs had been dropped, there was an "end of the world" in ways we have observed, yet the world still exists. And precisely in this end-of-the-world quality of Hiroshima lies both its threat and its potential wisdom.

Is Hiroshima, then, our text? Certainly as our *only* text, it would be quite inadequate. We know well that what happened there could not really represent what would happen to people if our contemporary nuclear warheads were used. When the Hiroshima and Nagasaki bombs were dropped, they were the only two functional atomic bombs in the world. Now there are approximately 50,000 nuclear warheads, most of them many times—some a hundred or a thousand or more times—the destructive and contaminating (through radiation) power of those first "tiny" bombs. While those early bombs initiated a revolution in killing power, we may speak of another subsequent technological revolution of even greater dimensions in its magnification of that killing power. The scale of Hiroshima was difficult enough to grasp; now the scale is again so radically altered that holding literally to Hiroshima images misleads us in the direction of extreme understatement.

Yet despite all that, Hiroshima and Nagasaki hold out important nuclear age truths for us. The first of these is the *totality of destruction.* It has been pointed out that Tokyo and Dresden were decimated no less than Hiroshima. But in Hiroshima it was one plane, one bomb, one city destroyed. And the result of the single bomb was the incalculable death and suffering we have noted.

A second Hiroshima truth for us is that of the weapon's *unending lethal influence.* Radiation effects were (and are) such that the experience has had no cutoff point. Survivors have the possibility of experiencing delayed but deadly radiation effects for the rest of their lives. That possibility extends to their children, to their children's children, indefinitely into the future—over how many generations no one knows. And we have seen how the physical and psychological blend in relation to these continuing effects.

A third truth, really derived from the other two, has to do with Hiroshima and Nagasaki survivors' identification of themselves as *victims of an ultimate weapon*—of a force that threatens to exterminate the species. This sense had considerable impact on Hiroshima survivors, sometimes creating in them an expectation of future nuclear destruction of all of humankind and most of the earth.

And there is still something more to be said about Hiroshima and Nagasaki regarding our perceptions of nuclear danger. The two cities convey to us a sense of *nuclear actuality.* The bombs were really used there. We can read, view, and if we will allow ourselves, *feel* what happened to people in them. In the process we experience emotions such as awe, dread, and wonder (at the extent and nature of killing, maiming, and destruction)—emotions surely appropriate to our current nuclear threat. Such emotions can transform our intellectual and moral efforts against nuclear killing into a personal mission—one with profound ethical, spiritual, and sometimes religious overtones. Hiroshima, then, is indeed our text, even if in miniature. And we have hardly even begun to take in what Hiroshima has to teach us.

The argument is sometimes extended to the point of claiming that this sense of nuclear actuality has prevented full-scale nuclear war; that in the absence of the restraining influence of Hiroshima and Nagasaki, the United States and the Soviet Union would have by now embarked upon nuclear annihilation. The claim is difficult to evaluate, and while I feel some of its persuasiveness, I do not quite accept it. In any case, one must raise a countervailing argument having to do with another dimension of Hiroshima's and Nagasaki's nuclear actuality: namely, the legitimation of a nation's using atomic bombs on human populations under certain conditions (in this case wartime). Once anything has been done, it is psychologically and in a sense morally easier for it to be done again. That legitimation can then combine with an argument minimizing the effects of the Hiroshima bomb: the claim that one has unfortunately heard more than once from American leaders that Hiroshima's having been rebuilt as a city is evidence that one can fight and recover from a limited nuclear war.

Here we may say that part of Hiroshima's value as a text is in its contrasts with our current situation. One crucial contrast has to do with the existence of an outside world to help. Hiroshima could slowly recover from the bomb because there were intact people who came in from the outside and brought healing energies to the city. Help was erratic and slow in arriving, but it did become available: from nearby areas (including a few medical teams); from Japanese returning from former overseas possessions; and, to some extent, from the American Occupation. The groups converging on Hiroshima in many cases contributed more to the recovery of the city as such than to that of individual survivors (physically, mentally, or economically). But they made possible the city's revitalization and repopulation.

In Hiroshima there was a total breakdown of the social and communal structure—of the web of institutions and arrangements necessary to the function of any human group. But because of the existence and intervention of an intact outside world, that social breakdown could be temporary.

Given the number and power of our current nuclear warheads, can one reasonably assume that there will be an intact outside world to help? I do not think so.

FOR FURTHER READING

Batchelder, Robert. *The Irreversible Decision, 1939–1950.* Boston: Houghton Mifflin Co., 1961. A historical analysis of the decisions to build and use the atomic bombs, with a focus on moral issues. Contains a careful examination of the decision to bomb Nagasaki.

Bernstein, Barton J., ed. *The Atomic Bomb: The Critical Issues.* Boston: Little, Brown and Co., 1976. This excellent reader is balanced and succinct. It is divided into four sections: the official explanation (statement and challenge); was the bomb necessary?; why was the bomb used?; and atomic diplomacy and the moral significance of Hiroshima.

Bernstein, Barton J. "Truman and the H-Bomb." *Bulletin of the Atomic Scientists* 40:3 (March 1984), pp. 12–18. A brief, yet comprehensive, analysis of the domestic political pressures that entered into the decision by the United States to build the hydrogen bomb.

Brown, Anthony Cave, and Dwight MacDonald, eds. *The Secret History of the Atomic Bomb.* New York: Delta, 1977. This valuable reference contains early official documents and reports, including the authoritative Smyth Report on the bomb development projects and lengthy excerpts from the Report of the Manhattan Project Atomic Bomb Investigating Group.

Caidin, Martin. *A Torch to the Enemy.* New York: Ballantine Books, 1979 (paperback). A detailed account of the incendiary bombing campaign against Japan that set the stage for the military use of the atomic bombs.

The Committee for the Compilation of Materials on Damage Caused by the Atomic Bombs in Hiroshima and Nagasaki. *Hiroshima and Nagasaki: The Physical, Medical and Social Effects of the Atomic Bombings.* Translated by E. Ishikawa and D. L. Swain. New York: Basic Books, 1981 (available in paperback). A comprehensive, carefully documented, technically detailed, yet readable reference work. Excellent coverage of physical and medical effects with some attention to psychological consequences.

Hachiya, M. *Hiroshima Diary: The Journal of a Japanese Physician, August 6–September 30, 1945.* Edited by W. Wells. Chapel Hill: University of North Carolina Press, 1955. A physician survivor's account of the physical and human damage caused by the first atomic bomb to be used in war.

Herken, Gregg. *The Winning Weapon: The Atomic Bomb in the Cold War, 1945–1950.* New York: Alfred A. Knopf, 1980 (available in paperback). A thorough study, utilizing recently declassified official documents, of the various factions within the U.S. government that struggled for the control of atomic weapons policy in the early postwar era. Herken identifies those who wanted to exploit the U.S. monopoly on nuclear weapons for military advantages, as well as those who advocated strenuous efforts to promote international cooperation before the arms race became uncontrollable.

Hersey, John. *Hiroshima.* New York: Alfred A. Knopf, 1946 (many recent paperback editions). A powerful and painful account of the Hiroshima bombing, written by a first-rate journalist and based on interviews with six survivors.

Holloway, David. "Entering the Nuclear Arms Race: The Soviet Decision to Build the Atomic Bomb, 1939–1945." *Social Studies of Science* 11 (1981), pp. 159–97. An excellent overview of Soviet atomic research between December 1938 and August 1945.

Japan Broadcasting Corporation. *Unforgettable Fire: Pictures Drawn by Atomic Bomb Survivors.* New York: Pantheon Books, 1981 (paperback). In response to a request by the Japan Broadcasting Corporation, hundreds of survivors of the Hiroshima and Nagasaki bombings sent in sketches and paintings of scenes they remembered from the days of the attacks and afterwards. Those selected for this book, and the accompanying narrative descriptions by survivors, provide vivid glimpses into the horror created by the bombs.

Kennett, Lee. *A History of Strategic Bombing.* New York: Charles Scribner's Sons, 1982. A concise historical overview of strategic bombing, beginning with hot-air balloons and extending to the atomic bombings of Hiroshima and Nagasaki.

Lifton, Robert Jay. *Death in Life: Survivors of Hiroshima.* New York: Random House, 1967 (reissued in paperback by Basic Books in 1982). The definitive study of the psychological and social aftermath of the atomic bombings by a psychiatrist who conducted in-depth interviews with more than sixty survivors.

Marx, Joseph. *Nagasaki: The Necessary Bomb?* New York: Macmillan Co., 1971. A detailed account of the atomic bombing of Nagasaki that questions its military necessity.

Sherwin, Martin. *A World Destroyed: The Atomic Bomb and the Grand Alliance.* New York: Alfred A. Knopf, 1975. An excellent analysis of the international and domestic considerations that entered into the decision to use the atomic bombs against Japan. Relying on declassified government documents, Sherwin explores Roosevelt and Churchill's desire to establish a British-American monopoly of atomic weapons after the war, even at the expense of ruining chances for international control. Sherwin also examines the roles of scientists, including those who opposed the use of the bomb against cities, as well as those who favored it.

Smith, Alice Kimball. *A Peril and a Hope: The Scientists' Movement in America, 1945–47.* Cambridge, Mass.: M.I.T. Press, 1970 (available in paperback). A detailed history of early attempts by many of the scientists who had been involved in the atomic bomb projects to inform the American public about the implications of atomic weapons. They also lobbied successfully to keep the new nuclear technology under civilian jurisdiction, rather than under military control. Traces the origins of several currently active public interest science organizations, for example the Federation of American Scientists.

———. "Manhattan Project: The Atomic Bomb." *The Nuclear Almanac: Confronting the Atom in War and Peace.* Edited by Jack Dennis, et al., pp. 21–42. Reading, Mass.: Addison-Wesley Publishing Co., 1984 (available in paperback). An excellent, succinct history of the development of the first U.S. atomic bombs.

Thomas, Gordon and Max Morgan Witts. *Ruin from the Air: The Atomic Mission to Hiroshima.* London: Hamish Hamilton, 1977. A detailed account of the planning and execution of the B-29 atomic bombing raid on Hiroshima as told by two accomplished British writers.

2

Nuclear Weapons and Their Effects

A basic understanding of the nature and effects of nuclear weapons is indispensible for evaluating critical issues involving the nuclear threat, such as whether nuclear war can be survived and "won," and how many and what kind of nuclear weapons are needed to assure our national security. These and other issues will be addressed in subsequent chapters.

The articles in this chapter examine three important dimensions of nuclear weapons. First, the *nature* of nuclear weapons is discussed: What are they? How do they work? How do they differ from so-called "conventional" or non-nuclear weapons? What are the differences between atomic, or A-bombs, like those used against Hiroshima and Nagasaki, and the hydrogen, or H-bombs, that constitute the bulk of current U.S. and Soviet nuclear arsenals? Second, the principal effects of nuclear explosions, both immediate and delayed, are explored. Third, an overview of the current nuclear arsenals of the United States, the Soviet Union, and other nuclear-armed nations is presented.

In his first selection for this chapter, "Types of Nuclear Weapons," Frank Barnaby explains how the Hiroshima and Nagasaki bombs worked and how they differ from contemporary hydrogen bombs. Just as atomic bombs were capable of vastly greater destruction than the conventional bombs that had destroyed the cities of Europe and Japan, hydrogen bombs are a thousand-fold more destructive than atomic bombs. The destructive power, or yield, of the atomic bombs dropped on Japan was measured in units called *kilotons,* or thousands of tons of TNT. (The Hiroshima bomb had a yield of approximately 12.5 kilotons.) In contrast, the yield of hydrogen bombs is customarily measured in terms of *megatons,* or *millions* of tons of TNT. Barnaby notes also that the modern nuclear weapons are far more efficient than the "crude" bombs used in Japan. Whereas the atomic bombs were so big and heavy that a specially modified, massive B-29 bomber was needed to deliver each to its target, modern nuclear weapons can be made so small and light that they can be delivered by 8-inch artillery shells.

The article by the U.S. Congressional Office of Technology Assessment (OTA), "General Description of Effects," explains that nuclear explosions release vast amounts of energy in several ways, including blast, heat, electromagnetic pulse, and radioactivity. The OTA emphasizes that it is important to recognize the long-term, as well as the short-term, effects of nuclear weapons. The OTA also stresses that assessing the long-term effects is fraught with difficulties. Indeed, the history of efforts to understand the effects of nuclear weapons has at times involved the belated appreciation of effects that had not been recognized by earlier researchers. For example, during the above-ground testing of hydrogen bombs by the United States in 1962, scientists were surprised to learn that a 1.4 megaton bomb detonated at a height of 248 miles disrupted electrical equipment in Hawaii 800 miles away. Power-line circuit breakers opened, street lights went out, and burglar alarms started ringing. Subsequent studies disclosed a previously unappreciated effect of nuclear explosions—an extremely powerful pulse of electrical energy (similar to, but far stronger than, lightning) that is now known as electromagnetic pulse (EMP). The implications of EMP proved to be quite astonishing and are still the subject of debate. A few hydrogen bombs exploded at high altitudes above the United States or the Soviet Union would destroy solid state electronic components over a range of thousands of miles, shutting down communications systems and possibly preventing military leaders from maintaining control over a nuclear war.[1]

Just as the destructive power of nuclear weapons has grown immensely since Hiroshima, so has the sheer size of the arsenals, particularly those of the United States and the Soviet Union. In his second article for this chapter, Barnaby indicates that the two superpowers currently possess more than 50,000 nuclear bombs and warheads on a wide variety of delivery systems, including intercontinental bombers, land-based ballistic missiles, nuclear-armed submarines, and long-range cruise missiles. He also notes that several nations now possess nuclear weapons, and yet others are striving to acquire their own.

The almost incomprehensible magnitude of current arsenals is suggested by Barnaby's calculation that they equal the destructive power of over 3 tons of TNT for every one of the more than four and a half billion people alive on earth. Another means of understanding this destructive power has been developed by one of our colleagues, Dr. Mike Casper of the Physics Department of Carleton College in Northfield, Minnesota. Casper converted the explosive force of current nuclear arsenals into "Hiroshima equivalents," that is, how many 12.5 kiloton Hiroshima explosions could be produced with present stockpiles. On the basis of weapons in place in 1983, Casper calculated that the 4800 warheads in the U.S. submarine force contain nearly 18,000 Hiroshimas; the nearly 2200 warheads in the U.S. intercontinental ballistic missile (ICBM) force contain approximately 27,000 Hiroshimas; and the 2588 bombs carried

[1] William Broad, "Nuclear Pulse (I): Awakening to the Chaos Factor," *Science* 212 (May 29, 1981), pp. 1009–10.

by U.S. strategic bombers contain more than 33,400 Hiroshimas! Soviet strategic nuclear forces are potentially even more destructive. Their 2000 submarine-launched warheads contain nearly 18,000 Hiroshimas; their 6384 ICBM warheads contain nearly 90,000 Hiroshimas; and their approximately 400 bomber-delivered nuclear weapons contain more than 7600 Hiroshimas.[2] Thus, each nation has enough nuclear weapons to destroy the other many times over. (In fact, as will be discussed in the next chapter, recent research suggests that even a small fraction of the present arsenal of either superpower could cause such devastating environmental damage that the attacking nation might eventually be destroyed—even if the attacked nation did not retaliate!)

Barnaby also examines ongoing and possible future developments in both American and Soviet nuclear weapons systems. He notes that such developments include both increases in the numbers of the weapons and improvements in the quality of the weapons, like greater accuracy. Such technical developments, in turn, lead to consideration of new policies for the actual use of the weapons. Some of these policies, Barnaby argues, are very dangerous. (We will return to this issue in Chapters 4 and 5, in which the debates over U.S. and Soviet nuclear weapons policies are examined, and in Chapter 6, which considers the question of how many nuclear weapons are enough.)

TYPES OF NUCLEAR WEAPONS
Frank Barnaby

Frank Barnaby is presently a Visiting Senior Fellow in the Harold E. Stassen Project for World Peace at the Hubert H. Humphrey Institute of Public Affairs at the University of Minnesota. Previously he served as Director of the Stockholm International Peace Research Institute. His many publications include *Arms Uncontrolled,* with Ronald Huisken, and *The Nuclear Arms Race: Control or Catastrophe?,* with G. P. Thomas.

Five countries—the USA, the USSR, the UK, France and China—are known to have nuclear weapons. Some believe that other countries—like Israel and South Africa—also have them but the evidence for this is inconclusive. What is certain, however, is that, of the nuclear-weapon powers, the nuclear arsenals of the USA and the USSR are enormous. In comparison, the other arsenals are pygmies. Whereas the superpowers deploy several tens of thousands of nuclear

[2] Barry M. Casper, "STOP VS. START." A slide show prepared for the Federation of American Scientists Nuclear War Education Project, available from the Nuclear War Graphics Project, 100 Nevada Street, Northfield, MN 55057.
Source: Frank Barnaby, "Types of Nuclear Weapons," in *The Nuclear Arms Race: Control or Catastrophe?,* ed. Frank Barnaby and Geoffrey Thomas (New York: St. Martin's Press, 1982), pp. 7–9. © 1982, Frank Barnaby and reprinted by permission of St. Martin's Press, Inc.

warheads, the British, French, and Chinese arsenals contain a total of a thousand or so nuclear weapons. Even though each of these smaller nuclear forces could wreak unimaginable damage, we will concentrate in this chapter on the American and Soviet nuclear arsenals simply because they are so huge that they totally dominate the others.

But before we discuss these arsenals in detail, we will describe the basic types of nuclear weapons which exist. The improvements being made in nuclear-weapon systems will then be explained and the consequences of them discussed. It will be suggested that the new nuclear military technologies themselves increase the probability of a nuclear world war. The possible ways in which such a war may occur are briefly described.

Atomic Bombs

The most basic nuclear weapon is the fission bomb (or A-bomb). A fission chain reaction is used to produce a large amount of energy in a very short time—roughly a millionth of a second—and, therefore, a very powerful explosion.

The fission occurs in a heavy material—specifically uranium or plutonium. The atomic bombs built so far have used the isotopes uranium-235 or plutonium-239 as the fissile material. A fission occurs when a neutron enters a nucleus of an atom of one of these materials, which then breaks up, or undergoes fission. When a fission occurs a large amount of energy is released, the original nucleus is split into two radioactive nuclei (the fission products), and two or three neutrons are released. These neutrons can be used to produce a self-sustaining chain reaction. A chain reaction will take place if at least one of the neutrons released in each fission causes the fission of another heavy nucleus.

There exists a critical mass of uranium-235 and plutonium-239—the smallest amount of the material in which a self-sustaining chain reaction (and hence a nuclear explosion) will take place. The critical mass depends on the nuclear properties of the material used for the fission (whether, for example, it is uranium-235 or plutonium-239), the density of the material (the higher the density the shorter the average distance travelled by a neutron before causing another fission and therefore the smaller the critical mass), the purity of the material (if materials other than fissile ones are present some neutrons may be captured by their nuclei instead of causing fission), and the physical surroundings of the material (if, for example, the material is surrounded by a medium like natural uranium, which reflects neutrons back into the material, some of the neutrons may be used for fission which would otherwise have been lost, thus reducing the critical mass).

The critical mass of, for example, a bare sphere of pure plutonium-239 metal in its densest phase would be about 10 kilograms, about the size of a small grapefruit. Using a technique called implosion, in which conventional explosive lenses are used to compress a slightly less than critical mass to a mass which is slightly greater than critical, a nuclear explosion could be achieved with less than 2 kilograms of plutonium-239. (A 2-kilogram sphere of plutonium-239 would have a radius of about 2.8 cm, smaller than a tennis ball.)

In a nuclear explosion exceedingly high temperatures (hundreds of millions of degrees Celsius) and exceedingly high pressures (hundreds of millions of bar) build up extremely rapidly (in about one-half of a millionth of a second, corresponding to the time taken for about 55 generations of fission). The mass of the fissile material expands, therefore, at very fast speeds (initially at a speed of about 1000 kilometres a second). In much less than a millionth of a second, the size and density of the mass of fissile material becomes less than critical and the chain reaction stops. The designer of a nuclear weapon must aim at keeping the fissile material together, against its tendency to fly apart, long enough to get sufficient generations of fission to produce an explosion strong enough for his purpose.

In the atomic bomb which destroyed Nagasaki, about 8 kilograms of plutonium (which contained more than 90 per cent plutonium-239) were used, in the form of two gold-clad hemispheres of plutonium metal. The plutonium was surrounded by a tamper which had two functions. Firstly, to reflect back into the plutonium some of the neutrons which escaped through the surface of the core, allowing some reduction in the mass of plutonium needed for a nuclear explosion. Secondly, and more importantly, because the tamper was made of a heavy material, its inertia helped hold together the plutonium during the explosion to contain the disintegration of the fissile material and obtain greater efficiency.

The plutonium core was surrounded by chemical explosives arranged as explosive lenses focused on the centre of the plutonium sphere. When these lenses were detonated the sphere was compressed uniformly, by the implosion. The compression increased the density of the plutonium so that the sub-critical mass was made super-critical.

The final component in the Nagasaki bomb was the 'initiator', used to initiate the fission reaction in the plutonium at precisely the right moment during the explosion of the chemical explosive lenses. The initiator consisted of a hollow sphere placed at the centre of the plutonium core. Inside the initiator was some polonium and berrylium, two elements which produce neutrons when intimately mixed. The two substances were placed separately on the opposite sides of the initiator. Explosive lenses were focused onto the surface of the initiator. At the moment of implosion the initiator was crushed, the berrylium and polonium mixed and a pulse of neutrons given off when the plutonium was super-critical.

The complete detonation of 1 kilogram of plutonium would produce an explosion equivalent to that of about 20,000 tons of TNT. The 8 kilograms of plutonium in the Nagasaki bomb produced an explosion equivalent to that of 22,000 tons of TNT. Its efficiency was, therefore, only about 10 per cent.

A major problem in designing this type of nuclear weapon for maximum efficiency is to prevent the chain reaction from being started before the greatest achievable super-criticality is reached, an eventuality called pre-initiation. If this occurs it will reduce the explosive power, or the yield, of the explosion and will also make the yield uncertain.

Pre-initiation is most likely to be caused by a neutron from spontaneous fission—fission that occurs without the stimulus of an external neutron—in the fissionable material. In 8 kilograms of plutonium-239 the average time between spontaneous fissions is only about three millionths of a second. The assembly of a plutonium bomb must, therefore, be rapid; implosion is necessary for such microsecond precision. In uranium, however, the average time between spontaneous fissions is much greater and so a gun method can be used to assemble a critical mass in a nuclear weapon.

In the Hiroshima bomb, for example, a sub-critical mass of uranium-235 was fired down a 'cannon barrel' into another sub-critical mass of uranium-235 placed in front of the 'muzzle'. When the two masses came together they formed a super-critical mass which exploded.

About 60 kilograms of uranium-235 were used in the Hiroshima bomb (of which about 700 grams underwent fission). The average time between spontaneous fissions was about one-fiftieth of a second—adequate for the gun technique. The yield of the Hiroshima bomb was equivalent to that of about 12,500 tons of TNT.

Although designs based on the Hiroshima and Nagasaki bombs might still be used by countries beginning a nuclear-weapon programme, they are crude compared with current American and Soviet nuclear warheads. The Nagasaki bomb, for example, was about 3 m long, 1.5 m wide, and weighed about 4500 kilograms. A modern American warhead weighs about 100 kilograms and has an explosive power of about 350,000 tons of TNT. Yield-to-weight ratios, the standard measure of the efficiency of a bomb, have gone from about 5000 for the Nagasaki bomb to about 3.5 million for today's best nuclear warheads. The latter figure is, in fact, close to the theoretical maximum attainable. Another indication of the sophistication of modern nuclear warheads is that they can be packed into 8-inch nuclear artillery shells.

H-Bombs

The next significant advance in nuclear warhead design after the Nagasaki bomb was the 'boosted weapon', in which fusion was used to obtain nuclear explosions with yields in the 100,000 ton (100-kiloton) range. The maximum explosive yield achievable by pure fission weapons is limited to a few tens of kilotons because the chain reaction can, in practice, be sustained for only a relatively short time.

The fusion process is the opposite to that of fission. In fusion, light nuclei are formed (fused) into heavier ones. In nuclear weapons the heavier isotopes of hydrogen—deuterium and tritium—are fused together to form helium. The reaction produces energy and is accompanied by the emission of neutrons. There is no critical mass for the fusion process and, therefore, in principle there is no limit to the explosive yield of fusion weapons—or H-bombs as they are often called.

Fission is relatively easy to start: one neutron of any speed will initiate a chain reaction in a critical mass of fissile material (such as uranium-235 or plutonium-239). But fusion is possible only if the component nuclei are given a high enough energy to overcome the repulsive electric force between them due to their like positive charges. In the H-bomb this energy is provided by raising the temperature of the fusion material. Hence H-bombs are also called thermonuclear weapons.

In order to make the deuterium-tritium fusion reaction work, a temperature of a hundred million degrees Celsius or so is required. This can be provided only by an A-bomb in which such a temperature is achieved at the moment of the explosion. An H-bomb, therefore, consists of a fission stage (the A-bomb which acts as a trigger), and a fusion stage (in which hydrogen is ignited by the heat produced by the trigger).

The energy released from an H-bomb comes from the fission trigger and the fusion material. But if the fusion weapon is surrounded by a shell of uranium-238 the high energy neutrons produced in the fusion process will cause additional fissions in the uranium shell (low-energy neutrons do not cause uranium-238 to undergo fission). This technique can be used to enhance considerably the explosive power of an H-bomb. Such a weapon is called a fission-fusion-fission device. On average, about a half of the yield from a typical thermonuclear weapon will come from fission and the other half from fusion.

H-bombs are much more difficult to design than A-bombs. The problem is to prevent the A-bomb trigger from blowing the whole weapon apart before enough fusion material has been ignited to give the required explosive yield. Sufficient energy has to be delivered to the fusion material to start the thermonuclear reaction in a time much shorter than the time it takes for the explosion to occur. This requires the energy to be delivered with a speed approaching the speed of light. It is this requirement that makes the design of an H-bomb much more sophisticated than that of an A-bomb.

H-bombs of very large yields have been exploded. For example, the Soviet Union exploded one in 1962 with a yield equal to that of 58 million tons of TNT (megatons), equivalent to about 3000 Nagasaki bombs. Such huge bombs, however, make little sense. The largest city would be completely devastated by an H-bomb of 10 megatons or so. . . .

THE EFFECTS OF NUCLEAR WEAPONS: GENERAL DESCRIPTION OF EFFECTS
Congressional Office of Technology Assessment

The Office of Technology Assessment (OTA) is a research arm of the U.S. Congress, given the mandate of undertaking nonpartisan research on issues involving science and public policy.

General Description of Effects

The energy of a nuclear explosion is released in a number of different ways:
- an explosive blast, which is qualitatively similar to the blast from ordinary chemical explosions, but which has somewhat different effects because it is typically so much larger;
- direct nuclear radiation;
- direct thermal radiation, most of which takes the form of visible light;
- pulses of electrical and magnetic energy, called electromagnetic pulse (EMP); and
- the creation of a variety of radioactive particles, which are thrown up into the air by the force of the blast, and are called radioactive fallout when they return to Earth.

The distribution of the bomb's energy among these effects depends on its size and on the details of its design, but a general description is possible.

BLAST

Most damage to cities from large weapons comes from the explosive blast. The blast drives air away from the site of the explosion, producing sudden changes in air pressure (called static overpressure) that can crush objects, and high winds (called dynamic pressure) that can move them suddenly or knock them down. In general, large buildings are destroyed by the overpressure, while people and objects such as trees and utility poles are destroyed by the wind.

Source: U.S. Congress, Office of Technology Assessment, "General Description of Effects," in *The Effects of Nuclear War* (Washington, D.C.: U.S. Government Printing Office, 1977), pp. 3–12.

For example, consider the effects of a 1-megaton (Mt) air burst on things 4 miles [6 km] away. The overpressure will be in excess of 5 pounds per square inch (psi), which will exert a force of more than 180 tons on the wall of a typical two-story house. At the same place, there would be a wind of 160 mph [255 km]; while 5 psi is not enough to crush a man, a wind of 180 mph would create fatal collisions between people and nearby objects.

The magnitude of the blast effect (generally measured in pounds per square inch) diminishes with distance from the center of the explosion. It is related in a more complicated way to the height of the burst above ground level. For any given distance from the center of the explosion, there is an optimum burst height that will produce the greatest overpressure, and the greater the distance the greater the optimum burst height. As a result, a burst on the surface produces the greatest overpressure at very close ranges (which is why surface bursts are used to attack very hard, very small targets such as missile silos), but less overpressure than an air burst at somewhat longer ranges. Raising the height of the burst reduces the overpressure directly under the bomb, but widens the area at which a given smaller overpressure is produced. Thus, an attack on factories with a 1-Mt weapon might use an air burst at an altitude of 8,000 feet [2,400 m], which would maximize the area (about 28 mi^2 [7,200 hectares]) that would receive 10 psi or more of overpressure.

Table 3 shows the ranges of overpressures and effects from such a blast.

When a nuclear weapon is detonated on or near the surface of the Earth, the blast digs out a large crater. Some of the material that used to be in the crater is deposited on the rim of the crater; the rest is carried up into the air and returns to Earth as fallout. An explosion that is farther above the Earth's surface than the radius of the fireball does not dig a crater and produces negligible immediate fallout.

For the most part, blast kills people by indirect means rather than by direct pressure. While a human body can withstand up to 30 psi of simple overpressure, the winds associated with as little as 2 to 3 psi could be expected to blow people out of typical modern office buildings. Most blast deaths result from the collapse of occupied buildings, from people being blown into objects, or from buildings or smaller objects being blown onto or into people. Clearly, then, it is impossible to calculate with any precision how many people would be killed by a given blast—the effects would vary from building to building.

In order to estimate the number of casualties from any given explosion, it is necessary to make assumptions about the proportion of people who will be killed or injured at any given overpressure. The assumptions used in this chapter are shown in figure 1. They are relatively conservative. For example, weapons tests suggest that a typical residence will be collapsed by an overpressure of about 5 psi. People standing in such a residence have a 50-percent

Table 3
Blast Effects of a 1-Mt Explosion 8,000 ft Above the Earth's Surface

Distance from ground zero (stat. miles)	(kilometers)	Peak overpressure	Peak wind velocity (mph)	Typical blast effects
.8	1.3	20 psi	470	Reinforced concrete structures are leveled.
3.0	4.8	10 psi	290	Most factories and commercial buildings are collapsed. Small wood-frame and brick residences destroyed and distributed as debris.
4.4	7.0	5 psi	160	Lightly constructed commercial buildings and typical residences are destroyed; heavier construction is severely damaged.
5.9	9.5	3 psi	95	Walls of typical steel-frame buildings are blown away; severe damage to residences. Winds sufficient to kill people in the open.
11.6	18.6	1 psi	35	Damage to structures; people endangered by flying glass and debris.

chance of being killed by an overpressure of 3.5 psi, but people who are lying down at the moment the blast wave hits have a 50-percent chance of surviving a 7-psi overpressure. The calculations used here assume a mean lethal overpressure of 5 to 6 psi for people in residences, meaning that more than half of those whose houses are blown down on top of them will nevertheless survive. Some studies use a simpler technique: they assume that the number of people who survive in areas receiving more than 5 psi equal the number of people killed in areas receiving less than 5 psi, and hence that fatalities are equal to the number of people inside a 5-psi ring.

DIRECT NUCLEAR RADIATION

Nuclear weapons inflict ionizing radiation on people, animals, and plants in two different ways. Direct radiation occurs at the time of the explosion; it can be very intense, but its range is limited. Fallout radiation is received from

Figure 1.   Vulnerability of Population in Various Overpressure Zones

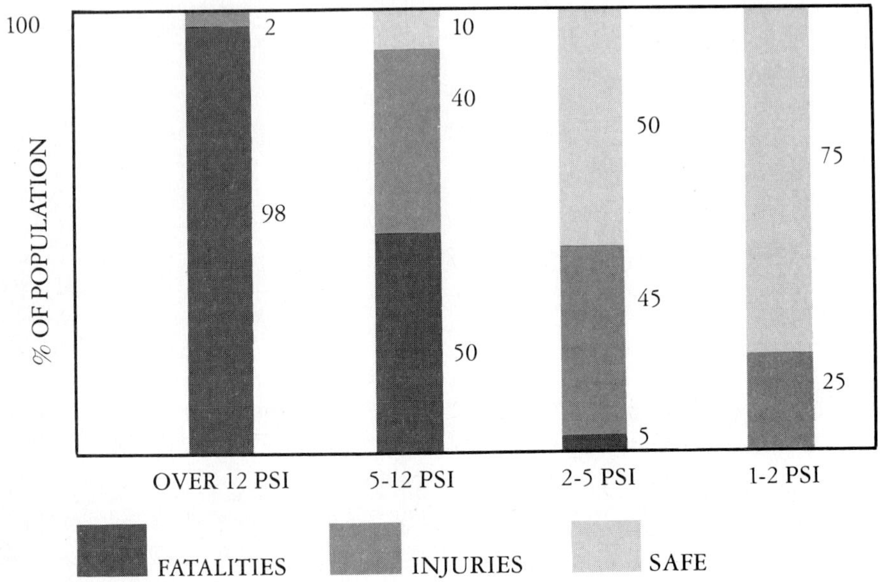

particles that are made radioactive by the effects of the explosion, and subsequently distributed at varying distances from the site of the blast. Fallout is discussed in a subsequent section.

For large nuclear weapons, the range of intense direct radiation is less than the range of lethal blast and thermal radiation effects. However, in the case of smaller weapons, direct radiation may be the lethal effect with the greatest range. Direct radiation did substantial damage to the residents of Hiroshima and Nagasaki.

Human response to ionizing radiation is subject to great scientific uncertainty and intense controversy. It seems likely that even small doses of radiation do some harm. To understand the effects of nuclear weapons, one must distinguish between short- and long-term effects:

- **Short-Term Effects.**—A dose of 600 rem within a short period of time (6 to 7 days) has a 90-percent chance of creating a fatal illness, with death occurring within a few weeks. (A rem or "roentgen-equivalent-man" is a measure of biological damage: a "rad" is a measure of radiation energy absorbed; a roentgen is a measure of radiation energy; for our purposes it may be assumed that 100 roentgens produce 100 rads and 100 rem.) The precise shape of the curve showing the death rate as a function of radiation dose is not known in the region between

300 and 600 rem, but a dose of 450 rem within a short time is estimated to create a fatal illness in half the people exposed to it; the
other half would get very sick, but would recover. A dose of 300 rem
might kill about 10 percent of those exposed. A dose of 200 to 450
rem will cause a severe illness from which most people would recover;
however, this illness would render people highly susceptible to other
diseases or infections. A dose of 50 to 200 rem will cause nausea and
lower resistance to other diseases, but medical treatment is not required. A dose below 50 rem will not cause any short-term effects
that the victim will notice, but will nevertheless do long-term damage.

- **Long-Term Effects.**—The effects of smaller doses of radiation are long
  term, and measured in a statistical way. A dose of 50 rem generally
  produces no short-term effects; however, if a large population were
  exposed to 50 rems, somewhere between 0.4 and 2.5 percent of them
  would be expected to contract fatal cancer (after some years) as a result. There would also be serious genetic effects for some fraction of
  those exposed. Lower doses produce lower effects. There is a scientific
  controversy about whether any dose of radiation, however small, is really
  safe. . . . It should be clearly understood, however, that a large nuclear war would expose the survivors, however well sheltered, to levels
  of radiation far greater than the U.S. Government considers safe in
  peacetime.

THERMAL RADIATION

Approximately 35 percent of the energy from a nuclear explosion is an intense
burst of thermal radiation, i.e., heat. The effects are roughly analogous to the
effect of a 2-second flash from an enormous sunlamp. Since the thermal radiation travels at the speed of light (actually a bit slower, since it is deflected by
particles in the atmosphere), the flash of light and heat precedes the blast wave
by several seconds, just as lightning is seen before the thunder is heard.

The visible light will produce "flashblindness" in people who are looking in the direction of the explosion. Flashblindness can last for several minutes, after which recovery is total. A 1-Mt explosion could cause flashblindness
at distances as great as 13 miles [21 km] on a clear day, or 53 miles [85 km]
on a clear night. If the flash is focused through the lens of the eye, a permanent retinal burn will result. At Hiroshima and Nagasaki, there were many
cases of flashblindness, but only one case of retinal burn, among the survivors.
On the other hand, anyone flashblinded while driving a car could easily cause
permanent injury to himself and to others.

Skin burns result from higher intensities of light, and therefore take place closer to the point of explosion. A 1-Mt explosion can cause first-degree burns (equivalent to a bad sunburn) at distances of about 7 miles [11 km], second-degree burns (producing blisters that lead to infection if untreated, and permanent scars) at distances of about 6 miles [10 km], and third-degree burns (which destroy skin tissue) at distances of up to 5 miles [8 km]. Third-degree burns over 24 percent of the body, or second-degree burns over 30 percent of the body, will result in serious shock, and will probably prove fatal unless prompt, specialized medical care is available. The entire United States has facilities to treat 1,000 or 2,000 severe burn cases; a single nuclear weapon could produce more than 10,000.

The distance at which burns are dangerous depends heavily on weather conditions. Extensive moisture or a high concentration of particles in the air (smog) absorbs thermal radiation. Thermal radiation behaves like sunlight, so objects create shadows behind which the thermal radiation is indirect (reflected) and less intense. Some conditions, such as ice on the ground or low white clouds over clean air, can increase the range of dangerous thermal radiation.

FIRES

The thermal radiation from a nuclear explosion can directly ignite kindling materials. In general, ignitible materials outside the house, such as leaves or newspapers, are not surrounded by enough combustible material to generate a self-sustaining fire. Fires more likely to spread are those caused by thermal radiation passing through windows to ignite beds and overstuffed furniture inside houses. A rather substantial amount of combustible material must burn vigorously for 10 to 20 minutes before the room, or whole house, becomes inflamed. The blast wave, which arrives after most thermal energy has been expended, will have some extinguishing effect on the fires. However, studies and tests of this effect have been very contradictory, so the extent to which blast can be counted on to extinguish fire starts remains quite uncertain.

Another possible source of fires, which might be more damaging in urban areas, is indirect. Blast damage to stores, water heaters, furnaces, electrical circuits, or gas lines would ignite fires where fuel is plentiful.

The best estimates are that at the 5-psi level about 10 percent of all buildings would sustain a serious fire, while at 2 psi about 2 percent would have serious fires, usually arising from secondary sources such as blast-damaged utilities rather than direct thermal radiation.

It is possible that individual fires, whether caused by thermal radiation or by blast damage to utilities, furnaces, etc., would coalesce into a mass fire that would consume all structures over a large area. This possibility has been intensely studied, but there remains no basis for estimating its probability. Mass fires could be of two kinds: a "firestorm," in which violent inrushing winds create extremely high temperatures but prevent the fire from spreading radially outwards, and a "conflagration," in which a fire spreads along a front. Hamburg, Tokyo, and Hiroshima experienced firestorms in World War II; the Great Chicago Fire and the San Francisco Earthquake Fire were conflagrations. A firestorm is likely to kill a high proportion of the people in the area of the fire, through heat and through asphyxiation of those in shelters. A conflagration spreads slowly enough so that people in its path can escape, though a conflagration caused by a nuclear attack might take a heavy toll of those too injured to walk. Some believe that firestorms in U.S. or Soviet cities are unlikely because the density of flammable materials ("fuel loading") is too low—the ignition of a firestorm is thought to require a fuel loading of at least 8 lbs/ft^2 (Hamburg had 32), compared to fuel loading of 2 lbs/ft^2 in a typical U.S. suburb and 5 lbs/ft^2 in a neighborhood of two-story brick rowhouses. The likelihood of a conflagration depends on the geography of the area, the speed and direction of the wind, and details of building construction. Another variable is whether people and equipment are available to fight fires before they can coalesce and spread.

ELECTROMAGNETIC PULSE

Electromagnetic pulse (EMP) is an electromagnetic wave similar to radio waves, which results from secondary reactions occurring when the nuclear gamma radiation is absorbed in the air or ground. It differs from the usual radio waves in two important ways. First, it creates much higher electric field strengths. Whereas a radio signal might produce a thousandth of a volt or less in a receiving antenna, an EMP pulse might produce thousands of volts. Secondly, it is a single pulse of energy that disappears completely in a small fraction of a second. In this sense, it is rather similar to the electrical signal from lightning, but the rise in voltage is typically a hundred times faster. This means that most equipment designed to protect electrical facilities from lightning works too slowly to be effective against EMP.

The strength of an EMP pulse is measured in volts per meter (v/m), and is an indication of the voltage that would be produced in an exposed antenna. A nuclear weapon burst on the surface will typically produce an EMP of tens of thousands of v/m at short distances (the 10-psi range) and thousands of v/m at longer distances (1-psi range). Air bursts produce less EMP, but high-altitude bursts (above 19 miles [31 km]) produce very strong EMP, with ranges of hundreds of thousands of miles. An attacker might detonate a few weapons at such altitudes in an effort to destroy or damage the communications and electric power system of the victim.

There is no evidence that EMP is a physical threat to humans. However, electrical or electronic systems, particularly those connected to long wires such as powerlines or antennas, can undergo either of two kinds of damage. First, there can be actual physical damage to an electrical component such as shorting of a capacitor or burnout of a transistor, which would require replacement or repair before the equipment can again be used. Second, at a lesser level, there can be a temporary operational upset, frequently requiring some effort to restore operation. For example, instabilities induced in power grids can cause the entire system to shut itself down, upsetting computers that must be started again. Base radio stations are vulnerable not only from the loss of commercial power but from direct damage to electronic components connected to the antenna. In general, portable radio transmitter/receivers with relatively short antennas are not susceptible to EMP. The vulnerability of the telephone system to EMP could not be determined.

FALLOUT

While any nuclear explosion in the atmosphere produces some fallout, the fallout is far greater if the burst is on the surface, or at least low enough for the fireball to touch the ground. . . . the fallout from air bursts alone poses long-term health hazards, but they are trivial compared to the other consequences of a nuclear attack. The significant hazards come from particles scooped up from the ground and irradiated by the nuclear explosion.

The radioactive particles that rise only a short distance (those in the "stem" of the familiar mushroom cloud) will fall back to earth within a matter of minutes, landing close to the center of the explosion. Such particles are unlikely to cause many deaths, because they will fall in areas where most people have already been killed. However, the radioactivity will complicate efforts at rescue or eventual reconstruction.

The radioactive particles that rise higher will be carried some distance by the wind before returning to Earth, and hence the area and intensity of the fallout is strongly influenced by local weather conditions. Much of the material is simply blown downwind in a long plume. . . . The plume would be longer and thinner if the winds were more intense and shorter and somewhat more broad if the winds were slower. If the winds were from a different direction, the plume would cover a different area. . . . Thus wind direction can make an enormous difference. Rainfall can also have a significant influence on the ways in which radiation from smaller weapons is deposited, since rain will carry contaminated particles to the ground. The areas receiving such contaminated rainfall would become "hot spots," with greater radiation intensity than their surroundings. When the radiation intensity from fallout is great enough to pose an immediate threat to health, fallout will generally be visible as a thin layer of dust.

The amount of radiation produced by fallout materials will decrease with time as the radioactive materials "decay." Each material decays at a different rate. Materials that decay rapidly give off intense radiation for a short period of time while long-lived materials radiate less intensely but for longer periods. Immediately after the fallout is deposited in regions surrounding the blast site, radiation intensities will be very high as the short-lived materials decay. These intense radiations will decrease relatively quickly. The intensity will have fallen by a factor of 10 after 7 hours, a factor of 100 after 49 hours and a factor of 1,000 after 2 weeks. . . .

Some radioactive particles will be thrust into the stratosphere, and may not return to Earth for some years. In this case only the particularly long-lived particles pose a threat, and they are dispersed around the world over a range of latitudes. Some fallout from U.S. and Soviet weapons tests in the 1950's and early 1960's can still be detected. There are also some particles in the immediate fallout (notably Strontium 90 and Cesium 137) that remain radioactive for years. . . .

The biological effects of fallout radiation are substantially the same as those from direct radiation, discussed above. People exposed to enough fallout radiation will die, and those exposed to lesser amounts may become ill. . . .

There is some public interest in the question of the consequences if a nuclear weapon destroyed a nuclear powerplant. The core of a power reactor contains large quantities of radioactive material, which tends to decay more slowly (and hence less intensely) than the fallout particles from a nuclear weapon explosion. Consequently, fallout from a destroyed nuclear reactor (whose destruction would, incidentally, require a high-accuracy surface burst) would not be much more intense (during the first day) or widespread than "ordinary" fallout, but would stay radioactive for a considerably longer time. Areas receiving such fallout would have to be evacuated or decontaminated; otherwise survivors would have to stay in shelters for months.

COMBINED INJURIES (SYNERGISM)

So far the discussion of each major effect (blast, nuclear radiation, and thermal radiation) has explained how this effect in isolation causes deaths and injuries to humans. It is customary to calculate the casualties accompanying hypothetical nuclear explosion as follows: for any given range, the effect most likely to kill people is selected and its consequences calculated, while the other effects are ignored. It is obvious that combined injuries are possible, but there are no generally accepted ways of calculating their probability. What data do exist seem to suggest that calculations of single effects are not too inaccurate for immediate deaths, but that deaths occurring some time after the explosion may well be due to combined causes, and hence are omitted from most calculations. Some of the obvious possibilities are:

- **Nuclear Radiation Combined With Thermal Radiation.**—Severe burns place considerable stress on the blood system, and often cause anemia. It is clear from experiments with laboratory animals that exposure of a burn victim to more than 100 rems of radiation will impair the blood's ability to support recovery from the thermal burns. Hence a sublethal radiation dose could make it impossible to recover from a burn that, without the radiation, would not cause death.

- **Nuclear Radiation Combined With Mechanical Injuries.**—Mechanical injuries, the indirect results of blast, take many forms. Flying glass and wood will cause puncture wounds. Winds may blow people into obstructions, causing broken bones, concussions, and internal injuries. Persons caught in a collapsing building can suffer many similar mechanical injuries. There is evidence that all of these types of injuries are more serious if the person has been exposed to 300 rems, particularly if treatment is delayed. Blood damage will clearly make a victim more susceptible to blood loss and infection. This has been confirmed in laboratory animals in which a borderline lethal radiation dose was followed a week later by a blast overpressure that alone would have produced a low level of prompt lethality. The number of prompt and delayed (from radiation) deaths both increased over what would be expected from the single effect alone.

- **Thermal Radiation and Mechanical Injuries.**—There is no information available about the effects of this combination, beyond the common sense observation that since each can place a great stress on a healthy body, the combination of injuries that are individually tolerable may subject the body to a total stress that it cannot tolerate. Mechanical injuries should be prevalent at about the distance from a nuclear explosion that produces sublethal burns, so this synergism could be an important one.

In general, synergistic effects are most likely to produce death when each of the injuries alone is quite severe. Because the uncertainties of nuclear effects are compounded when one tries to estimate the likelihood of two or more serious but (individually) nonfatal injuries, there really is no way to estimate the number of victims.

A further dimension of the problem is the possible synergy between injuries and environmental damage. To take one obvious example, poor sanitation (due to the loss of electrical power and water pressure) can clearly compound the effects of any kind of serious injury. Another possibility is that an injury would so immobilize the victim that he would be unable to escape from a fire.

CURRENT AND FUTURE NUCLEAR WEAPONS SYSTEMS
Frank Barnaby

In this next selection, Barnaby offers a more detailed look at current and future nuclear arsenals, and he includes in his discussion the newer tactical nuclear weapons. See also Appendix A for an updated look at current nuclear arsenals.

The Soviet and American Strategic Nuclear Arsenals

Current operational nuclear weapons have a vast range of explosive power, varying between 100 tons and at least 25,000,000 tons of TNT equivalent. (In practice, the minimum yield of a nuclear weapon is about 0.1 ton. This is because the chemical explosive needed for the implosion lens weighs at least about 100 kilograms. In principle, any amount of fission energy could be added to this yield. About 100 kilograms is also, of course, the minimum physical weight of a nuclear weapon. Some modern nuclear warheads, in fact, weigh little more than 100 kilograms.) To put these numbers into some sort of perspective, all of the bombs dropped in the eight most violent years of the Vietnam war totalled only about 4 million tons. *A single American B-52 strategic nuclear bomber can carry more explosive power than that used in all the wars in history.*

American strategic* nuclear forces carry about 9800 nuclear warheads, with a total explosive power equivalent to that of about 3400 million tonnes [metric tons] of high explosive. . . . Soviet strategic nuclear forces could deliver about 7000 nuclear warheads, with a total explosive power equivalent to that of about 4200 million tons of high explosive. . . . In the tactical nuclear arsenals there are probably about 35,000 nuclear warheads—about 20,000 American and about 15,000 Soviet—each on average several times more powerful than the Hiroshima bomb. These add another 4500 or so million tons of high-explosive equivalent to make a grand total of about 12,000 million

---

Source: Frank Barnaby, "Current and Future Nuclear Weapons Systems," in *The Nuclear Arms Race: Control or Catastrophe?*, ed. Frank Barnaby and Geoffrey Thomas (New York: St. Martin's Press, 1982), pp. 16–29. © 1982, Frank Barnaby and reprinted by permission of St. Martin's Press, Inc.

Editors' Note: Strategic nuclear weapons are those based in either the Soviet Union or the United States and used against the other's homeland. *Tactical* nuclear weapons are not targeted from one homeland to the other, as, for example, nuclear weapons designed for use on or around the battlefield in Europe.

tons—the equivalent of about 1 million Hiroshima bombs, or about 3 tons of TNT for every man, woman and child on earth.

Strategic nuclear weapons are deployed on intercontinental ballistic missiles (ICBMs), submarine-launched ballistic missiles (SLBMs), and strategic bombers. Soviet and American ICBMs have ranges of about 11,000 km, modern SLBMs have ranges of about 7000 km, and strategic bombers have ranges of about 12,000 km. Range is the main distinguishing feature between strategic and tactical nuclear weapons, the former having long (intercontinental) ranges.

Some ballistic missiles carry multiple warheads. Modern multiple warheads are independently targetable on targets hundreds of kilometres apart. These are called multiple independently targetable re-entry vehicles or MIRVs.

Strategic bombers carry free-fall nuclear bombs and air-to-ground missiles fitted with nuclear warheads. The most modern of these missiles is the American air-launched cruise missile (ALCM) which can fly over a range of about 2500 km.

The United States now has 1653 ballistic missiles (1053 ICBMs and 600 SLBMs) of which 1070 (550 ICBMs and 520 SLBMs) are fitted with MIRVs. Some 340 B-52s are operational as long-range strategic bombers.

The Soviet Union has deployed 2348 ballistic missiles (1398 ICBMs and 950 SLBMs), of which about 1010 (818 ICBMs and 192 SLBMs) are MIRVed. About 150 of its long-range bombers are probably assigned strategic roles.

Tactical nuclear weapons are deployed in a wide variety of systems, including howitzer and artillery shells, ground-to-ground ballistic missiles, free-fall bombs, air-to-ground missiles, anti-aircraft missiles, atomic demolition munitions (land mines), submarine-launched cruise missiles, submarine-launched ballistic missiles, torpedoes, naval mines and anti-submarine rockets. Land-based systems have ranges varying from about 12 km (artillery shells) to a few thousand km (intermediate range ballistic missiles). The explosive power of these warheads varies from about 100 tons to about a megaton.

The USA deploys tactical nuclear weapons in Western Europe, Asia, and the United States, and with the Atlantic and Pacific fleets. The USSR deploys its tactical nuclear weapons in Eastern Europe, in the Western USSR, and East of the Urals.

Future Developments in the Nuclear Arsenals

Although, according to present plans, there will be significant increases in the number of warheads in the Soviet and American arsenals over the next few years, mainly because of the deployment of more MIRVed ICBMs and SLBMs and cruise missiles, the most important developments in nuclear weapons in the foreseeable future will be qualitative improvements. There are so many nuclear weapons in the arsenals that any further increases in numbers will, in any case, make no sense, from a military or from any other point of view. This has been true for many years now.

The most important qualitative advances in nuclear weapons are those which improve the accuracy and reliability of nuclear weapon systems.

MODERNIZATION OF US AND SOVIET STRATEGIC NUCLEAR WEAPONS

The accuracy of a nuclear warhead is normally measured by its circular error probable (CEP), the radius of the circle centered on the target within which half of a large number of warheads, fired at the target, will fall. In both the USA and the USSR, the CEPs of ICBMs and SLBMs are being continually improved. In the USA, for example, improvements are being made in the computer of the NS-20 guidance system in the Minuteman III ICBMs, involving better mathematical descriptions of the in-flight performances of the inertial platform and accelerometers, and better pre-launch calibration of the gyroscopes and accelerometers. With these guidance improvements, the CEP of the Minuteman III will probably decrease from about 350 to about 200 metres. At the same time the Mark-12 re-entry vehicle and the W62 170-kiloton nuclear warhead were being replaced with the Mark-12A re-entry vehicle and the W78 350-kiloton nuclear warhead. The plan is to put the new warheads on 300 of the existing 550 Minuteman III missiles. The Mark-12A will have roughly the same weight, size, radar cross-section and aerodynamic characteristics as the Mark-12.

Mark-12A warheads with the higher accuracy will be able to destroy Soviet ICBMs in silos hardened to about 1500 psi (pounds per square inch) with a probability of about 57 per cent for one shot and about 95 per cent for two shots. Superior arming and fusing devices will provide more control over the height at which the warhead is exploded and, hence, the damage done.

The upgraded land-based ICBM force will significantly increase US nuclear war-fighting capabilities. These will be further increased by the MX missile system, now under development.

The MX system includes both a new ICBM and a related basing scheme. The guidance for the MX missile will probably be based on the advanced inertial reference sphere (AIRS), an 'all-attitude' system which can correct for movements of the missile along the ground before it is launched. A CEP of about 100 m should be achieved with this system. If the MX warhead is provided with terminal guidance, using a laser or radar system to guide the warhead on to its target, CEPs of a few tens of metres may be possible.

No decision has yet been made about the yield and other characteristics of the MX warhead but each missile will probably carry ten warheads.

The launch-weight of the MX will probably be about 86,000 kg, about 2.4 times more than that of the Minuteman III, and the throw-weight about 3500 kg. The three MX booster stages will use advanced solid propellants, very light motor cases, and advanced nozzles to produce nearly twice the propulsion efficiency of the Minuteman.

The MX missile, by design, could fit into the existing Minuteman silos. But, if deployed, a mobile basing system will probably be used. The first missiles will probably be operational in 1986.

The most formidable Soviet ICBM is the SS-18, or the RS-20 in Soviet terminology. This is thought currently to have a CEP of about 500 m. This accuracy will probably improve to about 250 m within a few years. Each SS-18 warhead probably has an explosive power equivalent to about 500 kilotons. With the higher accuracy, the warhead will have about the same silo-destruction capability as the new US Minuteman III warhead.

The USSR also has the SS-19 ICBM (the RS-18). This is thought to be more accurate than the SS-18 and to be equipped with a similar warhead. Some of both the SS-18s and -19s are MIRVed. So far, a total of 668 SS-18s and -19s have been deployed. If these are MIRVed to the extent allowed by the SALT II Treaty, they are equipped with a total of about 4500 warheads. The other Soviet MIRVed ICBM, the SS-17 (or RS-16), has been tested with four warheads. So far, about 150 SS-17s have been deployed. According to US sources, the USSR is developing at least two new types of ICBM.

The Soviet MIRVed strategic missile force is clearly an increasing threat to the 1000-strong US Minuteman ICBM force as the accuracy and reliability of the Soviet warheads are improved and their number increases.

STRATEGIC NUCLEAR SUBMARINES

The quality of strategic nuclear submarines and the ballistic missiles they carry is also being continuously improved. In the USA, for example, the present Polaris and Poseidon strategic nuclear submarine force is being augmented, and may eventually be replaced, by Trident submarines. The Polaris submarines now operating will be phased out by the end of 1982. Thirty-one Poseidon submarines are now operating.

Trident submarines will be equipped with a new SLBM, the Trident I, the successor of the Poseidon C-3 SLBM. Yet another SLBM, the Trident II, is currently being developed for eventual deployment on Trident submarines.

In the meantime, the Trident I missiles will also be deployed on Poseidon submarines. The first of 12 Poseidons to be modified to carry Trident I missiles went to sea in October 1979; the others should be ready by 1984.

The first Trident submarine, the USS Ohio, became operational in 1981. According to current plans, at least 8 Trident submarines (these have already been ordered) will become operational during the 1980s. But the ultimate size of the Trident fleet has yet to be decided.

The Trident displaces 18,700 tons when submerged. Its enormous size can be judged from the facts that it is twice as large as a Polaris/Poseidon submarine, which has a submerged displacement of about 8300 tons, and is as large as the new British through-deck cruiser (displacement 19,500 tons).

Each Trident will carry twenty-four SLBMs. The Trident I SLBM is designed to have a maximum range of 7400 km when equipped with eight 100-kiloton MIRVed warheads. Even longer ranges can be achieved if the missile has a smaller payload. The Poseidon SLBM, which it replaces, can carry up to fourteen 40-kiloton MIRVed warheads, but has a maximum range of only 4600 km. With the longer-range missile, Trident submarines will be able to operate in many times more ocean area and still remain within range of its targets. The long-range missiles will also allow Trident submarines to operate closer to US shores and still reach their targets, giving the submarines greater protection against Soviet anti-submarine warfare (ASW) activities.

Trident I, a two-stage solid propellant rocket, is provided with a stellar-aided inertial guidance system to provide course corrections. The CEP of the Trident SLBM is probably about 500 m at a maximum range, whereas that of the Poseidon SLBM is about 550 m, and that of the Polaris I SLBM is about 900 m. The development and deployment of mid-course guidance techniques for SLBMs and the more accurate navigation of missile submarines will steadily increase the accuracy of the missiles.

SLBM warheads may eventually be fitted with terminal guidance, using radar, laser or some other device to guide them onto their targets after re-entry into the earth's atmosphere. This could give CEPs of a few tens of metres. SLBMs will then be so accurate as to cease to be only deterrence weapons aimed at enemy cities, and will become nuclear war-fighting weapons.

The most modern Soviet SLBM is the 7400 km range SS-N-18, equipped with three 200-kt MIRVs. So far, 192 SS-N-18s have been put to sea, 16 on each of 12 Delta-class submarines, the most modern Soviet strategic nuclear submarines. The other main Soviet SLBM is the SS-N-8, with a range of 8000 km and a single 1-Mt warhead. Two hundred and ninety SS-N-8s are deployed on 22 Delta-class submarines.

The USSR also operates about 30 Yankee-class strategic nuclear submarines, each carrying 16 SS-N-6 SLBMs, a 3000 km range missile carrying either a 1-Mt warhead or two 200-kt warheads. In all, the USSR has 950 SLBMs, 192 of them MIRVed.

The USSR is developing a new ballistic-missile firing submarine—the Typhoon—which is apparently even bigger than the American Trident. A new SLBM, the SS-NX-20, is also under development, presumably for deployment on the Typhoon.

Soviet SLBMs are less accurate than are US ones. The SS-N-6 is thought to have a CEP of about 1000 m. But one can expect that the accuracy of Soviet SLBMs will be steadily improved and that more Soviet MIRVed SLBMs will be deployed.

Current US ballistic missiles carry 7033 independently targetable warheads. Of these missile warheads, 4880 are sea-based. US ballistic missiles have a total explosive yield of about 1820 Mt, of which about 330 Mt are carried by SLBMs. US sea-based strategic nuclear forces account, therefore, for about 70 per cent of the missile warheads. If all US strategic warheads, on bomber and missiles, are included, the sea-based forces account for about 50 per cent of the number.

Almost all Soviet strategic nuclear warheads are deployed on ballistic missiles; the USSR operates no more than 150 strategic bombers and there is no evidence that they are assigned an intercontinental role. There are said to be about 7140 independently targetable Soviet missile warheads. Of these, about 1300, or 20 per cent, are probably carried by SLBMs, while the rest are on ICBMS. The SLBM warheads probably have a total explosive yield of about 770 Mt out of a total missile megatonnage of about 4100 Mt. According to US sources, the Soviet Union normally has only about one-seventh of its strategic submarines (about ten boats) at sea at any one time. The land-based ICBM force is, at present, therefore, by far the most important component of the Soviet strategic nuclear arsenal.

CRUISE MISSILE

The US strategic bomber force, the third component of America's strategic triad, will be modernized by equipping B-52 strategic bombers with air-launched cruise missiles (ALCMs). The ALCM is a small, long-range, sub-sonic, very accurate, nuclear-armed, winged vehicle. ALCMs can be launched against Soviet targets by bombers penetrating Soviet defenses or from outside Soviet territory.

According to current plans, ALCMs should become operational in December 1982, when the first B-52G squadron is loaded with cruise missiles under the aircraft's wings. Full operational capability is planned for 1990, when all 151 B-52G aircraft will be loaded, each with 12 ALCMs under the wings and 8 in the bomb bays. ALCMs will about double the number of nuclear weapons these aircraft carry.

NEW TACTICAL NUCLEAR WEAPONS

Many of the 7000 or so tactical nuclear weapons in NATO countries in Western Europe were put there during the late 1950s and early 1960s. Since nuclear weapons have a lifetime of about 20 years, these are about due for replacement. In the meantime, new types of nuclear weapons have been developed and the plan is to replace the old nuclear weapons with some of these new types.

Among the new types planned for NATO are Pershing II missiles and ground-launched cruise missiles. These weapons are so accurate as to be perceived as nuclear war-fighting weapons. In December 1979, NATO decided to deploy 108 Pershing IIs and 464 cruise missiles, starting at the end of 1983.

Although less accurate than the American weapons, the Soviet SS-20 intermediate-range ballistic missile—a new type of Soviet tactical nuclear weapon—is accurate enough, or will soon be made so, to be regarded as a nuclear war-fighting weapon, given the large explosive yield of its warhead. About 250 were deployed in mid-1981, about 60 per cent targetted on Western Europe and the rest targetted on China.

THE SS-20

The Soviet SS-20, a two-stage mobile missile, was first deployed in 1977. The missile carries three MIRVs. With these warheads its range is said to be about 5000 km.

The yield of each SS-20 warhead is estimated by Western sources to be between 150 and 500 kilotons and the CEP is said to be about 400 m.

THE PERSHING II MISSILE

The Pershing II missile will replace the Pershing I missile, first deployed in 1962.

Pershing II will use the same rocket components as Pershing I. But there the similarity ends. Pershing II will be provided with a formidable new guidance system called RADAG. In the terminal phase of the trajectory, when the warhead is getting close to the target, a video radar scans the target area and the image is compared with a reference image stored in the computer carried by the warhead before the missile [is] able to penetrate a significant distance into the USSR: vanes . . . guide the warhead onto the target with accuracy unprecedented for a ballistic missile with a range of about 1700 km. The CEP of Pershing II is about 45 m.

Pershing II has double the range of Pershing I (750 km) because it has new rocket motors and uses a new highly efficient solid fuel. The missile is the only NATO ballistic missile able to penetrate a significant distance into the USSR: it could, for example, reach Moscow from the Federal Republic of Germany.

The replacement of existing tactical nuclear weapons with new types is likely to reduce somewhat the total number deployed but the reduction is unlikely to be very significant. Over the next few years, the number deployed in NATO countries in Western Europe may, for example, decrease from about 7000 to about 6000. A similar reduction may occur on the Warsaw Pact side.

THE GROUND-LAUNCHED CRUISE MISSILE (GLCM)

The GLCMs to be deployed in Europe will carry light-weight 200-kt nuclear warheads. These missiles are not only very accurate, with CEPs of about 40 m, but, although flying at sub-sonic speeds, are relatively invulnerable, having a very small radar cross-section.

FOR FURTHER READING

Note: The readings in this section focus on the *effects* of nuclear weapons. For readings on current nuclear arsenals, see the "For Further Reading" section of Chapter 7, "How Much Is Enough? Assessing the U.S.–Soviet Strategic Balance."

Cochran, Thomas B., William M. Arkin, and Milton M. Hoenig. "Nuclear Weapons Primer." In *Nuclear Weapons Databook.* Vol. 1, *U.S. Nuclear Forces and Capabilities,* pp. 22–36. Cambridge, Mass.: Ballinger Publishing Co., 1984 (paperback). An excellent introduction to fission and fusion weapons, with illustrations and photographs. The entire book is an invaluable reference on past and present U.S. nuclear weapons systems.

Foster, John S., Jr. "Nuclear Weapons." In *Encyclopedia Americana,* 1980. Vol. 20, pp. 518–28. An excellent overview of the history of nuclear weapons and how they work.

Glasstone, Samuel, and Philip J. Dolan, eds. *The Effects of Nuclear Weapons.* 3rd ed. Washington, D.C.: U.S. Department of Defense and Energy, 1977. An authoritative, highly technical reference work on the basic effects of nuclear weapons.

Goodwin, Peter. *Nuclear War: The Facts on Our Survival.* New York: The Rutledge Press, 1981 (paperback). An outstanding introduction to the nature and effects of nuclear weapons. Easy to read and contains many useful illustrations. Very good chapter on "How Radiation Affects People."

Morland, Howard. "The H-Bomb Secret: To Know How Is to Ask Why." *The Progressive* 43 (November 1979), pp. 14–25. A description of how hydrogen bombs work, derived from unclassified materials. Contains useful illustrations. The publication of this article created intense controversy, with critics arguing that it would expedite the development of H-bombs by other nations and defenders contending that it did not include data that were not already available. See also Morland's brief article, "Errata," in *The Progressive* 43 (December 1979), p. 36, for a discussion of additional details that had been omitted from the original article.

———. *The Secret That Exploded.* New York: Random House, 1981. Morland's account of how he discovered information about how H-bombs work and the government's efforts to suppress his articles.

Schroeer, Dietrich. *Science, Technology, and the Nuclear Arms Race.* New York: John Wiley and Sons, 1984 (paperback). Contains excellent chapters on fission and fusion bombs, as well as delivery systems.

Tsipis, Kosta. *Arsenal: Understanding Weapons in the Nuclear Age.* New York: Simon and Schuster, 1983. Chapter topics include "The Discovery of the

Nuclear Force," "The Physics of a Nuclear Explosion," and "The Physical Effects of a Nuclear Explosion."

————. "Inside the Mushroom Cloud." *Bulletin of the Atomic Scientists* 39 (February 1983), pp. 23–27. A concise, comprehensive primer on basic effects of nuclear explosions.

3

Can Nuclear War Be Survived?

We now turn to one of the most important—and controversial—issues to be examined in this book: Can nuclear war be survived? The articles in this chapter address this issue by considering two closely related questions. First, what are the probable consequences of different types of nuclear war? Second, is it possible to institute measures that could significantly reduce the severity of a nuclear attack and provide a reasonable chance for individual and societal recovery and long-term survival?

The importance of this issue derives from its military, economic, and political implications. Assumptions about the military role of nuclear weapons (that is, the kinds of weapons and policies needed to ensure national security) are likely to be influenced by attitudes about whether or not nuclear war can be survived. As we will see in the next two chapters, which analyze U.S. and Soviet nuclear weapons policies, policymakers disagree widely on this issue. Some analysts have concluded that survival in any meaningful sense is extremely unlikely and that, therefore, the only rational purpose for nuclear weapons is to deter other nations from using such weapons against the United States. According to this perspective, there would be no "winners" in a nuclear war. In contrast, others believe that proper preparations can keep the death and destruction caused by nuclear war to an acceptable level and that nuclear weapons can be reasonably used for a variety of purposes, including retaliation against non-nuclear aggression by an adversary. National security decision makers who believe that nuclear war is survivable may more readily entertain the possibility of actually using nuclear weapons than those who believe that any such use would inevitably lead to intolerable consequences.

Many millions of dollars have been spent by the United States since World War II in efforts to provide its citizens with protection in the event of nuclear attack. Such efforts have included identification and stocking of public fallout shelters, air raid sirens on the roofs of schools and other public buildings, and training tens of thousands of school children to quickly "duck and cover" (hide under the desks with their

hands over their heads) when they saw an unexpected "bright flash." [1]
Reagan administration plans have called for spending several billion
dollars during the coming years to reduce the casualties of a nuclear war
by means of a number of programs discussed below. Depending on one's
perspective, such expenditures can be seen either as necessary investments in national security or else as futile, destabilizing, and wasteful.

One's personal answer to the issue of nuclear war survival is likely
to lead to quite different political responses. If one concludes that nuclear war can in fact be survived, then support for present and even expanded governmental spending on civil defense is likely: however,
unjustified optimism about survivability may prevent potential victims
of nuclear war from appreciating their danger and taking actions to reduce it. On the other hand, awareness of the possibility that nuclear war
could result in the suffering and deaths of most, or all, of us might inspire individual and collective efforts to prevent nuclear weapons from
ever being used.

The issue of survivability is characterized by considerable controversy, in large part because definitive answers to the important questions
are difficult to obtain. As we saw in Chapter 2, serious methodological
difficulties confront researchers who attempt to precisely measure and
predict the effects of a single nuclear weapon. Such difficulties are compounded when the attempt is made to estimate the consequences of a
nuclear war in which vast numbers of weapons may be detonated.

Estimates of the probable consequences of a nuclear war are based
on several sources, including extrapolations from available data on the
Hiroshima and Nagasaki bombings, postwar studies of the effects of single nuclear weapons, and the researchers' assumptions about the number
and types of nuclear weapons used in the attack, the nature of the targets, prevailing weather conditions during and after the attack, civil defense preparations, and many other factors.

In the first selection for this chapter, "When the Bomb Falls,"
Leo Sartori examines three possible scenarios for the use of nuclear weapons. For his first scenario, Sartori cites a recent study conducted by the
U.S. Congressional Office of Technology Assessment (OTA), which indicates that a one-megaton airburst over Detroit could cause as many as
470,000 prompt fatalities and many thousands of serious injuries. Moreover, many of those injured would probably die because of delays in mobilizing a massive medical response.

His second scenario—a battlefield exchange of tactical nuclear
weapons in Europe—is particularly relevant in view of the present U.S.
policy of being ready and willing to use nuclear weapons in the event
that hostilities, either nuclear or non-nuclear, break out in Europe or
elsewhere in the world where U.S. tactical nuclear weapons are deployed. (See Chapter 7, "The Nuclear Dilemma in Europe.") Despite efforts by military leaders to avoid civilian casualties in such a European

---

[1] For a discussion of the "duck and cover" drills and other civil defense measures during the 1950s, see
Michael J. Carey, "The Schools and Civil Defense: The Fifties Revisited," *Teachers College Record* 84
(Fall 1982), pp. 114–27.

conflict, Sartori suggests that they could amount to a million or more. It should be noted that other analyses of tactical nuclear war scenarios have arrived at considerably more pessimistic results. For example, William Arkin, Frank von Hippel and Barbara G. Levi calculated that if nuclear weapons struck only about 170 targets in East and West Germany in an "exchange," the bombs could promptly kill as many as ten million people, and seriously injure another ten million, the vast majority of whom would be civilians.[2]

The third scenario—an "all-out" nuclear war between the United States and the Soviet Union—would cause death and destruction of vastly greater magnitude. Sartori cites a Department of Defense study that estimated that as many as 165 million Americans could be killed in such a war in the absence of any civil defense measures. Even with civil defense, many millions of people would be killed immediately, and millions more would die of untreated injuries in the post-attack world. The OTA study cited above estimated that even a so-called counterforce attack, in which only nuclear weapons installations of the United States were struck by Soviet warheads, could cause as many as 20 million prompt deaths, most of which would result from radioactive fallout many miles from the actual explosions. The OTA also estimated that a "large-scale" attack could kill as many as 160 million people in the United States and as many as 40 percent of the people in the Soviet Union.[3]

Some of the most eloquent and persuasive warnings about the consequences of nuclear war have come from physicians and other health care workers who have first-hand knowledge of the physical and mental vulnerability of human beings. In "Burn Casualties Among Survivors," physician John D. Constable shifts the perspective from the relatively abstract "scenarios" of nuclear war, with their incomprehensibly large casualty figures, to the more concrete level of the actual treatment of the serious injuries caused by nuclear weapons. Constable notes that treatment of severe burn injuries requires extensive medical resources over a period of months and years. However, even during peacetime, the treatment facilities of a given area can be readily overwhelmed by a catastrophe like an airplane crash or a hotel fire. A single nuclear weapon targeted against a city would simultaneously cause many thousands of severe burn injuries while destroying the medical resources needed to treat them. In a nuclear war in which many cities are attacked, Consta-

---

[2] William Arkin, Frank von Hippel, and Barbara G. Levi, "The Consequences of a 'Limited' Nuclear War in East and West Germany," *AMBIO: A Journal of the Human Environment* 11, no. 2–3 (1982), pp. 163–73.

[3] U.S. Office of Technology Assessment, *The Effects of Nuclear War* (Washington, D.C.: U.S. Government Printing Office, 1979). See especially "Three Attack Cases," pp. 63–106. A 1984 study, "Effects of Nuclear War on Health and Health Services," commissioned by the World Health Organization, arrived at even higher casualty estimates. The WHO research team calculated that a nuclear war in which about one-half of present U.S. and Soviet nuclear arsenals were employed would likely cause, on a world-wide basis, as many as 1.1 billion prompt deaths and an equal number of delayed deaths resulting from exposure to radioactive fallout, untreated burns and other injuries, and the lack of such necessities as food and water.

ble writes, "The medical facilities of the nation would choke totally on even a fraction of the burn casualties alone."

The severe psychological problems likely to afflict those who physically survive a nuclear war are addressed in the articles by psychiatrist Robert Jay Lifton and sociologist Kai Erikson. On the basis of studies of the atomic bombings and other mass disasters, the authors conclude that extreme mental paralysis, which they term "psychic numbing," would immobilize the survivors of nuclear war—significantly impairing their ability to cooperate in reconstructing what would be left of the society. The disruption of the social order, in turn, would exacerbate the psychological problems of individuals and create a dangerous, vicious cycle.

Despite such grim projections of unprecedented death tolls, untreated injuries, psychological trauma, and social disorganization noted above, high-ranking officials in past and present presidential administrations are on record as believing that nuclear war can be survived. For example, as a candidate for the presidency in 1980, Ronald Reagan was asked about his views on the survival issue by journalist Robert Scheer. Reagan replied: "Could we survive a nuclear war? It would be survival of some of your people and some of your facilities, but you could start again."[4] In January 1982, William Chipman, chief of the civilian defense section of the Federal Emergency Management Agency (FEMA)—which has overall responsibility for coordinating both peacetime and wartime disaster management—was asked by the same reporter if he thought the American political structure could survive a nuclear war. Chipman answered: "I think they would eventually, yeah. As I say, ants will eventually build another anthill."[5]

The article by Orr Kelly, "New Civil Defense Aim: Empty Major Cities," discusses Crisis Relocation Planning, a civil defense measure initiated by President Carter and continued and expanded by President Reagan. The plan, which calls for evacuating 145 million Americans from high-risk urban areas into rural "reception areas" during an international crisis, has generated a great deal of controversy. As this book goes to press, the Reagan administration has significantly reduced its efforts to implement crisis relocation planning and has instead supported a campaign to develop a system of space-based defenses against Soviet ICBM attacks, the Strategic Defense Initiative, popularly known as "Star Wars." The controversy surrounding the Strategic Defense Initiative is examined in Chapter 12.

While the debate continues, the federal government is proceeding with numerous, less visible, plans to protect key officials and functionaries should a nuclear war break out. One plan involves identifying over 30 federal agencies and departments whose activities are deemed "essential and uninterruptible," including the Selective Service System, the Federal Reserve Board, and even the Railroad Retirement Board. Each

---

[4] Quoted in Robert Scheer, *With Enough Shovels: Reagan, Bush, and Nuclear War* (New York: Random House, 1980), p. 58.

[5] Quoted in Robert Scheer, "U.S. Could Survive Nuclear War in U.S. Administration's View," *Los Angeles Times,* January 16, 1982.

of these agencies has been ordered to designate three teams of administrators, each capable of running the agency independently of the others.
In the event of an international crisis that could lead to nuclear war,
two of the teams would evacuate to specially prepared underground survival facilities, where they would wait out the attack and then help to
reconstitute the government when hostilities have ceased. The Soviet
government has made similar—in fact, more extensive—preparations.
High priority has also been given to protecting top military leaders by
the Department of Defense. Around the world, at least 96 "military
command centers" have been buried deep underground. Other plans include arrangements for the resumption of postal service after the war,
food rationing (coordinated by the Department of Agriculture), rein-
statement of the monetary system, and even the stockpiling of tons of
opium.[6]

Late in 1983, a major new dimension was added to the debate on
nuclear war survival when a team of scientists reported new findings on
possible long-term ecological and biological consequences of a nuclear
war. One of the team members, Carl Sagan, describes their ominous
findings in his article, "The Nuclear Winter." Sagan and his colleagues
discovered that the fires caused by nuclear explosions were likely to produce vast clouds of smoke that would blanket most of the Northern
Hemisphere, shutting out sunlight and plunging the temperatures on
the surface of the earth many degrees below their normal levels. One result, according to Sagan, would be that "virtually all crops and farm animals, at least in the Northern Hemisphere, would be destroyed, as
would most varieties of uncultivated and undomesticated food supplies.
Most of the human survivors would starve." The cold, dark "nuclear
winter" could last as long as several months, depending on the size and
nature of the nuclear war that precipitated it. Moreover, the researchers
found that even a "small" nuclear war fought with less than one percent
of the current world arsenals would be likely to produce a nuclear winter.

Predictably, the "nuclear winter" report aroused great controversy.
Critics of civil defense felt that their views had been strongly vindi-
cated. However, many proponents of civil defense remained undaunted
by the new data, either dismissing it as erroneous or else calling for
even more extensive civil defense precautions.

The controversy surrounding the possibility of a nuclear winter, as
well as its implications for nuclear weapons policy, will undoubtedly
continue as government agencies and other organizations conduct their
own research on this issue. As indicated in the article by R. Jeffrey
Smith, in late December 1984, an expert panel of the National Research
Council concluded that some form of a nuclear winter was in fact possible, though it stressed that extensive uncertainties make more specific
predictions questionable.

---

[6]Edward Zuckerman, "How Would the U.S. Survive a Nuclear War?" *Esquire* 97 (March 1982), pp. 37–
46.

WHEN THE BOMB FALLS
Leo Sartori

Leo Sartori is a professor of physics at the University of Nebraska, Lincoln. He served on the staff of the U.S. Arms Control and Disarmament Agency (ACDA) from 1978 to 1981 and was senior ACDA agent to the SALT delegation in 1979.

Most nuclear war scenarios entail the explosion of large numbers of weapons during a relatively short time, in a variety of settings that differ in many significant respects from test conditions. Any estimate of the consequences involves many assumptions and a great deal of modeling and extrapolation.

Although some aspects of the outcome can be predicted with fairly high confidence—for example, how many buildings in a given city would be destroyed by the blast from an explosion of specified yield—many others are much less certain. This is particularly true of the aftermath of a large-scale exchange, where much would depend on the behavior of human beings under unprecedented conditions. There is no way to model such a situation with any confidence.

In this article, I examine three possible settings in which nuclear weapons might be used—a single large weapon exploded on a major city, a tactical exchange in Europe, and an all-out strategic exchange—and discuss the likely consequences in each case. Obviously, many other scenarios are possible. My examples are intended to provide a general understanding of the kinds of effects that may be expected, of the possible dimensions of those effects, and of the uncertainties involved.

One Megaton on Detroit

Although it is unlikely that a nuclear "exchange" would be confined to a single shot, the single-city case is instructive since it serves as a basis for analysis of more extensive exchanges.

The Effects of Nuclear War, published by the Office of Technology Assessment, contains a detailed description of the effects of a one-megaton weapon exploded on downtown Detroit. I have drawn heavily on this study, but the results for any other major city would be quite similar.

If the weapon were exploded on the ground, it would leave a crater about 1,000 feet in diameter and 200 feet deep. Within a central region about 1.7

Source: Leo Sartori, "When the Bomb Falls," *Bulletin of the Atomic Scientists* (June/July 1983), pp. 40–49. Reprinted by permission of the *Bulletin of the Atomic Scientists,* a magazine of science and world affairs. Copyright © 1983 by the Educational Foundation for Nuclear Science, Chicago, IL 60637.

miles in radius virtually all structures would be destroyed and no one would be expected to survive. In a bordering region, between 1.7 and 2.7 miles from ground zero, individual residences would be destroyed, with only some foundations and basements remaining; stronger commercial buildings might remain standing, but with walls blown out. Some industrial buildings might remain nearly functional. Debris would be piled in the streets to depths between several inches and many feet. About half the people in this region would be killed, mostly as a result of buildings collapsing on them. Almost all the survivors would be injured.

In a third region, between 2.7 and 4.7 miles from ground zero, low residential buildings would be destroyed or severely damaged but large buildings would sustain less damage. The number of immediate deaths would be small, perhaps 5 percent, but about half the inhabitants would be injured. Finally, between 4.7 and 7.4 miles there would be only light damage to commercial structures and moderate damage to residences. In this region practically everyone would survive; about 25 percent would be injured. . . . During working hours many more people would be in the inner zones, and the expected number of fatalities would increase by some 130,000; and 45,000 more would be injured. The number of burn casualties would depend on the time of day, the season and the weather. The worst case would be a daylight attack on a clear summer day, when the most people would be outdoors. Under varying assumptions, the Office of Technology Assessment study found that of those who survived the blast, between 1,000 and 190,000 could be expected to die from burns; between 500 and 75,000 would be injured. With sufficient warning to allow people to get indoors, the number of direct burn casualties would be low.

Fire hazard would be most severe in the third band, since fire ignition and spread are more likely in partly damaged buildings than in completely flattened areas. The study estimated that perhaps 5 percent of the buildings in this region would be initially ignited, with spread to adjacent buildings highly likely where the separation is under 50 feet. Fires would continue to spread for at least 24 hours, with perhaps half the buildings ultimately consumed. There would be little attempt to fight these fires. Many survivors would be severely burned or suffer from smoke inhalation. Ironically, the number of casualties due to prompt radiation would be small, because most of the people close enough to receive a lethal dose would have been killed by blast or heat effects.

Early fallout, descending on the metropolitan area very soon after the explosion, would create dangerous levels of radiation and hamper emergency crews; some areas could receive as many as 300 rems during the first hour. Later fallout would affect a larger area, the location and extent of which would depend on wind patterns.

If the weapon were exploded in the air instead of on the ground there would be some significant differences in the outcome. There would be no crater and, more important, negligible fallout. People in the far suburbs . . . would be better off. But the regions of high blast damage would be larger than for a ground burst, and the number of casualties greater. The study estimates more than twice as many fatalities as for a ground burst (470,000 as against 200,000) and about 50 percent more injuries.

The injured would face bleak prospects. Most hospitals would have been demolished or severely damaged, and many doctors would themselves be victims. Perhaps 5,000 hospital beds in greater Detroit would remain usable, enough for only one percent of the injured. Rescue efforts by surrounding communities and federal and state governments would be severely hampered: by debris in the streets, making movement of vehicles difficult; by high levels of radiation due to fallout; and by the lack of electricity and phone service. Simply locating the injured would pose a major problem. Those who required immediate treatment would be unlikely to receive it.

Care of burn victims would be particularly taxing. Treatment of serious burns requires highly specialized facilities, which are rare; in the entire United States there are now only one or two thousand hospital beds dedicated to burn care. Even in a single-city attack a vast number of burn victims, who might have been saved, would probably die for lack of adequate treatment.

In time, the city could be rebuilt. Residual radioactivity would, however, last a long time. Authorities disagree on what constitutes a "safe" level of radiation; the long-term effects of small doses have not been sufficiently studied. A conservative definition is half a rem per year, about five times the natural background. It would be eight to ten years before such a level was reached in the inner city, and about three years in the outer regions.

A Battlefield Exchange

What would happen in a tactical nuclear exchange in Europe? The scenario most often cited begins with a massive Soviet attack, involving thousands of tanks, across the border between the two Germanys. NATO's declared policy is to employ tactical nuclear weapons to repel such an attack if it is unable to do so with conventional forces. The Soviets may be expected to reply in kind, and a tactical exchange would ensue, most of it on German territory.

Nuclear warheads are now deployed on a variety of weapons designed for battlefield use. They include short-range ballistic missiles such as the Lance (range about 75 miles), nuclear artillery (range about 10 miles), nuclear land mines and nuclear bombs carried by short-range aircraft. NATO currently has about 7,000 tactical weapons, with yields ranging from tens of kilotons down to a fraction of a kiloton. Low-yield weapons are intended to destroy battlefield targets while minimizing collateral damage to civilians and non-military structures in the vicinity, as well as to one's own forces. Among the likely targets are mechanized nuclear-capable and artillery units, but tanks are generally regarded as the principal targets. Weapons would be airburst to minimize fallout.

The controversial enhanced radiation warhead (neutron bomb), now being produced by the United States, is designed to make a tactical nuclear response more feasible. Because tanks can withstand considerably higher overpressures than can residential buildings, a weapon that relied on blast effects to destroy tanks in a given area would cause civilian casualties and property damage over a much larger area. An enhanced radiation warhead, however, releases a much greater fraction of its energy in the form of neutrons than does an ordinary fission weapon. As a result, the area in which prompt radiation is intense enough to incapacitate enemy tank crews exceeds that of severe blast damage. Through the use of these weapons, therefore, the extent of civilian casualties and property damage due to blast effects would be minimized.

In order to be effective militarily, a neutron bomb must incapacitate its victims quickly. This requires a very high dose, in the neighborhood of 8,000 rems. For a one-kiloton enhanced radiation warhead detonated at 1,500 feet, the required dose is produced within an area of about .8 of a square mile. There is, however, a considerably larger area (about 2.5 square miles) within which the dose, though still not enough to incapacitate quickly, can still cause radiation sickness and possibly death. Hence 2.5 square miles can be considered the lethal area of the weapon as far as civilians are concerned. Property damage would be confined to a much smaller region. In principle, even a fairly large tactical exchange could cause relatively light collateral damage if all detonations were confined to isolated areas with few civilians.

There are several reasons why such a scenario may be unduly optimistic. First, Western Europe is a densely populated region. The average distance between populated places in Germany is only a little over a mile, so there simply are not many places in the prospective battle zone where 2.5 square miles would not contain substantial numbers of noncombatants. Moreover, enemy tanks and troop convoys are likely to go through towns, perhaps even using them as shields. In the heat of battle, will NATO commanders refrain from attacking those towns? Some of the warheads may be mistargeted, unintentionally landing in populated places or on friendly troops; such accidents have happened in past wars, but with nuclear weapons the result would be catastrophic. Finally, even if NATO were successful in avoiding populated areas, there is little reason to suppose that Soviet commanders would exercise similar caution in targeting, particularly if the exchange were taking place on West German soil. (Soviet tactical weapons tend to have higher yields than do Western ones and to be less accurate, making selective targeting more difficult even if the Soviets attempted it.)

One can make a very rough estimate of the number of civilian casualties that might result from a tactical exchange. A large-scale Soviet invasion would involve something like 20,000 tanks. Those tanks would not be deployed in a closely packed formation, in which many could be destroyed by a single nuclear artillery shell. Study of Warsaw Pact field exercises suggest that no more than 10 to 20 tanks are likely to be within the effective area of one weapon. Hence, if a nuclear response by NATO is to have a significant impact on the military situation, at least several hundred tactical weapons would be required. Including the Soviet counterstrike, it is likely that 1,000 or more weapons would be exploded.

The average population density in the prospective battle zone is about 500 per square mile. Assuming that 1,000 weapons are detonated and that each one has a lethal area of 2.5 square miles containing 500 people per square miles, the total casualties come to 1.25 million. This may be overestimating, since NATO should be able at least to avoid the most heavily populated areas. On the other hand, some of the weapons used would be heavier than one kiloton. Hence it seems unlikely, therefore, that civilian casualties could be held below several hundred thousand.

Even a million civilian casualties would not exceed the toll of World War II, or the number of casualties likely to result from a large-scale non-nuclear conflict between NATO and the Warsaw Pact. Thus the consequences of a tactical exchange in Europe, if it could be confined to that, would not even remotely approach those of a strategic exchange. The major concern over this scenario is the danger that use of nuclear weapons might escalate beyond the battlefield. Once the nuclear threshold has been crossed, there may be irresistible temptation to launch nuclear attacks against major military installations, against the enemy's missile sites and control facilities, and ultimately to attack industrial centers and communication facilities. Both sides have large numbers of intermediate-range missiles and other nuclear weapons, with yields up to the megaton range, that could be devoted to such missions. As far as Europe is concerned, that would constitute a strategic exchange.

All-out Nuclear War

The most awesome possibility is an all-out strategic exchange. This is generally taken to mean a massive Soviet first strike against U.S. strategic forces, other military targets and major economic-industrial targets followed by a U.S. retaliatory strike against a similar set of Soviet targets. (The strikes could occur also in the opposite order.) Thousands of high-yield warheads would be used in such an exchange.

Several studies of the likely consequences of all-out nuclear war have been made. The results differ in details, but all the studies agree that the effects on both countries would be devastating no matter which side struck first. Even though it is assumed that civilian populations are not directly targeted, the proximity of many military and industrial targets to major population centers causes the number of expected fatalities to be extremely high. A 1977 study by the Department of Defense estimated that between 155 and 165 million Americans would be killed if no civil defense measures were taken and all the attacking weapons were ground burst. This is a "worst case," admittedly, but the numbers are appalling. A 1979 study by the Arms Control and Disarmament Agency found that between 65 and 95 percent of the key production capacity would be destroyed, and even non-targeted capacity would suffer 60 to 80 percent destruction from collateral effects. In the Agency's scenario the 200 largest cities in each country were destroyed and 80 percent of all cities with 25,000 or more people were attacked by at least one weapon.

If people made use of existing shelters near their homes, the Defense Department's estimate of fatalities drops to between 110 and 145 million. More significant reductions occur if urban populations are evacuated from high-risk areas. In this case the expected number of fatalities drops to between 40 and 55 million, and other studies give estimates as low as 20 million. The U.S. government is developing a large-scale evacuation plan in which host communities in lower-risk areas would receive people from large cities. The Soviets are reputed to have a similar plan, as well as an extensive civil defense program that includes shelters and the hardening of industrial facilities. Some have argued that the "civil defense gap" would give the Soviets a decisive advantage in case of war, but there are serious doubts about the effectiveness of such a program in an actual conflict, particularly with regard to carrying out massive evacuations, even with the required warning time.

Survivors would face formidable problems. Unlike the case of a single-city attack, devastated areas could not count on much help from outside, since neighboring communities are also likely to have been hit. Rescuing and treating the badly injured would be nearly impossible at first.

For perhaps a month, the major task would be simply to exist. Radiation levels would be very high throughout most of the country, particularly in the eastern half. . . . Survivors in those areas would have to spend most of their time in shelters under grim conditions. Many would be overcrowded. Supplies of food and water might not be adequate. Medicine is likely to be in short supply. Maintaining even minimal hygiene and sanitation would be difficult. Unless the shelter had a good filtration system the air would soon become clammy and malodorous. Sick people would vomit frequently, adding to the general discomfort. It might be too hot or too cold, depending on the location and time of year. People would not know how much radiation they had received and might panic at any symptom of radiation sickness. The level of stress in the shelters is likely to be high.

After radiation levels had subsided sufficiently people could leave the shelters and recovery efforts could begin, but under extremely adverse conditions. Millions would be homeless. Many essentials, including food, would be in short supply. Much of the livestock would have been killed by fallout. If the attack had come early in the growing season, crops would have been killed by radiation; if late in the season they could have been lost because of farmers' inability to harvest. Distribution of available food could also be a serious problem.

There is a high danger of infection and communicable diseases during the recovery period. Resistance to infection would be sharply lowered because of radiation, malnutrition, dehydration during the shelter period and general exposure and hardship. Poor sanitation, lack of refrigeration, and inadequate waste disposal would also encourage the spread of disease. Antibiotics would be in short supply, so epidemic diseases long under control, such as cholera, plague and typhoid fever, could re-emerge as dangerous threats. Hepatitis, salmonellosis and other diseases of the intestinal tract are likely to become more prevalent and deadly. Tuberculosis could also increase dramatically. Efforts to control epidemics would be difficult to implement.

Under such conditions the survivors would have to set about restoring the industrial plant, communications and transportation networks and commercial, medical-scientific and cultural systems—in short, practically every aspect of our complex society. Material and psychological obstacles would abound. Deficiencies in each component of society would hamper recovery in the others. Records and reference materials would have disappeared. The government would be hard put to maintain law and order and to establish and enforce priorities in the recovery effort. Significant changes in the political and social systems might come about.

Any estimate of how long it might take to restore conditions to something resembling their pre-war state cannot be much better than a guess. Some highly optimistic estimates predict recovery in as little as four years; others think society would never recover, or at least not for many decades or even centuries.

Some consequences of nuclear radiation will become apparent only months or even years after exposure. They include cataracts, leukemia and other forms of cancer, and genetic effects such as abortion due to chromosomal damage, deformed births and various mutations. Since all these effects can be induced by low-level radiation from late fallout, they would be manifested worldwide. The number of cancers and of genetic abnormalities that would be caused by a large-scale nuclear war are highly uncertain, but they are generally estimated to be in the millions—far fewer than the direct effects but not at all negligible.

A 1975 study by the National Academy of Sciences called attention to

the danger that the ozone layer in the stratosphere might be depleted by nitrogen oxides from high-yield nuclear explosions. Ozone is important because
it absorbs harmful ultra violet rays from sunlight; even a modest increase in
the amount of ultraviolet radiation reaching the Earth would produce dangerous sunburns and a variety of potentially harmful ecological effects. The
chemistry of the upper atmosphere is complex, and the likely extent of the
ozone depletion effect remains controversial.

Another potential disaster is the deposition of large amounts of smoke
in the atmosphere from fires in cities, forests, agricultural lands and oil and
gas fields. A recent study by P. Crutzen and J. Birks estimates that as a result, the average amount of sunlight reaching the ground in the Northern
Hemisphere would be reduced by a factor between two and 150 for many weeks,
perhaps months. This would strongly reduce and perhaps totally eliminate the
possibility of growing agricultural crops for an entire season, leading to widespread famine as well as causing a variety of other harmful ecological changes.

It is quite possible that there would be other hitherto unidentified effects
that could bring about significant changes, temporary or irreversible, in the
environment. Obviously one cannot estimate the magnitude of such unknown
effects, but their likelihood is yet another manifestation of the inherent uncertainty in trying to assess the consequences of nuclear war. About the only
thing one can predict with certainty is that it would be a disaster of unpar-
alleled dimensions.

BURN INJURIES AMONG SURVIVORS
John D. Constable, M.D.

John D. Constable is Associate Clinical Professor of Surgery at Harvard Medical School and Chief Consultant in Plastic Surgery at the Shriners Burns Institute in Boston.

The crash of a partially filled 30-passenger airplane on an island off the coast
of Massachusetts required the mobilization of all the emergency medical facilities of Greater Boston, a major surgical center. Yet we are asked to contemplate the possibility of ten thousand, or a hundred thousand, or even a million
severely traumatized victims of a military nuclear explosion. Adequate medical treatment for such survivors is an impossibility.

We can talk about how such injuries *should* be treated, but to transfer

Source: John D. Constable, "Burn Casualties Among Survivors," in *Last Aid: The Medical Dimensions of Nuclear War,* ed. Eric Chivian et al. (San Francisco: W. H. Freeman and Company, 1982), pp. 202–
210. Copyright © 1982.

this knowledge to the practical possibilities of treating the number of victims that have been predicted is categorically out of the question.

The injuries caused by a massive nuclear detonation would come from the various effects of such an explosion. People within and around buildings would suffer extensive traumatic injury, from being blown out of the buildings and from damage by debris. The initial blast effect of the explosion is characteristically followed by powerful winds rising to as much as 180 miles per hour, which would cause a number of severe traumatic injuries.

Most of those who have been crushed, cut, or blasted, but not burned, and who have survived initial injury and reached medical facilities would, in most cases, be expected to require only one major medical procedure. Although this might be very expensive in terms of time and material, including a great deal of blood and other support, the victims would then be expected to enjoy a relatively uncomplicated convalescence.

Such would not be the case for burns. Even though heat and light contain only some 35 percent of the total energy of a nuclear explosion, burns would consume a far higher percentage of the post-attack medical resources.

Let us consider the burn injuries that would result from a nuclear explosion and the treatment that would be required.

Patients suffering from anoxia, resulting from most of the atmospheric oxygen having been used up by the extensive fires (especially firestorms), would be rare. If the degree of thermal activity was sufficient to have caused anoxic damage, then usually there would be concomitant fatal incineration.

Both carbon monoxide poisoning and fire-induced anoxia must be distinguished from *pulmonary burns,* which remain one of the major therapeutic problems of thermal damage, one that is largely unsolved. This form of lung injury usually takes from 24 to 72 hours to develop and is not the result of direct thermal damage to the lung. If the heat around the patient's face is sufficient to actually destroy the trachea, bronchi, or lungs, there is almost invariably such devastating destruction of the face and other parts of the skin that the patient does not survive.

The generally accepted theory is that the damage to the lungs results from the chemical activity of noxious products of incomplete combustion. Consequently, this type of burn is characteristic of fires in closed spaces rather than the open spaces that would be more common with a major bomb. Among people confined to buildings, pulmonary burns would be a major lethal factor. In the Coconut Grove fire in Boston some 40 years ago, more than 400 people died, almost all without visible signs of burns. These deaths, which occurred mostly two, three, and four days after the fire, resulted from pulmonary damage now believed to have been from the fumes from the plastic in the artificial palm trees and furniture coverings.

Two kinds of direct thermal injury would occur from a nuclear explosion: one directly from the detonation, the other from the secondary fires following the ignition of available combustible material. These secondary fires would be of at least two sorts. One possibility is a firestorm. Much more certain is the development of a major conflagration, which would be essentially the sort of fire with which we are all too familiar, but enormously increased in scale. This fire would be associated with multiple smaller ones, starting from the breaking of gas mains, the failure of electrical pumps, the lack of water to put them out, and so on. The fires would be spasmodic over a very large area.

People would be exposed to the risks of thermal damage from the bomb itself and from its secondary fires. There is no essential difference in the nature of burns from these two etiologies. Burn damage to skin results from a combination of the amount of heat and the time of exposure, these factors being very much modified by the presence or absence of clothing, the moisture content of the atmosphere, and other factors. An explosion results in an almost instantaneous exposure to a very high heat level, with damage occurring over an incredible distance; but the nature of the injury is not different from other forms of thermal burns. It simply means that there can be much more severe damage in a very short time if the heat to which one is exposed is very great.

All people seriously injured by a nuclear explosion who also have had a significant amount of radiation injury would be more difficult to treat. Some survivors would have received sufficient radiation to result in death within a matter of weeks or months from the radiation alone. But even with those who received smaller doses of radiation, the damage to the immune system and to blood element regeneration would result in the patient being more prone to invasive sepsis, in less satisfactory healing, and in an increased risk of death from a thermal injury that might otherwise not have been fatal.

Experimental studies have shown that a burn from which a normal animal can be expected to recover becomes lethal if the animal has been previously or concomitantly exposed to non-lethal radiation.

First-degree burns at their very worst are equivalent to a severe sunburn. They may result in some transient dehydration, certainly considerable pain, but under any emergency conditions they require essentially no treatment and must be considered of no particular medical consequence.

Second-degree or partial-thickness burns (the latter term is much to be preferred) are, from the point of view of the surgical problems, almost as severe an injury as are third-degree or full-thickness burns. A deep partial-thickness burn requires essentially the same amount of resuscitative effort, the same difficult nursing, the same elaborate dressings, and the same extensive care during the first three to four weeks. Although these injuries heal from the base and therefore no skin grafting is required, and the eventual problems of resurfacing the patient are a great deal simpler, the immediate problem of care is almost as great as with a full-thickness burn. The two groups should be combined from the point of view of trying to evaluate the early load on the medical system.

Estimating accurately the extent and number of burn survivors in a population exposed to a nuclear explosion is very difficult. The figure might vary as much as a thousandfold, depending upon specific factors prevailing at the time of the explosion. Even a moderate degree of opacity in the air strikingly reduces the range of thermal damage. Other factors include the season, the time of day, and the extent to which the population had been warned. These conditions partly determine the amount of clothing being worn and whether people are outdoors or not.

For a one-megaton nuclear explosion, with 10-mile visibility, it has been estimated that third-degree or full-thickness burns might be expected within 5 miles; second-degree or partial-thickness burns within a 6-mile radius, and first-degree burns within 7 miles. If the atmosphere were sufficiently opaque to reduce visibility to 2 miles, then the second-degree zone would be reduced from 6 miles to something under 3 and the others changed proportionately.

Unfortunately, burns are the form of trauma that characteristically demand the largest amount of medical assistance. No injury can be counted on to use up more hospital facilities than a severe burn. Triage would be very difficult, and a great many patients treated for extended periods might still eventually die from their injuries.

The burn literature has been filled over the last ten years with reports of progress in salvaging the severely burned. Many new methods of infection control have come into use, including various surface antiseptic agents and topical antibiotics. The surface control of infection has prevented the conversion of partial-thickness to full-thickness burns by sepsis and has strikingly improved overall results in burn salvage. There also has been much effort to control systemic infection, both by the use of antibiotics and by elaborate isolation techniques. "Life islands," in which patients are isolated in a plastic enclosure, and laminar flow units, in which the air is regularly replenished and replaced so that bacteria are swept away, are recent innovations. All of these methods have helped reduce death from infection.

Another recent development is the early surgical excision of burns. Although it is usually not safe to excise more than one-fifth of the patient's body surface at one time, surgery may be carried out on the first or second day after the burn, and with maximum support again on the fourth, and so on, ending with as much as 80 to 90 percent of the skin being excised. Massive excision has been combined with immunosuppression to allow for the use of typed allografts taken from living donors or cadavers. Some dramatic results are possible with these methods, although they are still cosmetically relatively grotesque.

It is absolutely essential to recognize that any really severe burn may require as many as 30 to 50 operations, both immediate and delayed, and months and months of hospitalization. This care imposes immense strains on the medical facilities available. With the newer and more dramatic methods, there is at least the possibility, if sufficient material and personnel are poured in, of salvaging burns in the 85 to 90 percent range.

Triage is much more difficult when the physician is faced with an enormous group of patients sustaining 20 to 90 percent burns who might survive if treated. (Except for burns of the hands and face, I exclude burns affecting under 20 percent of surface because most of these can be treated relatively easily.) What is involved in treating large numbers of severe burns?

Some years ago the Shriners of North America, who had for years donated large sums to look after orthopedically crippled children, became interested in building specialized burn hospitals for children. Their plan was to start with three burn units and then to expand, possibly adding another 15 or so to match the number of orthopedic hospitals they were already maintaining. These initial three units were built in Boston, Galveston, and Cincinnati. In the 15 years since these three 30-bed hospitals were built, it has not been practical to build even one other unit, because the three burn units, with a total of 90 beds, consume a budget similar to that of nineteen orthopedic hospitals, most of which are of comparable size.

The cost of running a single 30-bed hospital, where half of the beds are reconstructive and where there would rarely be more than ten acute burn cases at one time, is in the neighborhood of $4 million per year. The United States has approximately 1000 to 2000 so-called burn beds in specialized institutions. Each burn patient requires specialized individual nursing for quite a long time. At most, one nurse can look after two patients.

Severe burns require not just one major operation but may need general anesthesia every other day and regular trips to the operating room for weeks or even months. Elaborate dressings and the application of antibiotics or at least antiseptic agents are necessary. The patients require large amounts of blood, albumin, and other human blood derivatives. They may need enormous areas of allografts, but after a nuclear war, obtaining sufficient quantities of these from cadavers may be difficult, because many of the dead would be in highly radioactive areas or be contaminated radioactively themselves.

Whereas most traumatic lesions are treated definitively immediately, and the victims either recover or die, burns are peculiar. The burn patient is not so ill during the first 12 to 24 hours. I have seen a number of older patients with 40 to 50 percent full-thickness, clearly fatal burns who, for the first 12 to 24 hours after their injury, appeared in reasonably good condition. They were capable of consulting their lawyers and doing whatever needed to be done. After this initial period the patient becomes sicker and sicker, and this critical hovering between survival and death may go on for weeks or months.

Once a burn has been initially resurfaced, it may need months or years of reconstruction. And even with all of this, anyone who is discriminating or humane would recognize that the end results are indeed pathetically poor. It is very difficult to estimate the cost of such cases in dollars because, to the best of my knowledge, no health program or insurance pays adequately for burn care. Blue Cross/Blue Shield and similar insurance programs admit that they cannot afford to pay the true cost. Nonetheless, it is reasonable to put the cost at anywhere from $200,000 to $400,000 for a severe surviving burn case.

Even though there are 30-bed burn units, such as the Shriners or those at large general hospitals, they can handle only two or three fresh severe burns at once. If a large group of such burns occurred in a major accident, they would have to be distributed for effective treatment.

Major burn disasters of recent years—the Coconut Grove and Hartford Circus fires—and various plane crashes have resulted in very few survivors of major burns. Initially following a nuclear attack, there would be thousands, or even tens of thousands, severely burned immediate survivors. Even the most conservative calculation of thermal injuries from an isolated one-megaton or "minimal" nuclear explosion, with hypothetical preservation of all U.S. medical facilities and the availability of immediate and perfect triage and transportation, shows that what we consider to be one of the most lavish and well-developed medical facilities in the world would be completely overwhelmed. It is impossible to imagine the chaos that would result from a larger explosion in which the hospitals themselves were partially destroyed and where there was no possibility of significant triage or inter-center transportation. The medical facilities of the nation would choke totally on even a fraction of the burn casualties alone.

Survivors of Nuclear War: Psychological and Communal Breakdown
Robert Jay Lifton and Kai Erikson

Robert Jay Lifton is Distinguished Professor of Psychiatry and Psychology at the City University of New York at John Jay College. Previously he held the Foundation's Fund Research Professorship in Psychiatry at the Yale University School of Medicine. Lifton won the National Book Award in the Sciences in 1969 for his study of the survivors of Hiroshima, *Death in Life;* his other works include *The Broken Connection: On*

Source: Robert Jay Lifton and Kai Erikson, "Survivors of Nuclear War: Psychological and Communal Breakdown," in *Last Aid: The Medical Dimensions of Nuclear War,* ed. Eric Chivian et al. (San Francisco: W. H. Freeman and Company, 1982), pp. 287–92. Copyright © 1982. All rights reserved.

Death and the Continuity of Life and *Indefensible Weapons: The Political and Psychological Case Against Nuclearism,* with Richard Falk.

Kai Erikson is Professor of Sociology and American Studies at Yale University and Editor of the *Yale Review.* He is a past president of the American Sociological Association. Among his publications are *Wayward Puritans: A Study in the Sociology of Deviants* and *Everything in the Path: Destruction of Community in Buffalo Creek.*

"Scenarios" about fighting, recovering from, or even "winning" a nuclear war tend to be remarkably vague about the psychological condition of survivors. Some simply assume that survivors would remain stoic and begin to rebuild from the ruins in a calm, disciplined way. Others seem to attribute that rebuilding to a mysterious, unseen hand. Usually absent is a reasoned estimate, on the basis of what experience we have, of how people might actually behave. Recently, physicians and other scientists have been making careful projections of the effects of nuclear war, and all raise severe doubts about general claims of recovery.

A 20-megaton bomb, for instance, if detonated over New York City, London, or Leningrad, would vaporize, crush, incinerate, or burn to death almost every person within a radius of 5 or 6 miles from the center of the blast—more than two million people. Within a radius of 20 miles, a million more or so either would die instantly or would suffer wounds from which they could not recover. If the bomb exploded on the ground, countless others who lived miles away, far beyond the reach of the initial blast and searing heat wave, would be sentenced to a lingering death.

But that picture, harsh as it seems, is inadequate even for a limited nuclear war and certainly for a full-scale one. New York City, for example, would be hit by many warheads, as would other cities, industrial centers, and military targets—hundreds of warheads, maybe thousands. Try to imagine 100 million or more people dead, and lethal amounts of radioactivity scattered over huge areas.

And the survivors? Would they panic? Would they help one another? What would they feel and do?

In Hiroshima, survivors not only expected that they too would soon die, they had a sense that *everyone* was dying, that "the world is ending." Rather than panic, the scene was one of slow motion—of people moving gradually away from the center of the destruction, but dully and almost without purpose. They were, as one among them put it, "so broken and confused that they moved and behaved like automatons . . . a people who walked in the realm of dreams." Some tried to do something to help others, but most felt themselves to be so much part of a dead world that, as another remembered, they were "not really alive."

The key to that vague behavior was a closing off of the mind so that no more horror could enter it. People witnessed the most grotesque forms of death and dying all around them but felt nothing. A profound blandness and insensitivity—a "paralysis of the mind"—seemed to take hold in everyone. People saw what was happening and were able to describe it later in sharp detail, but their minds, they said, were numbed.

Hiroshima and Nagasaki, however, can provide us with no more than a hint of what would happen in the event of a nuclear war. A single weapon today can have the power of 1000 Hiroshima bombs, and we have to be able to imagine 1000 of those exploding in the space of a few minutes. Moreover, in the case of Hiroshima and Nagasaki—and this is absolutely crucial—there was still a functioning outside world to provide help.

In a nuclear war, the process of psychic numbing may well be so extreme as to become irreversible.

Imagine the familiar landscape turning suddenly into a sea of destruction: everywhere smoldering banks of debris; everywhere the sights and sounds and smells of death. Imagine that the other survivors are wandering about with festering wounds, broken limbs, and bodies so badly burned that their features appear to be melting and their flesh is peeling away in great raw folds. Imagine—on the generous assumption that your children are alive at all—that you have no way of knowing whether the radiation they have been exposed to has already doomed them.

The suddenness and the sheer ferocity of such a scene would not give survivors any chance to mobilize the usual forms of psychological defense. The normal human response to mass death and profound horror is not rage or depression or panic or mourning or even fear: it is a kind of mental anesthetization that interferes with both judgment and compassion for other people.

In even minor disasters, the mind becomes immobilized, if only for a moment. But in the event of a nuclear attack, the immobilization may reach the point where the psyche is no longer connected to its own past and is, for all practical purposes, severed from the social forms from which it drew strength and a sense of humanity. The mind would then be shut down altogether.

The resulting scene might very well resemble what we usually can only imagine as science fiction. The landscape is almost moon-like, spare and quiet, and the survivors who root among the ruins seem to have lost contact with one another, not to mention the ability to form cooperating groups and to offer warmth and solace to people around them.

In every catastrophe for which we have adequate records, survivors emerge from the debris with the feeling that they are (to use the anthropologist Anthony Wallace's words) "naked and alone . . . in a terrifying wilderness of ruins."

In most cases—and this, too, is well recorded in the literature of disaster—that sense of isolation quickly disappears with the realization that the rest of the world is still intact. The disaster, it turns out, is local, confined, bounded. Out there beyond the periphery of the affected zone are other people—relatives, neighbors, countrymen—who bring blankets and warm coffee, medicines and ambulances. The larger human community is gathering its resources to attend to a wound on its flank, and survivors respond to the attention and caring with the reassuring feeling that there is life beyond the ruins after all. That sense of communion, that perception that the textures of social existence remain more or less whole, is a very important part of the healing that follows.

None of that would happen in nuclear war.

There would be no surrounding human community, no undamaged world out there to count on.

No one would come in to nurse the wounded or carry them off to hospitals. There would be no hospitals, no morphine, no antibiotics.

There would be no succor outside—no infusion of the vitality, the confidence in the continuity of life, that disaster victims have always needed so desperately.

Rather, survivors would remain in a deadened state, either alone or among others like themselves, largely without hope and vaguely aware that everyone and everything that once mattered to them had been destroyed. Thus, survivors would experience not only the most extreme forms of individual trauma imaginable but an equally severe form of collective trauma stemming from a rupture of the patterns of social existence.

Virtually no survivors would be able to enact that most fundamental of all human rituals, burying their own dead. The bonds that had linked people in connecting groups would be badly torn, in most cases irreparably, and the behavior of the survivors likely to become muted and accompanied by suspiciousness and extremely primitive forms of thought and action.

Under these conditions, such simple tasks as acquiring food and maintaining shelter would remain formidable for weeks and months, even years. And the bands of survivors would be further reduced not only by starvation but also by continuing exposure to radiation and by virulent epidemics.

For those who managed to stay alive, the effects of radiation might interfere with their capacity to reproduce at all or with their capacity to give birth to anything other than grossly deformed infants. But few indeed would have to face that prospect.

The question so often asked, "Would the survivors envy the dead?" may turn out to have a simple answer. No, they would be incapable of such feelings. They would not so much envy as, inwardly and outwardly, resemble the dead.

NEW CIVIL-DEFENSE AIM: EMPTY MAJOR CITIES

Orr Kelly

Orr Kelly, at the time this article was written, was a staff writer for
U.S. News and World Report.

Amid rising controversy over President Reagan's nuclear-arms policy, a White
House plan for a vast new civil-defense program has ignited a political firestorm.

The plan spelled out in late March [1982] calls, in case of a nuclear
showdown with the Soviet Union, for evacuating to the countryside the 145
million Americans living in 400 high-risk areas in big cities and near vital
military bases.

Key to the proposal is the assumption that risk of a nuclear war would
be obvious days before it actually began—not a surprise attack of the sort that
formed the basis of the last civil-defense program, which called for sending
people to nearby shelters.

Experts predict that an all-out nuclear attack today probably would kill
some 139 million of the nation's population of 231 million. Proponents claim
the new plan would cut the death toll to about 46 million.

"Our goal is to double the number of Americans that would survive from
a major Soviet attack on the U.S.," said Louis O Giuffrida, Director of the
Federal Emergency Management Agency.

STRATEGIC AIM

The plan also has a strategic purpose: To prevent a situation from developing
during an eyeball-to-eyeball confrontation in which the Soviets could empty
their cities but the U.S. could not, thus perhaps encouraging the Russians to
believe they could strike first and win.

Critics, some of them already at odds with the administration over the
issue of a nuclear-weapons freeze, retorted that the new civilian-defense program is part of an effort by the Reagan administration to convince Americans
that it is possible to fight—and win—a nuclear war. Merely putting the plan
into effect, opponents warned, would edge closer the possibility of an atomic
holocaust.

Source: Orr Kelly, "New Civil-Defense Aim: Empty Major Cities," *U.S. News and World Report* (April 12,
1982), pp. 45–46. Reprinted from *U.S. News & World Report* issue of April 12, 1982. Copyright
1982, U.S. News & World Report, Inc.

Others attacked the program on a pragmatic basis, arguing that monumental traffic jams and general chaos would result if officials tried to empty America's largest cities. Still other opponents contended that money could be better spent in other ways to increase the nation's defenses.

The new civil-defense scheme differs significantly from those put forward in the 1950s and 1960s, largely because of the enormous rise in the number of nuclear weapons now aimed at the U.S.

Once it was assumed that an atomic attack would destroy some cities but leave many others intact. Now the assumption is that 400 targets—all the U.S. cities of more than 50,000 population, the bomber and nuclear-submarine bases, the missile silos and other military and industrial sites—might be hit almost simultaneously.

The number of Americans living or working in those high-risk areas totals 145 million, and for them there would be no place to hide.

The new plan is to move them out into the countryside to host areas where they would be relatively safe from blast, heat and the initial burst of nuclear radiation. They would require protection—perhaps for weeks—from deadly radioactive particles carried by the winds.

The new approach is predicated on the conviction of civil-defense planners that the U.S. would get several days' notice of an impending Soviet nuclear attack during a period of growing tension, as occurred in the Cuban missile crisis of 1962. Aside from being tipped off by an exchange of demands and threats, officials count on the detection by intelligence sources of other signs of danger such as movement of ships and troops and a higher alert status for Russian nuclear forces.

RULED OUT: SURPRISE

Administration experts consider a bolt-from-the-blue surprise attack very unlikely, because this would bar evacuation of Soviet cities and leave the Russian population defenseless against a return blow from the United States. "Even if we have as little as 3 hours' warning, our program will save lives," says Giuffrida of FEMA. "If we have a week's warning, our program will be a significant benefit."

In contrast to earlier civil-defense programs that called for widespread civilian preparation in the form of fallout shelters and stocking of emergency supplies, the new plan requires virtually no involvement by most Americans until a nuclear war appears imminent. If that happens, this is how the plan is supposed to unfold:

- Each target city would have its own evacuation plan, with a corps of civil-defense workers trained to direct the exodus. Evacuation maps, along with instructions on where to go and what to do, would be printed in telephone books.

- When people from the cities reached the countryside, many would be put to work. Some would operate kitchens for mass feedings. Others would be handed shovels and told to stack dirt around shelters for protection against radiation from nuclear fallout.
- Evacuees would be housed in schools, churches and other public buildings, not in private homes. Engineering students hired during the summers already have checked out 975,000 of the 1.6 million shelters needed.
- Each person would be allotted an area of 40 square feet—about 6⅓ feet on a side. If a cloud of nuclear fallout were expected, evacuees would move into much more crowded fallout shelters.
- During peacetime, 20,000 shelter-management instructors would be trained. In a crisis, they would conduct crash courses to teach a million others.
- Seven million radiation devices would be available to tell survivors when they could leave the shelters and where they could safely travel.
- News and instructions would come from some of the 2,770 broadcast stations that would be protected from fallout and the disrupting effects of radiation given off by a nuclear explosion.

Critics of the plan seized on a comment by T. K. Jones, a longtime civil-defense advocate and now a deputy under secretary of defense, in an interview with the *Los Angeles Times.* "Everybody's going to make it if there are enough shovels to go around," Jones said. "Dig a hole, cover it with a couple of doors and then throw 3 feet of dirt on top. It's the dirt that does it."

Under angry questioning by members of the Senate Foreign Relations Committee on March 31, Jones said he did not mean to imply that a nuclear war is "winnable." But he insisted that the Soviet Union, using simple earthen shelters to protect its citizens, is much better equipped to survive an atomic exchange than the U.S.

BUDGET BOOST

The Reagan civil-defense plan is estimated to cost 4.2 billion dollars over seven years, not counting inflation. As a first step, Congress is being asked this year for 252 million dollars, nearly double the civil-defense spending in the 1982 budget.

Some administration spokesmen were more restrained than FEMA officials in describing the new program. Assistant Defense Secretary Richard Perle told members of Congress that the plan is "little more than insurance—insurance that in circumstances short of a central strategic exchange, some lives might be saved that would otherwise be lost."

Perle also gave a gloomy picture of what might happen if the plan were ever put into effect: "Evacuation would gravely deepen the crisis and would indeed be destabilizing. Evacuation would be accompanied by dread fear and most likely panic."

Others were far more critical. Senator Alan Cranston (D-Calif.) described the proposal as "faulty and perilous" and "a cruel and dangerous hoax on the American people."

Retired Vice Adm. Noel Gayler, whose naval career included a stint as deputy head of the staff that selects strategic targets in the Soviet Union, said the plan "generates a mind-set toward nuclear war."

It is impossible to hide from a nuclear attack, Gayler said, adding: "I've done the targeting. If you want to evacuate your cities, I'll target the evacuation areas."

Several communities—among them Cambridge, Mass.; Sacramento County, Calif.; Brattleboro, Vt., and Boulder County, Colo.—already have refused to take part in evacuation plans.

On April 1, the Senate Armed Services Committee dealt the plan a blow when it refused to provide the funds needed to get started on the program.

Twice before—in the early 1950s after the Soviets developed their own nuclear weapons, and again in the early 1960s when the Berlin and Cuban crises brought the threat of war—the U.S. set civil-defense plans in motion. In both cases, the drives faded out after the crises had passed.

In today's climate of rising worry over a nuclear conflict and concern over sharply increased budget deficits, Reagan's new attempt to overhaul U.S. civil-defense policy faces the toughest test yet.

THE NUCLEAR WINTER

Carl Sagan

Carl Sagan is David Duncan Professor of Astronomy and Space Studies and director of the Laboratory for Planetary Studies at Cornell University.

"Into the eternal darkness, into fire, into ice."

—Dante. *The Inferno*

Except for fools and madmen, everyone knows that nuclear war would be an unprecedented human catastrophe. A more or less typical strategic warhead

Source: Carl Sagan, "The Nuclear Winter," *Parade Magazine* (Oct. 30, 1983), pp. 4–7. Reprinted by permission of the author and the author's agents, Scott Meredith Literary Agency, Inc., 845 Third Avenue, New York, New York 10022.

has a yield of 2 megatons, the explosive equivalent of 2 million tons of TNT. But 2 million tons of TNT is about the same as all the bombs exploded in World War II—a single bomb with the explosive power of the entire Second World War but compressed into a few seconds of time and an area 30 or 40 miles across . . .

In a 2-megaton explosion over a fairly large city, buildings would be vaporized, people reduced to atoms and shadows, outlying structures blown down like matchsticks and raging fires ignited. And if the bomb were exploded on the ground, an enormous crater, like those that can be seen through a telescope on the surface of the Moon, would be all that remained where midtown once had been. There are now more than 50,000 nuclear weapons, more than 13,000 megatons of yield, deployed in the arsenals of the United States and the Soviet Union—enough to obliterate a million Hiroshimas.

But there are fewer than 3000 cities on the Earth with populations of 100,000 or more. You cannot find anything like a million Hiroshimas to obliterate. Prime military and industrial targets that are far from cities are comparatively rare. Thus, there are vastly more nuclear weapons than are needed for any plausible deterrence of a potential adversary.

Nobody knows, of course, how many megatons would be exploded in a real nuclear war. There are some who think that a nuclear war can be "contained," bottled up before it runs away to involve much of the world's arsenals. But a number of detailed analyses, war games run by the U.S. Department of Defense, and official Soviet pronouncements all indicate that this containment may be too much to hope for: Once the bombs begin exploding, communications failures, disorganization, fear, the necessity of making in minutes decisions affecting the fates of millions, and the immense psychological burden of knowing that your own loved ones may already have been destroyed are likely to result in a nuclear paroxysm. Many investigations, including a number of studies for the U.S. government, envision the explosion of 5000 to 10,000 megatons—the detonation of tens of thousands of nuclear weapons that now sit quietly, inconspicuously, in missile silos, submarines and long-range bombers, faithful servants awaiting orders.

The World Health Organization, in a recent detailed study chaired by Sune K. Bergstrom (the 1982 Nobel laureate in physiology and medicine), concludes that 1.1 billion people would be killed outright in such a nuclear war, mainly in the United States, the Soviet Union, Europe, China and Japan. An additional 1.1 billion people would suffer serious injuries and radiation sickness, for which medical help would be unavailable. It thus seems possible that more than 2 billion people—almost half of all the humans on Earth—would be destroyed in the immediate aftermath of a global thermonuclear war. This would represent by far the greatest disaster in the history of the human species and, with no other adverse effects, would probably be enough to reduce at least the Northern Hemisphere to a state of prolonged agony and barbarism. Unfortunately, the real situation would be much worse.

In technical studies of the consequences of nuclear weapons explosions, there has been a dangerous tendency to underestimate the results. This is partly due to a tradition of conservatism which generally works well in science but which is of more dubious applicability when the lives of billions of people are at stake. In the Bravo test of March 1, 1954, a 15-megaton thermonuclear bomb was exploded on Bikini Atoll. It had about double the yield expected, and there was an unanticipated last-minute shift in the wind direction. As a result, deadly radioactive fallout came down on Rongelap in the Marshall Islands, more than 200 kilometers away. Almost all the children on Rongelap subsequently developed thyroid nodules and lesions, and other long-term medical problems, due to the radioactive fallout.

Likewise, in 1973, it was discovered that high-yield airbursts will chemically burn the nitrogen in the upper air, converting it into oxides of nitrogen; these, in turn, combine with and destroy the protective ozone in the Earth's stratosphere. The surface of the Earth is shielded from deadly solar ultraviolet radiation by a layer of ozone so tenuous that, were it brought down to sea level, it would be only 3 millimeters thick. Partial destruction of this ozone layer can have serious consequences for the biology of the entire planet.

These discoveries, and others like them, were made by chance. They were largely unexpected. And now another consequence—by far the most dire—has been uncovered, again more or less by accident.

The U.S. Mariner 9 spacecraft, the first vehicle to orbit another planet, arrived at Mars in late 1971. The planet was enveloped in a global dust storm. As the fine particles slowly fell out, we were able to measure temperature changes in the atmosphere and on the surface. Soon it became clear what had happened:

The dust, lofted by high winds off the desert into the upper Martian atmosphere, had absorbed the incoming sunlight and prevented much of it from reaching the ground. Heated by the sunlight, the dust warmed the adjacent air. But the surface, enveloped in partial darkness, became much chillier than usual. Months later, after the dust fell out of the atmosphere, the upper air cooled and the surface warmed, both returning to their normal conditions. We were able to calculate accurately, from how much dust there was in the atmosphere, how cool the Martian surface ought to have been.

Afterwards, I and my colleagues, James B. Pollack and Brian Toon of NASA's Ames Research Center, were eager to apply these insights to the Earth. In a volcanic explosion, dust aerosols are lofted into the high atmosphere. We calculated by how much the Earth's global temperature should decline after a major volcanic explosion and found that our results (generally a fraction of a degree) were in good accord with actual measurements. Joining forces with Richard Turco, who has studied the effects of nuclear weapons for many years, we then began to turn our attention to the climatic effects of nuclear war. [The scientific paper, "Global Atmospheric Consequences of Nuclear War," is written by R. P. Turco, O. B. Toon, T. P. Ackerman, J. B. Pollack and Carl Sagan. From the last names of the authors, this work is generally referred to as "TTAPS."]

We knew that nuclear explosions, particularly groundbursts, would lift an enormous quantity of fine soil particles into the atmosphere (more than 100,000 tons of fine dust for every megaton exploded in a surface burst). Our work was further spurred by Paul Crutzen of the Max Planck Institute for Chemistry in Mainz, West Germany, and by John Birks of the University of Colorado, who pointed out that huge quantities of smoke would be generated in the burning of cities and forests following a nuclear war.

Groundbursts—at hardened missile silos, for example—generate fine dust. Airbursts—over cities and unhardened military installations—make fires and therefore smoke. The amount of dust and soot generated depends on the conduct of the war, the yields of the weapons employed and the ratio of groundbursts to airbursts. So we ran computer models for several dozen different nuclear war scenarios. Our baseline case, as in many other studies, was a 5000-megaton war with only a modest fraction of the yield (20 percent) expended on urban or industrial targets. Our job, for each case, was to follow the dust and smoke generated, see how much sunlight was absorbed and by how much the temperatures changed, figure out how the particles spread in longitude and latitude, and calculate how long before it all fell out of the air back onto the surface. Since the radioactivity would be attached to these same fine particles, our calculations also revealed the extent and timing of the subsequent radioactive fallout.

Some of what I am about to describe is horrifying. I know, because it horrifies me. There is a tendency—psychiatrists call it "denial"—to put it out of our minds, not to think about it. But if we are to deal intelligently, wisely, with the nuclear arms race, then we must steel ourselves to contemplate the horrors of nuclear war.

The results of our calculations astonished us. In the baseline case, the amount of sunlight at the ground was reduced to a few percent of normal—much darker, in daylight, than in a heavy overcast and too dark for plants to make a living from photosynthesis. At least in the Northern Hemisphere, where the great preponderance of strategic targets lies, an unbroken and deadly gloom would persist for weeks.

Even more unexpected were the temperatures calculated. In the baseline case, land temperatures, except for narrow strips of coastline, dropped to minus 25° Celsius (minus 13° Fahrenheit) and stayed below freezing for months—

even for a summer war. (Because the atmospheric structure becomes much more stable as the upper atmosphere is heated and the lower air is cooled, we may have severely *under*estimated how long the cold and the dark would last.) The oceans, a significant heat reservoir, would not freeze, however, and a major ice age would probably not be triggered. But because the temperatures would drop so catastrophically, virtually all crops and farm animals, at least in the Northern Hemisphere, would be destroyed, as would most varieties of uncultivated or undomesticated food supplies. Most of the human survivors would starve.

In addition, the amount of radioactive fallout is much more than expected. Many previous calculations simply ignored the intermediate time-scale fallout. That is, calculations were made for the prompt fallout—the plumes of radioactive debris blown downwind from each target—and for the long-term fallout, the fine radioactive particles lofted into the stratosphere that would descend about a year later, after most of the radioactivity had decayed. However, the radioactivity carried into the upper atmosphere (but not as high as the stratosphere) seems to have been largely forgotten. We found for the baseline case that roughly 30 percent of the land at northern midlatitudes could receive a radioactive dose greater than 250 rads, and that about 50 percent of northern midlatitudes could receive a dose greater than 100 rads. A 100-rad dose is the equivalent of about 1000 medical X-rays. A 400-rad dose will, more likely than not, kill you.

The cold, the dark and the intense radioactivity, together lasting for months, represent a severe assault on our civilization and our species. Civil and sanitary services would be wiped out. Medical facilities, drugs, the most rudimentary means for relieving the vast human suffering, would be unavailable. Any but the most elaborate shelters would be useless, quite apart from the question of what good it might be to emerge a few months later. Synthetics burned in the destruction of the cities would produce a wide variety of toxic gases, including carbon monoxide, cyanides, dioxins and furans. After the dust and soot settled out, the solar ultraviolet flux would be much larger than its present value. Immunity to disease would decline. Epidemics and pandemics would be rampant, especially after the billion or so unburied bodies began to thaw. Moreover, the combined influence of these severe and simultaneous stresses on life are likely to produce even more adverse consequences—biologists call them synergisms—that we are not yet wise enough to foresee.

So far, we have talked only of the Northern Hemisphere. But now it seems—unlike the case of a single nuclear weapons test—that in a real nuclear war, the heating of the vast quantities of atmospheric dust and soot in northern midlatitudes will transport these fine particles toward and across the Equator. We see just this happening in Martian dust storms. The Southern

Hemisphere would experience effects that, while less severe than in the Northern Hemisphere, are nevertheless extremely ominous. The illusion with which some people in the Northern Hemisphere reassure themselves—catching an Air New Zealand flight in a time of serious international crisis, or the like—is now much less tenable, even on the narrow issue of personal survival for those with the price of a ticket.

But what if nuclear wars *can* be contained, and much less than 5000 megatons is detonated? Perhaps the greatest surprise in our work was that even small nuclear wars can have devastating climatic effects. We considered a war in which a mere 100 megatons were exploded, less than one percent of the world arsenals, and only in low-yield airbursts over cities. This scenario, we found, would ignite thousands of fires, and the smoke from these fires alone would be enough to generate an epoch of cold and dark almost as severe as in the 5000-megaton case. The threshold for what Richard Turco has called The Nuclear Winter is very low.

Could we have overlooked some important effect? The carrying of dust and soot from the Northern to the Southern Hemisphere (as well as more local atmospheric circulation) will certainly thin the clouds out over the Northern Hemisphere. But, in many cases, this thinning would be insufficient to render the climatic consequences tolerable—and every time it got better in the Northern Hemisphere, it would get worse in the Southern.

Our results have been carefully scrutinized by more than 100 scientists in the United States, Europe and the Soviet Union. There are still arguments on points of detail. But the overall conclusion seems to be agreed upon: There are severe and previously unanticipated global consequences of nuclear war—subfreezing temperatures in a twilit radioactive gloom lasting for months or longer.

Scientists initially underestimated the effects of fallout, were amazed that nuclear explosions in space disabled distant satellites, had no idea that the fireballs from high-yield thermonuclear explosions could deplete the ozone layer and missed altogether the possible climatic effects of nuclear dust and smoke. What else have we overlooked?

Nuclear war is a problem that can be treated only theoretically. It is not amenable to experimentation. Conceivably, we have left something important out of our analysis, and the effects are more modest than we calculate. On the other hand, it is also possible—and, from previous experience, even likely—that there are further adverse effects that no one has yet been wise enough to recognize. With billions of lives at stake, where does conservatism lie—in assuming that the results will be better than we calculate, or worse?

Many biologists, considering the nuclear winter that these calculations describe, believe they carry somber implications for life on Earth. Many species of plants and animals would become extinct. Vast numbers of surviving humans would starve to death. The delicate ecological relations that bind together organisms on Earth in a fabric of mutual dependency would be torn, perhaps irreparably. There is little question that our global civilization would be reduced to prehistoric levels, or less. Life for any survivors would be extremely hard. And there seems to be a real possibility of the extinction of the human species.

It is now almost 40 years since the invention of nuclear weapons. We have not yet experienced a global thermonuclear war—although on more than one occasion we have come tremulously close. I do not think our luck can hold forever. Men and machines are fallible, as recent events remind us. Fools and madmen do exist, and sometimes rise to power. Concentrating always on the near future, we have ignored the long-term consequences of our actions. We have placed our civilization and our species in jeopardy.

Fortunately, it is not yet too late. We can safeguard the planetary civilization and the human family if we so choose. There is no more important or more urgent issue.

NRC PANEL ENVISIONS POTENTIAL NUCLEAR WINTER
R. Jeffrey Smith

R. Jeffrey Smith is a staff writer for *Science*.

An expert panel of the National Research Council (NRC) has concluded that a major nuclear war could potentially result in a substantial period of darkness and markedly lowered temperatures on the earth's surface, with a severe impact on surviving plants and animals, including man.

This scenario, which has come to be known as a "nuclear winter," was first envisioned only a few years ago. But since then, it has been a topic of intense scientific interest. Some military planners suggest that if true, it could render useless much civil defense planning, transform a nuclear first strike into a suicidal act, and eliminate hope of escaping the adverse effects of a major nuclear conflict anywhere on the globe (*Science*, 6 July, p. 30 [1984]). Consequently, "nuclear winter" has lately become a topic of increasing political

Source: R. Jeffrey Smith, "NRC Panel Envisions Potential Nuclear Winter," *Science* 226 (Dec. 21, 1984), p. 1043. Copyright 1984 by the American Association for the Advancement of Science.

controversy, with experts such as Edward Teller asserting that it is unlikely and others such as Carl Sagan suggesting that it is all but certain.

On 11 December [1984], the NRC [joined the] debate with a report that essentially endorses the notion that a "nuclear winter," created by the atmospheric injection of massive amounts of light-absorbing dust and soot from nuclear detonations, is possible. More than earlier studies, however, it emphasizes the extensive uncertainties behind existing predictions of the climatic aftermath of a nuclear war. As panel chairman George Carrier, a professor of applied mathematics at Harvard University, explains, "Our present knowledge is simply insufficient to make a definitive statement about the state of the atmosphere that would result from such an exchange. Nevertheless, when one makes plausible estimates, the results look very worrisome and one can't rule out the possibility that the impact might be very severe. Consequently, it has to be taken seriously."

Unlike most NRC panels, which usually analyze relevant literature, Carrier's group conducted its own research. Specifically, it envisioned that a major nuclear exchange could involve half of the world's present arsenals, or roughly 6500 megatons. It assumed that all of these weapons would be aimed at military, not civilian targets, but that one-fourth would detonate in cities that happened to contain such targets. It assumed that the resultant forest and urban fires would lift enormous quantities of dust and soot into the earth's atmosphere, and that some would linger there for anywhere from weeks to months.

"Estimation of the amounts, the vertical distributions, and subsequent fates of these materials involves large uncertainties," the panel says. "Furthermore, accurate detailed accounts of the response of the atmosphere, the redistribution and removal of the depositions, and the duration of a greatly degraded environment lie beyond the present state of knowledge." After incorporating its best estimates in a one-dimensional climatic model, however, the panel concluded that "there is a clear possibility" that much of the land areas of the northern temperate zone could suffer a temperature reduction of perhaps $10°$ to $25°C$, lasting for weeks, as well as subnormal—but less extreme—temperatures that might persist for months. "The impact of these temperature reductions and associated meteorological changes on the surviving population, and on the biosphere that supports the survivors, could be severe, and deserves careful independent study."

In its modeling, the panel made a particular effort to address a major criticism of earlier studies—namely, that the climatic models were implausible, either because they depicted deliberate targeting of cities or because they failed to consider geographical overlap between nuclear detonations. Carrier says that the panel was able to consult with several targeting experts on the panel itself, including two retired admirals and a former National Security Council staff member, as well as others. "The result is that our targeting scenario does conform to general military planning," he says. "I don't pretend that this is how a war will occur, but all of the elements here are realistic."

The panel deliberately omitted discussion of other worrisome consequences of a nuclear war, such as prompt radiation, blast, and thermal effects, as well as long-term radioactive fallout and an expected shortage of medical facilities. At the behest of its sponsor, the Defense Nuclear Agency, it also declined to assess the consequences of a more limited nuclear exchange. However, it noted that "any war scenario that subjects . . . city centers to nuclear attack, even one employing a very small fraction of the existing nuclear arsenal, could generate nearly as much smoke as in the 6500-megaton baseline scenario." In short, even a small exchange could potentially create some "nuclear winter" effects.

The report indicates that despite all the uncertainties, the postwar world would be decidedly grim. Large-scale fires would be prevalent in both urban and forested areas, emitting large quantities of carbon monoxide, nitrogen oxides, and organic compounds, as well as noxious chemicals, such as PCB's, dioxins, and dibenzofurans. The amount of soot expected to survive swift atmospheric scavenging is estimated by the panel at anywhere between 20 and 650 million metric tons, with an intermediate level of 150 million metric tons. Total darkness might result in some areas. Atmospheric ozone could be diminished by as much as 17 percent. "Although Southern Hemisphere effects would be much less extensive, significant amounts of dust and smoke could drift to and across the equator as early as a few weeks after a nuclear exchange," the panel says.

Richard Turco, an atmospheric scientist with R&D Associates in California and one of the principal authors of a less equivocal study of nuclear winter in *Science* last December, characterizes the NRC report as a "weak endorsement of our work. While it doesn't exactly confirm what we did, it indicates clearly that there were no oversights of a simple nature that would tend to explain all this away." The significance, he says, lies in the fact that it was prepared and reviewed by a group with diverse expertise and political orientation. "In a sense, it legitimizes this problem as a topic for additional research," he says.

Michael MacCracken, an atmospheric scientist at Lawrence Livermore National Laboratory, agrees. "It was easy for many people to dismiss the phenomenon of nuclear winter when it was first envisioned. This study will help pull people up to the current level of understanding: namely, that it is possible for this to happen, and that there is no fatal flaw that negates the work performed to date."

FOR FURTHER READING

Adams, Ruth, and Susan Cullen, eds. *The Final Epidemic: Physicians and Scientists on Nuclear War.* Chicago: Educational Foundation for Nuclear Science (distributed by The University of Chicago Press), 1981 (paperback). Contains several useful articles on the probable consequences of nuclear war.

Babyak, Blythe. "The Plane: Cruising to Armageddon." *Washington Monthly* (December 1978), pp. 32–36. Describes plans to save the President in the event of nuclear attack on the United States.

Beilenson, Laurence. "Selling Civil Defense." *Journal of Civil Defense* (December 1981), pp. 6–8. An argument, by a long-time and influential advocate, for far greater investment in civil defense preparations than past or present levels. Argues that the Soviet Union has a civil defense system vastly superior to that of the United States.

Beres, Louis René. "Subways to Armageddon." *Society* 20 (November 1983), pp. 7–10. A highly critical analysis of the proposed Crisis Relocation Plans of the Carter and Reagan administrations. In the same journal, this article is followed by several rebuttals. Collectively, they make a valuable pro–con discussion.

Chivian, Eric, et al., eds. *Last Aid: The Medical Dimensions of Nuclear War.* San Francisco: W. H. Freeman and Co., 1982 (paperback). A collection of articles by physicians from several nations examining effects of nuclear weapons and the physical and medical consequences of the atomic bombings of Japan and of a nuclear war. Very pessimistic about survival prospects.

Clayton, Bruce. *The Day After Doomsday: A Survivalist Guide to Nuclear War and Other Disasters.* New York: Doubleday, 1981. A detailed discussion of measures that can be taken to increase chances of survival. Guardedly optimistic about survival prospects.

Director of the Central Intelligence Agency. *Soviet Civil Defense.* Washington, D.C.: U.S. Central Intelligence Agency, 1978. Concludes that Soviet civil defense preparations would probably be overwhelmed by a nuclear attack.

Downey, Thomas K. "The Misguided Concept." *Worldview* (Jan./Feb. 1979), p. 44. U.S. Representative Downey argues against U.S. investment in Crisis Relocation Planning on the grounds that the existing Russian civil defense system would not enable its society to survive a nuclear war.

Drell, Sidney, and Frank von Hippel. "Limited Nuclear War." *Scientific American* (November 1976), pp. 27–37. Analyzes scenarios for a "limited" nuclear war in which attacks are confined to each side's strategic weapons; concludes that high number of casualties—with or without civil defense—would make the military value of such attacks doubtful.

Federal Emergency Management Agency. *Civil Defense Program Overview, FY 1983–FY 1989.* Washington, D.C.: Federal Emergency Management Agency, 1982, 23 pp. A detailed description of the "revised and improved National Civil Defense Program for the United States" as called for by President Reagan early in his first term in office.

Haaland, Carsten M. "Nuclear Winter and National Security." *Journal of Civil Defense* (February 1984), pp. 6–8. Haaland argues that the "nuclear winter" report overestimates the amount of soot that would be cast into the air and that it underestimates the capacity of "natural scavenging processes," like rain, to wash clouds of soot out of the air.

Jones, T. K. "Civil Defense for America Is No Laughing Matter." *L.A. Times* (March 15, 1985). A long-time advocate of extensive civil defense prepa-

rations argues that present Soviet civil defense capabilities require the
United States to develop its own.

Kaplan, Fred. "The Soviet Civil Defense Myth." *Bulletin of the Atomic Scientists,*
Part I (March 1978), pp. 14–20; Part II (March 1978), pp. 41–48. Argues that alleged Soviet civil defense capabilities are in fact greatly over-
rated and would not enable Soviet society to survive nuclear attack.

Katz, Arthur M. *Life After Nuclear War: The Economic and Social Impacts of Nuclear Attacks on the United States.* Cambridge, Mass.: Ballinger Publishing
Co., 1982. A richly documented analysis of several "attack cases" that
pays particular attention to social and psychological consequences.

Kincade, William. "Repeating History: The Civil Defense Debate Renewed."
International Security (Winter 1978), pp. 99–110. Views civil defense as
having both strategic and humanitarian functions. Reviews literature on
theory and practice of both U.S. and Soviet civil defense.

Leaning, Jennifer, and Matthew Leighton. "The World According to FEMA."
Bulletin of the Atomic Scientists 39 (June/July 1984), pp. 2S–6S. A skeptical, succinct, and thoroughly documented summary of the Federal Emergency Management Agency's assumptions about civil defense and nuclear
war survival. Reviews FEMA research studies, program planning, and
public education.

————, and Langley Keyes, eds. *The Counterfeit Ark: Crisis Relocation Planning
for Nuclear War.* Cambridge, Mass.: Ballinger Publishing Co., 1984
(available in paperback). A collection of articles by a variety of scholars
critical of the assumptions of Crisis Relocation Planning.

Lewis, Kevin. "Prompt and Delayed Effects of Nuclear War." *Scientific American*
241 (July 1979), pp. 35–47. A thorough yet concise analysis of the
probable consequences of a large nuclear war.

Postol, Theodore A. "Strategic Confusion—With or Without Nuclear Winter."
Bulletin of the Atomic Scientists 41 (February 1985), pp. 14–17. Good discussion of the implications of nuclear winter for nuclear weapons policy.

Powers, Thomas. "Is Nuclear War 'Impossible'?" *The Atlantic* 254 (November
1984), pp. 53–64. Argues that the "nuclear winter" phenomenon, if
proven valid, would render current Soviet and American nuclear weapons
policies obsolete.

Sagan, Carl. "Nuclear War and Climatic Catastrophe: Some Policy Implications."
Foreign Affairs 62 (Winter 1983/84), pp. 257–92. A readable, nontechni-
cal discussion of the "nuclear winter" phenomenon that also considers the
potential impact of the new data on current nuclear weapons policies.

Smith, R. Jeffrey. "DOD Says 'Nuclear Winter' Bolsters Its Plans." *Science* 227
(March 15, 1985), p. 1320. Reports on recent Pentagon studies of the
probability and implications of nuclear winter.

Weinstein, John M. "Civil Defense: Strategic Implications, Practical Problems."
In Robert Kennedy and John Weinstein, *The Defense of the West.* Boulder,
Colo.: Westview Press, 1984. Examines the Soviet civil defense program
and evaluates U.S. civil defense options.

Winkler, Allen. "A 40 Year History of Civil Defense." *Bulletin of the Atomic Scientists* 40 (June/July 1984), pp. 16–22. A brief, nonpartisan historical
overview of relevant federal agencies and programs.

World Health Organization. *Effects of Nuclear War on Health and Health Services.*
Geneva: World Health Organization, 1984. A report by an international

group of physicians and other health care professionals that estimates the short-term and long-term impacts of three possible scenarios of nuclear war. Arrives at pessimistic conclusions.

Zuckerman, Edward. *The Day After World War III*. New York: Viking, 1983. A carefully researched, fascinating description of the plans being made to reconstitute American society after a nuclear war. Includes details of the postwar postal system, survival facilities for national leaders, and many other aspects of ongoing plans.

4

The Debate Over U.S. Strategic Nuclear Weapons Policy

In this chapter, we turn to an examination of American nuclear weapons policy, and the debate over what U.S. policy should be. This requires us to think hard about basic issues: How does the existence of nuclear weapons affect the national security of the United States? What is the proper role for nuclear weapons in U.S. national security policy? Must nuclear war be avoided at all costs, or are there circumstances under which a nuclear war with the Soviet Union could be "limited," "controlled," or "won"? How politically and militarily "usable" are nuclear weapons?

As Jeffrey D. Porro points out in his article "The Policy War: Brodie vs. Kahn," these issues have driven the postwar debate about the impact of nuclear weapons on national security. This debate has focused around the conflicting ideas of two men. One, political scientist Bernard Brodie, had concluded as early as 1946 that nuclear weapons would be "usable" only insofar as they could threaten a potential attacker with devastating retaliation, and thus provide a credible deterrent to the first use of nuclear weapons. Because of the enormous destructive power of the new weapons, Brodie believed that it was illusory and dangerous to pursue such traditional military goals as defense or victory in a nuclear war.

In a series of books published in the 1960s, physicist Herman Kahn took issue with Brodie's view. Kahn acknowledged that nuclear weapons had rendered war prevention imperative and deterrence the overriding goal of strategy; and yet, he emphasized, deterrence could someday fail. In that event, Kahn argued, the United States should be prepared to fight nuclear war. From this perspective, he argued that nuclear weapons had not removed the need to think about defense, survival, and victory in war. Under the right circumstances, he contended, it would be possible for the United States to fight and win a nuclear war with the Soviet Union.

Both Brodie and Kahn are now dead, but as Porro illustrates, their writings and thinking have had important effects on the evolution of U.S. nuclear weapons policy. Although U.S. policymakers in the early 1960s flirted briefly with a strategy based on Kahn's notion that it was possible to fight and win a nuclear war, this gave way in the Johnson and early Nixon administrations to an emphasis on Brodie's approach, and the policy of threatening to retaliate and wreak "assured destruction" on Soviet society as a deterrent to a Soviet surprise attack. By the mid-1970s, however, U.S. policy had once more edged back toward Kahn's thinking. In 1974, then Secretary of Defense James Schlesinger announced a major reorientation in official U.S. policy on deterrence and nuclear war. In addition to maintaining an assured destruction retaliatory capability, Schlesinger revealed that the United States would develop additional, "flexible options" for the "limited" use of nuclear weapons below the level of all-out retaliation.

Schlesinger's ideas became the basis for U.S. nuclear weapons policy in the later Nixon and Ford administrations. Desmond Ball's contribution to this chapter, "PD-59: A Strategic Critique," explains how Jimmy Carter's Secretary of Defense, Harold Brown, took Schlesinger's revisions one step further. In his "countervailing strategy," Brown, like Schlesinger before him, underscored the importance of developing America's capacity to engage in limited nuclear strikes against the Soviet Union, and in particular, against Soviet nuclear forces. Brown also suggested that if deterrence failed, repeated but "controlled" nuclear "exchanges" with the Soviet Union might take place over a protracted period of time, in which case U.S. attacks would be intended to encourage a negotiated conclusion of hostilities.

Ball identifies several questionable technical and political assumptions which lie behind the "flexible nuclear options" or "limited nuclear warfighting" strategy, and concludes that these are untenable: nuclear war, once begun, could not be limited. He warns that the continuing infatuation of policymakers and strategists with a war-fighting strategy, by making nuclear war more "thinkable," may also make nuclear war more likely, thus increasing the risk of a holocaust which would be impossible to control.

It is only in this decade, however, that Herman Kahn's ideas have been fully rehabilitated. Perhaps the most influential and straightforward restatement of Kahn's views is the piece by Colin S. Gray and Keith B. Payne, "Victory is Possible." Like Kahn, Gray and Payne acknowledge the profound differences in destructive capability that separate nuclear from conventional high-explosive weapons, but nevertheless contend that traditional military concepts still retain their relevance in the discussion of nuclear strategy and nuclear war. In the prenuclear era, the ability of a country to deter invasion across its borders rested on its capacity for defense (that is, the use of non-nuclear forces to halt and defeat invading forces). In the nuclear age, according to Gray and Payne, so too does the credibility of *nuclear* deterrence rest on a willingness to use nuclear weapons effectively to defeat a potential enemy. They argue that a credible deterrent cannot be fashioned simply out of the ability to punish or "assuredly destroy" another nation following a first strike. A potential aggressor will only be deterred, they argue, if its leaders are convinced we can and will actually use our nuclear weapons to win a nuclear war. By this logic, Gray and Payne conclude that there exists a necessary connection between the United States' ability to "win" a nuclear war with the Soviet Union and our ability to deter the Soviets: The Soviet leadership would never start a nuclear war with the United States if the United States developed the capacity to first destroy a large portion of Soviet nuclear forces and then defend, or "limit damage" to, U.S. society against surviving Soviet weapons.

Primarily, Gray and Payne consider damage limitation and a "nuclear war-winning" strategy to be necessary for the support of U.S. foreign policy commitments. They note that the United States, to deter Soviet non-nuclear aggression against Western Europe, relies on the threat to use nuclear weapons first in the event of a European war. Additionally, the authors argue that the United States should be free to threaten the first use of nuclear weapons in future crises with the Soviet Union, and thus coerce the Soviets into retreating in these confrontations. According to Gray and Payne, only by being able to "dominate escalation" at the highest possible level of conflict—to win a strategic nuclear war with the Soviet Union—can U.S. leaders expect their nuclear threats to affect Soviet behavior.

Spurgeon M. Keeney, Jr., and Wolfgang K. H. Panofsky reject Gray and Payne's claim that nuclear war can be survived and won. In what is essentially a contemporary restatement of Bernard Brodie's ideas, they observe that for the present and foreseeable future, the Soviet Union and the United States will continue to exist in a world in which each retains thousands of nuclear warheads and bombs in its strategic arsenal. Under these conditions, even a defense that was 90 percent effective would fail to protect either country from catastrophic damage in nuclear war. Modern means of delivering nuclear weapons like ballistic missles are not only largely invulnerable to surprise attack, but impervious to defensive measures as well. Cities, on the other hand, remain extremely vulnerable to attack by these offensive nuclear weapons. New concepts for defense, which include space-based systems employing lasers, particle beams, or other "exotic" technologies, will not mitigate this essential and mutual vulnerability to nuclear retaliation, Keeney and Panofsky argue.

Keeney and Panofsky therefore use the term "mutual hostage relationship" in characterizing the nuclear dilemma faced by the superpowers. "Mutual assured destruction" is not a policy of choice, but a technological and political reality of Soviet-American relations. Part of coming to terms with that reality, the authors emphasize, is to recognize that nuclear weapons are inherently unusable for fighting, winning, or surviving nuclear war, and, for this reason, their diplomatic utility is limited as well: Nuclear weapons must be restricted to their proper and important role of deterring the first use of nuclear weapons against the United States or her allies.

In the "Reagan Nuclear Strategy," Robert C. Gray asks whether the Reagan administration has moved beyond the "limited" nuclear war-fighting strategy of the Nixon, Ford, and Carter administrations to embrace the full-fledged nuclear war-winning approach as discussed in "Victory is Possible." Gray concedes that various statements by senior Reagan national security officials and policy documents (like Defense Secretary Caspar Weinberger's "Fiscal 1984–1988 Defense Guidance") imply a shift to a war-winning strategy; yet he argues that the Reagan administration will simply continue the trend set earlier by Schlesinger and Brown: to acquire the counterforce and improved command and control forces necessary to wage a protracted (but "controlled") nuclear war—without endorsing the idea that such a war could actually be won.

Louis René Beres disagrees with this assessment of the Reagan nuclear strategy. In an interview, "U.S. Nuclear Strategy and World Order Reform," Beres terms the Reagan administration's approach to nuclear war "a significant departure from that of previous administrations." He contends that Reagan strategists have indeed adopted a nuclear war-winning strategy, citing as evidence the Reagan "strategic modernization program," which includes not only funding for counterforce weapons like the MX and sea-based Trident II missiles, but unprecedented investments in civil, air, and antiballistic missile defenses as well. In this sense, the administration's weapons programs are remarkably congruent with the kinds of initiatives Gray and Payne assert are necessary to achieve a nuclear war-winning capability. Beres, however, also makes a crucial point in observing that regardless of the semantical differences between them, the presence of either a war-*fighting* or a war-*winning* orientation in Washington may increase the risk of nuclear war, and thus reduce our security.

Although he believes both notions of controlling and winning nuclear war represent dangerous flights of fantasy, Beres is willing to endorse deterrence based on a "minimum" assured destruction capability as a legitimate U.S. goal—for the short to medium term. Over the long run, however, Beres fears the breakdown of deterrence and what he calls the "mutual threat" system of U.S.-Soviet security relations. To truly reduce the nuclear threat, he argues, the superpowers must strive for greater *global* security and equity, moderate their respective national impulses to pursue their own self-interests, and participate in a "global society of states."

THE POLICY WAR: BRODIE VS. KAHN

Jeffrey D. Porro

Jeffrey D. Porro is a former editor of *Arms Control Today,* the monthly journal of the Arms Control Association, a nonpartisan, Washington-based membership organization. He is coeditor with Marsha McGraw Olive of *Nuclear Weapons in Europe: Modernization and Limitation,* and with William H. Kincade, of *Negotiating Security: An Arms Control Reader.*

Fifteen years of public apathy about nuclear war have ended. Membership in arms control organizations is up. The nuclear freeze movement is growing. The national and local media regularly carry stories and features about arms control and the nuclear danger.

Most of the people newly concerned about arms control have, quite simply, been scared by the Reagan Administration. Vice President Bush's statement that a nuclear war is winnable, Secretary Haig's comments on a nuclear demonstration shot, President Reagan's musings on a European nuclear war, and recent quotes from Administration civil defense officials on the survivability of a nuclear war seem to add up to a radically new and dangerous policy.

People are right to be scared; the Administration's attitude is dangerous. But it is nothing new. Moreover, turning out the Reagan Administration will not, in itself, lessen the dangers of nuclear war.

American policy toward nuclear weapons has been shaped by a relatively small group of men, mostly civilians. During the last 20 years, most of these men have come to believe that we must think about nuclear war in the way we think about other kinds of war; that is, we must develop the plans and weapons necessary to fight. This nuclear warfighting strategy overlaps labels like Democratic and Republican, liberal and conservative.

This strategy has evolved from a conflict between the ideas of two men— Bernard Brodie and Herman Kahn. Educated as a political scientist at the University of Chicago, Bernard Brodie began his professional life before World War II with a number of well-received works on naval strategy. He turned his attention to atomic war after 1945, first at Yale and later at the RAND Corporation and the University of California at Los Angeles. The conclusions he drew about nuclear strategy were revolutionary.

Immediately after World War II, most strategists—civilian and mili-

Source: Jeffrey D. Porro, "The Policy War: Brodie vs. Kahn," *Bulletin of the Atomic Scientists* (June 1982), pp. 16–19. Reprinted by permission of the *Bulletin of the Atomic Scientists,* a magazine of science and world affairs. Copyright © 1982 by the Educational Foundation for Nuclear Science, Chicago, IL 60637.

tary—agreed that the atomic bomb had not altered military strategy fundamentally. But in a remarkable essay written within months of Hiroshima and
Nagasaki, Brodie took exception: "Thus far the chief purpose of our military
establishment has been to win wars. From now on its chief purpose must be
to prevent them. It can have almost no other useful purpose." [1] Brodie reasoned from Clausewitz's key insight that war is a *means* to a *political* objective.
If the costs of war outweighed the benefits of the political objective, war was
senseless.

In his early essays, Brodie focused on the likely costs of war. Since atomic
bombs could be acquired in large numbers and were so tremendously powerful, even if only a small percentage got through, hundreds of cities and millions of people would be destroyed. Brodie's conclusion: The costs to each side
in an atomic war would be so high they would far outweigh any meaningful
political goal. Neither side would be able to achieve "victory" in any valid
sense. Atomic weapons could be used only to prevent general war, not "win"
it.

To show just how atomic weapons should be used to prevent war, Brodie
dusted off an old concept, "deterrence." In the atomic age, Brodie said, the
key to deterrence was to guarantee that a potential attacker fear retaliation.

> If it must fear retaliation, the fact that it destroys its opponents'
> cities some hours or even days before its own are destroyed may avail it
> little. . . . Thus, the first and most vital step in any American security
> program for the age of atomic bombs is to take measures to guarantee to
> ourselves in case of attack the possibility of retaliation in kind. [2]

Throughout the 1950s, Brodie made it clear in his writings that deterrent strategy was very different from win-the-war strategies: The latter required superiority in numbers of weapons; deterrence did not. A relatively small
number of bombers and missiles—as long as they could survive—could damage an attacker enough to outweigh any conceivable political gain. In a war-
winning strategy, military might was used to destroy the enemy's weapons,
forcing him to surrender. In a deterrent strategy military might should be
directed against cities, not military forces, for two reasons:

- "Limiting damage" in any politically meaningful sense was impossible, given the destructive power of even a few nuclear weapons.
- More importantly, aiming at military forces could weaken deterrence
  and increase the chances of massive destruction. Any potential attacker "cares more for his cities intrinsically than he does for a few

---

[1] Bernard Brodie, "Implications for Military Policy," in *The Absolute Weapon,* ed. Bernard Brodie (New York:
Harcourt, Brace & Co., 1946), p. 74.
[2] Bernard Brodie, "Implications," pp. 73–76.

airfields."[3] . . . If the Soviets believed they would suffer only the loss of some military bases after they attacked us, they might be tempted. They would be much less tempted if they knew an attack would mean the loss of their cities.

Brodie's ideas—first published in 1946 and elaborated in the 1950s—dominated published works by civilian strategists until the early 1960s. But a significant minority of civilian strategic thinkers rejected them from the start. Many of these, interestingly enough, were Brodie's colleagues at RAND, but they also included some hard-line government officials like Paul Nitze, and Harvard's Henry Kissinger. Herman Kahn, however, most forcefully presented these anti-Brodie views.

Unlike Brodie, Kahn did not come to the analysis of nuclear warfare from studying military strategy in the pre-atomic era. Kahn studied physics and turned to strategy when he joined RAND in 1948. Kahn quantified and applied abstract logic to nuclear war. He translated deaths, destruction and even chromosome damage into columns of numbers, added up those on one side, compared them to those on the other, and decided who came out ahead. He dreamed up scenarios in which national leaders reasoned like chess players, trading off cities or millions of people, to place the enemy at a disadvantage on the board.

Kahn published *On Thermonuclear War* in 1960, resting his disagreement with Brodie on two points. First, nuclear war, like all other kinds of war, could be won or lost. Second, Brodie's version of deterrence was an insufficient strategy for the United States.

On his first point, Kahn claimed that, while a nuclear war was quite likely to be an "unprecedented catastrophe," it would not mean the end of civilization. In fact, "the limits of the magnitude of the catastrophe seem to be closely dependent on what kinds of preparations have been made, and how the war is started and fought."[4] As he said, "If proper preparations have been made, it would be possible for us or the Soviets to cope with all of the effects of a thermonuclear war in the sense of saving most people and restoring something close to the previous standard of living in a relatively short time."[5]

Since one side could cope better with nuclear war than the other, Brodie, according to Kahn, was wrong. Questions of victory or defeat were not irrelevant. The purpose of the military establishment remained what it always had been: to win the war.

Given this line of argument, it is not surprising that Kahn rejected Bro-

---

[3] Bernard Brodie, *Strategy in the Missile Age* (Princeton, New Jersey: Princeton University Press, 1965), p. 292.

[4] Herman Kahn, *On Thermonuclear War* (New York: Free Press, 1969) pp. 10–11.

[5] Herman Kahn, *On Thermonuclear War*, p. 78.

die's version of deterrence, which Kahn labeled Type I. Instead, Kahn called for what he labeled "Type II," deterring the Soviets by giving the United States the capability to fight and win a nuclear war. In Kahn's mind, there were a number of scenarios where the United States, if it lacked Type II deterrence, would be faced with a choice of "oblivion or surrender." One key example Kahn cited was a Soviet attack only on our nuclear forces, avoiding our cities.

The way out of this was for the United States to target our missiles not against Soviet cities but against their bomber and missile bases and—in some cases—to retain a first strike option. Kahn labeled a strike against the enemy's military forces "counterforce"; a strike against cities was "counter value." At the very least, a strategy based on a first strike option, plus counterforce, could spare cities, Kahn said. At the most it could allow the United States to win a nuclear war.

Throughout his work, Kahn the physicist never asked the questions that bothered Brodie: What possible political goal could justify the loss of a hundred cities or even a "few" million people? Could the people of a nation which suffered even "limited" nuclear damage be expected, in Brodie's words, to "show much concern for the further pursuit of political-military objectives?"

Not all experts, at RAND and elsewhere, who rejected Brodie's view of nuclear strategy agreed completely with Kahn. Some were much less sanguine about the prospects of recovery from nuclear war. But they agreed that Brodie's view of deterrence was insufficient, and that it would be more advantageous for us if our forces could fight a nuclear war by attacking the Soviet military.

The Kahn view was given a tremendous boost in 1960 with the election of John F. Kennedy and the appointment of Robert McNamara as Secretary of Defense.

McNamara was briefed on counterforce by the nuclear warfighters at RAND a few weeks after taking office. Impressed, he brought many of them to Washington. (Kahn was not invited, probably because he had become a lightning rod for public worry about nuclear war. Brodie was also conspicuously left behind.)

They began at once to work on a new strategy, which McNamara announced in early 1962. While McNamara, unlike Kahn, repeatedly stressed the terrible dangers of nuclear war, in the end, like the RAND people, he came down hard on Kahn's side of the argument:

> The U.S. has come to the conclusion that to the extent feasible, basic military strategy in a possible general nuclear war should be approached in much the same way that more conventional military operations have been regarded in the past. That is to say, principal military objectives, in the event of a nuclear war stemming from a major attack

on the Alliance, should be the destruction of the enemy's military
forces, not of his civilian population.[6]

Kennedy himself made statements implying that the United States might strike
first if its vital interest were threatened, and the Administration embarked on
a massive nuclear buildup.

The more McNamara studied nuclear war, however, the clearer it became to him that, with Soviet nuclear forces growing and becoming more difficult to destroy, it would not be possible to limit damage in a meaningful
way. Moreover, he found that a "damage-limiting" strategy helped the Air
Force drive for ever-larger strategic forces. In the middle 1960s, McNamara
began to move toward Brodie. By 1967 he could say, "It is our ability to
destroy an attacker . . . that provides the deterrent, not our ability to potentially limit damage to ourselves."[7] McNamara never completely abandoned
damage limitation; but the Brodie form of deterrence, now labelled "assured
destruction," was publicly given top priority by McNamara during his last
years.

Kahn's temporary victory had lasting effects, however. The United States
increased its submarine-launched ballistic missiles and ICBMs 18-fold, a buildup
which the Soviets soon began to match. A significant number of U.S. nuclear
weapons were now "counterforce targeted," that is, aimed not at Soviet cities
and economic assets, but at military targets including airfields and missile bases.

The boost from McNamara in the mid-1960s helped Brodie's views continue to dominate the writing and thinking of expert civilians. But the minority who supported a Kahn-like view, especially the analysts at RAND, was
stronger and more vocal.

The complete victory of Kahn's ideas came in the early 1970s, the result
of the public statements by another Secretary of Defense, James Schlesinger.

Schlesinger, who took office in 1973, had been at RAND during the middle and late 1960s, serving for a few years as Director of Strategic Studies. He
had published a number of scathing attacks on assured destruction, and soon
after he was appointed head of the Pentagon, he returned publicly to counterforce and nuclear warfighting. In 1973 and 1974 Schlesinger announced "a
change in the strategies of the United States with regard to hypothetical implementation of central strategic forces." In particular, the United States would
obtain "the forces to execute a wide range of options in response to particular
action by an enemy, including a capability for precise attacks on both soft and

---

[6] Quoted in Desmond Ball, *Politics and Force Levels: The Strategic Missile Program of the Kennedy Administration*
(Berkeley: University of California Press, 1980), p. 197.
[7] Robert S. McNamara, Statement before the House Armed Services Committee on the FY 1968–72 and
1968 Defense Budget, p. 39.

hard [military] targets, while at the same time minimizing unintended collateral damage."[8] Schlesinger's successor, Donald Rumsfeld, echoed Kahn even more clearly, rejecting the notion that nuclear war would inevitably wipe out a major portion of the American population and calling for a greater U.S. warfighting capability.

The Schlesinger-announced changes, like McNamara's, helped push the arms race forward. To allay Congressional worries about his new strategy, Schlesinger first said it required no higher levels of spending and no new nuclear weapons. But this announcement was soon followed by an increase in the number of U.S. warheads, a major improvement in the accuracy of U.S. ICBMs and the go-ahead for new, more powerful and accurate systems, including the MX.

Among civilian experts, Schlesinger's public move away from assured destruction provoked a storm of controversy, with the pendulum swinging Kahn's way.

The most influential blasts at views in agreement with Brodie's came from Paul Nitze. (Now the Reagan Administration's chief negotiator of nuclear weapons in Europe, Nitze had held high office in both the Defense and State Departments.) In 1975 and 1976, he published two articles using arguments that were basically "Kahn brought up to date," with more clarity and coherence.

Nitze began by attacking assured destruction. Like Kahn he argued that fighting nuclear war the right way, with correct preparations, could reduce damage significantly. He also argued that, in nuclear war, questions of victory or defeat were not irrelevant. The Soviets, Nitze said, knew this, but we did not. Since 1973, the Soviets had been "gaining the military capability to end an exchange in their favor." In spelling out exactly how the Soviets might do this, Nitze revived one of Kahn's scenarios. He feared the Soviets could avoid our cities and attack just our nuclear forces. Since the United States relied on assured destruction, Nitze claimed, it would then have to choose between suicide or surrender.[9]

To be sure, the supporters of Brodie's version of deterrence were far from silent during this period. But they no longer had their former impact, either on the non-government experts or on the Republican Administration. By late 1976, even the "moderates" writing about nuclear arms accepted the need for increased warfighting capabilities.

Some in what had become the minority Brodie school placed their hopes in the election of Jimmy Carter, and in Carter's appointment of Harold Brown

---

[8] James Schlesinger, "Flexible Strategic Options and Deterrence," *Survival* (March/April 1974), pp. 86–90.
[9] Paul Nitze, "Assuring Strategic Stability in an Era of Detente," *Foreign Affairs* (Jan. 1976), pp. 223–26.

as Secretary of Defense. As recently as 1975, Brown had warned that contingency planning to fight a nuclear war could "increase the likelihood of catastrophe." [10]

Before long, however, the new Secretary of Defense began to sound like the others. In 1978 he said: "We cannot afford to make a complete distinction between deterrence forces and what are so awkwardly called warfighting forces." [11] Over the next two years he elaborated what he called a "countervailing strategy" which meant having plans "to attack the targets which comprise the Soviet military force structure and political power structure, and to hold back a significant reserve." [12] The new strategy, codified in Presidential Directive 59, anticipated prolonged nuclear battles and required more accurate missiles and beefed-up civil defense.

To be sure, Brown and most of the others in the Carter Administration did not go as far in the direction of Kahn as did Nitze and some others. They were much less optimistic about the prospects of either side surviving a nuclear war and conceded it was unlikely that nuclear wars could remain limited. Nor did they support the same kind of arms buildup advocated by most of the vehement critics of assured destruction; and they strongly supported the SALT II Treaty. But they let Kahn-Nitze scenarios affect their thinking. In the end they agreed that the United States must develop plans and weapons that would allow us to avoid cities and strike Soviet military forces.

The Reagan Administration has not gone much further in Kahn's direction than did its predecessors. Indeed, by deciding to cut MX deployments from the Carter-planned level, they may have diminished U.S. warfighting capabilities. Yet Reagan officials have scared people simply because they have brought to public notice what nuclear war theorists have been saying for a long time.

As long as Kahn's ideas hold sway, the defeat of one President and election of a new one will not lessen the dangers of nuclear war. Democratic warfighters are no better than Republican ones. What is needed is a counterrevolution in nuclear strategy, a return to Brodie's ideas on nuclear war. This is the true challenge for the growing arms control movement.

---

[10] "Strategic Force Structure and Strategic Arms Limitation," *Civil Preparedness and Limited Nuclear War.* Hearings before the Joint Committee on Defense Production, (April 28, 1976), p. 133.

[11] Department of Defense *Annual Report, FY 1979*, p. 54.

[12] Department of Defense *Annual Report, FY 1981*, pp. 66–69.

PD-59: A STRATEGIC CRITIQUE
Desmond Ball

Desmond Ball is Professor of Political Science at Australian National University. Among his other works are *Can Nuclear War Be Controlled?* and *Politics and Force Levels: The Strategic Missile Program of the Kennedy Administration.*

It is fundamental to any evaluation of the new targeting policy formally adopted by the Carter Administration of 25 July [1980] to appreciate that, contrary to some media claims regarding the novelty of the concepts, they are really not all that new. There have been some changes of emphasis and priority, undertaken in a very evolutionary way, rather than any drastic revision of either the basic guidance for the employment of nuclear weapons in the event of a nuclear exchange with the Soviet Union (the NUWEP) or the actual targeting plans (the SIOP).

The SIOP has, at least since 1962, contained a range of options. The current SIOP, SIOP-5D, includes some 40,000 designated target installations which not only allows great scope for choice, but actually requires such choice since there are only 9,200 weapons in the SIOP force. These installations cover a variety of target types, divided into four general categories: Soviet nuclear forces, other military targets, political and military leadership facilities, and the Soviet economic-industrial base. The Soviet nuclear forces only became a separate target set in August 1950, but the other three categories had all been present in the war plans of the late 1940's. The fact that current planning requires that relatively less emphasis be accorded the destruction of the Soviet economic and industrial base and that greater attention be directed toward improving the effectiveness of our attacks against military targets should not obscure another fact that military targets already account for just over half the target installations in the SIOP—with the other 20,000 made up of 3,000 targets associated with the Soviet nuclear forces; 2,000 leadership targets; and some 15,000 economic-industrial targets.

Part of what *is* new is the appreciation that the choice of targets is as much an exercise in deterrence as the execution of the plans is in war-fighting. As one White House official stated in late 1977, as the NTPR got underway, "In the past nuclear targeting has been done by military planners who have basically emphasized the efficient destruction of targets. But targeting should not be done in a political vacuum.

"Some targets are of greater psychological importance to Moscow than

Source: Desmond Ball, "PD-59: A Strategic Critique," *F.A.S. Public Interest Report,* 33:8 (October 1980), pp. 4–5. Reprinted by permission of the Federation of American Scientists.

others, and we should begin thinking of how to use our strategic forces to play on these concerns." (New York Times, 16 Dec. 1977)

Hence there are some changes to exploit potential Soviet fears, such as threatening Moscow's food supply or making a target of Russian troops in the Far East ('kicking the door in!') so the Soviet Union would be more vulnerable to attack from China; and some consideration has been given to the adaptation of targeting to the dismemberment and regionalizations of the USSR, enhancing the prospect for regional insurrection during and after a nuclear exchange.

The most important consequence of this notion of targeting what the Soviets fear most, however, is the attention now being devoted to the targeting of the Soviet *assets for political control*—the Soviet state and its instruments of domestic and external coercion. But how realistic is this both as a strategy policy and as a targeting objective? Unless it is realistic, and is perceived by the Soviets as such, it has no value as a deterrent.

The second noteworthy aspect of the recent developments in targeting policy is the recognition that the current US *command, control and communication* (C^3) system is inadequate to support any policy of extended nuclear war-fighting. Hence the issue of Presidential Directives 53 and 58 and a wide range of other measures intended to improve the *survivability* and the *endurance* of the US C^3 system. But is it really possible to design a C^3 system that can operate in a nuclear environment in such a way and for a sufficient length of time to support the current US strategic policy of *escalation control?*

Let me address these two questions. First, how realistic is the concept of counter political control targeting? There seem to me to be several problems. One is that political control assets comprise, potentially at least, an extremely large target set. Political control in the Soviet Union emanates from the Kremlin in Moscow outward through the capitals of each of the Republics and down through those of the Oblasts and the Krays. Targeting the CPSU headquarters and other governmental and administrative buildings in each of these, as well as military headquarters and command posts and KGB centres throughout the Soviet Union could require many thousands of weapons. Already, the Commander of SAC has written to Secretary Brown to the effect that coverage of all these political control assets would require a major increase in the SIOP forces. To be effective, then, this policy could come into conflict with arms control objectives.

There is also the problem that the locations of many political control assets are not known. This is a tacit admission in the following statement by Secretary Brown in his *F.Y. 1981 Posture Statement:*

"Hardened command posts have been constructed near Moscow and other cities. For some 100,000 people we define as the Soviet leadership, there are hardened underground shelters near places of work, and at relocation sites outside the cities. *The relatively few leadership shelters we have identified* would be vulnerable to direct attack." *(italics added)*

Even where facilities have been identified, it would be difficult (if not impossible) to know exactly which elements of the leadership had dispersed to which facilities.

Moreover, the destruction of the political control facilities does not necessarily mean the destruction of the political control personnel. KGB officers are less likely to be in KGB buildings than dispersed among the population they are tasked with monitoring and controlling.

Indeed, this points to a larger problem. Many of the political and military leadership centres are located in or near major urban areas—particularly Moscow and the Republic capitals. Attacks on these would be virtually indistinguishable from counter-city attacks. Escalation control would be difficult to pursue following such attacks.

In fact, such attacks would probably mean the end of escalation control. As Colin Gray has pointed out (Naval War College Review, Jan.–Feb. 1980):

"Once executed, a very large strike against the Soviet political and administrative leadership would mean that the US had 'done its worst.' If the Soviet Government, in the sense of a National Command Authority, were still able to function, it is likely that it would judge that it had little, if anything, left to fear."

Finally, a counter political control strike would make it impossible for the Soviets to negotiate war termination.

The second question was: is it possible to design a C^3 system that is more survivable and has greater endurance than the strategic forces it is intended to support? It seems to me that, *a priori,* the answer to that must be "no," since C^3 systems are vulnerable to all the threats to which the forces could be subject plus a variety of additional ones. The strategic forces gain protection through hardening, proliferation, mobility and camouflage. Many C^3 systems, such as radar sites, VLF antennae and satellite sensor systems are necessarily relatively "soft;" some C^3 elements, such as the National Command Authorities, cannot be proliferated; major command posts, satellite ground stations and communication nodes are generally fixed; and radar sites and communication stations are extremely difficult to camouflage because of their electronic emissions. C^3 systems are generally more vulnerable to the blast effects of nuclear weapons than are the strategic forces, and have various peculiar vulnerabilities as well—susceptibility to electromagnetic pulse, electronic jamming, deception, etc.

There are five particularly noteworthy vulnerabilities:

(i)   the NCA
(ii)   the airborne C^3 systems
(iii)   satellite systems
(iv)   the "hot line" and
(v)   the communication systems for the FBM submarines.

These impose quite debilitating physical constraints on the situations in which escalation might be controlled, the time period over which control might be maintained, and the proportion of the SIOP forces that could be employed in a controlled fashion. The boundary of control in any militarily significant exchange (as compared to demonstration strikes) is unlikely to lie beyond either a few days or a few tens of detonations!

There is another problem with respect to the practicality of the concepts embodied in PD-59—control and limitation require that *all* the participants in the conflict be willing and have the capability to exercise restraints—in weapons, in targets, and in political objectives. It is most problematical as to whether the Soviets would "play the game." Despite some improvements in the capabilities for control, Soviet doctrine still seems to be that in the event of a nuclear exchange the Soviet forces would be used massively and simultaneously against a range of targets—nuclear forces, other military forces, the military-industrial base and, almost certainly, the US and NATO military, political, and administrative control centres.

Despite all the resources now being devoted to C^3, therefore, the uncertainties that inevitably remain make the use of nuclear weapons for controlled escalation no less difficult to envisage than their use in a massive retaliation.

MAD VERSUS NUTS: CAN DOCTRINE OR WEAPONRY REMEDY THE MUTUAL HOSTAGE RELATIONSHIP BETWEEN THE SUPERPOWERS?

Spurgeon M. Keeney, Jr. and Wolfgang K. H. Panofsky

Spurgeon M. Keeney, Jr., is Executive Director of the Arms Control Association in Washington, D.C. He served during the Kennedy and Johnson administrations on the staff of the National Security Council, and during the Nixon administration as Assistant Director of the U.S. Arms Control and Disarmament Agency (ACDA). He was Deputy Director of ACDA from 1977 to 1981.

Wolfgang K. H. Panofsky served between 1960 and 1965 as a member of the President's Science Advisory Committee and from 1977 to 1981 as a member of the General Advisory Committee of ACDA. He is a Professor of Physics at Stanford University and Director of the Stanford Linear Accelerator Center.

Since World War II there has been a continuing debate on military doctrine concerning the actual utility of nuclear weapons in war. This debate, irrespec-

Source: Spurgeon M. Keeney, Jr., and Wolfgang K. H. Panofsky, "MAD vs. NUTS," *Foreign Affairs* (Winter 1981/1982), pp. 287–91, 298–304. Excerpted by permission of *Foreign Affairs.* Copyright 1981/1982 by the Council on Foreign Relations, Inc.

tive of the merits of the divergent points of view, tends to create the perception that the outcome and scale of a nuclear conflict could be controlled by the doctrine or the types of nuclear weapons employed. Is this the case?

We believe not. In reality, the unprecedented risks of nuclear conflict are largely independent of doctrine or its application. The principal danger of doctrines that are directed at limiting nuclear conflicts is that they might be believed and form the basis for action without appreciation of the physical facts and uncertainties of nuclear conflict. The failure of policymakers to understand the truly revolutionary nature of nuclear weapons as instruments of war and the staggering size of the nuclear stockpiles of the United States and the Soviet Union could have catastrophic consequences for the entire world.

Military planners and strategic thinkers for 35 years have sought ways to apply the tremendous power of nuclear weapons against target systems that might contribute to the winning of a future war. In fact, as long as the United States held a virtual nuclear monopoly, the targeting of atomic weapons was looked upon essentially as a more effective extension of the strategic bombing concepts of World War II. With the advent in the mid-1950s of a substantial Soviet nuclear capability, including multimegaton thermonuclear weapons, it was soon apparent that the populations and societies of both the United States and the Soviet Union were mutual hostages. A portion of the nuclear stockpile of either side could inflict on the other as many as 100 million fatalities and destroy it as a functioning society. Thus, although the rhetoric of declaratory strategic doctrine has changed over the years, mutual deterrence has in fact remained the central fact of the strategic relationship of the two superpowers and of the NATO and Warsaw Pact alliances.

Most observers would agree that a major conflict between the two hostile blocs on a worldwide scale during this period may well have been prevented by the specter of catastrophic nuclear war. At the same time, few would argue that this state of mutual deterrence is a very reassuring foundation on which to build world peace. In the 1960s the perception of the basic strategic relationship of mutual deterrence came to be characterized as "Mutual Assured Destruction," which critics were quick to note had the acronym of MAD. The notion of MAD has been frequently attacked not only as militarily unacceptable but also as immoral since it holds the entire civilian populations of both countries as hostages.

As an alternative to MAD, critics and strategic innovators have over the years sought to develop various war-fighting targeting doctrines that would somehow retain the use of nuclear weapons on the battlefield or even in controlled strategic war scenarios, while sparing the general civilian population from the devastating consequences of nuclear war. Other critics have found an alternative in a defense-oriented military posture designed to defend the civilian population against the consequences of nuclear war.

These concepts are clearly interrelated since such a defense-oriented strategy would also make a nuclear war-fighting doctrine more credible. But both alternatives depend on the solution of staggering technical problems. A defense-oriented military posture requires a nearly impenetrable air and missile defense over a large portion of the population. And any attempt to have a controlled war-fighting capability during a nuclear exchange places tremendous requirements not only on decisions made under incredible pressure by men in senior positions of responsibility but on the technical performance of command, control, communications and intelligence functions—called in professional circles "c^3i" and which for the sake of simplicity we shall hereafter describe as "control mechanisms." It is not sufficient as the basis for defense policy to assert that science will "somehow" find solutions to critical technical problems on which the policy is dependent, when technical solutions are nowhere in sight.

In considering these doctrinal issues, it should be recognized that there tends to be a very major gap between declaratory policy and actual implementation expressed as targeting doctrine. Whatever the declaratory policy might be, those responsible for the strategic forces must generate real target lists and develop procedures under which various combinations of targets could be attacked. In consequence, the perceived need to attack every listed target, even after absorbing the worst imaginable first strike from the adversary, creates procurement "requirements," even though the military or economic importance of many of the targets is small.

In fact, it is not at all clear in the real world of war planning whether declaratory doctrine has generated requirements or whether the availability of weapons for targeting has created doctrine. With an estimated 30,000 warheads at the disposal of the United States, including more than 10,000 avowed to be strategic in character, it is necessary to target redundantly all urban areas and economic targets and to cover a wide range of military targets in order to frame uses for the stockpile. And, once one tries to deal with elusive mobile and secondary military targets, one can always make a case for requirements for more weapons and for more specialized weapon designs.

These doctrinal considerations, combined with the superabundance of nuclear weapons, have led to a conceptual approach to nuclear war which can be described as Nuclear Utilization Target Selection. For convenience, and not in any spirit of trading epithets, we have chosen the acronym of NUTS to characterize the various doctrines that seek to utilize nuclear weapons against specific targets in a complex of nuclear war-fighting situations intended to be limited, as well as the management over an extended period of a general nuclear war between the superpowers.

While some elements of NUTS may be involved in extending the credibility of our nuclear deterrent, this consideration in no way changes the fact that mutual assured destruction, or MAD, is inherent in the existence of large numbers of nuclear weapons in the real world. In promulgating the doctrine of "countervailing strategy" in the summer of 1980, President Carter's Secretary of Defense Harold Brown called for a buildup of nuclear war-fighting capability in order to provide greater deterrence by demonstrating the ability of the United States to respond in a credible fashion without having to escalate immediately to all-out nuclear war. He was very careful, however, to note that he thought that it was "very likely" that the use of nuclear weapons by the superpowers at any level would escalate into general nuclear war. This situation is not peculiar to present force structures or technologies; and, regardless of future technical developments, it will persist as long as substantial nuclear weapon stockpiles remain.

Despite its possible contribution to the deterrence of nuclear war, the NUTS approach to military doctrine and planning can very easily become a serious danger in itself. The availability of increasing numbers of nuclear weapons in a variety of designs and delivery packages at all levels of the military establishment inevitably encourages the illusion that somehow nuclear weapons can be applied in selected circumstances without unleashing a catastrophic series of consequences. . . . NUTS creates its own endless pressure for expanded nuclear stockpiles with increasing danger of accidents, accidental use, diversions to terrorists, etc. But more fundamentally, it tends to obscure the fact that the nuclear world is in fact MAD.

The NUTS approach to nuclear war-fighting will not eliminate the essential MAD character of nuclear war for two basic reasons, which are rooted in the nature of nuclear weapons and the practical limits of technology. First, the destructive power of nuclear weapons, individually and most certainly in the large numbers discussed for even specialized application, is so great that the collateral effects on persons and property would be enormous and, in scenarios which are seriously discussed, would be hard to distinguish from the onset of general nuclear war. But more fundamentally, it does not seem possible, even in the most specialized utilization of nuclear weapons, to envisage any situation where escalation to general nuclear war would probably not occur given the dynamics of the situation and the limits of the control mechanisms that could be made available to manage a limited nuclear war. In the case of a protracted general nuclear war, the control problem becomes completely unmanageable. Finally, there does not appear to be any prospect for the foreseeable future that technology will provide a secure shield behind which the citizens of the two superpowers can safely observe the course of a limited nuclear war on other people's territory. . . .

The thesis that we live in an inherently MAD world rests ultimately on the technical conclusion that effective protection of the population against large-scale nuclear attack is not possible. This pessimistic technical assessment, which follows inexorably from the devastating power of nuclear weapons, is dramatically illustrated by the fundamental difference between air defense against conventional and nuclear attack. Against bombers carrying conventional bombs, an air defense system destroying only 10 percent of the incoming bombers per sortie would, as a practical matter, defeat sustained air raids such as the ones during World War II. After ten attacks against such a defense, the bomber force would be reduced to less than one-third of its initial size, a very high price to pay given the limited damage from conventional weapons even when over 90 percent of the bombers penetrate. In contrast, against a bomber attack with nuclear bombs, an air defense capable of destroying even 90 percent of the incoming bombers on each sortie would be totally inadequate since the damage produced by the penetrating 10 percent of the bombers would be devastating against urban targets.

When one extends this air defense analogy to ballistic missile defenses intended to protect population and industry against large numbers of nuclear missiles, it becomes clear that such a defense would have to be almost leakproof since the penetration of even a single warhead would cause great destruction to a soft target. In fact, such a ballistic missile defense would have to be not only almost leakproof but also nationwide in coverage since the attacker could always choose the centers of population or industry he wished to target. The attacker has the further advantage that he can not only choose his targets but also decide what fraction of his total resources to expand against any particular target. Thus, an effective defense would have to be extremely heavy across the entire defended territory, not at just a few priority targets. The technical problem of providing an almost leakproof missile defense is further compounded by the many technical measures the attacking force can employ to interfere with the defense by blinding or confusing its radars or other sensors and overwhelming the system's traffic-handling capacity with decoys.

When these general arguments are reduced to specific analysis, the conclusion is inescapable that effective protection of the population or industry of either of the superpowers against missile attack by the other is unattainable with present ABM (anti-ballistic missile) defense technology, since even the most elaborate systems could be penetrated by the other side at far less cost. This conclusion is not altered by prospective improvements in the components of present systems or by the introduction of new concepts such as lasers or particle beams into system design.

These conclusions, which address the inability of ballistic missile defense to eliminate the MAD character of the strategic relationship, do not necessarily apply to defense of very hard point targets, such as missile silos or shelters for mobile missiles. The defense of these hardened military targets does offer a more attractive technical opportunity since only the immediate vicinity of the hardened site needs to be defended and the survival of only a fraction of the defended silos is necessary to serve as a deterrent. Thus, the technical requirements for the system are much less stringent than for population or industrial defense and a much higher leakage rate can be tolerated. When these general remarks are translated into specific analysis which takes into account the many options available to the offense, hard site defense still does not look particularly attractive. Moreover, such a defense, even if partially successful, would not prevent the serious collateral fallout effects from the attack on the population discussed above. Nevertheless, the fact that these systems are technically feasible, and are advocated by some as effective, tends to confuse the public on the broader issue of the feasibility of urban defense against ballistic missiles.

The United States has a substantial research and development effort on ballistic missile defenses of land-based ICBMs as a possible approach to increase survivability of this leg of the strategic triad. The only program under serious consideration that could be deployed in this decade is the so-called LOAD (Low Altitude Defense) system. This system, which would utilize very small hardened radars and small missiles with small nuclear warheads, is designed to intercept at very close range those attacking missiles that might detonate close enough to the defended ICBM to destroy it. This last ditch defense is possible with nuclear weapons since the defended target is extremely hard and can tolerate nuclear detonations if they are not too close. While such a system for the defense of hard sites is technically feasible, there has been serious question as to whether it would be cost-effective in defending the MX in fixed Titan or Minuteman silos since the system could be overwhelmed relatively easily. In the case of the defense of a mobile MX in a multiple shelter system, the economics of the exchange ratios are substantially improved if the location of the mobile MX and mobile defense system are in fact unknown to the attacker; however, there are serious questions whether the presence of radiating radar systems might not actually compromise the location of the MX during an attack.

Looking further into the future, the U.S. research program is considering a much more sophisticated "layered" system for hard site defense. The outer layer would involve an extremely complex system using infrared sensors that would be launched on warning of a Soviet attack to identify and track incoming warheads. Based on this information, many interceptors, each carrying multiple, infrared-homing rockets with non-nuclear warheads, would be launched against the cloud of incoming warheads and attack them well outside the atmosphere. The warheads that leaked through this outer exoatmospheric layer would then be engaged by a close-in layer along the lines of the LOAD last ditch system described above.

It has been suggested that the outer layer exoatmospheric system might evolve into an effective area defense for population and industry. Actually, there are many rather fundamental technical questions that will take some time to answer about the ability of such a system to work at all against a determined adversary in the time frame needed to deploy it. For example, such a system would probably be defeated by properly designed decoys or blinded by nuclear explosions and, above all, may well be far too complex for even prospective control capabilities to operate. Whatever the value of these types of systems for hard site defense to support the MAD role of the deterrent, it is clear that the system holds no promise for population or industry defense and simply illustrates the technical difficulty of dealing with that problem.

While the government struggles with the much less demanding problem whether it is possible to design a plausible, cost-effective defense of hardened ICBM silos, the public is bombarded with recurring reports that some new technological "breakthrough" will suddenly generate an "impenetrable umbrella" which would obviate the MAD strategic relationship. Such irresponsible reports usually rehash claims for "directed energy" weapons which are based on the propagation of extremely energetic beams of either light (lasers) or atomic particles propagated at the speed of light to the target. Some of the proposals are technically infeasible, but in all cases one must remember that for urban defense only a system with country-wide coverage and extraordinarily effective performance would have an impact on the MAD condition. To constitute a ballistic missile defense system, directed energy devices would have to be integrated with detection and tracking devices for the incoming warheads, an extremely effective and fast data-handling system, the necessary power supplies for the extraordinarily high demand of energy to feed the directed energy weapons, and would have to be very precisely oriented to score a direct hit to destroy the target—as opposed to nuclear warheads that would only have to get in the general vicinity to destroy the target.

There are fundamental considerations that severely limit the application of directed energy weapons to ballistic missile defense. Particle beams do not penetrate the atmosphere. Thus, if such a system were ground-based, it would have to bore a hole through the atmosphere and then the beam would have to be focused through that hole in a subsequent pulse. All analyses have indicated that it is physically impossible to accomplish this feat stably. Among other things, laser systems suffer from the fact that they can only operate in good weather since clouds interfere with the beam.

These problems involving the atmosphere could be avoided by basing the system in space. Moreover, a space-based system has the desirable feature of potentially being able to attack missiles during the vulnerable launch phase before the reentry vehicles are dispersed. However, space-based systems involve putting a very complex system with a large power requirement into orbit. Analysis indicates that a comprehensive defensive system of this type would require over a hundred satellites, which in turn would need literally thousands of space shuttle sorties to assemble. It has been estimated that such a system would cost several hundred billion dollars. Even if the control mechanisms were available to operate such a system, there are serious questions as to the vulnerability of the satellites to physical attack and to various measures that would interfere with the system's operation. In short, no responsible analysis has indicated that for at least the next two decades such "death ray weapons" have any bearing on the ABM problem or that there is any prospect that they would subsequently change the MAD character of our world.

Defense against aircraft further illustrates the inherently MAD nature of today's world. Although the Soviets have made enormous investments in air defense, the airborne component of the U.S. strategic triad has not had its damage potential substantially reduced. Most analyses indicate that a large fraction of the "aging" B-52 fleet would penetrate present Soviet defenses, with the aid of electronic countermeasures and defense suppression by missiles. It is true that the ability of B-52s to penetrate will gradually be impaired as the Soviets deploy "look down" radar planes similar to the much publicized AWACS (Airborne Warning and Control System). However, these systems will not be effective against the air-launched cruise missiles whose deployment on B-52s will begin shortly; their ability to penetrate will not be endangered until a totally new generation of Soviet air defenses enters the picture. At that time, one can foresee major improvements in the ability of both bombers and cruise missiles to penetrate through a number of techniques, in particular the so-called "stealth" technology which will reduce by a large factor the visibility of both airplanes and cruise missiles to radar.

In short, there is little question that in the defense-offense race between air defenses and the airborne leg of the triad, the offense will retain its enormous damage potential. For its part, the United States does not now have a significant air defense, and the limited buildup proposed in President Reagan's program would have little effect on the ability of the Soviets to deliver nuclear weapons by aircraft against this country. Consequently, the "mutual hostage" relationship between the two countries will continue, even if only the airborne component of the triad is considered.

It is sometimes asserted that civil defense could provide an escape from the consequences of the MAD world and make even a general nuclear war between the superpowers winnable. This assertion is coupled with a continuing controversy as to the actual effectiveness of civil defense and the scope of the present Soviet civil defense program. Much of this debate reflects the complete failure of some civil defense advocates to comprehend the actual consequences of nuclear war. There is no question that civil defense could save lives and that the Soviet effort in this field is substantially greater than that of the United States. Yet all analyses have made it abundantly clear that to have a significant impact in a general nuclear war, civil defense would have to involve a much greater effort than now practiced on either side and that no amount of effort would protect a large portion of the population or the ability of either nation to continue as a functioning society.

There is evidence that the Soviets have carried out a shelter program which could provide fallout and some blast protection for about ten percent of the urban population. The only way even to attempt to protect the bulk of the population would be complete evacuation of the entire urban population to the countryside. Although to our knowledge there has never been an actual urban evacuation exercise in the Soviet Union, true believers in the effectiveness of Soviet civil defense point to the alleged existence of detailed evacuation plans for all Soviet cities. Yet, when examined in detail, there are major questions as to the practicality of such evacuation plans. . . .

The U.S. Arms Control and Disarmament Agency has calculated, using a reasonable model and assuming normal targeting practices, that even with the general evacuation of all citizens and full use of shelters, in a general war there would still be at least 25 million Soviet fatalities. Such estimates obviously depend on the model chosen: some have been lower but others by the Defense Department have been considerably higher. The time for such an all-out evacuation would be at least a week. This action would guarantee unambiguous strategic warning and provide ample time for the other side to generate its strategic forces to full alert, which would result in a substantially greater retaliatory strike than would be expected from normal day-to-day alert. If the retaliatory strike were ground burst to maximize fallout, fatalities could rise to 40 to 50 million; and if part of the reserve of nuclear weapons were targeted against the evacuated population, some 70 to 85 million could be killed. Until recently little has been said about the hopeless fate of the vast number of fallout casualties in the absence of organized medical care or what would become of the survivors with the almost complete destruction of the economic base and urban housing.

Finally, there is no evidence that the Soviets are carrying out industrial hardening or are decentralizing their industry, which remains more centralized than U.S. industry. This is not surprising since there is nothing they can do that would materially change the inherent vulnerability of urban society in a MAD world.

In sum, we are fated to live in a MAD world. This is inherent in the tremendous power of nuclear weapons, the size of nuclear stockpiles, the collateral damage associated with the use of nuclear weapons against military targets, the technical limitations on strategic area defense, and the uncertainties involved in efforts to control the escalation of nuclear war. There is no reason to believe that this situation will change for the foreseeable future since the problem is far too profound and the pace of technical military development far too slow to overcome the fundamental technical considerations that underlie the mutual hostage relationship of the superpowers.

What is clear above all is that the profusion of proposed NUTS approaches has not offered an escape from the MAD world, but rather constitutes a major danger in encouraging the illusion that limited or controlled nuclear war can be waged free from the grim realities of a MAD world. The principal hope at this time will not be found in seeking NUTS doctrines that ignore the MAD realities but rather in recognizing the nuclear world for what it is and seeking to make it more stable and less dangerous.

VICTORY IS POSSIBLE

Colin S. Gray and Keith B. Payne

Colin S. Gray is President of the National Institute for Public Policy, and a member of the Reagan administration's General Advisory Committee to the Arms Control and Disarmament Agency. This article was written when he and Dr. Payne were on the professional staff of the Hudson Institute, and the views expressed therein do not necessarily reflect those of the Reagan administration. Dr. Gray has written widely on nuclear weapons and strategy issues, and is coeditor with Barry R. Schneider and Dr. Payne of *Missiles for the Nineties: ICBMs and Strategic Policy.* Among his other recent publications are *Nuclear Strategy and National Style.*

Keith B. Payne is Executive Vice-President and Director of National Security Studies at the National Institute for Public Policy. Dr. Payne was on the professional staff of the Hudson Institute at the time of this article's publication. He is a coeditor of *Missiles for the Nineties: ICBMs and Strategic Policy,* and author of *Laser Weapons in Space: Policy and Doctrine.*

Nuclear war is possible. But unlike Armageddon, the apocalyptic war prophesied to end history, nuclear war can have a wide range of possible outcomes. Many commentators and senior U.S. government officials consider it a nonsurvivable event. The popularity of this view in Washington has such a pervasive and malign effect upon American defense planning that it is rapidly becoming a self-fulfilling prophecy for the United States.

Recognition that war at any level can be won or lost, and that the distinction between winning and losing would not be trivial, is essential for in-

Source: Colin S. Gray and Keith B. Payne, "Victory is Possible," *Foreign Policy,* 39 (Summer 1980), pp. 14–27. Reprinted with permission from *Foreign Policy.* Copyright 1980 by the Carnegie Endowment for International Peace.

telligent defense planning. Moreover, nuclear war can occur regardless of the quality of U.S. military posture and the content of American strategic theory. If it does, deterrence, crisis management, and escalation control might play a negligible role. Through an inability to communicate or through Soviet disinterest in receiving and acting upon American messages, the United States might not even have the option to surrender and thus might have to fight the war as best it can. Furthermore, the West needs to devise ways in which it can employ strategic nuclear forces coercively, while minimizing the potentially paralyzing impact of self deterrence.

If American nuclear power is to support U.S. foreign policy objectives, the United States must possess the ability to wage nuclear war rationally. This requirement is inherent in the geography of East-West relations, in the persisting deficiencies in Western conventional and theater nuclear forces, and in the distinction between the objectives of a revolutionary and status quo power.

U.S. strategic planning should exploit Soviet fears insofar as is feasible from the Soviet perspective; take full account of likely Soviet responses and the willingness of Americans to accept those responses; and provide for the protection of American territory. Such planning would enhance the prospect for effective deterrence and survival during a war. Only recently has U.S. nuclear targeting policy been based on careful study of the Soviet Union as a distinct political culture, but the U.S. defense community continues to resist many of the policy implications of Soviet responses to U.S. weapons programs. In addition, the U.S. government simply does not recognize the validity of attempting to relate its freedom of offensive nuclear action and the credibility of its offensive nuclear threat to the protection of American territory.

Critics of such strategic planning are vulnerable in two crucial respects: They do not, and cannot, offer policy prescriptions that will insure that the United States is never confronted with the stark choice between fighting a nuclear war or surrendering, and they do not offer a concept of deterrence that meets the extended responsibilities of U.S. strategic nuclear forces. No matter how elegant the deterrence theory, a question that cannot be avoided is what happens if deterrence mechanisms fail? Theorists whose concept of deterrence is limited to massive retaliation after Soviet attack would have nothing of interest to say to a president facing conventional defeat in the Persian Gulf or in Western Europe. Their strategic environment exists only in peacetime. They can recommend very limited, symbolic options but have no theory of how a large-scale Soviet response is to be deterred.

Because many believe that homeland defense will lead to a steeper arms race and destabilize the strategic balance, the U.S. defense community has endorsed a posture that maximizes the prospect for self-deterrence. Yet the credibility of the extended U.S. deterrent depends on the Soviet belief that a

U.S. president would risk nuclear escalation on behalf of foreign commitments.

In the late 1960s the United States endorsed the concept of strategic parity without thinking through what that would mean for the credibility of America's nuclear umbrella. A condition of parity or essential equivalence is incompatible with extended deterrent duties because of the self-deterrence inherent in such a strategic context. However, the practical implications of parity may be less dire in some areas of U.S. vital interest. Western Europe, for example, is so important an American interest that Soviet leaders could be more impressed by the character and duration of the U.S. commitment than by the details of the strategic balance.

A Threat to Commit Suicide

Ironically, it is commonplace to assert that war-survival theories affront the crucial test of political and moral acceptability. Surely no one can be comfortable with the claim that a strategy that would kill millions of Soviet citizens and would invite a strategic response that could kill tens of millions of U.S. citizens would be politically and morally acceptable. However, it is worth recalling the six guidelines for the use of force provided by the "just war" doctrine of the Catholic Church: Force can be used in a just cause; with a right intent; with a reasonable chance of success; in order that, if successful, its use offers a better future than would have been the case had it not been employed; to a degree proportional to the goals sought, or to the evil combated; and with the determination to spare noncombatants, when there is a reasonable chance of doing so.

These guidelines carry a message for U.S. policy. Specifically, as long as nuclear threat is a part of the U.S. diplomatic arsenal and provided that threat reflects real operational intentions—it is not a total bluff—U.S. defense planners are obliged to think through the probable course of a nuclear war. They must also have some idea of the intended relationship between force applied and the likelihood that political goals will be achieved—that is, a strategy.

Current American strategic policy is not compatible with at least three of the six just-war guidelines. The policy contains no definition of success aside from denying victory to the enemy, no promise that the successful use of nuclear power would insure a better future than surrender, and no sense of proportion because central war strategy in operational terms is not guided by political goals. In short, U.S. nuclear strategy is immoral.

Those who believe that a central nuclear war cannot be waged for political purposes because the destruction inflicted and suffered would dwarf the importance of any political goals can construct a coherent and logical policy position. They argue that nuclear war will be the end of history for the states involved, and that a threat to initiate nuclear war is a threat to commit suicide and thus lacks credibility. However, they acknowledge that nuclear weapons cannot be abolished. They maintain that even incredible threats may deter, provided the affront in question is sufficiently serious, because miscalculation by an adversary could have terminal consequences; because genuinely irrational behavior is always possible; and because the conflict could become uncontrollable.

In the 1970s the U.S. defense community rejected this theory of deterrence. Successive strategic targeting reviews appeared to move U.S. policy further and further from the declaratory doctrine of mutual assured destruction adopted by former Secretary of Defense Robert S. McNamara. Yet U.S. defense planners have not thoroughly studied the problems of nuclear war nor thought through the meaning of strategy in relation to nuclear war. The U.S. defense community has always tended to regard strategic nuclear war not as war but as a holocaust. Former Secretary of Defense James R. Schlesinger apparently adopted limited nuclear options (LNOs)—strikes employing anywhere from a handful to several dozen warheads—as a compromise between the optimists of the minimum deterrence school and the pessimists of the so-called war-fighting persuasion. By definition, LNOs apply only to the initial stages of a war. But what happens once LNOs have been exhausted? If the Soviets retaliated after U.S. LNOs, the United States would face the dilemma of escalating further or conciliating.

Deterrence may fail to be restored during war for several reasons: The enemy may not grant, in operational practice, the concept of intrawar deterrence and simply wage the war as it is able; and command, control, and communications may be degraded so rapidly that strategic decisions are precluded and both sides execute their war plans. Somewhat belatedly, the U.S. defense community has come to understand that flexibility in targeting and LNOs do not constitute a strategy and cannot compensate for inadequate strategic nuclear forces.

LNOs are the tactics of the strong, not of a country entering a period of strategic inferiority, as the United States is now. LNOs would be operationally viable only if the United States had a plausible theory of how it could control and dominate later escalation.

The fundamental inadequacy of flexible targeting, as presented in the 1970s, is that it neglected to take proper account of the fact that the United States would be initiating a process of competitive escalation that it had no basis for assuming could be concluded on satisfactory terms. Flexible targeting was an adjunct to plans that had no persuasive vision of how the application of force would promote the attainment of political objectives.

War Aims

U.S. strategic targeting doctrine must have a unity of political purpose from the first to the last strikes. Strategic flexibility, unless wedded to a plausible theory of how to win a war or at least insure an acceptable end to a war, does not offer the United States an adequate bargaining position before or during a conflict and is an invitation to defeat. Small, preplanned strikes can only be of use if the United States enjoys strategic superiority—the ability to wage a nuclear war at any level of violence with a reasonable prospect of defeating the Soviet Union and of recovering sufficiently to insure a satisfactory postwar world order.

However, the U.S. government does not yet appear ready to plan seriously for the actual conduct of nuclear war should deterrence fail, in spite of the fact that such a policy should strengthen deterrence. Assured-destruction reasoning is proclaimed officially to be insufficient in itself as a strategic doctrine. However, a Soviet assured-destruction capability continues to exist as a result of the enduring official U.S. disinterest in strategic defense, with potentially paralyzing implications for the United States. No matter how well designed and articulated, targeting plans that allow an enemy to inflict in retaliation whatever damage it wishes on American society are likely to prove unusable.

Four interdependent areas of strategic policy—strategy, weapons development and procurement, arms control, and defense doctrine—are currently treated separately. Theoretically, strategy should determine the evolution of the other three areas. In practice, it never has. Most of what has been portrayed as war-fighting strategy is nothing of the kind. Instead, it is an extension of the American theory of deterrence into war itself. To advocate LNOs and targeting flexibility and selectivity is not the same as to advocate a war-fighting, war-survival strategy.

Strategists do not find the idea of nuclear war fighting attractive. Instead, they believe that an ability to wage and survive war is vital for the effectiveness of deterrence; there can be no such thing as an adequate deterrent posture unrelated to probable wartime effectiveness; victory or defeat in nuclear war is possible, and such a war may have to be waged to that point; and, the clearer the vision of successful war termination, the more likely war can be waged intelligently at earlier stages.

There should be no misunderstanding the fact that the primary interest of U.S. strategy is deterrence. However, American strategic forces do not exist solely for the purpose of deterring a Soviet nuclear threat or attack against the United States itself. Instead, they are intended to support U.S. foreign policy, to preserve Western Europe against aggression. Such a function requires American strategic forces that would enable a president to initiate strategic nuclear use for coercive, though politically defensive, purposes.

U.S. strategy, typically, has proceeded from the bottom up. Such targeting does not involve any conception of the war as a whole, nor of how the war might be concluded on favorable terms. The U.S. defense community cannot plan intelligently for lower levels of combat, unless it has an acceptable idea of where they might lead.

Most analyses of flexible targeting options assume virtually perfect stability at the highest levels of conflict. Advocates of flexible targeting assert that a U.S. LNO would signal the beginning of an escalation process that the Soviets would wish to avoid in light of the American threat to Soviet urban-industrial areas. Yet it seems inconsistent to argue that the U.S. threat of assured destruction would deter the Soviets from engaging in escalation following an LNO but that U.S. leaders could initiate the process despite the Soviet threat. What could be the basis of such relative U.S. resolve and Soviet vacillation in the face of strategic parity or Soviet superiority?

Moreover, the desired deterrent effect would probably depend upon the Soviet analysis of the entire nuclear campaign. In other words, Soviet leaders would be less impressed by American willingness to launch an LNO than they would be by a plausible American victory strategy. Such a theory would have to envisage the demise of the Soviet state. The United States should plan to defeat the Soviet Union and to do so at a cost that would not prohibit U.S. recovery. Washington should identify war aims that in the last resort would contemplate the destruction of Soviet political authority and the emergence of a postwar world order compatible with Western values.

The most frightening threat to the Soviet Union would be the destruction or serious impairment of its political system. Thus, the United States should be able to destroy key leadership cadres, their means of communication, and some of the instruments of domestic control. The USSR, with its gross overcentralization of authority, epitomized by its vast bureaucracy in Moscow, should be highly vulnerable to such an attack. The Soviet Union might cease to function if its security agency, the KGB, were severely crippled. If the Moscow bureaucracy would be eliminated, damaged, or isolated, the USSR might disintegrate into anarchy, hence the extensive civil defense preparations intended to insure the survival of the Soviet leadership. Judicious U.S. targeting and weapon procurement policies might be able to deny the USSR the assurance of political survival.

Once the defeat of the Soviet state is established as a war aim, defense professionals should attempt to identify an optimum targeting plan for the accomplishment of that goal. For example, Soviet political control of its territory in Central Asia and in the Far East could be weakened by discriminate nuclear targeting. The same applies to Transcaucasia and Eastern Europe.

The Ultimate Penalty

Despite a succession of U.S. targeting reviews, Soviet leaders, looking to the mid-1980s, may well anticipate the ability to wage World War III successfully. The continuing trend in the East-West military balance allows Soviet military planners to design a theory of military victory that is not implausible and that may stir hopes among Soviet political leaders that they might reap many of the rewards of military success even without having to fight. The Soviets may anticipate that U.S. self-deterrence could discourage Washington from punishing Soviet society. Even if the United States were to launch a large-scale second strike against Soviet military and economic targets, the resulting damage should be bearable to the Soviet Union given the stakes of the conflict and the fact that the Soviets would control regions abroad that could contribute to its recovery.

In the late 1960s the United States identified the destruction of 20–25 per cent of the population and 50–75 per cent of industrial capacity as the ultimate penalty it had to be able to inflict on the USSR. In the 1970s the United States shifted its attention to the Soviet recovery economy. The Soviet theory of victory depends on the requirement that the Soviet Union survive and recover rapidly from a nuclear conflict. However, the U.S. government does not completely understand the details of the Soviet recovery economy, and the concept has lost popularity as a result. Highly complex modeling of the Soviet economy cannot disguise the fact that the available evidence is too rudimentary to permit any confidence in the analysis. With an inadequate data base it should require little imagination to foresee how difficult it is to determine targeting priorities in relation to the importance of different economic targets for recovery.

Schlesinger's advocacy of essential equivalence called for a U.S. ability to match military damage for military damage. But American strategic development since the early 1970s has not been sufficient to maintain the American end of that balance. Because the U.S. defense community has refused to recognize the importance of the possibility that a nuclear war could be won or lost, it has neglected to think beyond a punitive sequence of targeting options.

American nuclear strategy is not intended to defeat the Soviet Union or insure the survival of the United States in any carefully calculated manner. Instead, it is intended to insure that the Soviet Union is punished increasingly severely. American targeting philosophy today is only a superficial improvement over that prevalent in the late 1960s, primarily because U.S. defense planners do not consider anticipated damage to the United States to be relevant to the integrity of their offensive war plans. The strategic case for ballistic missile defense and civil defense has not been considered on its merits for a decade.

In the late 1970s the United States targeted a range of Soviet economic entities that were important either to war-supporting industry or to economic recovery. The rationale for this targeting scheme was, and remains, fragile.

War-supporting industry is important only for a war of considerable duration or for a period of post-war defense mobilization. Moreover, although recovery from war is an integral part of a Soviet theory of victory, it is less important than the achievement of military success. If the USSR is able to win the war, it should have sufficient military force in reserve to compel the surviving world economy to contribute to Soviet recovery. Thus, the current trend is to move away from targeting the recovery economy.

To date, the U.S. government has declined to transcend what amounts to a deterrence-through-punishment approach to strategic war planning. Moreover, the strategic targeting reviews of the 1970s did not address the question of self-deterrence adequately. The United States has no ballistic missile defense and effectively no civil defense, while U.S. air defense is capable of guarding American air space only in peacetime. The Pentagon has sought to compensate for a lack of relative military muscle through more imaginative strategic targeting. Review after review has attempted to identify more effective ways in which the USSR could be hurt. Schlesinger above all sought essential equivalence through a more flexible set of targeting options without calling for extensive new U.S. strategic capabilities. Indeed, he went to some pains to separate the question of targeting design from procurement issues.

The United States should identify nuclear targeting options that could help restore deterrence, yet would destroy the Soviet state and enhance the likelihood of U.S. survival if fully implemented. The first priority of such a targeting scheme would be Soviet military power of all kinds, and the second would be the political, military, and economic control structure of the USSR. Successful strikes against military and political control targets would reduce the Soviet ability to project military power abroad and to sustain political authority at home. However, it would not be in the interest of the United States actually to implement an offensive nuclear strategy no matter how frightening in Soviet perspective, if the U.S. homeland were totally naked to Soviet retaliation.

Striking the USSR should entail targeting the relocation bunkers of the top political and bureaucratic leadership, including those of the KGB; key communication centers of the Communist party, the military, and the government; and many of the economic, political, and military records. Even limited destruction of some of these targets and substantial isolation of many of the key personnel who survive could have revolutionary consequences for the country.

The Armageddon Syndrome

The strategic questions that remain incompletely answered are in some ways more difficult than the practical problems of targeting the political control structure. Is it sensible to destroy the government of the enemy, thus eliminating the option of negotiating an end to the war? In the unlikely event that the United States identifies all of the key relocation bunkers for the central political leadership, who would then conduct the Soviet war effort and to what ends? Since after a large-scale counter-control strike the surviving Soviet leadership would have little else to fear, could this targeting option be anything other than a threat?

The U.S. defense community today believes that the political control structure of the USSR is among the most important targets for U.S. strategic forces. However, just how important such targeting might be for deterrence or damage limitation has not been determined. Current American understanding of exactly how the control structure functions is less than perfect. But that is a technical matter that can in principle be solved through more research. The issue of whether the Soviet control structure should actually be struck is more problematic.

Strategists cannot offer painless conflicts or guarantee that their preferred posture and doctrine promise a greatly superior deterrence posture to current American schemes. But, they can claim that an intelligent U.S. offensive strategy, wedded to homeland defenses, should reduce U.S. casualties to approximately 20 million, which should render U.S. strategic threats more credible. If the United States developed the targeting plans and procured the weapons necessary to hold the Soviet political, bureaucratic, and military leadership at risk, that should serve as the functional equivalent in Soviet perspective of the assured-destruction effect of the late 1960s. However, the U.S. targeting community has not determined how it would organize this targeting option.

A combination of counterforce offensive targeting, civil defense, and ballistic missile and air defense should hold U.S. casualties down to a level compatible with national survival and recovery. The actual number would depend on several factors, some of which the United States could control (the level of U.S. homeland defenses); some of which it could influence (the weight and character of the Soviet attack); and some of which might evade anybody's ability to control or influence (for example, weather). What can be assured is a choice between a defense program that insures the survival of the vast majority of Americans with relative confidence and one that deliberately permits the Soviet Union to wreak whatever level of damage it chooses.

No matter how grave the Soviet offense, a U.S. president cannot credibly threaten and should not launch a strategic nuclear strike if expected U.S. casualties are likely to involve 100 million or more American citizens. There is a difference between a doctrine that can offer little rational guidance should deterrence fail and a doctrine that a president might employ responsibly for identified political purposes. Existing evidence on the probable consequences of nuclear exchanges suggests that there should be a role for strategy in nuclear war. To ignore the possibility that strategy can be applied to nuclear war is to insure by choice a nuclear apocalypse if deterrence fails. The current U.S. deterrence posture is fundamentally flawed because it does not provide for the protection of American territory.

Nuclear war is unlikely to be an essentially meaningless, terminal event. Instead it is likely to be waged to coerce the Soviet Union to give up some recent gain. Thus, a president must have the ability not merely to end a war, but to end it favorably. The United States would need to be able to persuade desperate and determined Soviet leaders that it has the capability, and the determination, to wage nuclear war at ever higher levels of violence until an acceptable outcome is achieved. For deterrence to function during a war each side would have to calculate whether an improved outcome is possible through further escalation.

An adequate U.S. deterrent posture is one that denies the Soviet Union any plausible hope of success at any level of strategic conflict; offers a likely prospect of Soviet defeat; and offers a reasonable chance of limiting damage to the United States. Such a deterrence posture is often criticized as contributing to the arms race and causing strategic instability, because it would stimulate new Soviet deployments. However, during the 1970s the Soviet Union showed that its weapon development and deployment decisions are not dictated by American actions. Western understanding of what determines Soviet defense procurement is less than perfect, but it is now obvious that Soviet weapon decisions cannot be explained with reference to any simple action-reaction model of arms-race dynamics. In addition, highly survivable U.S. strategic forces should insure strategic stability by denying the Soviets an attractive first-strike target set.

An Armageddon syndrome lurks behind most concepts of nuclear strategy. It amounts either to the belief that because the United States could lose as many as 20 million people, it should not save the 80 million or more who otherwise would be at risk, or to a disbelief in the serious possibility that 200 million Americans could survive a nuclear war.

There is little satisfaction in advocating an operational nuclear doctrine that could result in the deaths of 20 million or more people in an unconstrained nuclear war. However, as long as the United States relies on nuclear threats to deter an increasingly powerful Soviet Union, it is inconceivable that the U.S. defense community can continue to divorce its thinking on deterrence from its planning for the efficient conduct of war and defense of the country. Prudence in the latter should enhance the former.

The Reagan Nuclear Strategy

Robert C. Gray

Robert C. Gray is Associate Professor and Chairman of the Department of Government at Franklin and Marshall College, Lancaster, Penn-
sylvania. He is a former International Affairs Fellow of the Council on
Foreign Relations and policy analyst in the Office of the Secretary of Defense. His other works include coauthorship with Stanley R. Sloan of *Nuclear Strategy and Arms Control: Challenges for U.S. Policy.*

The nuclear policy of the Reagan Administration has received an extraordinary amount of attention in the press for a number of reasons including the
projected $180 billion five-year strategic modernization program, the contin-
uing attempts to find an acceptable basing mode for the MX missile, and the
slow pace of arms control negotiations. But the most important cause of public interest in the Reagan nuclear strategy is also the root cause of the upsurge
in anti-nuclear activism in Europe and America—the incautious rhetoric about
nuclear war of the President, former Secretary of State Haig, Secretary of Defense Weinberger, and some lower-ranking officials at the National Security
Council and the Department of Defense.

Secretary of State Haig's casual reference to the use of nuclear weapons
in Europe inflamed sentiment there. President Reagan declared that "on balance the Soviet Union does have a definite margin of superiority." Secretary
of Defense Weinberger has repeatedly referred to "restoring the deterrence that
has kept the peace since World War II," suggesting that at the moment, the
Soviets are not deterred. And lower-ranking officials such as Richard Pipes of
the NSC staff and T. K. Jones, Deputy Under Secretary of Defense for Strategic and Theater Nuclear Forces, have clearly suggested that nuclear war is
winnable if we adopt the correct policies.

The Administration's national security policies richly deserve much of
the criticism they have received. Ronald Reagan's instincts toward the Soviet
Union have been excessively confrontational. It is indefensible that the Administration took 16 months to make a strategic arms control proposal. And
there are indeed people in responsible positions who hold extremist views on
nuclear policy.

If one looks carefully at the evolution of strategic nuclear policy, how-

Source: Robert C. Gray, "The Reagan Nuclear Strategy," *Arms Control Today* (March 1983), pp. 1–3, 9–
10. Reprinted by permission of Lexington Books, D. C. Heath and Company, from *The Race for
Security: Arms and Arms Control in the Reagan Years,* ed. Robert Travis Scott (Lexington, Mass.: Lexington Books, D. C. Heath and Company, forthcoming). Copyright 1985, D. C. Heath and Company.

ever, there are good reasons for believing that the press has over-stated the novelty of the Reagan Administration's policies. Before dealing with this argument, however, it is necessary to clarify the terms of debate over strategic nuclear policy. . . .

One source of confusion in discussing strategic nuclear policy today is that the terms of reference have shifted to the right in recent years. When Secretary of Defense James Schlesinger announced the move toward limited nuclear options in the mid-1970s, the ensuing debate was between advocates of assured destruction and those who believed that deterrence would best be preserved by increasing the flexibility and selectivity of nuclear plans (and, hence, the credibility of using nuclear weapons). Almost a decade later many observers still talk as if the debate were unchanged—assured destruction vs. warfighting deterrence, with the latter being viewed as an extreme position.

What has happened in the past decade, however, is that American strategy, force planning, and employment policy have all moved in the direction of a warfighting deterrent posture. Indeed, warfighting deterrence has become the new conventional wisdom, evolving from the Nixon and Ford Administrations through Carter and to Reagan. The new extremist position is the notion of *war-winning*, an idea associated most prominently with the writings of Colin Gray.

The question that should be asked about nuclear strategy under Reagan is not whether it is a warfighting one. Like that of previous Administrations, it certainly is. The key question is how far toward a *war-winning* strategy the Reagan planners will carry us. . . .

Assessing the strategic nuclear policy of the Reagan Administration is no simple task as of this writing (mid-January 1983), for there is no extensive description analogous to the detailed exposition in Secretary Brown's final *Annual Report.* The most interesting material about strategic nuclear policy has come in the form of leaks to the press from a classified document, the *Defense Guidance.* In a New York *Times* article of May 30, 1982, Richard Halloran reported that this document set a requirement for American forces to have the capability to "render ineffective the total Soviet (and Soviet-allied) military and political power structure." So as to prepare for "a protracted conflict period and afterward" emphasis was to be placed on c^3I. Halloran wrote that the views of the Reagan military planners "on the possibility of protracted nuclear war differ from those of the Carter Administration's military thinkers. . . ." As indicated above, however, Harold Brown referred explicitly to "a protracted conflict." Without knowing the details of the plans under Brown *and* seeing the Weinberger *Defense Guidance*, it is impossible to assess the validity of Halloran's assertion.

Secretary Weinberger's response to the leak of the *Defense Guidance* came in a speech at the Army War College on June 3. He defined the capability for a protracted response as essential for deterrence and declared that the notion that "nuclear war is winnable . . . has no place in our strategy." In an August letter to some seventy editors, Weinberger denied that the Administration was "seeking to acquire a nuclear 'war-fighting' capability." The latter statement was singularly inept, inasmuch as the warfighting trend in U.S. policy has been evident for almost a decade and was explicitly referred to in the statement by Secretary Brown quoted above.

In an attempt to rectify the cumulative damage of the diverse casual statements and leaks of the first two years, Secretary Weinberger submitted a prepared statement on "United States Nuclear Deterrence Policy" to the Senate Foreign Relations Committee on December 14, 1982. More professional than the August letter to the editors, the statement was nonetheless quite defensive. It reiterated the basis of deterrence, traced the evolution of policy with long quotations from McNamara, Schlesinger, and Brown, and summarized the Reagan strategic modernization program. The text set forth the case for a warfighting deterrent such as the countervailing strategy (without using that name). There was no mention of "protracted war" or "prevailing." It was a document designed to reassure the Senate Foreign Relations Committee that the ship of strategy had been put right.

Even this document designed to reassure raises more questions than it answers, however. It states that because we must think about the failure of deterrence,

> we must plan for flexibility in our forces and in our response options so that there is a possibility of *re-establishing deterrence at the lowest possible level of violence, and avoiding further escalation.* (Emphasis added)

The *Defense Guidance*, on the other hand, allegedly states

> that should deterrence fail and strategic nuclear war with the U.S.S.R. occur, *the United States must prevail and be able to force the Soviet Union to seek earliest termination of hostilities on terms favorable to the United States.* (Emphasis added)

The obvious difference in emphasis in these two passages is that the first, designed for public presentation, portrays the goal of an American response as re-establishing deterrence at the lowest possible rung on the escalation ladder, with no reference to prevailing. The second passage, presumably not designed for public release, emphasizes prevailing, with no reference to containing escalation. The problem facing the Reagan Administration is that, with the leak of a document which it feels it cannot responsibly discuss, it persists in making statements sufficiently at variance with that document as to raise questions about differences between its public statements and its actual policies.

It is possible, of course, that there is no contradiction between these two statements. One could argue that deterrence could not be re-established without "prevailing." And one could include in the seeking of the "earliest termination of hostilities on terms favorable to the United States" the subgoal of "re-establishing deterrence at the lowest possible level of violence." What the Reagan Administration should do is to formulate a public statement of some length and sophistication describing its concept of deterrence. Until that is done very little will be clear, and the possibilities for questioning the "real" policies of the Administration will be manifold.

Warfighting versus War-Winning: The Emerging Debate?

On the limited evidence available, strategic nuclear policy in the Reagan Administration seems to be an extension of the countervailing strategy it inherited from its predecessor. The nuclear force and c^3i improvements outlined in the strategic modernization program are consonant with a warfighting deterrent policy.

To be sure, some efforts have been made that would please advocates of the war-winning school of thought. Spending on civil defense (in the form of crisis relocation plans) is up. Air defense is being upgraded. Research and development on ballistic missile defense has been increased.

If one were to believe the more alarmist interpretations of the goal of "prevailing," one might suspect that a theory of victory was not far behind. And Colin Gray and others who believe nuclear war is winnable are associated with the Administration. Despite these developments, however, by far the most likely outcome is that the Reagan Administration will implement a warfighting deterrent strategy. More money will be spent than would have been by the Carter Administration, but the nuclear strategy may not be that different. Nuclear planning is highly incremental in nature. The labels describing policy change much more frequently than the actual war plans. It may even be that, within certain limits, nuclear planning has dynamics of its own. Jimmy Carter entered office wanting to eliminate nuclear weapons from the earth and ended up signing Presidential Directive 59. Even if Ronald Reagan entered office wanting to implement the war winners' every thought, budgetary limits, the moderating advice of some of the uniformed military who question spending large sums of money on such a remote contingency as protracted war, and the awesome responsibility of nuclear decision-making might well put him back somewhere near a warfighting deterrent (not a war-winning) nuclear strategy.

I could, of course, be wrong. If that is so—if the Reagan Administration were to adopt a war-winning position—the consequences could be grave. The Soviets might well perceive U.S. policy the way some Americans have viewed Soviet nuclear policy. It is the seeming congruence between aspects of Soviet declaratory policy, force size and characteristics, and employment policy that has motivated American decision-makers to formulate a warfighting strategy. If the Soviets perceived a similarly threatening congruence between a U.S. war-winning declaratory policy, forces with a first-strike capability, extensive defensive measures, and a supporting employment policy, it is difficult to believe that the United States would be in a more secure position in the world.

A more preferable outcome would be to convince the Soviets that there is no possibility of meaningful victory in nuclear war *and* that the United States will pursue arms control where possible and arms modernization where necessary. Implementation of a warfighting countervailing strategy without a willingness to engage in serious arms control/reduction negotiations would be dangerous. Adoption of a war-winning strategy, *or* operationalization of a warfighting countervailing strategy in such a way that it *appears* to the Soviets as a war-winning one, will almost certainly fail to bring about negotiated arms reductions and may well increase the risk of nuclear war.

It is inconceivable that the Reagan Administration would move policy back to assured destruction. All the key Reagan national security decision makers would oppose it. Moreover, developments during the last decade have institutionalized a declaratory policy that promises to deny victory to the Soviets, an employment policy that is decidedly warfighting, and an acquisition strategy that key decision-makers believe has made such a policy possible.

In the near term, the strategic debate may be between defenders of a warfighting deterrence/countervailing strategy and advocates of a war-winning one. "War winners" will argue that advances in ballistic missile defense technology, and improvements in the U.S.'s hard target kill capability make their strategy increasingly realizable. Those committed to assured destruction may have to temporarily join forces with defenders of warfighting deterrence to prevent the greater danger: the victory of those who would convert the illusion of winnable nuclear wars into national policy.

U.S. NUCLEAR STRATEGY AND WORLD ORDER REFORM

An interview with Louis René Beres

Louis René Beres is Professor of Political Science at Purdue University and has written widely on world order reform and nuclear weapons issues. His other publications include *Mimicking Sisyphus: America's "Countervailing" Nuclear Strategy; Nuclear Strategy and World Order: The U.S. Imperative;* and *Apocalypse: Nuclear Catastrophe in World Politics.*

In recent years, you have written widely on various aspects of the nuclear arms race and the growing danger of nuclear war. Your most recent work has focused on U.S. nuclear strategy. In what ways has current U.S. nuclear strategy contributed to the problem?

▶ Current U.S. nuclear strategy is enormously dangerous and misconceived. In rejecting minimum deterrence, it has produced a "counterforce syndrome" that gives unprecedented legitimacy to the idea of nuclear warfighting. Coupled with preparations for "victory" in a nuclear war, this strategy actually makes nuclear war much more likely.

At a time when myriad medical and scientific analyses point to the conclusion that nuclear war can never be tolerated, the Reagan Administration counsels a policy based on preparations for "rational" nuclear warfare. At a time when the Soviet Union reiterates its continuing rejection of the idea of "limited nuclear war," U.S. leaders codify a nuclear targeting policy that accepts such an idea as a critical starting point. At a time when the Commander-in-Chief of the U.S. Strategic Air Command openly doubts the prospects of launching an effective "countervailing" attack in the wake of a Soviet first-strike, the Reagan Administration reaffirms a "selective" nuclear strategy that is designed to fulfill military tasks at a level far exceeding the requirements of "assured destruction." And at a time when the need for collaborative de-escalation of the arms race must override all other considerations, the administration makes plans to deploy new strategic weapons with hard-target kill capabilities, a new generation of intermediate-range ballistic missiles that would threaten the Soviet homeland itself, and the neutron bomb.

If these plans were not enough to increase instability, President Reagan has gone ahead with the MX in a fashion that will have no bearing on the

Source: "U.S. Nuclear Strategy and World Order Reform," An interview with Louis René Beres, *Macroscope* (Spring 1982), pp. 3–6. Reprinted by permission of the World Policy Institute, 777 UN Plaza, New York, NY 10017.

alleged problem of ICBM vulnerability. Taken together with planned programs for ballistic missile defense (BMD), civil defense, c^3I (Command, Control, Communications and Intelligence) improvements, and anti-satellite weapons, the MX decision (with the resurrection of "linkage") is bound to make the Soviets increasingly fearful of a U.S. first-strike. Naturally, this means that the Reagan nuclear strategy *contributes* to the prospect of Soviet preemption.

How do you respond to those strategic experts who argue that these new weapons are needed to make deterrence more credible?

▶ To meet our deterrence objectives, we need to ensure that our strategic forces are sufficiently invulnerable and penetration-capable to assuredly destroy an aggressor after riding-out a first-strike attack. We do *not* need to take steps to threaten the other side's retaliatory forces in a manner that is exceedingly provocative. With this in mind, all of the administration's ongoing "improvements" in U.S. nuclear forces will have the effect of *undermining* this country's deterrence posture. This is the case because they will add nothing to the invulnerability/penetration capability requirements while they *will* heighten Soviet incentives to strike first.

Under President Reagan, this country's search for a "margin of safety" in strategic capability vis-a-vis the Soviet Union is making the world much less safe. After all, this search has now gone far beyond the reasonable requirements of reduced vulnerability and minimum deterrence to an institutionalization of unrestrained nuclear competition. Based on an exaggerated expectation of Soviet intentions, it has led to the expression of all the poison and impotence of U.S. foreign policy in the post-war period. In its drowning of any remaining hopes for long-term cooperative security with the Soviet Union, it offers a routinization of humancide that may ultimately project Armageddon from imagination to reality.

The Reagan administration's argument seems to be that the Soviet Union has developed a first-strike capability and that the U.S. must match them to keep the Soviets from gaining the upper hand in any conflict situation.

▶ Supporters of the MX counterforce targeting qualities argue that there is no reason to make such Soviet targets safe from U.S. ICBMs when comparable targets in this country are at risk from Soviet ICBMs. But this argument is based entirely on the confusion of survivability and targeting objectives, and substitutes "monkey-see-monkey-do" logic for a well-reasoned de-escalation of strategic competition. It may be true that Soviet modernization has placed U.S. ICBMs at some risk—although there is disagreement about this. But it is not true, even if our "worst case" assumptions are correct, that our assured destruction capability is in jeopardy or that U.S. security is best served by acting in an equally provocative or more provocative manner.

Curiously, nothing in our current nuclear strategy suggests a plausible relationship between nuclear war and politics. Why, exactly, are the Soviets believed to be getting ready to "fight and win" a nuclear war with the United States? What conceivable post-war prospect can be associated with alleged Soviet plans for a first-strike against the United States? Why should the Soviets be expected to disregard Clausewitz's principle that war should always be conducted with a view to sustaining the overriding "political object"?

The dangers of assessing Soviet nuclear intentions *in vacuo* are considerable. By assuming that their *Staatspolitik* offers no homage to plausible relationships between nuclear war and national political goals, our own nuclear policy creates a bewildering expectation of first-strike scenarios that in turn produces a staggering array of provocative tactics and deployments. The net effect of such United States strategic thinking is a heightened prospect of escalation and irrevocable collision.

The reasonableness of a second-strike counterforce strategy (i.e., America's current nuclear strategy) is contingent upon the expectation that a Soviet first-strike would be limited. This is the case because if the Soviet first-strike were unlimited, this country's retaliation would hit only empty silos. Yet, there is no reason why the Soviets would ever choose to launch a limited first strike against the United States. It follows that our current search for increasing hard-target kill capabilities may be geared to achieving a first-strike capability against the Soviets.

In response, of course, the administration argues that the Soviets have a refiring and reconstitution capability with their missiles and that even an unlimited first-strike would take place in several successive stages. Hence, United States counterforce, targeted warheads, used in retaliation, would not necessarily hit only empty silos. They would also hit silos that might otherwise spawn weapons to enlarge the damage of the Soviet first-strike.

Even here, however, the administration argument is devoid of intellect and understanding. Most obviously problematic, this argument is oriented entirely to issues of nuclear war *fighting*. Accepting the likely prospect of a nuclear war and the probable failure of nuclear deterrence, it concerns itself (in conjunction with plans for multilayer ballistic defense, air defense, and civil defense) exclusively with *intra-war* damage limitation. Yet, there would be very little of the United States left to protect after the first round of Soviet attacks had been absorbed (we must remember, in this connection, that we don't even target SLBMs). And the countervailing strategy makes such attacks more likely in the first place by undermining stable deterrence (i.e. by signaling U.S. first-strike intentions). Looked at in cost-benefit terms, therefore, it is abundantly clear that the alleged damage-limitation benefits that would accrue to the United States from its countervailing strategy during a nuclear war are greatly outweighed by that strategy's deterrence-undermining costs.

Finally, I must mention that current U.S. efforts for nuclear force "improvements" derive from an assumed need to be able to fight a nuclear war to victory. But why should this be correct? Is there any reason to suppose that the Soviets can be deterred effectively only by the prospect of all-out nuclear war? And even if there were such a reason, don't the Soviets (given their ideas about the implausibility of limited nuclear war) already calculate on the basis of total nuclear effort on both sides? The only consequence of the administration's new emphasis on nuclear warfighting potential as essential to deterrence is heightened Soviet insecurity concerning U.S. first-strike intentions. Moreover, the shift to an increasingly provocative configuration of counterforce targeting is apt to further *erode* our deterrence posture, since it is clear that a U.S. strategic second-strike against hard targets would produce substantially less damage to the Soviet Union than would extensive countervalue attacks.

The Reagan Administration's thinking on this issue, then, is a significant departure.

▶ Yes. In fact, the idea that the concept of "victory" has no place in a nuclear war is as old as the nuclear age. Yet, the administration's policies display no understanding of this idea. Even before the nuclear age, philosophers and military strategies probed the idea of victory with far greater sensitivity and prescience. Machiavelli, for example, recognized the principle of an "economy of violence" which distinguishes between creativity and destruction. Lacking Machiavelli's more insightful brand of *Realpolitik,* the administration is unable to grasp the difference between violence and power. This is the case, incidentally, not only in terms of nuclear strategy, but also in terms of our nation's increasingly insipid and simplistic approach to insurgency and human rights.

Still another problem with the idea of "victory" in a nuclear war is the arbitrariness or unpredictability intrinsic to all violence. Contrary to the anesthetized expectations of strategic "thinkers" who anticipate near-perfect symmetry between human behavior and their own rarified strategic plans, violence harbors within itself an ineradicable element of the unexpected. Entangled in metaphors and false assumptions, and unable to cope with the intellectually-demanding problems of synergy, the president and his strategic mythmakers display a singular failure to understand the non-rational springs of action and feeling, and an indefensible degree of faith in game-theoretic systems of rational explanation. If only our leaders could learn to appreciate how little humankind can control amidst the disorderly multitude of factors involved in war. If only they could learn to understand what presumptuous hazards are associated with a strategy that seeks to impose order on what must inevitably be a heightened form of chaos.

Aren't many of the risks you mentioned in current nuclear strategy also inherent in minimum deterrence?

▶ Yes, even a return to "minimum deterrence" would represent a continuation of grave danger. *Any* system based upon the threat of nuclear retaliation is fundamentally unstable. At one time or another, in one way or another, the manifestly catastrophic possibilities that now lie latent in nuclear weapons are almost certain to occur, either by design or by accident, by misinformation or miscalculation, by lapse from national decision or by unauthorized decision. The encouragement of a "counterforce syndrome" by the United States, however, is making a dangerous system even more dangerous.

What do you see as necessary for bringing this growing nuclear danger under control?

▶   There is a story by Jorge Luis Borges in which a condemned man, having noticed that expectations never coincide with reality, ceaselessly imagines the circumstances of his own death. Since they have thus become expectations, the man reasons, they can never become reality. Understood in terms of the overriding imperative to prevent nuclear war, this story points to the need for further confrontations with the imagery of extinction. Only by trying to understand and imagine the full import and likelihood of a nuclear war (and there is, already, an enormous literature on what would be involved) can we begin to take steps back to a durable peace. To do otherwise would be to accept the role of actors in a Greek tragedy who have lost command of their destinies, and who have foresaken the hope that human intervention can still be purposeful. In this connection, the motto for the Enlightenment, *sapere aude!*, dare to know!, suggested by Immanuel Kant, acquires a special meaning in the late twentieth century study of nuclear war. Just as repression of the fear of death by individuals can occasion activities that impair the forces of self-preservation, so we can impair our prospects for preventing nuclear war by insulating ourselves from reasonable fears of collective disintegration.

But isn't there the danger that the public is being prepared for nuclear war with routine discussions of civil defense, limited nuclear war, etc.?

▶   The growing prospect of nuclear war is tied very closely to the language that has been adopted by strategic mythmakers. Such euphemisms as "crisis relocation," "limited nuclear war," "countervalue" and "counterforce" strategies and "enhanced radiation warfare" are insidious to the cause of peace because they tend to make the currency of nuclear warfighting valid coin. Just as the barbarisms of the Nazis were made possible through such linguistic disguises as "final solution," "resettlement," "special treatment," and "selections," so do the euphemisms of the nuclear age make nuclear war more likely. To counter the current euphemisms that may etherize an unwitting humanity into accepting nuclear war, humankind must come to understand how much it has already lost in its own gibberish.

We must also come to understand that the growing number of formulations of livable post-apocalypse worlds are both nonsense and dangerous. This is the case because they interfere with the essential task of cultivating "end-of-the-world" imagery—imagery that must precede a durable peace. Without a fuller awareness of the effects of nuclear war, we will continue to stand outside the arena of mortality, unable to picture ourselves as victims.

Fortunately, the Administration's loose rhetoric about nuclear war has had quite the opposite effect and has prompted great public concern. The need to avoid nuclear war, only a few years ago a marginal tic of consciousness, is now the basis for a growing movement. Of course, heightened *awareness* is only the first step to preventing what the physicians now call "the final epidemic." Once such awareness has been generated, it is up to us to encourage the establishment of a new nuclear regime—one based upon such immediate measures as a return to minimum deterrence, agreement on a no-first-use pledge, a nuclear weapons "freeze," a comprehensive test ban, and additional nuclear weapon free zones. Each of these measures is described in some length in my WOMP working paper and in my forthcoming book, *Mimicking Sisyphus*. What I would stress here is that the essential arena of world reform must be *intranational*, with a special responsibility falling upon the United States to accept vital de-escalatory obligations. This means a rapid and farreaching disengagement from developing patterns of counterforce targeting and preparations for nuclear warfighting.

These are mostly short term goals. As you have pointed out, we cannot expect nuclear deterrence to work forever. What type of long-range changes should we be exploring?

▶ Without necessarily seeking fundamental changes in the prevailing state-centric structure of global authority, the two superpowers must learn to associate their own security from nuclear war with a more farreaching search for worldwide stability and equity. To prevent nuclear war between the superpowers, the prescribed nuclear regime must be augmented by a new awareness of the "connectedness" of states.

Ultimately the chances for a successful detachment from strategic arms competition will depend upon the specific steps needed to underscore the total disutility of a nuclear threat system. Implementation of these steps will require an early world summit of leaders from both rich and poor states to deal with international development and other pressing security issues. And these steps will depend upon a prior understanding, by the superpowers, that their own security interests are inevitably congruent with the security interests of the world as a whole. The balance of power between the Soviet Union and the United States can never be more stable than the balance of power in the whole of international society.

To prevent nuclear war that might occur through proliferation requires a nuclear regime that extends the principles of superpower war avoidance to the rest of international society. The centerpiece of this universal regime must be the cosmopolitan understanding that all states, like all people, form one essential body and one true community. Such an understanding, that a latent oneness lies buried beneath the manifold divisions of our fractionated world, need not be based on the mythical attractions of universal brotherhood and mutual concern. Instead, it must be based on the idea that individual states, however much they may dislike each other, are tied together in the struggle for survival.

Ultimately, then, what we should seek are more than the customary restraints offered by institutional and juridical modifications. Although such modifications are essential, they must be surrounded by a new field of consciousness—one that flows from a common concern for the human species and from the undimmed communion of individual states with the entire system of states.

Living at this juncture between world order and global disintegration, states must slough off the shackles of outmoded forms of self-interest. With the explosion of the myth of realism, the global society of states could begin to come together in a renewed understanding of the connection between survival and relatedness.

FOR FURTHER READING

Ball, Desmond. *Can Nuclear War Be Controlled?* Adelphi Paper 169. London: International Institute for Strategic Studies, 1981. The definitive critique of limited and controlled nuclear war, concluding that limited nuclear war is a "chimera."

Brodie, Bernard, ed. *The Absolute Weapon: Atomic Power and World Order.* New York: Harcourt, Brace, and Company, 1946. This collection of prescient essays, including Brodie's own piece stressing the importance of war prevention and heightened costs of conflict in the nuclear age, anticipated many of the issues and dilemmas we face today.

Fallows, James. "Theologians." In *National Defense.* New York: Random House, 1981. A trenchant critique of nuclear war-fighting strategies, with emphasis on the technical uncertainties and risks of malperformance that would attend the use of strategic nuclear weapons, and the lack of empirical evidence for the theories and claims made by nuclear strategists.

Freedman, Lawrence. *The Evolution of Nuclear Strategy.* New York: St. Martin's Press, 1981. A balanced and exhaustive history of postwar developments in western military strategy. Emphasis placed on American nuclear doctrine, but includes valuable discussion of European perspectives as well.

Gray, Colin S. "Nuclear Strategy: The Case for a Theory of Victory." *International Security* 4 (Summer 1979), pp. 54–87. A ringing critique of assured destruction advocates, this article helped set the tone of the current debate over U.S. strategic policy and nuclear doctrine, advocating the adoption of a "theory of nuclear victory" in U.S. policy.

Johansen, Robert C. *Toward an Alternative Security System.* New York: World Policy Institute, 1983. A critique of U.S. nuclear strategy and "realist" conceptions of world politics. Provides a step-by-step, concrete program for the achievement of nuclear disarmament and collective security.

Kahn, Herman. *On Thermonuclear War*. Princeton, N.J.: Princeton University Press, 1963. Kahn's original argument that victory and survival are possible in nuclear war.

Kaplan, Fred M. *The Wizards of Armageddon*. New York: Simon and Schuster, 1983. The fascinating inside story of American civilian strategists and how they have influenced the development of American nuclear strategy.

Paine, Christopher. "Nuclear Combat: The Five Year Plan." *Bulletin of the Atomic Scientists* 38 (November 1982), pp. 5–12. A detailed exposition and critique of the Reagan Administration's nuclear strategy.

Pringle, Peter, and William Arkin. *SIOP: Nuclear War from the Inside*. London: Sphere Books, 1983. A detailed description of the development and current status of America's plans and policies for the actual use of weapons, containing a valuable bibliographical essay.

Scheer, Robert. *With Enough Shovels: Reagan, Bush, and Nuclear War*. New York: Random House, 1982. A highly readable and startling analysis of the men and ideas that drive the Reagan Administration's nuclear weapons policies, highlighting the disturbing prevalence of "nuclear war-winners" within the senior ranks of the administration.

Yankelovich, Daniel, and John Doble. "The Public Mood: Nuclear Weapons and the U.S.S.R." *Foreign Affairs* 63 (Fall 1984), pp. 33–47. An analysis of the American public's views and misconceptions of U.S. nuclear strategy and arms control with the Soviet Union.

5

The Debate Over Soviet Nuclear Weapons Policy

Any comprehensive examination of the nuclear weapons issue must include a discussion of the Soviet Union's foreign and national security policies, for several reasons. The most obvious is that the Soviet Union is the only other country possessing a nuclear arsenal which rivals that of the Unites States. Equally salient are the political and ideological differences which constitute the principal sources of tension in Soviet-American relations. These antagonisms transform local conflicts in such regions as Latin America, Africa, and the Middle East into major sources of Soviet-American political tension; they also animate the ongoing superpower competition in nuclear arms. In their most aggravated form, these tensions could lead to nuclear war, and their constant presence threatens the security of both the Soviet Union and the United States.

A related consideration is that any effort to curtail and control this political and military competition will necessarily require the active participation of the Soviet Union. Because the Soviet Union *does* represent a threat to our security, and because the basic features of its social and political system are so very different from, and to most Americans, antithetical to our own system of government, any discussion of nuclear arms control and reducing the risk of a Soviet-American nuclear war is bound to require an examination of Soviet motives, capabilities, and behavior. As the Washington-based public education organization Ground Zero explains in its book, *What About the Russians and Nuclear War?*:

> *"What About the Russians?" has long been a stock response to the notion that the United States set limits on its nuclear weapons program. Whether the proposals be for unilateral action or for bilateral action, as in the case of the nuclear weapons freeze proposals on*

*so many ballots in legislative agendas in the early 1980's, the
question is the same. . . . The policies of the Soviet Union,
whether we like them or not, are fundamental when we think
about American security.*[1]

In this chapter we present a spectrum of views on the roles that nuclear
weapons play in Soviet foreign policy, as well as the degree to which
Moscow may be willing to cooperate with Washington in an effort to
reduce the costs and risks of the U.S.-Soviet nuclear arms competition.
The most pessimistic interpretation of Soviet intentions is put forward
here by Harvard historian Richard Pipes. Pipes, who spent two years as
the top Soviet specialist on the National Security Council staff during
Ronald Reagan's first term as President, believes that the Soviet leadership has a coherent "global strategy" for achieving world political domination.

Pipes cites three "expansionist tendencies" which he argues drive
Soviet foreign policy: Marxist-Leninist ideology, Soviet domestic politics, and traditional Russian territorial aspirations. Pipes argues that
military power plays a central role in achieving Soviet global objectives.
The cornerstone of Soviet military strategy is its strategic nuclear delivery capability, and a strategic doctrine which views nuclear war as a
winnable, survivable proposition, especially if the Soviet Union can succeed in landing the first blow in such a war. Pipes also argues that in
the 1970s, the Soviets used the Strategic Arms Limitation Talks (SALT)
process and the period of Soviet-American detente to enhance its capacity to undertake a nuclear first strike against the United States. (In an
earlier article, also published in *Commentary,* Pipes wrote "Why the Soviet Union Thinks it Could Fight and Win a Nuclear War."[2]) While
granting that the Soviet Union probably does not seek nuclear war,
Pipes believes that the Soviet leadership wishes to use what he views as
a growing Soviet advantage in nuclear war-fighting capabilities to extract political concessions from the United States, and weaken its resolve
to defend its vital interests in such areas as Europe, Japan, and the Middle East.

While agreeing that Soviet foreign policy reveals expansionist
tendencies, Marshall Shulman, in "What the Russians Really Want,"
asserts that these tendencies derive more from the Soviet's post-World
War II status as a great power than they do from a combination of revolutionary zeal, historical impulses, and domestic political imperatives.
Shulman also quarrels with Pipes' thesis that improvements in Soviet
military capabilities have "emboldened" the Soviet Union to become
more aggressive in the post-detente era. Neither side, he argues, possesses today a politically or militarily usable nuclear superiority over the
other. Nevertheless, he argues, the arms race continues because "neither
has had the self-confidence to regard a secure retaliatory force as sufficient." Thus, while not disagreeing with Pipes that certain elements of

---

[1] Ground Zero, *What About the Russians and Nuclear War?* (New York: Pocket Books, 1983).
[2] Richard Pipes, "Why the Soviet Union Thinks It Could Fight and Win a Nuclear War," *Commentary* 64
(July 1977), pp. 21–34.

Soviet strategic policy indicate an interest in acquiring options for actually using nuclear weapons in war, Shulman also points out that American strategic policy over the last decade and a half has revealed this same tendency. Shulman, unlike Pipes, sees scope for mutual accommodation and the potential for progress in achieving objectives of joint American and Soviet interest. The most critical area of obvious joint interest, he argues, is avoiding nuclear war. And in contrast to Pipes, Shulman regards past Soviet behavior as evidence that future progress in Soviet-American arms control is possible.

Richard Falk examines how "The Soviet Factor" has become "A Useful Enemy" for those in the United States who support unrestrained enhancements in American military capabilities and who generally oppose any steps towards negotiated arms agreements with the Soviet Union. Too often, Falk argues, the domestic legitimacy of American nuclear weapons policy derives solely from the American public's uncritical acceptance of "the Soviet challenge" as a rationale for greater American strength, and policymakers' ability to cultivate an image of the Soviet Union as the enemy.

Falk cautions us against blindly accepting this simplistic and stereotypical view of the Soviet Union as an implacable enemy with whom we share no common interests and concerns. True, we must recognize the politically unsavory and threatening aspects of Soviet policy, including both the repressive character of its social system at home and its ability to project military force abroad. But to acknowledge the Soviet Union as a potential security threat to the United States is a far cry from saying the Soviet Union is "hell bent on world conquest," and that any new U.S. nuclear weapons system, no matter how destabilizing, is justified and necessary if it will meet "the Soviet challenge." Falk, echoing Shulman's thoughts, argues that while a sober appreciation of the Soviet military threat is a necessary element in U.S. policy, "realism" must be "divorced from nuclearism," and each country must make the effort to overcome domestic opposition with the other and infuse the U.S.-Soviet relationship with greater military and political stability.

John Erickson's "The Soviet View of Deterrence: A General Survey" provides a glimpse into the debate over the character of Soviet nuclear weapons strategy and the way in which Soviet leaders think about the prospect of nuclear war with the United States. For almost a decade now, various western specialists in Soviet military policy have asserted that the Soviet leadership has a definitive strategy for fighting and winning a nuclear war with the United States, and that this strategy in turn guides Soviet strategic weapons development and deployment policy. As evidence, they cite suggestive passages written by Soviet military strategists in official Soviet military textbooks, journals, and newspapers that appear to confirm this view. Other analysts have disputed this interpretation, arguing that other statements drawn from these same sources indicate Soviet military and political leaders do recognize that under present circumstances, Soviet "victory" and "survival" in a nuclear war with the United States would not be possible.

Erickson, in commenting on this debate, makes a number of important points. Soviet strategists *have* written, in a very straightforward

manner, of the kinds of capabilities and operations the Soviets would
have to undertake in order to "defeat" the United States in a nuclear
war, emphasizing especially the need for a preemptive first strike counterforce capability and adequate strategic defenses, including civil defense. But as Erickson points out, *this is a far cry from saying that such a
strategy could be successfully implemented given the current size and invulnerability of American retaliatory capabilities,* which Soviet writers generally do
not. According to Erickson, "Soviet opinion seems to hold that nuclear
war is not a rational instrument of policy, for means and ends lose any
significance when the cost of destroying the enemy amounts to self-annihilation." Thus, while Soviet writers may refuse to endorse the western
concept of "deterrence," they appear to recognize each side's de facto
vulnerability to the other's retaliatory forces, and the *existence* of mutual
deterrence.

SOVIET GLOBAL STRATEGY
Richard Pipes

Richard Pipes is Baird Professor of History at Harvard University.
During 1981–82 he served as the ranking Soviet affairs specialist on the
staff of the National Security Council. Among his written works are *Survival Is Not Enough* and *U.S.–Soviet Relations in an Era of Détente.*

To begin with the ideological factors behind Soviet foreign policy: Marxism-
Leninism is by its very nature a militant doctrine, the child of the age of Social Darwinism, which views history as the record of uninterrupted class warfare and which advocates the continuation of class war as a means of abolishing,
once and for all, classes and the exploitation of man by man. The kind of
"stability" of which the President* speaks and which he implies to be the
desirable objective of all foreign policy can be attained, according to this doctrine, only *after* capitalism has been liquidated. The liquidation of capitalism,
however, calls for a long period of instability, including international wars,
which, according to Lenin, are an inevitable concomitant of capitalism.

Secondly, Marxism-Leninism is an international doctrine. As it perceives

Source: Richard Pipes, "Soviet Global Strategy," *Commentary,* 69:4 (April 1980), pp. 31–39. Reprinted
from *Commentary,* April 1980, by permission; all rights reserved.
* Editor's note: Here Pipes refers to former President Jimmy Carter.

them, the phases in the evolution of mankind are global in scope and cannot be contained (except transitionally) within the limits of the nation-state or served by its "legitimate security needs." The fundamental international, or, rather, supranational, character of the doctrine is symbolized by Communism's permanent slogan since 1847, "Proletarians of all countries, unite!" In 1917, the Bolsheviks (and this held true of the Socialist Revolutionaries and Mensheviks as well) were not fighting for a change of regime in Russia, but for a world-wide revolution. It deserves note that one of the earliest declarations of the Petrograd Soviet (then still firmly in the control of "moderate" socialists), issued in March 1917, was addressed to the "Peoples of the Entire World" and called on them to rid themselves of their "ruling classes." This attitude was never repudiated by Lenin; nor has it ever been repudiated by his successors.

Now it is possible to minimize such ideological considerations with the argument that history is replete with instances of movements which, having laid claim to universality, nevertheless adjusted themselves to more modest roles: several religions, including Islam, provide good examples. But apart from the fact that accommodations of this nature have always occurred as the result of a universalist movement running into resistance that it could not overcome, Communism is not only a faith, it is also the program of a powerful secular government. It is precisely this fusion of a universalist historical doctrine with the most mundane aspirations of a great imperialist power that lends Communist Russia's global ambitions such force. For behind the lofty ideals of a classless society loom also the very vulgar interests of a ruling elite which finds in them a rationale for power and privilege.

The most painful reality that the Soviet leadership confronts every day of its existence is that it has no generally acknowledged mandate to rule. It lacks the legitimacy of ancient tradition; nor can it derive its authority from the personal charisma of a great living leader. This committee of colorless, self-perpetuating civil servants pretends to rest on a popular mandate and to this end every now and then stages mock elections, but the ritual of choosing without having a choice surely deceives only simpletons. Such mandate as the Bolshevik regime can reasonably lay claim to derives entirely from history, namely, from the assertion that it represents the vanguard of the majestic force of progress whose mission it is to accomplish the final social revolution in human history. Once this particular claim is given up—as it would be were the Soviet government to acknowledge the international status quo as permanent and accommodate itself within its present sphere of influence—the question of legitimacy would at once crop up. For indeed, who has given the Communist part of the Soviet Union the right to monopolize the country's political authority as well as its human and material resources?—none other than the goddess of history who has challenged it to the noblest mission ever assigned to man. The regime, therefore, must press onward and outward, it must win, or at least appear to win, incessant victories against "capitalism" so as to maintain the illusion of a relentless forward movement, commensurate with its mission. The alternative is to risk having its political credentials subjected to scrutiny and possible disqualification.

In addition to its universalist ideology and the ordinary political self-interest of the ruling elite, Soviet expansionism also has solid roots in Russian history. Because of the inherent poverty of Russia, due to adverse climate, soil, and other related factors, the country has never been able to support a population at a level of density common in more temperate zones. Throughout their history, Russians have colonized areas adjacent to their homeland in the northern taiga, sometimes peacefully, sometimes by conquest. Of all European countries, Russia has not only the oldest and most persistent tradition of imperial expansion, but also the record of greatest tenacity in holding on to conquered areas.

Thus, ideology, political survival, and economic exigencies reinforce one another, impelling Russia toward conquest. Each new territory acquired becomes part of the national "patrimony" and is, sooner or later, incorporated into the homeland. Each demands a "buffer" to protect it from real or imaginary enemies, until it, too, becomes part of the homeland, and, in turn, requires its own buffer.

The theory of détente, promoted by the Soviet regime since the mid-1950's, would seem to contradict the thesis that expansionism and international class war are indispensable to Russian Communism. As presented to the West (the matter is handled quite differently within the country), the theory, calling for peaceful coexistence between diverse social systems, seems to accept the prospect of a nonviolent evolution and a common, "convergent" end-product. In reality, détente is merely a tactical adaptation of a general strategy, which does not run contrary to the principles enunciated above. To explain why this is the case, one must say a few words about the essential characteristic of Communist politics as formulated by Lenin and elaborated upon by his epigones.

Lenin's historic achievement is to have militarized politics. It has been aptly said that Lenin stood Clausewitz on his head by making politics the pursuit of war by other means: war is the aim, politics a means, rather than the other way around. This being the case, the application of political strategy and tactics is determined by an essentially military assessment of what is known as the "correlation of forces." The latter, in Communist theory, embraces not only those factors which in Western terminology are included in the concept of "balance of power" but also economic capabilities, social stability, and public opinion, i.e., elements that, although not military in the strict sense of the word, nevertheless have considerable bearing on a nation's ability to wage war.

From this point of view, the decision whether to press one's offensive against the "class enemy," internal as well as external, or to hold back, must be based on a cool appraisal of the contending forces. In a speech delivered in May 1918, in which he reiterated that "final victory is possible only on a world scale," Lenin admonished his followers not to rush headlong into battle under all circumstances:

> We possess great revolutionary experience, which has taught us that it is essential to employ the tactics of merciless attack when objective conditions permit. . . . But we have to resort *to temporizing tactics, to a slow gathering of forces* when objective circumstances do not favor a call for a general merciless repulse.[1]

In the eyes of the Soviet leadership, the phenomena which in the West are labeled "cold war" and "détente" and perceived as antithetical are merely tactical nuances of one and the same strategy, alternately applied, depending on "objective circumstances." In the case of the détente policy launched in the mid-1950's, the decisive objective circumstance was the enemy's complete nuclear superiority which placed him in a position to destroy much of the Soviet Union at will. This particular circumstance did not in the least obviate the necessity of waging international class war, but it did call for the adaptation of one's battle plans: confrontation had to be avoided and indirect methods of combat given preference—at any rate, until such time as America's nuclear threat could be safely neutralized.

The end objective of Soviet global policy is, of course, a world from which private property in the means of production has been banished and the constituent states are, with minor variations, copies of the Soviet state. It is only in a world so fashioned that the elite ruling Soviet Russia would feel secure and comfortable.

This objective does not, as is sometimes thought, require that the USSR physically occupy the entire world, a task which is beyond even the capabilities of its large military and security forces. The term "hegemony" conveys very accurately the kind of international arrangement with which the Soviet leadership would be satisfied. The concept is of Greek origin and was originally coined to describe the dominance enjoyed by one or another city state, and especially the Macedonian kingdom, over Hellas. Possession of "hegemony" did not then and does not now entail physical conquest: rather, it signifies the ability of the hegemonial power to assert its interest within the area

---

[1] V.I. Lenin, *Collected Works* (London, n.d.), XXVII, pp. 373, 377; emphasis added.

over which it claims hegemony by the threat of coercion, or, if that fails to produce the desired effect, by its actual application. Britain enjoyed hegemony over a good part of the globe in the 19th century; the United States had it between the end of World War II and its withdrawal from Vietnam. Germany launched two world wars in an unsuccessful attempt to obtain European hegemony. Andrei Gromyko, the Soviet Minister of Foreign Affairs, stated concisely the ultimate aspiration of Soviet policy in a speech to the 24th Congress of the CPSU in 1971 when he boasted, somewhat prematurely: "Today, there is no question of any significance which can be decided without the Soviet Union *or in opposition to it.*"[2] Implied in this statement is the rejection of the notion that Soviet interests are anything less than global in scope and can be confined within the boundaries of a national state or even a bloc of states. It goes without saying that the assertion of a similar claim by the United States would be rejected out of hand by the Soviet Union (as well as by American liberals) as a manifestation of the crassest imperialism. This is but one of many examples of the Soviet Union laying down the rules of international politics in a manner that entirely favors its own side.

If politics is warfare, then it requires strategic guidance. The strategy that one employs in the pursuit of global objectives cannot involve exclusively military weapons, but must embrace the entire spectrum of instrumentalities. Strategy of this type has been labeled "Grand" or "Total," and it suits a totalitarian country much better than it does a democratic one. The Soviet Union has indeed been organized by Lenin from the beginning for the waging of total war and it is to this end that the Soviet government has taken into its hands a monopoly of national powers and resources. There exists in the Soviet Union a mechanism of vertical and horizontal integration that not only enables but also compels the management of that giant political conglomerate to attempt a coordinated national and international policy. The proprietors of the Soviet Union have to seek to integrate politics, economics, and propaganda (ideology) to an extent inconceivable in the West where each of these realms is controlled by different groups and tends to pull in separate directions.

Let us cursorily survey the ingredients of Soviet Grand Strategy. Space precludes any discussion of the many aspects and nuances of Soviet *political* strategy. Its guiding principle, however, can be succinctly defined: it is to rely not so much on the forces at one's own disposal (i.e., foreign Communist parties and their "fronts") as on allies one is able provisionally and temporarily to detach from the enemy's camp on individual issues (e.g., nationalism, "peace," "racism," "anti-Zionism," etc.). This technique, originated by Rus-

---

[2] *XXIV S"ezd KPSS: Stenograficheskii otchet* (Moscow, 1971), I, p. 482; emphasis added.

sian opposition groups in the Czarist underground, has proved very successful when applied to international relations. Its essence can best be conveyed in the words of Lenin himself. In 1920 the Communist leader was faced with unrest over his cautious foreign policy from hotheads in the Third International. These people wanted a direct assault on the entire capitalist West. To them Lenin said bluntly:

> The entire history of Bolshevism, both before and after the October Revolution, is *full* of instances of changes of tack, conciliatory tactics, and compromises with other parties, including bourgeois parties!
>
> To carry on a war for the overthrow of the international bourgeoisie, a war which is a hundred times more difficult, protracted, and complex than the most stubborn of ordinary wars between states and to renounce in advance any change of tack, or any utilization of conflict of interest (even if temporary) among one's enemies, or any conciliation or compromise with possible allies (even if they are temporary, unstable, vacillating, or conditional allies), is that not ridiculous in the extreme? . . .
>
> After the first socialist revolution of the proletariat, and the overthrow of the bourgeoisie in some country, the proletariat of that country remains *for a long time weaker* than the [international] bourgeoisie. . . . The more powerful enemy can be vanquished only be exerting the utmost effort, and by the most thorough, careful, attentive, skillful, and *obligatory* use of any, even the smallest, rift between the enemies, any conflict of interests among the bourgeoisie of the various countries and among the various groups or types of bourgeoisie within the various countries, and also by taking advantage of any, even the smallest, opportunity of winning a mass ally, even though this ally is temporary, vacillating, unreliable, and conditional.[3]

The success of this policy has been in large measure due to the fact that the "international bourgeoisie" not only refuses to acknowledge the manipulative intentions behind Soviet conciliatory policies but feels confident of its own ability to fish in the political waters of the Soviet Union by pitting nonexisting "doves" against equally spurious "hawks."

The Soviet *economic* aresenal is not rich enough to serve as a major weapon of Soviet global strategy. In its expansion, the USSR consequently relies much less on investments and trade as a means of spreading influence than was the case with the other great powers in the classical age of modern imperialism. Soviet economic leverage is exercised mainly through military and economic assistance carefully doled out to countries judged to be of strategic importance. Aid of this kind creates all kinds of dependencies, including the willingness of the recipient to host Communist administrative personnel. It is very

---

[3] Lenin, *Collected Works*, XXXI, pp. 70–71.

instructive to analyze statistics of Soviet economic assistance to Third World countries because the figures give a good insight into the relative importance that Moscow attaches to them. On a per-capita basis, among the greatest beneficiaries of Soviet aid since 1954 have been South Yemen and Afghanistan. More recently, the USSR and its clients have poured vast sums of money into Turkey, a member of NATO, and Morocco. Significant increases in Soviet assistance are usually reliable indicators of Soviet strategic interests in a given area: judging by recent aid patterns, the Mediterranean enjoys very high priority in its mind.

In its relations with the advanced industrial powers, the Soviet Union is at a great disadvantage in attempting to exploit economic leverage, but even so it has had some success in making Western Europe and Japan dependent on its good will.

One form of leverage is the debts incurred in the West by the Soviet bloc during the period of détente. These are estimated today at $60 billion, one-quarter of it owed by the USSR, the remainder by the countries of Eastern Europe. The external indebtedness of the Soviet Union cannot be considered excessive, given that country's natural resources and gold reserves, but the same cannot be said of the "Peoples' Democracies" such as Poland, whose foreign obligations exceed those of its patron state. Western bankers have gladly lent vast sums to Eastern Europe on the assumption that any defaults would be made good by the Soviet Union. In so doing they have chosen to ignore official Soviet statements which repudiate any such obligation. Moscow's position on this issue, recently reiterated at an East-West conference held in Vienna, holds that "every country must repay its own debts."[4] Loans of this magnitude induce among Western bankers solicitude for the economic well-being and benevolence of their Eastern European debtors, and makes them beholden to détente, regardless of its political costs.

The other economic weapon is energy, of whose strategic importance the Soviet leadership has become aware long before it even dawned on Western politicians. In addition to placing itself in a position to impede the flow of Middle Eastern oil (of which more later), the USSR has sought to make Europe and Japan dependent on direct Soviet energy supplies, especially natural gas. To this end, it has established the practice of repaying in gas the costs of transmission pipes supplied by foreign concerns. West Germany is said to rely already for one-quarter of its natural gas on Soviet resources; and if negotiations now in progress for further cooperation in this field are successful, its dependence will increase further. What this development portends became apparent during the October 1973 war when the Soviet Union abruptly sus-

---

[4] *Neue Zürcher Zeitung*, October 10, 1979.

pended gas deliveries to Veba, Germany's largest energy company, apparently in order to pressure that country not to support Washington's pro-Israel policies.

A list of all the other instrumentalities which the Soviet Union employs in its global strategy would be long and diverse. Among them would have to be included such seemingly unpolitical matters as family relations. The broadening of contacts between relatives separated by the border between East and West Germany which followed the Helsinki accords, provides the Communists with useful political leverage, the fear of their disruption being often cited by Bonn circles as a strong reason for preserving détente.

Of all the instrumentalities at the Soviet Union's disposal, it is the military that occupies pride of place. Soviet imperialism (this also held true of Czarist imperialism) is a military phenomenon *par excellence*, and in proportion as Soviet combat power grows, both absolutely and in relation to the West's, it tends to push into the background the political manipulation on which the regime has had heavily to rely earlier. Increasingly, Soviet spokesmen call attention to the shift in the military balance in Russia's favor as a decisive fact of the contemporary world, and boast of the ability it gives their country to frustrate America's attempts to respond to Soviet initiatives.

It is sometimes difficult for people who are told of the low living standards of the Soviet Union's population and of the inefficiency of its economy to believe that such a country can present a serious military threat to the West. They ignore the fact that wealth and technical inventiveness, in which the West has an indisputable lead, do not make for military might unless they are harnessed in the service of defense. They further ignore that, conversely, a relatively poor country, as long as it has more than a minimal industrial-technical base, can offer more than a military match for its neighbors once it decides to allocate the necessary resources for war. Japan is an industrial and technological power of the very first rank. Yet because it has chosen to rely for its defense on the United States and forgo a military establishment commensurate with its economic power, its armed forces are one-half in size and a fraction in effectiveness of those of Israel, a country with one-thirtieth of Japan's population and one-fortieth of its GNP. As concerns the Soviet Union's low living standards, it should be obvious that when a country with its huge industrial plant cannot satisfy its population's needs for consumer goods, the reason must be sought not in incapacity but rather in the deliberate diversion of industrial resources to other than consumer needs. In other words, the fact that its population suffers a low living standard attests not to Russia's inability to threaten us militarily but rather to the opposite.

Russia has always tended to devote a disproportionate share of its resources to the upkeep of the armed forces: in the reign of Peter the Great, for example, more than nine-tenths of the state budget was allocated for that purpose. A large military establishment helped conquer new territories for Russia's growing population as well as to maintain order within the empire. High Czarist functionaries were well aware how much of the international influence that imperial Russia enjoyed was due to its ability to threaten small and great powers along its immensely long frontiers.

The principal weakness of pre-1917 Russian armies was a low level of supporting industry and transport, and all of those other non-military factors that World War I revealed to be of decisive importance in modern warfare. The lesson was learned by the Bolshevik leaders who studied with admiration Germany's extraordinary performance in that war; as soon as they seized power they put into effect the home-front mobilization measures initiated by Germany but made even more effective in Russia by the abolition of private property and the introduction of the universal obligation to render state service. Stalin's Five Year Plans, for all the noise about constructing socialism, were as thoroughly military in their intent as were Hitler's Four Year Plans.

The conglomerate nature of the Soviet regime makes it eminently suitable for purposes of military mobilization. If the Soviet government so decides, it can lavish on the defense sector of the economy manpower and resources in the quantities and qualities required, and let the consumer sector fend for itself. The mightier the industrial base, the more rapid under these conditions can be the expansion of the armed forces, inasmuch as the allocations to the civilian sector can be kept relatively constant while the bulk of the growing surplus is turned over to the military. And, of course, there are no recalcitrant legislatures or inquisitive media to raise questions about the need for such heavy defense outlays.

Thus it happens that neither détente nor the arms-limitation agreements accompanying it, SALT I included, have produced a dent in the upward curve of Soviet defense appropriations. A recent study by William T. Lee, a specialist with long CIA experience, estimates that the share absorbed by the defense sector of the Soviet Gross National Product has grown from some 12–13 per cent in 1970 to perhaps as much as 18 per cent in 1980; and since the Soviet GNP during this decade has also kept on growing, the absolute amounts given to the defense have risen yet more impressively.[5] Incidentally, in the same period (1970–79), U.S. defense expenditures as a share of the GNP have declined from 7.5 per cent to 4.6 per cent, and in constant 1972 dollars, from $85.1 to $65.0 billion.

Although the Soviet military seem determined to catch up to and surpass the United States in all the service branches, they assign the central role

---

[5] "Soviet Defense Expenditures in the Era of SALT," United States Strategic Institute Report 79-1 (Washington, D.C., 1979), pp. 10–11.

to strategic-nuclear weapons. These the Soviet military theorists regard as the decisive weapons of modern warfare. All the available evidence furnished by theoretical writings and observable deployments indicates that the Soviet General Staff does not share the prevalent U.S. view that nuclear weapons have no place in a rational strategy except as a deterrent. There exists a high degree of probability that in the event of general war the Soviet Union intends to use a part of its strategic arsenal in a devastating preemptive strike which would make an American retaliatory strike suicidal and possibly inhibit it altogether. The stress on large throw-weight combined with high accuracies of its ICBM's is a good indication that the Soviet Union intends to develop a first-strike capability.

The refusal of the American scientific community, which has been largely responsible for the formulation of U.S. nuclear strategy, to take seriously Soviet nuclear doctrine can charitably be described as an act of grave intellectual and political irresponsibility. Owing to it, in the coming decade the United States will find all three legs of its "triad" under growing threat which will not only make it difficult to respond to aggressive Soviet moves, but will also free the Soviet Union from those restraints which had inspired it to adopt the policy of détente in the first place. Once the nuclear balance will have become highly tilted, American crash programs will likely be discouraged by the same exponents of unilateral restraint who have helped bring the imbalance about, on the grounds that at this point any sudden moves would be "destabilizing" and could provoke the Soviet Union into a preemptive strike.

The strong Soviet commitment to the process of so-called "arms limitation" does not invalidate the contention that it operates on a first-strike doctrine. As has become evident since 1972, SALT I has had no significant influence on the development of Russia's strategic offensive forces. The same may be said of SALT II which, if ratified, would exert only a minimal effect on future Soviet deployments, while inhibiting and in some cases precluding important U.S. responses (such as long-range cruise missiles and protective shelters for the Minutemen missiles). Adopting for negotiating purposes the American "Mutual Assured Destruction" doctrine, the Soviet Union has been able to push through, at a relatively small price to its own deployments, severe restrictions on those of the United States.

Nuclear missiles, however, have not only a military utility: they are equally and perhaps even more useful as a means of political and psychological suasion. Russia's growing nuclear arsenal inculcates in influential Western circles a sense of all-pervasive fear which induces a spirit of accommodation. Once the view gains hold that there is no defense against nuclear weapons, it becomes not unreasonable to advocate avoidance of disagreement with another nuclear power as the highest goal of foreign policy. The following sentiments expressed by Congressman Jonathan Bingham of New York are quite typical of this body of opinion:

> *Above all,* we must remember that the Soviet Union remains the world's only other superpower—the only country in the world capable of destroying us. Maintaining good relations with the Soviet Union must be our *paramount* objective.[6]

I wonder whether Congressman Bingham has thought through the implications of his words. For he is, in effect, urging that we subordinate all our national interests as well as our ideals of freedom and human rights, and whatever else many of us regard as "paramount," to another criterion, namely, survival; and that in line with this criterion, we should seek accommodation with that country which can deny it to us. (Only we: there is nothing in this passage to suggest that the Soviet Union has a similar obligation toward us, the only country in the world capable of destroying it.) When this kind of thinking becomes prevalent, a nation loses the freedom to act in self-defense; psychologically, the white flag of surrender is up and sending unmistakable signals to the adversary. It takes little imagination to picture what effect this kind of thinking must have on the Soviet leaders: it virtually incites them to keep on increasing their nuclear preponderance, given that the greater their theoretical capability to destroy the United States, the louder the voices in the United States demanding that accommodation with the Soviet Union be made the "paramount" objective of national policy. . . .

To frustrate Soviet global strategy, it is necessary, first and foremost, to acknowledge that it exists. We must get rid of the notion, widespread among America's educated and affluent, that the Soviet Union acts out of fear, that its actions are invariably reactions to U.S. initiatives, and that it seizes targets of opportunity like some kind of international pickpocket. We are dealing with an adversary who is driven not by fear but by aggressive impulses, who is generally more innovative in the field of political strategy than we are, and who selects his victims carefully, with long-term objectives in mind.

Secondly, it is essential to overcome an attitude toward nuclear weapons which leaves us increasingly vulnerable to subtle forms of psychological and political blackmail. We once had a similar attitude toward cancer; it used to be thought that the mere mention of this disease brought it about. In fact, however, open discussion of cancer has led to early diagnosis and treatment, and considerably reduced the danger of death from it. Nuclear weapons are a

---

[6] Victor C. Johnson, co-author, *Foreign Affairs,* Spring 1979, p. 919; emphasis added.

kind of cancer of the international body politic. Awareness of their actual (rather than imaginary) dangers can lead to sensible measures being taken to reduce the risk of nuclear war breaking out and to keep casualties low should it nevertheless happen. Unless we are prepared to confront this danger, the growing Russian preponderance in strategic weapons will leave us in a position where we shall have no choice but to capitulate to Soviet demands whenever they are backed with the threat of war.

Thirdly, we should take an honest look at our alliance system which has deteriorated to the point where its utility seems more psychological than real. For some time now NATO has been a one-way street: the United States underwrites the security of Western Europe against Soviet attack, but its West European allies feel no particular obligation to support the United States in its confrontations with the Soviet Union in any other part of the world. This holds true even of the Middle East where Europe's interests are, if anything, yet more directly involved. Such behavior encourages the Soviet leaders to act aggressively in the Third World, in the knowledge that here the United States will be confronting them alone, and that such confrontations serve to exacerbate America's differences with its allies.

Fourthly, we must correct as rapidly as possible the skewed military balance, especially where strategic and naval forces are concerned. If a commensurate effort is undertaken by Western Europe and Japan, and if the mutual obligations of our alliance are made more equitable than they now are, then Soviet expansion into the Middle East and Africa ought to prove costlier and therefore less attractive.

The ultimate purpose of Western counterstrategy should be to compel the Soviet Union to turn inward—from conquest to reform. Only by blunting its external drive can the Soviet regime be made to confront its citizenry and to give it an account of its policies. It is a well-known fact of modern Russian history that whenever Russian governments suffered serious setbacks abroad— in the Crimean war, in the 1904–05 war with Japan, and in World War I— they were compelled by internal pressure to grant the citizenry political rights. We should help the population of the Soviet Union bring its government under control. A more democratic Russia would be less expansionist and certainly easier to live with.

WHAT THE RUSSIANS REALLY WANT: A RATIONAL RESPONSE TO THE SOVIET CHALLENGE

Marshall D. Shulman

Marshall D. Shulman has had extensive experience working on Soviet affairs in the U.S. government, inlcuding service as a special assistant to Secretaries of State Cyrus Vance and Edmund Muskie in the Carter Administration, with the rank of ambassador. He is currently Adlai E. Stevenson Professor of International Relations and Director of the W. Averill Harriman Institute for Advanced Study of the Soviet Union at Columbia University.

Like travelers who come upon an umarked fork in the road, we find ourselves obliged by the change in leadership in the Soviet Union to stop and think. The transition, with all the uncertainties it presents, compels us to consider where we are going in our fateful relationship with the Russians, and why, and whether we should be going in another direction.

Almost seven decades have passed since the revolution that led to the founding of the Soviet Union. For most of those years, relations between that country and our own have been animated by hostility, relieved only by brief intervals of abatement and passing hopes of some easement.

Each such interval, however, has been followed by an ever stronger expression of the conflict of power, beliefs, and purposes between the two nations. That conflict is now so deeply rooted and so intense that it evokes the destructive energies of both societies, weakening them and the fabric of the international system, threatening the possibility of catastrophe.

That hostility did not grow out of any natural antipathy between the peoples of the two countries, but with the passage of time each has come to be so persuaded of the malign intent of the other that it has become difficult to distinguish what is real and what is fancied in the perceptions each holds of the other.

In the conduct of our foreign relations, Walter Lippmann observed, we operate on the basis of "pictures in our heads." The images of the Soviet Union held most widely in this country are stereotypes, and they warp our thinking in a number of ways. They are simple caricatures of a complex society. They are static and do not take into account the changes that have taken place,

Source: Marshall D. Shulman, "What the Russians Really Want: A Rational Response to the Soviet Challenge," *Harper's Magazine* (April 1984), pp. 63–71. Copyright © 1984 by Harper's Magazine Foundation. All rights reserved. Reprinted from the April, 1984 issue by special permission.

particularly since the death of Stalin. They are based on prevalent assumptions that do not bear critical examination. They misrepresent the ways in which the Soviet people react to our actions and to our words. They do not distinguish between atmosphere and substance. Finally, as oversimple images informing oversimple policy, they make it difficult for us to resolve the dilemma of whether we should try to change the Soviet system or try to improve our relations with it.

After almost four decades spent studying the Soviet Union and about thirty trips there, what continues to strike me most forcefully is the sharp contrast between the complex reality of that country and the primitive perceptions of it that dominate our discussions, and the contrast between the way the world looks from Moscow and the way it appears from Washington. Even more troubling is the problem we face in bringing our values, our emotions, our apprehensions, and our judgments about the Soviet Union into some kind of reasonable balance with our relations with it.

To many Americans, including many specialists on the subject, it seems contradictory to recognize that the Soviet Union is repressive and expansionist and also to believe that we should seek to manage rationally the fundamentally competitive Soviet-American relationship. When has been absent from our thinking is the maturity to carry such apparently contradictory notions in our heads at the same time.

Good and reasonable people often come to hold fundamentally different views of the Soviet Union. There is much about that secretive society that we do not know. Into this uncertainty people tend to project either their fears or their hopes, according to their temperaments or their political prejudices or, perhaps, their experiences: a businessman who has been royally treated on his visits to the Soviet Union will have a different picture in his mind than an émigré who may have spent years in a labor camp or years battling bureaucrats for an exit visa; a military game theorist will see the Russians as the enemy, ruthless, omnicompetent, poised to attack.

The problems presented by the Soviet Union are serious. But stereotypes do not provide us with an adequate basis for responding intelligently. My purpose here is to suggest a way of thinking about these problems, beginning with a realistic view of the Soviet Union and its behavior and ending with some guidelines for the conduct of our relations with Moscow. Not everyone, and certainly not all of those who study Soviet behavior, will agree with what I regard as realistic or with my conclusions. But I believe that the time is overdue for us to address head-on some of the questions that underlie our present thinking about that country in order to contribute to a more rational discourse, beyond the level of partisan polemics.

One: In seeking to expand its power and influence around the world, are the Soviet Union's aspirations unlimited? Does it accept practical limitations on realizing its status as a superpower? Might it even become willing to live according to the norms of the international system?

Over the last sixty-seven years, we have witnessed the ascendancy of nation-state interests over revolutionary expectations and ideology as the primary motivation of Soviet foreign policy. It became apparent to the Soviet regime in its early years—and even more so after World War II—that the proletariat of the West was showing no signs of the revolutionary potential that Lenin had ascribed to it. In response to this fact, Soviet policy was adapted to address the bourgeoisie of both the Western industrial societies and the developing world for the purpose of influencing governments to act in ways favorable to Soviet interests. Although revolutionary ideology is still part of the official rhetoric and although it is bolstered by a bureaucratic apparatus that has a stake in it, it has been modified in such a way as to put off to the indefinite future the realization of apocalyptic goals. Peaceful coexistence, which to Lenin meant a breathing spell, has become a long-term political strategy of competition by means short of war.

While it is impossible to predict whether Soviet foreign policy will evolve in directions we would wish, it can be said that it has evolved more than is generally appreciated, largely as a result of Soviet efforts to adapt to changes in international politics, including options created by policies of the United States.

Coincident with this development—which has inclined Soviet policy toward favoring traditional balance-of-power maneuvers—has been a continuous movement away from the autarkic reliance on the Soviet economy promised by Stalin's commitment to "Socialism in One Country." In fact, the Soviet Union has become ever more deeply involved in the world economy, and the proportion of its gross national product derived from foreign trade has risen steadily.

While it does not seem likely that these trends will be reversed, it is clearly too much to say that they will necessarily lead to Soviet acceptance of the international system to the extent of being willing to act as a partner in preserving the system's stability. The Soviet Union has an interest in maintaining the status quo in Eastern Europe, but not elsewhere. A broader commitment would require a much greater departure from its residual faith that capitalist systems contain the seeds of their own destruction than any signs now indicate is likely.

Two: Are Soviet leaders, then, guided by the ideology of Marxism-Leninism?

If you were to ask them that question, their answer would be "Of course." None of them would say otherwise, and they seek sanction for every action, speech, article, or book by quoting from the storehouse of the writings of Marx, Engels, and, especially, Lenin.

Marxist-Leninist ideology, of course, is based on the prediction that captalist systems are doomed to decay and collapse, that they will seek to stave off this outcome by imperialist aggression, but that, in the end, "socialism" as the Soviet Union defines it will prove more effective and will emerge as the universal form of social organization. In practice, Soviet theoreticians have had to take into account the fact that these predictions from the nineteenth and early twentieth centuries have not received much confirmation. The lesson has not been lost on Soviet theoreticians, who have reinterpreted some parts of the ideology while clinging to others, seeking legitimacy in hoped-for improvements in performance, or what Khrushchev called "goulash communism." In truth, there is as much variance in the Soviet interpretation of Marxism-Leninism today as there is in American Protestantism.

To say that Soviet political figures and writers claim consistency with Marxism-Leninism is not to say that their actions are derived from ideology. Certainly the historical analysis of capitalism influences the way the older Soviet political elites interpret events, but the sacred texts offer less and less guidance for making the practical decisions demanded by the complex society that the Soviet Union has become. With rare exceptions, even those youths who aspire to become members of the Soviet establishment master their catechism with cynicism (the sound of shuffling feet during lectures on "diamat"—dialectical materialism—is reminiscent of the noise during lectures for GIs on social hygiene), suggesting that when they take the levers of power into their hands, the ideas that will shape their thoughts and guide their actions will bear only the slightest resemblance to the ideas that inspired the Revolution.

Three: Is the Soviet Union nevertheless inherently expansionist?

Some have argued that the answer to this question is yes. Should that be true, it would follow that in order to move Soviet behavior in the direction of greater restraint and responsibility it would be necessary to change the Soviet system in fundamental ways, and that this should be the primary objective of American policy. Those who take this position claim that it is only by external aggrandizement that the Soviet leadership can cement its power, claim legitimacy, and validate its view of history. Some even argue that there is a parallel between the Soviet Union and Nazi Germany, and that just as appeasement served to whet the Nazis' appetite, any accommodation with the Soviet Union can "only lead to disaster."

The study of Soviet behavior, however, suggests that Soviet actions are more consistently explained by reference to the pursuit of nation-state interests than by some inner compulsion related to the structure of the system. The leadership is strengthened by successes and weakened by failures, as is the case in any country, but there is no sign that Soviet adventures abroad have resulted in increased popular support. On the contrary, foreign adventures, whether in Hungary or Afghanistan, are regarded uneasily by Soviet citizens.

There is an expansive tendency in the Soviet Union behavior, but it is impelled not by the nature of the system but by the sense that the country has grown into a great power. Moreover, it has been activated by opportunities that the Soviet Union itself has not created, and it has been guided by a careful calculus of risks and gains as well as by a capacity for prudence. This was illustrated most recently by the absence of an immediate Soviet reaction to the attacks on Syria during the Israeli invasion of Lebanon.

The Nazi parallel is particularly misleading. Unlike the Nazis, Soviet leaders do not seek war. No one doubts that who has seen firsthand how fresh are the memories of the destruction and loss of life in World War II, or how universal is the appreciation of the consequences of nuclear war (much more universal than is the case in the United States). Soviet leaders have accepted and accommodated themselves to the practical constraints on their expansionist tendencies. They may hope that the future will bring more favorable opportunities, but faith in their historical inevitability has become ritualistic, and is advanced on national holidays with diminishing conviction.

Four: Even if the Soviet Union is not inherently expansionist, is it possible for us to maintain peaceful relations with it so long as it seeks to maximize its power and influence?

We have to accept the fact that the Soviet-American relationship is fundamentally competitive and is likely to remain so for the foreseeable future. What we must decide is whether it is in our interest to compete at a high level of confrontation or whether it is more sensible to manage the competition at lower levels of tension. If we seek to force the pace of military competition and to maximize pressure on the Soviet Union by cutting back diplomatic contacts, trade, and all forms of cooperation, the effect will be to increase the level of conflict and the risk of war and to push both societies toward greater, and destructive, militarization.

It is sometimes said in this country that the so-called détente of the early 1970s was a failure and a deception, and that it proved that the effort to moderate relations is bound not to work, leaving us at a disadvantage. But the principal reason why détente was not successful was that neither side fulfilled the two main requirements for reducing tensions. Those requirements are the management of the nuclear competition at lower and more stable levels and the codification of the terms of political competition in the Third World. On each side there were impediments to exercising the restraint that is essential to reducing the risk of war.

On the Soviet side, the main impediments to the stabilization of the nuclear competition appeared to stem from the influence of the military bureaucracy in Soviet politics; tendencies toward overinsurance in military matters; an inclination to think in prenuclear terms; a fear of the U.S. advantage in advanced military technology; a fear of appearing weak and therefore vulnerable to American pressure; and a mistaken belief that a strengthened military posture would make the United States more pliant in negotiations. In the Third World, the main impediment to restraint was the Soviet Union's commitment to expand its influence wherever it could do so at acceptable costs and risks, which it rationalized as support for what it chose to call national liberation movements. The increase in Soviet logistical capabilities and conventional weapons and forces made such interventions more tempting.

On the American side, the impediments to the stabilization of the nuclear competition included a lack of rationality in defense policy-making, as a result of which decisions were dictated by parochial economic and service interests; a residual commitment to superiority rather than parity as the basis for national security; a post-Vietnam fear of appearing to be weak; and a mistaken belief that a strengthened military posture would make the Soviet Union more pliant in negotiations. Moreover, a resurgence of nationalism, a universal phenomenon throughout the industrialized world, made any form of accommodation with the Soviet Union politically difficult. The basic impediments to stabilizing the U.S.–Soviet competition in the Third World were America's inexperience in international affairs, its parochialism, and its ignorance of the areas involved. That led the United States to regard countries of the Third World as abstract counters in the East–West competition, driving all radical movements into the Soviet camp, and to rely primarily on military instrumentalities for dealing with them.

In addition, there have been external impediments to a regulation of the competition. This period of international politics has been characterized by an extraordinary turbulence involving dramatic transformations in the industrialized nations, post-decolonization travails in the developing ones, and anarchy in the international system. Under the best of circumstances, it would have been remarkable if Soviet–American relations had not become roiled.

Five: Has Soviet foreign policy, emboldened by what some analysts see as military supremacy, become more aggressive in the years since détente?

There is a two-part answer to the military question. Certainly the improvements in the Soviet Union's conventional capabilities, the increase in the firepower and mobility of its forces, and its greater logistical capabilities—demonstrated in the impressive airlift of matériel to Ethiopia—have made it possible to intervene where it might not have been able to a decade ago. But despite the expanded Soviet strategic nuclear arsenal, it is wrong to speak of supremacy, and there are no grounds for believing that the strategic balance influenced the Soviet decisions to act as it did in Angola, Ethiopia, or Afghanistan.

The lack of restraint shown by the Soviet Union in exacerbating local conflicts cannot be justified, but its interventions have represented a continuation of its longstanding policy of seeking to exploit opportunities, whatever their cause. The 1975 intervention in Angola, for example, was a response to the collapse of the Portuguese position in Africa. (The Soviet Union was able to respond to that collapse more effectively than was the United States, tied as we were to our Portuguese ally and restrained as we were by the post-Vietnam inhibitions against foreign interventions.) In Ethiopia, it was Chairman Mengistu Haile-Mariam's alienation from the United States and his turning to the Soviet Union for support that created the Soviet opportunity, and there, as in Angola, the messianic mission of Fidel Castro gave the Soviet Union the benefit of Cuban soldiers. (In contrast, the Soviet invasion of Afghanistan was a response not to an opportunity but to a perceived threat; it can best be understood as a gross political and military miscalculation, reflecting Soviet paranoia about the security of its borders.)

Of course, even though these Soviet interventions were responses to opportunities rather than manifestations of a more aggressive policy, they are still a matter for concern. But it lies within our power to reduce such opportunities by understanding better what local factors generate upheavals and conflicts, and by responding to them more appropriately ourselves.

Six: Does the Soviet Union's military buildup indicate that is has accepted the risks of nuclear war?

The great increase in its conventional forces does raise the possibility that the Soviet Union is prepared to intervene in behalf of its newly acquired global interests. And in its production and deployment of nuclear weapons like the SS-18, an intercontinental missile capable of delivering ten warheads of 500 kilotons each with great accuracy, and the SS-20, an intermediate-range missile targeted on Europe and the Far East, it has not shown reasonable restraint and has aroused concerns in the West that have had the effect of reducing its own security. (In this respect, neither Soviet nor American defense policies have been marked by much rationality or foresight.) But it strains any plausible scenario to see Soviet strategic forces as capable of anything other than preventing a military attack or political intimidation.

Monetary measures of the Soviet Union's military effort have sometimes been used to show that its programs are alarmingly larger than ours, but these are not a reliable basis for comparison. The statistics cited in such comparisons are questionable: they depend on estimates of what it would cost us to produce Soviet weapons using American labor costs, and also on calculations of dollar-ruble equivalencies; they do not take into account the actual Soviet production costs; and even if it is argued that the percentage of the Soviet gross national product devoted to military programs is twice that of the United States, it must be borne in mind that the Soviet GNP is half our own. Moreover, the CIA has recently revised downward its estimates of Soviet military expenditures; those estimates now suggest that after annual increases of about 4 percent a year beginning in the early 1960s, the rate of increase began to level off in the mid-1970s, once the Soviet Union reached parity with the United States.

Judgments about parity are, of course, inexact, seeking as they do to compare quite different force structures (the Soviet Union has three quarters of its strategic force in land-based intercontinental missiles, compared with only one third of ours; the rest is in bombers and submarines). The Soviet Union fears that America's superior industrial technology may give us an edge in the future, and it continues to develop new weapons, duplicating our innovations when it can and compensating for others simply by doing more of what it can do. By any measure, however, it is apparent that given the destructiveness of nuclear weapons, neither side has or can hope to have usable military superiority over the other. But neither country has had the self-confidence to regard a secure retaliatory force as sufficient.

It has been said that Soviet military writings imply that Soviet leaders believe they can fight and win a nuclear war, but that argument reflects a superficial reading of the literature. Soviet military doctrine has evolved considerably since the time of Stalin, when nuclear weapons were discussed in pre-nuclear-age terms, and the authoritative statements of Yuri Andropov, Konstantin Chernenko, Minister of Defense Dmitri Ustinov, and Chief of the General Staff Nikolai Ogarkov have shown unequivocal awareness that nuclear war would be a danger to the security of their country.

Seven: Does it follow, then, that the Soviet Union is prepared to engage seriously in arms-control negotiations?

Arms-control negotiations about nuclear weapons seemed a radical idea to the Russians when they were first proposed in the Baruch plan in 1946. In the early years of the Strategic Arms Limitation Treaty negotiations, which began in November 1969, the Russians were obviously reluctant to consider entrusting their security to such arrangements—perhaps because they didn't feel strong enough, or their military was resistant, or they did not trust us any more than we trusted them. Most of the SALT proposals were advanced by the American negotiators, and many of the Soviet proposals (for nonaggression agreements, a ban on first use of nuclear weapons, and international conferences to discuss disarmament) had an agitprop character. Although the Soviet Union accepted the American proposal for strategic arms limitation talks, it did not appear to have accepted the fundamental SALT concepts: parity, mutual deterrence, and strategic stability.

But the situation has changed in two respects. We have changed. Despite our formal acceptance of deterrence as a guiding principle, we have moved toward developing war-fighting capabilities. Our defense plans are now based on the requirement that we be able to prevail in a prolonged nuclear conflict. In this respect, both the declaratory and the actual policies of the two countries have moved closer.

The Soviet Union has also changed: it became more than a passive partner in the negotiations. In the SALT II talks, it offered considerably more major concessions than did the United States; it was also prepared to agree that no new land-based intercontinental missiles be allowed, had we been willing to agree to what had originally been an American proposal. The Russians were stubborn bargainers, but they manifested a serious interest in limiting the nuclear competition.

Eight: What does this say about the belief that the United States must develop "positions of strength" in order to make the Soviet Union negotiate in good faith or accept our deterrent as credible?

To the Soviet Union, it appears that a military balance now exists and that American efforts to secure "positions of strength" mask attempts to achieve superiority. The Soviet reaction will be contrary to what is expected. Instead of feeling pressured to make concessions at the negotiating table, the Soviet Union will match every new American program with one of its own (as it has done in the past, for example when we introduced multiple-warhead systems). It is for this reason that the search for such "positions of strength" will lead to an upward spiral in the nuclear military competition, involving weapons that are less stable (the MX missile and the proposed space-based defense system) and less verifiable (cruise missiles) than those now in existence, with the consequence that it will be increasingly difficult to achieve any agreement.

Nine: Is the Soviet system capable of change?

It is here that we come to a question that is absolutely fundamental to the way we think about the Soviet Union, and it is here that our stereotypes are most strikingly out of date. Since the Revolution, the Soviet Union has evolved from a predominantly peasant society to one that is largely urban and industrializing. Although the process of industrialization has moved forward unevenly, and although large parts of the country do not seem to have changed in the past 100 years, the spread of education and the growth of cadres of specialists have made for a much more complex society, in which controls have been increasingly internalized and "privatization" stubbornly protects pockets of autonomy from intrusion by the central authorities. Leaving the intellectuals aside, for most people the system works, since they compare their living standards not with those of other countries but with their own in the past.

The engine of change is the emergence of new generations, with new expectations and experiences, and a vast generational shift is already in progress. Although it is not yet reflected in the composition of the top party leadership, it is to be seen at lower levels of the party, in the military, and in the various bureaucracies. The younger elite are well educated and competent. Not liberals in a Western sense, their thinking is nevertheless far more sophisticated than that of high-level party members, which has been characterized by parochial fundamentalism. They are free of the formative influences of the Revolution and the Stalinist terror and are relatively knowledgeable about the outside world and prepared to learn from it.

The prevailing Western images of the Soviet elite, based on monolithic totalitarian models, tend to stereotype Soviet officialdom, leading some observers to conclude that the system is brittle and cannot change without risk of collapse. This obscures the spectrum of views to be found even within the party establishment, which encompasses not only those who are careerists and bureaucrats supreme but also those who might be called "within-system critics," those who, within the bounds of loyalty to the system, possess and sometimes express unorthodox views about modernization. Because the changes they favor may provoke resistance, in the short run their activities may reinforce or even increase the authority of the political police. Whether in the long run such changes will moderate the repressiveness of the Soviet system may depend in part on the international climate.

In the end, one must wonder if the system will be able to cope with its enormous problems. That is a question no one can answer, not even the Soviet leadership. The decline in the country's growth rates is symptomatic of the contradiction between the rigidities of its political structure and the requirements of advanced industrialization. No one was more severe in cataloguing the deficiencies of the Soviet system than Yuri Andropov. The new leadership is also aware of the problems it faces. But it must deal with a profoundly conservative society, changing but resistant to change, fearful, above all, of the effects of reform on the party's control.

How these contending forces will resolve their differences is the most intriguing question of all, and the answer, when it becomes clear, will affect our thinking about our future relations with the Soviet Union.

There are, of course, other questions that we might wish to ask, but the issues we have already touched on point toward something that should be taken into account far more than has been the case: the factor of change. If instead of viewing the Soviet Union as a static system we view it as one in the midst of a historical transformation, then the starting point for thinking through our own policies should be to ask ourselves how they are likely to affect the processes of change in the Soviet system, Soviet conduct in the world, and opportunities for peaceful relations between the two countries.

Our capacity to influence the nature of change in the Soviet Union is limited. At the very least, however, we should exercise care lest our actions and words impair the prospects for changes we would like to see. It should be clear from past experience that if we are perceived to be bellicose, or if we declare our intent to undermine the Soviet order, we strengthen the backward elements in the Soviet political system.

It follows that our long-term policy should have an evolutionary purpose: it should be designed to encourage future generations of Soviet leaders to see that acting with restraint and enlarging the area of genuine cooperation between the United States and the Soviet Union serve their own self-interest. The main objective of our policy should therefore be to respond to the Soviet challenge in ways that will protect our security, our interests, and our values, rather than to try to force changes in the Soviet Union or to bring about changes in its foreign policy indirectly by seeking to undermine the Soviet system.

This does not mean that we are not interested in what happens inside the Soviet Union, nor that we should put aside our humanitarian concern about its repressive practices. None of us can remain unmoved by the cruelty with which the Soviet police apparatus deals with dissidents or with those who wish to emigrate. But we should have learned from our recent experience that it is counterproductive for our government to make the human rights issue an instrument in a political offensive against the Soviet Union and to engage the prestige of the Soviet leadership by frontal, public ultimatums, as it did with the Jackson-Vanik amendment and in the tragic cases of Andrei Sakharov and Anatoly Shcharansky. We should also remember that although decreased international tension may in the short run inspire campaigns of ideological vigilance designed to control the spread of bourgeois ideas within the Soviet Union, increased levels of international tension reduce the restraints on the Soviet police apparatus and encourage greater pressures for retrogressive movement toward neo-Stalinism.

Perhaps the best that can be hoped for in our relations with the Soviet Union, in the aftermath of the transition of the Chernenko leadership, is a Cold Truce, an improvement in the climate of confrontation that is now patently leading toward greater military competition and a greater risk of misperception and miscalculation in responses to local crises. Beyond the immediate period, we should recognize that the only sensible alternative to a relationship based on confrontation is one that seeks a *modus vivendi,* in order to manage the competition between us at a less destructive level of tension.

The most important aspect of such a policy is the military competition. Clearly, a military balance is required, but what kind, and at what level? If our political leaders and the public really accept the proposition that our security is better safeguarded by a stable nuclear balance than by unregulated competition, it follows that we should accept stability, parity, and mutual deterrence. We pay lip service to these concepts but have not been guided by them in practice. Their genuine acceptance would make possible serious negotiations that would take into account legitimate Soviet security concerns, as well as our own. Neither in the negotiations on strategic systems nor in those on theater nuclear weapons in Europe are the positions of the two sides so far apart that they cannot be bridged. That is also true of the negotiations on treaties for a comprehensive test ban and on the use of chemical weapons, among others. Meanwhile, it does not make sense for us to introduce systems that are destabilizing, systems that will make us more trigger-sensitive. There also must be a balance in conventional weapons. There, too, our long-term objective should be to seek a balance at a moderate level through negotiations, on the basis of the same kind of mutual deterrence that should guide our nuclear weapons policy.

In the political competition between the United States and the Soviet Union, containment by military force is clearly an inadequate response. There may be occasions when we will need sufficient forces on the ground to prevent Soviet intervention, but this is only a negative capability. More important, we must learn to respond to the causes of the strains and instabilities that create opportunities for exploitation by the Soviet Union. For example, we have allowed our relations with our allies among the industrialized nations to become strained by economic tensions and by their growing lack of confidence in the sobriety and wisdom of our leadership. Yet it ought to be the very heart of our policy to maintain the closest possible ties with them. In the Third World, we must show greater awareness of the sources of instability than we have so far. If we are prepared to deal with the causes of revolutionary change, to address the issues of health, food, literacy, and equity with more understanding, we will be able to respond to these problems before all hope of peaceful resolution is lost and the only solution becomes military arbitration between equally unsavory extremes.

In our relations with the Soviet Union we should rely on incentives as well as on constraints. This means that we must sustain a reasonable level of trade and exchanges and encourage limited measures of cooperation. Holding out the prospect of widening ties as the Soviet Union shows its readiness to act responsibly is a token of our hope that the relationship can move to a less dangerous stage. This, indeed, is the link to our longer-term policy. We cannot assume that Soviet behavior will evolve in this way, but we can let future generations of Soviet leaders know that if they do move in this direction we are prepared to accept this more productive relationship.

At the center of our thinking should always be the concern that the protection of our security and our values depends not only on the sensible management of relations with the Soviet Union but on the condition of the international system itself, on those fragile restraints on the behavior of nations that have been created so slowly and painfully over the years. It must be strengthened against the anarchy and chaos that now threaten it. To do this we must seek not to preserve the status quo but to codify processes of nonviolent change. We must work toward placing constraints on the use of force to produce or to prevent change, and we must be willing, ourselves, to live within these constraints.

One more thing needs to be said. Essential to a *modus vivendi* are diplomatic communications with the Soviet Union, firm but not bellicose, conducted with civility and common sense—recently so uncommon in American politics.

THE SOVIET FACTOR: A USEFUL ENEMY
Richard Falk

Richard Falk is Milbank Professor of International Law and Practice at Princeton University, and is the author of numerous works on international security and world order.

Hatred is like rain in the desert—it is of no use to anybody" is an African saying that speaks directly to our nature as human beings. Revealingly, hatred is of great use to the makers of foreign policy for powerful states. It builds a positive sense of "we" identity on the ground of our negative sense of "them." The image of sacrificing money, convenience, even life to oppose a common enemy has been used over and over again to summon a population to war and war preparations. To conceive of another people, members of the same species, as an enemy usually embodies elements of hatred and fear as well as issues of conflict and opposition. To the extent hatred and fear are present, peaceful relations are far more difficult to establish. Hatred, whether directed at another people, its leaders, or its ideology, may also be part of the essential moral and psychological preparation to wage nuclear war, implying a willingness to inflict and endure such severe suffering. As such it becomes essential to resist the manipulation of our emotions and the construction of our essential identity around the imagery of the hated enemy. In effect, the wisdom of the African saying should become a practical guide for international politics without, of course, any expectations that conflict will thereby disappear or that it will

Source: Richard Falk, "The Soviet Factor: A Useful Enemy," in *Indefensible Weapons: The Political and Psychological Case Against Nuclearism,* Robert Jay Lifton and Richard Falk (New York: Basic Books, 1982). © 1982 by Basic Books, Inc., Publishers. Reprinted by permission of the Publisher.

not continue to be necessary to oppose and defend against various political evils.

For Americans the presence of the Soviet Union in the world is enough to explain nuclear arms racing, making the nuclearist path seem inevitable, even if increasingly acknowledged as tragic. Presumably the architects of defense policy in the Kremlin see the world scene in reverse, confronted by a militarized United States poised to devastate the Soviet homeland if it were not for the constraining impact of Soviet armed might. Each side regards its own militarism as essentially reactive, as a defensive necessity given the character, designs, and capabilities of its rival. These mutually reinforcing images of an aggressive enemy are part of what makes nuclearism, a special aggravated case of militarism, such a rigid reality.

Historically it is useful to remember both that the United States and the Soviet Union fought together as allies against the common enemy of fascism and that virtually as soon as the enemy disappeared from the earth each victorious superpower began to treat the other as an enemy. Throughout the history of international relations states have seemed always to consider the main foreign states as either "allies" or "adversaries." This pattern of relations suggests that the idea of the enemy state may be strongly encouraged by the structure of international political life and that changes in this structure may be indispensable if there is to be any hope for building over time a world liberated from nuclearism.

Part of what keeps normal people—that is, people without any inclination to risk the nuclear death-trap—from deep questioning and opposition on matters of national security is their acceptance of the reality of the Soviet challenge. In effect, many Americans believe that unless we are prepared to surrender to Soviet tyranny, it is necessary to keep our nuclear defensive guard high. This means, at least, matching weaponry, and this produces, like it or not, a readiness for major war, a reliance on nuclear weapons, and an embrace of the nuclear arms race.

Often peace movement militants oppose the American reliance on nuclear weaponry and defense spending without seeming to take account of the existence of the Soviet challenge, and this disturbs many mainstream citizens who are worried by both the danger of nuclear war and the Soviet challenge. To this extent the movement can be dismissed as naive, pacifist, or utopian. The Soviet menace is generally perceived as real and must be addressed. In this regard most Americans continue to associate the security of their nation with a sufficiency of military prowess. For centuries such an image of security has been imprinted upon human consciousness. In relation to the Soviet Union it is specifically interconnected with the ideological legacy of more than sixty years of anti-Communist, anti-Marxist, antirevolutionary encounters and propaganda. To shape a politics of response to nuclearism requires us to include the Soviet Union in our appraisal of various risks and probabilities. And further, it is necessary, I think, to premise our concern with an acknowledgment that Soviet society and bureaucratic socialism more generally present us with an unpleasant version of collective life, something to be avoided for ourselves.

But to perceive the Soviet state in this manner does not further imply that Soviet leaders are hell-bent on world conquest, come what may. Currently Soviet leaders seem, on balance, more inclined to establish a moderate framework for international relations than do their American counterparts. There are several important reasons for this greater receptivity: The aged Soviet leadership tasted the bitterest fruits of war within its lifetime (20 million dead, 20 million wounded in World War II; famine, devastation of large areas; a cruel occupation); the Soviet Union started the nuclear arms race from a position of definite inferiority and has been untainted by the use or overt threat to use such weapons; Soviet defensive interests, partly because of geographical considerations, do not seem dependent on ever threatening first use of nuclear weapons (even along its contested China border); the absence of Soviet interests in the maintenance of the colonial order (except in East Europe) or of a favorable overseas climate for markets, investments, and multinational corporate activity puts their foreign policy into alignment with the phenomenon of national revolution that continues to sweep across the Third World (although Moscow's recent search for foreign bases and commitment to maintain Marxist-Leninist regimes once in power is producing an interventionary diplomacy as exhibited by its relationships with Cuba, Afghanistan, and Ethiopia).

Others, as you will see, evaluate the Soviet presence in the world in far more alarmist terms. The realistic prospects for reducing militarism and nuclear dependency depend critically on how we in the United States assess the Soviet challenge. This process of assessment is beset by ideological difficulties, as well as by a series of vested interests that find it useful to maintain the Soviet Union as our implacable "enemy." It is also beset by the strong appeal to common sense contained in the question "Well, what if you're wrong?" Nuclear arms racing, for all its costs, is viewed intuitively by many as a sort of ultimate insurance policy, overcoming reliance on the thin reeds of Soviet moderation or defensive dispositions and validated by the avoidance of nuclear war since 1945. The basic trouble with such justifications of nuclearism is that this form of insurance vastly increases the risks it is expected to alleviate and helps sustain conditions favorable to the occurrence of ultimate catastrophe.

Modern militarism is not a professional enterprise entrusted to small armies that carry out state policy. Since the Napoleonic wars of the early nineteenth century the prosecution of war has depended on the ideology of nationalism, on mass mobilization of support for costly war efforts, and, increasingly, on the blurring of combat distinctions between what is civilian and what is military. The image of "total war" expresses this essential development, and the strategic doctrines of the nuclear age represent a sort of terrorist culmination of prenuclear developments that extends its sway even to periods of so-called "peace." Beneath such phrases as "massive retaliation" and "mutual assured destruction" lies a *public* commitment to destroy with the push of a button an entire foreign society in a peculiarly horrifying way that includes long-lasting radiation effects, contamination of food and water for indefinite periods, and, quite possibly, irreversible environmental effects that pose a threat to the entire planet. Even the Nazis felt the necessity to keep "the final solution" hidden from their citizenry!

This American willingness to embrace a policy of genocide and ecocide has, to be sure, been presented as a defensive necessity, as the best that can be done given the nature of the challenge we face, given a world of rival states distrustful of one another. This selling of nuclearism has involved a subtle, complex, cumulative process that resembles, in its essential content, the original justification for using the bomb at the end of World War II. It goes back, in other words, to two intertwined realities: the absolute character of war (in the end, anything goes that helps achieve victory) and the unscrupulousness of the enemy (abstracted in such a way to minimize the concreteness of the victims and to discourage feelings of empathy across belligerent boundaries).

The ideological preparation for nuclear war centers on nurturing a hatred for "the enemy." This nurturing is especially necessary for the United States, with its democratic political forms that include the accountability of leaders by way of elections and with a cultural identity that emphasizes the goodness of the nation, sometimes described as American exceptionalism. In geopolitical terms the United States seeks to mask its "natural" identity as a leading state with an extensive global role and farflung interests by claiming that when it goes to war it is to destroy evil as well as to promote state interests. This mask was first loosened and then partially restored by the Vietnam experience; a large portion of the public, including those who were sent to fight, rejected "the mission" of the war and have been slow to accept that kind of mission again, as the lack of popular support for intervention in El Salvador demonstrates. This public reticence, also expressed by opposition to a revival of the draft, is what our militarists decry as "the Vietnam syndrome." At the same time, since the mid-1970s there has emerged a greater public willingness to fight for wealth as well as ideals. Even our leadership seems at a loss to find a moral rationale for the American military resolve to oppose revolutionary movements hostile to Western interests that might emerge in the oil-producing Persian Gulf. Nevertheless, the main reality is that the mobilization of resources and sentiments for war remains organized around the central idea of an enemy that is evil and whose evil will eventually encroach upon our independence, and even our territory, unless we are militarily prepared. Part of this composite image of evil incorporates the idea of "aggressor," as it is the enemy who endangers peace by threatening to launch a military attack. In that respect World War II provides a powerful text for this homily—it was Hitler who cast treaties aside, who trampled gleefully upon his Munich appeasers and resorted to war in the spirit of reckless expansionism, and it was imperialist Japan that attacked Pearl Harbor out of the blue. American leaders of all persuasion drew several central lessons from Munich and Pearl Harbor—appeasement doesn't work, aggression must be resisted with force of arms, and a foreign enemy will not hesitate to launch a surprise attack that is as crippling as possible. Under pre-1945 conditions even these lessons could have been absorbed without transforming the society, stage by stage, into a nuclear national security state, involving also the distortions of "a permanent war economy." Prior to nuclearism the United States indulged in "peace" without appearing to jeopardize its national security. The only plausible enemies were far away. We were protected from the recurrent ravages of war by our relative geographical isolation, and we often prescribed isolationism, at least in relation to Europe, as a source of both national virtue and national advantage (for instance, George Washington's celebrated edict against "entangling alliances").

Modern technology has deprived us of this possibility. Our oceans no longer offer us much of a buffer and, indeed, are an arena of danger, being patrolled by enemy submarines capable of delivering nuclear warheads to our cities in a matter of minutes. Since we are confronted by a powerful enemy we must remain constantly at the ready, especially as there is no way to protect our people or society from devastation no matter how many weapons we possess. Also, since any successful expansion by our enemy encourages the enemy's further expansion (aggression begets aggression; the recurrent imagery of falling dominoes), we must resist on a global scale to the extent practicable. And since the important factors in this competition are power and resources, the alignment of a foreign society with our enemy is as much a loss as if it was conquered on the battlefield. As a result, farflung alliances, military bases, and naval operations are all parts of our "defense," as is intervention in foreign civil strife.

Initially the Soviet menace has at various stages been intertwined with a broader ideological confrontation between capitalism and communism, between freedom and totalitarianism, between the modernized North and the developing South. From the moment of the Russian Revolution (at least the October Revolution), the United States joined in perceiving the ideology of communism as a mortal threat. We participated in an abortive effort, joining with several European allies, after World War I to destroy that revolution and for years afterward refused to enter even into normal diplomatic relations with the Soviet leadership, refused, in the parlance of international law, to recognize the Soviet Government. Later, and for decades, we did exactly the same thing in response to Mao's victory in China, including a prolonged arm-twisting foreign policy effort to deny the Communist government its natural place as China's representative in the United Nations.

During World War II we joined, of course, with the Soviet Union in an antifascist alliance, and it was the collapse of that alliance that set the stage for the current climate. There are many explanations of how the cold war got started, which side was primarily responsible, and what kind of conflicts of interest existed to threaten major war. Many sensitive interpreters of historical trends, going back at least as far as Alexis de Tocqueville, anticipated that a rivalry between the United States and the Soviet Union, because of their respective size, resource endowments, impenetrability, and strategic positions, would come to dominate international political life at some point. World War II undoubtedly accelerated the process, leaving the old European centers of power and conflict devastated and exhausted, unable even to hold onto their overseas colonial possessions. The Soviet Union was also badly bruised by the war itself, but its huge armies had swept to victory against Germany. The Soviet leadership transformed military occupation into political vassalage throughout Eastern Europe, which helped rekindle the anticommunism of the West, especially in the United States. Furthermore, the Soviet military presence in Eastern Europe threatened a helpless, broken Western Europe with invasion and subversion. These threats were magnified by the large Soviet-oriented Communist Parties in France and Italy. In a different dimension, the colonial order was collapsing under the rising pressures of national revolutionary movements. These anticolonial victories were largley seen by the United States as accretions to Soviet power, especially after Mao's 1949 victory in China. The United States saw itself confronted with an expanding monolithic world revolutionary movement orchestrated from Moscow, probing for weaknesses in Western defenses throughout the world.

Against this background the Cold War emerged, its initiation being often associated with the Truman Doctrine in 1947, declared in the context of a Western defense of the national integrity of Greece and Turkey in the face of alleged Communist subversion and external pressure. At this time also was enunciated the famous organizing image of "containment," given its original formulation in a famous dispatch ("the long telegram") written by George Kennan from his diplomatic post in Moscow. The important "moral" element in this dynamic of unfolding conflict was the perception of Soviet-led communism as an aggressive force in the world that could be "contained" only by defensive resistance. There have been learned discussions about whether Kennan meant the same thing by containment as did the various American political leaders who construed its mandate in largely military terms. Nevertheless, from the late 1940s American foreign policy has been supposedly organized around this central tenet of defensiveness.

Important, also, was the portrayal of evils of Soviet society, an inhuman political system that tormented its citizenry with cruelties and bureaucratic tedium. Gulag revelations of the extensiveness of the Stalinist death camps, post-Stalinist repression of dissidents, and periodic Soviet interventions in Eastern Europe to destroy the strivings of the people by way of restoring stability to Communist rule has lent credibility to the claim that our rival embodies evil in the primary sense that it is worth fighting and dying to avoid such a political fate for ourselves. In this regard it is not surprising that American leaders view as "contemptible" such European slogans as "better red than dead." Such a response to the threats posed by Communist expansionism is regarded as sure evidence of moral decadence by any committed cold warrior. Paul Nitze's formulation captures the spirit of the United States' image of the Soviet challenge: "The Kremlin leaders do not want war; they want the world. They believe it unlikely, however, that the West will let them have the world without a fight."[1] It is interesting that Nitze has been entrusted by the Reagan Administration with the task of negotiating a European arms control agreement with the Soviet Union, a choice that expresses the current official outlook.

It is against this background that the American public reliance on nuclear weaponry has been erected. It has been generally accepted, in large part, as a defensive necessity, given Soviet advantages of position and manpower in relation to the crucial sectors of the world outside the territory of either superpower (especially Western Europe and the Persian Gulf). In the background also are contentions about "the balance of power" and about the Soviet mentality. With respect to balance, it has been argued that any shift in alignment, especially with respect to Europe or the Persian Gulf, threatens world peace by upsetting the balance of power (of course, this is self-serving in the extreme as the balance is never disturbed by defections on their side) and, therefore, must be opposed by all possible means (including at times covert operations to prevent pro-Soviet governments from coming to power, if possible). The threat to inflict nuclear annihilation has been accepted as essential to keep Moscow in check, but to be effective altogether it must be reinforced by local capabilities that can resist low levels of Soviet military pressure and even by a willingness, as necessary, to engage in nuclear war-fighting.

This overall image of Soviet aggressiveness is, it is argued by the most militant on our side, rooted in Marxist-Leninist ideology. Soviet leaders have endorsed their commitment to the world revolutionary process, they lend support to "wars of national liberation," and they have, at great expense to their

---

[1]Paul H. Nitze, "Strategy in the Decade of the 1980s," *Foreign Affairs* 59 (Fall, 1980) p. 90.

own people, armed well beyond levels of armament required for prudent defense. Especially in the recent period since 1970, during the supposed time of détente, while the United States allegedly slowed its pace of arms racing, the Soviet Union has been portrayed as forging ahead in quest of strategic superiority.

With this sense of things, during the Carter presidency conservative forces in the United States mounted a blistering public relations offensive. As well documented by Jerry Sanders, a close student of special interest politics, in his forthcoming book *The Peddlers of Crisis,* very deliberate organized efforts were made by individuals with close Pentagon ties to make the American people feel that détente, the SALT process of arms control negotiations, nonmilitary priorities, and budgetary restraints were hobbling our capacity to deal with the growing threat of Soviet military power. This grim view was further reinforced among critics from the right by their belief that geo-political trends were definitely adverse. Colin Gray, professional strategist and skillful advocate of nuclear war-fighting preparations, argues the case for a Western military response:

> . . . the most pressing, dangerous, and potentially fatal fact of the real
> world—namely, that we are at the mid-stage of a shift in relative power
> and influence to the Soviet Union that is of historic proportions, and
> which promises, unless arrested severely, to have enduring significance.
> . . . The rise in Soviet standing in the world, which may be traced almost exclusively to the increase in relative Soviet military capabilities,
> both dwarfs other concerns in its immediacy and seriousness, and renders other problems far less tractable.[2]

The assessment was more or less accepted by pre-Reagan official documents of the United States Government, including the annual military posture statements issued by the Department of Defense after 1978. They pointed to the Soviet boldness of sending proxy Cuban troops to Ethiopia and Angola to assure Moscow-inclined victories in both countries, and subsequently they somehow connected the outcomes of the Iranian and Nicaraguan revolutions with Washington's absence of "resolve," a favorite word. And, finally, the Soviet invasion of Afghanistan in late December 1979 was seen as final confirmation of a new balance of forces in a strategic region, posing further threats to the oil-producing Persian Gulf, as well as a dangerous first use of Soviet troops in combat roles in a Third World country.

The active dissemination of this alarmist view of global developments was promoted from many sources—the Pentagon and its corporate allies, the strategic think tanks, the emergent "new" Right, the *Commentary* neo-conser-

---

[2]Colin Gray, *The Geopolitics of the Nuclear Era* (New York: Crane, Russak, 1977), p. 3.

vatives, a growing sector of Congress—and it was endorsed by such influential foreign policy heavyweights as Henry Kissinger and Zbigniew Brzezinski. Perhaps the most effective organ of cold war revivalism was the Committee on the Present Danger, organized in March 1976 by a grouping of prominent private citizens, most of whom had earlier served high up in the government, led by Paul Nitze, Eugene V. Rostow, and several retired generals, and who were to be returned to eminence by Reagan's 1980 electoral victory. The effect of this concerted campaign was to alter the public climate of debate in the late 1970s, putting the moderate approach of the early Carter years on the defensive. Big business also joined the chorus; reading the editorial columns of *The Wall Street Journal* meant receiving the same message as set forth in the handouts of the Committee on the Present Danger. *Business Week* devoted its entire March 12, 1979, issue to "the decline of American power," with a dramatic cover portraying a tearful Statue of Liberty.

It was in this atmosphere that Ronald Reagan, an effusive supporter of the Committee on the Present Danger, mounted his successful presidential campaign. A central theme of Reagan's appeal to the electorate was to cut social services and increase defense spending. This appeal was popular with both the middle classes and business, which believed that inflation and the declining productivity of American industry were associated with the defective economics and misguided ethics of the welfare state gone soft as well as with profit-eating environmental and antitrust regulation. Resurgent capitalists were determined to rebuild profit margins and growth rates by squeezing the poor, rolling back wages, and neglecting the environment. Reviving fears of a foreign enemy threatening our way of life was helpfully diversionary.

Whatever the causes, this revival of East-West tensions moves us closer to nuclear war, economic collapse, environmental crisis and, as such, contributes to the actuality of American decline and makes us, in objective and subjective terms, less, not more, secure. The picture being presented to the American people is put together with half-truths and the selective use of information and analysis. The Soviet Union is not, in any reasonable sense, riding the crest of history. Soviet power, as much as American power, is in a condition of decline. Soviet leaders are beset with an adverse set of circumstances that pose serious dangers to their current position. They are surrounded by enemies, the defection of China in the 1960s representing an enormous shift in the balance of power in a westward direction made credible by Chinese nuclear capabilities, huge armies, implacable hostility, and revisionist demands with respect to the four-thousand-mile long border. The Afghanistan invasion has turned into a Soviet nightmare with little light at the end of the tunnel. The Polish workers' movement has once again deeply exposed Moscow's morbid fear of genuine socialism, while once again discrediting Soviet claims of respect for the sovereign rights of the countries in Eastern

Europe. Soviet encouragement and support of martial law in Poland (imposed late in 1981) has both embarrassed and antagonized most Communist parties around the world, weakening the overall Soviet stature in the Third World. Even the Cuban role in Africa does not promise any permanent extension of Soviet influence. Of course, the Soviet Union is a global presence at this stage and as such will find favorable opportunities in various settings to extend its influence, but on balance its situation is precarious and deteriorating. In my judgment, the U.S.S.R.'s militarism, like ours, is a response to a perceived reality of overall political, economic, and cultural decline. Soviet leaders are likely to fear "the barbarians" at their gates at least as much as we do. And further, without excusing or ignoring the cruelty and grinding inefficiency of Soviet rule, there are no solid reasons to regard Soviet military power as anything more than a defensive capability that is designed, among other things, to deny us a free hand in areas of interest to them.

This conclusion seems especially persuasive with respect to nuclear weaponry. Remember that all along the Soviet Union has been "a poor second" straining to catch up, stay abreast, convince us of the futility of limited nuclear war; during this period of prolonged vulnerability the Soviet leadership was quite aware of the mutual suicide that would be the main result of nuclear war. Khrushchev and Brezhnev have repeatedly made clear their understanding of the importance of avoiding a superpower breakdown. It is the Soviets who have modified Marxist-Leninist thinking by insisting that "peaceful coexistence" is the proper relation of opposed political systems and ideologies in the nuclear age. George Kennan, among others, persuasively questions the view that "the Russians are such monsters" that they would, even if they could do so safely, "launch upon us a nuclear attack, with all the horrors and sufferings that that would bring." Kennan rejects the view, on the basis of his long observation of Soviet behavior, "that our Soviet adversary has lost every semblance of humanity and is concerned only with wreaking unlimited destruction for destruction's sake."[3] These observations are entitled to added weight, I think, because Kennan is not someone who has been oblivious to the Soviet danger (he is after all the father of containment, even if he has disowned the more militarist versions of his progeny) or someone with an idealist faith in the peaceful proclivities of human nature (indeed he cynically accepts spheres of influence as integral elements of international order and is skeptical about experiments in international cooperation).

Correlating American decline in a world setting with either the insufficiency of military power or with Soviet aggressiveness is sheer mystification. The main challenge to the preeminent position of the United States in the world is the continuing dynamic of national revolution and development in

---

[3]"Two Views of the Soviet Problem," *The New Yorker*, 2 November 1981, p. 62.

the Third World, rising energy costs, and the decay of critical sectors of American industry relative to European and Japanese competition. A militarist response in these circumstances represents a failure of analysis that actually worsens the American geopolitical situation. The current United States effort to crush the national revolutionary process in Central America is straining all credulity when it tries to justify American involvement by reference to Soviet arms provided revolutionary forces from Cuban sources. As has often been demonstrated, the outcome of civil strife depends overwhelmingly on internal factors, with the government forces usually having a big advantage when it comes to the scale and quality of weaponry. Whatever weapons a guerrilla movement gets from abroad are seldom likely to be a critical factor in the struggle for political control.

The Soviet dissident brothers Roy and Zhores Medvedev diagnose, correctly, I think, the collapse of détente and the rejection of the SALT II treaty: "We think the principal cause of the return to confrontation was the fact that SALT II did nothing to redress the disadvantages of the United States in the Third World, where America had suffered yet another setback after its failures in Indochina and Angola—the Iranian revolution."[4] Well, of course strategic arms control cannot help the United States in the Third World, even in the unlikely event that Moscow were inclined to link the two kinds of concerns. Moscow, too, lacks control over national revolutions, as events in Afghanistan suggest. Indeed the Soviet Union cannot even provide assured control over the revolutionary process in countries where a Marxist-Leninist leadership is in power, as the defection of Yugoslavia, China, and the various opposition movements in Eastern Europe suggest. In reaction to this basic pattern (alongside the proposed deployments of new missiles in Europe), West-West tensions have also risen. West German trade relations with the Soviet bloc have given them a major economic stake in détente. The ex-colonial powers increasingly believe that accommodation with the governments of successful national revolutionary movements is possible on a mutually acceptable basis. Indeed traditional allies of the United States, most notably France under Mitterand but also the Netherlands and the Scandinavian countries, are not willing to defer any longer entirely to American statecraft, even in Central America, as is evident in their sale of arms to the Sandinista government in Nicaragua despite vigorous opposition from Washington. Such European penetration of an American sphere of influence suggests the forming of new patterns of multipolar diplomacy (independent of either superpower) that will further obstruct the militarist approach currently prevalent in the United States. In addition, some richer Third World countries—for instance, Algeria and Libya—are extending support to the Sandinista government.

---

[4]"A Nuclear Samizdat on America's Arms Race," *The Nation,* 16 January, 1982, p. 44.

What seems evident is that the Soviet Union serves as no adequate excuse for continuing the nuclear arms race. There are wider human and global interests that should not be ignored. The Soviet challenge can and must be met without threatening first use of nuclear weapons or proceeding to develop further, even more destabilizing weapons systems. In a typical public statement the Soviet leader Leonid Brezhnev said, "It is madness for any country to build its policy with an eye to nuclear war"[5]. There is every reason to act as if the Soviet Union appreciates this madness, and the peace movement has prompted some comparable statements from Washington. Of course, appropriate deeds on both sides are called for at this stage. To remove the madness we do not have to trust the Soviet Union (nor they us), but we do require a political climate that challenges the entrenched positions of nuclear militarists on both sides. Such a challenge on the American side will almost certainly have to be preceded by a powerful grassroots movement outside the formal framework of politics; on the Soviet side the challenge will have to be mounted by a faction of the Politburo and then win wider support throughout the command structure of the topheavy Soviet bureaucracy.

In the end, more than challenging nuclearism is required. It will be necessary to work toward the adoption of new conceptions and structures of security that rest on a mutual disarming process. Such a process cannot occur unless realism can be divorced from nuclearism.

THE SOVIET VIEW OF DETERRENCE: A GENERAL SURVEY

John Erickson

John Erickson is Professor of Politics and Director of Defense Studies at the University of Edinburgh, and has published numerous books and articles on Soviet military affairs.

In the course of some recent exchanges on Soviet military science and Soviet military organisation, my perceptive colleague Professor Roger Beaumont from Texas A & M University enjoined me to read (or rather, to reread) an article on Russian military development by Edward L. Katzenbach, erstwhile consultant to the United States Air Force[1]. This proved to be a most revealing

---

[5]*New York Times*, 4 February, 1982, p. A1.

Source: John Erickson, "The Soviet View of Deterrence: A General Survey," in *The Nuclear Arms Race*, ed. Frank Barnaby and Geoffrey Thomas (New York: St. Martin's Press, 1982), pp. 73–94. © 1982, John Erickson and reprinted by permission of St. Martin's Press Inc.

[1]Edward L. Katzenbach, Jr, 'Russian Military Development', *Current History*, November 1960, pp. 262–6.

exercise, for while the article pointedly referred to 'a serious lag in Soviet strategic thinking'—lag which amounted to three years at least by this calculation—the markedly condescending judgment was supplemented by a platitude which deserved more attention, namely, that Russians do not necessarily think like Americans. Both these observations merit some closer inspection, for their relevance persists to the present day. The disdain shown towards the quality (or lack of quality) in Soviet strategic thinking was a marked feature of the 1960s, rooted in the supposed intellectual superiority of American sophistication in matters of 'deterrent theory' and encouraging the notion that during the SALT I process the Americans would perforce initiate the Russians into the mysteries of deterrent theory and the complexities of nuclear war. To general discomfiture, it soon became apparent that the Russians needed no tutoring in matters pertaining to war in general and nuclear war in particular, that there was a singular cogency to Soviet strategic thinking and that Russians did not necessarily think like Americans. While Western specialists in strategic theory refined their concepts of 'deterrence' into ever more complex (and arcane) theorems, a kind of nuclear metaphysics, the Soviet command had worked much more closely within classically configured military concepts, inducing at once a much greater degree of military and political realism into what in American parlance is termed their 'mind-set'. Belated though this recognition of Soviet realism was, it had one unfortunate aspect, that Katzenbach's platitude went unremarked. Not only Western terminology but also Western preferences were frequently superimposed on the Soviet scene, even to the point of interpreting Soviet weapons programmes in terms of a *Western* rationale for such programmes, particularly the transposition of the notion of 'first strike'.

This process, long established though now subject to some limited change, has had damaging, not to say dangerous results; and paradoxically it could be said that this most abstract of items—let us call it 'doctrine' by way of intellectual shorthand—may well prove to be the most potent factor in the strategic equation. Indeed, it is becoming ever more apparent that improved mutual understanding of doctrine is a prerequisite of effective arms limitation and arms control as opposed to confining the matter to technicalities of weapons systems. True asymmetry may lie in doctrine (and perceptions) rather than in disparate numbers of weapons and characteristics of their presumed performance. By the same token, the dovish argument that there is actual convergence in doctrine (where no such convergence exists and where insufficient recognition is accorded to the factor of sheer military weight in Soviet priorities) can be misleading, while paradoxically the hawkish deprecation of American political will and the exaggeration of American vulnerabilities is yet another damaging distortion, leading in turn to crude over-simplifications of Soviet doctrine, all duly transmuted into a form of strategic demonology. While it would be mistaken to regard Soviet doctrine as an absolute master-plan prescribing all strategic objectives—including winning a nuclear war—it is equally feckless to be dismissive about (or ignorant of) doctrine as an indicator of *Soviet* perceptions of the deterrence process, of threat profiles, force structures and military precautions so involved (what I called 'deterring against what, with what') and, finally, of that military-operational provision relevant to the collapse of deterrence.

That latter point is the nub of the matter. If Soviet realism and adherence to military orthodoxy has inculcated a persistent scepticism towards the metaphysics of deterrence, if Soviet political attitudes preclude placing any reliance on the goodwill (or rationality) of an adversary and if Soviet practice precludes any mutuality which would imply dependence on an adversary for even a particle of Soviet security, this is still some distance from postulating the rejection of deterrence as it might be generally understood in favour of viewing nuclear war as a rational instrument of policy and, moreover, as a process which is winnable. I am not suggesting that doctrine *tout court* will elucidate all problems inherent in Soviet strategic policies, but there is a case for some inspection of the more recent Soviet pronouncements and analyses. And therein lies a small irony, for if two decades ago Edward Katzenbach was pointing to the 'serious' lag in Soviet strategic thinking, at this juncture Soviet specialists point to the 'serious lag' in Western appreciation of Soviet doctrine; appreciation and evaluation which rely on sources which if not actually outmoded have become inevitably passé—for example, the stylised recourse to Marshal Sokolovskii's *Voennaya strategiya (Military Strategy)*[2]. The convenient myth of Soviet nuclear troglodytes seemingly died hard, only to be replaced by the equally distorted simulacrum of Soviet nuclear supermen.

Peace and War, Deterrence and Defence

It is impossible to evaluate Soviet perceptions of 'deterrence' without some brief inspection of general Soviet theories of armed conflict, what might be called 'official doctrine' designed to suggest guidelines for weapons programmes in time of peace and rules for the use of such force in wartime. Such a sustained effort has produced a voluminous and complex literature (little of which is known in the West) and in which the *leitmotif* is the insistence that while nuclear weapons have clearly changed the character of any future war, they have in no way altered the essence *(sushchnost)* of war as a *political* phenomenon, to be understood as such. While it is frequently said that the Soviet view is 'Clausewitzian', in fact Lenin modified Clausewitz's dictum to read *'imperialist* wars are a violent extension of the politics of imperialism', where the essence of imperialism must generate chronic conflict. In this search for

---

[2]See interview with Lt Gen. M. Milshtein, 'Moscow Expert Says US is Mistaken on Soviet War Strategy', *International Herald Tribune,* August 28, 1980. . . .

the 'laws of armed conflict' Soviet theory also departs from Clausewitz in refusing to regard wars as isolated phenomena: rather they have common features which inevitably involve 'the masses', as well as demonstrating various patterns in the relationship between war and politics.

Further to this search for laws and predictability, Soviet military doctrine *(voennaya doktrina)* is concerned specifically with disclosing 'the nature of contemporary wars which may be unleashed by the imperialists', as well as formulating the missions of the Soviet armed forces, specifying military-operational methods involved and estimating what is required in the way of defence preparations: Soviet military science *(voennaya nauka)* contributes analyses drawn from past wars and present weapons performance, while military art *(voennoe iskusstvo)* develops operational, battlefield methods. Thus, to the political awareness which is fundamental to the Soviet outlook must be added the infusion of military ideas which have a strongly orthodox cast about them. Both elements fuse in the notion that the essence of war has not been changed by nuclear weapons, that the nuclear weapon is not an absolute which has made war unthinkable—on the contrary, the situation must be thought through, into the situation where deterrence could well fail, or where it could be undermined by the malevolance of the imperialist camp. The nuclear weapon has not made conventional weapons superfluous; on the contrary, a flexible composition of military force is essential, exemplified in the Soviet 'combined-arms' concept. Whether any future war be long or short, large standing armies are indispensable: in what could well be a nuclear battle in the accepted sense of battle, the Soviet forces cannot remain inert, committed to absorbing an enemy strike and then lashing out in some indiscriminate punitive response—deterrence by punishment. And after the near catastrophe of June 1941 when German armies were launched against the Soviet Union, it is inconceivable that any Soviet leadership will countenance absorbing any initial strike.

It follows, therefore, that this outlook places a premium on defence in the first instance, so that defence and deterrence must go hand in hand: the massive Soviet programme of defence (both active and passive) needs little or no advertising, though it has been the cause of misgiving and misunderstanding. Ironically, the Soviet interest in defence, including an extensive civil defence programme, fuelled American fears that here was indeed a major ingredient of a first-strike policy (with the Soviet Union taking major steps to protect itself), while Soviet opinion saw in the lack of a defence programme in the United States more than a hint that American policy was essentially one of first strike, surprise attack, an annihilating blow which would perforce eliminate any retaliation, with the prime emphasis on offensive forces in a high state of alert.

It is here that Soviet reference to the possibility of 'victory' in the context of general nuclear war makes what to many is a disquieting, even alarming appearance. This is an issue which requires some careful consideration, beyond the rather simplistic assertion that such statements confirm absolute Soviet belief in surviving and winning a nuclear war, indeed might even encourage any Soviet leadership actually to think of nuclear war as a rational instrument of policy. Are we talking about 'victory' and 'survival' being synonymous, or as separate elements? It would seem that stereotyped statements affirming that in the event of an American/imperialist attack on the Socialist camp the latter system would prove superior and axiomatically survive, are little more than expressions of ideological conviction, or ideological rectitude. However, once the discussion closes more immediately on the operational features of any nuclear war, the tone changes. Soviet professional military writing (as opposed to that of the political officers) proclaims a much more cautious line, eschewing the notion that capitalist society will collapse like a pack of cards and demonstrating a ready appreciation of American second-strike capability to inflict a horrendous scale of damage on the USSR. By the same token, there is implicit recognition that rapid and total escalation is the most likely contingency arising from any so-called 'limited' war, speedily involving the full range of US strategic capabilities. This is the Soviet view.

Rhetoric and realism are obviously in conflict here. It is eminently understandable that political officers, responsible for moral and party-political education, should stress the superiority of the Socialist system and its potential for victory, but this is a far cry from asserting a military-operational reality. On the contrary, the military press stresses the unprecedented scale of damage following a nuclear attack, the huge volume of casualties and devastations of whole countries; observations supplemented very recently by the widespread publicity accorded to the exchanges between Soviet and American doctors on the effects of nuclear war, supplemented by the latest Ascot meeting. While it is certainly impossible to specify just what 'unacceptable damage' would mean in the Soviet context (with one Western argument using the figure of Soviet losses in 1941–5 as evidence that the Soviet Union is somehow inured to a higher level of unacceptable damage), informed Soviet opinion seems inclined to the view that the scale of damage and loss would be unprecedented.

We should return, however, to the point of nuclear war as a means of politics, a rational instrument of policy. The possibility of nuclear war is recognised in terms of the Marxist-Leninist theory relating to the causes of war at large, namely, as a *political* product of a society composed of antagonistic classes pursuing competitive aims. Thus, the question of the essence of any future nuclear war must be kept separate from the other issue, the acceptability (or otherwise) of nuclear war as an *instrument* of policy. On the whole, Soviet opinion seems to hold that nuclear war is not a rational instrument of policy, for means and ends lose any significance when the cost of destroying the enemy amounts to self-annihilation.

To take this logic a little further and returning to the fundamental tenet of the political essence of war, it is reasonable to infer that the sole contingency which could persuade any Soviet leadership of the 'rationality' of nuclear war in pursuit of policy would be the unassailable, incontrovertible, dire evidence that the United States was about to strike the Soviet Union: the political end would be the very survival of the Soviet Union through 'striking first in the last resort', to use Mr Malcolm Mackintosh's succinct phrase. Yet this form of 'rationality' is almost too fearsome to contemplate, hence the specific form of Soviet deterrence—to prevent the very emergence of that cataclysmic contingency.

In general, the role of military power is seen from the Soviet side as a major instrument in impressing on the 'imperialist camp' that military means cannot solve the historical struggle between the two opposing social systems, at the same time reducing (if not actually eliminating) the prospect of military gain at the expense of the Socialist camp. Putting this into the context of deterrent theory, while it might be said that the United States has embraced a concept of 'deterrence by punishment', the Soviet position is one of 'deterrence by denial'[3]. Obviously this is a somewhat simplified picture which must be developed in some detail, but it is worth noting that the terminology used in the Soviet Union to discuss deterrence tends to reflect this dichotomy. In the 1960s (and again in the 1980s) the Western deterrent concept has been defined as *ustrashenie* (which has a clear hint of threatening intimidation), while the Soviet stance is registered by the word *sderzhivanie* (conveying a sense of constraining and restraining an opponent, with even the word *oborona*—defence—used in a deterrence context). As we shall shortly see, this is more than mere semantic hair-splitting.

Some qualifications: While it is true that the Soviet leadership regards the capability to wage nuclear war—in terms of military preparation—as a major element of a visible deterrent, this does not indicate any preference for or inclination towards regarding nuclear war as a rational instrument of policy: even more, Soviet deterrent policies are designed to minimise the incentives for attacking the USSR and, above all, are aimed at preventing the outbreak of hostilities. This is 'denial' in an absolute sense. Certainly, this does imply reliance on Soviet capabilities rather than on enemy rationality or goodwill, the supreme importance of retaining the initiative and a certain scepticism about 'crisis management' when the crisis is (or could be) so apocalyptic. Thus, we have here not a commitment to 'war-avoidance' but to 'war-denial' (if that phrase can be admitted): at the same time, this does suggest some reduction in the notion of 'mutuality', where the Soviet Union is not willing to be dependent on an adversary for any element of its security, but, even more im-

---

[3]This distinction, which still retains its validity, was formulated by Glenn Snyder, *Deterrence and Defense,* (Princeton U.P., 1961).

portant, sees in the notion of mutuality in assured destruction nothing less than a disguise of what is essentially a US counter force (and first-strike) policy. Here we must return to the perception of the American notion of 'deterrence by punishment', which must be expanded to include 'compellence' which embraces 'escalation dominance' and connects military superiority with political, global dominance. Thus, the Soviet Union is to be 'deterred' into accepting this situation, where 'compellence' and 'extended deterrence' reflect an offensive military-political posture and commitment.

Mutuality is further diminished by the fact that while the Americans spoke of mutual assured destruction (MAD), in effect American policy was designed to increase counterforce capabilities: witness the MX missile programme, the Trident submarine-launched ballistic missile (SLBM) programme and the improvement in forward-based systems (FBS) which simply amounted to outflanking the SALT agreements. Even worse, Presidential Directive 59 (PD-59) allegedly reflected the real intent of US policy, reinforced and supported by the release of previously secret US documents such as the operational plan Dropshot[4]. US policy is designed to legitimise nuclear war by making the idea of limited nuclear war more feasible and thus more acceptable, resulting in a lowering of the nuclear threshold. A Eurostrategic nuclear war might then be pursued, leaving the USSR open to attack but giving sanctuary to the United States. Behind all this lies the intent of establishing (or re-establishing) escalation dominance and thus intimidating the USSR, or so the Soviet leadership reads the present situation.

While admitting the unremitting hostility of the adversary, Soviet military planners must take account in their deterrent calculations of the NATO theatre nuclear forces (TNF) modernization, which is seen as nothing less than a larger US design to regain military superiority. The idea is to tie NATO ever more closely into US strategic planning, to divert or to deflect Soviet counteraction towards Europe (rather than against the United States itself) and to adjust the overall strategic balance in American favour. More pertinently, the new weapons—above all, the Pershing II—can only be regarded as a first-strike counter force weapon, improving by a factor of ten the capabilities of Pershing I and capable of destroying not only inter-continental ballistic missile (ICBM) silos but also command and control centres[5]. What must impress Soviet military specialists is that the Pershing II has a flight time to target of only 4–6 minutes (as opposed to an ICBM which takes up to 30 minutes to reach its target): thus, with such a short flight time to target, the Pershing II nullifies any Soviet resort to launch under warning and even launch under at-

---

[4] For text see Anthony Cave Brown, *Dropshot: The United States Plan for War with the Soviet Union in 1957*, (New York, Dial Press, 1978). . . .

[5] See Doug Richardson, 'Pershing II—NATO's Small Ballistic Missile', *Flight International*, 8 August 1981, pp. 431–4. Richardson cites a range of 900 n.m. (1800 km) but, as I have noted, some Soviet sources increase this substantially. There is no official figure for Pershing II range, as far as I know.

tack[6]. Apparently the Soviet General Staff is prepared to regard the Pershing II range of 1500 miles (up to 2600 kms) as the truly effective range of the new missile, a figure which would mean much wider target coverage.

If we add the cruise missile, the Soviet sense of vulnerability can only deepen, leading to a denial concept without any measure of adequacy since it depends crucially on over-insurance—hence the preoccupation, not to say the obsession, with numbers and some numerical hedge of advantage. It is fair to comment here that this is not only a doctrinal requirement but one which also represents a number of bureaucratic and institutional interests (the Soviet equivalent of the military-industrial complex); yet by a fierce irony it is precisely this numerical fixation which will provide the coming crisis for Soviet deterrence policies. At the moment, the Soviet interpretation is that PD-59 plus NATO's TNF deployment plans amount to nothing less than an American push for superiority *tout court,* together with an attempt to implement a Eurostrategic variant for limited nuclear war.

The Soviet rejection of the idea of limited nuclear war is axiomatic, based as it is in the political notion that *political* objectives—not the performance of particular weapons—decree the essence or scope of war: it follows, therefore, that if American objectives are unlimited in the sense of regaining military superiority and escalation dominance over the USSR, then any war operation cannot be limited, whatever the technicalities of the weaponry involved. At the same time Soviet attention is concentrated on the offensive nature of US 'deterrent forces', where counter force targeting was—and has remained—a prime US interest, bringing Soviet nuclear delivery systems into the tight focus of such a targeting philosophy. 'Punishment' was allegedly only part of the story: American lack of interest in defence (active and passive) pointed to a singular approach to deterrence, with important destabilising implications, while American emphasis on mutual assured destruction seemed to be in sharp contradiction to the development of a counter force capability. The critical point for Soviet deterrence comes with the recognition that US counter force capability is not only expanding but will continue to expand in excess of a comparable Soviet capability. . . . A natural and inevitable scepticism pervaded the Soviet view of mutual assured destruction, not only because this ran counter to the principle of any dependence on a potential adversary for Soviet security, but more importantly because Soviet specialists perceived that the real issue was not MAD as such but rather that mutual deterrence in broad terms was being modified as the Americans moved away from deterrence via punishment and into greater emphasis on 'compellence', all with the aim of ensuring that

---

[6]With its 'Earth Penetrator', Pershing II is designed to attack command/control centres: this would inevitably force the Soviet command to 'launch on warning', but this requires high accuracy attack assessment and some estimates put this beyond the capability of Soviet computers—hence 'accidental launch' cannot be discounted with the danger of nuclear war by technological malfunction.

'US deterrence of the Soviet Union [will be] "more efficient" than Soviet deterrence of the United States'[7].

'Deterring against what, with what': threat profiles, force structures: In the United States and the 'imperialist camp' at large, the Soviet Union faces a formidable adversary, whose real purposes arguably are not disclosed by declaratory doctrinal positions (such as 'assured destruction' or even 'mutual assured destruction'). The reality in Soviet eyes lies in the American pursuit of war-waging counterforce capabilities with offensive strategic forces eminently capable of first strike: the 'punishment' concept has steadily given way to coercion and constraint, with counterforce capability growing constantly. American programmes, according to Professor Trofimenko (and others) are aimed at regaining unilateral deterrence, to which end the United States works to realign the balance in its own favour and to outflank the SALT agreements. As for counterforce capabilities and options, the Soviet side insists that their own recourse to such capabilities was a reaction to American initiatives and weapons programmes. In particular, the Schlesinger doctrine and more recently PD-59 are viewed as the development of a 'strategy of victory in a nuclear way through build-up of counterforce potential'.

In this counterforce context it is also important to recognize significant Soviet-American differences over what exactly comprises 'the balance': while Western sources evaluate the 'net balance' (ICBMs, SLBMs and long-range bombers as strategic weapons systems) Soviet reckoning perforce includes the Pershing II medium-range ballistic missile and the ground-launched cruise missile—due for deployment in Europe—as strategic components (if only because of the Soviet definition that any weapon which can strike the USSR is 'strategic', irrespective of its geographical basing). The same criterion is applied to the whole nexus of forward based systems (FBS), including land- and carrier-based aircraft. More pertinently, Pershing II with its high accuracy and extended range, is perceived not as a counterpart to restoring imbalance in theatre nuclear forces but expressly as a high-precision first-strike counterforce weapon: witness the 4–6 minute flight time of Pershing II to target, which effectively rules out launch on warning (assuming even rapid launch detection); and with strikes against Soviet missile silos and command and control centres, launch under attack will be hazardous if not actually impossible. In brief, the Soviet command sees itself facing the development of nothing less than a Eurostrategic nuclear capability associated with existing (and expanding) American offensive first-strike weaponry. . . .

---

[7][Professor Henry Trofimenko's study *Changing Attitudes towards Deterrence*, University of California ACIS Working Paper No. 25 (July 1980),] note 30 (p. 54) defines four threats facing the USSR: (1) from NATO, including British and French nuclear forces, plus US forward based systems (FBS), (2) from US strategic potential, (3) from China with 'its huge reservoir of manpower', and (4) from large US naval units in forward deployment.

Summary

To sum up, Soviet opinion from the outset was not inclined to accept what might be called the metaphysics of deterrence, or any arcane system of scholasticism which merely screened the American policy of containment: the Soviet Union was deterred and was intended to remain in that condition, all in the age of *ustrashenie* (the West's concept of deterrence). In the Soviet view, though American declaratory statements ostensibly committed US policy to concepts of nuclear sufficiency, in the real world—in the world of military procurement—the American build-up belied the notion of 'sufficiency' and American capabilities were being developed beyond those which could be identified with 'deterrence through punishment'. It was impossible, therefore, for the Soviet Union to subscribe to the mutuality of 'assured destruction' when military reality appeared to suggest further expansion of US counterforce capability: it was no part of Soviet policy to increase Soviet vulnerability nor to pinion the Soviet Union in a 'hostage' concept. As for mutual deterrence, it had to be a mutuality stripped of American attempts at coercion (compellance) and without resort to the reimposition of 'unilateral deterrence'. Yet another contradiction was that certain American attitudes professed war-avoidance and the 'unthinkability' of nuclear war, while the Soviet Union determined on war-prevention coupled with the acceptance of the possibility of nuclear war, an admixture which produced no small degree of confusion, acrimony and accusation in Western circles, certain of which insisted on the implacability of Soviet intentions in a quest for unchallenged military superiority—thus demolishing deterrence and undermining any mutuality.

It is too easy to dismiss deterrence as some kind of word-game or a form of nuclear mumbo-jumbo meant to obscure the significance of nuclear weaponry, a form of academic-intellectual conspiracy on the part of 'strategists' against humanity. But if there is a fault, it may well be not that we have paid too much attention to this phenomenon but too little, particularly in the matter of perceptions and, specifically, Soviet perceptions. These require at the very least close inspection, fair evaluation and due application of mutuality: as a very senior Soviet official put it in the course of our 'Edinburgh Conversations on Survival in the Nuclear Age' (a meeting held at Edinburgh in October 1981), what is sauce for the goose should be sauce for the gander. Whatever the dispute over Soviet intentions and capabilities, whatever the disparagement of deterrence as a moral or metaphysical hoax, it is nevertheless fair to state unequivocally that it is no part of rational Soviet design to see our collective goose cooked.

FOR FURTHER READING

Berman, Robert P., and John C. Baker. *Soviet Strategic Forces: Requirements and Responses.* Washington, D.C.: Brookings, 1982. A detailed history of the technical development of and strategic rationale for Soviet strategic nuclear forces. Includes introductory section on Soviet nuclear strategy.

Cockburn, Andrew. *The Threat: Inside the Soviet Military Machine.* New York: Random House, 1983. Describes the weaknesses in the Soviet military posture, concentrating on such "intangibles" as poor morale, poor training, the potential unreliability of Soviet allies, and the questionable technical reliability of Soviet weapons systems, factors often ignored or excluded from analyses of the East-West military balance.

Ground Zero. *What About the Russians and Nuclear War?* New York: Pocket Books, 1983. A highly readable, balanced introduction to the Soviet Union, its strengths, weaknesses, and the impact Soviet nuclear weapons policies have had on American security.

Hoffman, Erik P., and Frederic J. Fleron, eds. *The Conduct of Soviet Foreign Policy.* New York: Aldine, 1980. A reader/textbook on Soviet foreign policy with competing interpretations of the role ideology, national interest, military force, and arms control play in defining Soviet policy.

Holloway, David. *The Soviet Union and the Arms Race.* New Haven, Conn.: Yale University Press, 1981. An examination of the domestic and international political context of the Soviet Union's participation in the nuclear arms competition with the United States.

Kaplan, Fred M. *Dubious Spector: A Skeptical Look at the Soviet Nuclear Threat.* Washington, D.C.: Institute for Policy Studies, 1980. Disputes the claim that the Soviets are close to achieving nuclear superiority over the United States. Includes analyses of Soviet nuclear forces as well as Soviet military doctrine.

Kennan, George. *Nuclear Delusion: Soviet-American Relations in the Nuclear Age.* New York: Pantheon Books, 1983. A critique of U.S. policy towards the Soviet Union and America's overreliance on nuclear weaponry in its security policies, by the architect of America's postwar "containment" policy. Contains a compilation of Kennan's essays which span three decades.

Leebaert, Derek, ed. *Soviet Military Thinking.* London: George, Allen, and Unwin, 1981. A compilation of Western perspectives on Soviet nuclear and conventional military strategy.

Pipes, Richard. *Survival Is Not Enough.* New York: Simon and Schuster, 1984. The former Reagan NSC Soviet affairs specialist argues the Soviet social and economic systems are now in deep crisis, and that U.S. foreign policy should be directed at hastening the deterioration of this crisis and the eventual collapse "from within" of the Soviet state.

Talbott, Strobe. *Reagan and the Russians.* New York: Vintage Books, 1984. An examination of U.S.-Soviet relations during Ronald Reagan's first term as President of the United States, which explores the causes of the serious deterioration in superpower relations which occurred in this period.

Union of Soviet Socialist Republics. *From Whence the Threat to Peace.* Moscow: Military Publishing House, 1982. The Soviet Union's rejoinder to the United States Department of Defense's *Soviet Military Power* booklets, stressing U.S. advantages and military strength. Argues U.S. adheres to aggressive military and foreign policies.

U.S. Department of Defense. *Soviet Military Power 1985.* Washington, D.C.: U.S. Government Printing Office, 1985. An illustrated, comprehensive overview of Soviet military activities and the threat they pose to U.S. national security, stressing Soviet strengths and Western weaknesses. (1981, 1983 and 1984 editions also available.)

6

The Nuclear Dilemma in Europe

Throughout the post–World War II period, the security of Western Europe has been intimately linked to the United States' ability and willingness to use nuclear weapons on behalf of American allies in the region. If Western Europe were ever attacked by the Soviet Union or her allies, the United States has promised to respond, if necessary, with the use of nuclear weapons, even if the Soviets themselves do not employ such weapons in the original attack.

This American "first-use" of nuclear weapons policy is a legacy of the early postwar period, in which Soviet-American relations deteriorated rapidly following the defeat of Adolf Hitler and liberation of Nazi-occupied Europe. The need for such a policy grew out of the Western perception that the Soviet Union had continued to maintain a large standing army in the areas of Eastern Europe it controlled, in contrast to the United States, which had rapidly demobilized its own armies by 1948. In the context of the overall breakdown in U.S.-Soviet relations then in progress—and in light of the fact that these Soviet forces were believed to be well within striking distance of Western Europe—U.S. leaders treated this Soviet force as a potentially serious military threat to the West. The demobilization of American forces, moreover, was aggravated by the fact that the major West European members of the wartime "Grand Alliance"—Britain and France—were too weak in the immediate postwar period to contribute materially to any standing non-nuclear defense capability for Western Europe, a condition that persisted into the 1950s. It is not surprising, therefore, that American policy-makers viewed U.S. possession of the atomic bomb as a necessary counter to the perceived threat of a Soviet invasion during the early Cold War years.

But the first-use policy, which during the Eisenhower administration came to be known formally as the threat of "massive retaliation," made sense for another reason as well. The United States tested and used its first atomic weapons in 1945. The Soviets did not test their first A-bomb until 1949, and did not possess a delivery capability which

could threaten Western Europe with vastly more destructive thermonuclear weapons (first tested by the Soviet Union in 1953) until the latter
1950s. They would not achieve a survivable, intercontinental retaliatory
capability vis-à-vis the United States until the mid to late 1960s. By
the mid to late 1950s, by contrast, the United States had ringed the Soviets with bases from which hundreds of B-47 jet bombers could attack
military and industrial targets in the Soviet Union with multimegaton
thermonuclear weapons. Also in this period, the United States deployed
thousands of "tactical" nuclear weapons in Europe to be launched
on the battlefield at advancing Soviet troops if deterrence failed.

By virtue of this overwhelming U.S. nuclear superiority during
the 1950s, in which the Soviets were vulnerable to massive retaliation,
while Western Europe (for the moment) and the United States were not,
the first-use threat was a credible deterrent to a Soviet non-nuclear attack on the North Atlantic Treaty Organization (NATO), the United
States' alliance with the countries of Western Europe. The Eisenhower
administration was also interested in providing for the security of the
U.S. and its allies in the least expensive way possible. Nuclear forces
were viewed as cost-effective weapons which could yield "more bang for
the buck" than so called "conventional," or non-nuclear, forces. As importantly, the policy satisfied the concerns of West Europeans who
feared the consequences of another conventional war on their soil. They
believed that if the Soviet Union realized a conventional attack would
quickly lead to a massive nuclear response against them by the United
States, the risk of conventional as well as nuclear war in Europe could
be minimized.

In the early 1960s, however, American and West European perceptions of the deterrent value of nuclear weapons in NATO strategy began to part. The decisive factor in this divergence was the large
expansion in Soviet nuclear weapons delivery capabilities in the late
1950s and 1960s. At the onset of the Kennedy administration in 1961,
the new Defense Secretary, Robert McNamara, faced three important
changes in the U.S.-Soviet nuclear balance. First, the Soviets had already deployed a force of medium-range bombers and were deploying
medium- and intermediate-range nuclear missiles capable of destroying
all major West European cities from bases in the Soviet Union. Additionally, the Soviets had now equipped their own ground forces in Europe with tactical nuclear weapons. Finally, McNamara realized the
Soviet missile launch of the "Sputnik" satellite into earth orbit in 1957
foreshadowed a strategic future when the Soviets would possess a survivable land-based missile force which would threaten American cities.

All three of these developments served to undermine the credibility of the first-use threat. If the Soviets, for example, could respond to
NATO's first use of tactical nuclear weapons with their own "battlefield"
nuclear weapons, what military advantage could NATO possibly expect to
gain by using them? And wouldn't the Soviets' ability to respond
weaken deterrence? Similarly, if European NATO and American cities
were becoming vulnerable to retaliation, how could the Soviets be expected to be deterred by a threat of strategic "massive retaliation,"
which now appeared to represent a de facto threat by NATO to commit
suicide?

Convinced that Soviet nuclear weapons programs had or would soon neutralize the credibility of NATO's first-use policy, McNamara focused his attention on closing the perceived disparity between NATO's own conventional forces and those of the Soviet-led Warsaw Pact alliance (remember that it was this perceived imbalance in non-nuclear forces which had provided the strategic rationale for the first-use policy in the first place). With NATO cities now vulnerable to Soviet retaliation, McNamara reasoned, it was now necessary for NATO countries to bear the increased economic burden of shoring up its conventional forces—to the point where the alliance could defend its territory against a Warsaw Pact invasion without resorting to the first use of nuclear weapons. McNamara advocated the adoption of a "Flexible Response" policy, and tried to persuade America's European allies to rely on strengthened conventional forces to deter conventional attack, both to restore the credibility of NATO's deterrent and to reduce the likelihood that a European land war would escalate to an "exchange" between the Soviet Union and American nuclear arsenals, which would not only consume the superpowers but all of Europe as well.

But it was precisely this latter objective which the Europeans found the most dangerous element in McNamara's new strategy, and to which they objected the most strenuously. The goal of NATO military policy, they argued, should not be to prevent *nuclear* war in Europe, or *nuclear* war between the U.S. and Soviet Union, but rather to keep *any* kind of war—including a conventional war—from erupting again in Europe. The best way to do this, they maintained, was to convince the Soviets that any NATO–Warsaw Pact conflict would escalate to the use of nuclear weapons and involve the risk of nuclear destruction to Soviet society. They rejected McNamara's argument that improved conventional forces would provide for a "firebreak" between territorial defense and nuclear war, arguing instead that this simply would make conventional aggression less costly and therefore "safe" in the minds of Soviet military planners.

Though the name "Flexible Response" was adopted as the name of NATO's basic strategy in 1967, largely as a result of the reluctance of European leaders, and as a result of budgetary constraints facing the Western democracies on both sides of the Atlantic, McNamara's plan to significantly strengthen alliance non-nuclear forces was never fully implemented. The widespread Western perception that NATO's conventional forces are inferior relative to those of the Warsaw Pact remains. NATO continues to this day to rely on the threat to use nuclear weapons first as its primary deterrent to an attack by Warsaw Pact conventional forces, despite the fact that the credibility of such a strategy remains seriously in doubt, and its implementation would virtually ensure that any European conflict would escalate to global nuclear war.

In their article "Nuclear Weapons and the Atlantic Alliance," the so-called "Gang of Four" former U.S. national security policymakers— McGeorge Bundy, George Kennan, Gerard Smith, and Robert McNamara himself—argue it is time to reconsider the wisdom of such a policy. They note the "irrationalities" inherent in NATO's reliance on the first-use threat, and they emphasize in particular the Soviet's capacity for

retaliation in kind, the difficulty of controlling a nuclear war once begun, and the horrible destruction that would ensue if the threat ever
had to be carried out. NATO, they argue, should adopt an explicit
pledge not to introduce nuclear weapons into a conflict in Europe. Such
a "No First Use" policy, in their view, would have to be backed up by
strengthened NATO conventional forces, although they believe that So-
viet/Warsaw Pact advantages in non-nuclear forces have generally been
exaggerated. The key test of the policy's practicality, they stress, will be
whether the alliance can generate the necessary *political will* to undertake a reduction in NATO's reliance on nuclear weapons, which they concede may be difficult in light of West European concerns about
weakening the link between European security and a U.S. nuclear response.

Edward Luttwak offers a very different perspective on "How to
Think About Nuclear War." He argues that Bundy, et al. seriously underestimate the military, political, and economic obstacles which NATO
would have to overcome in order to implement a No First Use policy.
Chief among them, argues Luttwak, is the fact that NATO faces an opponent whose forces are numerically superior, more heavily equipped,
and thoroughly exercised in the tactics and strategy of *blitzkrieg* armored
warfare. NATO, he concludes, is seriously undermanned at the conventional level, a weakness that NATO cannot easily overcome, and that the
only equalizer at the West's disposal is the threat to use nuclear weapons in response to a Soviet attack. In contrast to Bundy et al., as well as
many other specialists in the field, Luttwak believes that the first use of
nuclear weapons would not necessarily precipitate an uncontrolled nuclear conflict that would engulf all antagonists. He asserts, rather, that
the most likely consequence of a NATO decision to use nuclear weapons
would be the rapid defeat of Soviet invasion plans and a negotiated conclusion of hostilities. In his mind, this justifies NATO's continued reliance on what he calls "by far the most important layer of deterrence,"
nuclear weapons.

Luttwak and P. Terrence Hopmann (whose article, "Negotiating
Security in Europe," we will consider shortly) both point out that many
West European defense specialists have reacted negatively to the No
First Use proposal. Luttwak observes that Europeans, and especially the
Germans, have a unique stake in this debate: If NATO and the Warsaw
Pact ever *were* to fight a war in Europe, it would almost certainly begin
on West German soil. As Karl Kaiser and three other senior German
foreign policy and military specialists have outlined in a *Foreign Affairs*
article—written in reply to the piece by Bundy et al.—European opposition to No First Use derives at least as much from political considerations as it does from military concerns.[1] In terms reminiscent of
European reactions to McNamara's call for strengthened conventional
forces under his Flexible Response proposal in the early 1960s, the German "Gang of Four" argues that a No First Use policy would "decouple"
the threat of an American strategic nuclear response against the Soviet
Union from the defense of Western Europe against a Soviet non-nuclear

---

[1] This article is cited in the suggested readings list at the end of the chapter.

attack. The result, they argue, would be to make Western Europe "safe" for Soviet conventional aggression, thus weakening deterrence and increasing the risk of a conventional conflagration fought on West European territory. They believe that the destructive effects of such an attack would be only marginally less catastrophic than those of a nuclear war. These German authors thus conclude that NATO should continue to rely on the threat to employ nuclear weapons first, in order to ensure the strongest form of deterrence possible.

Hopmann, in "Negotiating Security in Europe," contends that the military and political objections raised by Luttwak and the Europeans can be surmounted if a *mutual* U.S.-Soviet No First Use pledge is linked to and made conditional upon negotiated limits on NATO and Warsaw Pact conventional forces in Central Europe. According to Hopmann, such an arrangement could significantly reduce the risk of a Soviet conventional attack on Western Europe, thus allaying the concerns of Europeans that No First Use would by definition imply a weakening of deterrence of a non-nuclear European conflict. It would also ensure that a more stable and equal East-West conventional military balance is not purchased at the price of an intensified competition in conventional armaments in Europe.

Nuclear Weapons and the Atlantic Alliance

McGeorge Bundy, George F. Kennan, Robert S. McNamara, and Gerard C. Smith

McGeorge Bundy served as Special Assistant to the President for National Security Affairs in the Kennedy and Johnson administrations, and is currently Professor of History at New York University.

George F. Kennan has a distinguished record of service in the Foreign Service, and was Ambassador to the Soviet Union in 1952. He is the author of several books on Soviet foreign policy and U.S.-Soviet relations, and is currently Professor Emeritus at the Institute for Advanced Study at Princeton University.

Robert S. McNamara was U.S. Secretary of Defense from 1961 to 1968 and served as President of the World Bank from 1968 to 1981.

Gerard C. Smith was the head of the U.S. delegation in the SALT I negotiations and is author of *Doubletalk: The Story of SALT I*.

We are four Americans who have been concerned over many years with the relation between nuclear weapons and the peace and freedom of the members of the Atlantic Alliance. Having learned that each of us separately has been

Source: McGeorge Bundy, George F. Kennan, Robert S. McNamara, and Gerard Smith, "Nuclear Weapons and the Atlantic Alliance," *Foreign Affairs* (Spring 1982), pp. 753–68. Reprinted by permission of *Foreign Affairs* (Spring, 1982). Copyright 1982 by the Council on Foreign Relations, Inc.

coming to hold new views on this hard but vital question, we decided to see how far our thoughts, and the lessons of our varied experiences, could be put together; the essay that follows is the result. It argues that a new policy can bring great benefits, but it aims to start a discussion, not to end it.

For 33 years now, the Atlantic Alliance has relied on the asserted readiness of the United States to use nuclear weapons if necessary to repel aggression from the East. Initially, indeed, it was widely thought (notably by such great and different men at Winston Churchill and Niels Bohr) that the basic military balance in Europe was between American atomic bombs and the massive conventional forces of the Soviet Union. But the first Soviet explosion, in August 1949, ended the American monopoly only one month after the Senate approved the North Atlantic Treaty, and in 1950 communist aggression in Korea produced new Allied attention to the defense of Europe.

The "crude" atomic bombs of the 1940s have been followed in both countries by a fantastic proliferation of weapons and delivery systems, so that today the two parts of a still-divided Europe are targeted by many thousands of warheads both in the area and outside it. Within the Alliance, France and Britain have developed thermonuclear forces which are enormous compared to what the United States had at the beginning, although small by comparison with the present deployments of the superpowers. Doctrine has succeeded doctrine, from "balanced collective forces" to "massive retaliation" to "mutual assured destruction" to "flexible response" and the "seamless web." Throughout these transformations, most of them occasioned at least in part by changes in the Western view of Soviet capabilities, both deployments and doctrines have been intended to deter Soviet aggression and keep the peace by maintaining a credible connection between any large-scale assault, whether conventional or nuclear, and the engagement of the strategic nuclear forces of the United States.

A major element in every doctrine has been that the United States has asserted its willingness to be the first—has indeed made plans to be the first if necessary—to use nuclear weapons to defend against aggression in Europe. It is this element that needs re-examination now. Both its cost to the coherence of the Alliance and its threat to the safety of the world are rising while its deterrent credibility declines.

This policy was first established when the American nuclear advantage was overwhelming, but that advantage has long since gone and cannot be recaptured. As early as the 1950s it was recognized by both Prime Minister Churchill and President Eisenhower that the nuclear strength of both sides was becoming so great that a nuclear war would be a ghastly catastrophe for all concerned. The following decades have only confirmed and intensified that reality. The time has come for careful study of the ways and means of moving to a new Alliance policy and doctrine: that nuclear weapons will not be used unless an aggressor should use them first.

II

The disarray that currently besets the nuclear policy and practices of the Alliance is obvious. Governments and their representatives have maintained an appearance of unity as they persist in their support of the two-track decision of December 1979, under which 572 new American missiles of intermediate range are to be placed in Europe unless a satisfactory agreement on the limitation of such weapons can be reached in the negotiations between the United States and the Soviet Union that began last November. But behind this united front there are divisive debates, especially in countries where the new weapons are to be deployed.

The arguments put forward by advocates of these deployments contain troubling variations. The simplest and intuitively the most persuasive claim is that these new weapons are needed as a counter to the new Soviet ss-20 missiles; it may be a recognition of the surface attractiveness of this position that underlies President Reagan's striking—but probably not negotiable— proposal that if all the ss-20s are dismantled the planned deployments will be cancelled. Other officials have a quite different argument, that without new and survivable American weapons which can reach Russia from Western Europe there can be no confidence that the strategic forces of the United States will remain committed to the defense of Western Europe; on this argument the new missiles are needed to make it more likely that any war in Europe would bring nuclear warheads on the Soviet Union and thus deter the aggressor in the first place. This argument is logically distinct from any concern about the Soviet ss-20s, and it probably explains the ill-concealed hope of some planners that the Reagan proposal will be rejected. Such varied justifications cast considerable doubt on the real purpose of the proposed deployment.

An equally disturbing phenomenon is the gradual shift in the balance of argument that has occurred since the need to address the problem was first asserted in 1977. Then the expression of need was European, and in the first instance German; the emerging parity of long-range strategic systems was asserted to create a need for a balance at less than intercontinental levels. The American interest developed relatively slowly, but because these were to be American missiles, American planners took the lead as the proposal was worked out. It has also served Soviet purposes to concentrate on the American role. A similar focus has been chosen by many leaders of the new movement for nuclear disarmament in Europe. And now there are American voices, some in the executive branch, talking as if European acceptance of these new missiles were some sort of test of European loyalty to the Alliance. Meanwhile some of those in Europe who remain publicly committed to both tracks of the 1979 agreement are clearly hoping that the day of deployment will never arrive.

When the very origins of a new proposal become the source of irritated argument among allies—"You started it!"—something is badly wrong in our common understanding.

A still more severe instance of disarray, one which has occurred under both President Carter and President Reagan, relates to the so-called neutron bomb, a weapon designed to meet the threat of Soviet tanks. American military planners, authorized by doctrine to think in terms of early battlefield use of nuclear weapons, naturally want more "up-to-date" weapons than those they have now; it is known that thousands of the aging short-range nuclear weapons now in Europe are hard to use effectively. Yet to a great many Europeans the neutron bomb suggests, however unfairly, that the Americans are preparing to fight a "limited" nuclear war on their soil. Moreover neither weapons designers nor the Pentagon officials they have persuaded seem to have understood the intense and special revulsion that is associated with killing by "enhanced radiation."

All these recent distempers have a deeper cause. They are rooted in the fact that the evolution of essentially equivalent and enormously excessive nuclear weapons systems both in the Soviet Union and in the Atlantic Alliance has aroused new concern about the dangers of all forms of nuclear war. The profusion of these systems, on both sides, has made it more difficult than ever to construct rational plans for any first use of these weapons by anyone.

This problem is more acute than before, but it is not new. Even in the 1950s, a time that is often mistakenly perceived as one of effortless American superiority, the prospect of any actual use of tactical weapons was properly terrifying to Europeans and to more than a few Americans. Military plans for such use remained both deeply secret and highly hypothetical; the coherence of the Alliance was maintained by general neglect of such scenarios, not by sedulous public discussion. In the 1960s there was a prolonged and stressful effort to address the problem of theater-range weapons, but agreement on new forces and plans for their use proved elusive. Eventually the proposal for the multilateral force (MLF) was replaced by the assignment of American Polaris submarines to NATO, and by the creation in Brussels of an inter-allied Nuclear Planning Group. Little else was accomplished. In both decades the Alliance kept itself together more by mutual political confidence than by plausible nuclear war-fighting plans.

Although the first years of the 1970s produced a welcome if oversold détente, complacency soon began to fade. The Nixon Administration, rather quietly, raised the question about the long-run credibility of the American nuclear deterrent that was to be elaborated by Henry Kissinger in 1979 at a meeting in Brussels. Further impetus to both new doctrine and new deployments came during the Ford and Carter Administrations, but each public statement, however careful and qualified, only increased European apprehensions. The purpose of both Administrations was to reinforce deterrence, but the result has been to increase fear of nuclear war, and even of Americans as its possible initiators. Intended as contributions to both rationality and credibility, these excursions into the theory of limited nuclear war have been counterproductive in Europe. ·

Yet it was not wrong to raise these matters. Questions that were answered largely by silence in the 1950s and 1960s cannot be so handled in the 1980s. The problem was not in the fact that the questions were raised, but in the way they seemed to be answered.

It is time to recognize that no one has ever succeeded in advancing any persuasive reason to believe that any use of nuclear weapons, even on the smallest scale, could reliably be expected to remain limited. Every serious analysis and every military exercise, for over 25 years, has demonstrated that even the most restrained battlefield use would be enormously destructive to civilian life and property. There is no way for anyone to have any confidence that such a nuclear action will not lead to further and more devastating exchanges. Any use of nuclear weapons in Europe, by the Alliance or against it, carries with it a high and inescapable risk of escalation into the general nuclear war which would bring ruin to all and victory to none.

The one clearly definable firebreak against the worldwide disaster of general nuclear war is the one that stands between all other kinds of conflict and any use whatsover of nuclear weapons. To keep that firebreak wide and strong is in the deepest interest of all mankind. In retrospect, indeed, it is remarkable that this country has not responded to this reality more quickly. Given the appalling consequences of even the most limited use of nuclear weapons and the total impossibility for both sides of any guarantee against unlimited escalation, there must be the gravest doubt about the wisdom of a policy which asserts the effectiveness of any first use of nuclear weapons by either side. So it seems timely to consider the possibilities, the requirements, the difficulties, and advantages of a policy of no-first-use.

III

The largest question presented by any proposal for an Allied policy of no-first-use is that of its impact on the effectiveness of NATO's deterrent posture on the central front. In spite of the doubts that are created by any honest look at the probable consequences of resort to a first nuclear strike of any kind, it should be remembered that there were strong reasons for the creation of the American nuclear umbrella over NATO. The original American pledge, expressed in Article 5 of the Treaty, was understood to be a nuclear guarantee. It was extended at a time when only a conventional Soviet threat existed, so a readiness for first use was plainly implied from the beginning. To modify that guarantee now, even in the light of all that has happened since, would be a major change in the assumptions of the Alliance, and no such change should be made without the most careful exploration of its implications.

In such an exploration the role of the Federal Republic of Germany must be central. Americans too easily forget what the people of the Federal Republic never can: that their position is triply exposed in a fashion unique among the large industrial democracies. They do not have nuclear weapons; they share a long common boundary with the Soviet empire; in any conflict on the central front their land would be the first battleground. None of these conditions can be changed, and together they present a formidable challenge.

Having decisively rejected a policy of neutrality, the Federal Republic has necessarily relied on the nuclear protection of the United States, and we Americans should recognize that this relationship is not a favor we are doing our German friends, but the best available solution of a common problem. Both nations believe that the Federal Republic must be defended; both believe that the Federal Republic must not have nuclear weapons of its own; both believe that nuclear guarantees *of some sort* are essential; and both believe that only the United States can provide those guarantees in persuasively deterrent peacekeeping form.

The uniqueness of the West German position can be readily demonstrated by comparing it with those of France and the United Kingdom. These two nations have distance, and in one case water, between them and the armies of the Soviet Union; they also have nuclear weapons. While those weapons may contribute something to the common strength of the Alliance, their main role is to underpin a residual national self-reliance, expressed in different ways at different times by different governments, which sets both Britain and France apart from the Federal Republic. They are set apart from the United States too, in that no other nation depends on them to use their nuclear weapons otherwise than in their own ultimate self-defense.

The quite special character of the nuclear relationship between the Federal Republic and the United States is a most powerful reason for defining that relationship with great care. It is rare for one major nation to depend entirely on another for a form of strength that is vital to its survival. It is unprecedented for any nation, however powerful, to pledge itself to a course of action, in defense of another, that might entail its own nuclear devastation. A policy of no-first-use would not and should not imply an abandonment of this extraordinary guarantee—only its redefinition. It would still be necessary to be ready to reply with American nuclear weapons to any nuclear attack on the Federal Republic, and this commitment would in itself be sufficiently demanding to constitute a powerful demonstration that a policy of no-first-use would represent no abandonment of our German ally.

The German right to a voice in this question is not merely a matter of location, or even of dependence on an American nuclear guarantee. The people of the Federal Republic have demonstrated a steadfast dedication to peace, to collective defense, and to domestic political decency. The study here proposed should be responsive to their basic desires. It seems probable that they are like the rest of us in wishing most of all to have no war of any kind, but also to be able to defend the peace by forces that do not require the dreadful choice of nuclear escalation.

IV

While we believe that careful study will lead to a firm conclusion that it is time to move decisively toward a policy of no-first-use, it is obvious that any such policy would require a strengthened confidence in the adequacy of the conventional forces of the Alliance, above all the forces in place on the central front and those available for prompt reinforcement. It seems clear that the nations of the Alliance together can provide whatever forces are needed, and within realistic budgetary constraints, but it is a quite different question whether they can summon the necessary political will. Evidence from the history of the Alliance is mixed. There has been great progress in the conventional defenses of NATO in the 30 years since the 1952 Lisbon communiqué, but there have also been failures to meet force goals all along the way.

In each of the four nations which account for more than 90 percent of NATO's collective defense and a still higher proportion of its strength on the central front, there remain major unresolved political issues that critically affect contributions to conventional deterrence: for example, it can be asked what priority the United Kingdom gives to the British Army of the Rhine, what level of NATO-connected deployment can be accepted by France, what degree of German relative strength is acceptable to the Allies and fair to the Federal Republic itself, and whether we Americans have a durable and effective answer to our military manpower needs in the present all-volunteer active and reserve forces. These are the kinds of questions—and there are many more—that would require review and resolution in the course of reaching any final decision to move to a responsible policy of no-first-use.

There should also be an examination of the ways in which the concept of early use of nuclear weapons may have been built into existing forces, tactics, and general military expectations. To the degree that this has happened, there could be a dangerous gap right now between real capabilities and those which political leaders might wish to have in a time of crisis. Conversely there should be careful study of what a policy of no-first-use would require in those same terms. It seems more than likely that once the military leaders of the Alliance have learned to think and act steadily on this "conventional" assumption, their forces will be better instruments for stability in crises and for general deterrence, as well as for the maintenance of the nuclear firebreak so vital to us all.

No one should underestimate either the difficulty or the importance of the shift in military attitudes implied by a no-first-use policy. Although military commanders are well aware of the terrible dangers in any exchange of nuclear weapons, it is a strong military tradition to maintain that aggressive war, not the use of any one weapon, is the central evil. Many officers will be initially unenthusiastic about any formal policy that puts limits on their recourse to a weapon of apparently decisive power. Yet the basic argument for a no-first-use policy can be stated in strictly military terms: that any other course involves unacceptable risks to the national life that military forces exist to defend. The military officers of the Alliance can be expected to understand the force of this proposition, even if many of them do not initially agree with it. Moreover, there is every reason for confidence that they will loyally accept any policy that has the support of their governments and the peoples behind them, just as they have fully accepted the present arrangements under which the use of nuclear weapons, even in retaliation for a nuclear attack, requires advance and specific approval by the head of government.

An Allied posture of no-first-use would have one special effect that can be set forth in advance: it would draw new attention to the importance of maintaining and improving the specifically American conventional forces in Europe. The principal political difficulty in a policy of no-first-use is that it may be taken in Europe, and especially in the Federal Republic, as evidence of a reduced American interest in the Alliance and in effective overall deterrence. The argument here is exactly the opposite: that such a policy is the best one available for keeping the Alliance united and effective. Nonetheless the psychological realities of the relation between the Federal Republic and the United States are such that the only way to prevent corrosive German suspicion of American intentions, under a no-first-use regime, will be for Americans to accept for themselves an appropriate share in any new level of conventional effort that the policy may require.

Yet it would be wrong to make any hasty judgment that those new levels of effort must be excessively high. The subject is complex, and the more so because both technology and politics are changing. Precision-guided munitions, in technology, and the visible weakening of the military solidity of the Warsaw Pact, in politics, are only two examples of changes working to the advantage of the Alliance. Moreover there has been some tendency, over many years, to exaggerate the relative conventional strength of the U.S.S.R. and to underestimate Soviet awareness of the enormous costs and risks of any form of aggression against NATO.

Today there is literally no one who really knows what would be needed. Most of the measures routinely used in both official and private analyses are static and fragmentary. An especially arbitrary, if obviously convenient, measure of progress is that of spending levels. But it is political will, not budgetary pressure, that will be decisive. The value of greater safety from both nuclear and conventional danger is so great that even if careful analysis showed that the necessary conventional posture would require funding larger than the three-percent real increase that has been the common target of recent years, it would be the best bargain ever offered to the members of the Alliance.

Yet there is no need for crash programs, which always bring extra costs. The direction of the Allied effort will be more important than its velocity. The final establishment of a firm policy of no-first-use, in any case, will obviously require time. What is important today is to begin to move in this direction.

V

The concept of renouncing any first use of nuclear weapons should also be tested by careful review of the value of existing NATO plans for selective and limited use of nuclear weapons. While many scenarios for nuclear war-fighting are nonsensical, it must be recognized that cautious and sober senior officers have found it prudent to ask themselves what alternatives to defeat they could propose to their civilian superiors if a massive conventional Soviet attack seemed about to make a decisive breakthrough. This question has generated contingency plans for battlefield uses of small numbers of nuclear weapons which might prevent that particular disaster. It is hard to see how any such action could be taken without the most enormous risk of rapid and catastrophic escalation, but it is a fair challenge to a policy of no-first-use that it should be accompanied by a level of conventional strength that would make such plans unnecessary.

In the light of this difficulty it would be prudent to consider whether there is any acceptable policy short of no-first-use. One possible example is what might be called "No-*early*-first-use;" such a policy might leave open the option of some limited nuclear action to fend off a final large-scale conventional defeat, and by renunciation of any immediate first use and increased emphasis on conventional capabilities it might be thought to help somewhat in reducing current fears.

But the value of a clear and simple position would be great, especially in its effect on ourselves and our Allies. One trouble with exceptions is that they easily become rules. It seems much better that even the most responsible choice of even the most limited nuclear actions to prevent even the most imminent conventional disaster should be left out of authorized policy. What the Alliance needs most today is not the refinement of its nuclear options, but a clear-cut decision to avoid them as long as others do.

VI

Who should make the examination here proposed? The present American Administration has so far shown little interest in questions of this sort, and indeed a seeming callousness in some quarters in Washington toward nuclear dangers may be partly responsible for some of the recent unrest in Europe. But each of the four of us has served in Administrations which revised their early thoughts on nuclear weapons policy. James Byrnes learned the need to seek international control; John Foster Dulles stepped back somewhat from his early belief in massive retaliation; Dwight Eisenhower came to believe in the effort to ban nuclear tests which he at first thought dangerous; the Administration of John F. Kennedy (in which we all served) modified its early views on targeting doctrine; Lyndon Johnson shelved the proposed MLF when he decided it was causing more trouble than it was worth; and Richard Nixon agreed to narrow limits on anti-ballistic missiles whose large-scale deployment he had once thought indispensable. There were changes also in the Ford and Carter Administrations, and President Reagan has already adjusted his views on the usefulness of early arms control negotiations, even though we remain in a time of general stress between Washington and Moscow. No Administration should be held, and none should hold itself, to inflexible first positions on these extraordinarily difficult matters.

Nor does this question need to wait upon governments for study. The day is long past when public awe and governmental secrecy made nuclear policy a matter for only the most private executive determination. The questions presented by a policy of no-first-use must indeed be decided by governments, but they can and should be considered by citizens. In recent months strong private voices have been raised on both sides of the Atlantic on behalf of strengthened conventional forces. When this cause is argued by such men as Christoph Bertram, Field Marshal Lord Carver, Admiral Noel Gayler, Professor Michael Howard, Henry Kissinger, François de Rose, Theo Sommer, and General Maxwell Taylor, to name only a few, it is fair to conclude that at least in its general direction the present argument is not outside the mainstream of thinking within the Alliance. Indeed there is evidence of renewed concern for conventional forces in governments too.

What should be added, in both public and private sectors, is a fresh, sustained, and careful consideration of the requirements and the benefits of deciding that the policy of the Atlantic Alliance should be to keep its nuclear weapons unused as long as others do the same. Our own belief, though we do not here assert it as proven, is that when this possibility is fully explored it will be evident that the advantages of the policy far outweigh its costs, and that this demonstration will help the peoples and governments of the Alliance to find the political will to move in this direction. In this spirit we go on to sketch the benefits that could come from such a change.

VII

The first possible advantage of a policy of no-first-use is in the management of the nuclear deterrent forces that would still be necessary. Once we escape from the need to plan for a first use that is credible, we can escape also from many of the complex arguments that have led to assertions that all sorts of nuclear capabilities are necessary to create or restore a capability for something called "escalation dominance"—a capability to fight and "win" a nuclear war at any level. What would be needed, under no-first-use, is a set of capabilities we already have in overflowing measure—capabilities for appropriate retaliation to any kind of Soviet nuclear attack which would leave the Soviet Union in no doubt that it too should adhere to a policy of no-first-use. The Soviet government is already aware of the awful risk inherent in any use of these weapons, and there is no current or prospective Soviet "superiority" that would tempt anyone in Moscow toward nuclear adventurism. (All four of us are wholly unpersuaded by the argument advanced in recent years that the Soviet Union could ever rationally expect to gain from such a wild effort as a massive first strike on land-based American strategic missiles.)

Once it is clear that the only nuclear need of the Alliance is for adequately survivable and varied *second strike* forces, requirements for the modernization of major nuclear systems will become more modest than has been assumed. In particular we can escape from the notion that we must somehow match everything the rocket commanders in the Soviet Union extract from their government. It seems doubtful, also, that under such a policy it would be necessary or desirable to deploy neutron bombs. The savings permitted by more modest programs could go toward meeting the financial costs of our contribution to conventional forces.

It is important to avoid misunderstanding here. In the conditions of the 1980s, and in the absence of agreement on both sides to proceed to very large-scale reductions in nuclear forces, it is clear that large, varied, and survivable nuclear forces will still be necessary for nuclear deterrence. The point is not that we Americans should move unilaterally to some "minimum" force of a few tens or even hundreds of missiles, but rather than once we escape from the pressure to seem willing and able to use these weapons first, we shall find that our requirements are much less massive than is now widely supposed.

A posture of no-first-use should also go far to meet the understandable anxieties that underlie much of the new interest in nuclear disarmament, both in Europe and in our own country. Some of the proposals generated by this new interest may lack practicability for the present. For example, proposals to make "all" of Europe—from Portugal to Poland— a nuclear-free zone do not seem to take full account of the reality that thousands of long-range weapons deep in the Soviet Union will still be able to target Western Europe. But a policy of no-first-use, with its accompaniment of a reduced requirement for new Allied nuclear systems, should allow a considerable reduction in fears of all sorts. Certainly such a new policy would neutralize the highly disruptive argument currently put about in Europe: that plans for theater nuclear modernization reflect an American hope to fight a nuclear war limited to Europe.

Such modernization might or might not be needed under a policy of no-first-use; that question, given the size and versatility of other existing and prospective American forces, would be a matter primarily for European decision (as it is today).

An effective policy of no-first-use will also reduce the risk of conventional aggression in Europe. That risk has never been as great as prophets of doom have claimed and has always lain primarily in the possibility that Soviet leaders might think they could achieve some quick and limited gain that would be accepted because no defense or reply could be concerted. That temptation has been much reduced by the Allied conventional deployments achieved in the last 20 years, and it would be reduced still further by the additional shift in the balance of Allied effort that a no-first-use policy would both permit and require. The risk that an adventurist Soviet leader might take the terrible gamble of conventional aggression was greater in the past than it is today, and is greater today than it would be under no-first-use, backed up by an effective conventional defense. . . .

How to Think About Nuclear War
Edward N. Luttwak

Edward N. Luttwak is a consultant to the U.S. Department of Defense and a senior fellow at the Georgetown Center for Strategic and International Studies. Among his major works are *The Grand Strategy of the Soviet Union* and *Strategy and Politics*.

The "front" that the North Atlantic Treaty Organization sustains against the Soviet Union and its client-states divides not nations but political systems. On the one side there is the system of production of individual welfare and social amelioration, while on the other side there is a system that proclaims those same goals very loudly, even while subordinating them to the preservation of totalitarian control and the accumulation of superior military power.

If nuclear weapons were now disinvented, if all the hopes of the nuclear disarmers were fully realized, the Soviet Union would automatically emerge as the dominant power on the continent, fully capable of invading and conquering Western Europe and beyond if its political domination were resisted.

But why should that be so in a non-nuclear world? After all, our side has all the men and all the means that would be needed to outmatch the conventional forces of the other side. Already now, by the storekeeper's method

Source: Edward N. Luttwak, "How to Think About Nuclear War," *Commentary* (Spring 1982), pp. 21–28. Reprinted from *Commentary*, August 1982, by permission; all rights reserved.

of making up an inventory, the forces of NATO can appear as strong as or even stronger than those of the Soviet Union and its not-necessarily-reliable client-states.* Compare, for example, total manpower in uniform, on active duty: 4.9 million for NATO and the United States versus 4.8 million for the Soviet Union and its client-states (and remember that out of that total the Soviet Union must provide the large forces deployed against the Chinese). Compare total manpower in ground forces: 2.7 million for us versus 2.6 million for them (with the same Chinese qualifications, to make us feel even better). Compare total ground forces in Europe itself: 2.1 million on our side and only 1.7 million on the other (and one must make allowance for Polish, Hungarian, and other client-state troops that prudent Soviet military planners would not want to rely upon except to add sheer mass to a successful offensive). In naval forces, the U.S.-NATO advantage is large in almost every category, even if ships are counted by the prow as in Homer and not by tonnage (in which Western superiority is still greater).

If one delights in these comparisons, one can come up with more numbers that are comforting. But there are also some other numbers that are less reassuring. Tanks: 17,053 for NATO in Europe (U.S. included) versus a total of 45,500 on the other side, including 32,200 in reliable Soviet hands (Hitler had only some 3,000 in 1941 for "Barbarossa," the German invasion of Russia); artillery pieces: 9,502 versus 19,446; surface-to-surface missile launchers: 355 versus 1,224 for the Soviet camp (all the nuclear warheads are in Soviet hands exclusively); antitank guns (a rather antique category by conventional wisdom): 964 versus 3,614.

As for combat aircraft in Europe, the numbers go the same way: 2,293 fighter-bombers for NATO-Europe versus 3,255 in Soviet and Warsaw Pact air forces (but predominantly Soviet); fighters: only 204 on the NATO side (the U.S. Air Force believes in heavier multipurpose aircraft) versus 1,565 on the other side; interceptors (another depreciated category): 572 on the part of NATO versus 1,490 in Pact air forces.

Each set of numbers means little in itself. But ignoring all the details, there is one very striking fact that emerges—a fact that begins to tell us the real story about the "military balance" on which there is so much controversy now that McGeorge Bundy, George F. Kennan, Robert S. McNamara, and Gerard Smith have jointly proposed in an article in *Foreign Affairs* (Spring 1982) that NATO should renounce the "first use" of nuclear weapons to deter a nuclear invasion. That fact, indeed very remarkable, is that the rich are seemingly armed as poor men are armed, with rifles, while the poor are armed as rich men, with heavy weapons. Recalling that comparison of "total ground

---

*All the statistics following are from the 1982 edition of the *Military Balance*, published by the International Institute for Strategic Studies.

forces in Europe" in which NATO is shown with 2.1 million troops on active duty versus a mere 1.7 million for the Warsaw Pact—a ratio of 1.27:1 in favor of our side—we now discover that the ratios for the major weapons which modern ground forces need go the other way, in favor of the Soviet side: 2.65:1 for tanks; 2.05:1 for artillery; 3.45:1 for missile launchers; and so on.

More remarkable still, the poorer and less advanced have more combat aircraft, by ratios of 4.5:1 (bombers), 1.4:1 (fighter-bombers), 7.67:1 (fighters), 2.61:1 (interceptors), and so on. Never mind that on each side one should sort out old aircraft in each category, and never mind also that Soviet aircraft are judged inferior to their U.S. counterparts (though to take Israeli-Syrian combat outcomes as an index is totally misleading, since Soviet aircraft would do very nicely in Israeli hands, just as they performed quite well against our own fighter-bombers in Vietnam, and also in Indian hands against the Pakistanis). In spite of all qualifications large and small, the fact stands, and it is a great fact: the poor are far more abundantly armed, even in air power, which is the quintessential arm of the rich.

How can this be? What does this mean? How and why have the rich come to be poorly armed as compared with the Soviet Union (whose gross national product is now 60 percent of the American and a mere 25 percent of the U.S.-NATO total)? There is, of course, a very simple answer revealed by the statistics themselves. That famous number, the count of NATO ground forces in Europe in the amount of 2.1 million (as compared to 1.7 million for the Pact), is actually made up of 980,000 men in the armies of Western Europe and another 922,000 men in the Greek, Italian, and Turkish armies which mainly consist of lightly-armed infantry, disqualified by location, training, and equipment from fighting seriously against Soviet-style armored divisions.

But that too is no more than a circumstantial fact: it is not the ineluctable consequence of unalterable limits. NATO *could* have forces much larger *and* better equipped *and* in the right places, for it has a much larger population than the Pact, and also a far greater production. Why then do our richer allies in Western Europe fail to remedy the imbalance? Is it greed that dissuades them from spending enough, or is it perhaps defeatism? Both are in evidence in some degree. But the decisive reason is strategic: those in Europe who understand such matters know that an increased effort would not improve the balance unless it were truly huge, because there are two fundamental military factors at work which make NATO weak and the Soviet Union strong—and these are of such powerful effect in combination that they would nullify the benefits of any marginal increase in defense spending, just as they already outweigh every one of the disadvantages that afflict the Soviet Union, including the unreliability of some of its East European subjects, the hostility of China, and the technical inferiority of some Soviet weapons. Much more than the numbers, it is these two factors that truly determine the present military imbalance in non-nuclear strength, which is very great, and not at all the small matter that Messrs. Bundy, Kennan, McNamara, and Smith suggest (". . . there has been some tendency, over many years, to exaggerate the relative conventional strength of the USSR. . . .").

The first of the two fundamental military factors is, quite simply, that NATO is a defensive alliance—not just defensive in declared intent, as all self-respecting alliances will claim to be, but rather in actual military orientation. Specifically, the forces of NATO on the "central front"—the 600-kilometer line running from the Baltic Sea to the Austrian border—are incapable of offensive operations on a large scale. There are no plans for a NATO offensive against East Germany, there has never been suitable training, or any army-sized exercises for offensive action. In spite of the abundant claims to the contrary in Soviet propaganda at its most implausible, Soviet military planners must know that NATO could not launch an offensive against their front. The notion that Belgian, Dutch, British, German, and U.S. forces would suddenly march across the border to invade is quite simply fantastic.

This means that the Soviet high command can concentrate its own forces for offensive action without having to allocate significant strength for defense. To be sure, many Soviet divisions are either deployed on or assigned to the very long Chinese border. But there too the Soviet Union need not disperse its forces to provide a territorial defense, since the Chinese, for all their millions of troops and tens of millions of rifle-armed militiamen, have no real capacity to mount significant offensive operations. At the very most, at a time of great opportunity such as a Soviet attack upon the West might present, the Chinese could mount a very limited and very shallow move against some segment of the Trans-Siberian railway where it runs near their territory.*

The Soviet army, which was greatly diminished in size during the 1950's but which has grown again during the last two decades, can now mobilize so many divisions that it can cover the Chinese border very adequately; provide more divisions to maintain a threat against Iran, Eastern Turkey, and Pakistan; keep the forces now in place in Afghanistan; and still send more divisions against the "central front" than NATO could cope with.

Not counting at all the divisions of the East European client-states (even though some at least could in fact be used), the arithmetic runs as follows: if 10 more Soviet divisions are added to the Chinese "front" (in addition to the 46 stationed there already); and if a further 18 divisions are kept in reserve to deal with all the contingencies that a prudent and well-provided military leader can imagine; and if there is no reduction in the generous allowance of 26 divisions now deployed on the Soviet Union's "southern front" (opposite the un-

---

* That, incidentally, sets a firm ceiling to the strategic value of a U.S.-China alliance.

derequipped Turks, the chaotic Persians, and in Afghanistan); then, finally, the Soviet Union, upon mobilization, could launch 80 divisions against NATO in Central Europe—that is, against the West German border. And since NATO is a defensive-only alliance, the Soviet army could concentrate its forces in powerful offensive thrusts aimed at narrow segments of that front.

By another estimate, produced by the International Institute for Strategic Studies—nowadays a great favorite of Messrs. Bundy *et al.* owing to its far from hawkish positions—the Soviet army could send a total of 118 divisions against NATO, the greater number being obtained by assuming that no central reserve is maintained at all (the Soviet Union does after all keep 500,000 KGB and MVD troops, which are heavily armed) and that no reinforcement would be made to the Chinese "front."

As against this, NATO can claim a total of 116 divisions, only two fewer than the higher estimate of the Soviet divisions that could be sent against it—and actually 36 divisions more than the Soviet total estimated more conservatively.

But that is truly a hollow number, since NATO's 116 divisions include more than 16 American National Guard divisions that would have to be mobilized, remanned, reequipped (with what?), trained for weeks or months, and then transported to Europe by way of ports and airfields benevolently intact by Soviet forces. The 116 divisions include more than 29 Italian, Greek, and Turkish divisions that are stationed far from Central Europe and are neither trained nor equipped to fight on that front. And they include 9 other divisions of foot infantry of various kinds. Once all these make-weights are removed from the count, we discover that against 80 Soviet divisions, NATO might field no more than 58 divisions of its own, including more than 12 French divisions whose participation in a fight is uncertain but whose scant armament for such combat is unfortunately not in doubt.

In fact, we might estimate even more truly by measuring NATO forces in terms of *Soviet* division-equivalents, whereupon we obtain 35 divisions upon full mobilization and with the transfer of all earmarked U.S. forces. The numerical imbalance thus finally emerges and a sharp one indeed: 80 Soviet divisions versus 35 for NATO. And then the defense/offense asymmetry intervenes to make the true combat imbalance even greater, since the Soviet divisions can be concentrated during an offensive against few narrow segments of the front while NATO's divisions must defend all along the 600-kilometer border.

Under any circumstances, the numerical imbalance in real capabilities would make things very difficult for NATO. But it would not be decisive were it not for the second great factor that makes NATO weak, which arises from the very nature of armored warfare. Nowadays, there is only one army in the world that has actual hands-on expertise in the reality of armored warfare, in the

combined use of large numbers of tanks, troop carriers, and self-propelled artillery to stage offensives of deep penetration, whereby enemy forces are not
merely destroyed piecemeal by fire-fights but are defeated by being cut off and
forced into surrender—and that, of course, is the Israeli army. But if there is
one army in the world that seriously strives to overcome its lack of recent and
relevant combat experience, it is the Soviet army. It is the only one which
stages vast army-sized exercises to educate its officers and men in the broad
art and the detailed craft of armored warfare.

One reason Messrs. Bundy *et al.* are not much impressed by the strength
of the Soviet army is that they simply do not understand the meaning of armored warfare in a setting such as the NATO central front. The Soviet army
would not be lined up unit by unit along the 600 kilometers of the German
frontier, there to fight it out in head-on combat with the forces of NATO similarly arrayed (hence the worthlessness of inventory comparisons which imply
such front-to-front combat). Instead, its 80 divisions would be formed into
deep columns and multiple echelons poised to advance by swift penetrations
of narrow segments of the front. Having learned the art of armored warfare in
the hard school of war itself, at the hands of the best masters, and having
made the method at once simpler and much more powerful by employing the
sheer mass of great numbers to relieve the need for fancy German-style maneuvers, the Soviet army would not employ its forces to launch a set-piece
offensive on a preplanned line of advance (which would be detectable and vulnerable), but would instead seek to advance opportunistically, just as water
flows down a slope, its rivulets seeking the faster paths. Initially, the advance
regiments would probe for gaps and weak sectors through which a swift passage might be achieved. Any Soviet forces that could make no progress would
be left in place, to keep up the threat and prevent the NATO commands from
switching their forces to strengthen the front elsewhere. But Soviet reinforcements would only be sent where successful advances were being achieved in
order to add to the momentum. First more regiments, then divisions, then
entire "armies" would thus be channeled forward to keep up the pressure and
push deep into the rear of the NATO front.

By feeding reinforcement echelons into avenues of penetration successfully opened, the Soviet high command could obtain the full effect of the classic *Blitzkrieg* even without having to rely on the skill and initiative of regimental
officers, as the Germans once did. Instead of a fluid penetrating maneuver obtained by free improvisation, theirs would be an advance just as fast, achieved
by mass and momentum directed from above.

Soon enough, advancing Soviet columns would begin to disrupt the entire defensive structure of NATO, by cutting across roads on which Western
reinforcements and resupply depend, by overrunning artillery batteries, command centers, supply depots, and finally airfields—until the very ports of en-

try on the Atlantic shore would be reached. With NATO's front cut in several places, with Soviet forces already in their deep rear, the choices open to NATO formations in such non-nuclear combat would be either to stand and fight for honor's sake even without true military purpose, or else to retreat—thus opening further gaps in the front. In any case, the relentless advance would soon enough impose a broader choice at a much higher level of decision, for the Germans first and the others not much later: capitulation or military destruction.

Thus in the absence of nuclear weapons, it is not the numerical imbalance in itself that would bring the dismal results, but rather the fact that the Soviet army has a valid method of offensive war, while NATO for its part has no valid method of defense. For obviously the envisaged attempts to block Soviet advances by switching defensive forces back and forth along the line (right in front of Soviet forces which would have every opportunity to disrupt such lateral movement by fire and by their own thrusts) must fail. Indeed, it can be said that even if NATO had a perfect numerical equality, it would still find it impossible to match Soviet concentrations with its own, in order to block their advance right at the front line itself. The reason for this inherent defect is not any lack of military expertise on the part of NATO commanders and planners (although their unfamiliarity with modern armored warfare does show when some pronounce on the military balance by the bookkeeper's method). The defect rather is caused by the combination of NATO's defensive-only orientation and the character of large-scale armored warfare.

In the face of an offensive threat by an armored-mobile army (unless the defenders are *vastly* superior in sheer strength), one of two conditions must obtain to make a successful defense possible: either the defenders must be ready and willing to attack first, in order to disrupt an offensive preemptively; or else the defense must have considerable geographic space in which to maneuver and fight in a defense-in-depth strategy. If NATO had the political will, the training, and the organization to strike first in the face of massing Soviet forces, the latter could not safely form up in deep columns for the attack and would instead have to dilute their strength to form a defensive array of their own.

This option is purely theoretical in NATO's case. It is impossible to imagine that so many diverse governments would agree to let their national forces engage in a preemptive attack to anticipate a Soviet invasion before the outbreak of war. More likely, in the face of a Soviet mobilization and a build-up of divisions opposite NATO, there would be demands for negotiations to settle the crisis by what would no doubt be called "political means," i.e., eager concessions.

As compared with a wholly unrealistic strategy of preemptive attack, the second option, a defense-in-depth, may seem a feasible alternative; and it would offer the possibility of a very powerful defense indeed for NATO. Under such a strategy, Soviet invasion columns would *not* be intercepted by NATO's main defensive forces right in the border zone. Instead, advancing Soviet forces would encounter only a mere border guard along the frontier itself, thereafter being harassed, delayed, and clearly revealed by light and elusive forces as they continued to advance, being steadily weakened by the loss of momentum imposed by time, distance, breakdowns, mined barriers, multiple obstacles at river crossing points, canals, and towns—and also by successive battles with strongholds along the way. Then too, NATO air forces operating quite freely over their own territory, where Soviet air defenses would be very weak, could attack advancing Soviet forces heavily and frequently. Only then would the major combat on the ground finally take place, with fresh NATO divisions maneuvering to strike at the stretched-out and by then ill-supplied Soviet columns (air strikes would do much more damage to supply vehicles than to the Soviet armored forces themselves).

In such a setting, with a thin line of NATO covering forces on the border itself, with multiple barriers and strongholds in depth, and with the main line of resistance 100 or 200 kilometers to the rear, NATO could indeed have a very solid non-nuclear defense, and one which could moreover deter non-nuclear invasion all by itself—since any competent Soviet planner would have to estimate that defeat would be the most likely outcome. And that, of course, would be a defeat which would deprive the Soviet army of one-half of its divisions, and thus the Soviet empire of much of its gendarmerie as well as all of its prestige, no doubt triggering unrest at home and perhaps outright insurrection in the client-states.

But to imagine such a defense in depth for the NATO central front in Germany is not to consider a live option. It is, rather, to indulge in sheer fantasy—and malevolent fantasy at that. For that zone of deep combat happens to correspond to the territory where tens of millions of Germans live. Quite rightly, what the Germans demand is not merely an eventual ability to defeat an aggression at some ultimate point in time and in space, but rather an actual provision of security for themselves, their families, their homes, and their towns. The British, French, or Americans might obtain satisfaction from the defeat of an invading Soviet army in the depth of West German territory, but such a victory would be of little worth to the Germans themselves. What the European system of peaceful construction needs is a preclusive method of protection, not ultimate victory after much destruction and millions of deaths.

In the absence of an offensive capacity by NATO and a lively willingness to preempt invasion, such protection can only be assured by nuclear weapons—or more precisely, by the architecture of nuclear deterrence which is now in place. If the Soviet Union does attack, its offensive would be met in the first instance by a non-nuclear defense of the forward areas close to the border. If

NATO could not hold the front by non-nuclear combat, it would warn the Soviet Union that (small-yield) nuclear weapons would be used to strike at the invading Soviet forces. And then it would strike with such weapons if the warning went unheeded.

At that point the Soviet Union would realize that the alliance was standing up to the test, that it did have the will to defend itself in its moment of truth. One Soviet reaction might be to call off the war—a quite likely response if the invasion had been launched out of some hope to gain, but much less likely if it were the desperate last act of a crumbling empire.

Another Soviet reaction might be to respond to the threat by a wider threat against the cities of Europe, or else—and more likely—to reply in kind. With its own forces weakened by nuclear attack, it might employ nuclear weapons to make its invasion easier, by blasting gaps through the NATO defenses. Or else, the Soviet Union might want to avoid the intermediate steps, and try to impose a capitulation by threatening to attack European cities if any more battlefield nuclear weapons were used.

Such a verbal threat might in turn be averted by being answered in kind, in the first instance perhaps by the British and the French—assuming that their cities had also come under the threat. But a better response to such a Soviet threat would be possible if by then NATO had acquired its own theater nuclear forces which, like the Soviet forces that already exist in considerable numbers, would be suitable to threaten not merely cities indiscriminately, but rather such specific targets as political and military command centers, airfields, nuclear storage sites, and even large concentrations of ground forces— that threat being all the more credible for being less catastrophic.

Much more complex exchanges and many more variations can be envisaged. But by far the most likely outcome is that a war would end very soon if any nuclear weapons, however small, were actually to be detonated by any side on any target. The shock effect upon leaders on both sides—but especially on the Soviet leaders who had started the war—and also the devastating psychological impact upon the forces in the field, would most likely arrest the conflict there and then. It is fully to be expected that military units whose men would see the flash, hear the detonation, feel the blast, or merely hear of such things, would swiftly disintegrate, except perhaps for a handful of units particularly elite, and also remote from the immediate scene. The entire "software" of discipline, of morale, of unit cohesion and *esprit de corps* and all the practices and habits that sustain the authority of sergeants, officers, and political commissars, are simply not built to withstand such terror as nuclear weapons would cause—even if at the end of the day it were to be discovered that the dead on all sides were surprisingly few.

To believe—as Jonathan Schell insists in *The Fate of the Earth* and as Messrs. Bundy, Kennan, McNamara, and Smith imply—that the firing of small-yield nuclear artillery shells against an invasion force, or even the launch of some short-range battlefield missiles with kiloton-range warheads, would lead more or less automatically to successive nuclear strikes from one side and then the other, on a scale larger and larger, until finally European, Russian, and American cities would be destroyed, one has to believe that the instinct for survival would have been utterly extinguished in political leaders, and also that the armies in the field and their commanders, the air forces, the missile crews, and all the rest of mankind in uniform would behave as robots throughout. Just as a Roman legion trained to withstand all the terrors of the ancient world would surely break up and run if it came under machine-gun fire, so too a Soviet division that might otherwise fight and advance through artillery fire and close attack would almost certainly fall apart and retreat if its men came under nuclear attack. As for the politicians and the generals (who begin to resemble politicians when they reach the highest ranks), are we to believe that they would become so absorbed in the conflict-as-a-game that they would reply tit for tat, move by move, instead of stopping the war as soon as it had become nuclear, before it could destroy their own cities and their own families?

It is precisely this quality of nuclear weapons, their awesome, sinister, and only dimly known character, that makes them the fitting tools of deterrent protection in Europe. And yet Messrs. Bundy *et al.* hold that NATO should surrender its deterrent, except to deter a Soviet *nuclear* attack. They argue that NATO should renounce the first and by far the most important layer of deterrence, by repudiating its current and long-established policy whereby the alliance reserves the right to use nuclear weapons against a conventional invasion that could not be stopped by non-nuclear forces alone.

As we have seen, without a policy of "first use" there would no longer be a deterrent against a non-nuclear invasion and Western Europe would remain with only a dubious war-fighting defense which, even if greatly strengthened, could only yield at best some sort of ultimate victory—after much devastation and death.

But of course Messrs. Bundy, McNamara, Kennan, and Smith deny the bleak alternative. They do not believe that there is a gross imbalance, and indeed they confess that they have no sense of how one might estimate such a balance. Perhaps the four are too elevated to concern themselves with such lowly matters as the current Soviet method of armored warfare. And yet oddly enough a very specific technical suggestion is suddenly offered in the midst of the carefully crafted and indeed evasive political prose of their article. They suggest that the advent of "precision-guided weapons" might be weakening the Soviet army.

What Bundy *et al.* will only allude to most prudently others have proclaimed in black and white. The Soviet army, they say, is almost entirely made up of armored formations, and with the arrival of anti-armor missiles on the scene, its strength could now be nullified by the large-scale deployment of those cheap weapons—especially if the United States and NATO stop wasting their own funds on expensive and complex major weapons.

The prospect is most attractive: let the Soviet Union misuse its scant wealth on expensive tanks, obsolete playthings for nostalgic generals, since NATO can defeat their tanks, and their combat carriers too, and indeed all that relies on armor for its immunity, with cheap precision-guided weapons. Of late such things have been said or written by all manner of odd people, from the New York *Times* columnist who had never previously claimed the tactician's mantle, to that part-time physicist and full-time arms-control promoter, Hans Bethe—who has for so long used his Nobel Prize to demand authority on things very much larger than the very small particles which he has investigated. And then, of course, there is the usual array of Congressmen and assorted publicists who so readily assume that every military practice and every military choice must be the wrong-headed product of inert tradition and childish preference for large, and costly, weapons.

Reinforced by the sinking of British warships by "cheap" Exocet missiles, still sustained by lingering memories of the shell-shocked misreporting of the first days of the Yom Kippur war, hardly deflated by the outcome of that same war (decided by Israeli armor, inexplicably), or indeed by other experiences of missile combat before and since (the first use of anti-ship missiles dates back to 1943), the cheap-missile delusion lives on. In the new controversy over NATO's nuclear "first-use" policy, this delusion has attained an unprecedented currency by seemingly offering an alternative to the nuclear deterrence of invasion.

Imagine a Soviet tank approaching. A NATO soldier with his antitank missile can launch his weapon from three or four thousand yards away, he being well-hidden in the undergrowth while the tank stands clear as a very vulnerable target. The missile duly strikes and destroys the tank. That is the technical level of warfare—the only level that many scientists and all "techfix" enthusiasts readily comprehend.

But now broaden the picture somewhat. In a larger view we see more tanks and more NATO missile crews, but we also see the gathering of Soviet artillery—as concentrated as the Soviet armored columns themselves, to pound not all along the front but only those of its segments where breakthroughs are being attempted. Now the missile crews must see their targets through much intervening smoke (and when they cannot see them—if only for a second or two—their missiles will go off-course). But under the heavy artillery barrage many missile crews will be driven to seek refuge in the ground, or in the rear, and if not, they will be wounded or killed. They, after all, are entirely unprotected, unlike the advancing Soviet armor which can still move forward under artillery fire because of all that expensive armor protection. Now the weapon that had a 90 percent "kill-probability" in a technical estimate is revealed as much less powerful, and perhaps a 9 percent kill-probability becomes the more realistic estimate.

This is the tactical level of warfare, and one that quite a few believers in the missile illusion can still comprehend. Accordingly, they accept the analysis and merely point out that even if ten or more missiles must be purchased for each tank to be destroyed, the missile solution would still work—and would still obviate the need both for large budgets and for the "first use" of nuclear weapons. It is a matter of simple arithmetic. Armored vehicles are expensive, and even the Soviet army could scarcely have more than 40,000 or 50,000 for an invasion against NATO's central front (that being a huge number indeed, ultimately constrained by road capacities). Let NATO therefore deploy half-a-million missile launchers if need be—an enormous number (now there are 5,000) and yet still easily affordable, since for every planned $2.7-million tank that we give up we could obtain instead some 150 missile launchers (and we are planning to build thousands of those tanks).

But now finally broaden the picture still more, to embrace the full width of that 600-kilometer NATO front. Let the half-a-million missile launchers be deployed, and now finally at the strategic level of war we discover the true strength of offensive armored warfare: while the Soviet army would attack the front here and there at places of its own choosing in deep columns of concentrated strength, the infantry's missile launchers would be unable to move about to match the concentration. For even if some vehicles or other might be found for the weapons and crews, they would be kept from reaching the places of need by Soviet artillery fire—against which they would lack any armor protection. Now the arithmetic is suddenly overturned. Where it really counts, at the unpredictable places where the breakthrough battles would actually take place, the expensive and scarce armored vehicles would be many (because that is where they would be concentrated), while the antitank missiles would be few indeed once the initial array were scattered, suppressed, or destroyed by the devastating barrages of the abundant and concentrated Soviet artillery.

Just as at sea the cheap missile can destroy the expensive warship only so long as the latter's space and weight, crews and power sources are not properly used to accommodate countermeasures and counterweapons, so also the cheap missile can only destroy armored forces successfully if it is used against the unprepared and the underconcentrated. Otherwise it can only serve as one more weapon on the battlefield, undoubtedly useful, but not a substitute for large defense budgets, and still less for the necessity of nuclear deterrence. . . .

Negotiating Security in Europe

P. Terrence Hopmann

P. Terrence Hopmann is Professor of Political Science at the University of Minnesota and is the author of several articles on negotiation theory and practice.

The deployment of new intermediate-range nuclear missiles in Europe has brought an essential dilemma of Western security to centerstage. That dilemma results from NATO's reliance on the first use of nuclear weapons to counter Soviet conventional aggression in Europe. On the one hand, many Europeans question the reliability of the U.S. commitment to use nuclear weapons in their defense; on the other, they fear that America may be tempted to use nuclear weapons when Europeans would prefer greater restraint. The considerable strains this dilemma has created within the alliance call into question the future of the alliance itself.

As long as NATO relies so heavily on nuclear weapons to counter perceived conventional superiority of Warsaw Pact forces, these strains are likely to persist. Europeans will continue to be concerned either that the United States will not use its nuclear weapons to defend Europe, thus leaving it exposed to Warsaw Pact aggression and political blackmail, or that it will use its nuclear weapons to destroy Europe in order to "save" it. Although intended to reassure the allies on these points, the deployments have only aggravated their anxieties. The new missiles are widely perceived as another attempt to defend Europe inexpensively, not as a way to lessen European fears.

Seen in this light, the no-first-use proposal made in 1982 by four distinguished American specialists on defense and arms control—McGeorge Bundy, Robert S. McNamara, George F. Kennan, and Gerard Smith—is a sensible way out of the present dilemma. An agreement between NATO and the Warsaw Pact that neither would ever be the first to use nuclear weapons in a conflict in Europe would greatly reduce the risks that a limited conventional war might quickly escalate to the nuclear level. Under a no-first-use agreement, both the United States and the Soviet Union would be allowed to maintain their nuclear forces in Europe, but these weapons would be intended solely to deter the use of nuclear weapons by the other side. Thus their deployment and the strategic assumptions governing their use would be far different from at present. In the event of a conventional war, each side would be pledged to defend itself only with conventional weapons.

Source: P. Terrence Hopmann, "Negotiating Security in Europe," *World Policy Journal* (Winter 1984), pp. 23–41. Reprinted by permission of the World Policy Journal, 777 UN Plaza, New York, N.Y. 10017.

Despite its advantages over current NATO strategy, the no-first-use proposal has not gathered steam. It has received little serious attention in official circles in the West. Most West European and American officials have either dismissed the proposal outright or criticized it extensively. They have assumed that the defense of Western Europe cannot be guaranteed by NATO's conventional forces, which are thought to be inadequate to meet the challenge of a Warsaw Pact conventional attack. Substantial increases in NATO's conventional forces have thus been considered a prerequisite to any serious consideration of the no-first-use proposal.

Yet such increases, always politically unpopular in Europe, are even more so at a time of widespread economic trouble. Herein lies a major political obstacle to the no-first-use proposal. Although NATO conventional inferiority often is exaggerated, it is clear that the no-first-use proposal will not receive widespread public support until Western leaders are confident that a stable conventional balance in Europe has been reached and will be maintained. To date, this has meant politically unacceptable increases in defense spending.

But there is another way, often overlooked, to achieve and maintain a conventional balance in Europe. Rather than increase its conventional forces to try to stabilize the balance, NATO could more actively pursue an agreement with the Warsaw Pact to limit or reduce conventional forces on both sides to a level of parity. Negotiations were underway in Vienna for more than ten years to achieve just such an agreement until they were indefinitely suspended by the Soviet Union last December. Within the context of the Mutual and Balanced Force Reduction (MBFR) talks, both East and West had agreed in principle on the need for manpower parity in Central Europe, and progress had been made on issues of verification and associated measures, although numerous details still needed to be resolved.

A common ceiling on troop levels in Central Europe and a no-first-use agreement clearly are in the interest of the West. Yet neither, for different reasons, seems politically possible at present. This situation could be reversed, and progress made on both counts, if the two objectives were linked: Western interest in a no-first-use agreement could revive the stalemated MBFR talks, and success at these talks could make a no-first-use agreement more palatable to many critics in the West. A package linking a policy of no-first-use with conventional force ceilings in Europe not only would have tremendous economic, military, and political appeal, but could also, as this essay will suggest, go a long way toward resolving the deepening tensions within the alliance. . . .

Linking No-First-Use and Conventional Arms Control

To date, most serious discussion of the no-first-use proposal has presumed that NATO would have to increase its conventional forces in order to abandon its first-use option. On this, the authors of the original proposal were agreed.

They endorsed the call by NATO military commander, General Bernard W. Rogers, to increase defense expenditures by 4 percent over six years in order to give the alliance a credible conventional capability.

Yet it is clear that many members of the alliance, especially those facing severe domestic austerity measures, believe such increases cannot be justified in light of domestic priorities. In addition, several alliance members, such as France, Belgium, and Great Britain, believe that the conventional imbalance is so severe that increases of this magnitude cannot possibly redress it. In both cases, there is still a tendency to see nuclear weapons as a less expensive form of defense, especially when the risks of relying on them seem so abstract and unrealistic to most of the public.

But conventional force increases by NATO would be more than costly. They also would run the risk of stimulating an intensified conventional arms race in Europe. For this reason, although some modernization of NATO's conventional forces will almost certainly be necessary if the no-first-use proposal is to be adopted, a full-fledged conventional force buildup, with its attendant costs and risks, cannot be relied upon to make a no-first-use policy politically acceptable. A conventional arms race in Europe would be particularly likely if NATO adopted a more offensive-oriented conventional and nuclear strategy, such as the "Air-Land Battle 2000" strategy advocated by General Rogers. Thus it is conceivable that the conventional balance might remain unchanged, but at higher force levels that are even more expensive to maintain. Even worse, both sides might engage in mutually reinforcing buildups, emphasizing more provocative weapons and strategies that could deepen mutual hostility and reduce the security of both East and West.

The most promising way of stabilizing the conventional military balance, and thus of reaching a no-first-use agreement, is through arms control. That so little attention has been given to this idea is surprising. NATO and the Warsaw Pact have been engaged in such an effort at the Mutual and Balanced Force Reduction negotiations since 1973. These negotiations were adjourned last December with no date set for their reconvening, though the possibility that the talks might resume at any time was left open. Perhaps partly as a result of the lengthy and largely unsuccessful MBFR negotiations, the possibility of linking a no-first-use policy to conventional force reductions, though occasionally acknowledged, too frequently is dismissed as hopeless.

> The case would be different if through negotiations a conventional balance could be reached by reductions in Warsaw Pact forces. The authors [of the no-first-use proposal] do not explore this possibility, but the long years of as yet unsuccessful negotiations for mutual and balanced force reductions (MBFR) demonstrate the obstacles on this path.[1]

---

[1] Karl Kaiser, George Leber, Alois Mertes, and Franz-Josef Schulze, "Nuclear Weapons and the Preservation of Peace: A German Response," *Foreign Affairs,* Vol. 60, No. 5 (Summer 1982) p. 1163.

Yet some other German analysts have taken the arms control option far more seriously. For example, Egon Bahr of the Social Democratic Party has underscored the role of arms control in stabilizing the conventional balance in Europe.[2] Gert Krell, Thomas Risse-Kappen, and Hans-Joachim Schmidt have claimed that many Germans support a policy of no-first-use while opposing "conventional compensation, especially unilateral compensation attained by strengthening offensive capabilities. Changes in flexible response are likely, but they will not be large or sudden. Support for a de-emphasis of nuclear deterrence is more readily mobilized by appeals that emphasize reliance on so-called defensive technologies and arms control."[3]

The MBFR talks have focused largely on conventional force reductions in an area of Central Europe surrounding the two parts of Germany. Reductions in the West would take place in the Federal Republic of Germany, Belgium, the Netherlands, and Luxembourg, and in the East in the German Democratic Republic, Poland, and Czechoslovakia. All nations with forces stationed in these countries (except France, which does not participate) have been known as "direct participants." Thus the United States, the United Kingdom, Canada, and the Soviet Union all have been included. All other members of the two alliances have been allowed to participate "with special status," though Iceland and Portugal have not taken an active role. After ten years of negotiations, East and West have agreed on a common ceiling on troop levels in Central Europe and have reached a general agreement on the need for various forms of verification. The major differences between the alliances settled on two important questions: the first, how force reductions are to be defined; the second, how "associated measures," such as verification and confidence-building schemes, are to be designed. These two areas will be examined here in turn.

First, NATO and the Warsaw Pact disagree on how troop reductions should take place. The original NATO proposal called for equal ceilings on both sides at 700,000 ground manpower. Later, NATO proposed limiting air manpower to 200,000, which would create an overall ceiling of 900,000 men on each side. NATO thus sought to achieve equality of forces in an area where the Warsaw Pact was perceived to have a significant quantitative advantage. The Warsaw Pact, in contrast, initially proposed that no common ceiling be set, but that equal percentage reductions take place on both sides. It contended that equal ceilings would require the Warsaw Pact to make significantly greater reductions than NATO, whereas equal percentage reductions would maintain the current correlation of forces at lower levels.

---

[2] Egon Bahr, "Gemeinsame Sicherheit: Gedanken zur Entscharfung der nuklearen Konfrontation in Europa," *Europa Archiv,* Vo. 37, No. 14, July 25, 1982, pp. 421–30.

[3] Gert Krell, Thomas Risse-Kappen, and Hans-Joachim Schmidt, "The No-First-Use Question in West Germany," in John D. Steinbruner and Leon V. Sigal eds., *Alliance Security: NATO and the No-First-Use Question* (Washington, D.C.: The Brookings Institution, 1983), p. 169.

In 1978 the Warsaw Pact made a major concession on this issue. It accepted the proposed NATO ceiling of 900,000 combined ground and air manpower, with a subceiling of 700,000 ground troops on each side. It then submitted data on current force levels indicating that Warsaw Pact forces were approximately equal in strength to those of NATO in this region. These data not only contradicted its earlier statements, but they also meant that the East would have to cut back by only about 105,000 men to reach the common ceiling, only slightly more than the 91,000 by which NATO would have to reduce.

According to current NATO data, these most recent Eastern figures are significantly understated. NATO estimates that the Warsaw Pact has about 1,180,000 men in the region and thus would have to remove roughly 280,000 men to reach the common ceiling, more than three times the reduction that would be required of NATO. Although its estimates of Warsaw Pact forces have increased in recent years, these estimates are only slightly higher than those made in 1976 by the International Institute for Strategic Studies, which put the total at 1,103,000, and in 1978 by the Stockholm International Peace Research Institute, which put the total at 1,139,000 men.[4] The data presented by NATO and the figures tabled by the Warsaw Pact leave a discrepancy of up to 175,000. Discussions in Vienna have revealed that the disagreement centers largely on Polish and Soviet forces, especially some major Soviet combat units.

The West is not likely to accept any agreement until it is convinced that the Warsaw Pact will in fact reduce its forces to the prescribed level. So far, the Soviet Union has not had sufficient incentive to agree to such significant reductions. Perhaps its political leadership was willing to do so in 1978 when the proposed NATO ceiling was accepted. Since then, however, the Soviet military bureaucracy seems to have been able to block such asymmetrical reductions. Or it may be that Soviet leaders simply hoped the West would accept the new data and base an agreement upon them; having found NATO unreceptive to this possibility, they may simply have found no face-saving way to admit that their data understated Warsaw Pact troop strength in the region.

In principle, there are at least two ways to resolve this disagreement. The first is to obtain from the Warsaw Pact a revision of its data that would more or less accord with Western estimates. In this case, the negotiations would determine the precise number of troops that need to be withdrawn by each side to reach the common ceiling. Initial verification would focus on counting the number of troops withdrawn. More limited measures could then be used to ensure that troop levels were not subsequently increased. Permanent exit/entry

---

[4] See *The Military Balance: 1976–77* (London: International Institute for Strategic Studies, 1976), p. 104; and *World Armaments and Disarmament: SIPRI Yearbook 1978* (London: Taylor and Francis Ltd., 1978), p. 411.

posts supplemented by national technical means of verification, both accepted by the Warsaw Pact in July 1983, should be adequate to verify long-term compliance. For the Warsaw Pact, this proposal would have the advantage of minimizing intrusive verification procedures without calling for many provisions that it has not yet been prepared to accept. This option would, nonetheless, require a public admission of serious inaccuracies in the Warsaw Pact figures.

Even if an agreement cannot be reached on current force levels, a common ceiling might be specified anyway. In this case, verification would need to concentrate not on the number of troops withdrawn, but on the number of troops that remained. More intensive verification would be required to ensure that the ceilings had not been exceeded. For example, troop units might have to be selected randomly and then counted directly through on-site methods. Statistical procedures could then be employed to make reliable estimates of the number of troops each alliance has stationed within the region covered by the agreement. These procedures would need to be repeated regularly to assure that the ceiling was not later surpassed.

There is one clear advantage of verifying troop levels rather than troop reductions: the Warsaw Pact would be able to avoid admitting to possible errors in its data. Perhaps for this reason, Soviet representatives hinted at their interest in this option followwng the declaration issued at the Warsaw Pact Summit in Prague in January 1983. Of course, it is not yet certain that Soviet leaders would be willing to accept the more intrusive verification procedures that such an option would require. The measures they proposed in July 1983 fall short of making such a commitment, although they do indicate movement in this direction. In addition, the major Western opponent of such an option, West Germany, also hinted in 1983 that it might be ready to accept such intrusive verification measures.

The second issue disputed at the talks is closely related to the first. It concerns "associated measures," including provisions for verification, confidence-building, and non-circumvention. The Warsaw Pact long contended that any resolution of these issues would have to wait until an agreement had been reached on all other questions. In December 1979 NATO introduced a complex "associate measures" package intended to build mutual confidence and to facilitate the verification of other asepcts of the agreement. The package called for the prenotification of all military activities outside of normal garrisons by units of one division or more, including maneuvers and sizable troop movements. Under the NATO proposal, each side would have the right to send observers to these activities. Each side would also be required to give advance notification of movements by troops into and out of the area covered by the agreement. These movements would take place through fixed exit/entry points at which observers from each side would be stationed. In addition, information would be exchanged about the personnel strength and organization of forces left in the area, and provisions would be made for a specified number of annual inspections from the ground, the air, or both to ensure that force levels do not exceed the established ceilings. These provisions would thus build upon and strengthen the confidence-building measures established on a voluntary basis by the 1975 Helsinki Accords. NATO also proposed to set up a continuing consultative mechanism to help implement the agreement.

After several years of relative silence on the topic, the Warsaw Pact announced in 1983 that it would accept a number of the NATO provisions. Although the Eastern proposal remained vague on details, it appeared to endorse the creation of permanent observation posts at exit/entry points to verify force reductions. But because the Warsaw Pact also suggested that some measures remain voluntary, its proposal is likely to encounter some resistance. The voluntary aspects of the Helsinki Accords confidence-building measures have been widely criticized by Western and nonaligned delegations to the Madrid Review Conference on Security and Cooperation in Europe. Nonetheless, in agreeing to fixed observation posts, the Warsaw Pact removed one of the major obstacles to a MBFR agreement.

Before they were suspended, the negotiations dragged on for more than ten years, largely unwatched by the public and by political leaders. Progress at the talks was so slow, and the negotiations lasted so long, that areas of agreement, while genuine, often went unnoticed. Consequently, even well-informed observers are too readily inclined to dismiss the negotiations as hopeless.

But it is clear that the negotiations can be reopened and that an agreement can be reached, *if* both sides exert the political will needed to break through the few obstacles that remain. High-level political interest in the negotiations will be needed if an agreement is to be reached. The only way such attention can be generated is by an explicit acknowledgement of the inextricable link between the conventional balance and the role of nuclear weapons. To date, the MBFR talks have not been accorded the same status generally assigned to negotiations on nuclear weapons. A no-first-use proposal linked explicitly to the talks would confirm that a restored conventional balance can raise the nuclear threshold. But to make this clear, the West will need to take significant initiatives in Vienna. According to Jonathan Dean, former U.S. ambassador to the negotiations, in order for an agreement to be concluded,

> a sustained high-level political push from the Western participants will be necessary. Only this level of political engagement will elicit its counterpart on the side of the Soviet leadership, the engagement needed to override the resistance of the Soviet military establishment to decisive progress in the Vienna talks. If high-level political engagement can be achieved on both sides, completion of an agreement could follow within a year.[5]

---

[5] Jonathan Dean, "MBFR: From Apathy to Accord," *International Security*, Vol 7, No. 4 (Spring 1983), p. 137.

Political engagement, however, is unlikely to emerge from a vacuum. The West may need to take the initiative in order to convince the Soviet Union to resume talks and to accept such an agreement. Not only must Soviet political leaders, at a time of leadership transition, convince a reluctant military establishment to accept an agreement with the West, but they must also accept asymmetrical reductions in conventional manpower in Eastern Europe and either admit tacitly that previous data were in error or accept intrusive verification. A lever is needed, therefore, to overcome Soviet resistance to an agreement, and such a lever might well be provided most effectively by the no-first-use proposal.

This lever could work in several ways. The Soviet Union and its allies have long advocated a no-first-use policy, a position made public at the Second Special Session of the United Nations on Disarmament in 1982 and reaffirmed by the January 1983 Prague Declaration. The West has generally dismissed these proposals as cynical efforts by the Soviet Union to exploit its conventional superiority in Central Europe. Yet there is every reason to believe that Soviet leaders fear the consequences of a nuclear war in Europe. If so, they should be willing to make some compromises in order to reduce the probability that a conflict might escalate to the nuclear level.

The Soviet Union cannot fail to see the dangers entailed in an escalating arms race in Europe, in the deployments of intermediate-range nuclear missiles, and in the development of conventional "deep strike" capabilities. Soviet leaders clearly have an incentive to begin an arms control process in Europe that could make the deployment of new nuclear and provocative conventional forces by NATO far less likely. Indeed, an agreement on mutual force reductions and on a no-first-use policy might make an agreement on nuclear weapons easier to achieve, including the mutual reduction or elimination of intermediate-range nuclear delivery vehicles and the withdrawal of significant numbers of tactical nuclear weapons. Such a process could alleviate Soviet fears of a greater nuclear threat from Western Europe, and respond to Soviet concern about a substantial military buildup by West Germany. Finally, modest cost savings from reducing troop levels in Eastern Europe should provide an additional incentive for the Soviet Union to accept such a package agreement.

For these reasons, the Soviet Union might be willing to accept an agreement on conventional arms control if NATO were to propose a mutual no-first-use pledge. Such a bargain would have to include certain provisions. First, an agreement on real and verifiable parity of manpower in Central Europe would have to be reached. Second, sufficient confidence-building measures would be needed to assure each side that the other was not preparing a surprise conventional attack. If preparations for such an attack were detected, or if large numbers of troops above the limit were moved into the reduction zones, these measures should provide sufficient warning time for the other side to mobilize its conventional reinforcements. Third, in the event of massive violations of such an agreement, the other party would be released from its no-first-use pledge. Fourth, each side would have the right to maintain some nuclear forces in the zone, located away from the front line, to serve solely as a deterrent against their use by the other side.

The Benefits

Such a package agreement should provide greater stability and security in Central Europe than would either an agreement on conventional forces or a mutual no-first-use declaration taken individually. It would also overcome most political and military objections to the no-first-use policy raised in the West: it would establish conventional manpower parity in Central Europe and create confidence-building measures to ensure against undetected buildups and mobilizations of Warsaw Pact forces. A package agreement should thus be acceptable to leaders in both East and West.

First, and probably most important, the nuclear threshold would be raised. As long as nuclear weapons exist, nuclear war remains a possibility. A no-first-use agreement, while it would not guarantee that nuclear weapons would never be used, would force a change in the prevailing assumption that the first use of nuclear weapons would be likely and perhaps even necessary at an early stage of war in Europe. Changes in military equipment, tactics, and other operational measures would be required as a sign of commitment to the agreement. In particular, forward-based tactical nuclear weapons would need to be pulled back or withdrawn altogether to reduce pressures for rapid first use. The political climate between East and West would be improved as fears of rapid escalation to the nuclear level declined, along with the likelihood that panic, confusion, or misjudgment might cause leaders to resort to nuclear weapons at the outbreak of a conventional conflict. As a result, the possibility that limited conflicts over relatively minor issues might escalate into a nuclear conflagration would be greatly reduced.

An agreement on conventional parity in Central Europe, like a no-first-use policy, also would raise the nuclear threshold. Conventional manpower parity would imply that neither NATO nor the Warsaw Pact could launch a successful attack against the other without substantial reinforcements from outside the Central European zone. Thus deterrence at the conventional level would be maintained within the zone because neither side would possess the substantial superiority presumed necessary to launch an attack.

Especially worrisome to Western defense planners, however, is the possibility that Warsaw Pact troops might be mobilized and introduced into Central Europe along with large reinforcements from the western and southern military districts of the U.S.S.R. A conventional arms control agreement with significant confidence-building measures could reduce the threat of such an attack. Both the mobilization of reserves and the outside reinforcement of Warsaw Pact forces would constitute a clear and verifiable violation of the agreement. At present, Soviet reinforcements in Eastern Europe remain ambiguous, neither necessarily threatening nor necessarily benign. Under a major East-West arms control agreement, however, reinforcements above the ceiling would be a clear indication of hostile intent. Western military and intelligence analysts generally agree that such strategic warning could be crucial in preparing an effective NATO conventional defense against a surprise attack.

Furthermore, under such conditions, it would be far easier to gain political support for a Western military mobilization. At present, a comparable level of support could be generated only by an outright attack, in which case any military response might be too late. Almost all analysts of the European balance agree that the most serious threat NATO faces is the possibility that reinforced Warsaw Pact forces might attack before the West had time to countermobilize. Under an MBFR agreement, such an attack would either have to be launched with existing troops, in which case the attack almost certainly would fail, or it would have to be signalled in advance by a major mobilization which would give the defender an opportunity to mobilize in return. In either case, the ability of NATO to mount an effective conventional defense would be enhanced by an agreement. Not only would conventional deterrence be strengthened, but if war did break out in Europe, the existence of manpower parity there would make it easier to contain any conflict to the conventional level. While Europeans are correct to point out that a conventional war in Europe would do great damage, it is still far preferable that war, if it does come to Europe, be limited to conventional weapons. After a conventional war, civilization at least would have a chance to recover, albeit at great loss; after a nuclear war, even that chance might not exist.

Second, this proposal promises Europe a more effective, rational, and financially feasible defense policy, one with risks not grossly out of proportion to its ends. A major objection to the no-first-use proposal taken alone is that it would require either a reduction in the ability of Western Europe to defend itself against a conventional attack or substantial increases in Western defense expenditures. If an agreement were reached on manpower levels in Europe, one of the most expensive components of armed forces could then be reduced. Although some of the savings might be diverted to necessary improvements in training and equipment, these improvements might be made without major increases in Western defense budgets; and if the political climate permitted the funds could be rechannelled into the civilian economy or be used to meet other pressing governmental needs.

The no-first-use proposal, moreover, would require Western political leaders to take conventional defense, and all of its ramifications, more seriously than they do at present. They would no longer be able to view nuclear weapons as a quick and economical solution to all of their defense problems. They would have to develop military programs and strategies that give greater priority to an adequate conventional defense within the limitations imposed by an MBFR agreement. Because they could assume conventional manpower parity in Central Europe, their task would be easier than at present. In particular, NATO's fascination with high-technology hardware has often led to a serious neglect of less exotic conventional forces. Improvements in the quality of basic arms and equipment, better training, and longer terms of military service in some countries all could enhance the effectiveness of conventional deterrence, and at relatively low cost.

Third, this proposal would reduce either the likelihood or the extent of an arms race in Europe. If a no-first-use proposal were adopted, then at least some new nuclear weapons would not seem as necessary as they now do. The West would no longer need to rely as heavily on these weapons for its defense against a non-nuclear attack. A conventional arms control agreement in Vienna would make it less probable that a no-first-use agreement would be accompanied by an accelerating conventional arms race. Although some qualitative improvements in conventional weapons might take place, major quantitative increases would be severely limited. Furthermore, the precedent set by an agreement to limit manpower in Central Europe might encourage a second round of negotiations to limit conventional armaments there. An MBFR agreement would break the stalemate on conventional arms control which has lasted through the past decade and could lead to additional restraints on the conventional arms race in Europe.

Fourth, such a dual agreement would reduce some of the major tensions that now exist within the Atlantic alliance. Both a no-first-use policy and an agreement on conventional force reductions would be widely favored, especially by those in the peace movement. They might help to heal current domestic divisions, especially if they reduced simultaneously the danger of nuclear escalation in Europe and the dangers of a new race in provocative conventional armaments. At the same time, the linkage of a no-first-use agreement with a mutual manpower ceiling and improved confidence-building measures would tend to reassure those in Western Europe who now are hesitant to abandon the first-use option. It should also ease tensions with NATO about sharing the burdens of conventional defense without increasing the demands made on already tight budgets.

Although the dependence of Western Europe on American nuclear weapons would not be completely eliminated, it almost certainly would be reduced. Nuclear weapons would play a less central role in NATO strategy for at least two reasons. The no-first-use agreement would mean that these weapons could no longer figure prominently in NATO's plans to respond to a conventional conflict in Europe. In addition, an agreement to limit conventional forces would allow Western Europe greater confidence in its ability to defend itself conventionally in collaboration with U.S. conventional forces. Indeed, these forces would appropriately become a more central symbol of the American commitment to defend Europe. The continued presence of American troops there would serve to reassure the allies that the United States is psychologically, politically, and militarily committed to their defense, precisely because such a commitment would not entail risks for the United States as severe as those posed by the first-use option.

A dual agreement, moreover, because it would be negotiated in a forum that included the European allies, would give them a greater feeling of participation than would a bilateral no-first-use pledge by the superpowers. Because this pledge would be part of a binding, multilateral agreement involving the European members of both alliances, it would reduce fears of tacit or explicit agreements between the superpowers that might not serve the interest of the European members of either alliance.

Fifth, and finally, an agreement along the lines proposed here would reduce East-West tensions, which once again have become severe. A major East-West arms control agreement, after years of stalemate and the failure of the United States to ratify the SALT II treaty, would itself represent substantial progress in East-West relations. A mutual no-first-use pledge should calm the fears of nuclear war that haunt citizens and governments everywhere and that make cooperation on other, more mundane international issues very difficult to achieve. A conventional arms control agreement should also reduce fears of a surprise attack, which have grown in Europe in recent years. Even more important, an agreement that eased these fears could initiate a process of ever more significant measures of arms control and disarmament in Europe, perhaps culminating in the creation of a nuclear-free-zone in Central Europe.

The proposal to link a no-first-use policy with conventional force limitations in Europe represents not only a way to resolve the current strains within the Atlantic alliance, but also the first step in a process of negotiating a more durable security arrangement in Europe. It is a step that can be taken now, that builds on previous negotiations, and that may offer a way out of the present impasse. By promoting a positively reinforcing cycle of arms control and detente, it could make progress on arms control and disarmament easier in the years ahead. In the short run, it could enhance political, economic, scientific, and humanitarian cooperation between East and West. Any measure that offers hope that the arms race and the international and domestic tensions it both spawns and reflects may be curtailed, and eventually ended, deserves to be considered openly and seriously by political leaders in both East and West.

FOR FURTHER READING

European Security Study. *Strengthening Conventional Deterrence in Europe: Proposals for the 1980s*. New York: St. Martin's, 1983. The influential study directed by distinguished former European and American military and political leaders which argues that an improved NATO conventional defense capability is economically and strategically feasible, particularly if NATO exploits new non-nuclear weapons technologies in the context of a "deep-strike" interdiction strategy.

Evangelista, Matthew. "Stalin's Postwar Army Reappraised." *International Security* 7 (Winter 1982/1983), pp. 110–28. Based on recently declassified U.S. Government documents, this article argues that U.S. policymakers consistently exaggerated the Soviet non-nuclear military threat faced by Western Europe in the early Cold War period.

Kaiser, Karl, et al. "Nuclear Weapons and the Preservation of Peace: A German Response." *Foreign Affairs* 60 (Summer 1982), pp. 1157–70. Mainstream German national security specialists react to the Bundy, et al., No First Use proposal.

McNamara, Robert S. "The Military Role of Nuclear Weapons." *Foreign Affairs* 62 (Fall 1983), pp. 59–80. In a follow-up to the Bundy, et al., No First Use article, the former Secretary of Defense asserts that the military utility of nuclear weapons is limited only to the purpose of deterring the use of nuclear weapons by other countries.

Mearsheimer, John J. "Why the Soviets Can't Win Quickly in Central Europe." *International Security* 7 (Summer 1982), pp. 3–39. Analyzes the NATO–Warsaw Pact conventional military balance in Central Europe and concludes that NATO has good prospects of defending against a Warsaw Pact non-nuclear attack without resorting to the use of nuclear weapons.

Record, Jeffrey. *NATO's Theater Nuclear Force Modernization Program: The Real Issues*. Cambridge, Mass.: Institute for Foreign Policy Analysis, 1981. An analysis of NATO's "Two-tracked Decision" of 1979, underscoring the need to improve NATO's theater nuclear capabilities in order to redress Soviet advantages in long-range theater nuclear forces.

Sigal, Leon V. *Nuclear Forces in Europe: Enduring Dilemmas, Present Prospects*. Washington, D.C.: Brookings, 1984. Examines NATO's nuclear dilemmas, with special emphasis on intermediate nuclear force modernization issues, and the prospects for INF arms control.

Steinbruner, John D., and Leon V. Sigal, eds. *Alliance Security: NATO and the No First Use Question*. Washington, D.C.: Brookings, 1983. A survey of articles on critical issues related to the No First Use proposal, including an historical perspective on NATO strategy, and individual chapters on the prospects for effective conventional deterrence, Soviet theater military strategy, German views of No First Use, and other issues.

Ulman, Neil. "No First Use? Germans Answer Bundy and Co." *Wall Street Journal* (July 9, 1982). Discussion of the West German national security establishment's reaction to the No First Use proposal.

U.S. Congressional Budget Office. *Army Ground Combat Modernization for the 1980s: Potential Costs and Effects for NATO*. Washington, D.C.: U.S. Government Printing Office, 1982. Analyzes and evaluates prospects for improving NATO's conventional military forces, underscoring the weaknesses in NATO's current posture and the high cost of improving the situation.

Van Cleave, William R., and S. T. Cohen. *Tactical Nuclear Weapons: An Examination of the Issues.* New York: Crane Russak, 1978. The authors argue that NATO can develop "clean" battlefield nuclear weapons (like the "neutron bomb") which will make a tactical nuclear defense of Western Europe possible, thus compensating for NATO's non-nuclear weaknesses.

David S. Yost, ed. *NATO's Strategic Options: Arms Control and Defense.* New York: Pergamon Press, 1981. A collection of conservative perspectives on major strategic issues facing NATO.

7

How Much Is Enough?
Assessing the U.S.-Soviet Strategic Balance

This chapter has two objectives. One is to provide information about the various nuclear weapons programs the Soviet Union and the United States now have under way, and how these planned additions and qualitative improvements will affect strategic stability. A second is to examine the various ways in which analysts look at the strategic balance between the United States and the Soviet Union in trying to determine whether American nuclear forces are adequate to protect American security.

Perhaps the most important impression one should take away from a reading of the first two selections in this chapter is that each superpower is pursuing capabilities *far in excess* of what is necessary to provide a secure retaliatory deterrent capability. These levels of capability appear to express each country's desire to achieve the means to fight, and not merely to deter, a nuclear war with the other. Each country appears intent not only on developing the capability to strike at and destroy the other side's offensive nuclear weapons, but on devising means by which to actually defend against attack by the other country as well.

According to the U.S. Department of Defense's analysis of Soviet "Forces for Global Warfare," for example, the Soviet deployment of the ss-18/mod 4 and the ss-19/mod 3 ICBMs have provided them with at least a theoretical capability to destroy over 80 percent of the U.S. land-based Minuteman missile force. This Soviet counterforce capability, meanwhile, is complemented by continuing improvements in Soviet air defenses, as well as high levels of investment and research on ballistic missile defenses and civil defense. Similarly, the Center for Defense Information's report on "The Status of U.S. Nuclear Weapons Programs" describes American modernization programs which appear consistent with a nuclear war-fighting orientation. The Reagan administration wishes to deploy three new missiles—the MX and Midgetman ICBMs, and the Trident II SLBM, each of which will be theoretically accurate enough to destroy Soviet ICBMs in their hardened underground silos. The administration has also initiated efforts to improve U.S. air defenses, and has inaugurated, under the auspices of President Reagan's Strategic Defense Initiative, a major effort to develop and deploy a space-based, "leakage-proof" defense against ballistic missile warheads. (This issue will be examined in Chapter 12.)

The destabilizing aspects of this joint trend towards both offensive and defensive nuclear war-fighting capabilities will be examined in more detail in Chapter 8, when we examine possible "Paths to Nuclear War." At this point, we will only observe that these efforts to render ineffective the retaliatory forces of the other side, through some combination of counterforce offensive capabilities and effective strategic defenses, could *increase* each side's sense of vulnerability in a crisis, and in turn increase the risk of an intentional or accidental use of nuclear weapons by one side or the other.

Simultaneously, each country is now developing or deploying a variety of small, nuclear-armed, long-range, pilotless jet aircraft called *cruise missiles.* These are being developed as a hedge against what appears to be the growing vulnerability of existing nuclear delivery systems to prelaunch attack (as with silo-based ICBMs), or the other side's defenses (as with heavy bombers). Cruise missiles, because of their small size and high mobility, could eventually enhance the invulnerability and retaliatory potential of each side's offensive forces, thus counteracting the potentially destabilizing effects of the strategic weapons improvements discussed above. And yet these same characteristics will also make cruise missiles very difficult to locate and count for the purposes of verifying arms control agreements, so their widespread deployment woud pose costs and create uncertainties as well.

At a minimum, we can conclude from these two articles that there is tremendous momentum in each country's nuclear weapons programs, which threatens to make the world a more dangerous place in which to live. This dynamism also makes any effort to assess and compare the relative capabilities of the two countries at any one point in time somewhat problematic, because the composition and size of each side's force may change significantly in the space of a few years. Yet the state of the strategic balance is an important issue, one which bears directly on such critical areas of policy as weapons modernization and arms control. Generally speaking, if the strategic balance is deemed to be unfavorable to the United States, policymakers are likely to insist on some measure of arms modernization in advance of, or in conjunction with, the conclusion of arms control measures with the Soviet Union. Conversely, if U.S. nuclear forces appear adequate to carry out national policy, this makes negotiated, mutual arms restraints with the Soviet Union a more immediately feasible alternative.

This enterprise of "measuring" the U.S.-Soviet nuclear balance, however, should be approached with caution. In particular, students must be aware of the various approaches which can be taken in analyzing the strategic balance, and the advantages and disadvantages of each. As Marie Hoguet points out in "Beancounting and Wargaming: How to Analyze the Strategic Balance," one must be especially sensitive to the potential for distorting the relative nuclear capabilities of the two countries when simple "beancounts" of each side's forces are used for comparison. Too often, she argues, quantitative comparisons are stressed to the neglect of qualitative aspects of strategic capability. Another problem with "beancounts," she points out, is that many quantitative and qualitative aspects of military capability, like missile warhead yield and accuracy, can only be estimated, and are subject to potentially large uncertainties.

More illuminating and reliable, she argues, are studies which try to evaluate how each side's forces would actually fare in a nuclear war, using the techniques of computer simulation. Studies based on such "force-exchange" comparisons must also be scrutinized carefully, however. Particularly important is to examine the underlying assumptions of the force-exchange model employed. If these assumptions are unrealistic or are based on inadequate information, the model itself may be of no more value in gauging relative U.S. and Soviet strategic capabilities than simple "beancounts."

John Harris, in his "Assessing the Adequacy of U.S. Nuclear Forces," observes that differing interpretations of the strategic balance may be rooted in conflicting views about the "usability" of nuclear weapons, and the roles they should play in U.S. security policy. Students must not only be aware of the methodological problems discussed by Hoguet, he argues, but they must be sensitive as well to the *strategic assumptions* which lie behind an analyst's interpretation of the strategic balance, and sensitive to how these assumptions may affect his or her view of the issue.

THE STATUS OF U.S. NUCLEAR WEAPONS PROGRAMS

The Center for Defense Information

The Center for Defense Information is a Washington-based, non-profit public education organization which "supports a strong defense but opposes excessive expenditures and policies that increase the danger of nuclear war."

MX MISSILE

On April 19, 1983 President Reagan announced his endorsement of the recommendations of his Commission on Strategic Forces chaired by retired Air Force General Brent Scowcroft. The Scowcroft Commission was formed in January by the President to salvage the MX missile which was then facing Congressional defeat.

Source: The Center for Defense Information, "The Status of U.S. Nuclear Weapons Programs," *The Defense Monitor,* 12:7 (1983), pp. 6–15. Copyright © 1984 by the Center for Defense Information, Washington, D.C. Reprinted by permission.

The Commission's problem was primarily a political and public relations one of how to best sell the MX to a skeptical Congress and public so as to gain enough support to begin producing the missile. Their solution was to link the missile to arms control, promote it as a symbol of our national will, and recommend a follow-on small missile in the 1990's.

The MX has had a long and tortured history and the American people have good reason to be confused since they have been given so many contradictory rationales for why it is needed and how best to base it. For years a steady drumbeat of alarms was raised that our land-based missile force was vulnerable to a Soviet first strike. This alleged "window of vulnerability" had to be closed and MX was offered as the solution. More than thirty basing schemes were considered as solutions to the vulnerability problem and found flawed for cost, environmental, or arms control reasons. At different times officials have told the American people that the best plan for MX was to scatter 200 missiles amidst 4600 shelters in Utah and Nevada. Later the best plan was to concentrate 100 in a few square miles in a scheme called Dense Pack. Now the latest plan is to put at least 100 in the Minuteman silos we have been told for years were vulnerable.

Under questioning by Congress, Commission members were asked what happened to the "window." General Scowcroft responded with the argument MX critics had been making for years: "Whatever the Soviets conclude from their test data of missile firings, they have to have considerably greater skepticism about their ability to translate that into an operational maneuver, never before tried, never practiced, which has to work perfectly the first time." He also rediscovered our submarine and bomber forces where three-quarters of our strategic weapons reside, which had been conveniently forgotten when the window theory held sway.

Now that the "window of vulnerability" has gone the way of the "bomber gap" and the "missile gap," new rationalizations are offered. Prime among them is MX's warfighting potential. It is an ideal weapon to threaten and hit Soviet targets and the Pentagon is finally acknowledging it. Chairman of the Joint Chiefs of Staff General Vessey stated: "We have to look at the prospect of deterrence failing and actually having to fight a nuclear war. We want to tell you [Congress] that the hard-target kill capability of the MX has a usefulness there."

We have felt the weight of the Soviets threatening our targets, so the argument runs, and now we must do the same to them. How this contributes to stability, which was the Commission's stated main goal, is difficult to discern. General Vessey and Air Force Chief of Staff Gabriel indicated that we may be forced to a "launch on warning" policy and the Soviets have repeatedly stated that they will be forced to do the same.

A further rationalization for MX was to link it with arms control, a measure designed to gain Congressional support, though the exact relationship remains unclear. MX is sometimes presented as a "bargaining chip." However, while this strategy would seem to leave open the possibility of cancelling or limiting the missile, such is not the President's interpretation. He said in December 1982, that "even if we get the reductions of arms, this would not be the missile that would be taken out of circulation."

The Administration's real bargaining chip strategy is apparently to threaten the Soviets with *increased* deployments of MX (and Trident II) if they do not reduce their heavy and medium missile force from 800 to 210, the current Reagan proposal at the START talks in Geneva. Significantly, a secret Air Force planning document, dated May 11, 1983, referred to the "follow-on deployment" of a second 100 MX missiles.

The best estimate for the cost of the MX program, with the warheads, is $31.5 billion, or an average cost of over $300 million per operational missile.

MIDGETMAN

Entwined in the MX debate is the issue of a small ICBM (SICBM) or "Midgetman." The Scowcroft Commission recommended beginning research and development of a small single warhead ICBM to be ready in the early 1990's. The rationale for moving in this direction was belated recognition of the fact that MIRVed missiles are destabilizing.

The Air Force envisions a three stage, fifteen ton missile about 38 feet long with a nuclear warhead of 1,100 pounds and a range of over 6000 nautical miles. The Scowcroft Commission recommended a missile which could destroy Soviet missiles. As they said, it "should have sufficient accuracy and yield to put Soviet hardened military targets at risk." Yields of 200 kt, 470 kt, and 700 kt have been mentioned. It may be equipped with a terminal guidance system similar to the Pershing II which would give it an accuracy of 100 feet.

Many uncertainties exist over the number of missiles, how they would be based, and the cost. The most frequently mentioned number is 1000 Midgetman missiles, though 500, 3350, and 5000 have been suggested. Midgetman could be based in a variety of ways, though the two most frequently mentioned are in fixed hardened silos or on mobile armored vehicles stationed at military reservations. The mobile vehicles would be equipped with suction or corkscrew devices to anchor them in the ground so as not to be tipped over by nuclear blast during an attack.

The Department of Defense estimates that the cost for 1000 Midgetman missiles, depending on how they are based, will be $38–$70 billion. Some systems would need almost 50,000 personnel to operate, maintain and guard them, pushing costs to $3 billion a year.

It is difficult to assess the need for the proposed small ICBM without knowing factors such as arms control agreements and other nuclear forces. Incentives for a first strike in times of crisis would be lessened if both the U.S. and the Soviet Union "de-MIRVed" their ICBMs. Because an attacker would have to expend at least two warheads to be certain of knocking out a single missile they will have gained no advantage. In this respect Midgetman may lead to a reduction in the number of strategic nuclear warheads, but only if strategic forces as a whole are limited.

In other respects Midgetman poses major verification problems and would be inconsistent with several provisions of the SALT agreements.

TRIDENT SUBMARINES AND MISSILES

After many delays and cost overruns Trident submarines are finally entering the active fleet. The first two, the *USS Ohio* and the *USS Michigan*, are now on patrol and a third, the *USS Florida,* was commissioned in June. Through FY 83 ten Trident submarines have been authorized and funded. The FY 84 budget proposes $1.8 billion for an eleventh and initial money for a twelfth and thirteenth. In the long term the Navy envisions a force of 20–22 subs, though it could rise to 25 early in the next century. The present Trident programs are computed on the basis of 15 subs and with the missiles, warheads, and bases the total cost is $75 billion. If 20 Trident submarines are built the cost will be approximately $92 billion; if 25 are built it will cost $108 billion.

The Navy has just finished retrofitting twelve Lafayette-class submarines with Trident I missiles at an additional cost of $3.7 billion. Trident I missiles will temporarily be put on the first eight Trident subs. The Navy recently decided to begin installing longer range, more accurate Trident II (D-5) missiles on the ninth submarine, scheduled for delivery in December 1988. By 1996 the first eight would be retrofitted with D-5 missiles.

The Navy plans to buy 740 Trident II missiles for 15 subs. If 25 subs are bought more than a thousand missiles would be needed. Each missile will probably be MIRVed with 10 warheads. The recently chosen new reentry vehicle, called the Mark 5, will carry a 475 kiloton (W-87) warhead and be comparable to MX with accuracies of 400-500 feet.

The Navy foresees a peak ballistic missile submarine force in 1992 of 31 Lafayette-class subs and 14 Tridents carrying 832 MIRVed missiles with approximately 7700 warheads. If all Lafayette-class subs are retired at the end of their 30 year lifespans between 1993 and 1997 and if more Trident subs are built, by the year 2002 there would be 25 Trident subs carrying 600 Trident II missiles with approximately 6000 warheads.

The Navy also plans to buy fifteen new E-6A (modified Boeing 707) communication aircraft at a cost of $2.2 billion. These special planes, some always in the air, would relay nuclear firing orders to the submarines.

LONG-RANGE BOMBERS

The Reagan Administration is pursuing a variety of ambitious, costly, and redundant bomber programs.

B-52 Bomber. On a continuing basis the B-52s have been improved with more modern navigation, communication and electronic countermeasure systems and have been modified to carry various kinds of missiles, the most recent of which is the air-launched cruise missile (ALCM). The cost of these programs is upwards of $6 billion. There are conflicting assessments from the Pentagon of the B-52's ability to bomb the Soviet Union. Upon leaving office Secretary of Defense Harold Brown stated that with these improvements "the B-52 force can remain effective into the 1990s." Needing a reason to revive the B-1, the Reagan Administration has repeatedly questioned the B-52's viability. The recent edition of the Pentagon's booklet *Soviet Military Power* states that the "aging B-52G/H bombers will not be capable of effectively penetrating the Soviet air defenses in the mid-1980s."

B-1B Bomber. The B-1B has a long and controversial history. Cancelled by President Carter in 1977, it was revived by President Reagan in 1981 at four times the original cost. The Air Force has yet to clearly define what unique mission the B-1B could fulfill. The original rationale that it was needed as a penetrating bomber to replace the aging B-52s is suspect in view of recent Air Force comments that even the much smaller ALCM is now vulnerable to Soviet air defenses. The Pentagon is now touting the B-1B as a cruise missile launcher and conventional bomber. Neither mission requires a $400 million-per-copy plane.

The first 16 B-1B bombers are scheduled to go into operation at Dyess Air Force Base in Texas in the fall of 1986. The Air Force has already bought eight planes and is requesting ten this year at a cost of $6.9 billion, including research monies. Next year 34 will be requested at a cost of $8.5 billion.

The Air Force has made a firm promise to Congress to keep B-1B total costs at $28.3 billion for a fleet of 100. This may only be possible through creative bookkeeping and by omitting certain items. The Congressional Budget Office noted this technique and estimated the cost for complete airplanes at $40 billion.

Advanced Technology Bomber. The Advanced Technology Bomber (ATB), employing the latest advances in "stealth" technology, is supposed to be the U.S. bomber for the 21st century. Stealth technology encompasses assorted design configurations, engine modifications, electronic countermeasures, and non-metallic materials that reduce a plane's radar cross-section and infrared detectability to mask it from Soviet radar and sensors. The target date for fielding the first of a possible 132 Advanced Technology Bombers is 1991, but there has been talk of a crash program to produce a Stealth bomber as early as 1988. In the meantime the Air Force is incorporating some stealth features into the B-1B. While the exact amounts are classified one estimate for research costs for the next five years is over $6 billion. Judging by the B-1B program the cost of the ATB could approach $40-$50 billion.

CRUISE MISSILES

These miniature, jet propelled missiles can be launched from air, sea, or land platforms. The total cost of more than 9000 of three different varieties of cruise missiles will be $27 billion. Reportedly, a longer-term cruise missile program may encompass some 30,000 at a cost of over $63 billion.

Air-Launched Cruise Missiles (ALCM). Originally the Pentagon planned to build 4348 ALCMs at a total cost of $8.5 billion. As the FY 84 budget was being prepared it decided to limit the ALCM program to 1739 missiles and go directly to an Advanced Cruise Missile (ACM). The ALCM will equip 105 B-52G bombers with 12 missiles each at six bases. Two squadrons are already on alert, one at Griffiss Air Force Base, Rome, New York and the second at Wurtsmith Air Force Base, Oscoda, Michigan.

Little is known about the ACM program. General Dynamics has been chosen to build the missile. There are various reports on how many will be built. According to Secretary of the Air Force Verne Orr there has been no change from the 4348 total which would mean approximately 2600 ACMs. Other accounts put the number at half that. Though its funding has been hidden in a secret account one source puts the cost at $7 billion. What is known is that the new missile will have improved accuracy, greater range (4000–6000 miles as opposed to the ALCM's 1500), increased speed, and be less visible through stealth characteristics.

The fate of the ALCM program graphically illustrates how military technology advances so quickly that some weapons are obsolete even before being fully deployed. The Advanced Cruise Missile will not only be a more capable weapon, but a substantially different one. The ALCM could be viewed as "stabilizing" because its slow speed makes it an ineffective first strike weapon. The ACM, however, with its higher speeds and longer range could be a potential first strike weapon, if coordinated in large numbers with other weapons.

Ground-Launched Cruise Missile (GLCM). In December 1979 NATO agreed to deploy 464 GLCMs in Europe in a dual-track decision designed in part to counter the Soviet Union's deployment of SS-20 missiles if negotiations to reduce theater nuclear weapons proved unsuccessful. The GLCMs will be distributed and deployed as follows: 96 at RAF Greenham Common, U.K. beginning in December 1983; 112 at Comiso, Italy beginning in March 1984; 48 at Florennes, Belgium beginning in 1985; 96 at Wüschheim, West Germany beginning in 1986; 48 at Woensdrecht, Netherlands beginning December 1986; and 64 at RAF Molesworth, U.K. beginning in 1987.

The GLCM program has been plagued by technical and management problems and its schedule has slipped consistently. Nonetheless, the Pentagon is determined to meet its December 1983 deadline and is producing the GLCM concurrent with flight testing and fine tuning. As Rep. Joseph Addabbo, Chairman of the House Subcommittee on Defense Appropriations, has noted, such "high degrees of concurrency have led to high risks and in many cases, excessive costs." Indeed, the cost of the program has skyrocketed from $1.9 billion to $3.6 billion since initiated in 1977. If all missiles are sent to the six European bases, annual operating costs could be over $1 billion. The DOD is requesting $616 million in FY 84 to buy 120 GLCMs and another $172 million to construct bases in Europe.

Sea-launched Cruise Missiles (SLCM). The SLCM is the most costly of the Pentagon's cruise missile projects and a major component of President Reagan's naval buildup. The present $11.5 billion "Tomahawk" cruise missile package includes 593 short-range anti-ship, 758 nuclear land-attack, and 2,643 conventional land-attack missiles. The Navy has ordered 3,994 sea-launched cruise missiles for use on 76 surface ships and 80 submarines by the early 1990's. The ships and submarines designated to get SLCMs include: 31 Spruance- and 15 Burke-class destroyers; 4 battleships; 19 Ticonderoga, 1 Long Beach, 2 California and 4 Virginia-class cruisers; 37 Sturgeon, 41 Los Angeles, 1 Narwhal, and 1 Lipscomb-class attack submarines.

The SLCM program has encountered even rougher going than the GLCM project, with the conventional land-attack version in the worst shape. Testing and production of the 1500 mile conventionally-armed missile has slowed to a crawl while the contractor redesigns it. The 1,500 mile, 200-kiloton nuclear land-attack missile will go on attack submarines and surface ships beginning in June 1984. The 250-mile, conventionally-armed anti-ship SLCM is already on the attack sub "Guitarro" and it will be put on the destroyer "Merrill" in March 1984, some 15 months behind schedule. Thus far, out of a total of 106 Tomahawk test flights 28 have been failures, a poor record that has brought pressure from Congress. The Senate Armed Services Committee has served notice to the Navy that, unless test performances and program management improve it may cancel the program. In strong language the Committee noted the rise in cost, the unacceptable performance by the Navy and the contractors, and questioned the wisdom of placing nuclear SLCMs on surface ships, stating that the Navy had "not clearly formulated and articulated its strategic planning and concept of operations for the TLAM-Ns." As a result it cut back the number the Navy requested for FY 84 from 112 to 88 missiles.

There are other problems with SLCMs that should be addressed. The nuclear land-attack missile will pose serious verification problems in any arms control agreement. Once both the U.S. and the Soviet Union have huge arsenals of long-range SLCMs—and the Soviets are working on a program of their own—nearly every type of ship becomes a potential nuclear attack platform. Because the conventional and nuclear models are indistinguishable and the missile is so compact, verifying its presence and numbers will be virtually impossible.

The Navy is pusuing its own advanced cruise missile program. Once deployed, the sea-launched ACM will raise even more serious first-strike concerns than the air-launched ACM.

PERSHING II

The deployment of 108 Pershing II launchers was also part of the 1979 NATO decision. This December [1983] the first nine missiles (plus four spares) are scheduled to go to the U.S. battalion at Schwäbisch Gmünd in southern Germany. Over the next two years, the balance of the missiles will go there as well as to the other bases at Heilbronn, Neckarsulm, and Neu Ulm.

The Pershing II is a formidable weapon, much more capable than the Pershing Ia it is replacing. With a range of 1800 kilometers, this mobile missile will be able to deliver a 10-20 kiloton warhead to within 65–130 feet of its target. While it may not be able to reach Moscow, the Pershing II will still be able to strike many key targets such as hardened command bunkers and nuclear storage sites in the Western USSR. Because the Pershing warheads could hit them less than 10 minutes after launch, the Soviets have threatened to adopt a "launch on warning" policy in response to the first strike potential of these new missiles.

Originally the Army planned 216 missiles instead of 108, consigning a reload missile to each Pershing II launcher in Germany. When German Chancellor Helmut Kohl learned of this confidential plan he refused to accept any more than the agreed upon number. The Army was planning to buy approximately 380 missiles though now the number may be somewhat fewer. Extra missiles are generally purchased for spares, testing, and in this case for a Pershing training battalion stationed in the U.S.

Under the pressure of the December 1983 deadline, the original test program of 28 flights was compressed to 18, with a predictably high failure rate. Of the seventeen tests held thus far five have been failures. The cost of the program has risen to $2.7 billion, a billion more than the original estimate in 1979.

BATTLEFIELD NUCLEAR WEAPONS

Among the more controversial decisions made by the Reagan Administration was one to build—but not deploy—neutron weapons for the European battlefield. Last year 380 Lance missile neutron warheads were produced and are now likely stored in the Seneca Army Depot in upstate New York. Approximately 800 eight-inch neutron artillery shells are also being built.

Among military analysts and within NATO itself there is growing doubt as to the purpose and utility of neutron and other battlefield nuclear weapons. Often cited as the nuclear weapons most likely to be exploded first, many feel that once used, escalation to global nuclear war would be rapid. General Bernard Rogers, the Supreme Allied Commander-Europe, said he was "one of those who believes that certainly under current conditions there would be a very quick escalation to the strategic level."

There is strong sentiment within NATO to cut back on European nuclear battlefield weapons, one proposal calling for reductions by as many as 2,000. Most likely to be affected would be the nuclear Nike-Hercules air defense missile, nuclear land mines, and nuclear artillery shells. Some of these weapons would be replaced by conventional versions, but others would be supplanted by more modern nuclear weapons, such as the GLCM. A recent report by the North Atlantic Assembly calling for reductions said, "many of the systems lack accuracy . . . the warhead yields are too large for battlefield use" and "there is growing realization that the present tactical nuclear systems are effectively unusable and therefore NATO has little to lose and much to gain, particularly in a political sense, by reducing if not eliminating them."

A Senate committee recently stated that "the DOE and DOD have grave concerns about the safety and the military usefulness of [the 8-inch] atomic projectile."

No such doubts seem to have assailed the Army, which is asking for $64 million this year and twice that next year to begin developing 155-mm neutron artillery shells. Funded also in the DOE budget, the cost for approximately 1,000 could be $3 billion.

AIR DEFENSE

The Reagan Administration has undertaken a $7.8 billion program to upgrade continental United States (CONUS) air defense. In the early 1960's, the U.S. guarded against Soviet bomber attack with over 2,600 interceptor aircraft, 439 Bomarc surface-to-air nuclear missiles, hundreds of radars, ships and other aircraft staffed by over 200,000 military personnel. With the introduction of missiles which reach their targets within 8 to 30 minutes and against which there is no real defense, the United States gradually reduced its air defenses over the 1960's.

Now, citing a threat from the Soviet Backfire bomber, a future Soviet bomber code-named Blackjack, and future long-range cruise missiles, the Pentagon wants a variety of new programs. The Air Force plans to buy 144 F-15 fighters for use as air interceptors and, eventually, the Air National Guard would get new planes as well. In 1979, Airborne Warning and Control System (AWACS) aircraft went into use for CONUS air defense and the Air Force wants to buy an additional 12 AWACS between 1985–89. New radars which see over the horizon out to 2,000 miles are planned for the east and west coasts. About $600 to $700 million would be spent on upgrading the Distant Early Warning (DEW) line of radars stretching across Alaska, northern Canada, and Greenland. The Air Force wants to increase the current 31 radars to 50, of which 37 would not have on-site personnel.

This $7.8 billion CONUS defense program might well be but the tip of a very large iceberg. The Pentagon has estimated that the U.S. bomber and cruise missile buildup could force the Soviets to spend between $200 and $400 billion on air defense improvements. Now that the Soviets are striving to match our capability, we may find ourselves having to spend similar amounts to defend against their new weapons.

BALLISTIC MISSILE DEFENSE (BMD)

In what could be a far reaching shift in U.S. strategic policy and the arms race President Reagan on March 23, 1983 proposed a research effort to develop an anti-missile system. Two days later he signed National Security Decision Directive No. 85 entitled "Eliminating the Threat From Ballistic Missiles" which starts the implementation. The Secretary of Defense has set up a special committee which will report in the fall on funding recommendations and plans.

President Reagan, evoking a sense of inevitability about nuclear war, said that it was "inconceivable" that the U.S. and the Soviet Union could continue to threaten one another "each with a cocked gun, and no one knowing whether someone might tighten their finger on the trigger." The President's fears are well founded though his recommendation to alleviate it has brought forth widespread criticism from many sectors.

The scientific community has generally expressed skepticism about the technical feasibility of stopping ballistic missiles. The general consensus, given the vast destructiveness of nuclear weapons, is that there is no known defense against them. The offense can always overwhelm the defense. The present Administration's refusal to acknowledge this fact may lead us to embark on what former Secretary of Defense Harold Brown says "could well become the first trillion-dollar defense system."

The Administration has tried to gain the moral high ground with this new emphasis on defense, notwithstanding its own massive offensive buildup. Admiral James Watkins, Chief of Naval Operations, has recently said, "We must examine the possible contribution of *defensive* (his emphasis) systems to deter and provide for the security of the United States and our allies while making obsolete the large inventories of insidious nuclear bullets . . . Depending on retaliation—and accepting vulnerability—is neither a moral nor a sensible way for a God-fearing people to live when there is a rational, practical, and moral alternative."

The alternative may seem alluring to some who think that nuclear weapons have been less than revolutionary in their impact on warfare, but most experts have noted the destabilizing and dangerous consequences of proceeding with such systems. In concert with offensive warfighting weapons, a BMD could accelerate the likelihood of a U.S. first strike by blunting somewhat the impact of a Soviet retaliatory attack.

The DOD plans to spend almost $8 billion over the next three years for research on missile defense systems. . . .

ANTI-SATELLITE WARFARE

We stand at a crossroads in our use of outer space. The U.S. civilian space program, long a source of national pride, is being overtaken by rapidly expanding efforts to exploit space for military advantage. The Reagan Administration views space as an arena in which the U.S. must be prepared to fight a protracted nuclear war. It is the "high ground" which the United States must dominate.

Since the space systems described above have become so central to nuclear warfighting capabilities, it is not surprising that both superpowers are working on anti-satellite (ASAT) weapons to knock them out. While the U.S. abandoned its nuclear explosion ASAT system in the mid-1970's, the Soviet Union has been testing a non-nuclear orbiting "killer satellite" since 1968.

The U.S. has now developed a far more sophisticated ASAT, a rocket interceptor fired from a F-15 fighter plane. Sometime this fall the Air Force will begin conducting flight tests of the F-15 ASAT, which should be operational by 1987. While the U.S. ASAT program was originally supposed to cost $2.7 billion it is now estimated at $3.6 billion. The General Accounting Office has said that it may well cost "in the tens of billions of dollars." The FY 84 budget request is $333.4 million for continued R&D, limited production, and supporting C^3.

Soviet Military Power 1985: Forces for Nuclear Attack and Strategic Defense

U.S. Department of Defense

> The following article is excerpted from *Soviet Military Power,* an annual, illustrated publication of the U.S. Department of Defense that interprets the scope and nature of the Soviet military threat to the United States and her allies.

Forces for Intercontinental Attack

INTERCONTINENTAL BALLISTIC MISSILES

The operational Soviet ICBM force consists of some 1,400 silo launchers, aside from those at test sites. Some 818 of these launchers have been rebuilt since 1972. Nearly half of these silos are new versions of the original designs and have been reconstructed or modified in the past six years. All 818 silos have been hardened better to withstand attack by currently operational US ICBMs. These silos contain the world's most modern deployed ICBMs—the SS-17 Mod 3 (150 silos), the SS-18 Mod 4 (308), and the SS-19 Mod 3 (360). Deployment of these ICBMs began just six years ago.

The highly accurate SS-18 and SS-19 ICBMs carry more and larger Multiple Independently Targetable Reentry Vehicles (MIRVs) than the Minuteman III, the most modern US ICBM. The SS-18 Mod 4 carries ten MIRVs, and the SS-19 Mod 3 carries six, whereas the Minuteman III carries only three. The SS-18 Mod 4 was specifically designed to attack and destroy ICBM silos and other hardened targets in the United States. Each of its 10 warheads has more than 20 times the destructive power of the nuclear devices developed during World War II. The SS-18 Mod 4 force currently deployed has the capability to destroy more than 80 percent of US ICBM silos using two nuclear warheads against each. The SS-19 Mod 3 ICBM could be assigned similar missions and, in addition, could be used against targets in Eurasia. Although the SS-17 Mod 3 is somewhat less capable than the SS-19, it has similar targeting flexibility.

The remaining 580 Soviet ICBM silos are fitted with the SS-11—420 SS-11 Mod 2/3s, 100 SS-11 Mod 1s—and 60 SS-13 Mod 2s. These ICBMs of older vintage—1966 and 1973 initial deployment, respectively—are housed in less-survivable silos and are considerably less capable. Nevertheless, their destructive potential against softer area targets in the United States and Eurasia is significant in terms of many of the Soviet nuclear requirements outlined above.

Source: U.S. Department of Defense, *Soviet Military Power 1985* (Washington, D.C.: U.S. Government Printing Office, 1985), pp. 25–41, 43–49, 51–52.

The SS-16 is a three-stage, solid-propellant, single-RV ICBM that the Soviets claim has not been deployed. The system was first tested in 1972; the last known test took place in 1976. The SS-20 LRINF missile is closely related to the SS-16. The SS-16 probably was intended originally for both silo and mobile deployment, using equipment and a basing arrangement comparable to that used with the SS-20. The Soviet Union agreed in SALT II not to produce, test, or deploy ICBMs of the SS-16 type and, in particular, not to produce the SS-16 third stage, the RV, or the appropriate device for targeting the RV of that missile. While the evidence is somewhat ambiguous, it indicates that the SS-16 activities at Plesetsk are a probable violation of SALT II, which banned SS-16 deployment.

Deployment programs for all of the currently operational Soviet ICBM systems are complete. The command, control, and communications system that supports the Soviet ICBM force is modern and highly survivable, and the reliability of the ICBMs themselves is regularly tested by live firings from operational complexes.

Those ICBMs in the current force that the Soviets decide not to replace with modified or new ICBMs will, in accord with past practice, be refurbished to increase their useful lifetime. During this process, some system modifications could also be made. Through this capacity for refurbishment, the Soviets can sustain a higher level of confidence in system reliability over a longer term than would otherwise be possible.

Force Developments. Soviet research and development on ICBMs is a dynamic process involving many programs. The completion of current deployment programs probably marks the end of significant Soviet investment in the development of entirely new liquid-propellant ICBMs. Modified versions of the SS-18, however, are likely to be produced and deployed in existing silos in the future.

The Soviets appear to be planning on new solid-propellant ICBMs to meet future mission requirements, including a counterforce capability and ICBM force survivability. Two new solid-propellant ICBMs, the medium-size SS-X-24 and the smaller SS-X-25, are well along in their flight test programs from the range head at Plesetsk in the Soviet north. A mobile version of each of these systems will be deployed.

The SS-X-24 will probably be silo-deployed at first, with initial deployment expected in 1986. Rail-mobile deployment could follow by one to two years. Early preparations for the deployment of the SS-X-24 are already underway.

The SS-X-25 is approximately the same size as the US Minuteman ICBM. It will carry a single reentry vehicle. The SS-X-25 has apparently been designed for road-mobile deployment similar to that of the SS-20; as such it will be highly survivable with an inherent refire capability. Two bases, probably for the SS-X-25, are nearing operational capability. They consist of launcher garages equipped with sliding roofs and several support buildings to house the necessary mobile support equipment.

Recent activity at the Soviet ICBM test ranges indicates that two additional new ICBMs are under development. A new ICBM to replace the SS-18 is nearing the flight test stage of development. Additionally, a solid-propellant missile that may be larger than the SS-X-24 will begin flight testing in the next few years. Both of these missiles are likely to have better accuracy and greater throwweights than their predecessors.

SUBMARINE-LAUNCHED BALLISTIC MISSILES

The Soviets maintain the world's largest ballistic missile submarine force. As of early 1985, the force numbered 62 modern SSBNs carrying 928 nuclear-tipped missiles. These totals do not include 13 older submarines with 39 missiles currently assigned theater missions. Eighteen SSBNs are fitted with 300 MIRVed submarine-launched ballistic missiles (SLBMs). These 18 units have been built and deployed within the past 8 years. Over two-thirds of the ballistic missile submarines, including those equipped with MIRVed missiles are fitted with long-range SLBMs that enable the submarines to patrol in waters close to the Soviet Union. This affords protection from NATO antisubmarine warfare operations. Moreover, the long-range missiles allow the Soviets to fire from home ports, if necessary, and still strike targets in the United States.

Three units of one of the most modern Soviet ballistic missile submarine, the Typhoon, have already been built. Each Typhoon carries 20 SS-N-20 solid-propellant MIRVed SLBMs. The Typhoon is the world's largest submarine, with a displacement of 25,000 tons, one-third greater than the US Ohio-class. The submarine can operate under the Arctic Ocean icecap, adding further to the protection afforded by the 8,300-kilometer range of the SS-N-20 SLBM. Three or four additional Typhoons are probably now under construction, and, by the early 1990s, the Soviets could have as many as eight of these potent weapons systems in their operational force.

In accordance with the SALT I Interim Agreement, the Soviets have, since 1978, removed 12 Yankee I units from service as ballistic missile submarines. These units had to be removed as newer submarines were produced in order for the overall Soviet SSBN force to stay within 62 modern SSBN/950 SLBM limits established in 1972. These Yankees, however, have not been scrapped. Some have been reconfigured as attack or cruise missile submarines.

The Soviets may have begun to assign theater attack missions to some of the 21 remaining Yankee I submarines. However, Yankee patrols targeted against the United States continue.

Force Developments. The Soviets have launched two units of a new class of SSBN, the Delta IV, which will be fitted with the SS-NX-23 SLBM, now being flight tested. This large, liquid-propelled SLBM will have greater throwweight, carry more warheads, and be more accurate than the SS-N-18, which is carried on the Delta III SSBN. The SS-NX-23 is likely to be deployed on Delta IIIs as a replacement for the SS-N-18 as well as on the new Delta IVs.

The Soviets will probably begin flight testing a modified version of the SS-N-20. Additionally, based on past Soviet practice, they may initiate testing of a modified version of the SS-NX-23 before the end of the 1980s. Both modified versions of the SS-N-20 and SS-NX-23 are likely to be more accurate than their predecessors.

To ensure communication reliability, the Soviets emphasize redundant and timely command and control for their military forces, especially those for intercontinental attack. The Soviets are expected to deploy an extremely low frequency (ELF) communications system that will enable them to contact SSBNs under most operating conditions.

STRATEGIC AVIATION

Soviet strategic bombers and strike aircraft have been restructured to form five air armies subordinate to the Supreme High Command (VGK). The five armies are:

- Smolensk Air Army;
- Legnica Air Army;
- Venitza Air Army;
- Irkutsk Air Army; and
- Moscow Air Army.

These armies were established to place Soviet strategic aircraft on a footing in peacetime that would facilitate the transition to wartime. The armies are focused on potential conflicts in Europe, Asia, and the United States.

Strategic aviation assets include some 170 Bear and Bison bombers and about 250 Backfire bombers (including 120 Backfire bombers in Soviet Naval Aviation). The Soviets also have 360 medium-range Blinder and Badger bombers; 450 shorter range Fencer strike aircraft; and 530 tanker, reconnaissance, and electronic warfare aircraft. The Soviets have allocated these aircraft among the five air armies to provide support for specific theaters of military operations and to assure the flexibility to reallocate aircraft as necessary during wartime. The intercontinental Bear and Bison bombers are available for maritime and Eurasian missions, and the Backfire can be used against the United States. This flexibility allows the Soviets to focus their strategic air assets as circumstances require.

The Soviets have taken recent steps that indicate greatly increased interest in their long-range strategic bomber force. An entirely new variant of the Bear bomber—the Bear H—is now operational with the AS-15 long-range cruise missile. This is the first new production of a strike version of the Bear air-frame in over 15 years. In addition, older Bear aircraft configured to carry air-to-surface missiles (ASMs) are being reconfigured to carry the newer, supersonic AS-4 missile in place of the subsonic AS-3. Several of these reconfigurations (Bear G) have been completed. With the Bear H in series production, the decline in the inventory of Bear aircraft, characteristic of recent years, has been reversed.

The Backfire is the most modern operational Soviet bomber. The Soviets continue to produce this aircraft at a rate of at least 30 per year; this produc-tion rate is likely to be maintained at least through the end of the decade. The original design has been modified several times, and further modifications are likely to be made to upgrade aircraft performance. The Backfire is a long-range aircraft capable of performing nuclear strike, conventional attack, anti-ship, and reconnaissance missions. The Backfire can be equipped with a probe to permit in-flight refueling to increase its range and radius capabilities. It could be used against the contiguous United States on high-altitude subsonic missions. Its low-altitude supersonic dash capabilities make it a formidable weapon to support military operations in Europe and Asia as well.

The Soviets have some Fencer strike aircraft assigned to strategic avia-tion. The Fencer is a supersonic, variable-geometry-wing, all-weather fighter-bomber that first reached operational status in 1974. Three variants have been developed, the most recent introduced in 1981. The aircraft is still in pro-duction, and the number assigned to strategic aviation is likely to increase over the next few years.

Force Developments. The new Soviet long-range bomber, the Black-jack, is in the flight test stage of development. The Blackjack is larger than the US B-1B, probably will be faster, and may have about the same combat radius. This new bomber could be operational by 1988. The Blackjack will be capable of carrying cruise missiles, bombs, or a combination of both. It probably will first replace the much less capable Bison bomber and then the Bear A bomber.

A new aerial-refueling tanker aircraft, based on the Il-76/Candid, has been under development for several years. When deployed in the near future, the new tanker will support tactical and strategic aircraft and will significantly improve the ability of Soviet aircraft to conduct longer range operations.

LONG-RANGE CRUISE MISSILES

Current Systems and Force Levels. The AS-15, a small, air-launched, subsonic, low-altitude cruise missile, similar in design to the US Tomahawk, reached initial operational capability with the Bear H in 1984. The AS-15 has a range of about 3,000 kilometers. The system could also be deployed on Blackjack bombers when that aircraft becomes operational. The combination of the AS-15 and the new Bear H and Blackjack bombers will increase Soviet strategic intercontinental air power in the late 1980s. There are some 25 Bear H bombers operational at this time.

Force Developments. The Soviets are developing four other long-range cruise missile systems. Two of these are variants of the AS-15, and the other two are variants of a larger system probably designed for long-range operations. The latter have no US counterpart.

The two smaller cruise missiles are being developed for launch from sea- and ground-based platforms, respectively. The sea-based variant, the SS-NX-21, is small enough to be fired from standard Soviet torpedo tubes. Candidate launch platforms for the SS-NX-21 include: the existing Victor III nuclear-powered attack submarine (SSN), a new Yankee-class SSN and, the new Akula, Mike, and Sierra-class SSNs. The SS-NX-21 is expected to become operational this year and could be deployed on submarines near US coasts.

The ground-based SSC-X-4 variant of the small cruise missile may not be ready for operational deployment until late this year or next. Its range and the likelihood the Soviets will not deploy the system outside the USSR indicate that its mission will be in support of theater operations. The system will be mobile and probably follow operational procedures like those of the SS-20 LRINF missile.

The larger cruise missile is being developed as a sea-based system that has been designated the SS-NX-24. A newly converted Yankee-class nuclear-powered cruise missile attack submarine (SSGN) will be the test platform for the SS-NX-24. A ground-based variant of this missile may be in development. The SS-NX-24 could be operational within the next two years, and the ground-based version sometime after that.

When first deployed, these cruise missiles probably will be fitted with nuclear warheads and capable of attacking hardened targets. Depending on future munitions developments and the types of guidance systems incorporated in their designs, they could eventually be accurate enough to permit the use of conventional warheads. With such warheads, highly accurate cruise missiles would pose a significant non-nuclear threat to US and NATO airfields and nuclear weapons in a non-nuclear conflict. . . .

FORCES FOR THEATER ATTACK

With the initial deployment of the SS-20 LRINF missile in 1977, the Soviets launched a concerted effort to modernize and expand their intermediate-range nuclear force. Each SS-20 carries three MIRVs, thereby providing a significant force expansion factor even as the older single-RV SS-4 is withdrawn. The SS-20 also has significant improvements in accuracy and reaction time over the older missiles they are replacing.

About 400 SS-20s have been deployed, two-thirds of which are opposite

European NATO. Some shifting of the SS-20 force has recently been observed as the Soviets prepare for deployment of the SS-X-25 ICBM; however, no reduction in the SS-20 force is expected from this activity. The mobility of the SS-20 system enables both on- and off-road operation. As a result, the survivability of the SS-20 is greatly enhanced because detecting and targeting them is difficult when they are field deployed. Further, the SS-20 launcher has the capability of being reloaded and refired, and the Soviets stockpile refire missiles.

In addition to the SS-20 force, the Soviets still maintain some 120 SS-4 LRINF missiles. All of these missiles are located in the western USSR opposite European NATO. In addition to the land-based LRINF missile forces, the Soviets still maintain and operate 13 Golf II-class ballistic missile submarines. Each submarine is equipped with three SS-N-5 SLBMs. Six Golf II units are based in the Baltic, where they continue to pose a threat to most of Europe, while the remaining seven Golf IIs patrol the Sea of Japan, where they could be employed against targets in the Far East.

Future Force Developments. A modified version of the SS-20 is in flight test. This missile is expected to have even greater accuracy and other improvements over the current SS-20. . . .

SHORT-RANGE BALLISTIC MISSILES

Current Systems and Force Levels. Armies and fronts have missile brigades equipped with 12–18 SS-1C Scud SRBMs. Over 400 Scud launchers are opposite European NATO; over 100 are opposite the Sino-Soviet border and in the Far East; about 75 are opposite southwest Asia and eastern Turkey; and one brigade is in strategic reserve. The Scud is expected to be replaced by the SS-23, which has a longer range and improved accuracy. Initial deployment is anticipated opposite NATO and China. Each front commander may also have a brigade of 12–18 Scaleboard missiles available. They are more accurate than the SS-12 they replaced. Over 60 launchers are opposite European NATO and 40 are opposite the Sino-Soviet border in the Far East. There is one battalion opposite southwest Asia/eastern Turkey, and one brigade is in the Strategic Reserve military districts. The new generation of shorter range missiles can be employed effectively with conventional and improved conventional munitions warheads in light of their greatly increased accuracy.

In 1984, the Soviets, for the first time, forward deployed the Scaleboard short-range ballistic missile to Eastern Europe. These front-level missiles, which normally deploy with Soviet combined arms formations, are now in position to strike deep into NATO without having first to forward deploy.

Force Developments. It is likely that the Soviets will continue to seek improvements in their SRBM force. Improvements in guidance and control, warhead capabilities, and accuracies are expected. Such improvements will give the combined arms commanders enhanced non-nuclear targeting options and more flexible, reliable, and survivable SRBMs. These systems will be capable of delivering nuclear, chemical, or conventional warheads closer to the forward edge of the battle area and at greater depths within the military theater of operations.

TACTICAL MISSILES AND NUCLEAR ARTILLERY

Current Systems and Force Levels. At division level, the predominant weapon is the unguided Frog, found in a battalion of four launchers. The Soviets have begun to replace the Frog with the more accurate, longer range SS-21 in most divisions opposite NATO. Currently there are some 375 Frog and SS-21 launchers opposite NATO. Two hundred Frog launchers are opposite the Sino-Soviet border and in the Far East; about 100 are opposite southwest Asia and eastern Turkey; and about 75 are in the Strategic Reserve MDs.

In addition to Frog and SS-21 launchers, a division commander has some 800 nuclear-capable artillery tubes at his disposal. Two new self-propelled artillery pieces, 152-mm gun and a howitzer/mortar, are now entering the inventory. Both of these guns are nuclear-capable and will bring the total number of nuclear-capable artillery tubes to over 2,000 when fully deployed. An additional 4,000 152-mm howitzers have at least a potential nuclear capability.

Force Developments. As in all other nuclear attack forces, it is likely that the Soviets will improve the capabilities of their tactical missiles and nuclear artillery pieces. This improvement will be accomplished through incremental modernization of current systems and the introduction of entirely new systems. . . .

Strategic Defenses

LASER/ENERGY WEAPONS SYSTEMS

Soviet directed-energy development programs involve future Ballistic Missile Defense (BMD) as well as antisatellite and air-defense weapons concepts.

By the late 1980s, the Soviets could have prototypes for ground-based lasers for ballistic missile defense. Testing of the components for a large-scale deployment system could begin in the early 1990s. The many difficulties in fielding an operational system will require much development time, and initial operational deployment is not likely in this century. However, with high priority and some significant risk of failure, the Soviets could skip some testing steps and be ready to deploy a ground-based laser BMD by the early-to-mid-1990s.

Ground- and space-based particle beam weapons for ballistic missile defense will be more difficult to develop than lasers. Nevertheless, the Soviets have a vigorous program underway for particle beam development and could have a prototype space-based system ready for testing in the late 1990s.

The Soviets have begun to develop at least three types of high-energy laser weapons for air defense. These include lasers intended for defense of high-value strategic targets in the USSR, for point defense of ships at sea, and for air defense of theater forces. Following past practice, they are likely to deploy air defense lasers to complement, rather than replace, interceptors and surface-to-air missiles (SAMs). The strategic defense laser is probably in at least the prototype stage of development and could be operational by the late 1980s. It most likely will be deployed in conjunction with SAMs in a point defense role. Since the SAM and laser systems would have somewhat different attributes and vulnerabilities, they would provide mutual support. The shipborne lasers probably will not be operational until after the end of the decade. The theater force lasers may be operational sometime sooner and are likely to be capable of structurally damaging aircraft at close ranges and producing electro-optical and eye damage at greater distances.

The Soviets are also developing an airborne laser. Assuming a successful development effort, limited initial deployment could begin in the early 1990s. Such a laser platform could have missions including antisatellite operations, protection of high-value airborne assets, and cruise missile defense.

The Soviets are working on technologies or have specific weapons-related programs underway for more advanced antisatellite systems. These include space-based kinetic energy, ground- and space-based laser, particle beam, and radiofrequency weapons. The Soviets apparently believe that these techniques offer greater promise for future antisatellite application than continued development of ground-based orbital interceptors equipped with conventional warheads. The Soviets also believe that military applications of directed-energy technologies hold promise of overcoming weaknesses in their conventional air and missile defenses.

The USSR's high-energy laser program, which dates from the mid-1960s, is much larger than the US effort. They have built over a half-dozen major R&D facilities and test ranges, and they have over 10,000 scientists and engineers associated with laser development. They are developing chemical lasers and have continued to work on other high-energy lasers having potential weapons applications—the gas dynamic laser and the electric discharge laser. They are also pursuing related laser weapon technologies, such as efficient electrical power sources, and are pursuing capabilities to produce high-quality optical components. They have developed a rocket-driven magnetohydrodynamic (MHD) generator which produces 15 megawatts of short-term electric power—a device that has no counterpart in the West. The scope of the USSR's military capabilities would depend on its success in developing advanced weapons, including laser weapons for ballistic missile defense.

The Soviets have now progressed beyond technology research, in some cases to the development of prototype laser weapons. They already have ground-based lasers that could be used to interfere with US satellites. In the late 1980s, they could have prototype spacebased laser weapons for use against satellites. In addition, ongoing Soviet programs have progressed to the point where they could include construction of ground-based laser antisatellite (ASAT) facilities at operational sites. These could be available by the end of the 1980s and would greatly increase the Soviets' laser ASAT capability beyond that currently at their test site at Sary Shagan. They may deploy operational systems of space-based lasers for antisatellite purposes in the 1990s, if their technology developments prove successful, and they can be expected to pursue development of space-based laser systems for ballistic missile defense for possible deployment after the year 2000.

Since the early 1970s, the Soviets have had a research program to explore the technical feasibility of a particle beam weapon in space. A prototype space-based particle beam weapon intended only to disrupt satellite electronic equipment could be tested in the early 1990s. One designed to destroy satellites could be tested in space in the mid-1990s.

The Soviets have conducted research in the use of strong radiofrequency (RF) signals that have the potential to interfere with or destroy components of missiles, satellites, and reentry vehicles. In the 1990s, the Soviets could test a ground-based RF weapon capable of damaging satellites.

Soviet programs for the development and application of directed-energy technologies to strategic defense have been very vigorous in the past and will continue to be so in the future, irrespective of what the US does about new strategic defense initiatives.

In the area of kinetic energy weapons, using the high-speed collision of a small mass with the target as the kill mechanism, the Soviets have a variety of research programs underway. These programs could result in a near-term, short-range, space-based system useful for satellite or space station defense or for close-in attack by a maneuvering satellite. Longer range, space-based systems probably could not be developed until the mid-1990s or even later. . . .

BALLISTIC MISSILE DEFENSE

The Soviets are continuing a major upgrading of their ballistic missile defense capabilities. The Moscow missile defenses are being enlarged and equipped with a new generation of radars and interceptor missiles. Developments aimed at providing the foundation for widespread ABM deployments beyond Moscow are underway.

The new SA-X-12 surface-to-air missile, which incorporates ballistic missile defense capabilities, is nearing operational status, while research on directed-energy BMD technology continues apace.

The Soviets maintain around Moscow the world's only operational ABM system. This system is intended to afford a layer of defense for Soviet civil and military command authorities in the Moscow area during a nuclear war rather than blanket protection for the city itself. Since 1980, the Soviets have been upgrading and expanding this system around Moscow within the limits of the 1972 ABM Treaty.

The original single-layer Moscow ABM system included 64 reloadable above-ground launchers at four complexes for the Galosh ABM-1B, six TRY ADD guidance and engagement radars at each complex, and the Dog House and Cat House target-tracking radars south of Moscow. The Soviets are upgrading this system to the 100 accountable launchers permitted under the ABM Treaty. When completed, the new system will be a two-layer defense composed of silo-based, long-range, modified Galosh interceptors designed to engage targets outside the atmosphere; silo-based high-acceleration interceptors designed to engage targets within the atmosphere; associated engagement and guidance radars; and a new large radar at Pushkino designed to control ABM engagements. The silo-based launchers may be reloadable. The first new launchers are likely to be operational this year, and the new defenses could be fully operational by 1987.

The Soviets are developing a rapidly deployable ABM system to protect important target areas in the USSR. They have been testing all the types of ABM missiles and radars needed for widespread ABM defenses beyond the 100 launcher limit of the 1972 ABM Treaty. Within the next 10 years, the Soviets could deploy such a system at sites that could be built in months instead of years. A typical site would consist of engagement radars, guidance radars, above-ground launchers, and the high-acceleration interceptor. The new, large phased-array radars under construction in the USSR, along with the Hen House, Dog House, Cat House, and possibly the Pushkino radar, appear to be designed to provide support for such a widespread ABM defense system. The aggregate of the USSR's ABM and ABM-related activities suggests that the USSR may be preparing an ABM defense of its national territory.

In addition, the Soviets are deploying one surface-to-air missile system, the SA-10, and are flight testing another, the mobile SA-X-12. The SA-X-12 is both a tactical SAM and antitactical ballistic missile. It may have the capability to engage the Lance and both the Pershing I and Pershing II ballistic missiles. The SA-10 and SA-X-12 may have the potential to intercept some types of US strategic ballistic missiles as well. These systems could, if properly supported, add significant point-target coverage to a widespread ABM deployment.

AIR DEFENSE

The Soviets have deployed numerous strategic and tactical air defense assets that have excellent capabilities against aircraft flying at medium and high altitudes. Although their capability to intercept low-flying penetrators is marginal, they are in the midst of a major overhaul geared toward fielding an integrated air defense system much more capable of low-altitude operations. This overhaul includes partial integration of strategic and tactical air defenses; the upgrading of early warning and surveillance capabilities; the deployment of more efficient data transmission systems; and the development and initial deployment of new aircraft, associated air-to-air missiles, surface-to-air missiles, and airborne warning and control system (AWACS) aircraft.

Over the years, the Soviets have invested enormous resources in their air defense systems. This sustained effort has produced an array of weapons systems designed for a variety of air defense applications. For example, they have fielded 13 different surface-to-air missile systems, each designed to cover a specific threat regime.

The Soviets have made significant shifts in the subordination of their air and air defense assets. The reorganization has resulted in a streamlined organization that merged strategic and tactical air and air defense assets in most land border areas of the USSR. The air defense (APVO) interceptors became part of a new structure, the Air Forces of the Military District (MD), which also includes most of the assets of the former tactical air armies. The Air Forces of an MD include all air assets in their geographic area (excluding Strategic Aviation and transport assets). These assets can be used either offensively or defensively as the situation requires. The new structure improves defensive capabilities, but its most significant impact is on the capability to conduct massed offensive air operations. Technological advances in weapons systems and in command, control, and communications have made its implementation possible.

In terms of numbers alone, Soviet strategic and tactical air defense forces are impressive. Moreover, with the continuing deployment of new systems like the SA-10 SAM and impending deployment of the SA-X-12, these numbers are increasing along with capability. Currently, the Soviets have nearly 10,000 SAM launchers at over 1,200 sites for strategic defense, along with more than 4,000 launch vehicles for tactical SAMs, subordinated to nearly 445 launch units. More than 1,200 interceptors are dedicated to strategic defense, while an additional 2,800 Soviet Air Forces (SAF) interceptors could also be used. Further, the Soviets are continuing the Mainstay AWACS aircraft program and test and evaluation is underway. The Mainstay will substantially improve Soviet capabilities for early warning and air combat command and control, especially against low-flying aircraft. The Mainstay will also provide Soviet air defenses with overland and overwater capabilities to detect aircraft and cruise missile targets flying at low altitudes. Additionally, the Mainstay could be used to help direct fighter operations over European and Asian battlefields and to enhance air surveillance and defense of the USSR. Mainstay production could be about five aircraft per year.

The 1,200 all-weather interceptors assigned to strategic defense are primarily based in central air defense regions of the Soviet Union, in addition to fighter/interceptors subordinate to the military districts that are generally located on the periphery of the Soviet Union. The interceptor force is composed of a wide variety of aircraft with varying capabilities. . . .

PASSIVE DEFENSE

Soviet passive defense preparations have been underway in earnest for some 30 years and have, over time, expanded from the protection of such vital entities as the national Party and government leadership and Armed Forces to embrace the territorial leadership, national economy, and general population. The Soviets regard passive defense as an essential ingredient of their overall military posture and war planning. In conjunction with active forces, the Soviets plan for a passive defense program to ensure the survival and wartime continuity of:

- Soviet leadership;
- military command and control entities;
- war-supporting industrial production and services;
- the essential workforce; and
- as much of the general population as possible.

As this program has expanded, elements of it have been designated by the Soviets as "civil defense." Use of this term in its normal Western context does not convey the full scope of Soviet Civil Defense.

Extensive planning for the transition of the entire State and economy to a wartime posture has been fundamental to Soviet passive defense preparations. The Soviet General Staff and Civil Defense officials have supervised the development of special organizations and procedures to implement a rapid transition to war and have emphasized the mobilization and protection of all national resources essential to the successful prosecution of war and recovery.

The senior Soviet military establishment has also supervised the 30-year program to construct hardened command posts and survivable communications for key military commanders and civilian managers at all levels of the Party and government. Likewise, protective hardening, dispersal, and wartime production plans for Soviet industry have all been coordinated with the wartime requirements of the military and supervised by Civil Defense personnel. The protection of the general population through evacuation procedures and extensive sheltering in or near urban areas is the most visible aspect of the passive defense program. . . .

The annual military and civilian cost of four elements of the program— pay and allowances for full-time Civil Defense personnel; operation of specialized military Civil Defense units; construction and maintenance of facilities for these units; and shelter construction—is less than 1 percent of the estimated Soviet defense budget. If duplicated in the United States, these four elements would cost roughly $3 billion annually. The cost of construction and equipment for leadership relocation sites over the past 25 years is between 8 and 16 billion rubles, or $28–56 billion if acquired in the United States. . . .

BEANCOUNTING AND WARGAMING: HOW TO ANALYZE THE STRATEGIC BALANCE
Marie Hoguet

Marie Hoguet is the Educational Coordinator for the Arms Control Association in Washington, D.C.

Sooner or later most discussions of the arms race lead to the question of "who's ahead"—which side has more, or bigger, or better nuclear weapons; whose buildup has been more unprecedented; and what it all means for our defense policies. Many teachers and students have seen graphs and charts comparing the numbers of U.S. and Soviet intercontinental ballistic missiles (ICBMs), submarine-launched ballistic missiles (SLBMs), warheads, bombers and so on.

Comparisons of U.S. and Soviet nuclear forces are both inevitable and necessary in considering our relative strengths and weaknesses. But very often they are misleading because they omit so much relevant information and fail to disclose their underlying assumptions. They tend to give an incorrect impression of precision where in fact it is impossible to be precise.

There are two basic approaches to comparing U.S. and Soviet nuclear forces. The first and more familiar approach compares the characteristics and destructive potential of the two sides' weapons. Sometimes called "beancounting," it looks at specific weapons or characteristics of weapons and attempts to show, often in graphic form, what the U.S. and the Soviet Union each has in the discrete categories. This approach provides a static picture, a snapshot,

Source: Marie Hoguet, "Beancounting and Wargaming: How to Analyze the Strategic Balance," Arms Control Today (June 1984), pp. 6–9. Reprinted by permission of Lexington Books, D.C. Heath and Company, from The Race for Security: Arms and Arms Control in the Reagan Years, ed. Robert Travis Scott (Lexington, Mass.: Lexington Books, D.C. Heath and Company, forthcoming). Copyright 1985, D.C. Heath and Company.

of the various components of each side's forces at a particular time, in peace-time. Or it can provide a picture of the change in the quantity of these components over a certain period of time. This approach does not, and cannot, show how these components would interact in a war, or what extrinsic factors would affect their performance or importance in actual combat.

Let us look at one of the more frequently encountered comparisons—the one between U.S. and Soviet ICBMs and SLBMs—and note some of its limitations. A typical graph depicts a small forest of the many different kinds of Soviet missiles and a more modest array of the U.S. missiles. It will show that Soviet ICBMs and SLBMs are larger, more varied, and more numerous than their U.S. counterparts. One's intuitive conclusion, on seeing such a graph, would be that the Soviets are better armed and stronger.

But this sort of graph does not reveal that U.S. *Minuteman* missiles, which make up the vast bulk of our ICBM arsenal, are smaller because superior technology in miniaturizing explosive devices and guidance systems and in using more efficient, less bulky solid fuel propellants allowed the U.S. deliberately to scale down the size of its missiles. (If size itself were important, the U.S. would not be phasing out of its arsenal its largest ICBMs, the gargantuan *Titans*.) Nor does such a graph show that the variety of the U.S.S.R.'s ICBMs and SLBMs is in no small part attributable to the Soviets' persistent problems in producing one reliable model in which they have confidence. This graph gives no indication, moreover, of the qualitative differences between the Soviet and American ICBMs and SLBMs—differences which are at least as significant as differences in quantity, size and variety. For example, a submarine's ability to glide silently through the water and thus evade detection and destruction is a critically valuable feature. And the U.S.'s SLBM-carrying submarines can move much more quietly than Soviet submarines.

One frequently sees charts showing the relative increase in the number of U.S. and Soviet ICBMs and SLBMs over a particular span of time. This too can create a misleading effect. A graph showing the tremendous growth in the number of Soviet missiles and the much flatter growth of the U.S. arsenal from 1970 to 1980, for example, suggests a truly alarming Soviet build-up. However, a graph including the period from 1950, say, to 1980, would reveal that the U.S. too engaged in an enormous build-up—but in the decades preceding the Soviet effort. The point here is simply that the choice of period can radically alter the message of a graph comparing quantities of weapons over a span of time.

Another common way of comparing nuclear forces is by counting the number of warheads. Initially, both U.S. and Soviet missiles carried only one warhead apiece. Each missile could therefore be aimed at only one target. In the early 1970s, however, first the U.S. and then the Soviet Union mastered the technology of multiple independently-targetable reentry vehicles, or MIRVs, which allows one to load onto a single missile a number of warheads, each of which can be programmed to strike a different target. (The reentry vehicle of a missile basically contains the explosive device or warhead.)

By now, most of the superpowers' missiles are MIRVed, carrying between 3 and 14 warheads on each missile. Counting each side's ICBMs and SLBMs has therefore become an even less useful exercise than before, because it does not tell one how many bombs each side can deliver with these systems. So graphs comparing the number of deliverable warheads have become more common.

This measure, however, has its own limits. It is very difficult to determine just how many warheads the various delivery systems actually carry. The Strategic Arms Limitation Treaty of 1979 between the U.S. and U.S.S.R. (SALT II—signed, unratified by the U.S., but observed by both parties) put ceilings on the numbers of reentry-vehicles that ICBMs and SLBMs may carry. But in order to make their forces as versatile as possible, both the U.S. and the Soviet Union deploy their missiles with differing numbers of warheads, as well as differing megatonnage, range, and guidance systems. Thus in many cases missiles carry fewer than the maximum permitted them by SALT II. Bombers too vary in the amounts and kinds of warheads they carry. Comparisons of each superpower's warheads can therefore be based only on educated guesses.

Comparisons of numbers of warheads, like comparisons of delivery systems, also do not tell one about qualitative differences. The effectiveness—that is, the destructive potential—of a weapon is a function of the weapon's explosive power and its accuracy and must be judged in relation to the kind of target it is intended to destroy. A weapon with a certain combination of explosiveness and accuracy may be devastating against a "soft" civilian or military target such as a city or submarine base, but ineffective against a "hardened" target such as a missile silo or command-and-control bunker buried deep in reinforced concrete and steel. The importance of accuracy is thus especially great in relation to hard targets, which are built to withstand enormous explosions unless they occur almost precisely on point. *Accuracy,* therefore, is a key variable in comparing U.S. and Soviet forces.

Like the number and distribution of each side's warheads, however, accuracy can only be estimated. These estimates are based on observations of test firings of missiles. But there are too few tests for any particular model to permit an exact evaluation of its accuracy; the tests cannot be conducted over the path that the missile would have to follow if ever actually used; and weather and wartime conditions can also cause unpredictable variations. In addition, when observing Soviet missile tests, we cannot be sure how accurate the missiles are because we do not know the precise point at which they are aimed. And since estimates of accuracy are in turn used in other, more complex qualitative measurements of weapons' capabilities, the uncertainties inherent in assessments of accuracy are compounded in any subsequent measurements.

Beancounting and qualitative measurements can be useful when the limitations both of the underlying data and of the significance of the comparisons are kept in mind. As former Defense Secretary Harold Brown pointed out in the 1982 Annual Report of the Defense Department (DoD), however, these measures are isolated "from 'real world' factors inherent in any actual attack situation."

The second basic approach to weighing U.S. and Soviet nuclear forces seeks to approximate, in a very theoretical way, what could happen in "actual attack situations." It attempts to predict, through a series of calculations—computer wargames—how the superpower forces would interact in a nuclear war. These are often called *force exchange* comparisons, and they seek to measure the ability of the other side to retaliate, and the outcome of the exchange. Force exchange analysis allows a more sophisticated comparison of the two sides' forces, but depends entirely on the validity of the many underlying assumptions.

Sometimes these assumptions are stated explicitly. For example, one scenario seeks to determine the outcome of a surprise nuclear attack. It assumes that at the time of the attacker's initial strike, the other side's forces are on normal peacetime alert during which certain percentages of its ICBMs, SLBMs and bombers are kept fully readied to respond to the attack. Another scenario assumes that the other side has received warning of a likely attack and thus has readied a higher percentage of its forces to survive and retaliate. Many other factors, however, may enter into the calculations but are unlikely to be articulated.

Furthermore, as Harold Brown noted in the 1982 DoD Annual Report, force exchange analysis also omits from its calculations certain "real, important, yet hard-to-quantify factors such as leadership, motivation, C^3 (command, control and communication facilities), training and maintenance." It does not attempt to treat the military and political context in which such exchanges occur, or the military plans and tactics which would of course come into play in any real combat situation.

Beyond these important but unquantifiable factors is yet another range of very significant elements in comparing the military capabilities of the two superpowers. Alliances, industrial capacities, natural resources, population, geography, national morale, and political leadership and values all must figure in any realistic consideration of two potential adversaries' ability to wage war against each other. And although it is impossible to quantify these factors in a way that relates them meaningfully to an overall military balance assessment, they must nonetheless be borne in mind. Similarly, one must remember that while force exchange analyses have an artificial, even surrealistic, air, they are not merely theoretical constructs. Although abstract themselves, these analyses are based on real weapons—and weapons so powerful and so numerous that, if ever used, they would only serve, in Winston Churchill's oft-quoted phrase, to "make the rubble bounce."

This quick overview is intended only to suggest that the various ways of attempting to determine the relative strengths and weaknesses of the U.S. and Soviet nuclear forces all have limitations in both their methodology and their application. In the face of such uncertainties, how is the layman to regard such comparisons? It may be helpful to remember several general caveats.

First, no single quantitative measure or set of measures can give a true picture of the two sides' capabilities. At best they can be only pieces of a very large and complex mosaic. Second, the quantities themselves are in many cases subject to uncertainties, and often inherently so. Third, the scenario-based force exchange comparisons depend totally for their validity on their underlying assumptions, and unless one is aware of them—or at least of the fact that these assumptions loom under the surface—one has almost no way of knowing how meaningful the comparison is. Finally, it is always useful to ask what the purpose of the presentation of the chart or analysis is, and what message it is being used to convey.

With all these cautions, however, it is possible nonetheless to make some judgments about overall relative U.S. and Soviet nuclear capabilities. In the words of one authority, Raymond L. Garthoff,

> In the most basic sense, strategic parity between the United States and the Soviet Union has existed, and will continue to exist, so long as each has the recognized capability to deal the other a devastating retaliatory strike after receiving a first strike. The common wisdom that under such circumstance the leaders on each side will be deterred from starting a war or even knowingly courting high risks of war is more solid than the sophisticated assumptions of scenarios in which these leaders would be attracted by arcane calculations of theoretically possible residual advantages after the first, second, or third strategic exchange. This general existing parity of nuclear capacity, and the resulting mutual deterrence, is not the delicate balance sometimes depicted.

ASSESSING THE ADEQUACY OF U.S. STRATEGIC NUCLEAR FORCES
John B. Harris

John B. Harris is Assistant Professor of Political Science at Georgia State University.

Ronald Reagan is now well into his second term as President of the United States. As was the case during his first four years in the White House, nuclear weapons and their relationship to American national security persist as highly visible points of public debate. The *terms* of this debate, however, have shifted somewhat over the last two years. The nuclear weapons freeze is no longer the dominant issue in public discussions of nuclear war, as it was in the 1982–84 period, when the freeze became a major issue in the 1982 and 1984 national elections. Another change is that aside from the MX missile, which continues to face stiff opposition on Capitol Hill, public and congressional resistance to the administration's multi-weapon "Strategic Modernization Program," while sharp and vocal in Reagan's first term, has now significantly abated.

In the meantime, "Star Wars," as the administration's Strategic Defense Initiative (SDI) has come to be known, has largely transcended the freeze in public visibility. The controversy over "Star Wars" revolves around President Reagan's stated desire, as outlined in his televised speech to the nation in March 1983, to develop a system of defenses against nuclear attack which would make nuclear missiles "obsolete." The President's proposal has in turn sparked a heated debate over the technical feasibility and strategic wisdom of greatly expanding U.S. efforts to develop effective ballistic missile defenses, one to which the public, Congress, and the media have devoted increasing attention.

Despite the apparent shifting focus of these discussions, however, a very basic and unresolved issue remains with us from the nuclear weapons policy debate of Ronald Reagan's first term. Upon assuming office in 1981, senior Reagan national security officials—most prominently the President himself—declared that "a window of vulnerability" in American strategic nuclear capabilities had opened vis-à-vis those of the Soviet Union. The United States' ability to deter nuclear attack, these spokesmen warned, had been weakened by the policies of "unilateral U.S. restraint" which previous administrations had pursued. The new administration announced in October of 1981 its plans for a "strategic modernization program" which would provide for the development and deployment of a wide array of new, more sophisticated offensive and defensive strategic weapons systems. The modernization program, it was argued, was necessary to retrieve a "margin of safety" in U.S. capabilities relative to those of the Soviet Union, and to restore the credibility of America's strategic deterrent.

Simultaneously, the administration rejected out of hand any approach to arms control with the Soviet Union—including the idea of a U.S.-Soviet freeze on nuclear weapons testing, production, and deployment—which would interfere with key elements of the modernization program, claiming that weapons like the B-1B bomber, the MX ICBM, and the Trident II SLBM were vitally necessary to close the "window of vulnerability." The administration's own approach to arms negotiations with the Soviets, reflected both in its initial 1982 Strategic Arms Reduction Talks (START) proposal for missile and missile warhead reductions, and in its later flirtation with the idea of a "guaranteed build-down" in U.S. and Soviet forces, was to reduce numbers of strategic weapons while leaving each country free to "modernize" and improve the technical capabilities of its forces as it saw fit.

The Nuclear Weapons Freeze Campaign, the grass roots organization which swelled to national political prominence during Reagan's first term in office, was sharply critical both of the rationale for the strategic modernization program as well as the administration's approach to arms control talks with the Soviet Union. Freeze advocates contended that existing American nuclear forces, supplemented by only very modest modernization efforts (such as the replacement of existing missile-carrying submarines with newer models) would be more than adequate to preserve the United States' capacity to retaliate following a Soviet nuclear attack, and thus to preserve deterrence. For this reason, it was argued, a freeze on the testing, production, and deployment of new Soviet and American nuclear weapons would not damage U.S. security.

On the contrary, freeze supporters claimed, allowing a new generation of U.S. and Soviet weapons systems to be deployed—especially highly accurate, multiple-warhead ballistic missiles like MX and Trident II—would accelerate the arms race, increase the risk of nuclear war, and make future arms control agreements more difficult to achieve. Freeze advocates argued that U.S. security would ultimately be harmed if these new weapons developments were not arrested. A U.S.-Soviet nuclear weapons freeze was thus viewed by its proponents as a way to arrest these potentially destabilizing trends, while at the same time guaranteeing each side its essential security from nuclear attack or political intimidation by the other.

A central issue in this debate was the state of the U.S.-Soviet strategic balance. The administration and other critics of the freeze claimed that the existing balance of forces was demonstrably unfavorable to the United States, and would actually worsen under a freeze. President Reagan even went so far at one point to concede to the Soviet Union a "definite margin of superiority" in nuclear capability over the United States. In their own public education and organizing efforts, by contrast, the freeze campaign went to great lengths to prove the existence of a rough balance or "parity"in U.S. and Soviet nuclear forces, which they argued could be maintained under the terms of a comprehensive nuclear weapons freeze.

Public discussion of the strategic balance and its relationship to force modernization issues on the one hand, and to arms control on the other, generally served to sharpen the points of contention between the freeze campaign and the administration. At the same time, however, a full airing of the relevant issues was hampered by three problems which frequently plague efforts to assess the impact of the U.S.-Soviet strategic balance on broader issues of U.S. nuclear weapons and arms control policy: (1) the methodological weaknesses inherent in force comparisons which rely exclusively on so-called "static" assessments of the military balance; (2) the widespread tendency of politicians and analysts to ignore the presence of uncertainty in computer "models" of strategic nuclear warfare; and (3) the failure to identify the strategic assumptions which analysts bring to bear in judging the adequacy of U.S. nuclear forces. A brief examination of these problems should help to clarify some of the issues involved in the freeze debate, as well as to illustrate the importance of taking these three factors into account when making an assessment of the adequacy of U.S. strategic forces.

As in so many discussions of the strategic balance, various "static indicators," or measures of U.S. and Soviet forces "in-being," were brought forward by each side in the freeze debate to demonstrate the validity of its position. The Reagan administration produced chart after chart to illustrate large Soviet *numerical* advantages in land-based missiles, land-based missile warheads, and the total "throwweight," or lifting capacity, of its combined land- and sea-based missile forces. Freeze advocates, on the other hand, pointed to compensating U.S. advantages in the *quality* of its ballistic missile submarines, the greater reliability of U.S. missile systems, a large lead in submarine missile warheads, and an overall lead in total strategic "force-loadings" (that is, nuclear bombs and missile warheads). The use of such measures to compare U.S. and Soviet forces has certain advantages, not the least of which is that they represent relatively straightforward, concrete, and easily grasped indicators of military capability. [As Marie Houget points out in her contribution to this chapter, however, the use of static indicators, or "beancounts," to provide a "snapshot" of the strategic balance is fraught with interpretational and analytic hazards.]

To begin with, no single set of quantitative or qualitative measurements can give a true picture of the two sides' capabilities. Beancounts can quite easily be manipulated to justify a desired conclusion, especially if certain indicators are stressed in the analysis while others, because they would threaten or undermine the desired interpretation, are either deemphasized or simply excluded from consideration. Second, both qualitative and quantitative assessments of the kind employed by the protagonists in the freeze debate are subject to large uncertainties, which, in the case of such variables as warhead yield or missile accuracy (especially for Soviet weapons) are simply impossible to pin down with great precision.

Because the beancount approach simply compares the standing forces on each side, moreover, it fails to indicate any of the consequences for each country if these weapons were used. To overcome this liability of static comparisons, analysts have turned to computer modelling techniques, using assumptions about the likely performance of each side's forces to predict what the outcome of various kinds of U.S.-Soviet "strategic exchanges" would be. The central argument of the "window of vulnerability" thesis, for example, is that U.S. land-based missiles have become vulnerable to a first-strike by Soviet land-based missiles. This conclusion is derived from computer models which make assumptions about such critical variables as the "hardness" of American missile silos, and the yield, accuracy, and reliability of Soviet MIRVed missile warheads, fit these assumptions into a mathematical equation, and "predict" the outcome of a Soviet first strike on our land-based missiles.

Yet [as Howard Estes points out in his contribution to Chapter 8], these "force exchange" comparisons, although they may reveal more about the relative military capabilities of the two countries than do beancounts, are themselves based on uncertain information about each side's forces. These models, as noted above, incorporate assumptions about the *likely* performance of the two countries' strategic weapons in a given war scenario. The information provided by a force-exchange model is therefore highly dependent on, and is only as good as, the accuracy and realism of the model's underlying assumptions about human behavior and the performance of individual weapons. When these assumptions are inaccurate or unrealistic, or when they are left unstated (and therefore inaccessible to a reader who might challenge their validity), the force-exchange model approach is of no more use in providing an accurate picture of the strategic balance than the beancount method.

[Estes believes that this is precisely the problem with the analyses that were used to demonstrate the growing vulnerability of the U.S. Minuteman force to a Soviet first strike. The assessments of Minuteman vulnerability, he argues, may be based on unrealistic and exaggerated assumptions about the reliability and accuracy of Soviet missile systems, and therefore they fail to account for the large uncertainties regarding missile performance. Soviet planners would have to ignore such uncertainties, at their peril, in launching a first strike against U.S. ICBMs.]

There is a third and even more fundamental problem associated with comparing U.S. and Soviet strategic forces, however. Trying to arrive at some judgment about "the state of the strategic balance," and about whether U.S. strategic nuclear forces are inferior, equal, or superior to those of the Soviet Union, may in fact be to ask the wrong question. Arguably, the issue of inferiority, parity, or superiority may have lost its military and political significance when each superpower possesses several thousand strategic nuclear warheads. Rather, we should concentrate on the issue of whether U.S. nuclear forces are adequate to carry out the missions assigned to them in national policy. The existence of strategic "parity" does not guarantee that U.S. forces are sufficient to fulfill the goals of U.S. strategic policy, any more than sufficiency hinges on the maintenance of parity. Harold Brown, Defense Secretary to former President Carter, emphasized the importance of this distinction in his Fiscal Year 1981 posture statement when he wrote: "We may be able to obtain deterrence, and can achieve assured destruction or more without equivalence; it is by no means certain that equivalence alone will give us deterrence."

The distinction is necessary because a simple measurement of balance (or imbalance) fails to relate force comparisons to the concrete security problems faced by the United States. Only national strategic *policy*, and the United States' deterrent *strategy*, can provide the criteria by which to judge whether or not a given correlation of U.S. and Soviet strategic capabilities is sufficient to maintain the security of the United States. If we judge U.S. forces in this fashion, then we can establish whether or not they are adequate to the demands of national strategy. Moreover, it helps in policy to establish the relative weight to be given to nuclear force modernization on the one hand and arms control with the Soviet Union on the other. Broadly speaking, existing forces that are sufficient to fulfill the requirements of national strategy will provide greater scope for arms control initiatives with the Soviet Union, and generate less pressure for arms modernization, than will forces that fall short of those requirements.

The difficulty, of course, is that different groups and individuals may apply different strategic criteria to the problem. Frequently, disagreements over "how much is enough" are rooted in differing views about *what U.S. nuclear strategy should be.* The strategic forces necessary to support a "nuclear war-winning" capability [as outlined by Colin Gray and Keith Payne in Chapter 3, for example] are much more extensive than those required to maintain a second-strike (or "assured destruction") capability. A true nuclear war-winning capability would require that the United States be able to destroy a large portion of Soviet nuclear forces in a first strike "counterforce" attack, and to intercept or protect against surviving Soviet weapons with strategic defenses (that is, anti-ballistic missile, air, and civil defenses). An assured destruction posture, by contrast, demands neither a first-strike capability nor extensive strategic defenses. It simply requires that the United States possess enough survivable strategic nuclear weapons such that the Soviets could not attack without running a substantial risk of devastating retaliation in return. With these much more modest force requirements, the assured destruction posture generates far less pressure for weapons modernization, and creates greater scope for concluding mutual, negotiated restraints on new weaponry with the Soviet Union, than does a nuclear war-winning strategy.

This perspective can be applied to the Reagan-Freeze debate. The Reagan administration's differences with the freeze campaign appear to be rooted less in a disagreement over whether U.S. strategic forces are adequate to deter nuclear attack by the Soviet Union than they are in a dispute over the "usability" of nuclear weapons and over what kind of nuclear strategy is necessary to guarantee U.S. national security.

Freeze advocates have argued that the U.S. and Soviet Union each have enough nuclear capability because each already possesses many more individual strategic warheads than are necessary to maintain a secure retaliatory capability. On the other hand [as you read in Chapter 3], the Reagan administration is not satisfied with having a retaliatory force geared primarily to the mission of deterring nuclear attacks. Like the three administrations that have preceded it, the Reagan administration continues to search for ways in which nuclear weapons could be used in war without producing catastrophic consequences for the United States. The Reagan administration appears to endorse a policy of "war-fighting deterrence," and according to some interpretations, may actually be pursuing a nuclear war-winning capability. The United States currently possesses neither the capability to wage "limited" or "controlled" nuclear war (a requirement of "war-fighting deterrence"), nor the means to actually win and survive a nuclear war with the Soviet Union. Thus, a central element in the administration's opposition to the freeze campaign is the fact that a nuclear freeze would prohibit the major force improvements necessary to provide the United States with more credible nuclear war-fighting options.

As the *1984 Voter Options Guide for National Security* points out, however, the Reagan administration's view of the "usability" of nuclear weapons is not one which is shared by a majority of Americans. Most Americans agree with the proposition that the United States must possess a survivable force of nuclear weapons in order to deter their first use by the Soviet Union. What they do not endorse are the notions that nuclear war could be controlled or survived. As the *Voter Options Guide* also points out, however, a comparable majority of Americans does not understand that these concepts have crept into American nuclear strategy, and yet are seriously out of sync with their own view of the "usability" of nuclear weapons.

This fact underscores a point made earlier. How should we evaluate the strategic balance and its impact on the prospects for arms control with the Soviet Union? Citizens must do more than recognize the pitfalls of relying on static comparisons of U.S. and Soviet strategic capabilities; they must do more than acknowledge the uncertainties inherent in computer-generated projections of vulnerabilities in the U.S. TRIAD. They must also understand the strategic assumptions which lie behind "expert" assessments of the adequacy of U.S. nuclear forces and see how conflicting assessments of the strategic balance, leading to diverging views on the priorities and urgency of arms control, result from conflicting conceptions of the "usability" of nuclear weapons.

FOR FURTHER READING

International Institute of Strategic Studies. *The Military Balance 1984–1985*. London: IISS, 1984. Country-by-country descriptions of national military forces around the world, with special sections on the U.S.-Soviet nuclear balance, and the East-West nuclear and conventional military balances in Europe. A basic reference, published annually.

Polmar, Norman. *Strategic Weapons: An Introduction*. New York: Crane Russak,

1982. An illustrated account of the development of U.S. and Soviet strategic nuclear forces, with a separate chapter on the nuclear forces of Britain, France, and China.

Richelson, Jeffrey T. "Static Indicators and the Ranking of Strategic Forces." *Journal of Conflict Resolution* 26 (June 1982), pp. 265–82. A good summary of the pitfalls of relying on static measures of military capability to determine the strategic balance.

Schroeer, Dietrich. "Nuclear Deterrence and Stability." In *Science, Technology, and the Nuclear Arms Race,* pp. 194–216. New York: John Wiley and Sons, 1984. An analysis of the U.S.-Soviet strategic balance, based on strategic and technical aspects of the U.S. deterrent posture.

Scowcroft, Brent, et al. "Report of the President's Commission on Strategic Forces." Washington, D.C.: U.S. Department of Defense, Office of Public Affairs, 1983. Commissioned by President Reagan to examine the issue of U.S. ICBM vulnerability and the MX missile system, this report raised doubts about the vulnerability of U.S. deterrent forces and the credibility of the administration's "window of vulnerability" thesis. Nevertheless, it recommended the continuation of all the offensive strategic nuclear weapons programs envisioned in the Reagan "Strategic Modernization Program."

Speed, Roger D. "The Survivability of U.S. Strategic Forces." In *Deterrence in the 1980s.* Stanford, Ca.: Hoover Institution, 1980. An analysis of U.S. deterrent forces, highlighting potential Soviet military threats to their survivability.

Stockholm International Peace Research Institute. *World Armaments and Disarmament 1984.* Stockholm: SIPRI, 1984. Analysis of worldwide military activities, including extended examinations of trends in the nuclear policies of the superpowers and other special topics. A basic reference, published annually.

United States Joint Chiefs of Staff. *United States Military Posture, Fiscal Year 1986.* Washington, D.C.: U.S. Government Printing Office, 1985. The official view of the United States' military leadership in the U.S.-Soviet military balance. Published annually.

Weinberger, Caspar W. *Annual Report of the Secretary of Defense to the Congress for Fiscal Year 1986.* Washington, D.C.: U.S. Government Printing Office, 1985. Presented annually to the Congress, provides a comprehensive overview of the U.S. military program for the coming fiscal year. Includes sections on nuclear strategy and nuclear weapons programs.

8

Paths to Nuclear War

A U.S.-Soviet nuclear war could start in several ways. Some of these potential paths to nuclear war can be traced directly to the present nuclear
weapons policies and postures of the United States and the Soviet
Union. Examples of such paths include a premeditated attack by one
superpower on the other, an accidental launch caused by a technical malfunction in the forces of one side or the other, and an attack precipitated by human error or irrationality. Other foreseeable scenarios have
their roots in causes which may not be directly linked to superpower
policies. Examples of such scenarios include a crisis in a conflict-ridden
region of the world (like the Middle East) escalating into a Soviet-American nuclear "exchange," and a regional nuclear war which spirals out of
control and engulfs the superpowers. In this chapter we offer an overview of some of the more threatening trends in U.S.-Soviet relations and
international politics—trends which appear to be increasing the risk of a
nuclear war.

In our view, one of the most dangerous trends over the last decade
has been the gradual shift in the attitude of political leaders toward the
possible use of nuclear weapons. As you learned in Chapter 4, many
U.S. leaders have come to accept the idea that under the right circumstances, nuclear war could be limited or controlled. Officials of the Reagan Administration have even given indications that they believe the
United States could "prevail" in a nuclear war with the Soviet Union.
There are disturbing signs that some Soviet strategists, as you learned in
Chapter 5, may also share the belief that, under the right circumstances, nuclear war could be won and survived.

Paralleling these trends, both nations have increasingly emphasized the acquisition of nuclear war-fighting capabilities. The Soviet
Union has augmented its traditional attention to air and civil defense in
recent years by deploying "fourth generation" ss-18 and ss-19 MIRved
ICBMs. Some Western analysts now believe these weapons threaten the
survivability of the U.S. Minuteman ICBM force. Similarly, the desire of
defense officials in the Nixon, Ford, and Carter administrations to acquire "prompt hard-target" counterforce capabilities has been broadened
by the Reagan administration. President Reagan's "Strategic Defense

Initiative" embodies a quest for a defensive ballistic missile shield against Soviet nuclear missile warheads.

The most threatening of these developments may be each side's apparent intention to develop the capability to destroy the land-based ICBMs of the other side. This is a particularly vexing problem for the Soviet leaders, whose ICBMs account for roughly 75 percent of their strategic power. The American Minuteman force, by contrast, carries only about 21 percent of U.S. strategic warheads. The prospective vulnerability of Soviet ICBMs to advancing American counterforce improvements is therefore likely to be of as much or more concern to Soviet leaders as the theoretical vulnerability of Minuteman is to American policymakers.

In responding to the deployment of U.S. counterforce-capable missiles like the MX and "Midgetman" ICBMs, or the Trident II (D-5) SLBM, the Soviets may adopt policies which would increase the risk of a Soviet-American nuclear war. To avoid losing their weapons to a U.S. first strike, the Soviets could adopt a policy of "launch on warning." Alternatively, they might plan to deal with a crisis by launching a preemptive surprise attack in anticipation of an American attack. Either one of these policies would increase the risk of nuclear war. If the Soviet Union builds its own counterforce capabilities,thereby rendering large portions of the U.S. TRIAD vulnerable, these risks will apply to U.S. behavior in future crises as well. (Examples of a Soviet counterforce could include a sea-based hard-target capability to simultaneously destroy both the U.S. heavy bomber and ICBM forces, or a "strategic" anti-submarine warfare capability to hunt down and destroy our missile submarines.)

The real danger, however, may not lie in the technical characteristics and theoretical war-fighting capabilities of each side's current and future arsenals. The danger may lie rather in the way policymakers *think* about the "usability" of nuclear weapons systems. As Howard Estes argues in "On Strategic Uncertainty," because modern strategic nuclear weapons systems are complex, and because it is infeasible to test them under anything close to "operational" conditions (that is, in an actual or simulated attack), there are large doubts about how these weapons will actually perform.

The problem is that policymakers often *exaggerate* the technical capabilities of various weapons systems. Yet, because of uncertainty, it is unreasonable and risky for policymakers—regardless of the "on-paper" capability of a ballistic missile to execute a first strike—to assume the virtually perfect performance that would be required. Overestimating the level of performance could lead to disastrous consequences for the attacker *and* the attacked. What if, for example, the U.S. or Soviet leadership believed they had a disarming first-strike capability (when in fact they did not), and under the pressures of a crisis, proceeded to order such an attack anyway? Not only would the attacked party suffer great damage as the consequence of being struck first, but it would also possess a sufficiently large retaliatory capability to destroy the attacker in return as well.

Another potential source of "crisis instability" in the U.S.-Soviet nuclear relationship is the vulnerability of U.S. and Soviet command and control systems. These are the command posts, communications links, and procedures through which the superpowers try to ensure that nuclear weapons are never used without a command from the proper authority. However, if nuclear weapons have to be used in retaliation, the command to launch a retaliatory strike promptly and reliably reaches the crews in missile launch control centers, missile submarines, and heavy bombers. The latter function plays a key role in maintaining the credibility of a second-strike deterrent posture: Without the ability to command surviving forces to retaliate, these forces, regardless of their own ability to ride out a first strike, lose credibility as a deterrent.

Yet, as Jeremy J. Stone observes in "Command and Control: Use It or Lose It?", the command and control facilities of both countries are highly vulnerable to attack. This mutual vulnerability of command and control assets on each side could induce a "use it or lose it" mentality within each country's leadership during a crisis. This disturbing possibility is lent credence when one considers the amount of attention Soviet strategists have paid to the role which attacks on command and control facilities can play in paralyzing an opponent. On the U.S. side, Secretary of Defense Caspar Weinberger's "Defense Guidance" document for fiscal years 1984–88 indicates that the Reagan administration is basing its strategy for nuclear conflict with the Soviet Union on the idea of "nuclear decapitation." This strategy calls for attacks on Soviet command and control centers, which would cripple the Soviets' ability to retaliate. This mutual emphasis on attacking command and control targets could undermine deterrence in a crisis. It also suggests a principal weakness of "limited" or "controlled" nuclear war-fighting theories: If nuclear weapons are ever used, "control" over the conflict could erode quickly if each side's vulnerable command and control facilities were attacked.

Richard Thaxton, in "Nuclear War by Computer Chip," points to another potential source of instability: a malfunction in the strategic warning system of either superpower. Thaxton describes how technical "errors" in the U.S. strategic warning system have led to false warnings of a Soviet missile attack. As Thaxton observes, fortunately in noncrisis conditions we have the luxury of taking the time to check several sources of information in order to determine whether a warning of attack is real or not. In a highly charged confrontation with the Soviet Union, however, the time span for decision-making may be dramatically shortened. In turn, the risk of an accidental launch of nuclear weapons would be severely aggravated, particularly if either superpower had been forced by the counterforce deployments of the other to adopt a "launch-on-warning" posture, in order to ensure that its vulnerable retaliatory forces could be launched before a surprise attack hit.

Lester Grinspoon, in "Crisis Behavior," outlines the various frailties in human decision-making processes that could compound "crisis instability." Grinspoon begins with the possibility that "group paranoia" aboard a submarine could lead a small segment of the crew to launch its nuclear missiles without authorization. He then describes the various forms of cognitive malfunctioning that the pressures and stress of a crisis can induce in decision-makers, including "misperception, impulsiveness, and a tendency to jump to conclusions." Time pressures, fear, and the phenomenon called "groupthink" are other potentially dangerous sources of decision-making irrationality in a crisis. "Anyone whose confidence ultimately depends on a belief in reliable human functioning at all levels, and in the prudence and restraint of national leaders in an unprecedented situation," he warns, "is merely avoiding anxiety by indulging in wishful thinking."

Leonard Spector, in "Nuclear Proliferation: The Pace Quickens," explains that the "horizontal spread of nuclear weapons to other countries is increasing the risk that nuclear weapons will be used in conflict-ridden regions of the world." According to Spector, although no new nation testes a nuclear weapon in 1984, there are disturbing signs in the Middle East, Southwest Asia, Latin America, and Southern Africa that certain "threshold" nations are making steady, concerted progress toward a nuclear weapons capability. This, in turn, has added a new dimension to the risk that a local conflict could become the "catalyst" for a nuclear war between the U.S. and Soviet Union. Although the superpowers have managed since 1945 to avoid a direct military conflict with one another, analysts have long worried about the risk that they might be drawn into a regional war, however hard they tried to avoid doing so. Many analysts, moreover, contend that a "catalytic" nuclear war is at least as likely a scenario for a Soviet-American nuclear war as a full-blown strategic exchange prompted by a technical malfunction or strategic miscalculation. This argument gains more force, moreover, when one considers the areas of the world like the Middle East, the Persian Gulf, and Central America, where U.S. and Soviet interests collide against a background of persistent and intense regional conflict.

As Richard Halloran explains in his "Spread of Nuclear Arms Is Seen by 2000," the prospect that other countries in these regions may soon develop (or, in the case of Israel, already possess) their own nuclear weapon has already had an important effect on U.S. strategic calculations. Based on a recent intelligence estimate that 31 countries could produce nuclear weapons by the year 2000, U.S. military planners are even now contemplating a world in which "nuclear engagements with adversaries other than the Soviet Union" might have to be fought to defend vital U.S. national interests in areas like the Middle East.

On Strategic Uncertainty

M. Howard Estes

M. Howard Estes is a retired Major General in the United States Air Force who currently holds the position of Director of Strategic Analysis for the BDM Corporation in Albuquerque, New Mexico.

Minuteman silo survivability is expected to be as low as 10 per cent for several years before the planned MX development. . . .

—Harold Brown

Nothing has been put forward which technologically supports the belief that we (or the Soviets) could, with any degree of confidence, expect to hit one silo at ICBM range, let alone 1,000 of them. . . .

—Arthur G. B. Metcalf

The above statements appeared during the debate on the merits of a multiple protective shelter (MPS) basing scheme for the MX missile and on the existence, or lack thereof, [of] a "window of vulnerability" for U.S. ICBMs. The basic controversy has been rekindled by President Reagan's proposal of a . . . deployment of the MX.

Three aspects of the statements cited bear mention. The first, obviously, is the disparity between the two survivability estimates. The second is that the lower estimate came from a gentleman who has not generally been regarded as an alarmist about the Soviet threat, while the upper estimate was rendered by someone who has a reputation for regarding that threat very seriously, indeed. The third is that, after the publication of these statements, no data (as differentiated from rhetoric) were forthcoming in the public press to prove that either was wrong.

The purpose of this article is to suggest that, in a certain sense, both gentlemen were "right" and then to pursue the implications of this suggestion for U.S. strategic doctrine and strategic force planning.

Statistics and Uncertainty

The field of statistics offers many techniques for dealing with uncertainty. Some of the more useful deal with the establishment of upper and lower bounds on a parameter the true value of which is unknown. The size of the uncertainty range defined by these bounds will depend upon the amount and quality of the available relevant data. It can be argued that what Drs. Brown and Met-

Source: M. Howard Estes, "On Strategic Uncertainty," *Strategic Review* (Winter 1983), pp. 36–43. Copyright © 1983 United States Strategic Institute, *Strategic Review*, Winter 1983.

calf have done with their statements is to provide us with estimates of the lower and upper bounds of Minuteman survivability, thus yielding a range of uncertainty from 10 to 100 per cent. Since this range is quite wide, clearly high-quality, relevant data must be in short supply.

Let any statisticians among the readers rest assured that the author is fully aware that the preceding paragraph is, from the standpoint of statistical theory, nonsense. Uncertainty bounds and data quality measures are, of course, supposed to be computed by a statistician using well-defined mathematical operations on specified data sets, not inferred from verbal assertions by different authors, however eminent. When the frame of reference is shifted to the consideration of current strategic problems, the paragraph does contain a kernel of truth. Different strategic experts *have* put forth, without convincing contradiction, widely differing assessments of the possible outcomes of strategic engagements. The reason they can do this is that the uncertainty ranges in the analytical results that underlie the assessments are quite wide. The reason that the ranges are wide is the paucity of good data to make them narrower.

One product of the debate over the "window of vulnerability" has been a reasonably thorough airing of the unsatisfactory state of the U.S. (and, by inference, the Soviet) data base on ballistic missile effectiveness in destroying hard targets such as ICBM silos. The detailed discussions that have been presented of such things as the uncertainties in missile-guidance accuracy, weapons effects, actual target hardness, reentry vehicle fratricide, etc., will not be repeated in this article. It suffices to say that these discussions, and the conclusions drawn from them, of which Metcalf's and Brown's are exemplary, have demonstrated clearly that prediction of the possible outcome of an attack by ICBMs (either U.S. or Soviet) on a set of hard targets is a process that is characterized by considerable imprecision.

A fact that has not been emphasized in the debates is that analogous uncertainties exist in estimates of the effectiveness of the other strategic systems in the U.S. and Soviet inventories. The lethality of submarine-launched ballistic missiles (SLBMs) against hard targets is subject to the same questions raised about ICBMs. To this are added the uncertainties of anti-submarine warfare (ASW) in the effectiveness. Manned bombers, with or without cruise missiles, introduce additional uncertainties into the effectiveness calculus, notably those in pre- and postlaunch survivability. Similar remarks can be made about strategic defensive systems: air and ballistic missile defenses and civil defense measures.

The Sources of Uncertainty

A logical question to ask is: Where did all this uncertainty come from, since it had not been a significant feature of previous debates on strategic issues? A short answer is that it did not "come from" anywhere; rather, it has been with us for decades and stems primarily from two sources. The first relates to the technical, geographical and political constraints on the testing of strategic nuclear weapons. These constraints make it impossible to perform the kinds of "all-up," "end-to-end" system tests that are routine, and mandatory, for other military hardware. As a result, the United States (and the Soviet Union) have acquired, and are acquiring, strategic nuclear weapons on the basis of operational test data that are less realistic than those produced for the purchase of aircrew flashlights or UHF radios. This situation is unlikely to change.

The second source of uncertainty is the fact that no nation has ever fought a strategic nuclear war. There is no historical data base of combat experience to guide, restrain or calibrate the predictions of the various theorists. . . .

Magnified Uncertainties of Strategic War

The central thesis of this article is that uncertainty is an intrinsic and important feature of today's strategic scene and must be explicitly considered in the formulation of strategic doctrine and in strategic force planning. A likely reaction to this statement from any student of the history of warfare would be the observation that warfare has always been the most uncertain of human activities. History is replete with accounts of how unforeseen factors have had decisive effects on the outcome of combat. Military theorists from Sun Tzu onward have warned that doctrine and planning must take account of the imponderables inherent in war. What is new or different where strategic nuclear war is considered?

Nothing is new, in the sense that the lessons of history and the dicta of the great military theorists are still relevant. Yet, at least three things seem different.

The first is that the magnitudes of the uncertainties in strategic analysis are greater, and so are also perforce the chances of wrong choices in formulating strategic doctrine or in strategic planning. Some effects of the lack of adequate technical and historical data bases have already been mentioned. Two more points should be made. First, as was noted in the earlier discussion, one benefit of extensive "end-to-end" operational testing of weapon systems is that it should narrow the uncertainty bounds on what have been called the "known unknowns." These are characteristics such as the guidance-system bias of given weapons, ICBM silo hardness, bomber penetration probability, etc. It is generally acknowledged that these parameters cannot be predicted precisely. The only arguments are over the degree of precision that can be attained.

A second benefit of testing, which has received little attention in the current literature, is that it also offers the best chance of surfacing the "unknown unknowns" before the system is fielded. An "unknown unknown" is an event for which no probability of occurrence can be determined. The most critical of these are in the "fatal flaw" category. No matter how much testing a weapon receives prior to deployment, there is always some possibility of a major failure to perform as predicted in combat. This has happened a number of times. The performance of U.S submarine torpedoes in the early days of World War II—and of U.S. air-to-air missiles, Soviet surface-to-air missiles and the M-16 rifle in the Vietnam conflict—are a few examples. Obviously, no examples exist for combat failures of U.S. strategic nuclear systems. However, there are accounts of a "fatal flaw" in the Polaris A-3 SLBM which was not detected until well after deployment and which would have resulted in a 75 per cent failure rate if the missiles had ever been launched in anger. Therefore, an additional detrimental effect of the constraints on testing of strategic weapons should be to raise the probability of occurrence of a "fatal flaw" in combat.

The second point is that an analogous conclusion can be drawn from the absence of a historical data base. A highly relevant maxim is that "good judgment comes mostly from experience, and experience comes mostly from bad judgment." In the field of strategic nuclear war, the level of experience suggests that the potential for bad judgments in formulating doctrine and strategy is high. "Fatal flaws" can also occur in these activities. French defense doctrine in 1940 and American doctrine for the role of the battleship in 1941 come to mind. In each case, the error made was not a marginal miscalculation, but a total misapprehension of the situation. These errors were committed despite considerable historical data bases on conventional war in Europe and on aircraft operations in naval warfare. Unless one accepts the theory that formulation of strategic nuclear doctrine and plans is improved by the lack of any data base of prior experience, it seems safe to predict that mistakes—and possibly bad ones—will occur.

The second difference between strategic nuclear war and past conflicts is that the penalties for material failures or for wrong doctrinal and strategic decisions will probably be more severe and will be exacted more promptly, and the chances for remedial action will be far less. Past conventional wars provided the best possible "proving grounds" for evaluating weapons and doctrine. The pace and levels of destructiveness of most of the conflicts allowed the combatants to fix or replace weapons and doctrine that did not work, and to fight on. If the opinions of most experts are correct, this situation would not obtain in a strategic nuclear war.

A third difference is that, unlike conventional warfare, strategic nuclear war admits of easy, and intellectually titillating, analysis. For a first-order analysis, a nuclear exchange can be treated as a short, cataclysmic artillery duel. The mathematics are simple. The amount of input data required is minimal, and the outcome can be specified by very few numbers (e.g., warheads surviving on both sides) with as many significant digits as the conscience of the analyst allows. Much more complex analyses, using large digital computers, can also be performed. Such arcana as game theory and the calculus of variations can be invoked to produce "optimal" solutions. Best of all, there is no possibility of the analyst being embarrassed by history.

This situation was epitomized by a lecture this writer once attended at the National Defense University. The lecturer was the head of Systems Analysis in the Office of the Secretary of Defense. He stated that, while his office was able to do an excellent job of analyzing and determining strategic force structure, it did a poor job in analysis of conventional forces, thus establishing an interesting inverse relationship between the perceived quality of an analysis and the amount of real data available on the subject to be analyzed.

All of this is amusing, but it also has a serious aspect. The seductive ease with which strategic wars can be "fought" in the computer room—and the spurious air of accuracy provided by printouts of results tabulated to eight (or more) significant figures—have led some people (who should know better) to believe, or to act as if they believed, that it is possible to predict with considerable certainty the outcome of a strategic nuclear war. Outstanding examples of this are the charts presented in Secretary Brown's last two *Annual Reports,* which purported to show, year by year, the precise outcomes of possible strategic nuclear exchanges between the United States and the Soviet Union. Only one uncertainty was allowed to intrude, and that concerned the number of reentry vehicles that the Soviets might deploy on a new ICBM. Other examples, displaying equally precise results, abound in the strategic literature.

Improvements in Operational Testing

Thus far, it has been argued: 1) that the uncertainties attending the employment of strategic nuclear forces are unavoidable and are at least as large, and probably larger, than those associated with conventional forces; 2) that the nature of strategic nuclear war makes the assessment of these uncertainties a more critical function than it is for conventional war; and 3) that, in many cases, this assessment function is being performed poorly, or not at all. The next question is: What, if anything, can be done to improve the situation?

The first, and hardest, task will probably be that of getting acceptance by decisionmakers of the idea that something should be done. A dramatic seachange in attitudes will be required. Uncertainty is anathema to most leaders in the military and in government. Any analyst who told a general, or a Congressional committee, that a weapon system would have survival probability of between 10 per cent and 100 per cent would be drummed out of the analysts' corps, and his viewgraphs would be burned to avoid spreading the infection. Probably the best line of argument to use against this dislike of uncertainty is to point out that, whether acknowledged or not, uncertainties exist, will be operative during war, and therefore the more we know about them, the better. This should be followed with a "self-answering question."

If better information on the extent and possible effects of the uncertainties were available, could better decisions be made with its use or without?

If it is accepted that explicit consideration of the U.S. uncertainties in strategic nuclear war is a sensible idea, the next step would be to establish that consideration of the uncertainties facing the Soviets is equally sensible. Their lack of relevant data is almost as large as ours, and they face much the same problems that we do in pondering the outcomes of possible nuclear wars. Analyses of Soviet uncertainties will be more difficult, and conjectural, than examining our own, but this is a necessary step in coming to grips with such knotty questions as the perceptual basis for deterrence and tenable positions for START negotiations.

A third action would be, where possible, to attempt to reduce U.S. uncertainties by appropriate operational testing of strategic weapons and support systems. For the weapons only marginal improvements are possible, but some useful tests might be conducted. For example, some of the Minuteman flights used for crew training and follow-on testing could be conducted from operational silos in the ICBM fields, using procedures as close to the "real thing" as safety considerations permitted.

The United States has never conducted a successful launch of an ICBM from an operational silo. Some years ago, an Operational Base Launch program to do this was proposed, but it was never carried out—although it was declared to be quite feasible and to have a very low probability of any injuries or fatalities from impact of the spent lower stages. Such firings would do nothing to help resolve the arguments over missile guidance system bias that are at the heart of the "window of vulnerability" debate. They would, however, if conducted properly—i.e., by exercising the whole chain from the surveillance systems through to the Launch Control Center—provide additional confidence that the National Command Authority could get the missiles out of their silos if it had to.

Data relevant to the ballistic missile accuracy question could be obtained by the firing of SLBMs and ICBMs on varying launch azimuths. Flights over the north polar regions would not be possible, but some light would be cast on the question of variation in bias with launch azimuth. Whether the value of the data obtained would be worth the large costs involved in providing the many missiles required to obtain statistically valid results and the necessary range instrumentation is a question best decided by the experts.

One area where the uncertainties are significant, and probably most critical, is command, control and communications. The geographical and political constraints on permissible operational testing of strategic C^3 components and systems are less severe than for strategic weapons testing. As a matter of fact, one of the reasons behind a general acceptance of the notion that the United States is today in serious trouble in the strategic C^3 area has to do with the ominous results obtained in operational tests. Activities such as full-scale system tests to determine the susceptibility of airborne command posts and surveillance satellites to electromagnetic pulses are not cheap, but reasonably credible data can and should be obtained.

The Need to Quantify the Uncertainties

The fourth thing that must be done is a concerted effort by statisticians and analysts to use the data now available and those forthcoming from future tests to produce the best possible (which may not be very good) quantitative description of the various uncertainties on both sides of the strategic equation. For the decisionmaker, analysis can provide illumination of the issues that can be of immense help, as long as the presentation of the analysis includes clear exposition of its limitations.

It is probable that some of the most significant uncertainties will not be susceptible to quantification. By definition, the "unknown unknowns" fall in this category. These cases will have to be treated qualitatively, with as much objectivity and precision of logic as can be mustered.

The contemplated product of the recommended analysis effort would be a presentation of: 1) what is known "for sure" about various aspects of strategic nuclear war (this is likely to be a small, perhaps empty, set); 2) what is known imprecisely, with discussions of the sources of the imprecision, and estimates of the magnitudes of the imprecision in the various parameters of interest; 3) what is not known at all; 4) the possible effects of these uncertainties and their criticality to the tasks of doctrine formulation and strategic force planning.

It is quite possible that the first pass through this analytical process would produce ranges of uncertainty in the output data so wide that they would appear to have no utility for the decisionmaker. In this case, the urgings to "shoot the messenger" should be resisted. If the strategic situation facing the United States really is unsatisfactorily uncertain, this itself would be a useful (if discouraging) piece of information. If the initial ranges of uncertainty were too wide, there would be at least two remedial actions to consider. Additional weapons system tests might be applicable. Another measure would be a critical examination of the logic used in compounding the various uncertainties to produce the final outputs. Strategic analysts in general, and military strategic analysts in particular, are inclined to consider "worst cases" when given a choice. Uncritical application of this philosophy to the problem under discussion could yield very large uncertainty ranges.

A possible objection to the foregoing prescription is that it seems to presuppose an unrealistic level of objectivity on the part of those who would order, and those who would perform, the required analytical efforts. The objective of much of the analysis that is performed today is not to seek the "truth," but to buttress the position already taken by a given set of advocates. If the recommended effort were undertaken, a likely result would be not one analysis with universally acceptable conclusions, but rather several, each reflecting the preconceived views of a different faction in the strategic debate. It can be argued that such a result, although less satisfying intellectually than one unified view of the "truth," would be most beneficial. The process of preparation and approval of the analysis would force analysts and decisionmakers to think about matters hitherto ignored, and comparison of the results of the various analyses would provide a better frame of reference for the debates on strategic issues.

Translation into Force Posture

Once a reasonable, if not universal, consensus on the strategic uncertainties had been produced, the next step would be a concerted effort to incorporate the analytical results into the formulation of U.S. strategic doctrine and into our strategic force planning. The principal objective of this effort would be to determine the "match" between the various doctrinal and force options and the inherent uncertainties.

For example, whatever else can be said of the doctrine of assured destruction, it appears quite likely that the United States (or the USSR) could carry out the actions called for. The number and diversity of U.S. nuclear weapons that would be available, even after a devastating Soviet first strike, and the vulnerability of the target set are such that the United States, even with a highly degraded C^3 system and weapons that did not work very well, could destroy Soviet society, and the USSR could do nothing to prevent it. Assured destruction, therefore, could be termed a "highly certain" (though possibly suicidal) doctrine.

At the opposite pole would be a doctrine based on the type of preemptive, disarming, first-strike attack that is the principal stock-in-trade of the "window of vulnerability" theorists. The attacking weapons would have to work very well indeed, and even if they did, the attack could be negated by the use of launch-on-warning tactics by the victimized power. A preemptive doctrine is thus a highly uncertain one.

The various "flexible response" doctrines, of which Harold Brown's (and, presumably, Caspar Weinberger's) Countervailing Strategy is the latest example, lie somewhere between these two extremes. Depending upon the target sets specified, the performance required from the surviving C^3 facilities, etc., the doctrines would appear to range from moderately to highly uncertain.

In advance of the performance of the requisite analysis, it is difficult to predict in detail how this exercise of "matching" doctrine and strategy options to the uncertainties would come out. It should be an interesting, and, if successful, illuminating process. One action that should follow any success should be a general agreement among U.S. decisionmakers that no strategic doctrinal or force structure option would be considered, much less adopted, without explicit formulation, and display to the decisionmakers concerned, of the effects of the relevant uncertainties. . . .

If the analytical efforts recommended in this paper are undertaken, and done right, one of two things will occur. The results could show that the uncertainties in strategic nuclear war are really much smaller and less critical than has been alleged above. This would invalidate the central thesis of the paper, but it would be good news, indeed, for U.S. decisionmakers and would provide them with much useful ammunition for the next joust over the "window of vulnerability." On the other hand, more likely results would be the production of some useful data and the establishment of a more rational analytical framework for U.S. decisionmakers to use in thinking about strategic issues.

One benefit of this could be a U.S. strategic doctrine more closely aligned with the possibilities of implementation in the event of war. A second could be a more sensible view of the Soviets' ability to do the same. Benefits may also accrue in the area of strategic weapon system acquisition. The need explicitly to consider the uncertainties in system performance might result in greater, and earlier, attention during system development to the trade-offs between reliability and complexity. Test and evaluation activities should receive a new, and traumatic, orientation, since the objective would be not only to determine whether the system met its original specifications, but also to produce, and provide to the Secretary of Defense and the Congress, quantitative and statistically sound estimates of how well, and how badly, the system might perform in combat. One result of the process might be more robust strategic hardware. Another might be greater candor by those involved in the weapons acquisition process. There is today a surfeit of neither.

The course of action recommended above could founder at any point in the sequence of activities described. Political, psychological and technical "rocks and shoals" abound. However, the benefits of even a partial attainment of the objectives sought would justify the expense and pain incurred. More succinctly, it is worth a try.

COMMAND AND CONTROL: USE IT OR LOSE IT?

Jeremy J. Stone

Jeremy J. Stone is the Director of the Federation of American Scientists, a Washington-based scientific lobbying and public education organization.

Nothing ought to be of more concern to arms controllers than the growing disproportion between the extraordinarily good ability to command, control, and communicate (C^3) with strategic forces before they are attacked, and the very poor ability thereafter.

A nation that strikes first with strategic forces does so with its command structure, control mechanisms, and communication devices wholly intact, alerted and ready. Each and every telephone line, satellite, and antennae is functioning and every relevant person is alive and well. By contrast, the nation which seeks to launch a retaliatory attack may find its chain of command highly disrupted, its telephone lines dead, its satellites inoperative, its radio signals interfered with, and its communications officers out of action.

This always dramatic disproportion is today increasing. The *unattacked* forces have ever more flexible first-strike capabilities. They can be retargeted with many options, and have ever increasing accuracy against hardened targets such as missile silos or command bunkers. Accordingly, no fixed land-based target, or set of targets numbering in tens of hundreds, can be expected to survive a deliberate attack. Indeed, as a result of MIRV, strategic forces have the capacity to strike thousands of targets which means, in particular, that airspace could be barraged making even airborne command posts of uncertain survivability.

EMP From Only A Few Bombs

Worst of all . . . the effects of such electrical phenomena as electromagnetic pulse could be used with devastating effect, with only a few nuclear weapons, to put satellites out of action while affecting the communications of an entire enemy continent. Considering that tens of nuclear weapons could be spared for this purpose alone, and that a handful might suffice, the feasibility of highly organized retaliation in response to a massive attack is questionable.

Source: Jeremy J. Stone, "Command and Control: Use It or Lose It?" *Federation of American Scientists Public Interest Report* (October 1980), pp. 1–3. Reprinted by permission of the Federation of American Scientists.

It has long been argued by arms controllers that vulnerable strategic forces, such as ICBMs built in exposed ("soft") locations, were a form of "instability" precisely because they were effective if fired first but—because vulnerable to attack—useless in retaliation. Such a disproportion between their value on first and second strike, respectively, was considered both a temptation to enemy attack and an inducement to one's own preemption. In a crisis, it would lead military officers to recommend to political authorities that it was "now or never." (As a latent form of this recommendation phenomenon, observe that the Strategic Air Command chief wrote Secretary Brown on April 9, 1979, that the countervailing strategy options could only be exercised if the United States fired its missiles at the first sign of an attack or attacked first. See Washington Post, August 21, 1980.)

But nothing has the extraordinary "use it or lose it" quality of command, control and communications under modern conditions. And precisely because the strategic forces of the two sides include nuclear submarines, whose basing is highly invulnerable to direct attack, the vulnerability of what is termed C^3 may be insufficient for controlled responses. That neither side is likely to be able to control its forces once more than some tens of nuclear weapons have been fired is probably the most decisive argument against limited nuclear war, and the best argument that it would surely escalate.

A Conclusion For Arms Controllers

Perhaps the single most important conclusion for arms controllers in confronting this subject is the importance, for each side, of avoiding attacks on command, control, and communication (including satellites) if, somehow, nuclear forces are deliberately or accidentally fired. Preparations to attack C^3 are, in effect, a kind of supercounterforce and correspondingly destabilizing. Should either side carry out deliberate efforts to attack the C^3 of the other, it appears almost certain that a spasm war would result in which the attacked nation gave its military commanders either by prior agreement or last desperate message, the authority to fire at will. As its ability to communicate gave out, it could and would do no less than use its last communications channel for the final order.

To get some idea of the dimensions of the problem, the United States C^3 involves the following very short (and vulnerable) list of military command centers. One Soviet nuclear weapon could put both Washington (with all 16 civilian successors to the President) and the Pentagon (the major command post) out of action. The Alternative National Command Post at Fort Ritchie is vulnerable also to direct nuclear attack in an era in which the accuracy of Soviet missiles with large warheads is approaching one-tenth of a mile. The Strategic Air Command headquarters in Omaha would not survive a direct attack. Nor would the headquarters of the Commander-in-Chief of our force in Europe (CincEur), the Pacific (CincPac) and the Atlantic (CincLant).

True, the latter three headquarters have airborne command posts ready to take off with their commanders, but would they do it on time? Just as the Afghanistan invasion started on Christmas Eve, and the Yom Kippur war on Yom Kippur, even attacks induced by crises would be expected to occur at night or unexpected times. Would the military leadership be able, for example, to get into its plane in less than a half an hour (or even 15 minutes) to escape the atomic cloud?

The Strategic Air Command's "Looking Glass" headquarters *is* permanently in the air. Thus, it has a certain amount of what is termed "location uncertainty." But consider . . . that a single explosion detonated in the atmosphere about 300 miles above Chicago would produce an electromagnetic pulse coverage of 25,000 volts per meter over the entire United States and adjacent waters! Aircraft are vulnerable to these effects at ranges "very dependent on many factors" according to an article in Signal Magazine of January, 1980. See also "Doomsday Plans Are Vulnerable To N-Pulse" in which Joseph Albright of the *Atlanta Constitution* (24 September, 1980) says even the electronically hardened Boeing 747 (E-4Bs) which have not yet replaced the electronically vulnerable command posts (E-4As) would lose 26% of all critical circuits if flooded with an 800-volt electromagnetic pulse. Thus, there is a real chance that even airborne command posts might not be operative. Here is what the Defense Department says about EMP:

> The effect of nuclear weapon detonations, particularly those occurring at high altitudes, is of continuing concern . . . Such detonations can cause electromagnetic pulse (EMP) and radio propagation blackout over wide areas of the earth from only a few suitably located explosions, *not necessarily relatable to an act of war. (italics added)*

The United States also maintains certain Minuteman missiles with radio transmitters, rather than warheads, which it proposes to launch into a very high ballistic missile orbit from which the transmitters would scream out a last message for about one half hour. Whether these missiles can be safely hidden amidst the other 1,000 armed Minuteman missiles is a question only the U.S. Air Force (and/or Soviet intelligence) are qualified to guess. But, obviously, attacks on all Minuteman missiles would, presumably, have a reasonable probability of destroying the handful devoted to message carrying.

Would The Messages Arrive?

In addition to attacking these C^3 nodal points, a calculated attack could be expected to try to cut the links between the points so that messages to them even if they survived, would not arrive.

Some tentative conclusions upon which FAS members are encouraged to comment for the December Report seem to be as follows:

We should improve the survivability of our C^3 to the point where it does not tempt attack in crises as a way of neutralizing our entire strategic force.

But we ought not talk of attacking Soviet command and control lest we simply encourage the Soviet Union to devolve nuclear authority in advance on ever more junior officers. Further, we ought not, in fact, launch such attacks, unless *our* command and control is attacked lest we lose all chance of war-termination. In particular, Soviet leadership bunkers ought not be attacked except in some final parting salvo as an alternative to attacking Russian innocents in cities.

We ought not kid ourselves that we are prepared to fight a protracted nuclear war when no plausible improvement in C^3 is likely to permit it; countervailing strategies with numerous complicated options that cannot, in fact, be carried out could become an expensive kind of self-delusion.

In particular, as General Ellis pointed out above, these options require more and more warheads (that is, if they are going to be carried out *in retaliation*) and thus the options could and will dominate our procurement planning for a long time if we permit our war plans to be built around such ambitious possibilities.

NUCLEAR WAR BY COMPUTER CHIP: HOW AMERICA ALMOST LAUNCHED ON WARNING

Richard Thaxton

Richard Thaxton is the pen name of a Washington journalist.

Fittingly enough, *Dr. Strangelove* was showing at the Capitol Hill Cinema in Washington June 6 [1980] when a false alarm of a massive Soviet attack—the second in a week and the third in seven months—started the countdown for an American nuclear strike against Russia.

In *Strangelove,* it took a mad SAC general, a Soviet doomsday device, and a bizarre series of accidents and miscalculations to ignite World War III.

The two most recent false alarms were set off by something far simpler—a short-circuit in a computer chip the size of a dime and worth less than half a dollar. In both alerts, the error was detected in three minutes, but not before U.S. nuclear armaments were unsheathed.

Source: Richard Thaxton, "Nuclear War by Computer Chip: How America Almost Launched on Warning," *The Progressive* (August, 1980), pp. 29–30. Reprinted by permission from *The Progressive,* 409 East Main Street, Madison, WI 53703. Copyright © 1980, The Progressive, Inc.

Could the Pentagon's errant, forty-six-cent computer chip actually have triggered doomsday with a premature warning that it had come? Defense Secretary Harold Brown answered this question with an emphatic "no." He said the warning system's safeguards require absolute verification of any attack and prevent machines from usurping the ultimate decision to retaliate.

Unfortunately, Brown's assessment seems much too sanguine in light of the escalating U.S.-Soviet rift, the march of nuclear weapons technology, and his own admission that false alarms of atomic attack are likely to recur.

Herbert Scoville is one of several defense experts who believe the two June false alarms were considerably more dangerous than the one that occurred last November 9. Tension had heightened over the months because of the Soviet invasion of Afghanistan and President Carter's warning that the United States would resort to force—possibly nuclear force—if the Russians were to move on the Persian Gulf.

Some officials say the intense preparations for war taken during the brief June false alarms suggest the United States is on a higher level of alert than in November—that the situation is now "hair trigger."

The November 9 alarm, also caused by a computer error, lasted twice as long as the two in June. Yet SAC nuclear bomber pilots were not even instructed to board their B-52s and get them safely into the air, according to Government officials.

The attack warning gave U.S. military commanders barely five minutes to react before the first Russian missiles—supposedly launched from submarines—were to hit targets, including all the SAC bomber bases, Government sources say. Yet it was not until a minute after these warheads were to have struck that Air Force technicians discovered the alert had been triggered by a computerized war game gone awry—a simulated attack tape had somehow gone out as the real thing. Nevertheless, neither President Carter nor Secretary Brown was informed.

Meanwhile, the sources say, the pilot and crew of Carter's E-4 jet command center (on runway alert at Andrews Air Base to allow a President to escape the initial holocaust and direct retaliation from the skies) dashed into the aircraft and took off without having heard from the President.

In June, the reaction was much more vigorous—frighteningly so. According to Pentagon and other Government officials, here is what happened in those two cases:

Air Force officers deep underground at the North American Air Defense Command near Colorado Springs were routinely monitoring warning apparatus.

Suddenly, the fluorescent display screens connected to a "Nova" Data General computer flashed a warning: A large-scale Soviet missile attack of land-based and submarine missiles had just been launched.

The computer warned that Soviet missiles had been fired on a "depressed trajectory" from submarines positioned close to American shores. They would strike their targets here in as few as three minutes (the period of time it took to discover the error).

SAC was alerted and, at airfields across the United States, pilots and crews of 116 B-52 nuclear bombers on runway alert scrambled into their planes, gunned the engines, and began taxiing for takeoff. Nuclear submarine commanders also were alerted.

Inside underground launch centers near silos housing American ICBMs, missile launch officers strapped themselves into jolt-resistant swivel chairs, unlocked strongboxes, removed "attack verification codes" and launch keys, and inserted the keys into slots.

(When two keys ten feet apart are twisted within two seconds of each other, the warheads blast toward the Soviet Union.)

Shortly after the false alarm came to light, as unlikely a critic as Senator John Tower of Texas rejected the Pentagon's assurances that nothing dangerous had occurred. He predicted a Congressional investigation. The left wing of Britain's Labour Party expressed shock and called for a Parliamentary debate on the issue. And the Soviet Union accused the United States of harboring a "nuclear persecution complex."

Some critics are most concerned with what might happen if a false alarm were to recur in an even more tense East-West climate.

For instance, Bruce Blair of the Brookings Institution—an expert on nuclear attack warning systems and a former Air Force missile launch officer—suggested the following scenario:

The United States and the Soviets are on the brink of war because of a crisis in the Middle East, Africa, Western Europe, or all of the above. At this most inopportune time, the U.S. warning system decides to emit a false alarm of a Soviet atomic attack.

U.S. bombers take to the skies to avoid being blown to bits, and missiles are primed for quick launch.

Meanwhile, the Soviets, through their satellite sensors, detect that U.S. bombers have been launched. Fearful that submarine missiles and ICBMs are soon to follow, and that their own missiles will be destroyed in their silos, the Soviets unleash at least some of their warheads—not at our missile silos, which they fear would be empty, but at other military targets, quite possibly in heavily populated areas.

But, still fearing that U.S. missiles are the targets of a Russian first strike, we "retaliate" against the Soviet "retaliation" against the nonexistent American first strike, in order to save our own warheads from destruction. Apocalypse, close behind, obliterates the confusion.

Pentagon spokesman Thomas Ross refused to comment on such a scenario, but argued that a computer error could never prompt "retaliation" against a nonexistent attack. Attack warnings are verified or shown false through U.S. satellite sensors, he said. But the problem is that the sensors, too, have been known to fail, occasionally reporting sunspots as missiles. Blair recalled a 1973 incident in which a computer misinterpreted sensor data about a Soviet test missile fired from a site near Iran. The computer predicted the missile would land in California, and sparked an alert. But the missile landed where it was aimed, in Kamchatka, Siberia.

In the above scenario for doomsday, the flashpoint was reached because each side was convinced its missiles were about to be destroyed on the ground. Indeed, the vulnerability of missiles has become almost an obsession with many in the military establishment because technological developments seem to have made the "hardened" missile silo obsolete.

But many of those more concerned with the vulnerability of the human race to accidental war than with the fate of hardened silos believe a grave danger is posed by U.S. strategy for deterring the Soviets from launching a first strike against American missiles.

The strategy, known as "launch-on-warning," has been embraced by Secretary Brown. He has warned the Soviets that the United States may well launch some or all of its warheads upon electronic detection that the Russians have launched theirs. General David Jones, chairman of the Joint Chiefs of Staff, assured the House Armed Services Committee last year that the United States has the capacity both to detect an attack and to retaliate before it arrives.

But given the demonstrated fallibility of electronic detection, the dangers of launch-on-warning are all too obvious.

Many are convinced that launch-on-warning may soon be transformed from an option in the American war plan into an imbedded doctrine. Partly as a result of the waning support for the MX missile concept of deploying missiles amid a cluster of empty silos for protection, the military establishment is seeking a "quick fix" for the problem of missile vulnerability.

Among the many objections to launch-on-warning is that, in effect, it relegates decision-making power to machines. Many defense analysts believe Soviet submarine missiles can hit their U.S. targets in as few as three minutes from first detection. ICBMs take fifteen or twenty minutes. In any event, there is little time for leaders to reflect on the course to take if they want to preserve the ability to launch on warning. So faulty information from machines could easily determine their decisions.

We may be approaching the point where a computer chip could assume the role of Commander-in-Chief and decide whether to go to war.

CRISIS BEHAVIOR

Lester Grinspoon

Lester Grinspoon is Associate Professor of Psychiatry, at Harvard Medical School in Boston, Massachusetts.

Predictably, many who read or hear of the TTAPS paper with its forecast of a nuclear winter will not accept its conclusions. Too often, people cannot risk being overwhelmed by the anxiety which might accompany a full grasp of the present world situation and its implications for the future.

If they cannot fault the assumptions, data and computational protocols that lead to these conclusions, they may dismiss the possibility of extinction on the ground that the human species would never allow it to happen. But in some TTAPS scenarios, as little as 100 megatons of explosive power, in the form of airbursts over cities, can produce desperate climatological and ecological conditions.

The catastrophic effects of nuclear war can be initiated by a small fraction of the world's nuclear arsenals. The reality is that we have created a system which demands perfection if it is to guarantee the safety of humankind. And because human beings are involved at every level, the system is fallible from bottom to top.

At the bottom, there are dangers of accident, human error and psychopathology. More than 50 serious accidents involving nuclear weapons have occurred in the West alone since 1950. The U.S. Nuclear Weapons Reliability Program requires screening and evaluation for all personnel who have access to nuclear missiles and bombs or who control entry to a nuclear weapons area, as well as for those who can order a launch at the battalion or squadron level or control sealed orders, messages and computer tapes. About 120,000 people are subject to this screening.

The Department of Defense says that these procedures, plus other controls such as the rule which permits no one unaccompanied access to nuclear weapons, make the danger of human error or aberration minimal. But there is no psychiatric screening system, however elaborate, which can predict with assurance who will or will not behave rationally. And there are reports that screening in the Nuclear Weapons Reliability Program is grossly inadequate or even perfunctory. In 1975 and 1976, 4 percent of the personnel admitted

Source: Lester Grinspoon, "Crisis Behavior," *Bulletin of the Atomic Scientists* (April 1984), pp. 27–31. Reprinted by permission of the *Bulletin of the Atomic Scientists,* a magazine of science and world affairs. Copyright © 1984 by the Educational Foundation for Nuclear Science, Chicago, IL 60637.

after screening had to be transferred out for substance abuse, negligence, aberrant behavior and criminal convictions.[1]

It is no surprise that there are frightening stories to tell. In August 1969 an Air Force major was suspended for keeping three men with "dangerous psychiatric problems" as nuclear missile guards at a base in San Francisco; one of them had gone berserk with a loaded carbine. The major said he needed the men because he was short-handed. Later that year, men with access to nuclear-capable missiles near Miami were arrested for possession and sale of LSD. In late 1974 the Milwaukee Journal reported an Army code specialist as saying that soldiers in Germany were sometimes intoxicated on alcohol or drugs while attaching nuclear warheads to missiles.[2]

Drug and alcohol abuse is a persistent problem in the armed forces, regarded by both enlisted men and officers as a detriment to discipline, morale, combat readiness and job performance. In 1979, according to reports of Navy medical officers, alcohol was involved in 15 to 20 percent of major aircraft accidents.[3] According to a questionnaire survey conducted in 1980 for the Department of Defense, 21 percent of all respondents had drunk eight or more 12-ounce glasses of beer at least one day a week for the preceding year. Seven percent were alcohol-dependent; 36 percent had used an illicit drug in the previous year, 27 percent in the past month. About 10 percent had been high while on duty on 40 or more days.[4]

Certain features of military life contribute to this problem: monotonous work, poor living conditions, lack of recreational facilities, overcrowding and, on bases in foreign countries, culture shock, isolation and homesickness. But in general, servicemen use drugs and alcohol about as much and for the same reasons as civilians of the same age. The trouble is that drinking and drug use, relatively harmless in civilian life, can be extraordinarily dangerous in the presence of powerful weapons.

To avoid the dangers created by mentally unstable, intoxicated, or negligent individuals, nuclear weapons commands rely heavily on group decision-making. The U.S. defense system and presumably the Soviet one as well rely on many-person controls as a way to avoid the danger that some lone madman will set off a nuclear war. But the system becomes too cumbersome to be effective if too many simultaneous participants are required for each action.

The problem is where to draw the line, and the question is whether the

---

[1] Lloyd J. Dumas, "Human Fallibility and Nuclear Weapons," *Bulletin* (Sept. 1980), pp. 15–19.
[2] *Ibid.*
[3] "Drug Abuse in the Military," Hearing before Select Committee on Narcotics Abuse and Control, U.S. House of Representatives, Sept. 17, 1981 (Washington, D.C.: Government Printing Office, 1981).
[4] Marvin P. Burt and Mark M. Biegel, *Highlights from the Worldwide Survey of Nonmedical Drug Use and Alcohol Use among Military Personnel* (Bethesda, Maryland: Burt Associates, 1980).

line has been drawn at numbers that are too low. We do not know the exact arrangements for delegating to a submarine commander the authority to launch nuclear weapons; but neither do we know that submarine officers cut off from direct communication with higher authority would not be capable of launching missiles on their own. A single Trident submarine has enough warheads to wipe out all the major cities of the Soviet Union. One report also claims that as few as four officers in a Minuteman squadron of 50 missiles could set off a world war.[5]

There is a form of madness known as shared paranoid disorder, in which two or more persons who live for a long time in intimate association develop a common delusion, transmitted by the dominant member of the group. It happens especially when they live in relative isolation.

People who are otherwise quite normal may develop a shared paranoia under the influence of a charismatic individual who suffers from persecutory delusions. For example, a very careful psychiatric examination of one of the women convicted of murder along with Charles Manson failed to establish that she was suffering from any serious psychopathology either before she came under Manson's influence or after the Manson "family" broke up. There were several dozen members, but probably no more than two or three of them had displayed obvious psychopathology before the family came into existence. No screening program could have predicted that the others had the potential to develop a shared paranoid disorder of the kind that led to the Tate and La Bianca murders.

We do not know for certain the size of the smallest group that, under some circumstances, could autonomously launch missiles. What we do know, however, gives no reason for complacency. It would perhaps require more than individual or group psychopathology to bring about an unintentional massive nuclear exchange. But in a moment of extreme international tension and paranoia, with all the superpowers' warning systems on alert for attacks, the act of an insane person or group could set off a nuclear exchange which might or might not escalate.

The greatest danger is at higher levels of authority, where we have to deal with what might be called the normal pathology of nuclear arms strategy and of individual and group decision-making in a crisis. It is argued that no one would be so mad as to launch a first strike. But war games undoubtedly include simulations of preemptive or preventive nuclear war. Systems like the Trident submarine and the MX missile are potential first-strike weapons.

The increasing number of nuclear weapons heightens the danger that someone in power will think it possible to achieve a first strike. It is also said

---

[5] Ted Wye (pseudonym), "Will They Fire in the Hole?," *Family,* supplement of *Air Force Magazine* (Nov. 17, 1971).

that even if one superpower were irrational enough to launch a full-scale nuclear attack, the leaders of the target nation would be too sensible to retaliate. Whatever bluffs and threats they might consider strategically necessary, they presumably understand the paradox of deterrence: once a large-scale nuclear attack has occurred, it becomes irrational by any standard to carry out the threat that was supposed to prevent it. Victory becomes impossible, and retaliation only decreases the world's chance of recovery.

Thus the idea that we can count on the paradox of deterrence to save humanity from nuclear extinction requires many false assumptions about the commitments involved in nuclear arms strategy and about behavior under extreme pressure and uncertainty. Common sense is unlikely to prevail either during the time of rising international tension that would precede a nuclear war or amid the panic and chaos following a nuclear attack.

That is hardly surprising, since common-sense rationality has not dominated the nuclear arms buildup itself. The doctrine of mutual assured destruction commits both sides, coldly and deliberately, to profound irrationality. Even if the kind of strategic reasoning that is thought to rule now persists through a nuclear crisis, there is no cause to believe that it would protect us from disaster. Consider only the launch-on-warning or launch-under-attack scenarios now being proposed in war rooms. They would in effect create a doomsday machine, eliminating the possibility of a decision not to retaliate once electronic sensors indicated an attack.

Officials on both sides say they have no such plan, but there is evidence that it has been considered as a response to the threat of so-called counterforce weapons which would destroy enemy missiles and command centers. One of the dangers of the Pershing missiles, which can reach the Soviet Union in five or six minutes, is the possibility that the Soviets will adopt a launch-on-warning policy in response.

The most likely way for a world-devastating war to begin is not a surprise first strike but a period of international tension developing into a more or less gradually escalating exchange of nuclear weapons. Human behavior in such a crisis is unpredictable. Because military scenarios almost never work out as intended, the only safe prediction is that a nuclear conflict will not go the way the strategists have planned it.

Technical factors will make it hard to contain a nuclear conflict once it breaks out. Command, control and communications systems are likely to fail, especially if anti-satellite weapons are developed, making it hard for leaders to tell what is happening. Leadership might not survive a first strike, in which case there would be no one to countermand a fixed policy of continued nuclear exchanges. Communications between the adversaries would probably be interrupted soon after the first exchange of weapons, again making it difficult, even impossible, to read each other's intentions.

Above all, the normal pathology of crisis decision-making will come into play. As Daniel Frei puts it:

> Substandard performance by decision-makers in crisis situations is particularly common: more than two decades of crisis research have provided ample evidence of all kinds of individual and organizational failures, such as misperceptions, erratic behavior under stress, the improper handling of information, the escalation of hostilities by mirror-image mechanisms, the hazards of "group-think," the failure to implement decisions due to their overwhelming complexity, confusion due to organizational bottlenecks and the inflexibility of standard operating procedures. . . .
>
> It must therefore be asked whether the political leaders of the countries concerned, in the hectic situation of a crisis emergency, will still be capable of deciding and acting fully in accordance with the requirements of the complex and infinitely subtle logic of nuclear crisis strategy. Decision-makers may become victims of urgency and commit all kinds of mistakes, miscalculations, and misperceptions.[6]

High levels of stress reduce cognitive capacity and individual effectiveness. Incomplete or overwhelmingly confusing information, as well as uncertainty about the effects of one's actions, make it hard to resolve ambiguities and sort out the relevant from the irrelevant. The results are misperception, impulsiveness and a tendency to jump to conclusions.

Picture the situation of a national leader faced with what appears to be a massive nuclear attack which has come after a period of rising international tension. The chief decision-maker is overloaded with responsibility, probably tired and deprived of sleep, losing alertness, possibly aging or ill. He has about a half-hour to make a decision on which the fate of humanity may depend— or only a few minutes if the missiles are launched from submarines off Cape Hatteras or from Pershing II launch complexes in Western Europe.

Extreme time pressure is a deadly foe of rational decision-making. Studies show that people given very short notice of overwhelming danger tend to act more irrationally than when they have no warning at all. They are likely to manifest a state called hypervigilance, which in its extreme form becomes panic. Time pressure promotes cognitive rigidity and repetitive thinking, especially in older people whose cognitive processes tend to be slower; such people occupy many national leadership positions. The most obvious recourse will be to rely on programmed routines and carry out a retaliatory plan.[7]

At the same time, fear brings feelings down to a primitive level and distorts perception. The fear turns to anger when power is intact: a leader

---

[6] Daniel Frei, *Risks of Unintentional Nuclear War* (Totowa, New Jersey: Allanheld, Osmun, 1983).
[7] Irving L. Janis and Leon Mann, *Decision Making* (New York: Free Press, 1977); Irving L. Janis, "Preventing Pathogenic Denial by Means of Stress Inoculation," in S. Breznitz, ed., *The Denial of Stress* (New York: International Universities Press, 1983).

whose country has just been struck by nuclear weapons will not feel like a mortally wounded creature but like a cornered one, with claws and teeth intact. That leader is likely to come under the influence of what Jonathan Schell termed the real-world substitute for the missing rational motive for massive retaliation.[8] His instinct will be to strike back in revenge, especially against an enemy who has been presented as the embodiment of evil. The desire to destroy the enemy may become greater than the desire to stay alive, and it will be hard to stay calm and wait. There will be a strong desire for action to relieve the tension and punish the foe.[9]

Another danger is group thinking. Groups in leadership positions often develop shared illusions of invulnerability, collective rationalizations to discount warnings, a sense of inherent righteousness that leads them to ignore the moral consequences of their actions, and stereotyped attitudes toward the enemy as weak, evil or stupid. They tend to be biased in processing information, surveying choices, risks and goals inadequately. Subordinates are reluctant to question their superiors, and dissenters are under strong pressure to conform.[10]

Isolated groups, especially, are often more reckless in their decisions than individuals. Experiments show that group decision-making increases risk-taking because each person feels less responsible for the result.[11] Members of a political leadership group, deep underground in a fallout shelter with their families, are in a particularly poor position to understand emotionally the consequences of their actions. Shared paranoid disorder is an extreme and pathological form of group thinking. But in the greatest crisis that humanity will ever face, even the ordinary deficiencies of group decision-making are likely to be magnified to a pathological degree.

The conduct of leaders during the Cuban missile crisis may be a warning. Both the Soviet decision to emplace the missiles and the belligerent U.S. response can be seen as dangerous and unnecessary. Secretary of Defense Robert McNamara argued that the importance of missiles in Cuba should be minimized because they advanced only slightly the date of strategic parity between the United States and the Soviet Union.[12] But he was ignored, and the world was brought to the brink of nuclear war over little more than a test of national resolve and toughness. If leaders were willing to do this, how can they be trusted to act with restraint in a full-scale nuclear crisis?

---

[8] Jonathan Schell, *The Fate of the Earth* (New York: Alfred A. Knopf, 1982).

[9] Jerome D. Frank, *Sanity and Survival: Psychological Aspects of War and Peace* (New York: Random House, 1967).

[10] Alexander L. George, "Adaptation to Stress in Political Decision Making: The Individual, Small Group, and Organizational Contexts," in George V. Coelho, David A. Hamburg and John E. Adams, eds., *Coping and Adaptation* (New York: Basic Books, 1974).

[11] Daniel Frei, *Risks.*

[12] Elie Abel, *The Missing Crisis* (Philadelphia: Lippincott, 1968).

It is possible that any use of nuclear weapons would not escalate into a war of extinction. But the fact is that a limited degree of rationality and morality has been displayed so far in nuclear matters. Taking into account the conditions that would probably prevail during a nuclear attack, anyone whose confidence ultimately depends on a belief in reliable human functioning at all levels, and in the prudence and restraint of national leaders in an unprecedented situation, is merely avoiding anxiety by indulging in wishful thinking.

NUCLEAR PROLIFERATION: THE PACE QUICKENS

Leonard Spector

Leonard Spector is a senior associate at the Carnegie Endowment for International Peace in Washington, D.C., and is author of *Nuclear Proliferation Today*.

For those dedicated to curbing the spread of nuclear arms, 1984 was a bad year. This year could be much worse.

Although no new nation tested a first nuclear device during 1984, and none of the nuclear weapons threshold countries appears to have acquired for the first time the nuclear material needed to manufacture nuclear explosives, virtually all of the threshold countries appear to have taken steps, in some cases significant, toward developing or expanding nuclear weapons capabilities. These overall trends are likely to continue in 1985. Moreover, it appears highly probable that one more nation, Pakistan, will acquire the capability to assemble nuclear weapons, joining the ranks of India, South Africa and, presumably, Israel. This event would have severe repercussions for the entire non-proliferation regime. Coupled with challenges to the Non-Proliferation Treaty expected at the Treaty review conference in September, the year is likely to be a gloomy one for non-proliferation.

Events in 1984 suggest that India and Pakistan may be on the verge of a serious nuclear arms race. In January, the head of Pakistan's enrichment program, Abdul Qadir Khan, announced that Pakistan had mastered the uranium enrichment process at its Kahuta plant and baldly declared that his team of

Source: Leonard Spector, "Nuclear Proliferation: The Pace Quickens," *Bulletin of the Atomic Scientists* (January 1985), p. 2. Reprinted by permission of the *Bulletin of the Atomic Scientists,* a magazine of science and world affairs. Copyright © 1985 by the Educational Foundation for Nuclear Science, Chicago, IL 60637.

scientists would have little difficulty in building nuclear weapons if called upon to do so by Pakistan's political leaders.

According to a June 21, 1984 speech by Senator Alan Cranston, 1,000 centrifuge units were operating at the Kahuta facility, enough to produce 15 kilograms of highly enriched uranium per year, adequate for a single, carefully designed device. On July 26, the *Washington Times* quoted senior Reagan Administration sources as stating that Pakistan had, in fact, produced an unspecified quantity of weapons-grade uranium, although other Administration sources have subsequently questioned this.

That report came on the heels of other U.S. press accounts in June, now widely accepted as accurate, that within the past several years China has transferred nuclear weapons design information to Pakistan and is helping it run the Kahuta plant. Indeed, this continuing Chinese aid caused the Reagan Administration to postpone the formal signing of the U.S.-China nuclear trade agreement, initialed during the president's trip to Peking in April.

Finally, in July three Pakistani nationals were indicted in Houston, Texas, for attempting to export illegally 50 high-speed electronic switches (krytrons), items apparently used in the triggering mechanisms of nuclear devices. The episode seems to leave little doubt that the overall objective of the Pakistani nuclear program is to produce weapons at the earliest time. Although close, indeed, to this goal, Pakistan is unlikely to test a device in the near term, to avoid jeopardizing the $3.2 billion in U.S. aid it is now receiving.

How India will respond to these developments remains uncertain. According to news reports, some U.S. intelligence officials apparently believe India is readying a preemptive strike against Pakistan's more provocative nuclear facilities, but New Delhi has denied this. Of perhaps greater concern is that India may reactivate its nuclear explosives program, apparently dormant since 1974. In 1981 and again in 1983, there were reports in the press that India was preparing an additional nuclear test, and a number of Indian defense analysts have openly called for a nuclear arsenal.

India's capacity for producing plutonium not subject to International Atomic Energy Agency (IAEA) safeguards—and thus legally available for nuclear explosives—grew substantially during 1984 with the inauguration of the Madras atomic power plant. Spent fuel from this unsafeguarded installation could be reprocessed at the Tarapur reprocessing plant, without IAEA supervision, to produce over 60 kilograms of plutonium per year, possibly enough for 12 nuclear weapons annually, depending upon the quality of their design. Currently Tarapur is reprocessing safeguarded spent fuel from the Rajasthan reactors.

In addition, India has apparently completed the refurbishing and expansion of its reprocessing plant at the Bhabha Atomic Research Center, although it is not clear whether this facility has begun operating. The installation is intended to reprocess spent fuel from India's Canadian-supplied CIRUS reactor, which produced plutonium for the 1974 test, and from the soon-to-be-commissioned R-5 reactor, at 100 megawatts approximately two-and-a-half times the size of CIRUS. None of these three facilities is covered by safeguards, leaving India free to use any plutonium they produce for nuclear arms.

These various plutonium production capabilities, when combined, will permit India to produce about 150 kilograms per year of the material, many times in excess of the announced needs of its nuclear energy and research program. A reasonable conclusion is that the underlying purpose of the facilities is to expand India's nuclear weapons potential.

Despite these trends and increasing Indo-Pakistani tensions, if Pakistan does not engage in a nuclear test it is possible that India will simply tolerate its neighbor's establishing an undeclared nuclear weapons capability since, in addition to conventional military superiority, India would retain a nominal nuclear lead as a result of its 1974 detonation. This would avoid the high economic and diplomatic costs of a serious nuclear weapons program. Domestic political pressures for such a program are likely to intensify, however, and may well tip the balance against continued restraint, once the turmoil from Prime Minister Indira Gandhi's assassination has subsided.

In the middle east, while no state passed a significant milestone in the pursuit of nuclear arms during 1984, movement toward that goal continued. Iraq's nuclear ambitions were gravely set back by Israel's destruction of the Osiraq reactor in 1981, but its interest in acquiring a nuclear weapons capability apparently remains strong. In June, Italian authorities reported that Baghdad had for several years been seeking to purchase 34 kilograms of plutonium from an Italian black market arms-smuggling ring whose leaders, including former Italian intelligence service officials, were expected to be indicted shortly.

Iraq also continues to hold 12.5 kilograms of highly enriched uranium fuel that France had supplied for Osiraq. Especially if combined with similar fuel at the Soviet-supplied IRT-2000 reactor, this would be more than enough for a single, carefully designed nuclear weapon, if Baghdad were prepared to violate its commitments under the Non-Proliferation Treaty. These commitments have been rendered less certain by Iraq's blatant violation of its pledges under atomic weapons through the Italian arms smuggling ring mentioned earlier. When the leaders of the ring indicated that such weapons were available on the black market, Syria was reported to be the country most interested in their purchase. As in the case of the 34 kilograms of plutonium said to have been offered to Iraq, it is not likely that atomic weapons were actually available for sale. But Syria's apparent interest in acquiring such arms is significant.

Movement toward acquisition of nuclear weapons capabilities in Argentina and Brazil has also apparently continued. In Argentina, many had hoped that the newly elected government of Raul Alfonsin would modify the nuclear policies of his predecessors, but his administration has continued to support completion of the Ezeiza reprocessing plant, scheduled to start up in 1986, and the Pilcaniyeu enrichment facility, scheduled for completion in 1985.

Both facilities could provide access to nuclear weapons material, although any plutonium produced at Ezeiza would be subject to IAEA safeguards since Argentina currently lacks a source of unsafeguarded spent fuel. What is not clear is whether the necessary funds have in fact been budgeted for completion of these plants. According to one account the Argentine Atomic Energy Commission suffered an 80 percent budgetary reduction in 1984.

The Alfonsin government has also backed away from pre-inauguration statements that it would support ratification of the Tlatelolco Treaty on the Prohibition of Nuclear Weapons in Latin America. In February, Argentine Foreign Minister Dante Caputo outlined a number of unattainable preconditions to Argentina's embracing the accord, and in April, President Alfonsin rejected Mexican President Miquel de la Madrid's calls for its ratification, made during a state visit to Buenos Aires.

In Brazil, the year's most important development appears to have been the intense reaction to Argentina's late 1983 announcement of its previously secret Pilcaniyeu enrichment facility. Responding to the strategic implications of this plant, in December 1983 and throughout the early part of 1984, a number of senior Brazilian military leaders openly declared that Brazil would acquire its own nuclear weapons capability by 1990—highly unusual statements for officials of an emerging nuclear state.

The principal focus of efforts to achieve this goal are uranium enrichment programs at two research centers, the Institute for Nuclear and Energy Research in São Paolo, and the Brazilian air force's Aerospace Technical Center in São Jose dos Campos. The Center is investigating the laser process, while Institute researchers are developing gas centrifuges, with a laboratory-scale facility to be completed by 1987 and a semi-industrial unit able to produce highly enriched uranium due for completion by 1990.

These activities, which are not subject to international safeguards, are totally separate from Brazil's efforts to implement its 1975 nuclear pact with West Germany, all of which is subject to IAEA monitoring. Under the 1975 accord, West Germany is assisting Brazil in building a pilot enrichment plant at Resende (based on the Becker jet-nozzle enrichment process) and is also building two nuclear power plants, Angra II and III, as well as providing technology for a reprocessing plant at the Resende site. Progress on all of these facilities has been slow, however, and the enrichment and reprocessing plants are subject to strict controls which will limit their proliferation potential.

Little seems to have changed last year in South Africa's nuclear posture or capabilities. It continues to maintain its unsafeguarded pilot enrichment plant at Valindaba, thought to be capable of producing 50 kilograms of highly enriched uranium per year, perhaps enough for two or three weapons.

One important factor not previously considered in estimating South Africa's nuclear weapons potential, however, is the possibility that in 1980 or 1981 Pretoria received from China substantial quantities of low-enriched uranium which is not subject to IAEA safeguards. Press accounts quoting U.S. intelligence sources state that such a transaction took place when Pretoria was seeking to obtain fuel for the Koeberg nuclear power plants. South Africa is known to have obtained initial loads from Belgian and Swiss sources with the aid of U.S. uranium brokers. This raises the possibility that South Africa could now use any low-enriched uranium it obtained from China as feed for its Valindaba pilot-scale enrichment plant, possibly tripling its annual output of highly enriched uranium. China has denied making the sale.

The events of 1984 provide obvious warning as to the potential danger points in 1985: Pakistan's acquisition of a nuclear weapons capability, India's response, new efforts by the Middle East Arab states to match Israel's presumed nuclear arsenal, and intensified efforts in Latin America to build unsafeguarded enrichment and reprocessing capabilities. To this must be added the risk that the September Non-Proliferation Treaty review conference will result in a serious erosion of support for that critically important accord.

The 1980 review conference was unable to produce a consensus statement concerning Treaty implementation, largely because of controversy over the failure of the United States and the Soviet Union to make progress in reducing their own nuclear arsenals, as called for in Article VI of the pact. Given the expansion of the superpowers' nuclear weaponry since then and the current suspension of nuclear arms control negotiations, the antagonisms seen at the 1980 conference are likely to be intensified. American officials fear that some parties may threaten to withdraw from the Treaty unless specific measures to end the U.S.-Soviet arms race are taken by a specified date. Even if not implemented, the corrosive effect of such threats on the consensus underlying the Treaty could be substantial.

If sometime during 1985, it becomes clear that Pakistan has acquired a nuclear weapons capability and that an act of proliferation has actually taken place, the international non-proliferation regime is likely to suffer a still more grievous blow. The consequences could extend well beyond India's possible revival of its nuclear explosives program, as grave as this might be, because, at bottom, a Pakistani nuclear capability would mean that the non-proliferation regime had proven impotent.

In contrast to the acquisition of such capabilities by Israel, India and South Africa, Pakistan's intentions and its efforts to realize them have been widely understood for years, certainly since the late 1970s. Yet despite intensive efforts by the United States and other interested nations to thwart Islamabad's nuclear ambitions through diplomatic pressure, strengthened export controls and, occasionally, economic sanctions, Pakistan would have succeeded in achieving its nuclear objectives. That Pakistan could do so under these circumstances—which include its repeated flouting of nuclear-supplier-country export controls—can only be seen as evidence of the declining vitality of the international non-proliferation regime and of the loss of political will by the United States and others to make the regime effective.

Such a clear failure, along with increased questioning of the Treaty, could well make 1985 a year of severe challenge to the institutions built up for more than three decades to curb the spread of nuclear arms.

SPREAD OF NUCLEAR ARMS IS SEEN BY 2000
Richard Halloran

Richard Halloran is a security affairs correspondent for the *New York Times*.

A recent United States intelligence survey asserts that 31 countries, many of them engaged in longstanding regional disputes, will be able to produce nuclear weapons by the year 2000, according to military analysts.

The analysts said that because of this, American military forces would have to be prepared to engage in nuclear battles with countries other than the Soviet Union, even though American military planners put most of their attention today on the possibility of nuclear war with the Soviet Union.

Defense Guidance, a classified five-year plan of strategic direction for the armed forces, reflected that appraisal, saying that "a continued effort should be made to reduce the spread of nuclear weapons capability, particularly to nations hostile, or potentially hostile, to United States interests."

But the military planners who wrote the guidance for the signature of Secretary of Defense Caspar W. Weinberger were clearly aware of the pros-

Source: Richard Halloran, "Spread of Nuclear Arms Is Seen by 2000," *New York Times* (November 15, 1982).

pects for nuclear armaments to spread, saying, "As nuclear capabilities spread, additional measures will be required to protect United States forces and interests."

Leading Role for Marines. Nuclear engagements with adversaries other than the Soviet Union would most likely require small tactical nuclear weapons rather than the large strategic missiles aimed at the Soviet Union, the analysts said.

In line with that, the guidance instructed the armed services that "Priorities should be directed toward achieving improved survivability, endurance, and communications, command, control, and intelligence capabilities of our tactical nuclear forces."

The guidance particularly directed the Marine Corps to "take the lead in developing a nuclear operations concept for its AV-8B," or Harrier "jump jet."

The military analysts said the intelligence survey was based on assessments of each nation's scientific and technical capabilities, the industrial base, probable access to nuclear materials and financial status.

They said the analysts who worked on the survey paid special attention to the potential of each nation to receive technical and financial help from other nations and particularly to the possibilities for converting peaceful nuclear facilities into producers of weapons.

The United States, the Soviet Union, France, Britain, China, and India have produced nuclear weapons.

Israeli Production Suspected. In the Middle East, Israel has long been thought capable of producing nuclear weapons and has been suspected of having done so. Among the Arab nations, Egypt, Saudi Arabia and Iraq were named. Other Moslem nations named were Iran and Pakistan.

South Africa was the only sub-Saharan nation on the list, the analysts said.

In Asia, South Korea, Taiwan and the Philippines are candidates as nuclear powers. Japanese scientists have said Japan could acquire nuclear arms within a year of a decision to do so.

Potential nuclear powers in Latin America, the analysts said, are Mexico, Brazil and Argentina.

In Europe, those with the potential for producing nuclear arms include West Germany, Sweden, Italy and Spain. Other Western possibilities included Canada and Australia.

FOR FURTHER READING

Aldridge, Robert C. *First Strike.* Boston: South End Press, 1983. An analysis of U.S. strategic programs. The author argues the programs are intended to give the United States a first-strike capability vis-à-vis the Soviet Union.

Beres, Louis Rene. *Apocalypse: Nuclear Catastrophe in World Politics.* Chicago: University of Chicago Press, 1980. Examines those trends in world politics that, the author argues, are increasing the risk of nuclear wear—including the possibility of an accidental or unauthorized use of nuclear weapons in a crisis.

Bracken, Paul. *The Command and Control of Nuclear Forces.* New Haven, Conn.: Yale University Press, 1983. Warns that the "organizational routines" developed by the U.S. and Soviet Union to control both their strategic and European-based nuclear forces could precipitate, rather than dampen, escalation of a crisis into a nuclear conflagration.

Dumas, Lloyd J. "Human Fallibility and Weapons Systems." *Bulletin of the Atomic Scientists* 36 (November 1980), pp. 15–19. A disturbing description of how the increasing sophistication and complexity of nuclear weapons systems contribute to the risk that human and technical errors may produce disaster.

Dunn, Lewis A. *Controlling the Bomb: Nuclear Proliferation in the 1980s.* New Haven, Conn.: Yale University Press, 1982. A comprehensive discussion of the technical, political, and strategic factors which may drive additional countries to acquire a nuclear weapons capability. Analyzes the dangers of nuclear proliferation, and possible means to slow its pace.

Falk, Richard, et al. "How a Nuclear War Could Start." *Bulletin of the Atomic Scientists* 35 (April 1979), pp. 21–27. A series of short articles describing possible scenarios for the outbreak of nuclear war, adapted from papers originally presented at the "First Nuclear War Conference" held in Washington, D.C., in early 1979.

Ford, Daniel. *The Button.* New York: Simon and Schuster, 1985. A disturbing revelation of the many weaknesses in the U.S. strategic command and control system, and their impact on the Air Force's planning for nuclear war with the Soviet Union.

Frei, Daniel. *The Risks of Unintentional Nuclear War.* Totowa, New Jersey: Allanheld, Osmun, and Co., 1981. Discusses possible triggers for nuclear war, including crises, nuclear weapons accidents, and proliferation.

Griffiths, Franklyn, and John C. Polanyi, eds. *The Danger of Nuclear War.* Toronto: University of Toronto Press, 1979. A reader on nuclear weapons issues that includes several articles on potential paths to nuclear war, originally presented at the 30th International Pugwash Symposium held in May 1978.

George, Alexander L. *Presidential Decision-Making in Foreign Policy.* Boulder, Colo.: Westview Press, 1980. A breakdown of various possible psychological and organizational sources of stress and irrationality in foreign policy decision-making.

Ground Zero. "Thinking About Preventing Nuclear War." Washington, D.C.: Ground Zero, 1983. A sixteen-page pamphlet that identifies potential sources of nuclear instability and suggests means to reduce or remove them.

The Harvard Nuclear Study Group. "The Shattered Crystal Ball." In *Living With Nuclear Weapons,* pp. 47–70. New York: Bantam Books, 1983. A case-by-case description of various scenarios that could lead to nuclear war, with commentary on their varying degrees of probability.

Spector, Leonard. *Nuclear Proliferation Today.* New York: Vintage Books, 1984. A region-by-region examination of the increasing dangers and probability of the spread of nuclear weapons to other countries.

9

Past Efforts to Control Nuclear Weapons

In this chapter, we turn to an examination of past Soviet and American efforts to control their competition in nuclear arms. As detailed in the Union of Concerned Scientists' synopsis, "Arms Control Treaties Now in Effect," the two countries have concluded a seemingly impressive array of nuclear arms control treaties. These include treaties or agreements which place direct limits on each side's weaponry, like the Strategic Arms Limitation Talks (SALT) agreements, and others which aim to improve the two countries' ability to avoid rash and irrevocable decisions in a crisis, like the 1963 Hotline Agreement. The other articles present several different perspectives on the degree to which these efforts have succeeded in curtailing the costs and risks of the Soviet-American nuclear competition.

G. Allen Greb and Gerald W. Johnson, in "A History of Strategic Arms Limitations," provide a valuable historical perspective on the genesis and evolution of SALT. They examine the major issues which divided Soviet and American negotiators in the course of the SALT I, SALT II, and the more recent Strategic Arms Reduction Talks (START), and they analyze how the SALT I and SALT II agreements have affected the nuclear arms race.

Greb and Johnson readily concede that these negotiations have largely failed to fulfill the traditional "objectives of arms control": to reduce the risk of nuclear war; to reduce the costs of maintaining security; and to reduce the costs of war, should war occur. Since the advent of the SALT negotiations in 1969, both Soviet and American nuclear weapons capabilities have grown enormously in number and in lethality. And, as we saw in Chapter 7, both countries are now investing enormous resources in new weapons systems which threaten to destabilize mutual deterrence. A superpower nuclear war today would be even more destructive than it would have been fifteen years ago.

SALT may not have created these circumstances, but it has certainly done little to prevent them. True, there have been some successes. In the 1972 SALT I ABM Treaty, the U.S. and Soviets did agree to drastically restrict the deployment and testing of anti-ballistic missile systems. The SALT I Interim Agreement on Offensive Systems also succeeded in setting overall limits on offensive missile launchers, limits which in the SALT II Treaty were extended to include bombers and multiple warhead systems. Neither agreement, however, dealt satisfactorily with the problem of offensive force modernization. In particular, SALT I failed to control the deployment of multiple, independently-retargetable reentry vehicles (MIRVs), while neither SALT I nor SALT II set any meaningful limitations on the two countries' ability to improve the qualitative sophistication of their respective arsenals.

These disappointments are compounded by the fact that the negotiating process itself has now ground largely to a halt. The 1979 SALT II Treaty remains unratified by the United States. Meanwhile, the Reagan administration's effort to pursue "deep reductions" in each side's forces has come to naught. Both START and the U.S.-Soviet negotiations on Intermediate Nuclear Forces (INF, see below), collapsed in late 1983 after the Soviets "walked out" of the negotiations in response to the initial U.S. deployment of ground-launched cruise missiles and Pershing II ballistic missiles to Europe that December.

Despite these problems, Greb and Johnson believe the SALT process has been of value to the United States. Most importantly, SALT, by establishing ground rules for verification and definitional categories for various weapons systems, has provided the United States more knowledge about Soviet military programs than would have been possible without SALT. A second important accomplishment of SALT was the creation of the Standing Consultation Commission, which since SALT I has evolved into an important forum in which Soviet and American representatives can air and have resolved disagreements about whether one or the other side is violating the terms of a treaty.

Seymour Weiss sees the Soviet-American arms control process from a very different perspective. In "The Case Against Arms Control," Weiss offers a ringing, conservative denunciation of the entire enterprise. In terms similar to those of Richard Pipes, Weiss views SALT as a tool which the Soviets have used to pursue its "fundamental" political objectives: "the extension of Soviet power and influence, normally at the direct expense of the West." In SALT, Weiss argues, this has been manifest in Soviet efforts to promote political differences between the U.S. and its allies; to lull the American public into complacency about the need for adequate nuclear modernization programs; to reduce U.S. advantages in military technology; and to exploit ambiguities and loopholes in agreements for unilateral advantage. Weiss concludes that the United States should dispense with all efforts to achieve negotiated solutions to the problem of nuclear war with the Soviet Union, and rely instead on its own national military resources to guarantee its security.

Liberal arms control critics have adopted precisely the opposite view, arguing that SALT has not gone nearly far enough in curbing the nuclear war-making capabilities of the Soviet and American national security establishments. In contrast to Weiss, these critics place much of the blame on SALT's failure to control the nuclear arms race on U.S. strategic nuclear policy. In Chapter 12, for example, Senators Edward

Kennedy and Mark Hatfield—who advocate that the United States and Soviet Union take the dramatic step of "freezing" the further production, testing, and deployment of nuclear weapons—describe in their article how SALT has failed to curtail defense expenditures, to curb destabilizing weapons improvements, and to lower the number of weapons deployed on each side.

Lawrence Freedman, in "Negotiations on Nuclear Forces," highlights another problematic aspect of SALT. As SALT came to focus exclusively on the "central strategic weapons systems" (that is, land-based ICBMs, SLBMs, and long-range bombers), a large number of nuclear weapons systems of potential "strategic" capability went largely ignored in the negotiations. These included U.S. "Forward-Based Systems" (FBS) like F-4 and F-111 fighter-bombers based in Western Europe, and carrier-based A-6 and A-7 aircraft, all of which could attack targets in the Soviet Union with nuclear weapons, as well as Soviet intermediate- and medium-range systems like the SS-5 and SS-4 missiles which, from their bases in the western USSR, could reach most of the major cities in Western Europe. In addition, SALT did not consider a variety of medium- and intermediate-range missile and bomber systems deployed by Britain, France, and China which could reach targets in the Soviet Union.

As Freedman explains, concern over these so-called "intermediate nuclear forces" (INF) began to mount following the Soviet deployment of the intermediate-range, MIRVed SS-20 missile and Backfire medium bomber in the late 1970s. This concern intensified in the wake of NATO's "Two-Tracked Decision" of 1979, in which 572 new U.S. missiles—108 Pershing II MRBMs and 464 Tomahawk ground-launched cruise missiles (GLCMs)—would be installed in Western Europe beginning in 1983 if the Soviets refused to accept negotiated limits on their own INF forces. Yet, Freedman argues, by the time negotiations on these weapons started in November 1981, Soviet and American negotiating positions had already congealed to the point where agreement was probably impossible.

One particularly thorny issue was the fact that the Soviet SS-20, SS-5, and SS-4 force was already deployed, while the Reagan administration, in its "Zero Option," was asking the Soviets to scrap these existing systems in return for an American promise not to deploy its new weapons, the Pershing II and GLCM, which it had not yet fielded. Another sticking point was the existence of French and British INF forces which were quite obviously pointed at the Soviet Union, and which Soviet negotiators argued should be accounted for in the negotiations. The British and French governments insisted, however, that their "national deterrents" should left be completely out of the discussions, a view in which the Reagan administration readily concurred.

The one serious attempt to mediate these differences in the U.S. and Soviet negotiating positions in the INF Talks—the so-called "Walk in the Woods" by Soviet negotiator Yuli Kvitsinsky and his U.S. counterpart, Paul Nitze, in July 1982—resulted in a compromise which was summarily rejected by both governments. Negotiations collapsed when the Soviets "walked out" of the talks in December 1983 as deployment of the new U.S. missiles to Europe commenced as scheduled, a break-down which was clearly the product of each side's intransigence. In the meantime, deployments of the Pershing II and GLCM have proceeded apace, and the European-based force of Soviet SS-20s has swelled to number some 243 missiles and 729 warheads.

In the "Verification Spectrum," Glenn Buchan discusses the ongoing debate in the United States over whether the Soviets have violated existing SALT agreements, an allegation levied by Weiss in his article. As Buchan points out, whether or not one believes the Soviets have failed to adhere to the terms of previous arms control agreements depends on the perspective one adopts towards the requirements of arms control verification. Should arms agreements, for example, be designed to prevent undetected Soviet cheating that could harm U.S. national security? Should arms agreements be viewed "legalistically," where *any* Soviet infringement, no matter how minor, is treated as a serious violation? Or should they be interpreted "metaphysically," where any Soviet behavior that is inconsistent with the U.S. interpretation of an agreement is viewed as a sure sign of Soviet duplicity and unreliability? Buchan argues that the Reagan administration's interpretation of Soviet treaty compliance behavior, which has surfaced publicly now in recent reports to the Congress detailing several alleged Soviet "violations" of past agreements, reflects the administration's adherence to this latter view.

ARMS CONTROL TREATIES NOW IN EFFECT
Union of Concerned Scientists

The Union of Concerned Scientists (UCS), based in Cambridge, Massachusetts, is a coalition of scientists, engineers, and other professionals that undertakes studies and educational efforts to reduce the risk of nuclear war. Its recent publications include *No First Use* and *The Fallacy of Star Wars.*

Agreements to Prevent the Spread of Nuclear Weapons

ANTARCTIC TREATY

1 December 1959
Signatories: 25 states
Twenty-five nations, including the United States and the Soviet Union, have agreed to make the Antarctic continent a nuclear-free, demilitarized zone. The Treaty bans any military use of this continent and prohibits nuclear tests and

Source: Union of Concerned Scientists, "Arms Control Treaties Now in Effect," in *Solutions to the Nuclear Arms Race: A Briefing Manual* (Boston: Union of Concerned Scientists, 1982), pp. 59–63. © Union of Concerned Scientists, 1982.

nuclear waste disposal, as well as nuclear weapons storage. The fundamental goal of promoting scientific cooperation and peaceful use of the continent's resources has been attained.

OUTER SPACE TREATY

27 January 1967
Signatories: 81 states
The treaty bans the deployment of "weapons of mass destruction" (e.g., nuclear weapons) in orbit, in outer space, and on the moon or other celestial bodies. It also requires that the moon and other bodies be used and explored only for peaceful purposes. This treaty has been observed thus far, but it could be endangered by the rapid development of space-based and space-directed weapons.

TREATY OF TLATELOLCO

14 February 1967
Signatories: 22 states
Initiated as a result of the Cuban Missile Crisis of 1962, this treaty establishes all of Latin America as a nuclear-free zone. It prohibits the testing, manufacture, production, acquisition, or use of nuclear weapons by the signatories, both directly and indirectly. Argentina, Brazil, Chile, and Cuba have not signed the Treaty.

NON-PROLIFERATION TREATY

1 July 1968
Signatories: 118 states
Under the terms of this treaty, nuclear-weapons states pledge not to transfer nuclear weapons or nuclear weapons technology to non-weapons states; these states also agree to negotiate in good faith to control the arms race and to reduce their own arsenals. Other signatories pledge not to acquire nuclear weapons. Nations with non-military nuclear facilities, such as power reactors, promise to allow international inspections of such facilities by the International Atomic Energy Agency. France, China, and at least twenty states capable of producing nuclear weapons in the near future are not signatories.

SEABED TREATY

11 February 1971
Signatories: 70 states
Prohibits deployment of nuclear weapons on the world's seabeds beyond a twelve-mile wide coastal zone. Verification is by national technical means.

Agreements to Limit the Risk of Nuclear War

HOTLINE/MODERNIZATION AGREEMENTS

20 June 1963
Signatories: U.S.-U.S.S.R.
The Cuban Missile Crisis demonstrated the importance of direct and prompt communications between American and Soviet leaders in the event of an international crisis. As a result, the two governments agreed to establish direct wire-telegraph and radio-telegraph links between Washington and Moscow. The system was modernized in 1972. The value of the hotline was shown again during the 1967 and 1973 Middle East wars, when it was used to clarify American and Soviet intentions and maneuvers in the region.

ACCIDENTAL MEASURES AGREEMENT

30 September 1971
Signatories: U.S.-U.S.S.R.
The danger that nuclear war could start by accident or as the result of some unauthorized act has worried nuclear weapons specialists and individual citizens for many years. Under the terms of this treaty, American and Soviet leaders pledged to improve safeguards against this danger, to use the hotline promptly when needed, and to provide advance notification of certain weapons tests.

AGREEMENT ON THE PREVENTION OF NUCLEAR WAR

22 June 1973
Signatories: U.S.-U.S.S.R.
This agreement sets forth general principles of conduct for both the United States and the Soviet Union, and contains mutual pledges for joint governmental consultation when a danger of nuclear confrontation arises.

Agreements to Limit Nuclear Testing

LIMITED TEST BAN TREATY

5 August 1963
Signatories: 111 states
This first important step toward limiting nuclear weapons testing was initiated, at least in part, as a response to widespread public concern over the dangers of nuclear fallout. The Treaty prohibits nuclear weapons tests in the atmosphere, outer space and underwater, and prohibits underground explosions which cause the release of radioactive debris beyond the national borders of the testing state. The parties agreed to continue talks for final negotiation of a comprehensive nuclear test ban treaty.

THRESHOLD TEST BAN TREATY

3 July 1974
Signatories: U.S.-U.S.S.R. (Unratified)
In this follow-on to the Limited Test Ban Treaty, the U.S. and the Soviet Union agreed to ban underground nuclear weapons tests having a yield of more than 150 kilotons (150,000 tons of TNT). More importantly, the parties agreed to exchange scientific data to facilitate verification. Information on number and location of tests, and geologic data for the test sites, would have greatly increased the level of confidence for verification of treaty compliance; unfortunately, data exchange is not to occur until after ratification of the agreement. The United States has not ratified the TTB Treaty, and has stated a desire to re-negotiate certain of the Treaty's verification and compliance provisions.

PEACEFUL NUCLEAR EXPLOSIONS TREATY

22 June 1976
Signatories: U.S.-U.S.S.R. (Unratified)
This treaty regulates nuclear explosions for peaceful purposes should either party wish to engage in such activity. It bans "group explosions" with an aggregate yield exceeding 1500 kilotons and requires on-site observers for group explosions with a yield over 150 kilotons.

COMPREHENSIVE TEST BAN TREATY

Negotiations suspended.
Negotiators: U.S., United Kingdom, U.S.S.R.
In 1977, the United States, United Kingdom, and Soviet Union began trilateral negotiations for a comprehensive nuclear test ban treaty. By 1980, when talks were suspended, most of the more difficult provisions had been resolved: nuclear weapons explosions would be prohibited, tamper-proof seismic stations would be established on signatories' territory, on-demand on-site inspection would be permitted. The Reagan Administration has declined to resume negotiations, expressing difficulties with treaty verification.

Agreements to Limit Nuclear Weapons

SALT I INTERIM AGREEMENT

26 May 1972
Signatories: U.S.-U.S.S.R.
Designed to stabilize the arms race until a permanent treaty could be negotiated, the Interim Agreement froze ICBMs and SLBMs at their 1972 levels. Asymmetries between U.S. and Soviet force structures made the negotiation

of equivalent limits difficult and controversial. At the time of the treaty, the Soviet Union had a lead in ICBMs (1600 to 1054), while the United States enjoyed leads in strategic bombers and MIRV technology. Treaty verification would be by national technical means, i.e., reconnaissance satellites and other remote monitoring devices. The SALT I Treaty was superceded by the SALT II Treaty.

TREATY TO LIMIT ANTI/BALLISTIC MISSILE SYSTEMS

26 May 1972
Signatories: U.S.-U.S.S.R.
The ABM Treaty effectively bans the deployment of extensive ABM systems. The Treaty allows the construction of no more than two ABM systems for each nation, each to consist of no more than 20 radars, 100 launchers, and 100 missiles. The development, testing, and deployment of sea-based, space-based, and mobile ABM systems are prohibited, as are multiple launch systems. Parties agreed to consultations prior to development of ABM systems based on physical principles other than radar/launcher/missile technology.

ABM PROTOCOL

3 July 1974
Signatories: U.S.-U.S.S.R.
Further limitations on ABMs were adopted: each state is allowed to construct only one ABM system, either around the national capitol or at another specified site.

SALT II TREATY

18 June 1979
Signatories: U.S.-U.S.S.R. (Unratified)
This successor to SALT I is the most comprehensive strategic arms limitation treaty ever negotiated. It sets important quantitative and qualitative limits on a wide range of nuclear weapons and weapon delivery systems. Although ratification was prevented by the American reaction to the Soviet invasion of Afghanistan, each state has agreed to abide by the treaty's provisions as long as the other signatory continues to do so. Specific treaty provisions include:

- Initial aggregate level of 2400 strategic systems, to be reduced to 2250 during the term of the treaty.
- A sublimit of 1320 MIRVed ICBM/SLBM launchers and aircraft equipped with long-range cruise missiles.
- A sublimit of 1200 MIRVed ballistic launchers.
- A sublimit of 820 MIRVed ICBM launchers.
- Restrictions on testing and deployment of new-type ICBMs.

- Limits on the number of MIRVs permitted on new and existing ICBMs and SLBMs.
- Within the numerical limits set by the Treaty, freedom to determine force-mixes.

Many of the verification provisions established in SALT I are continued in SALT II. As in the earlier agreement, compliance verification is by "national technical means." Interference with those means, or deliberate concealment that would interfere with the ability to verify compliance, is prohibited. SALT II also enhances verification capabilities by establishing precise counting rules designed to overcome certain problems associated with the use of national technical means of verification. For example, in order to simplify the counting of ICBM and SLBM warheads, any missile ever tested with MIRVs will be counted as a MIRVed missile carrying the maximum number of warheads with which [it] has been tested.

A HISTORY OF STRATEGIC ARMS LIMITATIONS
G. Allen Greb and Gerald W. Johnson

G. Allen Greb is a research historian in the Program in Science, Technology, and Public Affairs at the University of California, San Diego.

Gerald W. Johnson is on the Senior Technical Staff of TRW and was the personal representative of the Secretary of Defense to the SALT II and Comprehensive Test Ban negotiations, 1977–79.

SALT I, the Vladivostok accord, SALT II, START—more has been said and written about these superpower forays into arms control than any other set of agreements or negotiations of the nuclear era. Included in this vast literature are several book-length accounts by participants, volumes of Congressional testimony and analyses by government experts and scholars.

Yet, while familiar with the acronyms, most Americans would be hard pressed to discuss the substance of these efforts to limit strategic nuclear arms. Our aim here is to help demystify this historic set of negotiations.

Although the Strategic Arms Limitation Talks (SALT) constitute the most important, most intense and longest-running attempt to curb the arms race, they do not stand alone. In fact, SALT would not have come into existence at all if its most famous antecedent, the so-called Baruch plan, had been imple-

Source: G. Allen Greb and Gerald W. Johnson, "A History of Strategic Arms Limitations," Bulletin of the Atomic Scientists (January 1984), pp. 30–36. Reprinted by permission of the Bulletin of the Atomic Scientists, a magazine of science and world affairs. Copyright © 1984 by the Educational Foundation for Nuclear Science, Chicago, IL 60637.

mented. On June 14, 1946, at the very outset of the nuclear age, the United States introduced this plan to ban forever all atomic weapons and place nuclear technology under international control. The men behind the plan were a diverse group of scientific and government experts: the atomic scientist Robert Oppenheimer, who originally conceived it; U.S. Atomic Energy Chairman David Lilienthal and Secretary of State Dean Acheson, who substantially modified it; and financier Bernard Baruch, who presented it before the United Nations.

The proposal called for the creation of an international nuclear development authority. This authority would have the power to control all atomic energy activities and to establish inspection procedures not subject to U.N. Security Council veto. The United States promised to dismantle its nuclear bombs once this agency was established. The Soviet reply, presented by Deputy Foreign Minister Andrei Gromyko, came only five days later; because the United States enjoyed a nuclear monopoly, the Soviets called for the destruction of existing atomic arsenals *before* any discussion of inspection and control procedures could take place. This fundamental difference blocked all progress toward any form of arms control or disarmament for a dozen years.

The roots of this U.S.-Soviet failure went deeper than disagreement on the specifics of the Baruch plan. Growing tension between East and West rendered any agreement on atomic energy highly unlikely. The authors of the plan, especially Oppenheimer, were well aware of this hostile political climate. They believed, however, that the uniqueness and magnitude of the problem demanded extraordinary measures:

> The program we propose will undoubtedly arouse skepticism when it is first considered. It did among us but thought and discussion have converted us.
>
> It may seem too idealistic. It seems time we endeavor to bring some of our expressed ideals into being.
>
> It may seem too radical, too advanced, too much beyond human experience. All these terms apply with peculiar fitness to the atomic bomb.
>
> In considering the plan . . . one should ask oneself, "What are the alternatives?" We have, and we find no tolerable answer. [Chester I. Barnard et al., *A Report on the International Control of Atomic Energy,* prepared for the Secretary of State's Committee on Atomic Energy (Washington, D.C.: March 16, 1946), p. 31.]

These words proved all too prophetic. As many anticipated, the Soviet Union soon acquired the bomb. The Cold War deepened and intensified, and the nuclear arsenals of both sides grew in both numbers and sophistication. It was two stormy decades before the superpowers could again address the issue of arms limitation, if only partially, through the medium of SALT.

An early approach to negotiation proposed by Secretary of War Henry

Stimson to President Harry Truman and the Cabinet one month after the nuclear attacks on Hiroshima and Nagasaki has recently come to light. Although Truman did not follow Stimson's suggestion, it did outline a bold and possibly attractive alternative to the Baruch plan. Stimson suggested that the United States, in concert with the United Kingdom, enter into direct discussions with the Soviet Union, warning that a multinational approach could create the impression of "ganging up" on the Soviets. He noted that the atomic bomb was a uniquely dangerous weapon that must be brought under control, and that traditional diplomatic procedures might not suffice to meet the challenge. In his view, *when* the Soviets acquired the bomb—whether it be four or 20 years—was less important than the superpowers having a peaceful cooperative relationship when they did.

In November 1969, the United States and the Soviet Union in essence adopted such an approach, formally initiating bilateral negotiations on strategic nuclear arms. This followed a number of abortive overtures and initiatives made during the 1950s and 1960s: one by Soviet Premier Nikolai Bulganin in 1955 and several by U.S. President Lyndon B. Johnson. In 1964 Johnson proposed a "verified freeze" on strategic weapons; in 1966 a limit on antiballistic missile (ABM) deployment and in 1967 restrictions on both offensive and defensive systems. Finally, in mid-1968, each side publicly committed itself to enter negotiations. But that summer the Soviet Union invaded Czechoslovakia. As so often has happened in the history of SALT, it was an unrelated political action, but it rudely changed the course of events. The 1968 presidential elections made for further delay. Talks formally began on November 17, 1969, after President Nixon and his special assistant Henry Kissinger reviewed and approved the SALT idea.

What put arms limitation on the political and diplomatic agendas of each side at this time? One fact stands above all others: stockpiles of nuclear weapons and the means to deliver them had reached such levels that Soviet and U.S. leaders independently concluded that their national security lay in some degree of mutual arms restraint. Washington and Moscow cited both the risks of nuclear war and the prohibitive cost of carrying on an unbridled strategic competition.

Each side had its own variations of this common theme. For the United States, arms limitation had become more attractive because of a fundamental change in the global strategic environment. For the first time, U.S. nuclear dominance was clearly and irrevocably ended, as a result of a determined Soviet buildup following the Cuban missile crisis of 1962. Each side now possessed—or perceived itself and the other to possess—a nuclear retaliatory force that could inflict unacceptable damage after a first strike. This tenuous balance seemed to promise new possibilities in arms control.

The person primarily responsible for rethinking and retooling U.S. strategic goals in light of this new international reality was President Lyndon Johnson's Defense Secretary, Robert S. McNamara. Backed by an army of "systems analysts," McNamara persuasively demonstrated to the President and the Joint Chiefs of Staff the absurdity of engaging in a strategic arms competition that no one could win. He also successfully conveyed his concerns about anti-ballistic missiles (ABMs). This developing technology, he argued, offered no sure guarantees of safety and might completely destabilize the deterrent system by acting as a stimulus to offensive countermeasures. ABM curbs became the prime target of the U.S. negotiating position.

For the Soviet Union, catching up with the United States in nuclear weaponry made negotiations attractive for different reasons. The Soviets had always been haunted by feelings of inferiority in comparison with their capitalist adversaries. The leaders who took over in the wake of the 1962 Cuban fiasco, Leonid Brezhnev and Alexei Kosygin, were, in the view of prominent Kremlinologists, particularly "obsessed by the notion of inequality." And SALT offered confirmation of their country's status as a superpower. The Brezhnev-Kosygin regime also saw an opportunity to check the U.S. technological lead in new weapons systems, including ABMs, even though the Soviets had been first to deploy these, and multiple independently-targeted re-entry vehicles (MIRVs). American advances in multiple warheads in particular threatened to undermine the hard-fought Soviet gains in the numerical strength and capabilities of its Strategic Rocket Forces.

Beyond these strategic considerations, domestic pressures played a major role in both U.S. and Soviet decisions to negotiate. In the United States, negative reaction to the Vietnam War and a growing public and Congressional interest in national security matters produced demands for reductions in defense spending. Some officials worried that Congress would legislate unilateral restraints on strategic forces in the absence of mutual agreements. For the Soviet Union, discussion and negotiation became a way to avoid costly global confrontations while consolidating power at home and within the Soviet sphere. The deepening Sino-Soviet breach, dating from the late 1950s and fully confirmed after 1964; persistent nationalism in East European countries; and the allure of trade and credits with the West caused the new Kremlin regime to initiate what Brezhnev and Kosygin termed an "opening to the West."

Both superpowers were also motivated by the desire to build upon a series of arms control agreements achieved during the previous decade: the Antarctic Treaty, the Hot-Line agreement, the Limited Test Ban Treaty, the Outer Space Treaty and the Non-Proliferation Treaty. Article VI of the 1968 Non-Proliferation Treaty, for example, specifically committed the two giants "to pursue negotiations in good faith on effective measures relating to cessation of the nuclear arms race."

Thus, with the strategic forces and psychology of both countries "in phase," as the chief U.S. negotiator, Gerard Smith, put it, SALT began. Neither side, however, entered into these initial negotiations with much optimism. "Although overall political relations had mellowed slightly in the 1960s," Ambassador Smith remembers, "American and Soviet SALT negotiators were under no illusions that they were involved in anything but an adversary relationship, representing two superpowers tentatively searching for a less risky and costly way to maintain the balance of nuclear terror." Nevertheless, after two-and-a-half years of hard bargaining involving both formal negotiations and important behind-the-scenes maneuvering between Henry Kissinger and Soviet Ambassador A. F. Dobrynin, Washington and Moscow forged two accords, together known as SALT I.

The 1972 ABM Treaty and its companion 1974 Protocol severely restrict ballistic missile defense systems, allowing each side only one deployment site and placing qualitative restraints on ABM technology. Considered by many to be the most significant result of SALT, the Treaty was described by one expert as "a classic case of both sides agreeing not to build something that neither side wanted but that each would have probably ended up building in the absence of an agreement." Though of unlimited duration, the pact is subject to review every five years. Each side reaffirmed its support for the Treaty at the 1982 review, but ballistic missile defense is again being considered seriously. President Reagan in fact recently announced a long-term research and development program to explore all possible non-nuclear avenues to provide for an effective missile defense.

The SALT I interim Agreement on Offensive Arms essentially imposes a five-year quantitative freeze on the superpowers' intercontinental ballistic missiles (ICBMs) and submarine-launched ballistic missiles (SLBMs), the first set of actual limits on strategic hardware ever achieved. Much more controversial and difficult to negotiate than the ABM Treaty, the Interim Agreement is a series of compromises—or trade-offs—between adversaries. The agreement left the Soviet Union with several hundred more launchers than the United States had—2,347 to 1,710. And within this aggregate, the Soviets were allowed about 300 "modern large" or "heavy" ICBMs while the United States had none. The U.S. research and development community much earlier had turned away from large missiles in favor of Minuteman, a smaller, more accurate, more efficient rocket. But this discrepancy worried many Pentagon planners nonetheless.

For their part, the Soviets could point to a number of important compromises which compensated for asymmetries in the aggregate force level: First, it was significant that they accepted *any* restrictions on their offensive missiles. The Kremlin had resisted including such forces for a year and a half, an indication of internal pressure from the military establishment. Even more important, the Soviets agreed to defer consideration of several key issues: U.S. technological superiority, U.S. forward-based systems capable of delivering a nuclear attack on Soviet territory from outside the United States and the U.S. advantage of approximately three-to-one in long-range strategic bombers.

Neither side was fully satisfied by the Interim Agreement, but both recognized it as a temporary measure, with the potential to produce more meaningful future limits on strategic forces. In addition, both governments welcomed it and the ABM Treaty as significant political achievements. During the negotiations SALT acquired an institutional life of its own that has fundamentally altered the superpower relationship.

> Soviet and American officials sat across from each other at long tables, sipped mineral water and discussed military matters that used to be the stuff that spies were paid and shot for. . . . The process was the product. There emerged SALT bureaucrats in Washington and SALT *apparatchiks* in Moscow. SALT became a career in the civil service. The process acquired an institutional mass . . . that served as a kind of deep-water anchor in Soviet-American relations. [Strobe Talbott, *Endgame: The Inside Story of SALT II* (New York: Harper and Row, 1980), p. 20.]

The American public and Congress also greeted SALT I with much initial enthusiasm, reflected most vividly in the Senate ratification vote of 88-to-2. Gerald Ford, then a Congressman, best summarized the national mood: "What it all comes down to is this," Ford told a middle-America audience in June 1972. "We did not give anything away, and we slowed the Soviet momentum in the nuclear arms race." Support was not unconditional, however. Congress overwhelmingly approved the SALT I accords in September but added an amendment sponsored by Senator Henry Jackson requesting "the President to seek a future treaty that . . . would not limit the United States to levels of intercontinental strategic forces inferior to the limits provided for the Soviet Union."

Foreshadowed by the Jackson amendment and the debate over Soviet "superiority," the problems rather than the promise of SALT dominated the next phase of discussions. Between November 1972 and November 1974, the negotiations stalled over familiar issues: What systems to include in a permanent, comprehensive agreement; how to deal with qualitative as well as quantitative limits, especially with regard to MIRV; and how to keep outside political events—"linkage" —from influencing the discussions.

By far the greatest impediment to progress in this period was the continued improvement of Soviet and U.S. strategic nuclear forces within SALT I limits. During the 1970s the military, industrial and scientific bureaucracies on both sides kept pressure on policy-makers to modernize strategic systems. Working from worst-case analyses, they warned about the possibility of technological "breakout" and worried about the uncertainties and unknowns of a possible SALT II agreement, all of which created a difficult and uncomfortable situation for SALT negotiators.

The Soviet military buildup was particularly dramatic, especially in the eyes of U.S. defense planners. Of gravest concern was a new generation of hardened Soviet ICBMs with improved accuracy, increased throw-weight (payload capacity), and MIRV capabilities. The Soviets also introduced new submarine-launched ballistic missiles; a new intermediate-range ballistic missile, the SS-20; and a new bomber, the Tu-22M Backfire. And they continued to improve air defense and civil defense systems. According to political analyst Thomas Wolfe, during the 1970s the "Soviet R&D establishment . . . was continuing to operate at its own cyclical rhythm, little affected by SALT." [*The SALT Experience* (Cambridge, Mass.: Ballinger, 1979), p. 123.]

Reacting to these moves, President Nixon's defense secretary, James R. Schlesinger, suggested in 1974 that the Soviets were creating a "major one-sided counter-force [hard-target] capability against the United States ICBM force" that was "impermissible from our point of view." This became the major justification for the continuing modernization of U.S. nuclear forces. In addition to proceeding with MIRV deployment, which helped maintain the substantial U.S. advantage in numbers of warheads, Washington expanded the existing Trident missile and B-1 intercontinental bomber programs and initiated numerous other research and development projects. These included the MX missile, the long-range cruise missile, the increased yield MK-12A warhead, and MARV, a maneuverable re-entry vehicle that was the technological successor of MIRV. Wolfe's observation about Soviet research and development could as easily apply to U.S. programs.

Negotiators also found themselves adversely affected by the deterioration of international relations. SALT I had bolstered U.S.-Soviet political accommodation, but SALT II fell victim to political trouble between the superpowers. The Soviets' backing of the October 1973 Arab attack on Israel and their adventurism elsewhere in the Third World noticeably strained the Geneva negotiations.

Still, both sides had a great deal invested in SALT and the preservation of detente. Hence the talks continued, surviving the shifts in the U.S. Administration after Watergate. Finally in November 1974, President Gerald Ford and General Secretary Brezhnev met at Vladivostok where they hammered out an "agreed framework" for SALT II. Henry Kissinger, utilizing his talents at personal diplomacy, was largely responsible for engineering this major breakthrough.

Like SALT I, the Vladivostok accord was a mixture of superpower compromises. Meeting a central U.S. concern, the Kremlin accepted the principle of equal overall ceilings on delivery vehicles and agreed to drop the contentious forward-based-systems issue. However, the specific force level aggregate set by Ford and Brezhnev—2,400 strategic nuclear delivery vehicles, including for the first time, strategic bombers—was higher by about 300 than the United States would have preferred. Within this aggregate, moreover, each side would be permitted to mix and modernize its forces in any way it saw fit (which left unresolved the issue of Soviet heavy missiles). Also, bowing to U.S. pressure for "parity," the two leaders established a sub-ceiling of 1,320 MIRVed missile launchers for each side, but placed no specific limits on throw-weight, in which the Soviets had a large advantage.

Despite having a treaty "90 percent" completed by the end of 1975, according to Kissinger, and despite a January 1976 "near miss" by Kissinger to find that 10 percent solution, SALT II would not be signed for another three years. There were several reasons for this renewed stalemate. For the sake of agreement, the negotiators at Vladivostok once more left the hardest strategic questions for future discussion. They underestimated the dynamism of new technology. And they met a formidable roadblock in the U.S. political process.

The two particularly controversial new technologies were the Soviet Backfire bomber and the U.S. long-range cruise missile. The Backfire is a modern supersonic airplane intended for use primarily as a medium-range bomber but which could also be employed for strategic missions. The modern cruise missile is a small, pilotless aircraft. It can be launched from the air, land or sea, and its sophisticated guidance system permits it to fly at very low altitudes. The fact that the Backfire bomber and the cruise missile are both capable of strategic as well as tactical roles made each attractive to their respective military establishments, even while posing almost insurmountable difficulties for negotiators. Whether to include the Backfire as a strategic system and how to count cruise missiles in a new SALT agreement became the almost impossible arms control task.

In 1977 the Carter Administration came to power, deeply committed to arms control and determined to resolve the difficult remaining SALT issues. In March Carter sent Secretary of State Cyrus Vance to Moscow with a comprehensive package of SALT proposals they were confident would break the impasse. In a typically bold but rash move, Carter and his national security advisor, Zbigniew Brzezenski, had included several provisions that went far beyond the Vladivostok equal-aggregates formula. As Paul Warnke, the Administration's chief arms negotiator, later recalled, Carter and Brzezinski hoped "to shortcut the arms control negotiating process and move in one single giant step toward very significant reductions in numbers and toward a whole series of qualitative restraints." Predictably, the proposal shocked Soviet bureaucrats who had a built-in distaste for surprises or changes. Brezhnev summarily rejected it.

Thus, what seemed at first to be a giant leap toward arms limitation turned out to be [a] step backward. But despite continuing Soviet uneasiness over Carter's idealism, his open style of diplomacy and his unpredictability, the two sides narrowed their differences and adopted a compromise negotiating framework in September 1977. At the same time, they issued unilateral statements agreeing to abide by the SALT I Interim Agreement while the SALT II process continued. On June 18, 1979 Carter and Brezhnev met in Vienna and signed the three-part SALT II accords.

What is SALT II? At first glance, the accords appear to be a complex mass of documents describing the minutiae of nuclear arsenals. They include the basic Treaty on the Limitation of Strategic Offensive Arms to run through 1985, a protocol of three years' duration, and a bewildering jumble of Joint and Agreed Statements, Common Understandings and Memoranda totalling more than 100 pages. Buried in this legalistic and technical jargon, however, is a working, viable agreement.

At the heart of the Treaty are the aggregate numerical limits and sub-limits: on total launchers (2,400 initially, 2,250 within a year, which would require the Soviets to dismantle 250 existing systems); on MIRV launchers, including missiles and cruise-missile-carrying bombers (1,350); on MIRVed missiles alone (1,200); on MIRVed land-based ICBMs alone (820); and on "heavy" ICBMs (308). The Treaty also established limits on numbers of warheads or reentry vehicles per missile (10 for each MIRVed ICBM, 14 for each SLBM) and on the number of long-range cruise missiles per heavy bomber (an average of 28). The parties also agreed to several important bans: on the flight-testing or deployment of new types of ICBMs, except for one new type of "light" missile for each side; on heavy mobile ICBMs and heavy SLBMs; on the construction of additional fixed ICBM launchers; and on rapid reload systems. Restrictions on the Backfire bomber are less clear, but the Soviets did add an official statement that limits its production rate to 30 per year. Finally, the agreement includes detailed definitions and counting rules for the weapons systems it covers as well as an agreed data base.

The spirit of compromise was very evident in the Treaty. The Joint Chiefs of Staff explicitly recognized this in 1979 and consequently supported SALT II as a "modest but useful step in a long-range process which must include the resolve . . . to maintain strategic equivalence coupled with vigorous efforts to achieve further substantial reductions." [David C. Jones, Chairman, Joint Chiefs of Staff, "SALT II: The Opinion of the Joint Chiefs of Staff," *Vital Speeches of the Day* 45 (Aug. 15, 1979), p. 655.] Many former national security officials and members of Congress, however, did not see it this way. Led by Senator Henry Jackson and Paul Nitze, a former SALT I negotiator and co-founder of the Committee on the Present Danger, domestic critics mounted a massive campaign against SALT II during 1978 and 1979 which intensified during the ratification process.

Nitze became the intellectual driving force behind the anti-SALT movement. He and his Committee on the Present Danger attacked the Treaty itself as "fatally flawed" and President Carter as soft on national security issues. Nitze emphasized the persistent question of the Soviet heavy missile advantage, stressing the hypothetical threat it posed for U.S. ICBMs and creating ingenious scenarios in which the Soviets might use this advantage in a post–SALT II world for political blackmail. Nitze, Jackson and other Treaty detractors noted another "fatal flaw"—the non-inclusion of the Backfire bomber as a strategic system—and also raised questions about the ability to monitor Soviet compliance with the treaty.

Political analysts and Senate-watchers were still giving SALT II at least a 50-50 chance of ratification when a series of world events in the latter months of 1979 threw the agreement into limbo. In August, the United States discovered a Soviet troop brigade in Cuba; in November, Iranians seized the U.S. Embassy in Teheran; and in December, the Soviet Union invaded Afghanistan. The overall effect of these actions was to both divert attention from SALT and deepen public distrust of the Soviets. In January 1980, Carter asked the Senate to "delay consideration" of the Treaty.

The present U.S. Administration has yet another approach to arms limitation. President Reagan came to office with a strong public mandate to "get tough" with the Soviets. He initially took his mandate to heart, adopting a policy of "arms now—talk later" in his dealings with the Soviets. For nearly a year and a half, high-level Administration officials paid almost no attention to the issue of arms control. But responding in part to a growing international and national anti-nuclear movement, Reagan's advisors have expressed renewed interest in arms control even while emphasizing the need to bolster the military.

What does this mean for SALT? Nearly all members of the national security team, including the President, have been extremely critical of the SALT agreement. Eugene Rostow, former director of the Arms Control and Disarmament Agency, for example, has stated that the benefits of SALT I and SALT II "have turned to ashes in our mouths." [*Los Angeles Times,* Jan. 24, 1982.] Thus when forced to formulate their own policies and goals, these advisors proposed going beyond the SALT regime to achieve "truly substantial" reductions in nuclear arsenals. SALT became START—Strategic Arms Reduction Talks—and was conducted in coordination with the new intermediate Range Nuclear Forces talks, dealing with European theater systems.

The START deep-cut strategy envisions downgrading the importance of equal numbers of delivery vehicles and emphasizing instead restraints on the "destructive capacity" of strategic weapons—throw-weight, megatonnage, warhead and missile accuracy. Whether this approach can actually lead to agreement is questionable. As a Carnegie Endowment Study notes, the task is formidable: "Any scheme must deal with the wide differences in current forces and consider how to move from the current regimes toward a significantly different one without creating new instabilities." [Carnegie Panel on U.S. Security and the Future of Arms Control, *Challenges for U.S. National Security: Nuclear Strategy Issues of the 1980s,* Third Report (Washington, D.C.: Carnegie Endowment for International Peace, 1982), p. 68.] Still, the Soviets have not rejected the Reagan proposals outright (as they did Carter's in 1977), and talks have resumed.

The Reagan Administration first proposed at START to cut each side's total force of submarine and land-based missiles to 850. Warheads on those missiles would be reduced to 5,000 each, with no more than 2,500 on land-based ICBMs. This would cut U.S. missiles by half and Soviet missiles by two-thirds. Moscow countered with an offer to make an overall reduction in the missile and strategic bomber forces to 1,800 for each side, but Soviet negotiators carefully avoided proposing restrictions on any of the separate strategic weapons systems. Responding to the Scowcroft Commission report and congressional suggestions on arms control, Reagan has since slightly modified the original U.S. START position. While maintaining the proposed 5,000-warhead limitation, the President has directed negotiators to abandon the ceiling of 850 missiles for each side and called for "measured flexibility" in the negotiations.

SALT II survives as a *de facto* observance by both sides. But Reagan's defense officials continue to explore the ICBM vulnerability problem in ways that threaten to unravel existing elements of SALT—for example, using ABMs to protect the MX, which would require abrogation or "technical adjustment" of the 1972 ABM Treaty. "Dense pack" would also have been inconsistent with the terms of SALT II.

What do we stand to lose if SALT I and SALT II are gradually eroded or even scrapped? To be sure, SALT has left both sides with huge nuclear arsenals. And certain negotiating tactics that can be traced back to the Nixon-Kissinger years have actually accelerated weapons procurement. The utilization of "bargaining chips"—new weapons systems employed to gain negotiating leverage—is perhaps the most disturbing of these practices. "The bargaining chip," one study notes, "cannot always be cashed in." Or as another puts it, "Weapons initially justified as bargaining chips soon become building blocks—weapons systems which become permanent parts of the arsenal."

Benefits from SALT far outweigh its costs, however. Apart from the specific restrictions of individual agreements which act as a control mechanism, however imperfect, on the East-West arms race, the overall SALT process has resulted in some general benefits to U.S. security. Heading this list are advances in verification procedures and apparatus which both increase our knowledge about the other side and build mutual confidence. The 1972 agreements explicitly legitimize, and SALT II reaffirms, the unimpeded use of "national technical means of verification," a euphemism for satellite reconnaissance and other non-intrusive information-gathering techniques, such as radar and electronic monitors. SALT II builds upon this basic achievement with several new verification measures: "counting rules" for hard-to-inspect systems, among them MIRVed missiles (adopting the standard "once tested [as a particular type], always counted"); "type definitions" of systems, for example, of "heavy" missiles; and an "agreed data base" on ten categories of strategic forces to be updated at regular intervals.

Together these provisions represent a significant gain for U.S. intelligence and a marked change in Soviet attitudes about secrecy. After agreeing to the data base exchange, for example, chief Soviet negotiator Vladimir Semyenov reportedly said to Paul Warnke that 400 years of Russian history had just been "repealed." "But on reflection," he added, "maybe that's not a bad thing." Not only have Soviet leaders agreed to reveal more to the West; they have in the process opened a flow of information within their own bureaucracy. Apparently, the military is no longer the sole custodian of strategic facts and doctrine. New constituencies, in particular foreign policy experts, have taken their place in the internal decision-making process through the negotiations themselves, and such special SALT bodies as a jointly-run ad hoc group within the Ministry of Defense.

Another valuable product of the SALT process is the Standing Consultative Commission. Set up originally by the ABM Treaty to monitor problems and complaints about compliance, the Commission has quietly evolved into an important force for continuing dialogue and accommodation on nuclear issues. Since its inception in 1973, it has met at least twice a year in Geneva, in sessions completely separate from the formal negotiations. In the past, the U.S. delegation has been represented by a civilian commissioner from the Arms Control and Disarmament Agency, a military deputy and a staff of advisors from various government agencies. Today both top officials are military officers. The Kremlin also has civilian and military personnel on its delegation, led since the outset by Major General G. I. Ustinov of the General Staff and Viktor P. Karpov of the Ministry of Foreign Affairs, who now also heads the START negotiations. According to one SALT scholar, the Commission's most significant contribution to date has been the "successful . . . defusing [of] several public accusations of Soviet cheating by American critics of the SALT process." This confidence-building role will expand under SALT II and START since the Commission will be responsible for maintaining the data base, supervising any dismantling of strategic weapons that may be called for, and even considering new arms limitation strategies.

Thus, each side is now playing the strategic armaments game by a new set of rules which make the game more predictable and enhance stability. They should not be sacrificed or discarded in the interests of short-term military goals. SALT is not a panacea for our national security problems; neither is it the main cause of U.S. strategic deficiencies. Rather, it provides a valuable framework in which the superpowers can work toward further progress in negotiated arms limitation.

THE CASE AGAINST ARMS CONTROL
Seymour Weiss

Seymour Weiss served as director of the State Department's Bureau of Politico-Military Affairs and is coauthor with John Lehman of *Beyond the SALT II Failure.*

In one sense the case against arms control is not difficult to make. One might simply ask just what evidence exists that recent nuclear-arms-limitations agreements with the USSR have actually contributed to U.S. security. Yet in spite of the fact that no such evidence can be found, emotional attachment to the hoped-for benefits, together with the presumption that arms control is politically attractive, has created what Albert Wohlstetter has sardonically described as the mad momentum of arms control. It is this emotional attachment that makes the task of rational assessment more difficult. There is an undeniable and understandable yearning among our people, reflected in Congress and certainly echoed by our allies, for a cessation of the tensions that have accompanied the years of confrontation with the USSR.

That yearning nevertheless sometimes takes forms which misperceive reality: the idea, for example, that arms control is necessary to stop the "arms race"; or that it helps to avoid wasteful military expenditures; or that it is essential to the prevention of nuclear war. Each of these pleas on behalf of arms control has been made (and no doubt will be made over and over again). But can these problems—the arms race, wasteful military expenditures, or the drift toward nuclear war—be attenuated or corrected by arms control?

To begin with the arms race: arms control cannot stop it for the simple reason that in no real sense has there been any such thing as an arms race. As Assistant Secretary of Defense Richard Perle stated in recent congressional testimony, the number of U.S. nuclear weapons has been "declining rapidly" for two decades. Thus the U.S. has over 8,000 fewer warheads and a fourth less megatonnage today than it had in the 1960's. This reduction in U.S. inven-

Source: Seymour Weiss, "The Case Against Arms Control," *Commentary* (November 1984), pp. 19–23. Reprinted from *Commentary*, November 1984, by permission; all rights reserved.

tories has been the result of a modernization program, designed in part to put safer as well as more effective weapons in the U.S. inventory. It is not the product of agreements reached with the Soviet Union.

In any case, during the same period, which also marked the apex of détente and arms control, the Soviet Union, for its part, has added enormously both to the quantity and quality of its nuclear arsenal. A U.S. government study conducted in the late 1970's compared 41 categories of U.S. and Soviet nuclear capabilities (warhead numbers, megatonnage, delivery systems, and the like) for the year 1962 (the Cuban-missile-crisis period) with the late 1970's and early 1980's. It found the U.S. ahead significantly in every category in 1962 and behind in all but two by the late 1970's (with the lead in those two projected to disappear in the early 1980's).

There has, in short, been no arms race so far as the United States is concerned; conversely, arms control has not prevented the Soviets from forging ahead in their military programs.

How about saving money? Have past agreements not saved otherwise needless expenditures for arms, and might not additional savings be achieved through arms control in the future? The answer is a clear "no" to the former and an "almost certainly not" to the latter. Take the jewel in the arms-control crown, the ABM Treaty of 1972. One argument advanced at the time this agreement was negotiated was that it would spare the nation a wasteful and massive expenditure for a ballistic-missile defense. Some estimated that such a system might cost as much as $10 billion; other estimates ran considerably higher. Moreover, by precluding ballistic-missile defenses, each side would be saved the expenditure that would otherwise be required for offensive forces designed to overcome these defenses. The nation got an ABM treaty, but did it save itself the projected expenditures? It did not.

It is true that projected expenditures were cut back when we failed to finish the deployment of the ABM defense that was under way. At least in part as a result of that decision, however, we are proposing to spend tens of billions on the MX missile and perhaps tens of billions more on the so-called Midgetman missile in order to avoid the total vulnerability of our ICBM force—the very problem which the ABM system was expressly designed to solve. Furthermore, President Reagan has suggested that we reopen the issue of strategic defense, and specifically of ABM defense. While a sound suggestion on the merits, such a program, if adopted, could cost additional billions over time. Thus, it is possible that had we deployed an ABM defense in the early 1970's, we might have had a less costly, and not incidentally a more effective, defense posture than is now the case. (Surprisingly, some of the most vocal supporters of arms control advocate the adoption of a launch-on-warning strategy as a means of overcoming the vulnerability of our land-based forces. While this would indeed preclude the necessity for costly new programs of the MX or Midgetman type or of ABM's designed to protect such land-based systems, the danger to U.S. security of relying on such an unstable strategy ought to be apparent. The "cost" to the nation's security of such a strategy must surely be deemed to outweigh the costs of reconstituting our land-based forces whose vulnerability was in some measure increased by earlier arms-control agreements.)

In general, as most students of the subject will testify, savings have not resulted from arms-control agreements with the Soviets. Indeed, some have charged that arms control actually results in larger expenditures. For one thing, in order to gain the support of those directly responsible for providing for U.S. military security and who worry about the effect of arms control on the capacity for self-protection, other new and costly military programs must be promised. In addition, expensive new intelligence-monitoring systems must be developed. (It is arguable that certain military and intelligence programs might not have gained approval on their own merits without the pressures to provide for special safeguards generated by arms-control proposals.)

Finally, arms control, by constraining the kinds of systems we can have, as well as the numbers, increases the difficulty of providing for our security. Unless there is a commensurate reduction in the forces on the other side, the effect may be to raise the cost or endanger the security or both. The record clearly demonstrates that there has not been such a reduction.

The charge that the alternative to arms-control agreements is nuclear war would hardly warrant refutation were it not voiced at one time or another, directly or by implication, by a host of esteemed statesmen. On sober reflection, it is probable that so sweeping an assertion is not intended to be taken literally. Yet in the heat of political battle, when cherished policy objectives are being contested, extravagant statements do tend to be made.

In reality, the relationship between arms-control agreements and the avoidance of nuclear war is complex. Some even maintain that an inverse relationship exists—that arms-control agreements, by making it more difficult to provide for our security, may thereby have increased the ultimate danger of war. One need not go so far. Still, the positive relationship between recent agreements designed to limit nuclear arms and the prevention of nuclear war itself is anything but clear and direct.

It is, then, not hard to fault arms control on the merits. Nevertheless, no U.S. President has come out flatly against arms control. Why? There are several reasons having greater or lesser weight, depending upon the individual President. First, arms control is thought to be so politically popular (a notion fanned by the media despite polls which seem to demonstrate deep suspicion on the part of the public over agreements made with the Soviets) that no one seeking office can afford to oppose it in principle. Secondly, European support of and pressure for arms control must be reckoned with if the U.S. wants a politically viable alliance. Thirdly, no President can possibly take office without feeling the heavy burden placed upon him by the very existence of nuclear weapons, and he is therefore predisposed to embrace the view that arms control at least offers some hope of relief from a risky and burdensome arms competition.

Every recent President, every national leader, whether of liberal or conservative persuasion, has thus announced in favor of arms control. Some may have demurred on the terms of particular proposals, as was the case, for example, during the SALT II debates, but none challenged the principle. None rejected the notion that arms control was good (most said "essential"); the key was to find the right formula. But the unfortunate truth is that there can at present be no "right formula."

The reason lies in the nature of our conflict with the Soviet Union. Arms control is no more an end in itself than the national-defense efforts which nations undertake to provide for their security. Each is a means to an end. (Thoughtless advocates of nuclear arms-control agreements frequently lose sight of this fact; for such people arms control is an imperative, unlinked to other aspects of the U.S.-Soviet relationship.)

The development of a nation's military forces, moreover, is an expression of a national concern for the preservation and advancement of a vision of the national interest. What gives impetus to the development of military power is the existence of *seriously opposed* national interests. The U.S. force posture is not designed to cope with Canada or France or Japan, even though we may have some differences with these nations. For these differences are minor compared with our common interests. This is not so for the Soviet Union. In addition to pursuing interests inimical to our own, the USSR is a major military power. The constitutional requirement to provide for the common defense and protect the national welfare could in consequence not be fulfilled without offsetting military capabilities.

But could it not be argued that this is precisely what makes seeking arms-control measures a practical imperative? Cannot limitations of arms by each of the two sides substitute for a build-up? Exactly the contrary is true. The Soviet Union, at enormous material and political expense, has developed a massive conventional, theater-nuclear, and strategic-nuclear arsenal in order to advance its view of a desired international order, one dominated by Moscow. For the Soviets see military power as a precondition to maintaining a "favorable correlation of forces." Whether it is the physical suppression of freedom in Eastern Europe, the invasion of Afghanistan, the projection of Soviet forces and equipment into the Syrian-Middle East tinderbox, the use of proxies in the Third World to foment and support revolution (in the Soviet lexicon, "wars of national liberation"), or simply the exercise of political blackmail against Western Europe, military power plays the key role in advancing the Soviet view of a desirable international order.

Given all this, what is the basis for believing that the Soviets will ever agree to limit or reduce the very military power they require to maintain and advance their national objectives? What leads us to imagine that the Soviets might be willing to negotiate away their hard-won military advantages in an arms-control agreement? Why would the Soviets hand over at the negotiating table what they see no prospect of being forced to surrender in the ongoing political contest with the West, or—should it come to that—in a contest of arms?

Nothing suggests any such outcome—certainly not the recent history of U.S.-Soviet arms-control negotiations. On the contrary, those negotiations and the few significant agreements that have emerged from them point to precisely the opposite conclusion. The Soviet Union will sign arms-control agreements with the West only if such agreements are consistent with its fundamental political objectives—that is, only if they contribute to the extension of Soviet power and influence, normally at the direct expense of the West.

Past agreements have been used by the Soviets to achieve this end in a variety of ways:

- They have been designed to sow political discord between the U.S. and its allies, in the hope of promoting the dissolution of the postwar Western alliance. If an agreement can properly be seen as limiting U.S. power to support friendly states desirous of resisting the extension of Soviet power, it has served a vitally important Soviet objective. This is especially pertinent in the case of nuclear weapons, the U.S. having made solemn political commitments to employ them, if required, in defense of allies.

- If an agreement can lull the U.S. into believing that arms control reduces—or even removes—the need for self-help military measures, this contributes to Soviet purposes. In a strikingly candid warning, the Soviet leader Brezhnev told President Nixon at the time of the signing of SALT I that the USSR intended to maximize its military power within the constraints permitted by those accords. Mr. Nixon, in revealing this Soviet warning to the American people, no doubt hoped that, being so forewarned, the Congress and the public would respond by maximizing the military programs permitted the U.S. It was a vain hope, revealing a lack of comprehension of the mind set of Western society. There never was a realistic possibility that Congress, once a highly publicized and much lauded "arms-control" agreement was concluded with the USSR, would appropriate vast sums for military preparedness. And so the predictable happened. While the USSR, true to Brezhnev's word, developed a military arsenal of unprecedented dimensions during the late 60's and 70's, a period paralleling the SALT negotiations, the United States failed to keep pace, thus permitting the military balance to shift adversely both in fact and in the perception of most of the world.

- If an agreement disrupts the development of U.S. military technology while permitting the Soviets to close an important gap, it also serves Soviet purposes. One agreement which has had precisely this effect is the ABM Treaty of 1972. At the time of its signing, the U.S. held a major technological advantage in ballistic-missile defense. In the decade since the signing, the Soviets have pursued a massive development program in, and at least a partial deployment of, ballistic-missile defense. U.S. efforts during the same period limped along at a pitifully inadequate level. (Why, it was repeatedly asked by the Congress and the press, should we invest in ABM research and development when deployment of an ABM system was prohibited by treaty?) The result is that, by most public accounts, the Soviets are now capable of deploying an extensive ballistic-missile defense far more rapidly than is the U.S. Thus was the ABM Treaty utilized by the Soviets to nullify an important U.S. lead in military technology.

- If an arms-control agreement is clearly either unverifiable or unenforceable, it serves Soviet purposes. The U.S., by virtue of the nature of its society, can be expected to adhere to a strict interpretation of the terms of agreement. Indeed, examples abound whereby the U.S. exercised self-denial, fearing that a proposed arms development or production initiative *might* lead to an interpretation of inconsistency with an arms-control agreement. The Soviets, by contrast, have blatantly violated agreements. While insisting on arms-control provisions that are ambiguous, thus making verification inherently difficult, they are, in the last analysis, disdainful of the requirement to adhere even to *un*ambiguous agreements. Yet no U.S. administration has acted forcefully in the face of such violations. Even the Reagan administration, which to its credit has charged the Soviets with violations of treaty obligations, has not taken action to follow up on this charge. For the suggestion of retributive action would invoke the wrath of arms-control advocates who would deplore such action on the grounds that it would worsen U.S.-Soviet relations, as if it were the act of discovering Soviet cheating that was reprehensible rather than Soviet perfidy itself. It would appear that the Soviets' knowledge of the Western democratic process leads them to conclude (accurately) that Washington will resort to rationalizations of Soviet misbehavior to preserve arms-control agreements (and, when selling such agreements, will portray them in fictitiously favorable terms).

Can this deterioration be arrested? It is difficult to say. Arms control in the West has developed a dynamism and momentum of its own. Because of the false hopes concerning its putative benefits, most segments of Western society, ignoring the history of past agreements, call for more, not less, arms control. If SALT I worked contrary to our interests, negotiate SALT II. If the Soviets violate the Biological Arms Treaty, negotiate another treaty on any one of several subjects. If, as is occasionally the case, a U.S. proposal is advanced which might have the effect of reducing a Soviet military advantage and which is thus predictably rejected by the USSR, the cry goes up for more U.S. "flexibility" (a euphemism for making additional concessions to the Soviets).

Are there, then, any conditions that would permit an equitable agreement to limit nuclear arms? Two suggest themselves: first, fundamental Soviet political objectives might change. That is, the Soviets might abandon their quest for the advancement of a "socialist" international order responsive to Moscow. Clearly this is not a realistic prospect. Second, the U.S. might establish so formidable a level of military power that the Soviet Union would have no other alternative than to seek genuinely equitable agreements. This too seems remote. U.S. efforts to reestablish military might have a long way to go, despite the large defense budgets of the Reagan administration. (The notion that the U.S. might even try to reestablish military superiority, a condition which prevailed up until the mid-to-late 60's, is denounced by the U.S. press for reasons which remain obscure.) Moreover, the Soviets will try very hard to maintain military advantages where they have them. It is by no means clear that they would be unable to measure up in such a competition.

But if, in the broader sense, U.S. and Soviet political objectives are in radical conflict, what of those more narrowly defined interests that are presumed to emanate from successful arms-control negotiations—stability and equivalence?

Stability has generally been taken to apply to two issues: the so-called arms race and the management of crisis. As we have already seen, the arms race is largely an American illusion. American interest in and efforts at constraint are not shared by the Soviets. (Former Secretary of Defense Harold Brown once noted that "Soviet defense spending showed no response to U.S. restraint. . . . When we build, they build, when we cut, they build. . . .") The Soviet interest in constraint seems to be limited to U.S. military technology. In any event, more than a decade of arms control has seen the Soviet Union, with a much smaller GNP than the U.S., succeed in out-distancing the U.S. in a wide range of military (including nuclear) armaments. It would appear that the Soviets do not see such competition as fundamentally destabilizing.

Even less do they appear to share U.S. concern with crisis stability. Years

of effort to persuade the Soviets that fixed MIRVed ICBM's are inherently destabilizing have been unavailing. U.S. analysts have emphasized that during a
time of intense crisis such fixed systems would be so vulnerable to preemptive
attack that the temptation would be great to fire the missiles before they could
be destroyed. Moreover, once dispatched toward their targets, these missiles,
unlike bombers, are not recallable. The Soviets, however, have shown little
propensity to acknowledge the validity of these arguments, perhaps because
they are not entirely unhappy with the vulnerability of our ICBM's to a
preemptive strike.

Nor is seeking equivalence between the two strategic forces an apparent
Soviet interest. In the SALT I negotiations, according to Ambassador Paul Nitze,
the U.S. recognized that the asymmetrical characteristics of U.S. and Soviet
strategic systems would require the two sides to develop certain formulas which,
if accepted, would create equivalence between their respective military capabilities. But the negotiations demonstrated that the Soviets did not share the
U.S. desire to seek such an equivalence. Instead the Soviets sought a condition
they described as "equal security." As defined by the Soviets, equal security
meant that they must be permitted military forces in the aggregate superior
to those maintained by *all* other potential adversaries. So defined, "equal security" is closer to the now outdated U.S. concept of strategic superiority than
to the U.S. arms-control concept of strategic equivalence.

We have seen that fundamentally incompatible political objectives logically preclude arms-control arrangements which by U.S. standards are fair to
both sides. Yet it now appears that even on narrower grounds involving arms-
control objectives like stability and equivalence, there is little reason to project a commonality of interest. As George Kennan once said:

> There is no use trying to swing Russians into line by referring to com-
> mon purposes to which we may both have done lip-service at one time
> or another. . . . For them it's all a game. And when we try to come at
> them with arguments based on such common professions, they become
> doubly wary.

Suppose, for the sake of argument, that the case made here against arms
control is essentially correct. The indictment would be a powerful one. The
only possible conclusion one could draw would be that contemporary nuclear
arms-control agreements with the Soviet Union have been contrary to U.S.
national interests. Even so, no issue as complex as this one is likely to lead to
so simple and direct a conclusion. Might there be a consideration not yet addressed that would impart to the arms-control efforts of the last two decades
something more than a passing redeeming value? May it not be that even if
the agreements were "flawed" in some respects, *the process itself* was—and is—
of great value? For whatever one may think of the substantive merit of any
particular agreement, the process keeps U.S. and Soviet officials in direct con-

tact, exchanging views on nuclear strategy, weapons capabilities, and the intentions of the two sides. Surely, in the nuclear age, nothing can be of greater importance than the continuing contact that the arms-control process provides.

But is it really true that a better comprehension of an adversary's purpose offers promise of more tranquil relations? Not necessarily. Reviewing the history of the early 1930's, especially the arms-control efforts made at the time, one discovers that despite ample contact and a continuing process, Europeans whose vital interests were being challenged nevertheless deluded themselves about the purposes of the Third Reich. As Richard Perle wrote in 1981:

> After all, the political and bureaucratic elite in prewar Britain believed itself to be clear-eyed and hard-headed in matters of international politics and diplomacy. Its members believed in arms control and thought that it could stabilize the military balance in Europe in the 1930's. But they approached arms control with claims of prudence and caution that ring not so very different from those heard during the 1970's.

For example, Perle points out, the British Imperial Defense Committee in 1932 declared:

> The military forces of the nations . . . should be limited in such a way as to make it unlikely for any aggressor to succeed with a "knockout blow." The committee went on to urge an end to what is called "disarmament by example," a notion that Paul Warnke could be found advocating some forty-five years later.

Yet when the British government proposed a modest increase in the Royal Air Force over a five-year period beginning in 1934, "the Labor and Liberal opposition brought a censure motion regretting that: 'His Majesty's Government should enter upon a policy of rearmament . . . certain to jeopardize the prospects of international disarmament and to encourage a revival of a dangerous and wasteful competition.' "

Additional examples from British history in the 1930's could be cited, but the message is clear. It appears not only possible, indeed it may be the norm, for Western democracies to understand that they are confronting a serious adversary, to observe concrete evidence of military preparation whose purpose (given the opposed political objectives of the two sides) can only be political intimidation or aggressive military action, and yet to rationalize all this away. Such self-delusion is not surprising when the consequences of facing reality are so challenging and require hard sacrifice and courageous political leadership. How much easier it is to project an image of hope for a brighter future, free of these burdensome considerations. Under such circumstances, arms control has been, and continues to be, a longed-for panacea.

Self-delusion of the sort described here has little or nothing to do with lack of information due to inadequate contact with the adversary. British officials up to and including the Prime Minister met repeatedly with Hitler and his associates, but proximity did not breed a general comprehension of reality. Conversely, Winston Churchill required no intimate contact to perceive the truth. Here we have the essence of the matter. The process itself offers little hope for benefit when the parties bring divergent purposes to the table.

But still, is it not better to "talk than fight"? Consider the answer of Dean Acheson to this question:

> I have heard people who should know better . . . say happily, "As long as they are talking they are not fighting." Nothing could be more untrue; they are fighting. . . . To our minds international conferences and international negotiations are so completely means for ending conflict that we are blind to the fact that they may be and, in the hands of experts, are equally adapted to, continuing it. . . . "There is no alternative to negotiations with the Russians" is the constant theme of a well-known columnist and a prominent politician in this country. . . . This is, of course, silly. For if there is no alternative, and if the Russians will only negotiate, as is now the case, on their own terms, then there is no alternative to surrender. . . .

Nothing that has happened since has affected the truth of these words, and much that has happened since has strengthened the case against arms control. It does not serve our security, it does not save money, and it does not lessen the risk of war. Arms control is certainly politically popular, but it is just as certainly the repository of false and dangerous hopes.

Negotiations on Nuclear Forces
Lawrence Freedman

Lawrence Freedman is Professor of War Studies at King's College, London, and is author of *Britain and Nuclear Weapons* and the *Evolution of Nuclear Strategy*.

It is easy to believe that the current problems besetting nuclear arms control in Europe are simply the result of an inflexible U.S. or Soviet stance. However, a backward look at the history of these problems provides no evidence that negotiators operating in a more favorable political environment found them much more tractable. These "gray area" weapons have dogged strategic arms

Source: Lawrence Freedman, "Negotiations on Nuclear Forces," *Bulletin of the Atomic Scientists* (December 1983), pp. 22–28. Reprinted by permission of the *Bulletin of the Atomic Scientists,* a magazine of science and world affairs. Copyright © 1983 by the Educational Foundation for Nuclear Science, Chicago, IL 60637.

control from the start and often have been removed as an obstacle only by being deferred to a later stage in the negotiations.

It is also clear that if at last they can be encompassed in the agreement, a deal at Geneva will be less radical than the rhetoric surrounding the negotiations might suggest. This, in turn, casts doubt on the role that arms control negotiations can play in rationalizing force structures.

When the SALT talks began in November 1969, there were grounds for believing that nuclear weapons in Europe played a small and declining role in the strategic calculations of the United States and the Soviet Union. Nevertheless, these weapons raised a series of awkward questions which made it likely from the start that they would complicate the negotiations.

The first question was that of the scope of the talks: was the concern with weapons of a particular range, able to travel intercontinental distances, or with weapons capable of reaching the territory of a superpower? Taking the first view allowed for a cut-off point by range, with due allowance for submarine-launched systems. This was favored by the United States but was unacceptable to the Soviet Union, which felt directly under threat from British, French and Chinese systems, and from U.S. weapons based in Europe as well as from U.S. intercontinental systems.

This raised the question of responsibility to allies. The Soviet view of the scope of the talks challenged the United States to negotiate on behalf of other countries and to accept restrictions on weapons that played a major role in the basic security guarantees it had made to its allies. Yet the Soviet Union was not offering restrictions on its forces which directly threatened these allies. An added difficulty was the knowledge that the numbers and types of systems based in Europe were of a sort that would frustrate negotiations.

At the start of SALT neither side accepted the difficulties of setting limits to the negotiations. Both proposed partial limits on some of the other side's European systems. The initial U.S. SALT proposal, developed prior to the start of the negotiations, advocated a freeze on medium-range ballistic missiles (which only the Russians still maintained) and a ban on mobile versions thereof.

The Soviets argued that U.S. fighter-bombers in Europe—the so-called forward-based systems—had the range to reach the Soviet Union and so were strategic and should be withdrawn before the talks could proceed. On similar grounds they argued for the removal of U.S. forces in the Far East and on aircraft carriers. The exclusion of their own theater forces was justified on the grounds that these could not reach the United States and were needed for defense against third countries. This latter point, of course, made it difficult for the Soviets to argue for inclusion of third-country forces. Yet it did so, in a muted way. The lack of conviction behind the effort was illustrated by the concentration on only submarine-based forces and the neglect of British and French aircraft.

The U.S. and Soviet proposals on theater forces led to an impasse and were responsible for a lack of progress at the talks. The Americans eventually proposed, in August 1970, that forward-based systems and medium-range missiles both be excluded, to permit progress on the basic issue of central strategic systems. This was supported by the allies. Whatever the West European view a decade later, at the time far greater priority was attached to keeping the U.S. forward-based systems out of the negotiations than getting the Soviet missiles in. The Soviets dropped only their demand for the withdrawal of forward-based systems, but still insisted that these systems be properly "taken into account" in the main agreement.

This was not explicitly granted in the SALT I agreement of May 1972, but a number of tacit concessions may have been made by the United States in return for Soviet deferral of the forward-based systems issue. The agreement was far more limited than originally proposed and allowed the Soviets numerical superiority in offensive missiles. The Soviet Union also seemed to think that it had been given some allowance for British, French and Chinese systems. In a unilateral statement of May 1972, which was not accepted by the United States, the Soviet team argued that any additional British or French missile-carrying submarines, in addition to the nine then deployed or planned, would justify a comparable Soviet increase in submarine numbers.

As the forward-based systems had not been formally included in SALT I, they were still available as a Soviet bargaining chip for SALT II. Once again the Soviets raised the issue. The November 1974 Vladivostok *aide-memoire* between Presidents Ford and Brezhnev excluded these systems but once again there were suspicions that some form of quid pro quo had been obtained by the Soviet heavy bombers and the abandonment of attempts to reduce the Soviet heavy-missile arsenal.

Throughout this period, the issue of nuclear weapons in Europe was not dealt with head-on. It was seen as peripheral to the main concerns of SALT and the weapons themselves as something of a relic of a bygone age. For the Soviets, leaving the forward-based systems issue unsettled kept it available as a bargaining chip, while formal agreement might legitimize the U.S. presence in Europe and draw attention to the imbalance in theater forces. The Americans, for their part, wanted to keep forward-based systems out of the talks because of potential difficulties with allies. While justifying their exclusion by reference to the Soviet position on its own theater forces, there was little disposition to push the linkage so as to achieve a clear trade between Soviet missiles and U.S. aircraft. Thus, over the first few years of SALT, the issue declined rather than grew in importance.

The trend moved dramatically in the opposite direction during SALT II. The main reason for this was the advent of a new category of weapons—known as "gray area" systems—that could not be properly termed either strategic or theater. The principal weapons in this category were the Backfire bomber and the cruise missile. The Backfire problem was rather like that of forward-based systems in reverse, in that the aircraft was primarily intended to fulfill a theater mission but was technically capable of striking the opposing homeland.

Throughout 1975, the United States pressed for Backfire to be included in SALT, while the Soviets remained adamantly opposed. Primitive cruise missiles were still around from the early stages of the nuclear race, and prompted some ironic exchanges in SALT before the modern potential of the weapon was recognized. In 1969, the United States had proposed a freeze on submarine-launched cruise missiles, which only the Soviets then retained. The chief Soviet negotiator, intent on ridiculing U.S. concern, compared cruise missiles to "prehistoric animals of the Triassic period."

The U.S. program in the 1970s focused initially on submarine-launched cruise missiles, comparable to those of the Soviet Union, but the emphasis soon shifted to air-launched programs. It became clear that the new weapons could be extraordinarily versatile, performing strategic or theater roles, delivering nuclear or conventional munitions from a variety of platforms and with phenomenal accuracy. A worse complication from the arms control point of view was that the range and payload of any given type seemed impossible to verify. The initial SALT involvement with cruise centered on the twin issues of range restrictions and counting rules. The Soviets used an imprecise statement in the Vladivostok accords to press for a ban on all cruise missiles over 600 kilometers in range. The United States, while prepared to forego systems which had intercontinental range in their own right, was wary of any greater constraints.

The issues of Backfire and cruise were the principal obstacles to progress in SALT II for nearly three years after the Vladivostok summit. It was natural, then, that a tradeoff should be attempted to break the deadlock. On two occasions, once in February 1976 and again a year later, the United States proposed that the twin problems be deferred to SALT III to enable an interim agreement to be reached. The Soviet Union, however, was not prepared to leave cruise missiles unconstrained, and it became obvious that some more complex solution to the gray area problem was required.

In the end, in SALT II, Backfire was not made subject to major constraints. The Soviet Union had steadfastly resisted U.S. demands that it should count as a heavy bomber, or that its deployment should be limited to "peripheral" areas such as Europe. All the United States obtained was a written promise not to increase the Backfire production rate from 30 per year (a level which it has not at any rate met in recent years) nor to convert the aircraft to an intercontinental role. One way in which the United States reconciled itself to this setback was to assert its right to counter the Backfire by a similar U.S. system, the FB-111.

The United States accepted limits on the air-launched cruise missile, in terms of effective numerical ceilings. The ground- and sea-launched versions were viewed by the Soviets as much more threatening, but a protocol to the Treaty which prohibited their deployment for three years did no more than state a physical fact. This protocol served as a device to put off difficult issues for future negotiations, while putting down a marker for the content of those negotiations, reinforced by a declaration of principles on SALT III.

Moscow expected, or at least hoped, that the protocol would set a precedent for the future, and U.S. and European critics were anxious that this might be so. Washington described the protocol as virtually meaningless, but President Carter was forced to give a positive assurance that the weapons could be deployed in Europe once the three-year period expired.

Far from setting a precedent, the protocol helped precipitate the modernization decision. More paradoxically still, European worries over the cruise missile helped to prejudice the very arms control process which was fast becoming a political necessity for the success of the theater nuclear force program.

The real root of increased NATO sensitivity was the shift from stagnation in the theater stockpile to an accelerating arms race. The Europeans did not want SALT to prejudice any weapons system which might conceivably be needed to counter the new Soviet buildup. Europeans were worried that, because of its preoccupation with its own vulnerability, the United States would leave the *theater* capabilities of Backfire and SS-20 unconstrained by SALT, while bargaining away any Western response.

Meanwhile, by codifying a sort of symmetry at the strategic level, SALT was enhancing the importance of asymmetries lower down the line. Last, but by no means least, it was believed by many defense planners that, irrespective of what the Soviets were up to with the SS-20, NATO had to improve its own theater forces because of the age of existing capabilities, in particular the F-111 and the Vulcan bomber.

There was a growing consensus in the late 1970s that theater nuclear weapons should be directly involved in future arms control negotiations. The development which forged this consensus was that the two blocs at last were prepared to pay for restrictions on opposing theater nuclear forces by accepting constraints on their own arsenals:

- The Americans were concerned that the technological ambiguity of gray area systems, together with the resurrection of the forward-based systems issue, would prevent any further progress in SALT unless the theater nuclear forces problem was tackled head-on.
- The Europeans wanted to remove or to counter the growing threat

posed by Backfire and SS-20 and had learned from the furor over the neutron bomb that any program for new nuclear deployments had to be accompanied by substantive proposals for arms control.

- The Soviets were extremely worried about the military and political implications of having cruise and Pershing missiles stationed in Western Europe.

In December 1979 NATO ministers approved a program to base 464 Tomahawk cruise missiles and 108 Pershing II ballistic missiles in Europe during the 1980s. The opportunity to justify the modernization program by reference to the SS-20 was too good to miss, and the future of the two programs was seen to be linked. This encouraged the view that it was necessary to produce an arms control proposal in "parallel" to the plans for force modernization. The agreed proposal involved the following conditions:

- Any future limitations on U.S. systems designed principally for theater missions should be accompanied by appropriate limitations on Soviet theater systems.
- Limitations on U.S. and Soviet long-range theater nuclear systems should be negotiated bilaterally in the SALT III framework in a step-by-step approach.
- The immediate objective of these negotiations should be the establishment of agreed limitations on U.S. and Soviet land-based long-range theater nuclear missile systems.
- Any agreed limitations on these systems must be consistent with the principle of equality between the sides. Therefore, the limitations should take the form of *de jure* equality both in ceilings and in rights.
- Any agreed limitation must be adequately verifiable. Adopting SALT as the most appropriate forum acknowledged that cruise missiles were already bound up with SALT, and that completely separate talks on central and theater systems could symbolize a break in the link between the major U.S. nuclear arsenal and the defense of Europe. The unwillingness of the British and French to expose their small nuclear forces confirmed the bilateralism. Only U.S. missiles from the NATO side were to be discussed. Restricting future negotiations to "land-based missiles" reflected the popular perception of the issue at hand. It would also keep matters simple by excluding aircraft. There was, however, a disposition against regional ceilings, on the grounds that only a global ceiling could take in most of the relevant SS-20s.

The actual substance of the proposal reveals the preoccupation with parity. The use of the term *de jure* equality indicated that NATO would be more interested in establishing a right to equal ceilings than in actually creating an equality in practice.

The problem lay in combining two conflicting objectives. The culture of arms control and popular perceptions of the issues stressed the importance of missile parity. Yet the military objective had not been to match the ss-20, missile for missile, but merely to provide a credible response, reflecting established requirements. More important in doctrinal terms, the notion of a separate regional balance implied by parity reflected exactly the sort of uncoupling from the central strategic balance that West Europeans had been trying to prevent.

After the NATO decision it was unclear whether the Soviets would agree to talk at all. The initial reaction was that the "basis" for talks had been destroyed, but by July, and the visit of West Germany's Chancellor Schmidt to Moscow, a new basis had been found. The new Soviet position was stated in *Pravda* on July 7, 1980:

> Without withdrawing the proposals put forward earlier, [the Soviet Union] could also agree to a discussion of issues relating to medium-range weapons even before ratification of SALT II. At the same time, the discussions must involve not only medium-range missiles, but also U.S. forward-based nuclear weapons. Both these problems must be discussed simultaneously and in organic connection. . . . Possible accords could be implemented only after the SALT II Treaty comes into force.

From October to November 1980, preliminary discussions between U.S. and Soviet teams on theater nuclear arms control took place in Geneva. In May 1981 Secretary of State Alexander Haig agreed, in Rome, that negotiations should resume before the end of the year; the time would be settled when he met Soviet Foreign Minister Andrei Gromyko at the U.N. General Assembly in September.

Before the start of the negotiations proper in November 1981, it was possible to identify the problems that would create the greatest difficulties.

- NATO wanted to concentrate solely on missiles, whereas the Soviet Union wished to include aircraft. The United States argued that its F-4s and carrier-based A-6s and A-7s were dual-capable and generally unsuitable for strikes into Soviet territory.
- The Soviet Union wished to confine discussions to forces actually based in Europe. The United States could not accept that: at a minimum, the ss-20s able to cover both Western Europe and China in sites just east of the Urals would have to be included.
- NATO envisaged limitations on relevant systems currently facing China. The Soviets held that these ss-20s and bombers have nothing to do with the European theater, but from the NATO perspective, these systems could be turned against it, either as a result of a Sino-Soviet rapprochement or just through reinforcement measures in an emergency. It has been suggested that ss-20s could be transported to new sites by air.

The Soviet Union had always seen itself as *demandeur* on the issue of nuclear weapons in Europe, because of the importance it attached to weapons that could attack Soviet territory as against those which could merely attack the territory of its allies. If Soviet weapons of [a range comparable] to the U.S. forward-based systems were included, then a comparison of U.S. and Soviet inventories put the Soviet Union far ahead in numbers. Thus, if the argument were to be phrased in terms of "equality," the Soviets would have to make all the concessions.

It was too much for the Kremlin to move from a situation where the United States had to make all the concessions to one where the onus was on the Soviet Union. The Soviet leadership therefore argued that the basic position was equal and that the two sides should make equal reductions and eschew one-sided increases: parity existed and had to be preserved.

NATO had, in the past, resisted notions of separate European balances, but the culture of arms control and the logic of its own arguments was forcing it toward such a balance. The initial negotiating offer reflected the history of European systems being seen as complicating factors in the central strategic balance, to be dealt with either as part of a broader "deal" or as a once-and-for-all trade between two equally awkward—if not strategically comparable—systems. This depended on being able to view cruise/Pershing and the ss-4, -5 and -20 in isolation from other systems in Europe.

Such a position might have been possible while negotiations on central systems provided the dynamic to arms control; but it was hopeless once these theater negotiations had to stand on their own. Given the long-standing Soviet position on forward-based systems, the inclusion of aircraft was inevitable. NATO, too, was being forced to argue for equality in Europe, despite all its doctrinal misgivings about such a course. To justify extra missiles coming in on the NATO side, it could not be accepted that parity existed; for NATO, parity was now desirable, but had to be created.

Negotiations began in November 1981. It has become a truism that the United States and the Soviet Union have been gearing their statements as much to Western public opinion as to the other side. The Soviet Union has had grounds for hoping that the cruise/Pershing program would be scuttled through domestic opposition—so obviating the need for concessions on its part. The United States, for its part, assumed that it was only when it seemed likely that the NATO program would go ahead that Soviet concessions would be forthcoming. Its positions have thus been designed to secure support from domestic opinion, even if they were unacceptable to the Soviet Union.

Despite initial promises from the negotiating teams of discreet, businesslike diplomacy, the continual playing to the gallery by the national leaders has undercut traditional diplomacy. Bold statements demanding quick rebuttals are rarely conducive to the solution of complex issues. In fact, the process of public debate has served to reinforce the original positions which can now probably only be reconciled, if at all, through intensive private diplomacy.

The opening U.S. position was the so-called "zero option," by which NATO would forego the cruise and Pershing program if the Soviets abandoned all of its ss-4s, -5s and -20s, including those in the Far East. The episode demonstrated the European governments' preoccupation with getting the Americans to provide a negotiating spectacle, especially one that appropriated the slogans of the disarmament movement, without devoting much thought to the content of the negotiations. This approach was always vulnerable to a Soviet veto, which could deny the image of "negotiability" to any position. This fate befell the zero option and is now likely to be suffered by the new compromise—the "interim solution." In the latter, both sides have equal numbers of missile warheads, at a level as close as possible to zero but probably around 300. In doctrinal terms this is more acceptable but no more negotiable, and carries with it the strong suggestion that somewhere, somehow, cruise and Pershing missiles will have to be installed. In September 1983 President Reagan moved some way toward easing a few secondary points of contention: by offering compromise solutions on Soviet systems based East of the Urals (a U.S. right to match Soviet numbers with a promise not to exercise it); by acknowledging that one day aircraft will have to be included; and hinting—but not promising—a possible compromise on the European balance (maybe something less than parity such as disproportionate cuts of Pershing).

The basic construction of the Soviet position is bogus. It claims an existing equality of aircraft and missiles in Europe—at just under 1,000 apiece. However, it can only construct this equality by disregarding its own counting rules at difficult moments. Thus it imposes a geographical restriction to keep out of negotiations its own aircraft and systems facing China (which *could* be moved to face Western Europe in a crisis); yet it wishes to include U.S. FB-111 aircraft, plus A-6 and A-7 aircraft or carriers, both based outside of its own guidelines area.

The Soviets set a minimum range of 1,000 kilometers, which would exclude U.S. F-4s but include the Soviet SU-19 Fencer; yet it tries to bring in the former and keep out the latter by playing games with calculations of combat range. (They do this essentially by suggesting that the U.S. F-4s need not worry about Soviet air defenses and could fly at a continual high altitude, while the Soviet SU-19s *would* have to worry about their own defenses and fly continually from base to a low altitude!) And finally, Moscow wants to include British and French submarines, even though, by its own previous arguments as well as those of the countries concerned, these should be discussed, if at all, as strategic forces.

The Soviet position as laid down in a draft treaty of May 1982 would have the two sides going down to 300 aircraft and missiles within five years of the treaty coming into force. In terms of their calculation, the Soviets could keep a reasonably healthy ss-20 and Backfire force while all U.S. aircraft would be expelled from Europe and there would even have to be a reduction in the number of U.S.-based FB-111's.

In December 1982 Yuri Andropov modified the formula to allow for a specific deal, relating the number of ss-20s to the 162 British and French missiles. The offer underlined the Soviet preoccupation with getting the Americans out of Europe rather than cutting the European forces. For the first time Moscow offered a specific limit on numbers of ss-20s, but it did not involve a move away from the previous position, which included aircraft. Aircraft would still have to be reduced.

In April 1983 Andropov offered to count warheads rather than launchers. This would have been a concession if combined with a greater concession on accepting new U.S. missiles in Europe, but as an extension of the established Soviet proposal it seemed to reach exactly the same conclusion as before. The same was true of an August offer which later seemed to be qualified, to "eliminate" ss-20s later from Europe rather than move them east of the Urals. Anything else would have been preposterous. What is notable is that there has been no movement from the refusal to sanction any new U.S. missiles. The preoccupation with British and French missiles has also become something of a fixation. The speed of Andropov's rejection of President Reagan's September 1983 compromise does not suggest a willingness to legitimize the new U.S. missiles even though the Kremlin must now know their arrival is inevitable.

This saga provides an illustration of how not to go about arms control. The problem might have been more tractable in the early 1970s when the forces seemed reasonably settled. Whatever opportunity there might have been was lost through the natural disposition to put off awkward issues of low salience. By the time it had become impossible to defer the issue any longer the political, strategic and arms control context had become much less propitious. As with many other areas of political activity, attitudes are often struck more with regard to immediate pressures and short-term effect than with regard to long-term considerations. The history of arms control is littered with lost opportunities, as weapons still at the early stage of development, or issues of great potential relevance but of slight contemporary interest, passed by.

It may be that until arms control can escape the dead hand of parity there is always the possibility of a repeat performance. Parity is a natural concept for diplomats. In practice it involves attempting to match complex force structures that may be essentially similar in broad functions and overall capability but are not at all comparable in detail. The effort to squeeze these distinct forces into contrived categories is not only extraordinarily difficult but it is also controversial and can create for more bad feeling than any success can dissipate. Already many in the field want to entangle battlefield nuclear weapons in the arms control net. Obviously, these weapons are not wholly benign and deserving of protection from interference; but arms control, as now conceived and practiced, with its neat but arbitrary accounting methods is the least promising method for addressing the problems that they create.

It is not possible to turn the clock back and restart the arms control enterprise on the basis of more modest and clearer ambitions. With the INF (intermediate-range nuclear forces) negotiations now bearing an enormous political burden—for the state of alliance cohesion as well as of East-West relations—there is a need for a fix of some sort.

It is unlikely that the formal position of either side can serve as a basis for a future agreement. At some point the structure of an eventual deal is not hard to work out; it would probably follow the famous Nitze-Kivitsky "walk in the woods" compromise of July 1982. The basic arrangement in that deal was that the Soviets gained the cancellation of Pershing and a freeze instead of reduction in its Far Eastern deployments, while the United States was allowed some 300 cruise missiles in Europe with a reduction of SS-20s to 75, with 225 warheads. Conceding the introduction of any new NATO missiles will be difficult for Moscow, as will tolerating a further delay in dealing with aircraft. For Washington, the main difficulty may be in accepting the abandonment of Pershing. It is a better missile, though not as dramatic in its implications as suggested in Soviet propaganda.

If an agreement were to be reached, it would not be equivalent to a treaty. Given the vexed issues of definition, non-circumvention and verification, which will all take months to sort out, all one can hope for in 1983 is an agreed framework, à la Vladivostok, with a promise to expedite consideration of the details.

As I have argued, the attempt to construct a separate framework for a European nuclear balance was, if anything, an aberration. It was a result of the exhaustion of the negotiations on central strategic systems, political enthusiasm for an INF negotiating effort, doctrinal absentmindedness by the West Europeans, and a crude misrepresentation of the existing balance by the Soviet Union.

Even if the attempt is sustained, there are many years of fruitless wrangling ahead, continuing to poison European politics, in order to achieve an elusive and artificial construction of minimal strategic significance. The concentration on Europe suggests the importance and distinctiveness of the relevant systems. The great disparities born of the Soviet Union's more consistent interest in intermediate and medium-range systems cannot be readily overcome by compromise even if the will was there to compromise. Moving into aircraft offers no relief. The disparities remain and even get worse as the range is lowered. The problems are aggravated by difficulties of definition and restriction with dual-capable systems. Battlefield systems will inevitably be drawn in, rendering counting and verification even more difficult, adding to the chaos. For the longer term, therefore, the need is to draw a clear line to avoid further complications from further systems.

The Americans should acknowledge that their F-111s, FB-111s and sea-launched cruise missiles will have to fit in, in return for inclusion of the Soviet Backfire, Badger and Blinder aircraft. Having identified these extra systems—along with the ground-launched cruise missile and ss-4s, ss-5s and ss-20s—it should be made clear that all other systems—including U.S. Phantoms and Soviet Fencers—are unsuitable for traditional methods of arms control. The designated systems should then be put back into the strategic arms pot where they have always belonged.

Although it is possible to design schemes for this remerger the position has been greatly complicated by the sorry state of strategic arms control and the various complicated formulas being advanced by the United States at the START negotiations (now being revamped following the Scowcroft Report on the basing of the MX). It is possible that warheads will emerge as a sole unit of account which is fine for missiles but causes immense problems for aircraft. Although the asymmetries in START are by no means as marked as in the INF negotiations, each specific issue tends to carry with it great domestic baggage in the United States. There can thus be no confidence that INF or START can be merged with, as it were, balanced books on either of the sides, let alone both sides. Whether a merger between two confused and incomplete negotiations would intensify or ease the agony will depend on the political circumstances of the time. It is not a matter for dogmatism. What is clear is that if nuclear arms control is ever again to prosper, some overall framework must be found.

THE VERIFICATION SPECTRUM
Glenn C. Buchan

Glenn C. Buchan is on the research staff of the Institute for Defense Analyses in Alexandria, Virginia.

The "ability to verify" an arms control agreement is obviously a pivotal question in any negotiation. Yet there is no consensus on this fundamental issue. At least three schools of thought on verification can be identified: *substantive, legalistic* and *metaphysical.*

Source: Glenn C. Buchan, "The Verification Spectrum," *Bulletin of the Atomic Scientists* (November 1983), pp. 16–19. Reprinted by permission of the *Bulletin of the Atomic Scientists,* a magazine of science and world affairs. Copyright © 1983 by the Educational Foundation for Nuclear Science, Chicago, IL 60637.

- The *substantive* school holds that an arms control treaty can be adequately verified if neither side could alter the strategic balance by undetected cheating. This was essentially the position of the Carter Administration and others favoring SALT II. And, indeed, the substantive view has undeniable appeal for several reasons. One is that it takes advantage of the relative insensitivity of the strategic balance to any of the areas that have so far been constrained by SALT. To make any real difference strategically, violations would have to be so massive that detection would be virtually certain. Another is that information requirements closely approximate those of the normal intelligence collection and evaluation process. Multiple sources of intelligence can be used; judgments can be made based on the weight of all evidence; emphasis can be placed (in principle, at least) on things that matter. Also treaty provisions can be somewhat looser. For example, various types of limits on weapons system testing become attractive as arms control measures, on the assumption that new or improved weapons could have little impact on the strategic balance unless their reliability and performance could be demonstrated through adequate testing. If the substantive view of verification were generally accepted, verification would probably never have been a major issue in the SALT II debate and might at least be manageable in the future.
- The *legalistic* school takes a much narrower view of verification. Its adherents regard a strategic arms limitation treaty essentially as a legal contract and consider violations to be serious issues per se regardless of their relative strategic significance. Such a "strict constructionist" view tends to equalize all elements of a treaty. SALT II opponents took this tack in charging the Soviets with "massive violations" of SALT I, lumping together assorted ambiguities and possible minor violations with little regard for their relative significance. The intelligence collection burden is clearly much greater under the legalistic interpretation since the resolution of even relatively trivial ambiguities can become important. For example, when the United States alleged that the Soviets had violated the Anti-Ballistic Missile Treaty by testing an air defense radar "in an ABM mode," the intelligence community was faced with a much more delicate and difficult task than if it had merely been asked to monitor Soviet capability to upgrade their air defense system to provide an effective ballistic missile defense. Moreover, the "rules of evidence" to be used in assessing treaty compliance appear to be much more limited if the legalistic view prevails.

The SALT process stressed verification by "national technical means." Thus, the rules of the game demand that allegations of violations be supported by evidence that plausibly could have been obtained using national technical means, thereby excluding, at least in a formal way, consideration of evidence from other intelligence sources. Nor is any future treaty requiring "cooperative measures" likely to help much in solving this particular problem, although conceivably, a provision for something like on-site inspection might allow either side to "prove its innocence" in ambiguous situations. An example is the famous flap at SALT II over the environmental covers on Minuteman silos at Malmstrom Air Force Base. When we chided the Soviets over verification problems posed by particular idiosyncracies of their ICBM deployment, they countered with charges that *we* were interfering with *their* ability to employ national technical means of verification. It might be possible to write a future treaty with verification provisions that would prevent such sticky problems.

Having signed such a treaty, neither side is likely to be incompetent enough to commit violations that could be easily detected. Given the will to do so, even treaties that include on-site inspection provisions can usually be circumvented. The net effect, then, of the legalistic view is to make verification more difficult and to risk deterioration of U.S.-Soviet relations because of relatively trivial matters.

- The *metaphysical* school is the most difficult of all to satisfy in terms of verification. Its concerns go well beyond the letter of any strategic arms agreement, insisting in effect that the Soviets conform to some unspoken behavior code and interpreting Soviet actions as measures of intent and "character." A classic illustration was the flap that occurred when the Soviets began encrypting telemetry from missile tests. There was an immediate cry of anguish from those who felt that the Soviets were violating SALT I by interfering with U.S. national technical means of verification. Since nothing in SALT I required telemetry to verify, the objections to encryption represented a demand for an openness in Soviet weapons development far beyond anything formally agreed to up to that time.

This reasoning could lead to measures that might be considered even more intrusive than on-site inspection, requiring *ultimately* that each side deny the other nothing about its strategic weapons development program. In the case of telemetry encryption, for example, there are testing procedures available for many weapon systems that do not require the use of telemetry. Would failure to use telemetry at all be considered a sin comparable in magnitude to encrypting telemetry? Even the United States has some military secrets that it would prefer to keep and it is not clear how to draw the line other than by using explicit language in a treaty.

Implicit insistence on adherence to a "code of behavior" to demonstrate good will, trustworthiness and so on begs the question of whether both sides understand the rules of the game in the same way. Some of the hair-splitting over treaty language has obviously resulted from efforts by one side or the other to protect specific new weapons programs—possibly a necessary condition for internal acceptance of a SALT treaty. The United States made a point of protecting the MX, ICBM and various cruise missile programs during the SALT II negotiations. And in retrospect, it seems likely that the definitional problems regarding "heavy" ICBMs encountered during the negotiations derived at least in part from a Soviet desire to protect the SS-19 program, and that the Soviets took some pains to make sure that deployment of that missile would not violate the letter of the Interim Agreement. Given the difficulty of achieving both internal consensus and mutual acceptance by the United States and the Soviet Union on treaty language, the notion that even strict compliance with some provisions could be interpreted as "sinister" could render arms control through formal agreement virtually impossible. The concept of verification would become meaningless.

Should consensus emerge on what verification actually means, it will almost certainly be an amalgam of the three schools. The relative weight that the views of each school would receive in this amalgam remains an open question, but one that should be of vital concern to arms control advocates.

Something might have come out of the SALT II debate had it been allowed to continue; the battle lines were already being drawn. For example, a Senate Intelligence Committee report on SALT II verification concluded the obvious: The United States could verify Soviet compliance with the quantitative provisions of the treaty with relatively high confidence, but verifying the qualitative restraints such as the limits on new types of missiles would be much harder. When the report first leaked to the press, it was interpreted by some as an endorsement of the treaty—a statement that it was "adequately verifiable." The opposition on the Senate Intelligence Committee was having none of that, however, and the ensuing debate made it clear that there was no consensus on even definitional issues involving verification. (The report itself carefully avoided making any value judgments about whether the treaty was or was not adequately verifiable.)

It soon became clear that the treaty had no chance of ratification and it was difficult to sort out true positions from political posturing. Some senators who represented potential "swing" votes and who could probably have been counted as nominal supporters of arms control in general expressed various reservations about details of the treaty. In particular, some identified verification as a particular concern, which was somewhat ironic since verification was really less of a substantive issue on SALT II than it had been on SALT I or is likely to be on any future START agreement. But senators can almost always get away with citing verification problems as an excuse for voting against a treaty that they actually oppose on other grounds. (To their credit, some senators—Barry Goldwater among them—deliberately dismissed verification as an issue and took positions on the treaty based on their view of its fundamental merits.) The picture that emerged in the latter stages of the SALT II debate made it difficult to draw any conclusion about which school of verification theology, if any, was gaining the upper hand. And the 1980 election only added to the uncertainty.

Obviously, most arms controllers would prefer to see the substantive school emerge victorious. It is hard to argue, however, that entry into a formal treaty would not place some extra burden on the parties to behave acceptably, thus inevitably tightening verification requirements. President Carter tacitly recognized the concerns of the legalists by stating publicly that the United States would consider any violations of the SALT II agreement to be a serious matter that could lead to Washington's abrogation of the treaty. Of course, there would still have been room for considerable internal bureaucratic bickering over whether a particular Soviet act constituted a "violation." Predictably, the SALT II provision dealing with "new types" of ICBMs, particularly the 5 percent limit on changes in selected physical parameters of new missiles, caught the attention of the legalistic school during the Senate debate. Had the debate continued, the degree of acceptance that the "new types" provision eventually received might have provided some measure of the legalists' clout at the time.

The metaphysical school may get its due as well. Even in the Carter days, it had an impact. For example, the United States leaned heavily on the Soviets to include a ban on telemetry encryption in the SALT II treaty. The eventual treaty text did explicitly include limitations on telemetry encryption—a forensic triumph for the U.S. side—but only in cases where encryption would directly impair the ability to verify. Since such encryption would presumably be banned in any case by provisions relating to non-interference with national technical means, it is not clear that the specific language added much substance. However, the Carter Administration's demonstrated concern over the encryption issue and its rhetoric about not trusting the Soviets to abide by the terms of any SALT agreement was presumably intended to counter criticism from the metaphysical school.

With the ascendancy of the Reaganites, the stock of the metaphysical school will inevitably go up. High-level Reagan appointees in the Arms Control and Disarmament Agency and the Pentagon have publicly complained about past Soviet behavior in abiding by the letter but not, in their view, the spirit of earlier arms limitation agreements—the very credo of the metaphysical school. They have served notice that Soviet behavior on arms control-related matters will be interpreted as a measure of their intent in the international arena, and vice versa. This view of enhanced linkage can hardly fail to increase tension between the United States and the Soviet Union and will necessarily complicate any future arms control negotiations.

The ultimate test of any definition of verification is the degree to which attention can be focused on important factors and diverted from minor flaps. Wide acceptance of an approach to verification that focuses on trivia could endanger the arms control debate by creating further tensions between Moscow and Washington. If that should occur, the net effect on arms control prospects could be more negative than positive and arms control advocates might be obliged to look for other avenues.

Assuming that the definitional problems surrounding verification can be resolved satisfactorily, the larger question remains of how the verification issue is likely to affect prospects for achieving meaningful arms control in the future through the formal treaty process. While it is probably premature to try to provide definitive answers, it seems appropriate to raise a few specific issues for the arms control community to consider.

First, there is the matter of substance. In any future negotiations, it is likely that many potential treaty elements that would be of most interest to arms controllers—further constraints on cruise missiles or limits on "gray area" systems, for example—may prove to be legitimately unverifiable. Similarly, any requirement on monitoring production facilities, which might be part of either the Reagan proposals for overall reductions or some versions of the nuclear freeze, is likely to be either difficult or impossible to accomplish to the satisfaction of all. If that should be the case, one of several results—all unfavorable from an arms control point of view—might ensue. Among these might be:

- a truly unverifiable treaty, the net effect of which would probably be increased tension resulting from mutual suspicion;
- a verifiable treaty that did little to control arms;
- a verifiable treaty that was actually destabilizing and counterproductive.

The last possibility is particularly disturbing and not without precedent, in SALT. Consider, for example, the case of mobile ICBMs. As strategic weapons go, they are relatively stabilizing since they are hard to target and less sensitive to qualitative improvements or quantitative changes in force size than their silo-based cousins. Unfortunately, precise force size verification is a formidable task which has continued to muddle already difficult negotiations. The U.S. side was sufficiently concerned about the possibility of the Soviets deploying a mobile version of the ss-16, even though the ss-16 is the least capable of the new Soviet ICBMs, that it argued for—and eventually got—a ban on any further development, testing or deployment of the ss-16 for the duration of the SALT II treaty. By contrast, treaties involving silo-based ICBMs, which are vulnerable and therefore destabilizing, are reasonably easy to write and verify. Even treaties that do not rely solely on satellites for verification are likely to be inadequate in this area. The danger is that the need for *veri-*

fication inherent in an arms control *treaty* might very well produce results that are contrary to the legitimate objectives of arms control.

Next, there is the degree to which verification issues muddle, and are muddled by, already complex political problems. For example, the much-publicized loss of intelligence monitoring sites in Iran and the resulting compromise of a new U.S. satellite system have created a climate in which it is easy to raise doubts about U.S. capability to verify arms control agreements even though nobody has yet demonstrated convincingly that these intelligence setbacks have substantially weakened our verification capability.

According to information available from open sources, the main arms-control-related impact of the loss of the Iranian stations would be the difficulty in obtaining accurate data on booster operation during tests on new Soviet ICBMs. In terms of monitoring SALT II, this would have been relevant only to monitoring the "new types" restrictions on increasing booster size. On substantive grounds, this is not very important, although the legalistic school would be incapable of conceding such a judgment. In any case, the lost intelligence-gathering capability can eventually be replaced.

Presumably, it was the Carter Administration's need to foster a measure of public confidence in our ability to verify SALT II that prompted its proposal to Turkey that the United States be allowed to use its territory and air space for U-2 flights. The whole sequence of events—the public offer, the statement by the Turkish government that the Soviets would have to approve of the plan, hints of the political price demanded by the Turks for their acquiescence, the eventual Soviet refusal to endorse the plan—was truly bizarre. Subsequently, a similar U.S. proposal to establish electronic monitoring sites in Norway met the same fate.

Only slightly less bizarre was the Chinese offer to operate monitoring stations in China with equipment supplied by the United States, an offer that was ultimately accepted by the United States. Joint intelligence ventures are not in themselves particularly unusual, but U.S.-Chinese cooperation in such an enterprise no doubt raised an eyebrow or two. It was the public nature of the whole operation that marked a significant departure from the usual norms of international diplomacy.

These episodes serve to highlight some of the additional complexities that SALT in general, and verification problems in particular, have already introduced into the international arena and, conversely, the political prices that the evolving SALT process may require and the sensitivity of that process to events that are beyond our control. Even the relatively straightforward bilateral elements of SALT have the potential for all manner of mischief, depending on how the principals decide to play the game. It is possible that each side would try to avoid questionable actions and ambiguities that could be misconstrued by the other. But it is also possible that either side might deliberately choose to commit actual or apparent violations to test the other's intelligence capabilities and political responses, or to send political "signals." The principal danger is heightened political sensitivity resulting from nuances of SALT/START and the strategic balance. Since making international relations less sensitive to nuclear weapons-related issues and reducing tension between the United States and the Soviet Union are among the primary objectives of arms control, the formal process might ultimately fail to serve the aims of arms controllers.

Finally, some elements of the verification bureaucracy could stand further examination. In particular, the role of the intelligence community is somewhat ambiguous. Its dual role in building and operating intelligence collection systems on the one hand, and assessing verification matters as part of the Special Coordination Committee on the other appears to represent a potential conflict of interest. In his institutional role, the director of Central Intelligence is likely to have a vested interest in building more and better technical collection systems and SALT/START verification could provide a useful rationale for these systems. Moreover, there is always the temptation for the intelligence community to promote treaty provisions that make intelligence collection easier, regardless of their direct relevance to arms control issues.

The Central Intelligence director might well have a vested interest in the formal SALT/START process per se, since treaty verification is likely to be viewed almost universally as a beneficial activity, unlike some other enterprises in which the intelligence community indulges. Its high profile role in the verification process, however, also entails political risks. There will be increasing pressure on the director to make essentially political judgments on verification matters and institutional pressures on him to take an "intelligence conservative" view in the councils of government, particularly in the drafting stages of treaties. Again, the danger is that none of this may serve the interests of arms control.

Achieving a balance at this point is difficult. SALT has made some information easier to get by forbidding interference with technical collection systems and establishing some sets of rules about testing and so on. Moreover, the treaties' existence probably places some burden on each side to demonstrate that it is living up to its end of the bargain. There may be little incentive to cheat in the first place, given low payoffs and significant political risks—the other side of the "metaphysics" argument, if you like.

In the long run, these benefits of SALT/START could prove more symbolic than substantive, but even that might be of some value. Yet SALT is already vulnerable to a number of arms control-related criticisms: failure to make any significant progress toward arms reductions; failure to reduce arms spending; the political necessity for imposing a large measure of symmetry on U.S. and Soviet strategic force structures, instead of taking advantage of asymmetries that might have useful arms control implications. And there are others. Unless an acceptable consensus on verification requirements emerges soon, or if the need for verification and the objectives of arms control diverge too sharply, the arms control community might do well to give more attention to alternatives to formal negotiations, such as the "buy what you need" approach, or informal agreements.

FOR FURTHER READING

Blacker, Coit D., and Gloria Duffy, eds. *International Arms Control: Issues and Agreements.* 2nd ed. Stanford: Stanford University Press, 1984. A comprehensive text on the theory, practice, and history of arms control.

Johansen, Robert C. *SALT II: Illusion and Reality.* New York: World Policy Institute, 1979. A world order reform advocate critiques the U.S.-Soviet SALT process, emphasizing its failure to significantly restrain U.S. and Soviet strategic programs.

Kincade, William H., and Jeffrey D. Porro, eds. *Negotiating Security: An Arms Control Reader.* Washington, D.C.: Carnegie Endowment for International Peace, 1979. An edited reader on arms control issues, with short articles on SALT, nuclear proliferation, non-nuclear arms control, nuclear strategy and weapons, tactical nuclear weapons, regional arms control, and arms control decision-making.

Myrdahl, Alva. *The Game of Disarmament: How the Superpowers Run the Nuclear Arms Race.* New York: Pantheon, 1982. A heavily critical discussion of U.S.-Soviet efforts to control nuclear weapons, and the demonstrated inability of the superpowers to curb their mutual competition in and dependence on nuclear arms.

Newhouse, John. *Cold Dawn: The Story of the SALT.* New York: Holt, Rinehart & Winston, 1973. The background to and history of the first Strategic Arms Limitation Talks.

Russett, Bruce M., and Bruce G. Blair, eds. *Progress in Arms Control?* San Francisco: W. H. Freeman and Company, 1979. A compilation of articles dealing with SALT I and II, and the global politics of arms control—with special emphasis upon the impact of new nuclear weapons technologies on the prospects for arms control. (A new edition is planned for publication in 1985.)

Scott, Robert Travis. *The Race for Security.* Lexington, Mass.: Lexington Books, 1985 (forthcoming). An edited compilation of short articles on arms control and related issues first printed in *Arms Control Today,* the monthly journal of the Washington-based Arms Control Association.

Smith, Gerard C. *Doubletalk: The Story of SALT.* Garden City, New York: Doubleday, 1980. From the head of the U.S. negotiating team, the "inside" account of U.S. policymaking during the SALT I negotiations.

Talbott, Strobe. *Endgame: The Inside Story of SALT II.* New York: Harper and Row, 1980. The definitive history of the SALT II negotiations.

———. *Deadly Gambits: The Reagan Administration and the Stalemate in Nuclear Arms Control.* New York: Alfred A. Knopf, 1981. A revealing account of arms control policymaking in the Reagan Administration's first term, and the U.S.-Soviet START and INF negotiations.

Starr, Richard F. *Arms Control: Myth Versus Reality.* Stanford, Ca.: The Hoover Institute, 1984. A collection of conservative perspectives on arms control, introduced by a critique of past U.S.-Soviet efforts to control nuclear arms by William R. Van Cleave.

Wolfe, Thomas W. *The SALT Process.* Cambridge, Mass.: Ballinger, 1976. An analysis of SALT through the signing of the Vladivostok Accord in 1974, with perspectives on both Soviet and American policymaking goals and procedures.

10

Obstacles to Reducing the Nuclear Threat

From the very beginning of the nuclear era, individuals and organizations have tried to warn humanity about the grave risks posed by nuclear weapons. As indicated in the previous chapter, there have been numerous attempts to restrain the arms race and to reduce the danger of nuclear war. However, as also noted, there is a wide range of opinion on how effective such efforts have been. Advocates of arms control argue that without such measures as the ABM Treaty and SALT, the arms race would be even more dangerous than it is at present. Critics counter that arms control treaties tend to lull Americans into a false sense of security that prevents them from properly appreciating the Soviet menace and from supporting measures needed to maintain a strong deterrent force. And even many of those who believe in the value of past arms control efforts acknowledge that the danger of nuclear war continues to be intolerably high. In view of the growing momentum towards nuclear war, it is difficult to escape the conclusion that past efforts to reduce the nuclear threat, while very necessary, have been grossly insufficient.

The inadequacy of past efforts to reduce the threat of nuclear war reflects the magnitude, diversity, and even irrationality of the political and psychosocial forces that perpetuate and intensify the problem. As Herbert York, a distinguished scientist and former defense policymaker, notes, ". . . a vicious spiral has been created that gives the arms race a 'mad momentum' of its own and drives it forward blindly and faster than necessary with regard to, and in spite of, the absurd situations that have steadily arisen from it."[1]

This chapter explores some of the forces that contribute to the momentum of the nuclear arms race and that create obstacles to efforts to reduce that momentum. The readings that follow disclose such obstacles at three levels of analysis—international, intranational, and psychological.

---

[1] Herbert York, *Race to Oblivion: A Participant's View of the Arms Race* (New York: Simon and Schuster, 1970), p. 237.

At the international level, some observers have noted that a reciprocal political and military competition between the United States and the Soviet Union (also referred to as an action-reaction process) has provided a great deal of the impetus for the nuclear arms race. Each superpower blames the other for successive rounds in an arms race that threatens the security of both. Moreover, as Swedish Nobel Peace Laureate Alva Myrdal notes, from the perspective of much of the rest of the world, both nations have been guilty of unilaterally aggravating the arms race either by deploying destabilizing new weapons or by refusing to compromise in arms control negotiations.[2]

A theory of technological determinism has also been offered as a means of accounting for the momentum of the arms race. There can be little doubt that the constant invention of new weapons systems seriously complicates the struggle to bring the arms race under control. As Frank Barnaby has noted: "Such huge resources—manpower and money—have been devoted to military science for so long that the momentum of military technology is now well-nigh irresistible."[3] However, it is important to avoid the assumption that technology can somehow develop a momentum of its own *independently* of the human beings who invent, maintain, and utilize it. To appreciate the role of technology in the nuclear dilemma, it is necessary to acknowledge the economic, political, and psychological forces involved in the creation of the technology, the development of vested interests in it, and our continued and expanded reliance upon it.

Other analysts focus on domestic political pressures that fuel the arms race. Such intranational forces are examined in the readings by Adams, Holloway, Markusen and Harris, Frank, and Peattie.

The notion that individuals and organizations in the United States have developed vested interests in high levels of defense spending was first articulated in 1961 by President Dwight Eisenhower, former Commander in Chief of Allied Forces in Europe during World War II, during his farewell address to the American citizenry. Eisenhower warned about the "total influence—economic, political, even spiritual. . . ," of the "military-industrial complex."[4] The validity of Eisenhower's warning is underscored by Gordon Adams in his article, "The Iron Triangle." Noting that the trend toward ever-increasing levels of defense spending "seems irreversible," Adams argues that an important force behind this trend is a "small, incestuous, mutually supporting group" consisting of the Pentagon, industries that are heavily involved in defense contracts, and key Congressional committees. This "Iron Triangle," asserts Adams, has developed both powerful interests in high defense spending and powerful means (financial and political) of defending those interests. The influence of the Iron Triangle extends into communities across the nation which depend on defense-related industries as vital sources of jobs and local economic growth. While he does acknowledge the existence of

---

[2] Alva Myrdal, "A History of Lost Opportunities," in her *The Game of Disarmament: How the United States and Russia Run the Arms Race,* pp. 55–110. Revised and updated ed. (New York: Pantheon, 1982).

[3] Frank Barnaby, "Military Scientists," *Bulletin of the Atomic Scientists* 37 (June/July 1981), p. 11.

[4] Dwight Eisenhower, "Liberty is at Stake: A Farewell Address," Jan. 17, 1961, *Public Papers of the President* (Washington, D.C.: U.S. Government Printing Office, 1961), p. 1038.

countervailing interests, like the U.S. Arms Control and Disarmament Agency, Adams suggests that their power is far weaker than that of the Iron Triangle.

David Holloway, in excerpts from his book, *The Soviet Union and the Arms Race,* describes the structure of defense policymaking in the Soviet Union and addresses the question of whether a powerful military-industrial complex has developed within that society. While Holloway states that "the formal policy-making structure" is ". . . not very different from what it was under Stalin," he does note that present leaders are more likely to heed the advice of experts in military matters, science, and industry than was Stalin, who autocratically determined policy at all levels. Like their counterparts in the United States, defense industries in the Soviet Union benefit from close connections with the political leadership. They receive the best machinery, have priority in the allocation of supplies and materials, and their workers receive higher pay than workers in the civilian sector. Moreover, as Holloway notes, "the managers of the defence industry form a cohesive group with interlocking careers." However, Holloway cautions against simplistic assumptions about monolithic power over defense policy in the Soviet Union. While the military has grown quite powerful, the Party still makes the final decisions.

Markusen and Harris, in their selection "The Institutionalization of Nuclearism and the Erosion of Democracy," examine a number of psychological and social forces that interfere with the ability to think clearly about the nuclear threat, both among individuals directly involved with nuclear weapons and among members of the general citizenry. Markusen and Harris also argue that the reliance on nuclear weapons by the United States tends to weaken the very democratic political system that the weapons are supposed to defend. They discuss the tendency for citizens to be excluded from the nuclear policymaking process, as well as the concentration of unprecedented power in a relatively tiny circle of decision makers. Such circumstances create a vicious cycle in which the worsening problem of the nuclear threat actually *reduces* the ability of both individual citizens and the entire society to confront and respond to the problem. It should be noted that similar processes undoubtedly occur in the Soviet Union, and to a considerably greater extent, since the Soviet system lacks the democratic checks and balances that still operate in the United States.

Psychiatrist Jerome Frank, in his article, "Nuclear Arms and Pre-Nuclear Man: Sociopsychological Aspects of the Nuclear Arms Race," analyzes several psychological processes which "facilitate perhaps the most important psychological source of the arms race—the tendency to cling to reassuring but outmoded modes of thought and behavior in the face of a novel threat." Frank also examines the ways in which very negative "images of the enemy" held by leaders of the United States and the Soviet Union can create obstacles to cooperative efforts to reduce a danger that threatens both nations. Frank argues that the present system of deterrence "is guaranteed to provoke recurrent states of high emotional tension in national leaders," which further impair their abilities to devise means of reducing the nuclear threat.

Finally, the reading by Lisa Peattie makes disturbing comparisons

between the perpetration of the Holocaust—the Nazi attempt to exterminate the Jews of Europe—and the preparations for nuclear war,
which, as noted in Chapter 2, would probably destroy the combatant
nations and could possibly extinguish our species. In both cases, notes
Peattie, certain psychological and social processes have enabled individuals to "normalize the unthinkable." Such "normalization" occurred
among both the perpetrators and the victims of the Holocaust. It also
characterizes both those who are currently making the preparations for
nuclear war and those who would be the victims, should nuclear war occur.

While such obstacles are undeniably powerful, it would be a grave
mistake to conclude that the threat of nuclear war is insurmountable.
Apathy and fatalism create a self-fulfilling prophecy by allowing dangerous forces to go unchecked and permitting dangerous policies to continue unchallenged. Past efforts *have* played a vital role in preventing
the danger of nuclear war from becoming even greater than it is at present. And, as is discussed in Chapter 12, there are a number of potentially valuable and feasible proposals currently under consideration.
Furthermore, the citizens of the United States have only recently begun
to confront and respond to the nuclear threat on a significant scale. If
this citizen involvement persists and widens, the likelihood of a significant reduction of the nuclear threat will increase dramatically.

THE IRON TRIANGLE
Gordon Adams

Gordon Adams is an independent economic policy analyst in Washington, D.C. He served formerly as Director of the Military Project of
the Council on Economic Priorities. Among his written works are *The
Iron Triangle: The Politics of Defense Contracting* and the *B-1 Bomber: An
Analysis of Its Strategic Utility, Cost, Constituency, and Economic Impact.*

During the next five years, the Reagan Administration proposes to spend $1.5
trillion on defense—or more than $6,500 for every American citizen. Even if
the cuts now being considered in Congress are made, military spending authority for the next fiscal year will probably exceed $220 billion—$1,000 per
person.

This huge buildup, which is even larger than what took place during
the Vietnam War, will restock and modernize the entire American arsenal from
strategic missiles to conventional forces. A new generation of weapons will be

Source: Gordon Adams, "The Iron Triangle," *The Nation* (Oct. 31, 1981), pp. 425, 441–444. Reprinted
by permission of *The Nation.*

introduced: MX missiles with ten warheads each; Trident submarines; B-1 bombers; advanced F-16 and F-18 fighters; precision-guided battlefield weapons; intermediate-range nuclear missiles like the ground-launched cruise and Pershing 2, and the M-1 battle tank.

The tide of spending seems irreversible. The few protesting voices in Congress are drowned out as the pack in full cry follows the Administration's commands to "catch up with the Russians" and "rearm America." The fiscal curmudgeons, those watchdogs of waste and golden fleecings, are out of style, and any proposals of sensible alternatives that might purchase national security at a lower cost, such as the proposal to cancel the B-1 and develop the Stealth bomber instead, go unheard.

The magnitude of the Reagan budget explosion has caused us to lose sight of the workings of the military-industrial money machine, which goes on increasing defense spending in good times and bad, during times of détente and times of confrontation. Save for a few years during the 1970s when the military budget remained constant in real dollars, the graph line of defense spending has etched a steadily rising trajectory.

There are various explanations for this phenomenon. One theory, advanced by economists and journalists like Seymour Melman, Richard Kaufman, J. Ronald Fox, A. Ernest Fitzgerald and James Fallows, focuses on the workings of the defense bureaucracy; it posits rival fiefdoms vying for status and power and driven to spend ever larger sums on ever more complex and costly (and often unworkable) weaponry. From different theoretical vantage points, both Keynesians and neo-Marxists reach the conclusion that defense spending serves as essential pump-priming for the U.S. economy. Still others, including a substantial portion of the national security establishment, argue that the defense budget is simply responding to the imperatives of foreign policy and national security.

There is some truth in all of these explanations, but they all omit a crucial factor—the inner workings of the defense policy apparatus, the "Iron Triangle" of the Pentagon, the defense industry and the armed services and military appropriations committees in Congress. This small, incestuous, mutually supportive group decides what weapons will be made, before they are even on the drawing boards in research and development labs. The Iron Triangle sets the priorities that are ultimately reflected in the defense budget.

One side of the Iron Triangle consists of the defense contractors. Through lobbying and sophisticated "government relations," they influence policy and procurement decisions. The defense industry exists in a state of economic dependence on the Federal government, its main customer. The second side, the Defense Department, in turn relies on private industry to supply most of its weapons. The third side, the Congressional committees, approves the funding.

Money, influence and information are the essential ingredients of power within the Iron Triangle. The defense contractors, for example, seek access to the bureaucracy and Congress in order both to sway their decisions and to gain vital information. And the information they provide to the planners and the Congressional money men influences their decisions. The triangle preserves its monopoly on information and control over policy through secrecy; it fends off critics of defense spending and blocks legislation hostile to its interests.

Let us step inside this closed world where weapons decisions are made. The process begins with the awarding of research and development contracts. Here, removed from public view and Congressional oversight, industry and the Defense Department devise the weapons systems of the future. Today's multiple, independently-targetable warheads and laser-guided projectiles were once items buried deep in the R&D budget.

A review of the research and development contracts awarded to the nation's eight leading defense contractors—Boeing, General Dynamics, Grumman, Lockheed, McDonnell Douglas, Northrop, Rockwell International and United Technologies—shows that they received $23 billion from the Defense Department and the National Aeronautics and Space Administration during the past decade. In addition, between 1973 and 1978, these eight companies were reimbursed by the D.O.D. for $1.3 billion in corporate R&D investments through a little-known program called Independent Research and Development/Bids and Proposals [see Adams and Christopher Paine, "The R&D Slush Fund," *The Nation,* January 26, 1980].

This program enables contractors to develop weapons that will ultimately be sold to the Defense Department without risking their own money. It means that ideas for new weapons originate with the firms that stand to gain if these weapons are produced. At this crucial early stage, ideas are freely exchanged between industry and government, giving contractors ample opportunity to influence decisions. Major contractors are well represented on the roughly fifty nongovernmental committees and hundreds of subcommittees that advise the D.O.D. or NASA—most notably the Defense Science Board and the scientific advisory groups of each branch of the military. Access to these key committees gives the contractors a further chance to affect new weapons policies long before the public or Congress has even heard of them.

The close ties between industry and government are reinforced by a steady flow of employees back and forth. In the 1950s, Congressional studies revealed that more than 1,000 retired military personnel had taken jobs in the defense industry. In the 1960s, this number rose to about 2,000. Between 1969 and 1974, the Council on Economic Priorities reported, the figure reached 2,000 for the top 100 D.O.D. contractors. A study of the eight leading defense contractors previously mentioned showed that 2,000 of their employees transferred either from industry to government or from government to industry in the 1970s. Of the nearly 500 civilians in this group who moved in either direction during this period, 34 percent worked in the key R&D offices in the Army, Navy, Air Force and the Office of the Secretary of Defense.

Many individuals circulate at the highest levels of industry and government. Gen. Alexander Haig, for example, moved from the Army to the presidency of United Technologies to Secretary of State. United Technologies employs other government alumni. Clark MacGregor, head of the company's Washington, D.C., office, is a former member of the House of Representatives. Hugh Witt, a government relations specialist, was in the Office of the Secretary of the Air Force and subsequently director of the Office of Federal Procurement Policy in the Office of Management and Budget.

Tom Jones, a former deputy program manager for Boeing, became staff assistant to the Defense Department delegation for the SALT talks in 1971, went back to Boeing in 1974 as a program and products evaluation manager and recently returned to the Defense Department. Seymour Zeiberg, appointed Deputy Under Secretary of Defense for Strategic and Space Systems in 1977, joined Martin Marietta in 1981 as a vice president for research. Walter LaBerge, formerly Deputy Under Secretary of Defense for Research and Engineering, is now executive assistant to the president of Lockheed Missiles and Space Company.

This movement and the familiarity it breeds provides contractors with a unique access to the defense policy-making process. *The Wall Street Journal* reported on February 29, 1979, that Boeing had obtained information about plans for a land-based missile from a Boeing employee "on leave to work in the Pentagon's Weapons Research and Development Office." Once the report had been read, its substance was telexed to a former D.O.D. employee working at Boeing's headquarters in Seattle. *The Journal* concluded: "The movement of weaponry experts between industry and government jobs, frequently on the same project, facilitates the easy flow of information and tends to blur the distinction between national security and corporate goals."

A company with this inside access has a major advantage in winning future contracts. As one defense industry official described it: "Your ultimate goal is actually to write the R.F.P. [Request for Proposals], and this happens more often than you might think." As contractors acquire favored access to Defense Department offices and originate specific weapons, all pretense of competitive bidding is dropped. Today, 90 percent of all prime defense contracts are awarded on a negotiated basis.

Once research and development on a weapon has begun, it becomes difficult for the government to cancel it, and defense contractors use the lobbying resources of their government relations departments to keep the ball rolling. The contractors' Washington offices serve as nerve centers for these campaigns. From 1977 through 1979, the same eight leading defense companies employed 200 people in their Washington offices, including forty-eight registered lobbyists. It is difficult to obtain information about the cost of such operations, but according to figures provided by the Defense Contract Audit Agency to Common Cause in 1981, Boeing, General Dynamics, Grumman, Lockheed and Rockwell International spent $16.8 million on their Washington offices in 1974 and 1975, or an average of $1.6 million per year each. Rockwell alone spent $7 million from 1973 through 1975.

These Washington offices perform many functions, including keeping track of program developments in the Pentagon and NASA, following the progress of legislation, lobbying on Capitol Hill, handling public relations, funneling information back to the company and handling negotiations with foreign buyers. Virtually all of the nonentertainment expenditures of these offices, including lobbying activities, are billed as administrative expenses on their defense contracts. (And money spent on entertainment that is a legitimate business expense is, of course, tax deductible.) The Defense Department tried to halt this practice whereby taxpayers subsidize lobbying by defense contractors, but abandoned the plan under industry pressure in 1978. This month, the department announced plans to renew its enforcement efforts.

Defense contractors also use political action committees. In fact, according to data gathered by Prof. Edwin Epstein of the University of California at Berkeley, these PACs are among the leaders in spending. The eight leading contractors have channeled more than $2 million into their PACs since the late 1970s.

The biggest spender was General Dynamics, which had total outlays of $500,000; Grumman spent the most on national races—$338,000. The bulk of the contributions went to Congressmen representing states where the companies operate or to members of the defense policy and appropriations committees in both houses of Congress. Congressmen receiving sizable contributions included Senators Strom Thurmond, John Tower, John Warner and Sam Nunn and former Representatives Charles Wilson, Jim Lloyd, Mendel Davis and Bob Wilson. (Bob Wilson is now a government relations specialist in Washington representing, among others, Rockwell International.)

The influence of the Iron Triangle reaches outside Washington into the hinterlands. Defense contractors' employees, the communities where the companies are located, their stockholders, subcontractors and suppliers are all part of the network, and may indeed depend on it for survival. Leading unions, such as the United Auto Workers and the Machinists and Aerospace Workers, have a large number of members who work in defense industries and their locals often follow the company's call to support weapons systems with lobbying in Washington.

In the mid-1970s, for example, Rockwell International mounted a grass-roots effort on behalf of the B-1 bomber program, which was on the brink of cancellation. The company urged its 114,000 employees and the holders of its 35 million shares of stock to write their Congressmen. More than 3,000 sub-contractors and suppliers in forty-eight states were also asked to tell their Congressmen about the adverse impact scrapping the B-1 would have in their districts. Rockwell admitted that it spent $1.35 million on such efforts from 1975 through 1977, an amount that opponents of the B-1 could not have hoped to match.

The interlocking ties within the Iron Triangle, and the steady flow of personnel, resources, information and influence through it, create a community of interest in which it becomes almost impossible to tell who controls whom. In time, Iron Triangle members become prisoners of their own isolation, identifying their private gain with the national interest.

In Congress, members of defense-related committees jealously guard their power over legislation and appropriations, and other members tend to follow their leadership. Other Congressional groups that deal with defense policy have little influence. The Joint Committee on Defense Production, the Joint Economic Committee and the government operations committees in both houses have regularly debated defense and procurement issues but have had little effect on actual legislation and appropriations bills. The Joint Committee on Defense Production was abolished in 1978 as part of committee reform in Congress, and its functions were absorbed by the banking committees, eliminating an important forum for discussion of alternative approaches to defense procurement policy.

Within the executive branch, resistance to the power of the Iron Triangle is minimal. The Defense Department's Office of Economic Adjustment, which was set up to help communities adjust to base closings and contract terminations, has limited authority and little influence over procurement decisions. The Arms Control and Disarmament Agency has become a weak reed.

Even David Stockman recently found it almost impossible to cut defense spending because of the Iron Triangle's clout in the White House. His Office of Management and Budget has final say over the budget requests of all agencies save one—the Defense Department. The department can appeal to the President, who frequently overrules the O.M.B. As Philip Hughes, former Deputy Director of the Budget Bureau (O.M.B.'s predecessor) put it:

> The most relevant consideration is, in blunt terms, sheer power—where the muscle is—and this is a very power-conscious town, and the Secretary of Defense and the defense establishment are a different group to deal with, whether the Congress is dealing with them or whether the Budget Bureau is dealing with them.

The development of the Iron Triangle has blurred the traditional arm's-length relationship between business and government in the defense sector. Now we have a situation in which, according to Murray Weidenbaum, chairman of the Council of Economic Advisers:

> The close, continuing relationship between the Department of Defense and its major suppliers is resulting in convergence between the two, which is blurring and reducing much of the distinction between public and private activities in an important branch of the American economy.

Under the Reagan Administration, the Iron Triangle has enjoyed a resurgence. Debate prior to making informed choices among weapons has been all but abandoned in an unrestrained burst of spending. Effective cost control, difficult in the best of times, is disappearing altogether. The defense budget grows monolithically with no thought given to its potential impact on inflation, capital supply and employment. National security is equated with whatever the Defense Department and industry demand.

The Iron Triangle must be broken. While the suggestion by John Kenneth Galbraith and others that the defense industry should be nationalized is sound, it is not realistic at this time. Short of that, the debate must be opened up and more information on defense contracting made available to Congress and the public. Committees in Congress now excluded from the Iron Triangle can and should assert their right to contest defense spending that impinges on their own legislative programs. A true, open political triangle needs to be built— one that combines a concern with social needs and economic health with a properly defined national security and defense policy.

THE DEFENCE ECONOMY
David Holloway

David Holloway is lecturer in the Department of Politics at the University of Edinburgh in Great Britain. He has written widely on Soviet nuclear weapons policies and domestic aspects of Soviet military policy. This piece was excerpted from his *The Soviet Union and the Arms Race.*

The Soviet state was born in revolution and civil war; and after twenty years of social and political upheaval it was subjected to the test of a terrible war

Source: David Holloway, "The Defense Economy," and "The Politics of Military Power," in *The Soviet Union and the Arms Race* (New Haven, Conn.: Yale University Press, 1983), pp. 109–115, 117–20, 169–72. Copyright 1983 by Yale University Press.

with Germany. Stalin claimed in 1946 that victory over Germany proved that his policies of collectivization and industrialization had been correct, and he proceeded to build up the power of the state again, arguing that it would take at least until 1960 for the Soviet Union to be ready for 'all contingencies'. In 1960, however, the Soviet Union adopted a new military doctrine for the nuclear age and in the years since then has built up its forces to prepare for the contingencies of nuclear war, and to support its foreign policy.

The Central Policy-Making Bodies

Control of defence policy rests in the hands of the Party leaders. It is in the Politburo that the main lines of policy are determined, the major resource allocation decisions taken, and the most difficult issues resolved. The Politburo normally meets once a week, but in the early 1970s it met in special session on several occasions to consider American arms control proposals. Its role in foreign and defence policy was strengthened in 1973 when the Ministers of Defence and Foreign Affairs and the head of the KGB were included as full members.

The main specialized body for defence policy-making is the Defence Council, which, according to the 1977 Constitution, is a state and not a Party institution. It appears to consist of a handful of Politburo members, including the Minister of Defence; other military and political leaders may be called to attend when necessary. Like the Politburo, the Defence Council is chaired by Brezhnev, who claimed to speak with the authority of that office when he said in October 1979 that the number of medium-range nuclear delivery systems in the Western part of the Soviet Union had not been increased over the previous ten years. The Defence Council's responsibilities are wide: it deals with 'questions of military development and of strengthening the might and combat readiness of the Soviet Armed Forces'.[1]

The precise relationship between the Defence Council and the Politburo is not clear. The Defence Council may handle detailed matters of policy for which the Politburo has not time, while leaving major issues to that body. Alternatively, it may consider all major issues and make recommendations to the Politburo, in which case it may be an effective instrument for ensuring Brezhnev's domination of defence policy. The constitutional status of the Council, and Brezhnev's position as Chairman of the Presidium of the Supreme Soviet—which decides on the composition of the Council—suggests that the latter role is possible. But there is no reason to suppose that the balance of influence between the Politburo and the Defence Council always remains the same. . . .

---

[1] *Sovetskaya Voennaya Entsiklopediya,* vol. 1, Moscow: Voenizdat, 1976, p. 588.

The formal policy-making structure is not very different now from what it was under Stalin, especially during the war with Germany. The Defence Council is modelled on the State Defence Committee, which exercised supreme power in the state during the war, and it may be intended to play a similar role in the event of war. The Main Military Council of the Ministry of Defence would provide the basis for the *Stavka*, the Headquarters of the Supreme High Command, while the General Staff would serve as the chief instrument of command and control.

But the style of policy-making has changed in important ways since Stalin's rule. Stalin dominated, in a ruthless fashion, the Party-State bureaucracy his policies helped to create. His authority in military matters was unquestioned in the latter part of his rule. He took advice, but could ignore it when he wished. He took a detailed part in all aspects of defence policy-making. After the war, for example, he saw Kurchatov almost every day to discuss nuclear weapons development, and played a major part in making decisions about other weapons programs. He also controlled the discussion of military strategy, and barred any assessment of the impact of nuclear weapons on the conduct of war, just as he prevented any critical study of the events of 1941.

Khrushchev's style was different, for even at his most powerful he did not control the policy-making process in the way that Stalin did. Ultimate authority for defence policy still rested with the Party leadership. In his memoirs Khrushchev reports several discussions of specific matters in the Politburo; for example: rejection of a plan from Admiral Kuznetsov (Commander-in-Chief of the Navy) for warship construction; a decision to scrap the Mya-4 *Bison* bomber; and a decision to convert the Tu-95 *Bear* bomber into the Tu-114 civil airliner.[2] But the confused politics of the early 1960 suggests that Khrushchev did not always get his way, as for example, in the case of the manpower cuts he proposed in January 1960. Moreover, Stalin's death led to more open discussion about nuclear weapons and the history of the war. Although Khrushchev tried to turn these discussions to his own advantage, he was not always able to impose his own views.

The Brezhnev Politburo has adopted a style of policy-making that is apparently more responsive to the advice of the different elements in the Party-State bureaucracy. Power has been diffused at the centre, and more effort made to base policies on the support of the relevant bureaucracies. In the Soviet Union this change has been described as a shift towards a more scientific form of leadership—an approach that recognizes the claims of professional competence and special expertise. This appears to give professional advice a greater role in decision-making, in military as in other affairs. The greater role for

---

expertise results in part from the increasing complexity of decisions. During the May 1972 summit meeting in Moscow, Brezhnev showed that he had not completely mastered the characteristics of Soviet missiles. And at the final stage in negotiating the Interim Agreement, Smirnov, the head of the Military-Industrial Commission, was brought in to settle the technical details.

A great deal remains unclear about the arrangements for defence policy-making. The existence of the Defence Council was revealed only in May 1976, when Brezhnev was given the rank of Marshal of the Soviet Union; his position as Chairman of the Council was made public at the same time. In October of the following year an article in *Voennyi Vestnik*, the journal of the Ground Forces, mentioned in passing that Brezhnev was Supreme Commander-in-Chief of the Armed Forces; this is the only reference the Soviet press has made to his holding that office.

It is not clear how long the Defence Council has existed, or how long Brezhnev has been Supreme Commander-in-Chief. These arrangements may go back to the late 1960s, or to the early 1970s; or the fact of their being announced in 1976 and 1977 may indicate that Brezhnev and the Defence Council were given new responsibilities at the time. Such disclosures are rarely accidental in the Soviet Union. It may therefore be significant that Brezhnev was made Marshal of the Soviet Union, and that his chairmanship of the Defence Council was revealed, less than a month after the death of Marshal Grechko and his replacement as Minister of Defence by Ustinov. Since then the Party's dominant position in defence policy-making has been strongly emphasized, and the defensive rationale for Soviet military power spelled out. . . .

The Defence Sector of Soviet Industry

The defence sector is both an integral part of the Soviet economy, sharing many of its general characteristics, and the highest priority sector in Soviet industry, with special features of its own. Like other production ministries, those in the defence industry have their own research institutes, design bureaus and production plants, and their output is planned and coordinated by higher economic agencies. But the high priority of the defence sector has helped to make it different from the rest of Soviet industry. It has tended to receive the best machinery and instruments. Pay is higher than in civilian production, and the defence industry can offer its workers more benefits—for example, in housing and medical care; the quality of the workers may therefore be higher. High priority is reflected also in the arrangements for day-to-day management. Defence plants have the power to commandeer what they need from civilian industry, and this must be an important advantage in an economy where supply problems are chronic. Economic planning agencies will deal more quickly with requests and orders from the defence industry, and this too must be an advantage in a system where bureaucratic delays can be considerable.

The priority system was established, and remains in existence, to shield the defence industry from shortcomings in the rest of the economy. One consequence of this attempt to protect the defence industry has been, ironically, to encourage a tendency that is found elsewhere in the economy: the pursuit of autarky by ministries, through the creation of supply industries under their own control. This tendency appears to be very strong in the defence industry group. In the 1930s the defence industry commissariats had their own metallurgical base and machine-tool production. In the early 1960s, 90 to 95 per cent of all aviation production (airframes, aeroengines, instruments, avionics) was concentrated in the enterprises of the Ministry of the Aviation Industry. In the mid-1970s the Ministry of the Electronics Industry had to produce hundreds of materials and components it needed because it could not rely on outside suppliers (i.e. on other ministries) to meet its quality requirements. This pattern may show that the defence industry has high priority, since it has been given its own supply industries. But it also shows that the priority system is not wholly effective in ensuring that other branches supply the defence industry with what it needs—otherwise it would not need its own supply industries.

The powerful position of the customer is another important feature of the defence industry. The Ministry of Defence takes part in planning the programs of weapons development and production, and it also exercises considerable control over the execution of those programs. One instrument of Ministry supervision is the system of military representatives in design bureaus and production plants. These have three major functions: to prevent production bottlenecks by speeding up the supply of materials and parts; to supervise the pricing of military products; and to ensure that military production meets quality standards. These representatives give the Armed Forces a degree of consumer power unusual in the Soviet Union. . . .

A Military-Industrial Complex?

Military power has been of central importance for the Soviet state and its survival, but this has not given the Armed Forces or the defence industry a political position of commensurate significance. The early Bolsheviks, who saw strong parallels between the French Revolution and their own, were suspicious of any sign of 'Bonapartism' and took steps to ensure that the Red Army remained subordinate to the Party. Stalin, although he built up the Red Army during the 1930s, destroyed the Army's command in the military purge of 1937. After the war with Germany, he appropriated to himself the glory of victory. In July 1946 he removed Marshal Zhukov from his position as Commander-in-Chief of the Ground Forces and gave him the much less important post of Commander of the Odessa Military District. This (along with harsher treatment meted out to lesser figures) warned the High Command against making any attempt to convert the popularity they had gained during the war into an independent base of political power.

Since 1953, the High Command has emerged as a more active force in politics. In each case of leadership change—Beria's arrest and execution in 1953, Malenkov's defeat by Khrushchev in 1955, Khrushchev's victory over the 'anti-Party group' in 1957, and Khrushchev's fall in October 1964—members of the High Command have played some role. But their influence was one factor among many, and probably not the decisive one. Such intervention was made possible only by divisions in the Party leadership, and on no occasion has a situation arisen in which Party leaders were ranged on one side, and the High Command on the other. The Party and military leaderships are too closely intertwined for that.

In October 1957, only months after helping Khrushchev to defeat the 'anti-Party group' of Molotov, Malenkov et al. in the Central Committee, Zhukov was removed from the Politburo and from his post as Minister of Defence. This shows that engaging in leadership politics can be a risky business for soldiers. He was accused of undermining the position of the Main Political Administration and of cutting back political education in the Armed Forces. He was also charged with wanting to pursue an adventurous foreign policy; even the spectre of Bonapartism was raised. Khrushchev exploited divisions within the High Command, calling on Zhukov's old rivals, notably Marshal Konev, to disparage him and his achievements. Whatever the justice of the charges against Zhukov (and his rehabilitation after 1964 suggests that while he may have posed a political threat to Khrushchev, he did not plot to overthrow Party rule), Khrushchev's action did underline the Party's determination to retain its supremacy over the Armed Forces.

Although Party-military relations have not been completely harmonious, the principle of Party supremacy has never seriously been threatened. The Party maintains its control through a variety of institutions. It controls appointments through the *nomenklatura* system. It has its own structure of Party and Komsomol (Young Communist League) organizations in the Armed Forces, thus supplementing military discipline with Party discipline. The Main Political Administration and its political officers try to instill a positive commitment to the Party and to sustain the morale of the troops. Finally, the KGB is active in rooting out any political opposition.

It is not so much the formal mechanisms of Party and secret police control that explain the political quiescence of the Armed Forces, however, as the way in which military interests have been given priority in Party policy. This is not to ignore Stalin's brutal treatment of the Red Army or to deny that Khrushchev pursued policies that the High Command opposed. But the Party, by stressing the importance of conflict between states and the need for cohesion and solidarity at home, has provided an ideology that gives clear purpose to the Armed Forces' existence. Party policy has given the officer corps a good standard of living and high status, and has furthered their professional interests by allocating generous resources to defence. Finally, the Party has provided capable and cautious leadership (with some glaring exceptions) in foreign policy, avoiding risky adventures that might provoke war.

Since 1953 power has been diffused at the centre of the Soviet state; no individual has dominated policy-making in the way that Stalin did. The resulting political system has been called 'institutional pluralism', on the grounds that policy is now formed in the competition of different institutions and interests inside the Party-State apparatus. This is a useful description as long as it is clear that this is not the pluralism of groups in civil society. Moreover, like any pluralism, this one is imperfect in the sense that some groups and institutions have more power than others. The Armed Forces have been well placed to take advantage of this diffusion of power. The Ministry of Defence and the General Staff are institutions of undisputed competence, and their monopoly of professional military expertise makes it difficult for others to challenge them. They seem to have benefited from the Brezhnev Politburo's emphasis on taking account of expert and technically competent advice. Besides, key elements of military policy are shrouded in secrecy, and this limits criticism of the resources devoted to defence and of the way in which those resources are used.

The defence industry too has occupied a privileged position, as a result of the high priority the Soviet leaders have given to building up military power. The managers of the defence industry form a cohesive group with interlocking careers. Many have held their positions for a long time. Ustinov, for example, became People's Commissar of Armament in 1941. Ye. P. Slavskii, the present Minister of Medium Machine Building (in charge of nuclear weapons development and production) has held that position since 1957 and first started to work in the nuclear weapons program in 1946. Yet in spite of the fact that these men form a clearly identifiable group, there is no evidence that they have an independent power base, or that they constitute a clearly defined lobby.

The one occasion on which the defence industry ministers seem to have acted together was in the period from 1957 to 1963, when they took part, with some success, in the resistance to Khrushchev's decentralization of the economic system. In April 1963, after some recentralization had taken place, Khrushchev complained about the inefficiency of the defence sector. It is not clear, however, exactly what was in dispute. Specific weapons programs—in particular the ICBM program—may have been at issue. Or the defence industry ministers may have felt—along with other economic managers and some members of the Party leadership—that Khrushchev's reforms were weakening the economy and hampering their own operations.

Can one speak then of a Soviet 'military-industrial complex'? The Soviet Union certainly possesses a large defence industry and powerful Armed Forces, and the ties between them are close and numerous. But the mere existence of such institutions does not mean that they can dictate a government's policy. It cannot plausibly be argued, for example, that Stalin was forced to pursue the policies he did by pressure from the Red Army or the defence industry. They were his instruments, and he helped to create them in order to make the Soviet Union a powerful state. He controlled these institutions. He was not their prisoner—as his imprisonment of so many soldiers, designers and managers shows.

The question arises, however, whether the diffusion of power since Stalin's death has changed that relationship. The answer is that it has, but not to the extent of removing the power of final decision from the Party leaders. Military influence has grown in the making of defence policy, but it is still the Politburo that has to make the major decisions about resource allocation, and to reconcile the competing claims of defence, consumption and investment. No doubt the defence industry and the military do propose new weapons and ask for a greater defence effort, but it is the Politburo that disposes of the resources. Close ties exist between the military and the defence industry, but it is still the vertical relationships, culminating in the Party leadership, that predominate: it is far more important for the military to have allies in the Party leadership than in the defence sector. The Armed Forces and the defence industry do embody an historic commitment to military power, and would doubtless resist a major change in priorities. Such resistance might have considerable political significance if the Party leaders were divided on the issue. But priorities have been changed since Stalin's death (for example, in the greater investment in agriculture), and this suggests that while the old structures may make it difficult to adopt new priorities, they do not make it impossible. In other words, whatever momentum Soviet military policy may have acquired over the years, the build-up of military power since the late 1950s must be seen as the product of conscious political choices, and not only as the result of pressure from a military-industrial complex. . . .

Economic Choices

In 1961 the Communist Party adopted a Program which proclaimed that the Soviet Union would surpass the United States in production per head of population before 1970, and build the material-technical basis of a communist society by 1980.[3] These economic hopes have not been fulfilled. The rate of economic growth has declined steadily since the 1950s, whether measured in

---

[3] The 1961 Party Program, in Leonard Schapiro (ed.), *The USSR and the Future,* New York: Praeger, 1962, p. 284.

Soviet national income statistics, or in Western estimates of Soviet GNP. From 1956 to 1960 Soviet national income (produced) grew at 9.1 per cent a year; from 1975 to 1979 it grew at an annual rate of 4.5 per cent.[4] According to CIA estimates, Soviet GNP grew at an annual rate of 5.8 per cent from 1956 to 1960; from 1976 to 1980 the rate was 2.8 per cent a year.[5] The decline in the growth rate has been secular, and neither the 11th Five Year Plan for 1981–5 nor the projections of Western observers point to a major reversal of the trend. The 26th Party Congress in 1981 called for a new Program to be drawn up, and this is likely to make fewer specific promises than Khrushchev's Program did.

In the late 1950s Khrushchev believed that growing Soviet strategic power would enable him to make important gains in foreign policy, and in 1960 he claimed that the Soviet Union would maintain its lead over the United States in ICBMs. But his foreign policy led to the debacle of the Cuban missile crisis; and by 1965 the United States had a very substantial numerical and technological lead in strategic forces. Since then, however, the Soviet Union has built up its military power, though at considerable cost. During the Brezhnev years, Soviet military expenditure has risen at an annual rate of 4–5 per cent, according to the CIA estimate.[6] The proportion of GNP devoted to defence remained at about 11–13 per cent for most of this time, but rose to 12–14 per cent, in the CIA estimate, as the military effort continued to increase alongside the slowdown in economic growth. Some Western analyses argue that the rate of growth of military expenditure was even higher; and that it absorbs a greater share of the GNP. Others claim that the CIA overstates the growth rate of military outlays and the proportion of GNP devoted to defence. But there seems, in any event, to be little disagreement that Soviet military expenditure has grown steadily for twenty years or more.

For most of the post-Stalin period the Soviet leaders have been able to combine the growth in military expenditure with steady improvements in the standard of living and a continuing high rate of investment. By the late 1970s, however, they were no longer able to sustain this pattern. The rate of growth of capital investment was cut in the 10th Five Year Plan (1976–1980) and is to fall further in the 11th Plan.[7] In the 1970s, especially towards the end of the decade, the rate of growth of per capita consumption fell off considerably, compared with the 1960s. Of the three major categories of resource use, only

---

[4] Philip Hanson, *Trade and Technology in Soviet–American Relations*, New York: Columbia UP, 1981, p. 32, and Abram Bergson, 'Soviet Economic Slowdown and the 1981–85 Plan', in *Problems of Communism*, 1981, p. 26.

[5] *Ibid.*

[6] CIA: National Foreign Assessment Center, *Estimated Soviet Defense Spending: Trends and Prospects*, SR 78-10121, June 1978, p. i.

[7] Bergson, *loc. cit.*, p. 26.

defence has so far been protected against the effects of the economic slow-down.

The choices facing the Soviet leaders are not likely to become easier. A leading economist and member of the Party Central Committee wrote after the 26th Congress that

> in the '80s we will have to solve simultaneously such large-scale tasks as further raising the standard of living of the people, continuously increasing the economic and scientific-technical might of the country, reliably ensuring its security. And these tasks have to be solved, as was emphasized at the Congress, in conditions that are far from easy, since several factors which complicate economic development will be operative. Among them are the reduction in growth of labour resources, the increasing cost of exploiting the East and the North, expenditure on preserving the environment and on the infrastructure, above all transport and communications, and the necessity for more rapid renewal of productive funds.[8]

Energy will be more expensive to produce, because mineral fuels are becoming harder to extract. The growth rate of the labour force will diminish. Increases will come primarily in Central Asia and the Transcaucasian Republics, whose people seem reluctant to emigrate, and not in the European part of the Soviet Union, where labour is most needed. The government may have to direct industrial investment to the south.

The Soviet leaders face declining rates of growth in both labour and capital, but they nonetheless intend the 11th Five Year Plan to halt the economic slowdown and improve the lot of the consumer. They hope, no doubt, for better weather and better harvests than in the last Five Year Plan period; their hopes on this score were disappointed in 1981, however. They are continuing to try to improve the workings of the system of economic planning and management, and they have stressed the need for more effective technological innovation. There are no signs, however, that the current effort to improve planning and innovation will yield far-reaching results, and that is why even the modest goals of the 11th Five Year Plan may prove difficult to achieve.

The CIA's estimate of the economic burden of military expenditure can be read in two ways. It can be taken, first, as indicating that the Soviet leaders are seriously committed to increasing their military power and therefore likely to ignore the economic costs. It is clear (and from better evidence than Soviet military outlays) that the Soviet leaders have been committed to making their country a great military power. They have also been committed to making it a great economic and technological power. They have been more

---

[8] N. Inozemtsev, 'XXVI s''yezd KPSS i nashi zadachi', *Mirovaya Ekonomika i Mezhdunarodnye Otnosheniya*, 1981, no. 3, p. 7.

successful in pursuing the former goal than the latter, but there is no evidence that they have abandoned the pursuit of economic growth and technological progress. Since the 1920s Soviet policy has been based on the assumption that military power must rest on a strong economic and technological foundation. It seems improbable, therefore, that the Soviet leaders would put the economic basis of their military power in jeopardy in order to maintain the rate of growth of military expenditure (though it is not clear at what point they might decide that that was the effect of their policy). Furthermore, both Khrushchev and Brezhnev have made the improvement of living standards a central element in their political strategy, in order to secure popular support for their rule. The targets in the 11th Plan suggest that this remains an important priority. To say that the Soviet leaders are firmly committed to military power does not tell us what choices they will make, for they are committed to other objectives too.

The economic burden of defence can be interpreted, secondly, as showing that the cost of the military effort is high and might have to be cut if other objectives are to be met. It is not clear, however, what impact a cut in military expenditure—or in its rate of increase—would have on the rest of the economy. How great the benefit would be depends on what resources—skilled labour, scarce materials, or scientists and engineers—were released, and how quickly they could be absorbed into the civilian economy. Besides, it would also depend on how efficiently the resources would be used in comparison to the way in which they are being used now. These factors make it difficult to estimate the effects a change in expenditure might have. A cut in the rate of growth might have an immediate effect by loosening supply constraints and thus alleviating bottlenecks in the civilian economy. For any perceptible effect on investment or consumption, however, five years might be needed. In the longer term, the effects would be greater: a decision taken in 1982 to reduce the rate of growth in military expenditure would show up in economic performance at the end of the decade. An actual cut in outlays would presumably have a more profound impact, more quickly.

The level of military expenditure has been, presumably, a factor in the Soviet economic slowdown. But it is by no means the only one; many other obstacles to growth have been identified by Soviet and foreign economists alike. In the 1930s the 'war economy' enabled the Soviet Union to build up its industry and its military power by concentrating high levels of investment and a rapidly growing industrial labour force in key sectors. Now, however, the planning system, which is unchanged in its basic features, has become a brake on economic growth, and in particular on technological progress. This is a serious problem because innovation has become a more important factor in economic growth as the opportunities for increasing the labour force and capital investment have diminished. In the 1930s the planning system served both industrial and military policy equally well. But now a contradiction has emerged between the two, for while the system hinders progress in civilian industry, it allows the state to protect the defence sector and ensure that it is more successful in pursuing technological progress.

In the 1960s many economists, both Soviet and foreign, assumed that the Soviet Union would have to undertake a major reform in order to improve its economic performance. The cause of reform was set back, however, by the crisis in Czechoslovakia in 1968, because political developments in that country were widely interpreted as resulting from the economic reform of 1966. Full-scale reform now looked politically risky. After 1968 Brezhnev adopted several partial measures to try to improve economic performance: one was to use the defence industry as a technological dynamo for the economy as a whole (another was to place more stress on buying foreign technology). In 1971 he told the 24th Party Congress that 'taking into account the high scientific-technical level of the defence industry, the transmission of its experience, inventions and discoveries to all spheres of our economy acquires the highest importance'.[9] In the piecemeal reforms of the 1970s some of the defence industry's organizational features and management techniques—especially in the area of R&D—have been transferred to civilian industry. At the October 1980 Plenary Session of the Central Committee Brezhnev returned to the same theme when he called for the mobilization of the country's 'strongest scientific collectives', which he defined as the Academy of Sciences and scientists and designers in the defence sector, to improve civilian machine-building.[10]

This approach to reform has not had a dramatic effect on economic growth. This is partly because not all the conditions that explain the better technological performance of the defence sector can be reproduced in civilian industry: the powerful role of the military customer, for example, cannot be transferred to civilian production. Further, a very clear redefinition of priorities is needed if the inertia of day-to-day management is to be overcome.

The 9th Five Year Plan (1971–5) called—for the first time since plans were instituted—for a faster rate of growth for Group B industries (those producing consumer goods) than for Group A industries (those producing the means of production). But the traditional priorities were not in fact reversed. One of the reasons why was suggested by an article in *Literaturnaya Gazeta* in 1972, which pointed out that in numerous ways—in prestige, in the priority given by other ministries (for example, in construction projects), in wages, in cultural and housing facilities, in labour turnover—Group B industries fared worse than those in Group A. One of the letters provoked by the article claimed that

---

[9] *Materialy XXIV s''yezda KPSS*, Moscow: Politizdat, 1971, p. 46.
[10] *Pravda*, 22 October 1980.

> the best conditions are given to the so-called 'leading' branches. Then
> we have the remaining enterprises in Group A. Last in line are the
> Group B enterprises. Naturally, the most highly skilled cadres—work-
> ers, engineers, or technicians—find jobs or try to find them where the
> pay is highest, so they are concentrated in the 'leading' branches of in-
> dustry. What is more, these branches receive the best materials, the
> most advanced technology, the latest equipment, etc. etc. . . .

There is little doubt that within Group A the defence industry occupies the
position of highest prestige and therefore shows these features to the highest
degree. The 11th Plan once again reverses the traditional priorities between
Group A and Group B; it remains to be seen whether the new priority will
be realized in practice.

A shift of resources from defence would require, to be effective, a clear
redefinition of priorities. The question of priorities could raise once again the
issue of economic reform, since the present planning system seems to favour
the defence sector over civilian industry. If that happened, a change of priorities might become more difficult because it would be more far-reaching in its
consequences. It is possible, therefore, that military expenditures will become
the focus of a broad and bitter argument about the future of Soviet policy—
an argument that could be as significant as the industrialization debate of the
1920s.

NUCLEARISM AND THE EROSION OF DEMOCRACY

Eric Markusen and John B. Harris

Eric Markusen is Assistant Professor of Sociology at Old Dominion
University, Norfolk, Virginia.

John B. Harris is Assistant Professor of Political Science at Georgia
State University, Atlanta, Georgia.

The Institutionalization of "Nuclearism"

"Nuclearism," according to Robert Jay Lifton and Richard Falk, is the "psychological, political, and military dependence on nuclear weapons, the embrace of the weapons as a solution to a wide variety of human dilemmas, most

---

Source: Eric Markusen and John B. Harris, "The Role of Education in Preventing Nuclear War," *Harvard
Educational Review* 54:3 (1984), pp. 282–303. Copyright © 1984 by President and Fellows of Harvard College.

ironically that of 'security.'"[1] They observe that both individuals and organizations develop incentives to maintain the status quo of basing national security on the search for nuclear superiority and upon the readiness to wage
nuclear warfare. To the extent that such individuals and organizations attain
significant power in the political structure of the nation, nuclearism becomes
institutionalized.

As a psychiatrist, Lifton has examined the writings and statements of
numerous individuals who have played important roles in the development of
nuclear weapons and policies; he noticed that some tended to become psychologically identified with the weapons and to regard both the weapons and
themselves as saviors of our freedom and security:

> The ultimate contemporary deformation is a condition we may call *nucle-*
> *arism:* the passionate embrace of nuclear weapons as a solution to death
> anxiety and a way of restoring a lost sense of immortality. Nuclearism is
> a secular religion, a total ideology in which "grace" and even "salva-
> tion"—the mastery of death and evil—are achieved through the power
> of a new technological deity. This deity is seen as capable not only of
> apocalyptic destruction but also of unlimited creation. And the nuclear
> believer or "nuclearist" allies himself with that power and feels com-
> pelled to expound on the virtues of his deity. He may come to depend
> on his weapons to keep the world going.[2]

In extreme cases, such as that of Edward Teller, the "father" of the hydrogen
bomb, this nuclearism can lead to a crusade on behalf of building more and
better weapons. It can also, as has been the case with Teller, lead to distortion
of evidence in support of the crusade.

Others who are perhaps less centrally and less passionately involved with
nuclear weapons may still develop dependencies and rationalizations. Both their
personal equanimity and their financial security may depend upon their ability
to believe in the need for such weapons and in the validity of existing policies.
To question such weapons and policies may be tantamount to questioning their
own integrity. As York describes such individuals:

> Nearly all . . . have had a deep long-term involvement in the arms
> race. They derive either their incomes, their profits, or their consultants'
> fees from it. But much more important than money as a motivating
> force are the individuals' own psychic and spiritual needs; the majority
> of the key individual promoters of the arms race derive a very large part

---

[1] Lifton and Falk, *Indefensible Weapons: The Political and Psychological Case Against Nuclearism* (New York:
Basic Books, 1982), p. ix.

[2] Lifton, *The Broken Connection: On Death and the Continuity of Life* (New York: Simon & Schuster, 1979), p.
369.

of their self-esteem from their participation in what they believe to be an essential—even a holy—cause.[3]

The psychological tendency towards nuclearism may be intensified by the nature of the milieu in which nuclear weapons work is done. As psychiatrist John E. Mack suggests, "the madness of the arms race is not primarily in individuals but in the context of the problem. There are individuals, especially in the two superpowers, who bear responsibility for the arms race, but policymakers and strategists seem to be caught up in a structure, a system in which the interlocking parts activate one another, but which no one controls. There is a state of mind, a mental 'set,' which accompanies this system."[4]

While individuals may enter the milieu of nuclear weapons work with an "open mind," they may soon encounter pressures to conform their thinking to the status quo. In order to advance, junior members may align their images, beliefs, and so forth to those of their superiors. Those who are unwilling or unable to do so may find themselves passed over for promotion. At worst, a dangerous process which Irving L. Janis and Leon Mann have termed "groupthink" may emerge, in which "members use their collective cognitive resources to develop rationalizations supporting shared illusions."[5]

Most of the work on nuclear weapons policy and on the weapons themselves takes place within large bureaucratic contexts that affect the intellectual and emotional functioning of those who work within them. Looking back at his participation in target selection for nuclear war, Henry T. Nash states: "I and my colleagues, with whom I shared a large office, drank coffee, and ate lunch, never experienced guilt or self-criticism. Our office behavior was no different from that of men and women who might work for a bank or insurance company. What enabled us to calmly plan to incinerate vast numbers of unknown human beings without any sense of moral revulsion?"[6] Among the features of the workplace milieu that helped Nash and his colleagues narrow their thinking about the nature and implications of their work were the "strong technological orientation" of the tasks, the anonymity of the human beings at whom the weapons were aimed, and the compartmentalization of knowledge that enabled each worker to focus on his or her job and avoid thinking about the larger context. "Obscuring the 'big picture,'" Nash notes, "helped promote peace of mind."[7]

---

[3] York, *Race to Oblivion* (New York: Simon and Schuster, 1970), p. 235.
[4] Mack, "Psychosocial Effects of the Nuclear Arms Race," *Bulletin of the Atomic Scientists,* 37 (April 1981), 20.
[5] Janis and Mann, *Decision Making: A Psychological Analysis of Conflict, Choice, and Commitment* (New York: Free Press, 1977), p. 129.
[6] Nash, "Bureaucratization of Homicide," *Bulletin of the Atomic Scientists,* 36 (April 1980), 24.
[7] Nash, "Bureaucratization of Homicide," p. 25.

Organizational dynamics may reinforce the tendency not to question prevailing policies and standard operating procedures. In his analysis of war planning during the Vietnam period, Daniel Ellsberg, who was a nuclear war planner during the Kennedy administration, notes several impediments to rational policymaking and open-minded analysis. He writes:

> There was a whole set of what amounted to institutional, "anti-learning" mechanisms working to preserve and guarantee unadaptive and unsuccessful behavior: the fast turnover in personnel; the lack of institutional memory at any level; the failure to study history, to analyze or even record operational experience or mistakes; the effective pressures for optimistically false reporting at every level for describing "progress" rather than problems or failure, thus concealing the very need for change in approach or for learning.[8]

In a recent analysis of nuclear weapons policymaking, Major General Howard M. Estes, Jr., USAF (Ret.), formerly with the Air Force Systems Command and the Space and Missile Systems Organization, points out a similar phenomenon, stating that "the objective of much of the analysis that is performed today is not to seek the 'truth,' but to buttress the position already taken by a given set of advocates."[9]

Indirect evidence of the power of institutionalized nuclearism is provided by the many individuals who become outspoken critics of prevailing policies only after leaving active involvement with weapons work and policymaking. The presence of factors that inhibit an open mind while on the job might help explain what Lifton has termed the "retirement syndrome," that is, the tendency for certain influential figures within the national security establishment to question or even repudiate their former work once they have left active involvement. A recent example of the retirement syndrome is Admiral Hyman Rickover, the father of the nuclear navy, who was forced to retire at the age of eighty-one. Rickover went before a joint session of Congress and reflected on his life's work. Lifton notes that Rickover "declared that both nuclear weapons and nuclear power should be outlawed. He further declared that these weapons would probably be used in a future war because history showed that nations employ whatever weapons are at hand; that 'I think we'll probably destroy ourselves'; and that 'I'm not proud of the part I played.'"[10]

In sum, attempts to question and change prevailing policies and practices involving nuclear weapons are likely to be firmly—even passionately—resisted by those who are responsible for the weapons and policies. Individuals

---

[8] Ellsberg, *Papers on the War* (New York: Simon & Schuster, 1972), p. 18.
[9] Estes, "On Strategic Uncertainty," *Strategic Review*, 11 (Winter 1983), 41.
[10] Rickover, quoted in Lifton and Falk, *Indefensible Weapons*, p. 96.

at all levels of the power structure may develop strong psychological, political, and economic incentives for maintaining the status quo and for denying the possibility that they may be on a course heading for disaster.

U.S. Nuclear Weapons Policy and the Erosion of Democracy

An important consequence of U.S. reliance upon nuclear weaponry as the keystone of its post–World War II defense policies has been a massive erosion of the democratic processes that ostensibly govern U.S. policymaking.[11] The erosion of democracy reflects two mutually reinforcing tendencies: first, the general citizenry tends to be excluded from meaningful participation in the nuclear policy process; second, power is concentrated among a very small number of individuals and organizations. Most of the nuclear era has been characterized by the persistent failure of U.S. citizens, through inability or unwillingness, to demonstrate to their political leaders a concern for the costs and dangers of nuclear weapons. We have not demanded from those leaders policies designed to reduce our reliance upon these weapons for security. This political paralysis, in turn, is rooted in a constellation of psychological factors—both emotional and intellectual—that prevent citizens from facing and responding to such a threat to their survival.

Many people, for example, are simply unable to cope with the reality of the nuclear threat and resort to denying its existence. When the mind is confronted with images or ideas that are extremely unpleasant and threatening, it tends to engage in various defenses against full awareness and feeling. Foremost among these defenses are denial—simply shutting out the unpleasant reality from the conscious mind—and what Lifton has termed "psychic numbing"—the diminishment of feelings. Consciously and unconsciously, many people simply do not want to think about the nuclear threat because they find it so disturbing. The tendency to resist thinking about nuclear war and related issues is exacerbated by a sense of helplessness and despair. As John Kenneth Galbraith observes, "the mind resists involvement with horror as, in a normal person, it resists preoccupation with death. And in consequence we leave the issue of nuclear arms, their control and their consequences, to the men who make horror their everyday occupation. It is reckless, even fatal, delegation of power."[12]

Many people who recognize the significance of the nuclear threat are bewildered by the complexity of the issues, by the esoteric jargon used by the "experts" to discuss the issues, and by the fact that apparently equally quali-

---

[11] Lifton and Falk, *Indefensible Weapons*, p. 139.

[12] Galbraith, "Economics of the Arms Race—and After," in *The Final Epidemic*, ed. Ruth Adams and Susan Callen (Chicago: Educational Foundation for Nuclear Science, 1981), p. 50.

fied "experts" hold diametrically opposed views on many of the issues. Often, when the president announces a new policy or deployment, the papers are filled with the voices of authorities, some defending the decision and others challenging it. The average citizen is driven to despair with feelings of intellectual futility and helplessness. Citizens reason that the problem lies beyond their intellectual abilities and that they must therefore defer to experts and let them determine policy.

Apathy towards influencing policy, in turn, breeds ignorance. Having abdicated their opportunity—and their responsibility—to influence governmental policy on nuclear weapons issues by deferring to the experts, citizens see little reason to *be informed about* government policy. Thus many U.S. citizens today remain unaware that the Carter administration's strategic policy ultimately came to embrace the concept of "controlled" or limited nuclear warfighting, or that the stated objective and responsibility of U.S. strategic forces under the Reagan administration is to be able to "prevail" over the Soviet Union in a protracted nuclear war.

Symptomatic of this ignorance is what Harold Feiveson has called the separation of nuclear weapons experts and strategists from the "root common sense" of the American public. The experts have gradually turned U.S. policy away from the notion that nuclear warfighting makes no sense, and that U.S. nuclear weapons are possessed only for the purpose of maintaining a deterrent by the threat of retaliation in kind. The public, out of ignorance, has failed to comprehend these shifts in U.S. strategic doctrine and remains convinced that policy still reflects their root common sense that nuclear weapons are inherently unusable instruments of mass destruction.

Government officials, in turn, have exploited this ignorance by dissembling the true nature of U.S. nuclear strategy before the public. For example, in select forums where few citizens read or hear statements by the administration (as in the annual report of the Secretary of Defense, strategic journals, and congressional hearings), senior Reagan administration spokesmen have stressed our ability to terminate nuclear war on "terms favorable to the United States." Yet, when writing for millions of citizens in his August 1982 open letter to U.S. newspaper editors, Secretary of Defense Caspar Weinberger felt constrained to emphasize that "there is nothing new about our policy. . . . We do not believe there could be any 'winners' in a nuclear war" and that U.S. weapons were deployed only to demonstrate a convincing threat of retaliation.

The distractions of day-to-day life compound this denial, apathy, and ignorance. People are preoccupied by more immediate problems, such as paying bills, finding a job, and—in much of the world—finding enough to eat. Fred Ikle, currently the undersecretary of defense for policy, made a perceptive observation that is as true today as it was in 1973.

> We all turn away . . . from the thought that nuclear war may be as
> inescapable as death, and may end our lives and our society within this
> generation or the next. We plan and work every day for the workers
> saving for retirement, as a nation that seeks to preserve its physical en-
> vironment, its political traditions, its cultural heritage. For this larger
> horizon—encompassing for the younger generation simply the common
> expectation of a healthy life—we do in fact assume "nuclear immortal-
> ity." We believe, or we act as if we believe, that thanks to a certain in-
> ternational order, the existing arsenals of nuclear weapons with their
> almost incomprehensible destructiveness will never be used.[13]

It is *only* when nuclear weapons policies have threatened the immediate, everyday interests of citizens that they have become involved in the policy-making process. For example, it was the health risks posed by long-term global radioactive fallout that prompted worldwide public opposition to further atmospheric nuclear testing in the mid- and late-1950s and led policymakers to consider negotiated restraints on nuclear testing. This process eventually resulted in the Limited Test Ban Treaty (LTBT) of 1963 among the Soviet Union, the United States, and Great Britain.

Similarly, it was the outcry against "bombs in our backyards" by urban and suburban dwellers in several of the major cities slated for the siting of nuclear-armed antiballistic missile (ABM) complexes in the late 1960s that led to the demise of the Nixon administration's Sentinel ABM system and, in an indirect way, to negotiations on the SALT I ABM Treaty. As Joel Primack and Frank von Hippel point out, arguments about the dangers inherent in an uncontrolled arms race made little headway with local citizens during the ABM debate. More effective were descriptions of the destruction that might result if a nuclear warhead were to detonate accidentally at the Sentinel base planned for construction near their homes. Primack and von Hippel conclude that "the most important reason for success of the Sentinel opposition lies in the fact that the arguments against 'bombs in the backyard' struck a responsive chord with the public. . . . Only when the nuclear arms race threatened to become a concrete local reality were suburbanites prodded into action."[14]

Although these efforts clearly had some success in restraining the development and deployment of new weapons systems, it was precisely the limited focus of these movements that prevented them from curbing the larger dangers of an uncontrolled arms race. Two adverse effects of the narrow focus of past citizens' efforts merit close attention. First, because these efforts were parochial and directed at achieving limited objectives, policymakers—the president most importantly—felt obliged to address only those issues of immediate popular concern, and felt free to avoid others of more direct relevance

---

[13] Ikle, "Can Nuclear Deterrence Last out the Century?" *Foreign Affairs*, 51 (Jan. 1973), 267.
[14] Primack and von Hippel, *Advice and Dissent: Scientists in the Political Arena* (New York: Basic Books, 1974), pp. 189–92.

to the larger question of Soviet-U.S. nuclear competition. One consequence of the LTBT was described by Glenn Seaborg: "Ironically, the end of the fallout menace may have had a negative effect on the achievement of the treaty's other objectives. The fear of radioactive fallout . . . was the primary basis of popular concern about nuclear testing. . . . With the fallout worry put aside by the treaty, nuclear tests ceased to be a burning public issue. . . . The elimination of concern about fallout make the continuation of uninhibited weapons developments politically respectable."[15]

Partial steps like the Limited Test Ban and the two SALT agreements also tend to lull the public into a false confidence and sense of security that, in fact, policy-makers *are* handling the nuclear weapons issue in a safe, rational manner. As Ikle observed in 1973, there is a strong tendency among the public to believe that the nuclear dilemma has been "solved" in the aftermath of arms control agreements which, at best, place only minimal constraints on the nuclear arming behavior of the Soviet Union and the United States.

This combination of psychic numbing, apathy, ignorance, parochialism, and the distractions of everyday living has until recently prevented most U.S. citizens from becoming actively involved politically on nuclear weapons issues. If there has been one distinguishing feature of the domestic politics of nuclear weapons in the United States, nominally the most democratic country in the world, it has been the virtual absence of effective political participation by its citizens on these questions. The lack of a political constituency for arms control has resulted in numerous valuable ideas and proposals having little chance of being seriously considered by policymakers and political leaders. Marshall Shulman of Columbia University's Russian Institute and special advisor on arms control issues to the State Department under the Carter administration, emphasizes that

> lobbying efforts on arms control considerations are often ingenious and involve a lot of energy and enthusiasm, but for the most part they are very weak in comparison with lobbying efforts on behalf of particular weapons systems. . . . A candidate can easily be defeated on an arms control issue; I doubt he can be elected on an arms control issue. This is a major fact in the politics of national security, that there is no effective political constituency with a national interest point of view in regard to arms control.[16]

The erosion of democracy in the United States, which begins with the lack of citizens' political voices on nuclear weapons issues, is in turn exacerbated both by the character of the national security decisionmaking process

---

[15] Seaborg, *Kennedy, Khrushchev, and the Test Ban* (Berkeley: Univ. of California Press, 1981), pp. 286–87.

[16] Shulman, "The Process of Governmental Policy-Making in This Area," in *The Role of the Academy in Addressing the Issues of Nuclear War,* ed. Harmon Dunathon (Geneva, NY: Hobart and William Smith Colleges, 1982), p. 34.

and by the very nature of the nuclear weapons technology itself. These factors combine to create an unprecedented concentration of power in such crucial areas of policy as weapons procurement, arms control, and decisions regarding the actual use of nuclear weapons. As a result, policy choices affecting the lives of millions are largely made within and among a highly circumscribed set of individuals and organizations.

In the United States, the nuclear weapons policymaking process has been described as a "game" of competition, bargaining, and compromise among various "players" whose parochial interests will be either enhanced or injured, depending on the outcome of the game. The players in this game include the principal national security actors—the president, the National Security Council, the Departments of Defense and Energy, the uniformed services, various quasi-governmental agencies like the national nuclear weapons laboratories, and private corporate actors with vested economic interests in the disposition of nuclear weapons policies. Thus, decisions about specific weapons usually emerge as the result of many "random and parochial pressures" that bear on decision-makers. The object of the game, according to arms control analyst Steven E. Miller, is simple and straightforward: "Each of the [actors] involved will seek, within the limits of its influence and effectiveness in the bureaucratic politics of the situation, to preserve its own interests or, at the least, to avoid having them badly violated."[17]

The troubling aspect of this process is that actors with a predilection towards greater reliance on military—and often nuclear—force have vastly greater political and financial assets than those seeking a political, negotiated *modus vivendi* with the Soviet Union based on the control and reduction of nuclear weaponry. As a consequence, the policymaking process moves relentlessly forward with a bias towards the development and deployment of new weapons systems. This happens because these weapons satisfy the preferences of those who dominate the process in the absence of, in Shulman's terms, "an overarching political judgment about how the national interest is to be served."[18] Shulman implies that this bias will persist as long as citizens are unwilling to impress upon their duly elected political leaders the "overarching political judgment" that the national interest can be best served by controls and reductions in nuclear weapons.

A second consequence of this situation is that arms control initiatives are constrained or undermined by these power centers which dominate the national security process. Shulman's observation that arms control efforts between the Soviet Union and the United States are characterized by negotiations, "not only *between* the nations involved but *within* the nations involved" (em-

---

[17] Miller, "Politics Over Promise: Domestic Impediments to Arms Control," *International Security*, 8 (Spring 1984), 80.
[18] Shulman, "Government Policy-Making," p. 34.

phasis added), is particularly apropos. Invariably, arms control agreements with
the Soviet Union come at the price of presidential assurances to the domestic
power centers that avenues of weapons development left unconstrained by the
particular agreement will be fully exploited by the United States. For example, in order to obtain the support of the Joint Chiefs of Staff (JCS) for the
LTBT in 1963—whose support was necessary to ensure Senate ratification of
the treaty—President John Kennedy was forced to commit himself to the four
"safeguards" which the Joint Chiefs insisted upon as the price for their approval of the test ban. The most important of these safeguards was the requirement that Kennedy, in the aftermath of the atmospheric test ban
negotiations, pursue a vigorous program of underground nuclear testing.

Thus, at the very same time that public interest in test ban issues began
to wane due to the public's feeling that the atmospheric ban had reduced the
risks of radioactive fallout, intragovernmental pressures for aggressive underground testing began to mount. Moreover, Seaborg has pointed out that Kennedy's assurances to the Joint Chiefs about a vigorous post-LTBT underground
program have been carried out by Kennedy's successors up to the present day,
and that the Soviet leadership has been equally aggressive. Out of the 654
nuclear tests conducted by the United States between 1945 and 1981, 361
(55 percent) took place after the LTBT was in force. Of the 307 Soviet tests
through 1981, 177 (57 percent) were conducted after 1963. The cost of this
competition over years, as Seaborg notes, has been that "since 1963 both sides
have added significantly to the variety and sophistication of their nuclear
weapons." [19]

Similarly, one reason the Nixon administration probably resisted efforts
to include limitations on Multiple Independently Targetable Reentry Vehicles
(MIRVs) in the SALT I negotiations was its fear that such a limitation would
result in the loss of the high-level political support necessary to underwrite
the treaty's passage through the domestic ratification process. [20] The exclusion
of MIRVs from the SALT I Interim Agreement had destabilizing consequences:
Soviet and U.S. strategic warheard totals grew enormously during the 1970s
as each side MIRVed their intercontinental ballistic missiles (ICBMs) and submarine-launched ballistic missiles. Equally serious were the fears promoted about
ICBM vulnerability, as each country began in the latter half of the decade to
deploy high-yield, very accurate MIRVs theoretically capable of destroying
hardened ICBM silos.

More recently, during the SALT II negotiations, the JCS agreed to lend
their support to the treaty only after President Jimmy Carter had agreed to
develop the MX missile and a variety of other strategic programs. The overall
implication of this brief historical look at U.S. arms control policymaking is

[19] Seaborg, *Kennedy, Khrushchev, and the Test Ban*, p. 288.
[20] John Newhouse, *Cold Dawn: The Story of SALT* (New York: Holt, Rinehart and Winston, 1973), p. 181.

that without adequate popular support for arms control measures, as well as information needed to properly evaluate such measures, the "domestic politics" of arms control will continue to be driven by the ability of the JCS and other national security actors to extract prior concessions from any president intent on achieving significant negotiated agreements with the Soviet Union.

The ultimate concentration of power involves the decision processes governing the actual use of nuclear weapons. Such decisions involve only very small numbers of individuals. The decision to attack Hiroshima and Nagasaki was made by President Harry Truman after consultation with only his very closest advisers—without either the knowledge or consent of Congress. During the Cuban missile crisis of 1962, the fates of millions were in the hands of two small groups of tired men in Washington, D.C., and in Moscow. And, as Jeremy [J.] Stone, director of the Federation of American Scientists, points out, there continues to be no formal constitutional restraint on the president's ability to initiate the use of nuclear weapons: "Under the War Powers Resolution, the President can engage in hostilities for up to sixty days unless Congress votes to prevent him from continuing. And nothing in that act refers to the tactics or the weapons that he may use. He may turn an undeclared conventional war into a full-scale nuclear war without any legal requirement to consult Congress."[21]

Viewed in this manner, nuclear weapons in conjunction with the political passivity of the U.S. public, corrupt democracy by creating a condition of permanent readiness for war that tends to disrupt the system of checks and balances upon which democratic government relies.

NUCLEAR ARMS AND PRE-NUCLEAR MAN: SOCIOPSYCHOLOGICAL ASPECTS OF THE NUCLEAR ARMS RACE

Jerome D. Frank

Jerome D. Frank, M.D., Ph.D., is Professor Emeritus of Psychiatry at the Johns Hopkins University School of Medicine. Among his many publications is *Sanity and Survival: Psychological Aspects of War and Peace.*

A good point of entry for our inquiry is the strange, almost incomprehensible behavior of the leaders of the nuclear powers. All agree intellectually that an

---

[21] Jeremy J. Stone, "First Use Deserves More Than One Decision Maker," *Federation of American Scientists Public Interest Report* 28:7 (1975), pp. 1–2.

Source: Jerome D. Frank, "Nuclear Arms and Pre-Nuclear Man: Sociopsychological Aspects of the Nuclear Arms Race," from *Nuclear War and Nuclear Weapons* edited by Christine Cassell, MD, Michael McCally, MD, and Henry Abraham, MD. Copyright © 1983 Praeger Publishers. Reprinted and adapted by permission of Praeger Publishers.

all-out nuclear exchange would be an incalculable, perhaps irretrievable, catastrophe for all nations involved; yet they pursue a competition in nuclear arms that steadily increases its likelihood. In trying to accumulate more and better nuclear weapons than their adversaries, they continue to cling to the outmoded reliance on superior military power as the ultimate source of security, although this is no longer achievable.

This is an example of the fact that mere intellectual insight is virtually powerless to change maladaptive behaviors, especially when it has been ingrained over years, linked to a biological drive, in this case self-preservation, and supported by strong emotions. Unfortunately, in contrast to intellectual cognitions, which we can easily modify to fit changing circumstances, emotions are mediated by the autonomic nervous system, which is a very slow learner. Psychotherapists have painfully discovered that mere intellectual insight into the nature of a problem in living accomplishes very little unless accompanied by a "corrective emotional experience" (1). Our intellect may tell us what we should do, but our emotions too often prevent us from doing it.

Efforts to modify our emotional reactions to nuclear weapons run into two formidable obstacles. The first is the psychological unreality of the danger; the second, the difficulty in relinquishing ways of perceiving and behaving that we have relied on for feelings of security.

Although we have an excellent intellectual grasp of the enormous destructiveness of nuclear weapons, they lack emotional impact because they are psychologically unreal. Their destructiveness is so huge that it baffles our moral imagination. . . . A further source of the unreality of nuclear weapons is that, except for the dwindling ranks of the survivors of Hiroshima and Nagasaki, no one has directly experienced their effects. No national leader, to my knowledge, has even witnessed an atmospheric nuclear test. I might add that perhaps some Americans can speak so calmly about limited, contained nuclear war because no living American has experienced the devastation wrought by any weapon of war on American soil.

As Charles Osgood has pointed out, words that gain their meaning only by reference to other words, such as megatonnage, have little if any emotional impact. "The gap between words and things increases with remoteness of things from immediate, individual experience. . . . We have immediate knowledge of what a *knife* can do, our knowledge about what a *nuclear missile* can do is rather remote and gutless. Thus, irrationally, knowing that one's city is targeted by a 10-megaton nuclear missile ten thousand miles away is not as threatening psychologically as knowing that a madman with a carving knife is loose in the city streets" (2). Single nuclear weapons poised for annihilation

[1] Alexander, F., & French, T. M. *Psychoanalytic therapy*. New York: Ronald Press, 1946.
[2] Osgood, C. E. Conservative words and radical sentences in the semantics of international politics. In G. Abcarian & J. W. Soule (Eds.), *Social psychology and political behavior*. Columbus, Ohio: Merrill, 1971, p. 103.

in distant countries cannot be seen, heard, smelled, tasted or touched, they elicit only spasmodic emotional responses. As a result, although intellectually we may know that we are in the nuclear age, emotionally we remain in the days of spears and clubs.

When the horrors of nuclear weapons sporadically do force themselves into awareness, a common psychological mechanism for dealing with the resulting anxiety has been termed denial or defensive avoidance. This refers to the exclusion from awareness of certain aspects of reality which, if allowed to enter consciousness, would create strong anxiety or other painful emotions. Denial is a normal and appropriate response to threats about which one can do nothing, such as one's own eventual death, but it is life-threatening when facing the danger would enable the person to prevent or escape it. Many persons have died of curable illnesses because they "denied" that they were ill and therefore failed to seek appropriate treatment until too late.

Denial is facilitated by adaptation. Humans, like all living creatures, stop attending to stimuli which persist unchanged over a period of time. Survival in the wild required not only the ability promptly to detect tiny, novel environmental stimuli, but also to ignore them if they continued without anything happening. If an animal kept attending to every stimulus, its capacity to sense new dangers would be swamped; therefore, it adapts to continuing stimuli—that is, it soon stops attending to them. They simply become part of the background. Similarly, the first atomic bomb dropped on Hiroshima created a worldwide shock wave that stimulated intense efforts to ban atomic weapons. Atmospheric tests elicited some attention, especially with the leap from fission to fusion bombs, but as testing has gone underground, the nuclear threat has slipped out of attention and elicits only occasional flurries of concern. Nuclear stockpiles have become part of the background of our lives.

A psychophysical concept may be relevant to this failure to react to the increase in nuclear weapons, the "just noticeable difference." The smallest difference between two stimuli that an observer can detect is proportional to the intensity of the stimuli—the stronger the stimuli, the greater the size of the difference between them required to become detectable. If even a very large increase occurs so gradually that successive increments remain below the just noticeable difference, we fail to detect it. This has been happening with nuclear weapons—although each additional nuclear missile may add thousands or millions of tons of TNT equivalent, in comparison with the astronomical size of the nuclear stockpile itself these increments are too small to flag attention.

Denial and adaptation facilitate perhaps the most important psychological source of the arms race—the tendency to cling to reassuring but outmoded modes of thought and behavior in the face of a novel threat. Humans guide their behavior by their interpretations of events. . . . Fortunately what we say about reality ordinarily coincides closely with objective reality so that our behavior is not seriously maladaptive. Furthermore, thanks to humans' extraordinary powers of symbolization, when objective reality changes they are usually able to adjust their perceptions and behavior sufficiently promptly to avoid disaster.

When humans are faced with an unprecedented danger, however, they may try to make it appear like a familiar one that can be overcome by methods that succeeded in the past, thereby preserving their feelings of security. This can create a dangerous gap between perceived and objective reality. All of today's national leaders climbed to power in a reality dominated by conventional weapons, so their feelings of security rest on their mastery of the pre-nuclear game of negotiations, deterrence, and—if these failed—war as the final resort. To prepare for this recurrent eventuality, nations sought to acquire a more powerful arsenal than any adversary. By this means, they hoped to reassure themselves, intimidate actual or potential enemies, and hold the loyalty of their allies. Although there have been exceptions, this policy has been heavily reinforced by success—that is, the side that entered a war with the biggest military machine won.

With strategic nuclear weapons, this policy will no longer work. As Harold Brown, a former United States secretary of defense, wrote: "Comprehensive military supremacy for either side is a military and economic impossibility" (3).

National leaders attempt to deny this new reality by conjuring up scenarios of limited, controlled nuclear warfare which would somehow be ended by mutual agreement when "our" side is ahead. The notion that a nuclear war can be limited presupposes a tight, minute-by-minute control of operations maintained despite the disruption of electronic command and control systems through the electromagnetic pulses emitted by nuclear weapons. Furthermore, while the fighting was actually going on, both sides, operating with different information, different weapons, and diametrically opposed objectives, would have to agree to accept the same outcome. Merely to state these conditions indicates how impossible they would be to meet. As a matter of fact, even with conventional weapons, wars involving approximately equal powers arouse such strong passions that they have almost always escalated until one side has thrown every weapon it possessed at the other, including atomic weapons. All that has saved humanity so far has been that even the most powerful weapons were relatively weak. Nuclear weapons have removed this safeguard.

Nuclear weapons have abruptly and permanently broken the connection between weaponry and strength in one respect, but not in another. Perceived and actual reality still coincide in that strategic nuclear weapons in the hands of one adversary gravely menace the other. They differ sharply, however, in

---

[3] Brown, H. Quoted in *Defense Monitor*, 1980, 9(8): 3.

that beyond a certain point the more a nation possesses the more strong and secure it and other nations perceive it to be, whereas in actuality the reverse is true.

Beyond a level long since passed by the U.S. and the USSR, accumulating more powerful and sophisticated strategic nuclear weapons increases the danger to all nations, including the possessor. It stimulates the spread of these weapons to nations that do not now possess them and also assures that they will eventually fall into the hands of terrorists within countries. The more persons who have hands on these weapons within and among nations, the greater the likelihood that one will be fired by malice or by accident, thereby triggering the computers programmed to launch a strategic nuclear exchange (4). With these weapons, one cannot afford a single mistake.

Perceiving them simply as larger nonnuclear ones, however, enables everyone to preserve the comforting illusion that increasing the nuclear arsenal increases their nation's power and security. Unfortunately, as long as the world's leaders perceive nuclear weapons as simply bigger conventional ones, the country that has a smaller or less technically advanced stockpile will see itself as weaker and will be seen as weaker by its opponents and allies. So it will act as if it actually were weaker; that is, it will be more easily intimidated, will act less decisively in crises, and will be in danger of losing its allies and tempting its opponents to seize the initiative. As Admiral Stansfield Turner put it: "But whatever we do, it must not only correct the actual imbalance of (nuclear) capability; it must also correct the perception of imbalance. . . . Changing the world's perception that we are falling behind the Soviet Union is as important as not falling behind in fact" (5). In other words, the pursuit of security through illusory nuclear superiority is in reality more a race for prestige than actual strength. The nuclear arms race turns out to be an especially costly and dangerous form of psychological warfare.

The impetus to arms races is, of course, a perceived enemy. An enemy is a threat to the welfare, or even the existence, of the group to which one belongs. As social creatures, humans can survive only as members of organized groups. Groups provide protection against hostile environments and outside enemies. They also provide a sense of psychological security in that, since all members share the same customs and norms, they can readily understand each other's behavior, and the group carries the values that give meaning and significance to their lives. Thus a threat to the group's integrity strikes at the very basis of its members' psychological, as well as biological, survival.

That many experience the thought of submission to an alien ideology and social system as more intolerable than death itself may be a major reason

[4] Dumas, L. J. Human fallibility and weapons. *Bulletin of the Atomic Scientists,* November 1980, 15–20.
[5] Turner, S. Why we shouldn't build the MX. *New York Times,* March 29, 1981.

for the escalation of wars. This attitude is summed up in the American slogan "Better dead than Red" (for which I'm sure the Russians must have a counterpart).

Humans share with all social animals the predisposition to fear and distrust members of groups other than their own. When two groups compete for the same goal, this distrust rapidly escalates into the mutual perception of each other as enemies. The image of the enemy is always the same, no matter who the enemies are, and they mirror each other—that is, each side attributes the same virtues to itself and the same vices to the enemy. "We" are trustworthy, peace-loving, honorable, and humanitarian; "they" are treacherous, warlike, and cruel.

Furthermore, the image of the enemy readily forms and dissolves depending on the changing relationships between the groups. This is illustrated by the findings of repeated surveys of Americans concerning their characterizations of people of other countries. In 1942 and again in 1966 respondents were asked to choose from a list of adjectives those that best described the people of Russia, Germany, and Japan. In 1942 the first five adjectives chosen to characterize both Germans and Japanese (enemies) included warlike, treacherous, and cruel, none of which appeared among the first five describing the Russians (allies) (6); in 1966 all three had disappeared from American characterizations of the Germans and Japanese (allies), but now the Russians (no longer allies, although more rivals than enemies) were warlike and treacherous. Data were reported for the Mainland Chinese in 1966 and, predictably, they were seen as warlike, treacherous, and sly. After President Nixon's trip to China in 1972, these adjectives disappeared from the American characterization of the Chinese, whom they now saw as hardworking, intelligent, artistic, progressive, and practical (7).

The image of the enemy creates a self-fulfilling prophecy by causing enemies to acquire the evil characteristics they attribute to each other. In combatting what they perceive to be the other's cruelty and treachery, each side becomes more cruel and treacherous itself. The image hostile nations form of each other thus more or less corresponds to reality. Although the behavior of the enemy may be motivated by fear more than aggressiveness, nations that failed to recognize that their enemies are treacherous and warlike would not long survive.

Unfortunately, these mutual perceptions, however justified they may be, aggravate mutual hostility and impede resolution of the conflict in several ways. They lead to progressive restriction of information, which can result in a fail-

[6] Gallup Poll. Image of Red powers. *The Santa Barbara News-Press*, June 26, 1966.
[7] *Gallup Poll, Public Opinion 1959–71*, Vol. 111. New York: Random House, 1972, p. 2015; and *Gallup Poll, Public Opinion 1972–77*, Vol. 1, 1972–75. Wilmington, Del.: Scholarly Resources, Inc., 1978, p. 20.

ure of empathy, often manifested by an attacker's underestimation of the target's determination to resist. This may be a major psychological source of the outbreak of wars (8). The enemy image also acts like a distorting lens which overemphasizes confirming information and filters out incompatible information. This increases the likelihood of serious misunderstandings of the enemy's intention. Thus the mass media play up incidents of an enemy's treachery or cruelty and ignore examples of humanitarian or honorable behavior. Along the same lines, the same behavior is seen as in the service of good motives if performed by our side and in the service of bad ones if performed by an enemy. For example, although in wartime both sides always commit atrocities, the enemy's atrocities are evidence of his evil nature, whereas ours are portrayed as regrettable necessities.

Since the enemy is unmitigatedly wicked, he becomes a convenient scapegoat for the domestic and international problems besetting both sides. By projecting the blame for these on the enemy, each side protects its own self-esteem from the realization that it cannot solve them. Thus the rising tide of violence all over the world is caused primarily by collapsing standards of living—the result of increasing population pressure on limited resources, aggravated by the economic dislocations caused by huge arms budgets. Although other nations may seek to use the resulting unrest to their own advantage, they are not its basic cause. Yet both the USSR and the U.S. blame turmoil in their client states mainly on the subversive machinations of the other. This intensifies the mutual enemy image by exacerbating mutual antagonisms, while diverting attention from the real causes of the problem.

Finally, because anything the enemy wants must by definition be bad for us, the enemy image blinds both sides to interests they might have in common. Thus when the Soviet Union stresses the horrors of nuclear war, many Americans perceive this as a ruse to cause us to stop our nuclear arms buildup. They cannot entertain the possibility that mutual reduction of nuclear stockpiles would benefit both countries. I shall return to other more constructive parallel interests later in another context.

Faced with an adversary perceived as treacherous and implacably malevolent in a world without effective international peace-keeping institutions, a nation's only recourse has been to confront him with superior force in the hope that this will deter hostile acts through threat of retaliation or defeat him should deterrence fail.

Since resort to nuclear weapons would be suicidal, nuclear powers are forced to rely on the hope of maintaining deterrence indefinitely. There are strong psychological grounds for believing that such a hope will continue to be vain in the future, as it always has been in the past.

---

[8] White, R. K. Empathizing with the rulers of the USSR. *Political Psychology,* 1983, 4(1): 121–137.

The essence of deterrence is the attempt of one party to control another by threat of punishment should the latter attempt to perform a forbidden act. This creates an inherently unstable social system. Since it depends on rational calculations of both parties as to the relative benefits and costs of performing or refraining from the act in question, it breaks down when one of the parties calculates, correctly or incorrectly, that the potential benefits of the forbidden action outweigh the probable costs, as in Hitler's invasion of Poland, or when the emotional tensions reach such a pitch that leaders stop calculating and throw caution to the winds. Thus at the onset of World War I the Kaiser said, "Even if we are bled to death, England will at least lose India," and the Japanese war minister in ordering the attack on Pearl Harbor said, "Once in a while it [is] necessary to close one's eyes and jump from the stage of the Kiyomizu Temple" (a favorite Japanese form of suicide) (9). This is the point when, as Bertrand Russell put it, the desire to kill one's enemies becomes greater than the desire to stay alive oneself.

Since meaningful superiority in nuclear weapons is objectively unattainable, deterrence has come to rely primarily on projecting the appearance of strength and resolution to the deterring nation itself, its allies, and its enemies. Nuclear deterrence thus puts a premium on bluffing. Former Secretary of State Henry Kissinger wrote, "Deterrence depends above all on psychological criteria. . . . For purposes of deterrence a bluff taken seriously is more useful than a serious threat interpreted as a bluff" (10). Thus each nuclear power is faced with the virtually impossible task of trying to make credible an essentially incredible threat.

Recently technological advances in the power and accuracy of international ballistic missiles have caused a shift from deterring an adversary by threatening to destroy his cities to threatening to destroy his weapons. By putting a premium on striking first, thereby shortening decision time, this intensifies mutual fears and thereby the danger of triggering a nuclear holocaust through accident or misjudgment.

A policy of mutual nuclear deterrence, in short, is guaranteed to provoke recurrent states of high emotional tension in national leaders. If the previous analysis is correct, this would cause them to cling more tenaciously to the comforting illusion that nuclear weapons are simply larger conventional ones, to be managed in the same way.

In the grip of strong emotions, a person's thinking becomes more primitive—that is, he perceives fewer alternatives, simplifies issues, and focuses exclusively on combatting the immediate threat without considering remote

---

[9] Holsti, O. R. The value of international tension measurements. *Journal of Conflict Resolution,* 1963, 7: 611.
[10] Kissinger, H. J. Central issues in American foreign policy. In K. Gordon (Ed.), *Agenda for the nation.* Garden City, N.J.: Doubleday & Co., 1968, p. 501.

or long-term consequences. Strong emotion also impels to impulsive action. There is nothing harder when under emotional stress than to do nothing (11).

We can, perhaps, derive some comfort from the recognition that national leaders would not have reached the top unless they were able to preserve good judgment under stress. Yet the graveyard of history is littered with the remains of societies whose leaders' judgment failed under emotional pressure. As Robert Kennedy indicated in his book on the Cuban missile crisis, even some of the "best and brightest" can reach a breaking point: "some (of the decision-makers) because of the pressure of events, even appeared to lose their judgment and stability" (12).

The fact that major decisions concerning national policy are made by small groups rather than individuals does not protect these decisions from irrationality. On the contrary, groups may be more prone to rash actions under some circumstances than individuals. To be sure, a group has access to information from more sources and provides opportunities to express more viewpoints, which should help steady its judgments, and a group member may be restrained by others who do not share his perspective; but group members may also reinforce each other, or even egg each other on, especially if emotion runs high. This mutual reinforcement is strengthened by what I. Janis has termed "Groupthink" (13). The more a group feels threatened, the more its members are impelled to maintain group solidarity by agreeing with each other and the leader, even at the expense of their individual judgments. The Bay of Pigs was an instructive example.

Normalizing the Unthinkable
Lisa Peattie

Lisa Peattie is Professor of Urban Anthropology at the Massachusetts Institute of Technology. She has worked with the MIT Disarmament Group and is coauthor of *Women's Claims*.

An Environmental Protection Agency study of "Evacuation Risks" argues energetically against the "panic image" of human behavior in an emergency situation: "People will often stay in a potentially threatening situation rather

---

[11] Group for the Advancement of Psychiatry. *Psychiatric Aspects of the prevention of nuclear war*. Report No. 57. New York: Group for the Advancement of Psychiatry, 1964.
[12] Kennedy, R. F. *Thirteen days*. New York: W. W. Norton, 1969, p. 31.
[13] Janis, I. L., & Mann, L. *Decision making*. New York: Free Press, 1977.
Source: Lisa Peattie, "Normalizing the Unthinkable," *Bulletin of the Atomic Scientists* (March 1984), pp. 32–36. Reprinted by permission of the *Bulletin of the Atomic Scientists*, a magazine of science and world affairs. Copyright © 1984 by the Educational Foundation for Nuclear Science, Chicago, IL 60637.

than move out of it," the report declares. "Human beings have very strong tendencies to continue on-going lines of behavior in preference to initiating new courses of action."[1]

Current planning for the management of a nuclear war in itself constitutes an exemplary confirmation of this principle. The situation which the planners address is the most dreadful conceivable. It involves at the minimum the deaths of a substantial number of the human beings whom we love and with whom we share a common fate, the destruction of the physical places where we live and to which we are attached, the disorganization of our society. It may mean the end of human life on Earth, and thus the very sensibleness of planning. But the tone of the planning studies is entirely normal and normalizing.

One approach is to work from analogies with the familiar. A study of the consequences of "incidents" involving nuclear power plants draws from human actions and reactions in floods, fires and earthquakes. The data are deaths from motor vehicle accidents; costs for food and housing; salaries and wages for National Guardsmen, policemen and firemen; loss of wages per day per evacuee.[2] Such analogies appear also in planning for nuclear war.

Nuclear war, however, even in the world of civil defense research, appears somewhat off the scale of analysis by analogy to the ordinary. Therefore resort is made to rendering the situation playfully, via models and games. One study, for example, declares that "Like war games and business games the post-attack problems for which a single city model might be used are characterized by both rich environments and incomplete sets of decision rules."[3] Such a gaming approach deals in "weapons impacts," "resource availability," "cumulating costs of items or modules damaged beyond repair" and "vulnerability indexes." Dividing reduced resources by a greatly reduced population, it is possible to conclude that "Considering resources alone, a moderate level attack on the nation might reduce consumption to the equivalent of that of the Great Depression."[4]

The principle is correct. There appears to be no situation so abnormal—experientially, socially, morally—that human beings, if not totally stunned out of all reactivity, will not at least strive to assimilate it to normal practice. . . .

Let us consider what we know of human behavior in the concentration camp. Jean François Steiner's account of life in Treblinka describes how, even as the scale and atrociousness of the extermination process advanced, the in-

---

[1] Environmental Protection Agency, "Evacuation Risks—An Evaluation" (EPA 520/6-74 -002), p. 45.
[2] Ibid.
[3] John Dewitt Norton, *Economic Models: Methods, Uses, Prospects* (Washington, D.C.: National Planning Association, Economic Programming Center, 1969), p. viii.
[4] Ibid, p. 111.

stitutions and social organization of the camp came more and more to parallel those of a normal society.[5] The technology improved; the original clumsy experiments with killing Jews by exhaust fumes in the trucks which brought them from Warsaw were supplanted by the developed technology of the gas chambers. The Germans found it inconvenient to work with a perpetually inexperienced labor force. Thus, from an initial strategy of gassing those who had been forced to strip their fellow victims of clothing, valuables, hair and gold teeth, they established a set of longer-term workers who would only at extended intervals be sent to the chambers.

Relationships, both bureaucratic and personal, came into being. The longer-term inmates found particular niches in the organization and learned to work the system for their own personal well-being and protection and, when they could, to protect their friends. A prisoners' orchestra was formed, and when the trains unloaded a new set of victims, musicians were pulled out of the ranks to join the music makers. Prizefights became another form of entertainment, and another principle of selection. A park and zoo were built.

Toward the end, when the Germans began to realize that they were likely to lose the war, a goal became that of concealing the evidence. The prisoner-workers were set to digging up, by heavy machinery, bodies which had been piled into deep pits, so that they could be burnt. It took a little time to evolve the techniques for cremating this mountain of bodies, but eventually a regular procedure was developed, and the slow, smoky burning of the old bodies became part of the normal functioning of the camp.

Meanwhile, a new institution came into being: a cabaret, shared by the Germans and some of the more established, and therefore privileged, inmates. Weddings were held and celebrated with festivities.

In the latter period of the camp's operation, the long-term inmates, now able to function on a more extended basis, began to organize an uprising. In Steiner's account of this process—which ended with a bloody battle and the capture and death of almost all of those prisoners who had escaped—the most painful part of the story is the difficulty experienced by the leaders in starting the revolt.

They kept putting it off, although they knew that time was running out for them. They made calculations: the original Jewish population of Warsaw; the thousands who passed through the gas chambers; the numbers that must be left; the weeks it would take to process the remaining Jews into extinction. They knew that at the moment the death factory ran out of raw material they too would go into the gas chambers. But no given day seemed quite right. Steiner wrote that it was as though they were stuck in a dream: the dream of the daily routine, of the normality of ordinary behavior. The camp, with its

---

[5] Jean François Steiner, *Treblinka* (New York: Simon and Schuster, 1967).

bureaucracy, its personalities, its roles, its smoking bodies, had become normal.

Steiner's description of Treblinka is particularly rich in recording the normalizing of an atrocious institution, but the theme is in all the personal accounts of concentration camp experience by those who survived for any time in one or the other. There was the daily routine of blows and roll call and soup. There was the barter economy of bread, turnips, scraps of cloth, gold teeth. There were specializations: prison plumbers laid the water pipe in the crematorium and prison electricians wired the fences. The camp managers maintained standards and orderly process. The cobblestones which paved the crematorium yard at Auschwitz had to be perfectly scrubbed.

Germany was not a backward country. On the contrary, it was a world leader in modern music, philosophy, high technology and the social institutions we call the welfare state. Thus, to normalize the unthinkable, the world of the concentration camp had available to it not only the simple techniques of every human society—the establishment of routine, of social ties and of exchange relationships muting conflict through shared commitment and individual rewards for participation. It also had the sophisticated techniques of technological elaboration and bureaucratic rationality. The inhabitants of Treblinka were able to normalize the atrocious by elaborating around it not only music and art but also technology and management. . . .

When we hear of "scientific" experiments performed on inmates in the concentration camp setting we tend to recoil in horror. But is the pretense of science any more horrifying than the rest of it? Indeed, it seems that we must understand these experiments as arising not out of pure sadism, but out of that same human tendency to normalize any setting that generated the concentration camp infirmaries, to which they were often connected. It was quite in keeping with the spirit of it all that these "experimental" tortures constituted the basis for papers read at scientific meetings where, although the source of the data must have been evident, apparently no protest was made. "Science" in the concentration camp was yet another manifestation of the human normalizing tendency, both noble and horrifying, which came to link victims and torturers in the creation of a shared society based on the production of death.

Are we not today engaged in a similar enterprise?

The ss men watched the crumbling of the German Reich, and the prisoners counted the numbers of Jews in the transports and calculated how many weeks it must be before their turn would come. Yet together, day by day, they scrubbed the cobblestones or ordered the cobblestones scrubbed; went to roll call to count and be counted, maintaining the world of Treblinka. Like them, we collaborate day by day in maintaining the institutions of the warfare state which seems more and more plausibly set to destroy us. We are caught in the human endeavor to create daily life: to normalize the unthinkable.

The devices which we use are roughly similar: the division of labor, which separates, in understanding and potential for collective organization, what it makes interdependent in functioning; the structure of rewards and incentives which makes it to individuals' personal and familiar interest to undermine daily, in countless small steps, the basis of common existence; and the legitimating use of bureaucratic formalism and of scientific and technological elaboration.

The division of labor serves most obviously to normalize the atrocious when it takes the form of institutions specialized for purposes which we must assume that normal people would abhor. We might be somewhat less inclined to out-of-hand rejection of the claims of "good" Germans that they did not know what those crematoria were burning when we consider that Bishop Leroy Matthiesen—now a particularly outspoken opponent of the nuclear arms race—served for nine years as a parish priest, two miles from the Pantex plant at Amarillo, Texas, without realizing that its output is nuclear bombs. Pantex covers 10,000 acres and employs 2,400 people; it does final assembly of the entire nuclear arsenal.[6]

But even within the institutions of death, the division of labor continues in a multitude of ways to normalize operation. At the structural level, it divides participants in the organization into groups with specialized interests, less likely to combine against the higher authorities. So at Treblinka an absolute separation of work, housing and communication was maintained between the group of workers who received the Jews from the trains and marshalled them into the gas chambers and those at the other side who removed hair and gold teeth and disposed of the bodies.

A more central issue for war planners is the separation of planning from execution. Adolph Eichmann was a thoroughly responsible person, according to his understanding of responsibility. For him it was clear that the heads of state set policy. His role was to implement, and fortunately, he felt, it was never part of his job actually to have to kill anyone.[7]

There are gradations of distance from execution which constitute varying levels of protection from responsibility and render the moral problem exceedingly fuzzy. During the debates in the late 1960s at MIT with respect to its role in weapons development, the head of the main military research laboratory argued that their concern was development, not use, of technology. The university administration eventually undertook to sever operational weapons

---

[6] "The Bishop at Ground Zero," *Life*, 5, No. 7 (July 1982), pp. 62–66.
[7] Hannah Arendt, *Eichmann in Jerusalem: A Report on the Banality of Evil* (New York: Viking Press, 1964).

systems research from the Institute but it still permitted on-campus work, which was funded mainly because of its potential military application.[8]

Even while diffusing responsibility by separating planning from execution and one element of execution from another, the division of labor produces complicity through the functional interdependence of the specializations. In Treblinka "the Jews themselves had to become responsible for output as well as for discipline." "Experience with the ghettos had taught [the Germans] that a man who had knowingly compromised himself did not revolt against his masters, no matter what idea had driven him to collaboration: too many mutual skeletons in the closet."[9]

The division of labor brings with it an organizational sociology of specialization, hierarchy and differential rewards. Material rewards are allocated on the basis of active and skillful participation in the system. Defense contractors can bid for the most highly skilled engineers and scientists and pay them handsomely. Weapons research and war planning become the path to material success. In the underworld of the concentration camp, the "low numbers"—those who had survived for relatively long periods—were all specialists. Only they ate enough to keep alive.

The work-Jews at Treblinka ate well and were well-clothed because of the goods which came with the "transports"; there are accounts of storerooms knee-deep in valuables. The transports of persons to the gas chambers were also the camp's lifeline. . . .

Along with material success comes prestige. Salaries and positions translate into dinner parties with important people, heads that turn when one enters the conference room. A former research analyst at the Department of Defense recalls:

When I was "chosen" for a special clearance, my immediate feeling was one of achievement and pleasure. I also remember the earlier feeling when I was not cleared for special intelligence and how important it seemed to me to be one of the three or four who were cleared among the twenty or so analysts in the Political and Economics Section.[10]

Primo Levi brags at Auschwitz: "In the whole camp there are only a few Greeks who have a [food pot] larger than ours. Besides the material advantages, it carries with it a perceptible improvement in our social standing."[11]

[8] Dorothy Nelkin, *The University and Military Research: Moral Politics at MIT* (Ithaca, New York: Cornell University Press, 1972).
[9] Steiner, *Treblinka,* pp. 68, 69. Levi, *Survival,* p. 102. Gitta Sereny, *Into That Darkness: An Examination of Conscience* (New York: Random House, 1982), pp. 212–13.
[10] Henry T. Nash, "The Bureaucratization of Homicide," *Bulletin,* 36 (April 1980), pp. 22–27.
[11] Primo Levi, *Survival in Auschwitz* (New York: Collier Books, 1961).

Specialization brings with it the possibility of developing the peculiarly human satisfactions in problem-solving, expertise and the exercise of skill. High technology is the creative frontier. The development of the atomic bomb is one of the great dramas of creativity of our time, and the subsequent elaboration of the technology has provided, and continues to provide, opportunities for the intellectual excitement of stretching the mind to its limits.

In 1947, James Killian, then vice president of MIT and later its president, said of the Institute during wartime:

> The concentration of war research on its campus, the presence here of a great assemblage of gifted scientists from hundreds of institutions and the remarkably varied activities of its own staff contributed . . . to the establishment of a fresh and vigorous post-war program. . . . No one at MIT during this period can fail to be impressed by the ferment of ideas.[12]

The concentration camp may seem like an unpropitious environment for skill and discovery, but even there it had its role in the experiments on human subjects. At Treblinka, when they solved the problem of how to burn the bodies, they broke out champagne; it was a technological breakthrough. And in the underworld of the prisoners, Primo Levi boasts again from Auschwitz: "And I would not like to be accused of immodesty if I add that it was our idea, mine and Alberto's, to steal the rolls of graph-paper from the thermographs of the Desiccation Department."[13]

Paul Loeb, studying the community developed around plutonium production at Hanford, Washington, shows how organizational process within the enterprise, and family and community life around it, give the production of bombs the most peaceful of settings. As one informant explained:

> We were proud to work for a major company like General Electric. We felt we were part of a well-run industrial enterprise with good management practices, good cost control and a good competitive feeling because the AEC [Atomic Energy Commission] would be comparing our cost and productivity figures with those of Savannah River. Some of us even went on recruiting trips, visiting different colleges along with other people from GE divisions around the country—and we explained plutonium as simply our product, just as light bulbs or turbines were someone else's.[14]

---

[12] Quoted in Dorothy Nelkin, *The University*, p. 17.
[13] Levi, *Survival*, p. 98.
[14] Paul Loeb, *Nuclear Culture: Living and Working in the World's Largest Atomic Complex* (New York: Coward, McCann and Geoghegan, Inc., 1982).

In his work on Treblinka, Steiner makes a general point which seems strongly relevant to the movement toward nuclear war. It is not simply the attachment to going concerns which makes it difficult to stop; it is the very seriousness of the situation. An outcome of sufficient dreadfulness becomes, in effect, inconceivable. "One fact played into the hands of the 'technicians': the monstrosity of the truth. The extermination of a whole people was so unimaginable that the human mind could not accept it."[15] Similarly, nuclear war has been designated "the unthinkable."[16] . . .

There are those who argue that preparation for nuclear war is necessary for reasons of national security. I believe, and have tried to show, that the continuation of weapons production and military planning can be explained without recourse to any argument involving national interest. And about the argument as it relates to national purpose, I would say that:

- there now exists descriptions of the consequences of nuclear war sufficiently apocalyptic to show that there is no conceivable national purpose for which the triggering of nuclear war would be sufficient justification;
- the continuing institutionalized preparation for nuclear war brings us continually closer to the precipice of its occurrence;
- we ought to move immediately to eliminate preparation for nuclear war from its current place as an instrument of national policy. Even the brutalized and complicitous prisoners of Treblinka eventually rose up against normalization of the unthinkable.

Some of us, confronted with our present situation, are ready to consign the very notion of national purpose to the dustbin of history, along with Hitler's Third Reich.

FOR FURTHER READING

Adams, Gordon. *The Iron Triangle: The Politics of Defense Contracting.* New York, Council on Economic Priorities, 1981 (paperback). A critical analysis of defense spending policies. Meticulously documents interconnections among key Congressional committees, the Department of Defense, and major defense contractors; examines the means employed by defense contractors to gain influence with government agencies; contains profiles of such contractors as Boeing, General Dynamics, and others.

Allison, Graham T., and Frederick Morris. "Exploring the Determinants of Military Weapons." In Franklin A. Long and George Rathjens, eds., *Arms, Defense Policy, and Arms Control,* pp. 33–45. New York: Norton, 1975. A concise, yet comprehensive discussion of some of the organizational dy-

---

[15] Steiner, *Treblinka,* p. 136.
[16] Herman Kahn, *Thinking about the Unthinkable* (New York: Horizon Press, 1962).

namics and vested interests that influence the defense policymaking process.

DeWitt, Hugh E. "The Nuclear Arms Race Seen from Within a Nuclear Weapons Laboratory." *Science and Public Policy* 9 (April 1982), pp. 58–63. The author, a physicist with the Lawrence Livermore Laboratory—one of the two federally sponsored nuclear weapons labs—argues that "the nuclear weapons labs are indeed the wellsprings of the nuclear arms race."

Gansler, Jacques S. *The Defense Industry.* Cambridge, Mass.: M.I.T. Press, 1982. Detailed analysis of the U.S. "military-industrial complex." Avoids polemics while assessing problems, examining approaches of other nations, and making recommendations for reform.

George, Alexander L. "Psychological Aspects of Decisionmaking: Adapting to Constraints on Rational Decisionmaking." In *Presidential Decisionmaking in Foreign Policy: The Effective Use of Information and Advice.* Boulder, Col.: Westview Press, 1980 (paperback). Identifies common impediments to the efficient processing of information and other factors that may compromise the rationality of the decision-making process.

Harvard Nuclear Study Group. "Nuclear Lessons: What Have We Learned?" In *Living with Nuclear Weapons* (New York: Bantam Books, 1983), pp. 30–36. Identifies five theories that attempt to explain the persistence of the arms race: (1) genuine security requirements; (2) uncertainty and misperception; (3) domestic political pressures; (4) technological determinism; and (5) international political rivalry.

Janis, Irving L. *Groupthink: Psychological Studies of Policy Decisions and Fiascoes.* Boston: Houghton Mifflin Co., 1982. Innovative analysis of the psychological and social forces that can distort the judgment of policymakers operating under conditions of uncertainty and stress. Includes several detailed case studies, including the Cuban Missile Crisis of 1962.

Kovel, Joel. *Against the State of Nuclear Terror.* Boston: South End Press, 1983 (paperback). Creative analysis of psychological, political, and economic forces that perpetuate the nuclear threat. Excellent analysis of the antidemocratic implications of nuclear weapons. Contains a valuable section on principles and practices of antinuclear politics.

Lifton, Robert Jay, and Richard Falk. *Indefensible Weapons: The Political and Psychological Case Against Nuclearism.* New York: Basic Books, 1982. Written by a psychiatrist and a political scientist/legal scholar. Excellent analysis of the psychological and political factors that have prevented potential victims of nuclear war from more effective efforts to reform existing policies. Analyzes how to surmount psychological and political obstacles to reform.

Lifton, Robert Jay. "Scientists and Nuclearism." In *The Broken Connection: On Death and the Continuity of Life.* New York: Simon and Schuster, 1979 (available in paperback). Provocative psychological analysis of how some scientists develop a strong belief in the need for more and better nuclear weapons, despite evidence to the contrary. Examines autobiographical writings of Robert Oppenheimer, Leo Szilard, Edward Teller, and other important scientists closely associated with nuclear weapons.

Mack, John. "Resistances to Knowing in the Nuclear Age." *Harvard Educational Review* 54 (August 1984), pp. 260–71. Identifies both individual and collective tendencies to avoid thinking and learning about the nuclear threat. Discusses the implications of such tendencies.

Macy, Johanna Rogers. *Despair and Personal Power in the Nuclear Age.* Philadelphia: New Society Publishers, 1983. Discusses prevalence and implications of feelings of despair about the nuclear threat and approaches to reducing such despair.

Miller, Steven. "Politics over Promise: Domestic Impediments to Arms Control." *International Security* 8 (Spring 1984), pp. 64–80. Convincingly argues that 'the promise of arms control as an instrument of national security policy has been stunted as much by domestic political factors as by any other." Identifies vested interests in the United States promoting the deployment of more weapons and resisting the efforts of arms control to constrain such deployments.

Myrdal, Alva. *The Game of Disarmament: How the United States and Russia Run the Arms Race.* Revised and updated edition. New York: Pantheon Books, 1982 (paperback). Written by a Nobel Peace Prize-winning Swedish diplomat, this book asserts that *both* superpowers have unilaterally escalated the arms race by deploying destabilizing new weapons and by refusing to compromise in arms control negotiation. Contains excellent "History of Lost Opportunities." Discusses proposals for reducing the nuclear and conventional threats.

Nash, Henry. "Bureaucratization of Homicide." *Bulletin of the Atomic Scientists* 36 (April 1980), pp. 24–30. Excellent account, by a former strategic target planner, of psychological and organizational dynamics in defense bureaucracies that prevent workers from thinking about the nature and implications of their work.

Pringle, Peter, and James Spigelman. *The Nuclear Barons.* New York: Holt, Rinehart, and Winston, 1981. Historical account of development of nuclear technology by present nuclear-armed nations. Argues that the governments of these nations—including the democracies—have deliberately concealed crucial information from their citizens in order to prevent popular resistance to pronuclear policies.

Rathjens, George. "The Dynamics of the Arms Race." *Scientific American* (April 1969), pp. 35–46. Discusses the destabilizing implications of the plans to deploy ABM and MIRV systems. Excellent case studies of the action-reaction dynamic of the arms race.

Russett, Bruce. "Why Do Arms Races Occur?" In *The Prisoners of Insecurity: Nuclear Deterrence, the Arms Race, and Arms Control,* pp. 69–96. San Francisco: W. H. Freeman and Co., 1983 (paperback). Concise review of theoretical and empirical literature on international and domestic causes of arms races. An excellent introductory treatment of the subject.

11

Costs of the Arms Race

The earlier chapters in this reader have shown how the nuclear arms race between the United States and the Soviet Union is rapidly escalating; a similarly escalating race in conventional weapons is also under way.
Each nation justifies its activities in the name of national security. Proponents of new and better nuclear weapons argue that, given the wide range of threats facing sovereign nations in an unstable world, the nation that fails to prepare for nuclear war runs the risk of having its security threatened or even destroyed.

However, a growing number of people—"experts" and "ordinary citizens" alike—have reached a different conclusion about the nuclear arms race. They maintain that the uncontrolled arms race actually *endangers* national security by rendering the world even less stable. According to this perspective, the most evident and dangerous cost of the nuclear arms race is the growing risk of nuclear war.

In this chapter, we will examine costs of the arms race as identified by some writers—although others have questioned their assumptions. Depending on one's perspective, some of these costs may be less, or more, burdensome than the commentators allege. Other critics would regard these costs as necessary prices that must be paid to assure security. The articles selected for this chapter examine four such costs: the economic burden imposed by high levels of defense spending; the psychological impact of living under the threat of nuclear annihilation; the weakening of democratic political processes; and the ethical dilemmas created by our reliance on nuclear weapons and our readiness to wage nuclear warfare.

Considerable controversy surrounds the question of how nuclear spending affects the overall economy. (It has been estimated, for example, that the United States will spend well over one trillion dollars on defense during the next four years.) Lloyd J. Dumas, in "The Military Albatross: Arms Spending Is Destroying the Economy," asserts that "over the last several decades military spending has been the predominant cause of the deterioration of the U.S. economy. . . ." Dumas cites four reasons for this allegation, including the economically non-productive nature of military goods, the exorbitant "cost plus" system of defense contracting, the trade imbalance created by military exports, and the declining rate of civilian technological progress caused by diversion of scientific and engineering expertise into military projects. One result of such conditions, argues Dumas, will be a continuing high level of inflation.

An alternative perspective is provided by the excerpt from the U.S. Congressional Budget Office (CBO) study, "Defense Spending and the Economy." In contrast to Dumas, the CBO concludes that current and projected levels of defense spending do not "pose much risk of rekindling inflation in the near term." Nor is the CBO worried about high levels of military spending adversely affecting employment in civilian industries. It states that money spent on defense creates about the same number of jobs as money spent in nondefense areas. However, the CBO does express concern about possible long-term effects of the expanding defense budget, particularly the potential increase to the federal deficit. While the short-term situation may appear reassuring, current trends in defense spending may create serious problems for the future.

Concern about another cost of the arms race—the possible psychological trauma to the young—is expressed in psychiatrist John Mack's statement—submitted to a recent Hearing of the Select Committee on Children, Youth, and Families of the U.S. House of Representatives. Mack surveys a number of studies and concludes that many children are aware of, and worry about, the prospects of a nuclear war in their lifetimes. He says that many children think that the world is out of control and that they have serious doubts about their futures. Many of the children say they have no one with whom they can talk about their feelings and fears concerning nuclear weapons and nuclear war. Referring to a recent study of teenagers in the Boston area, Mack notes that "there were vivid expressions of terror and powerlessness, grim images of nuclear destruction, doubt whether they will ever have a chance to grow up and an accompanying attitude of 'live for now.' Some expressed anger toward the adult generation that seemed to have so jeopardized their futures."

Such pessimistic views have not gone unquestioned. For example, in a recent article in *Commentary*, Joseph Adelson and Chester F. Finn, Jr., argue that the data cited by Mack were methodologically flawed and that Mack and other "experts" have been motivated by political sympathy to the nuclear freeze movement to exaggerate the psychological problems of youth presumed to be caused by nuclear fears. (See the reference in "For Further Reading," page 429.)

It should be noted, however, that recent public opinion polls have indicated that many young people *are* concerned about the danger of nuclear war. For example, in a poll conducted recently by the firm of Yankelovich, Skelly, and White, 50 percent of the respondents under the age of thirty indicated a belief that, within the next ten years, "all out nuclear war" is either "very likely" or "fairly likely."[1] A poll conducted in 1982 in the state of Minnesota found that more than half of the graduating class of a suburban high school felt that World War III was going to occur within their lifetimes. In contrast, when the class of

---

[1] Daniel Yankelovich and John Doble, "The Public Mood," *Foreign Affairs* (Fall 1984), p. 37.

1962 had been asked the same question, 58 percent answered that World War III *would not* occur while they were alive.[2] Thus, while the precise extent, as well as the psychological implications, of nuclear fears remain the subject of debate, a case can be made that such fears are pervasive among the young.

Nor are adults immune to disturbing feelings about the nuclear threat. Clinical psychologist Johanna Rogers-Macy suggests that many adults as well as youth experience a profound sense of despair about the nuclear predicament. They are painfully aware of the gravity of the nuclear threat, but they feel there is nothing they or anyone else can do to prevent or escape it. The feeling of powerlessness is one of the symptoms of despair. Other symptoms include estrangement from other people, doubts about one's own sanity, and psychic numbing. Such despair can create a vicious circle: Apathy and inaction allow the threat to worsen, while the worsening threat intensifies the despair. Fortunately, Rogers-Macy and others who have explored these psychological processes believe that it is possible to "work through" despair. Confronting the validity of the fears, involvement with other people who share similar concerns, and direct action are among the means that Rogers-Macy recommends.[3]

A third "cost" of the arms race is addressed by Robert Karl Manoff in "The Media: Nuclear Secrecy vs. Democracy." Manoff argues that government-imposed secrecy about nuclear weapons has been a feature of the nuclear era since the first atomic bombs were dropped on Japan. The U.S. press, on which citizens depend for vital information, succumbed to government pressure to withhold facts that would have enabled the American public to appreciate the unprecedented nature of the atomic bombs. Thus the public has not understood subsequent developments in nuclear weapons and policies. The result of such secrecy, Manoff asserts, has been the weakening of democracy. (Antidemocratic effects of nuclear weapons are also examined by Markusen and Harris in their article in Chapter 10.)

The fourth cost to be considered in this chapter involves the moral and ethical dilemmas created by a national security posture that relies on the willingness to wage nuclear war. As John Gardiner states in his essay, "Deterrence: The Deadly Paradox," such a willingness to engage in mass destruction of human beings has been justified as the only way to deter the use of nuclear weapons against the United States. In other words, both the Soviet Union and the United States have found themselves in the predicament of having to *prepare for* nuclear war in order to *prevent* it from occurring. Gardiner argues, however, that such preparations can be morally justified only if they do in fact succeed in deterring nuclear war. He also suggests that the very nature of deterrence may create tensions that could actually *increase* the risk of nuclear war.

This intrinsic paradox of deterrence has stimulated a great deal of debate about the moral aspects of nuclear weapons policies in recent years. During 1982 and 1983, the National Conference of Catholic

---

[2] "Minnesota Poll," Minneapolis *Tribune* (Nov. 21, 1982).

[3] Johanna Rogers-Macy, *Despair and Personal Power in the Nuclear Age* (Philadelphia: New Society Publishers, 1983).

bishops generated intense controversy with their Pastoral Letter, *The Challenge of Peace: God's Promise and Our Response*. After considerable deliberation, the bishops concluded that, while the *use* of nuclear weapons would be straightforwardly immoral, the *possession* of them, in order to deter an adversary from using its nuclear weapons against the United States, is "conditionally" morally tolerable, as an interim measure, pending negotiations to reduce the arsenals of both nations. However, the bishops have been criticized on a number of grounds. Spokespersons for the Reagan administration contend that the realities of the present nuclear-armed world morally require the United States not only to *possess* nuclear weapons, but also to be ready and willing to *use* them under certain circumstances. (See, for example, the article by Elliot Abrams listed in "For Further Reading.") Others argue that the bishops, by even *conditionally* tolerating the possession of nuclear weapons, are morally compromised. For example, Kermit D. Johnson, a retired Army Major General and Chief of Chaplains, argues that nuclear deterrence itself is immoral. "The time has come," he asserts, "when the churches acting in concern and in the spirit of repentance must withdraw *all* moral sanction from the strategy of nuclear deterrence."[4]

In the final article for this chapter, Jonathan Schell, in an excerpt from his controversial and widely read book, *The Fate of the Earth*, reflects on the moral implications of the recent "nuclear winter" studies. After reviewing many of the known potential consequences of a nuclear war, Schell writes, "one must conclude that a full-scale nuclear holocaust could lead to the extinction of mankind." It is true that the facts do not permit the assumption that extinction would be certain. However, given the stakes involved, Schell believes that "although, scientifically speaking, there is all the difference in the world between the mere possibility that a holocaust will bring about extinction and the certainty of it, morally they are the same, and we have no choice but to address the issue of nuclear weapons as though we knew for a certainty that their use would put an end to our species."

Throughout this book, we have tried to present a balanced debate on the various issues surrounding nuclear weapons, not only in the selections we have made, but also in our comments on them. We would like to step outside that objective role, however, to elaborate on the moral issue that Schell has just raised.

The United States is not the only nation to base its national security on nuclear weapons. Nor is it the only nation to contribute to the arms race. We feel, however, that American citizens have a unique moral obligation to prevent nuclear weapons from ever being used. First, the majority of Americans are morally guided by the Judeo-Christian ethical tradition, which places primary value on the sanctity and dignity of human life. Built into our Constitution is a reverence for life and human rights. Second, the United States was the first nation to build nuclear weapons and the first and only nation to use them against

---

[4] Kermit D. Johnson, "The Morality of Nuclear Deterrence," in Gwyn Prins, ed., *The Nuclear Crisis Reader* (New York: Vintage Books, 1984), p. 150. Emphasis in original.

human beings. Moreover, as is evident from readings in earlier chapters, the United States unilaterally initiated some of the most dangerous and destabilizing developments in the arms race, including the hydrogen bomb and MIRVed missiles. Finally, as citizens of a participatory democracy, we are directly responsible for our leaders and their decisions about nuclear weapons. They are, in effect, our "paid employees." Our taxes also support the development and deployment of nuclear weapons. Unlike the citizens of our principal adversary, the Soviet Union, American citizens possess the ability to seriously question and reform existing policies, despite obstacles discussed in the preceding chapter. This ability, in our opinion, confers upon us a moral responsibility to become involved in efforts to evaluate and change policies that presumably exist to assure our security.

THE MILITARY ALBATROSS: HOW ARMS SPENDING IS DESTROYING THE ECONOMY
Lloyd J. Dumas

Lloyd J. Dumas is associate professor of Political Economy and Economics at the University of Texas, Dallas, and a member of the Nuclear Weapons Steering Committee of the American Association for the Advancement of Science. Among his publications are *The Political Economy of Arms Sales*.

I believe that over the last several decades military spending has been the predominant cause of the deterioration of the U.S. economy, which has, in turn, been largely responsible for our simultaneously high unemployment and inflation. There are four major reasons why this is true.

The first reason is the economic nature of military goods; the second is the nature of military procurement; the third, the balance of payments problem; and the fourth, the effect on civilian technological progress.

The Economic Nature of Military Goods

Whatever else you say about military goods, they have no economic usefulness. They cannot be worn, eaten, or lived in; they make no direct contribution to the material standard of living. Nor do they contribute to an economy's capacity to produce goods and services which do contribute to the standard of living, as do products like industrial machinery and factory buildings.

Source: Abridged selection in Lloyd J. Dumas, "The Military Albatross: How Arms Spending Is Destroying the Economy," in Jim Wallace, ed., *Waging Peace: A Handbook for the Struggle to Abolish Nuclear Weapons* (New York: Harper and Row, 1982), pp. 100–105. Copyright © 1982 by Sojourners. Reprinted by permission of Harper & Row, Publishers, Inc.

People who produce military goods and services are, however, paid like everyone else, and the money they receive will be spent by the employees on consumer goods or by the business firms on industrial goods. But these people do not produce a corresponding supply of the consumer or industrial goods which would absorb their money. Taxes have not been raised enough to offset this excess spending power, and inflation has resulted.

Military Contract Practices

The second reason relates to military contract practices. Since World War II, these contracts have in practice become "cost plus," which means that the contractor gets paid whatever it costs to produce plus some amount for profit. The higher the cost, then, the higher the revenues. So contractors interested in bringing more money into the firm simply produce inefficiently, that is, at high cost.

Motivated by this kind of incentive system and backed by a very rich customer, the Department of Defense, these firms have bid resource prices up in order to get the resources they needed. That bidding up of resource prices has contributed to the inflation rate. More importantly, though, the purchasing power of the military industry has enabled it to preempt important parts of key economic resources from the civilian sector.

The Balance of Payments

The third reason is the situation surrounding the balance of payments. From 1893 until 1970, the U.S. had a yearly balance of trade surplus, which meant that exports were greater in value than imports. If that had been the only thing going on in the United States' international economic interactions, the U.S. dollar would now be the strongest currency in the world. We know that hasn't happened. The United States' balance of payments has been in deficit for quite a long time. Why?

During the 20 years from 1955 to 1974, U.S. military expenditures abroad alone were 10 percent greater than the entire balance of trade surplus. So the outflow of dollars related to the support of military establishments and military foreign aid helped to destroy what would otherwise have been a positive balance of payments for the United States.

The pressure generated by the balance of payments deficit is first an inflationary pressure. When the dollar is worth less in exchange for, say, the Swiss franc, a product whose price in Swiss francs has not changed becomes more expensive to U.S. consumers. The United States now imports a great many of its important industrial commodities, including oil and steel. By having to pay more for these imported goods, the U.S. is feeding rising costs into its economic system at its base.

The balance of trade has also turned against the United States in the last few years because the competitive ability of U.S. industry has declined as a result of the technological retardation of U.S. civilian industry, which is in turn a direct result of the military emphasis in the economy. Blaming the non-competitiveness of U.S. industry on the high wages of U.S. labor is nonsense. U.S. wages have been higher than wages in most of the rest of the world for 50 to 100 years, and until very recently the U.S. had no particular difficulty in competing in world markets.

The problem is that large numbers of engineers and scientists are required for the design and manufacture of military products. Estimates of the fraction of all U.S. engineers and scientists engaged in military and military-related work range from about 30 percent to about 50 percent. Pulling this many of them out of civilian work has devastating effects on the rate of civilian technological progress.

Civilian Technological Progress

Technological progress is critical to an economy's ability to offset the rising cost of inputs; that is, as wages, fuel prices, and the costs of raw materials rise, the only way product prices can be held down is to find more efficient ways of producing.

Technological progress is the result of setting engineers and scientists to work on particular problems to solve those problems and develop improved techniques. A large fraction of the engineers and scientists in this country have been working on military-related problems and looking for military applications and solutions, and that's exactly what they've found.

The U.S. is probably the most technologically advanced producer of nuclear submarines, ICBMS, etc., in the world. But when it comes to things like building trolley cars or better railroad cars or better housing, or even finding better techniques for producing steel, the U.S. is not as advanced as some other countries.

Deterioration of civilian technological progress has meant that much of U.S. industry has lost the ability to offset higher labor, fuel, and materials costs, which are passed along to consumers in the form of higher prices. This process has progressively priced U.S. industries out of world markets, and led to a worsening in the balance of trade. It has also priced U.S. industries out of the domestic markets.

In addition, engineering and scientific educational institutions have oriented their curricula toward training people for the available jobs. Military technology is highly specialized. It is so much at the frontiers of knowledge that it requires many people, each of whom is an expert in a very small area. This overspecialization is carried through into curricula, and now even the people who have been graduated from our major engineering schools, but who do not go into defense work, have not necessarily had the most appropriate kind of training for work in civilian technological development.

For example, in 1974 I met the president of an energy consulting firm which advises businesses in conserving energy. In 1974 his business was booming, and he wanted to hire more engineers to take care of this additional business. He put an ad in *The New York Times*.

He told me later that he thought he could have built a spacecraft with the people who applied for the jobs. The master designer of the solar panels on one of the major satellite systems asked for work. But my friend couldn't find anyone in that whole group who knew anything about the design or even the operation of an industrial boiler. In fact, one fellow said to him, "You mean they still use boilers in industry?" He finally got the energy engineers he wanted by importing them from Britain.

Clearly, the non-competitiveness of U.S. industry due to this technological retardation has not only generated inflation, but also unemployment. When U.S. industries lose markets, U.S. workers lose jobs.

The Solution: Conversion from Military to Civilian Orientation

Now, the question is what we do about this. A revitalization of U.S. industry is required, which takes a piece-by-piece conversion of U.S. industry from a military to a civilian orientation. This means putting serious money, labor, and technological resources into civilian activity. . . .

The benefits of carrying out such a conversion are substantial. It is no longer just an idealist's dream or a peacenik's vision. It is the only real hope of revitalizing the U.S. economy on a permanent and enduring basis, of getting us out of the economic mess in which we find ourselves.

DEFENSE SPENDING AND THE ECONOMY
U.S. Congressional Budget Office

The U.S. Congressional Budget Office (CBO) is a nonpartisan government agency that provides research and analysis to the Congress of the United States on important and controversial public policy issues.

Summary

The Administration has proposed a succession of large increases in the defense budget for fiscal years 1984 through 1988, following substantial increases over the last several years. The Administration's plan would increase real (inflation adjusted) budget authority for the Department of Defense (DoD) by about 6.9 percent annually for 1984–1988. The 1981–1983 growth av-

---

Source: U.S. Congressional Budget Office, "Summary," in *Defense Spending and the Economy* (Washington, D.C.: U.S. Government Printing Office, 1983), pp. xi–xvi.

eraged about 10 percent annually. The plan emphasizes investment (which includes weapons procurement, military construction, and research and development); after adjustment for inflation, growth in these investment accounts would average 13 percent a year for the entire 1981–1988 period.

When the United States has expanded its arsenals this rapidly in the past, it has also experienced a substantial increase in inflation. The inflation rate rose an average of 3.7 percentage points during the last four major military buildups. Some influential economists have warned that the currently proposed buildup could have similarly deleterious effects on inflation and on productivity.

The choice of appropriate levels of defense spending essentially is a question of priorities, reflecting assessments of the requirements for national security and evaluations of the importance of alternative uses of resources. This choice probably should not be influenced unduly by the effects of defense spending on the economy, since those effects can, in principle, be offset or achieved by other policies. It is, nonetheless, important to be mindful of the economic effects of defense spending, since that knowledge can help in shaping appropriate overall budgetary and monetary policies. This report helps to identify the effects of higher defense spending on inflation, employment, and productivity over the next several years.

Few Economic Risks from Buildup in the Short Term

According to the results of this study, the Administration's proposed defense buildup should neither rekindle inflation nor stunt employment growth over the next few years. This conclusion rests on an assessment of the near-term economic outlook, which is influenced by all aspects of federal budgetary and monetary policies.

Most macroeconomic forecasters currently foresee a sluggish cyclical recovery and continued economic slack that, together, will contribute to a continued gradual slowing of inflation during the next few years. The Congressional Budget Office (CBO) forecast, for example, projects that inflation, as measured by the implicit price deflator for gross national product (GNP), will decline from about 6 percent in calendar year 1982 to less than 5 percent in 1985. This outlook suggests that neither the military buildup nor the stimulative posture of overall fiscal policy should pose much risk of rekindling inflation in the near term. On the contrary, the risk that appears most acute is that growing deficits and tight credit conditions will choke off interest-sensitive spending, thereby stalling the recovery. . . .

Labor Availability. An evaluation of probable labor-market developments similarly shows no inflationary wage pressures. The defense buildup may contribute to future shortages of some scientists, engineers, skilled machinists, and tool-and-die makers—categories of workers that are heavily employed in defense production. But, in the next few years, these will be exceptional cases in a generally bleak labor market. Less than 3 percent of the work force falls into these categories, and current employment and unemployment data suggest that labor-market tightness is not pervasive even in these occupations.

Employment Growth. Increased defense spending should not adversely affect overall employment. Contrary to the assertions of some observers, the results of this analysis suggest that additional dollars spent on defense should provide more or less the same employment as additional dollars spent on most nondefense products. Simulations performed on econometric models suggest that an additional $10 billion in defense spending in fiscal year 1983 could create up to 250,000 additional jobs; the same $10 billion spent on purchases of nondefense goods and services could also create almost 250,000 jobs. An additional $10 billion spent entirely on defense purchases might induce an additional 210,000 jobs. The smaller effect from this added spending reflects the greater proportion of highly paid workers in defense industries.

Some Risks Posed by Buildup

Although the foregoing analysis suggests that the defense buildup should not contribute much to increased inflation or lower employment during the next few years, the buildup does raise some economic risks. These risks may grow as time passes and as more is known about the projected economic recovery.

INCREASES IN WEAPONS PRICES

Although bottlenecks in major defense-related industries seem unlikely, some may occur in smaller industries specializing in defense production. Such bottlenecks are unlikely to spawn widespread inflation, but they could drive up some weapons prices and increase the costs of the defense buildup.

Growth rates will be high in many specialized defense-intensive industries. After adjustment for inflation, median annual growth from calendar years 1983 to 1985 could be 7.5 percent in the 100 small industries that are most involved in defense production. This is more than double the 3.6 percent growth rate CBO projects for the economy as a whole. For some of these industries, annual real growth rates may run as high as 20 percent over these years. Production is currently depressed in many of these industries, however, and thus these high growth rates might not lead to bottlenecks.

Unfortunately, available data on industrial capacity are too aggregated to permit careful analysis of possible bottlenecks in these smaller industries. Nonetheless, when compared to production trends in the recent past, projected growth rates suggest that 36 of the 100 industries will be well above their production trends by 1987. These 36 industries include predominantly ordnance, aerospace, selected segments of the electronics and instruments industries, specialty metals, and metal fabrications important for defense, particularly forgings. Together, the industries that could be well above trend account for only 3.7 percent of GNP, which suggests that they would not contribute to widespread inflation. Defense production by these industries, however, accounts for 37 percent of all industrial defense production. This suggests that tightness in these industries could substantially raise defense weapons prices, but not the overall price level.

REDUCTIONS IN PRODUCTIVITY

The defense buildup could also adversely affect increases in productivity in the late 1980s. A strong surge in private demand for capital goods might occur in those years as a result of economic recovery, pent-up demands for business and consumer capital goods, and investment incentives embodied in current tax laws. In such circumstances, the proposed rapid increase in military spending on procurement, construction, and research and development (R&D) could contribute to shortages of capacity to produce capital goods and to shortages of industry engineers and scientists. Nondefense demands might be curtailed disproportionately in the resulting competition for limited resources, resulting in lower private investment and R&D and, hence, lower productivity. The associated imbalances in markets for capital goods and for technically trained personnel could contribute to a slowdown in economic activity that, in itself, could delay private-sector productivity gains. Note that these risks hinge on the possibility that shifts in demand might be unusually sudden or large, rather than on the theory that defense spending invariably retards productivity. The statistical evidence for this latter proposition is ambiguous.

INCREASED INFLATION THROUGH FASTER ECONOMIC GROWTH

The analysis thus far has assumed that the economy will recover sluggishly, in line with the CBO forecast. The future always holds surprises, however. If the private economy recovers more rapidly than currently forecast, then the proposed buildup could increase risks of renewed inflation and of crowding out of private borrowing in financial markets.

The economy might, for example, experience an average cyclical recovery. This would entail real GNP growth of more than 6 percent in 1983 and about 16 percent cumulatively for the 1983–1985 period, compared with the CBO forecast of only 2.1 percent in 1983 and about 11 percent cumulatively from 1983 through 1985. If this more robust recovery occurred, capacity utilization in manufacturing would edge above the 85 percent level associated with full employment by the end of 1985. Capacity utilization in each of the seven major, defense-intensive manufacturing sectors, except steel, would exceed historical averages by a wide margin. The outlook for business investment is particularly important. A surge in investment—which is characteristic of an average cyclical recovery—could overextend the high-technology industries which are already forecast to be operating at rather high rates in 1985.

SERIOUS RISK IN LONGER RUN IF BUILDUP FINANCED WITH DEFICITS

In the longer run, as the economy approaches full employment of resources, deficits caused by the defense buildup and other fiscal policies could pose a serious risk. Risks would derive, in part, from budget initiatives taken over the last two years. The Administration and the Congress have boosted defense spending while reducing tax burdens and curbing growth in nondefense spending. The combination of higher defense spending and lower tax revenues, even after offsetting tax increases in 1982, added more to the deficit than nondefense spending reductions cut from it. As a result, CBO projects that—without further Congressional action—the unified federal deficit will remain around $200 billion through fiscal year 1985 and increase to nearly $270 billion by 1988. Even measured at high-employment levels of income and employment, the deficit is projected to increase from $90 billion in fiscal year 1984 to $130 billion in 1985 and to more than $200 billion in 1988. This suggests that, without changes in current policies, fiscal policy will remain stimulative, with attendant inflationary pressures, as the economy approaches full employment.

The nature of the growing defense budget—with its emphasis on procurement—increases long-run concerns. The Congress, in appropriating money for defense procurement, commits funds years in advance of actual spending. Indeed, one dollar in an average defense procurement contract produces outlays of only about 12 cents in the first year, and outlays from that contract may continue over five years or more. If the Congress commits itself to high levels of defense procurement spending, it could have difficulty moderating fiscal stimulus in the future when the economy approaches full employment of resources.

These observations suggest that some combination of prospective reductions in defense or nondefense spending or increases in taxes are critical to avoid over-stimulating the economy after 1985. Without them, higher inflation would, in time, be likely. If inflation was restrained by monetary rather than fiscal policy, then high interest rates and sluggish economic growth would be probable.

Conclusion

The ultimate decision on procurement and other defense spending principally should depend on considerations of national security and priorities for the use of resources. Current forecasts suggest that the proposed rapid defense buildup need not rekindle inflation in the near term. The buildup could, nonetheless, contribute to tightness in some particular industries that do a great deal of defense work. This could raise risks of cost growth and delivery delays in weapons systems. Moreover, a defense buildup financed by large federal deficits that continue even after the economy recovers could damage economic performance in the longer run.

THE PSYCHOLOGICAL IMPACT OF THE NUCLEAR ARMS COMPETITION ON CHILDREN AND ADOLESCENTS
John E. Mack

Jack E. Mack, M.D., is Professor of Psychiatry at Harvard Medical School and a member of the American Psychiatric Association Task Force on the Psychosocial Impacts of Nuclear Developments. Among his many writings is the biography, *A Prince of Our Disorder: The Life of T. E. Lawrence,* for which he won the Pulitzer Prize in 1977.

INTRODUCTION

I wish to thank the Committee and its Chairman for the opportunity to speak with you this morning. This is a subject which, I expect, is disturbing for all of us, whether or not we have children of our own. Social psychologist M. Brewster Smith in an address delivered in Eugene, Oregon in October, 1982 noted how little research has been done "on the impact of the nuclear age on children and youth" considering "the human centrality and scientific interest of the issue." President Reagan in his address of November 23, 1982 on nuclear strategy expressed concern about "the effects the nuclear fear is having on our people." He described in particular upsetting letters "often full of terror" he was receiving from school children telling their fear of a nuclear holocaust. In my comments this morning I will summarize the information available to date on the impact of the nuclear threat on children and adolescents and offer some suggestions about further work that is needed.

Three types of study have been done to date: surveys given to a broad sample; more detailed questionnaires given to particular communities; and interview studies. In addition, there are media reports and films, and anecdotes reported by children and their families, teachers and others.

Source: John E. Mack, "The Psychological Impact of the Nuclear Arms Competition on Children and Adolescents," statement prepared for the Select Committee on Children, Youth, and Families, U.S. House of Representatives, *Congressional Record* (Sept. 20, 1983), pp. 47–51.

LARGE SCALE QUESTIONNAIRES

The only survey to address specifically the concerns of young people about nuclear war was conducted by Jerald G. Backman and his colleagues at the Institute for Social Research of the University of Michigan. From 1975 to 1982 they administered questionnaires to 16–19,000 seniors from 130 public and private high schools across the country. To the question "of all the problems facing the nation today, how often do you worry about the chance of nuclear war," Bachman found a fourfold increase from 1975 to 1982 of those who worry "often." Bachman and his co-workers also found a 61 percent increase during this period of those who agreed or mostly agreed with the statement "nuclear or biological annihilation will probably be the fate of all mankind within my lifetime." Psychiatrist Daniel Offer has been using self-administered questionnaires since 1962 to assess teenagers' views of themselves and their worlds. He found that the samples of young people in the early 1960's expressed more hope and a greater belief in the future than those questioned from 1979 to 1981, which may or may not be related to the nuclear issue as Offer did not ask specifically about it. Survey specialist Daniel Yankelovich, summarizing the available data in December, 1982, reported a mood of despair and gloom in Western Europe and the United States. He related this mood to "a sense of the future as being very threatening, as perhaps there not being a future, a future of grimness, of shortages, of greater difficulty, a closing in of horizons."

QUESTIONNAIRE STUDIES

The first questionnaire studies were performed by psychologist Sibylle Escalona and Milton Schwebel and were begun in response to the Cuban Missile Crisis. Both were published in 1965. Escalona examined 311 children from widely different socio-economic groups and ranging in age from 10 to 17. Schwebel sent questionnaires to 3,000 junior and senior high school students of various socio-economic backgrounds and asked questions such as "Do you think there is going to be a nuclear war?" "Do I care?" "What do I think of fallout shelters?" Both Escalona and Schwebel found a greater degree of fear of war and uncertainty about the future than they had anticipated. Escalona observed, "The profound uncertainty about whether or not mankind has a foreseeable future exerts a corrosive and malignant influence upon important developmental processes in normal and well-functioning children."

No studies performed between 1963 and 1977 have come to our attention. In 1977 the American Psychiatric Association appointed a Task Force to study the psychosocial impact of nuclear advances.

Among the subjects to be studied was the impact of nuclear developments on children and adolescents. One thousand one-hundred and fifty one

(1,151) questionnaires were administered to children from the 5th through 12th grades in the Boston, Los Angeles and Baltimore areas. More detailed responses were obtained from 75 children in two high schools in the Boston area where the examiners spent additional time in the classroom with the teenagers. The questionnaires were administered in 1978, 1979 and 1980. The results were gathered by Dr. William Beardslee and myself and published in the Task Force Report in 1982. Questions asked included, "what does the word 'nuclear' bring to mind?" "How old were you when you were first aware of nuclear advances?" "What do you think about Civil Defense?" "Do you think that you could survive a nuclear attack?" "Have thermonuclear advances influenced your plans for marriage, having children or planning for the future?" and, "Have thermonuclear advances affected your way of thinking? (about the future, your view of the world, time?)." The questionnaire underwent some revisions between 1978 and 1980 in order to facilitate quantitative scoring. Approximately 40 percent of the total group reported they were aware of nuclear developments before they were 12. Although the majority of the overall group studied thought that civil defense would not work, a considerable percentage considered it essential. Approximately 50 percent of the 1979 sample of 389 high school students reported that nuclear advances had affected their thoughts about marriage and their plans for the future. A majority reported that nuclear advances affected their daily thinking and feeling.

Among the more detailed responses of teenagers from high schools in the Boston area there were vivid expressions of terror and powerlessness, grim images of nuclear destruction, doubt about whether they will ever have a chance to grow up and an accompanying attitude of "live for now." Some expressed anger toward the adult generation that seemed to have so jeopardized their futures.

Beardslee and Mack, as Escalona had done before, raised questions about the impact of the nuclear threat on the development of personality. They wondered in particular about the effect of the formation of stable ideals or values, which depends upon a sense of human continuity and confidence in the future. They asked what happens to the formation of such ideals when the adult generation to whom young people turn for models, and to whom their futures are entrusted, cannot protect them and may even be seen as jeopardizing the future.

In the last two years there have been several additional questionnaire studies. High school senior Jon Klavens administered a modified version of the APA questionnaire to 950 students at Newton North High School in Newton, Massachusetts. Thirty-four percent of the students thought nuclear war would occur in their lifetime while 52 percent were unsure. Sixty-two percent thought the threat of nuclear war was increasing. Over half reported that the threat had affected their thinking about the future and their sense of time.

Family practitioner Stephan D. Hanna administered the APA questionnaire early this year to 700 11- to 19-year old students in the Akron, Ohio area. A higher percentage than in the Beardslee/Mack [study] associated the word nuclear with destructive imagery as opposed to peacetime uses. The intensity and pervasiveness of expressions of fear, helplessness and cynicism and anger toward the adult generation was also greater than in the APA study.

Psychologist Richard L. Zweigenhaft in conjunction with the Greensboro-Guilford County Emergency Management Assistance Agency administered a 51-item questionnaire in November 1982 to 938 adolescents and adults living in this area, including 372 high school students. Sixty-two percent of the total sample expected nuclear war to occur in their lifetimes while 66 percent were worried or very worried about the use of nuclear weapons. Sixty-three percent thought that nuclear war was prophesized in the Bible. The Greensboro-Guilford County study also disclosed troubling ignorance about fundamental nuclear realities. Only 70 percent of high school students knew which country has used nuclear weapons in war; 192 minutes was the mean estimate of how long it would take Soviet nuclear missiles to reach this country. There was much misinformation disclosed about what the post nuclear attack world would be like, although the great majority expressed the wish for more information.

In October 1982 Educators for Social Responsibility sponsored a day long symposium on nuclear issues called "Day of Dialogue." Many thousands of questionnaires containing questions similar to those in the initial APA study were distributed to high school students across the country. The results of 2,000 randomly selected responses were examined from among a larger number collected in Massachusetts, Wisconsin, Oregon and California. Eighty percent of those responding thought that there would be a nuclear war in the next 20 years and 90 percent of these reported that if such a war occurred, the world would not survive. Eighty-one percent said that the threat of nuclear war affected their hopes for the future, while 34 percent said it was having an impact on having a family or planning to get married.

Psychologist Scott D. Haas administered a questionnaire to students from four parochial private and public schools in the Hartford, Connecticut and Dearfield, Massachusetts area in which he attempted to separate the impact of the nuclear threat from other fears and concerns of adolescence such as the economy, employment and energy shortages. Although the nuclear issue was listed as the first concern more frequently than any other issue, less than half listed this first.

Psychologist Ronald M. Doctor and his co-workers at California State University have administered a questionnaire developed by pediatrician John Goldenring to 913 junior and senior high school students in Los Angeles, San Fernando Valley and San Jose areas. In order to overcome methodological bias, or disclosure of the examiner's agenda which takes place when specific questions are asked about the nuclear issue, these researchers have embedded the nuclear war question among twenty items. Doctor et al. found that 58.2 percent of the sample were worried or very worried about nuclear war, with this concern ranking fourth, behind a parent dying, getting bad grades and being a victim of a violent crime, but ahead of such matters as getting a job, parental divorce, pollution, cancer, world starvation and their own deaths. When asked their "greatest worry" the students ranked nuclear war second behind their parents dying.

INTERVIEW STUDY

The only interview research conducted to date is a pilot study conducted by psychology student Lisa A. Goodman with psychiatrist John E. Mack and coworkers at The Cambridge Hospital, Harvard Medical School. The purpose of the study was to begin to learn in greater depth how teenagers perceive the nuclear threat and to gain knowledge about their attitudes toward the political process.

Teachers, parents and counselors helped Goodman locate students from several communities in the Boston metropolitan area. Seventeen girls and fourteen boys ranging in age from 14 to 19 were interviewed in July and August 1982. The teenagers were from diverse religious and socio-economic backgrounds. As was revealed in the questionnaire studies, Goodman and her colleagues found widespread fear, sadness, helplessness, cynicism and anger among the teenagers. Each interviewee thought that nuclear war would come in his or her lifetime. Some seemed to live on two levels, planning as if there were a future, while believing nuclear annihilation to be inevitable. Civil defense was dismissed by all of these teenagers as useless, while none believed that a nuclear war would remain limited. Nuclear weapons seemed to offer little sense of security, although the interviewees would not wish to live in a situation where the Soviets had nuclear weapons and America did not. Some of these adolescents resisted stereotyping of the Soviet Union, acknowledging that they are "supposed to be our enemy." Some distinguish the Soviet government or "system" from its people. Both superpowers are held responsible for the arms race, which is perceived as dangerously out of control with a momentum of its own. Some see technology as having wrested control from man. One 15-year-old boy was unsure who would have responsibility for initiating a nuclear war. "I think that's who does it—a computer, or the President. I'm not sure. I think it's a computer." Many expressed the desire for more knowledge, especially about the Soviet Union. In offering solutions to the impasse these students emphasize better communication between the leaders of the superpowers and express the desire for a greater chance to participate in the decision-making process, which is also seen as a way of overcoming the sense of terror and helplessness.

ANECDOTES, MEDIA REPORTS AND FILMS

There is a steady flow of information which reaches researchers and others from newspaper and television reports, films and anecdotes relayed by word of mouth on the subject of children, adolescents and the nuclear threat. These data are often difficult to evaluate as sources because they have been selected to illustrate a point of view, or passed on because of their emotional impact on the person reporting or the anticipated impact on an audience. As a frequent "audience" myself of such reports, and an individual clearly concerned about this issue, I can only offer a few personal impressions. It seems that younger and younger children are expressing their fears about this issue. An eleven-year-old girl recently asked her parents if she would have time to commit suicide in the interval between learning that nuclear bombs were on the way and their actual detonation. Children as young as five and six are expressing fears to their parents and teachers about nuclear destruction and not growing up. Young children, ages 6–9, seem particularly afraid that they will be abandoned and left alone in a nuclear war, i.e., that they will survive while their family and friends are killed. This observation reminds us of the fact that reports of what children and adolescents express about the nuclear threat, especially in the case of pre-adolescent children, must be considered in relation to other developmental issues and concerns. Some children voice curiosity about what it is like to experience different age periods, as they do not expect to reach them themselves. The obsession with video games, in which nuclear destruction comes inevitably after a period of defensive success, seems to be both an effort to master the nuclear fear as well as a preparation for nuclear annihilation that is seem as inevitable.

CRITIQUE OF STUDIES TO DATE

The data available so far about what American children and adolescents think and feel about the threat of nuclear war is limited. There are methodological limitations in the size and percentage of compliance in the studies and in the age, geographic and socio-economic distribution of samples. The studies have been largely performed by people who are themselves personally concerned about this issue and may at times reflect a researcher bias.

There is only one pilot interview study with few on the way. There have been no studies devoted specifically to pre-teenage children. Questionnaire studies on an emotionally laden topic such as this suffer from the fact that the complex thoughts and feelings which the subject elicits can not be simply categorized. For example, many young people seem not to be involved by the nuclear threat. Does this mean they are truly not involved or are they defending themselves emotionally? Some children's concerns seem to be below the surface. An eleven-year-old boy in my neighborhood after he was interviewed by a teacher about his thoughts on the nuclear issue said that until that time he had not known "how much it was on my mind." One ninth grader in responding to a question as to whether the nuclear threat had affected his plans for the future wrote "No, No, No" in letters over an inch high. How are we to categorize such a response—as a yes or a no? Teenagers and young adults seem in record numbers to be moving ahead conscientiously to plan careers. Does this mean that they are not troubled about the future in the ways these studies suggest? Perhaps. On the other hand, Brandeis sociologist, Gordon Fellman, asked one of his students a few weeks ago why students are so conscientious these days about their work. "It's the only alternative to despair when the world can blow up at any moment," was the reply.

SUMMARY AND CONCLUSIONS

In summarizing I will set forth what I believe may be objectively concluded from the findings themselves and add to that interpretations and conclusions of my own that I believe may be derived from these data.

Summary of the Data

1. Many children in different parts of the country are concerned about the threat of nuclear war and experience troubling feelings of fear, sadness, powerlessness, and rage.
2. The meaning of this concern and its issues varies according to the developmental level of the young persons.
3. Worry about the nuclear threat has increased in the period 1975–1983, as the nuclear arms competition has appeared to become increasingly out of control.
4. An important part of this sense of things being out of control is the perception that authority for nuclear war has slipped out of human control and has been taken over by technology.
5. Children and adolescents seem less defended than adults and more able to perceive the reality of what nuclear weapons can do and what nuclear war would really mean for them, their families and the world.
6. There are great variations in the amount of information children and adolescents receive. Television appears to be the chief source of information.
7. Many children feel they have no one [with] whom they can discuss the nuclear problem. They feel alone with their fears and abandoned, isolated and unprotected by the adult generation, including their nation's leaders. This adds to the sense of hopelessness and creates cynicism.
8. Many young people express uncertainty about whether there will be a future. This futurelessness has raised questions for a number of investigators about the possible impact of the nuclear threat on personality

development in childhood and adolescence. There is no systematic data on this subject.

Personal Conclusions. The distress and questions of many of our children and adolescents should lead us to a broader consideration of security than that to which we have been accustomed. Security relates to a sense of certainty or uncertainty about one's safety and existence. It is, in this sense, a state of mind. From this point of view we are failing as a society to provide security for large numbers of our children. One can go further. We have left our children alone with this problem, to learn what they can from the media and each other. We have provided neither reliable information through our schools nor the opportunity for open and considered discussion with responsible adults— parents, teachers and religious, community and government leaders.

The problem of security in the nuclear age cannot be resolved by technological means alone, no matter how ingenious. The nuclear threat is largely the creation of human beings who cannot resolve their relationships with one another in the political realm. Our young people know this and they know too that the work of securing the future requires new ways of approaching relationships in the political and cultural domain, just as improvement in the emotional climate in a household is brought about by changing the quality of relationships among members of a family.

RECOMMENDATIONS

1. Further careful research is needed to learn about the impact of the nuclear arms competition on the children and adolescents.
2. Educational programs are needed which provide accurate information about nuclear science and technology and the political, historical and cultural realities of the arms competition, including the objective study of the history and psychology of enemies and potential enemies.
3. We need to create opportunities for young people to be able to talk about these troubling matters with responsible adults in their homes, and in their schools and communities, so they can participate appropriately in the national dialogue relating to nuclear weapons.
4. There is a need to broaden our conceptions of security to include considerations of health and, in the case of the impact of nuclear weapons on children and adolescents, psychological health and well being as well.
5. New approaches to achieving security are needed, which include examination of the dimension of human relationships in war and peacemaking in addition to purely military and technological considerations if we are to create for our children the confidence in the future, and the freedom from fear, which President Reagan called for in his speech a few months ago.

THE MEDIA: NUCLEAR SECRECY VS. DEMOCRACY

Robert Karl Manoff

Robert Karl Manoff is a contributing editor of *Harper's* magazine. Research for this article was supported by a Hibakusha Travel Grant Fellowship.

It is best to start at the beginning, and the beginning, of course, is Hiroshima. The world is quite familiar, I suppose, with what a primitive atomic device accomplished on the quiet and sultry morning of August 6, 1945, with how thousands of people simply disappeared in an instant, with the pictures of the city laid waste, with those blurry photos snapped from the suburbs by startled children and eager amateurs, those pictures that show, sometimes from a distance and sometimes from almost beneath it, that tremendous, churning, roiling cloud sucking up whole acres of the city now made into dust. And I suppose we are familiar with the silence of the grave that Hiroshima had now become, and with the scores of thousands of people, dazed, shattered, more animal than human in their instinct to flee, who picked themselves up, dug themselves out, and for hours afterward clogged the streets of the city with a procession of burned and bloody survivors, their skin hanging off them in giant rolls, begging for water, shuffling—trotting, those who could manage it—until they found the rivers of this delta city where they plunged or fell or waded in, there to drink and there, in the thousands and thousands, to die.

That, I suppose, is the familiar part.

What may be unfamiliar is the fact that quite literally before the dust had settled, before a hundred minutes had passed, three journalists who had escaped their death had paid a boatman, piled into his leaky vessel and had been rowed, the first argonauts of the atomic age, down one of those rivers so choked with the dead and dying that the boatman had difficulty getting his oar into the water. The three were named Nakamura, Katashima and Mayahara, and they were reporters for Domei, the Japanese news agency, whose motto, it should be noted, was "Patriotism Through Journalism."

I met Katashima in Hiroshima last summer [1983], and we talked about that day and about Nakamura, the bureau chief, who was his boss. "His priority was to get the story first," Katashima recalled. "In that sense he was a real

Source: Robert Karl Manoff, "The Media: Nuclear Secrecy vs. Democracy," *Bulletin of the Atomic Scientists* (January 1984), pp. 26–29. Reprinted by permission of the *Bulletin of the Atomic Scientists*, a magazine of science and world affairs. Copyright © 1984 by the Educational Foundation for Nuclear Science, Chicago, IL 60637.

reporter. He just told me to go out and write what I saw. We had no idea what had happened, so one of us thought of reporting that it was a new type of bomb." This is precisely the expression that Nakamura used when he patched together telephone lines and a radio connection to file the first story on the bombing of Hiroshima, less than three hours after it occurred. Two bombs, he told his Tokyo editors, floated down by parachute, had destroyed the city.

This is what Nakamura has said about his boat trip down the river:

> There were thousands of dead bodies bobbing all around. They were so burned and scorched that you couldn't even tell whether they were men or women. I thought I was floating down a river in hell. Suddenly a burnt arm stuck up out of the water and the hand grabbed onto the side of the boat. We couldn't ignore it and tried to pull it up. But the skin came off in sheets. It was a soldier, and he sank back into the river without his skin. Big fish were floating in the river, too. Multitudes were crying for help. I wanted to help them, but we couldn't. I asked their forgiveness in my heart, and we went on.

A photographer for the *Chugoku Shimbun*, Hiroshima's newspaper of record, was also looking for absolution that morning. Dazed but uninjured by the bomb, Yoshito Matsushige first saw to his family and then set out on an eight-hour odyssey through the city. By the end of it he had taken five pictures—the only ones taken in Hiroshima on the day of the blast—but he had taken none at all of the dead. He couldn't bring himself to shoot them, he told me, and the people he did shoot, after hours of walking around the city, he shot through a veil of tears and to the sound of his own prayers for forgiveness.

This was the extent of journalism in Hiroshima that day and for some days and months to come. The *Chugoku Shimbun* was wrecked, 113 of its 300 employees dead. It would not publish until November. And imagine this: All the paper in the city had been vaporized or burned. Journalism couldn't exist because there was nothing to write on. What was left of the newspaper staff just went into the streets to shout out the news. Journalism was one of the first casualties of the atomic bomb.

Journalism in Japan, and of course particularly in Hiroshima, has never been the same. The president of the *Chugoku Shimbun*, now the ninth largest newspaper in the country, describes his daily, using the Japanese word for those who survived the atomic bombing, as the world's first *Hibakusha* newspaper. The paper is overtly, proudly, persistently anti-nuclear. The news director of the Nagasaki Broadcasting Company tells me: "Nuclear weapons should not exist. That concept underlies all our activities." The managing editor of the *Asahi Shimbun*, the New York Times of Japan, launches a peace campaign and writes all foreign bureaus that the newspaper "must lead the way to the establishment of public opinion favorable to disarmament." Not all news executives feel this way, of course, but Japanese journalism as a whole has developed in response to the Japanese experience of nuclear war.

I believe the same is true of U.S. journalism: It, too, has been profoundly, deeply, lastingly influenced by the American experience of nuclear warfare. Our knowledge, however, unlike that of the Japanese, is indirect. We have never experienced the bomb, or, most of us, known anyone who has. We know what we are told. We know, after all is said and done, what we read in the papers. As a result, it seems to me, we don't appear to know very much. Henry Steele Commager noted last spring, for example, that the "pages of the [New York] *Times* erupt almost every day with eloquent and solemn discussions" about the advisability of a no-first-use policy, as though the question had not been answered "once and for all (and twice and for all) in August 1945."

We are talking here about habits of inquiry and discourse that were developed over 40 years ago, although the facts about the bombing of Japan were but the first of many that were to be mislaid in the great and rambling temple of American democracy. Such misadventures have shaped the American nuclear experience, and this is what is reflected in American nuclear reporting. Let me sketch what I have in mind:

- The Manhattan Project itself, conceived in wartime, established secrecy and internal security as one of its highest priorities. The atom bomb, in fact, became a symbol of success through secrecy.
- The U.S. mass media voluntarily censored all nuclear news during World War II. The term "atomic energy" did not appear in the U.S. press. Neither did the word "uranium." Neither did certain place names, such as Los Alamos, which either disappeared from the journalistic gazetteer or were never entered in it in the first place.
- The bombing of Hiroshima was managed as a modern media event. Seeking what he called an "objective touch" in his publicity materials, General Leslie Groves, commander of the Manhattan Project, borrowed William L. Laurence, the New York Times's Pulitzer-prize-winning science reporter, to supervise the writing of the president's announcement, all other official declarations and the pounds of press releases that were distributed at the August 6 press conference at which the bombing of Hiroshima was announced. All other communication about the event was expressly forbidden by the Secretary of War. In other words: Everything the American people learned about the bombing from its newspapers on August 7, and for days and weeks to come, had been prepared for it by the War Department, which set and controlled the journalistic agenda during those first crucial moments of the atomic age.

- Both the Japanese and U.S. governments, each for its own reasons, made immediate efforts to suppress details of the story. Nakamura's scoop, for example, did not get by the Japanese military censors. The next day's *Asahi Shimbun* merely reported that two B-29s had caused "a little" damage to the city. When it subsequently became clear that it would be impossible to deny the disappearance of Hiroshima, the story was allowed to break into the papers, but always to serve the government's particular political purposes: to warn, rouse, encourage the population and to excoriate the enemy.

  This has also been true of U.S. coverage. The bomb, it is important to remember, was a demonstration shot. It was meant to demonstrate to the Japanese that resistance was impossible, to the Soviets that world revolution was impractical, to the Allies that U.S. leadership was inevitable, and to the Congress, which had approved the $2 billion bill, and to the American people, who had paid it, that they had all gotten their money's worth.

  These were precisely the themes that most press accounts tended to support. More independent evaluations, it should be emphasized, were not encouraged. After the first Western journalist to enter Hiroshima reported, in the London *Daily Express* of September 5, that 30 days after the bombing, "people are still dying, mysteriously and horribly . . . from an unknown something which I can only describe as an atomic plague," General Douglas MacArthur's army of occupation tried to expel him from Japan and placed Hiroshima off limits to civilian journalists. All similar reports, pointing to what we now know was radiation sickness, were flatly and repeatedly denied. The idea that the bomb could continue to kill for days, weeks and months after it was dropped, was, the press reported to the American people, "Japanese propaganda."

- Finally, once the Occupation had taken full control of Japan, MacArthur's general headquarters promulgated a so-called press code which effectively banned all coverage of the devastation and suffering caused by the atom bomb. Under this code, both the manuscripts and finished copies of all printed material had to be submitted to the scrutiny of military censors. No sign of censorship was allowed to appear in the publications, and the censorship itself could not be mentioned. Sadako Kurihara, a writer whose work on Hiroshima ran afoul of the censors, remarked to me that the American democrats developed a far more sophisticated and successful censorship system than had the Japanese militarists they replaced.

  Writers such as Kurihara continued to create under the press code, even if they were unable to publish. Journalists, for their part, answering to a lesser calling, merely gave up. Denied access to the facts, the Japanese public was left in ignorance of its fate. The American public learned even less of the truth about life after nuclear war.

In general, then, where the Japanese had a direct experience of nuclear warfare, the U.S. experience was indirect and mediated by the U.S. press. The press, in turn, was dependent upon the government, responsive to its needs and sensitive above all else to the government's own perceptions of its interests. When, therefore, I repeat that American journalism has been deeply and lastingly influenced by the American nuclear experience, I mean to say that the American press, like the American people, has had neither direct experience of the facts nor the kind of freedom necessary to compensate for the absence of direct experience. American journalists cannot understand the commitment of Japanese journalists to real nuclear peace because we have never, most of us, been able to come to grips with the actual meaning of nuclear war.

The American nuclear experience has been shaped by inadequate knowledge and constrained inquiry. The entire nuclear regime, in fact, is both an organization of violence and an organization of knowledge. It is a system that maintains deterrence by mobilizing science, technology, industry and politics. But it is also a system that sustains itself by organizing the knowledge that all this other activity requires. The nuclear regime, in other words, has its own epistemological structure, its own set of possibilities for acquiring and disseminating knowledge. This structure was designed by the Manhattan Project, strengthened at the time of the Hiroshima bombing, and cemented every year since.

The cognitive possibilities structured by the nuclear regime have established what may be known and by whom; a definition of secrecy and accessibility; a politics of information and a media politics; concepts of what is and what is not expert knowledge, technical knowledge, general knowledge, and therefore concepts of what are technical decisions and what are political decisions, what are matters of technical competence, and what matters of general, popular, political competence. The epistemological structure defines fields of inquiry and determines their relationship one to the other. It sets the agenda for scientific and medical research. It establishes the limits and opportunities of journalistic initiative. It establishes priorities. It even establishes the criteria for determining what is and what is not fact, opinion and knowledge itself.

As it has developed over the last four decades, the actual epistemological structure of the nuclear regime is both rigid and restrictive. Since it is this structure that sets the parameters of knowledge in journalism, science and politics, I think we must conclude that the cognitive history of the nuclear era is the history of the relative restriction of socially available knowledge even as the possibilities for its expansion have in fact increased.

Thirty-eight years after Hiroshima, it is time to come to grips with the central political fact of modern American life: The epistemological structure of the nuclear regime is incompatible with the epistemological structure of democracy itself. Nuclearism and democracy embody antagonistic ideals of knowledge. They foresee different patterns for its dissemination. They contemplate entirely different consequences for social action and political participation.

This suggests a disturbing but unmistakable conclusion: The United States cannot long endure as both nuclear and democratic. This country cannot be nuclear and democratic at the same time, for one system is closed and the other is open; one system requires secrecy, the other, in the finest sense of the word, publicity; one system must concentrate control, the other exists in order to diffuse it.

Nuclear war or not, whether or not deterrence "fails" and precipitates Armageddon, or "succeeds" and condemns us to a permanent hair-trigger peace, whether or not our inventory of nuclear warheads is built up, or built down, whether or not it is to be the most pessimistic scenarios of nuclear proliferation or the most optimistic ones of arms control which are to be validated by history—regardless of what happens, this country has *already* been transformed by its absolute commitment, a commitment made years before most Americans were born and reaffirmed almost every month of their lives, to the waging and the winning of nuclear war.

Nuclear weapons have not been and will never be an inert presence in American life. Merely by existing they have already set off chain reactions throughout American society and within every one of its institutions. Journalism, the press, the media, the entire communications industry, have been no exception. Despite loose talk about adversary journalism, the press has proved exceedingly pliant in yielding to the requirements of the nuclear regime. During the war it killed the atomic story. It rewrote and printed the Hiroshima press releases. It dismissed the radiation story, just as the government told it to. It faithfully bought the idea that there was a single atomic secret to be guarded, that the Soviets would be a decade at least in discovering it, that the Super should be built, that the bomber gap existed, that the missile gap existed, and, later, that a vulnerability gap existed, that the Limited Test Ban Treaty was an arms control measure (when, as Alva Myrdal has pointed out, it did little but improve the drinkability of our milk), that Mutual Assured Destruction was really the operational targeting doctrine of U.S. strategic forces, that MIRVs were a good thing, that SALT II died because the Soviet Union invaded Afghanistan, and, until recently, that the MX was a necessary weapon, even if the basing-mode fiasco did have a certain comic quality (except, of course, that the people of Nevada weren't laughing).

Make no mistake about it: The press has become an essential component

in the epistemological apparatus of the nuclear regime. It has proved responsive above all to government news leadership and to the consensual nuclearism
of elite opinion. Grassroots movements do not interest the press until they
begin to throw their weight around and until those with real power begin to
take notice. On that day the grassroots story moves from the category of human interest to that of politics, and out of obscurity and onto page one.

Given the fact that an overwhelming majority of the American people
want real arms control, and given the fact that the U.S. government, over a
period of decades, has failed to produce it, it is only fair to conclude that
administration after administration, Congress after Congress, have passed, in
this respect at least, out of the control of their constituents. If I may para-
phrase what Oxford historian Michael Howard has written about World War
I, the government and the people of this country are now very nearly at cross-
purposes.

Not until this conflict has been resolved, not until democratic values
reassert their primacy over nuclear ones, will elite and governmental priorities
shift, and, along with them, the cognitive possibilities of science, politics and
the press. The journalism we get, in short, is the journalism we deserve. And
so we must be prepared to act in the midst of a paradox: A vibrant democracy
will produce a vibrant press that will make the vibrant democracy possible.

DETERRENCE: THE DEADLY PARADOX
Robert W. Gardiner

This selection is taken from Robert W. Gardiner's 1974 analysis of
the political, psychological, and moral implications of modern weapons
technology.

Since 1945, the existence of weapons of potentially unlimited destructiveness
has forced into the consciousness of nations the concept of weapons as instruments essentially for preventing rather than waging or winning of war. The
very magnitude of existing nuclear weapons threatens, in their prospective use,
a destruction so massive as to be unbearable. Hence their possession by the
great powers is assumed to impose upon them a deterrent factor of extremely
high efficacy: each side is "deterred" from using its own nuclear arsenal, or
from otherwise grossly overstepping the boundaries of acceptable international

Source: Robert W. Gardiner, "Deterrence: The Deadly Paradox," in *The Cool Arm of Destruction: Modern Weapons and Moral Insensitivity* (Philadelphia: Westminster Press, 1974), pp. 37–44. Copyright ©
1974 The Westminster Press. Reprinted and used by permission.

behavior, by the prospect of drawing upon itself a retaliatory strike of potentially unlimited devastation. Thus, in essence, the purpose of deterrent policy is, by *threatening* destruction, to *avoid* the necessity of imposing it. In other words, to reduce, to the zero point if possible, the likelihood of a general war by making general war too horrendous to be acceptable as a live option to either side.

Deterrence is by no means a new concept. All weapons contain a deterrence factor, since their possession threatens potential enemies with unwanted damage in the event of aggression. But deterrence has never in the past functioned with more than a limited efficacy. When the desired political objectives to be achieved from the initiation of armed conflict are accorded greater weight than the undesired costs entailed by such conflict, deterrence no longer deters. Like the threat of police action in a society, its major function has been to increase the cost of unacceptable behavior and thus to raise the boundary above which such behavior is likely to be attempted.

Nuclear deterrence, however, imposes a new factor: it radically escalates the cost of misbehavior. Both sides recognize that the massive destruction of their society is a consequence in which any conceivable objectives would simply be swallowed up. In this sense, nuclear deterrence "works": it motivates both sides to avoid initiating a major conflict that they recognize would destroy all the possible objectives in whose behalf such conflicts have traditionally been fought.

There has not been a general war since 1945. It is impossible to determine whether or not the policy of nuclear deterrence is solely responsible for this, since there is no way of empirically testing past events, yet it is possible that the inescapable danger of nuclear exchange contained in any direct military confrontation has caused the United States and Russia to avoid such confrontations. If so, the effect of nuclear deterrence has been to drive the conflict down to lower levels, where the danger of a nuclear response is less serious.

"Deterrence strategies," as Jerome Frank observes, "are intended to achieve a posture that without heightening international tension or provoking the adversary into further arming clearly signals determination to retaliate if he attacks." [1] The ideal deterrent, in other words, would find just that level of strength necessary to deter but not to provoke. It would be such as to indicate certain retaliation in the event of attack, but *only* in the event of attack. Needless to say, such an ideal deterrent has not been found. Even the best deterrent strategy available, within the boundaries of current imagination, contains built-in flaws which erode its viability as a permanent policy. Nuclear deterrence "works" in the short run, but I believe there is some question as to whether it will do so in the long run.

---

[1] Jerome Frank, *Sanity and Survival: Psychological Aspects of War and Peace*, p. 139.

The major limitation of all deterrence systems, nuclear or otherwise, is their tendency to deter and to provoke at the same time. They achieve their objectives by promoting on each side an awareness of itself as being threatened by the other. All such threats, explicit or implicit, promote a certain element of mutual mistrust. Each side is conscious of itself as targeted by the other's weapons, and neither side can ever be entirely certain what the other side will or will not do with those weapons. Thus the appeal of deterrence essentially is to fear, and through fear, to hostility. Deterrence requires for its successful functioning mutual perceptions that maintain bad relations and undercut the search for accommodation. Continuing bad relations, in turn, perpetuate the need to maintain the deterrent, thus leading to a self-reinforcing spiral. Continuing bad relations perpetuate the possibility of crisis, in which the danger of escalation is always present.

Thus there is a degree of instability in all deterrence systems. This instability is complicated by further instabilities inherent in the nature of modern technology. Weapons technology, like all modern technology, is itself unstable: it develops at an extremely rapid pace. Therefore the stalemate on which successful deterrence depends is always in danger of being upset. The fear that prevents each protagonist from initiating hostilities *also* impels him to reduce the threat to his own society by seeking to develop a deterrent of his own that will nullify that of his adversary. Each side, in the interest of its own security, must seek to make itself significantly less vulnerable than the other. Yet the very achievement of such an objective—actual or seeming— would be self-defeating, for it would substantially increase on both sides the pressure toward the *use* of the weapons hitherto deployed only for deterrence. The temporarily disadvantaged nation, in self-defense, would be tempted to strike before the first nation could exploit its advantage; the nation that made the breakthrough, seeing its temporary advantage, would be tempted to strike while that advantage was still its, or more probably because it feared that the other nation might strike in the fear that *it* would do so.[2]

Any human dynamic based on fear contains an element of paradox. Even as it "works," elements within it tend to sabotage its full success. Thus the effect of the nuclear deterrent has been, so far, to forestall direct U.S.-Soviet military confrontations, in the interest of more indirect, circumscribed methods of conflict. Yet the dangers of such conflict are enhanced by the continual temptation to persist more stubbornly in the pursuit of one's objectives, using

---

[2] It ought to be noted that the instability inherent in nuclear deterrence as such is in danger of being increased by the deployment of MIRVs (Multiple Independently Targetable Reentry Vehicles). Since it is, of course, much easier to knock out a single warhead than it is to knock out five or six, there is pressure, in the event of crisis, to destroy MIRVs while they are still on the launch pad and their multiple warheads are still contained in a single package. Thus the deployment of MIRVs is a provocative act, which increases the advantage of a first strike by the adversary.

the nuclear threat as a source of pressure toward their attainment. Thus, as John Bennett observes, it is often assumed

> that if we are resolute enough to make our deterrent credible, the other side will always yield. Much of the willingness to defend the use of nuclear weapons is based upon the assumption that if the people on our side show enough toughness, enough readiness to use them, they never will have to be used.[3]

Interestingly, this assumption works—at least it has worked so far (since we are still here). Yet the game is extremely dangerous, because it is a game that both sides can play. If "we" persist, in the assumption that "they" will yield, and if "they" persist, in the assumption that "we" will yield, the game can have only one possible conclusion. Thus the dynamic of this game is to invest even limited objectives with potentially unlimited consequences. Every confrontation becomes, potentially, a nuclear confrontation.

Moreover, success in playing this game could multiply the dangers inherent in it. It could lead to arrogance and recklessness. It could be resorted to with increasing readiness, in the interest of ever more limited objectives. Such recklessness is clearly the very opposite of the type of response that deterrence strategies intend.

Thus it is clear that while all forms of deterrence are to some degree paradoxical, nuclear deterrence, by its own special nature, is paradoxical in a fashion peculiar to itself. This paradox is derived from the potentially "absolute" nature of the weapons involved. Its effect is to introduce a grotesque disproportion between any possible objectives that might be sought or defended and the price that their attainment might require.[4] To limited political objectives (and all political objectives are limited) is attached a price tag that is potentially *un*limited. The price tag itself is paradoxical: to *avoid* paying it, we must be *willing* to pay it; and if we do end up having to pay it, we have thereby cancelled completely the objective on whose behalf it was paid.

Putting it another way: nuclear weapons, by their very dreadfulness, act as a powerful deterrent against major war; yet their very existence makes major war possible, and the dreadfulness which deters also insures that, if it comes, war will be that much worse than it otherwise would have been. Nuclear weapons, as a deterrent, function to preserve civilization from the scourge of

---

[3] John C. Bennett, *Foreign Policy in Christian Perspective*, p. 113.
[4] This is perceived, for example, even by Herman Kahn, who on one occasion wrote: "Aside from the ideological differences and the problem of security itself, there does not seem to be any objective quarrel between the United States and Russia that justifies the risks and costs that we subject each other to." Stanford Research Institute *Journal*, 1959, cited by Robert F. Drinan, S.J., *Vietnam and Armageddon: Peace, War and the Christian Conscience*, p. 159.

a major conflict; yet if deterrence fails and the nuclear weapons are used, "they will destroy all that their possession is intended to defend."[5] Thus the very instruments through which war is prevented would serve to make war, if it comes, so terrible as, in retrospect, to nullify the justice of the policy which, by seeking (unsuccessfully) to prevent it, had actually brought it about.

The paradox defined here may be translated into the language of social and political options by means of such questions as the following:

1. Is it right to defend valid social values by means of a policy which, if unsuccessful, is likely to destroy those values even more completely than they would have been destroyed with no defense at all?

2. Is it right to choose a policy involving (for the time being) a low risk of unlimited evil, as opposed to a policy involving the high risk of lesser evils?

3. Is it right to preserve *limited* values by incurring the risk of *unlimited* cost—especially when the cost must be carried by millions of people who have not been consulted about the choice?

4. Is it right, for the sake of its short-run benefits (if they *are* benefits), to pursue a policy that is likely to be *unsuccessful* in the long run—especially when there is no way of knowing just how long, or how short, that "long run" will be?

Questions of this kind expose rather concretely the moral paradox implicit in all nuclear deterrence strategies. It is a paradox because it links together two contradictory conditions: deterrence appears to be a genuinely moral option as long as it works; yet it can be said truly to work only if it works *perfectly*—only, that is, *if it never breaks down.* But that judgment can never be rendered, for the working of deterrence is always strictly a *past* event—there is no way of knowing whether, or how long, it will continue to work in the future. And its failure to work at some future date would, by destroying even more completely all that it had sought to defend, thereby have absolutely nullified any and all moral claims that it had made for itself up to that time.

The paradox of weapons whose *non*-use can be assured only by their readiness for *use* is ultimately a paradox of intention. Deterrence functions effectively only if we are able to communicate a willingness to *use* the weapons whose use deterrence is designed to *prevent.*[6] Thus, in order to prevent a war that both sides know is utterly disproportionate to any conceivable objective, we must be *willing,* if necessary, to launch such a war—and we must make certain that this willingness is well understood as an international fact. Such

---

[5] Bennett, *op. cit.,* p. 113.

[6] Most strategists believe that for such an expressed willingness to be fully credible it must be actual: a stated willingness that was not actual would be eventually detected, through security leaks, etc. See, for instance, Herman Kahn, *On Thermonuclear War,* p. 185.

a stated willingness entails two serious consequences: (1) It establishes the possibility that such a war could actually occur—thereby tending to sabotage the very purpose (i.e., deterrence) of the willingness itself. (2) It establishes, in the words of James Douglass, "an essential conflict between the apparently moral acts of deterring or limiting warfare and their fundamentally immoral means in the nuclear age: the intention to wage thermonuclear genocide."[7] Or, to put it more simply: an apparently moral act (deterrence) seems to require for its successful operation the maintenance and the vigorous proclamation of a grossly immoral intention (the intention, if necessary, to wage thermonuclear genocide).

I fail to see how the maintenance and the proclamation, by national states over a long period of time, of a grossly immoral intention can have any other effect than the morally corrupting one of enhancing the generally perceived legitimacy of such intentions as a normal dimension of policy. This, in fact, is precisely what has taken place. Thus, in the long run, the logic of nuclear deterrence has been to contribute to the spread of moral sensitivities that perceive the willing—and, by extension, the doing—of genocide as morally acceptable.

THE FATE OF THE EARTH
Jonathan Schell

Jonathan Schell is a staff writer for the *New Yorker*. What follows is an excerpt from his book, *The Fate of the Earth*. His other works include *The Village of Ben Suc*, *The Military Half*, *The Time of Illusion*, and *The Abolition*.

In recent years, scientists in many fields have accumulated enough knowledge to begin to look on the earth as a single, concrete mechanism, and to at least begin to ask how it works. One of their discoveries has been that life and life's inanimate terrestrial surroundings have a strong reciprocal influence on each other. For life, the land, oceans, and air have been the environment, but, equally, for the land, oceans, and air life has been the environment—the conditioning force. The injection of oxygen into the atmosphere by living things, which led to the formation of an ozone layer, which, in turn, shut out lethal ultraviolet rays from the sun and permitted the rise of multicellular organ-

---

[7] James W. Douglass, *The Non-Violent Cross: A Theology of Revolution and Peace*, p. 161.
Source: Jonathan Schell, *The Fate of the Earth* (New York: Alfred A. Knopf, 1982) pp. 91–96. Copyright © 1982 by Jonathan Schell. Reprinted by permission of Alfred A. Knopf. Originally appeared in the *New Yorker*.

isms, was only one of life's large-scale interventions. The more closely scientists look at life and its evolution, the less they find it possible to draw a sharp distinction between "life," on the one hand, and an inanimate "environment" in which it exists, on the other. Rather, "the environment" of the present day appears to be a house of unimaginable intricacy which life has to a very great extent built and furnished for its own use. It seems that life even regulates and maintains the chemical environment of the earth in a way that turns out to suit its own needs. In a far-reaching speculative article entitled "Chemical Processes in the Solar System: A Kinetic Perspective," Dr. McElroy has described the terrestrial cycles by which the most important elements of the atmosphere—oxygen, carbon, and nitrogen—are kept in proportions that are favorable to life. He finds that in each case life itself—its birth, metabolism, and decay—is chiefly responsible for maintaining the balance. For example, he calculates that if for some reason respiration and decay were suddenly cut off, photosynthesis would devour all the inorganic carbon on the surface of the ocean and in the atmosphere within forty years. Thereafter, carbon welling up from the deep ocean would fuel photosynthesis in the oceans for another thousand years, but then "life as we know it would terminate." Dr. McElroy also observes that the amount of ozone in the stratosphere is influenced by the amount of organic decay, and thus by the amount of life, on earth. Nitrous oxide is a product of organic decay, and because it produces nitric oxide—one of the compounds responsible for ozone depletion—it plays the role of regulator. In the absence of human intervention, living things are largely responsible for introducing nitrous oxide into the atmosphere. When life is exceptionally abundant, it releases more nitrous oxide into the atmosphere, and may thus act to cut back on the ozone, and that cutback lets in more ultraviolet rays. On the other hand, when life is sparse and depleted, nitrous-oxide production is reduced, the ozone layer builds up, and ultraviolet rays are cut back. These speculative glimpses of what might be called the metabolism of the earth give substance to the growing conviction among scientists that the earth, like a single cell or a single organism, is a systemic whole, and in a general way they tend to confirm the fear that any large man-made perturbation of terrestrial nature could lead to a catastrophic systemic breakdown. Nuclear explosions are far from being the only perturbations in question; a heating of the global atmosphere through an increased greenhouse effect, which could be caused by the injection of vast amounts of carbon dioxide into the air (for instance, from the increased burning of coal), is another notable peril of this kind. But a nuclear holocaust would be unique in its suddenness, which would permit no observation of slowly building environmental damage before the full—and, for man, perhaps the final—catastrophe occurred. The geological record does not sustain the fear that sudden perturbations can extinguish all life on earth (if it did, we would not be here to reflect on the subject), but it does suggest that sudden, drastic ecological collapse is possible. It suggests that life as a whole, if it is given hundreds of millions of years in which to recuperate and send out new evolutionary lines, has an astounding resilience, and an ability to bring forth new and ever more impressive life forms, but it also suggests that abrupt interventions can radically disrupt any particular evolutionary configuration and dispatch hundreds of thousands of species into extinction.

The view of the earth as a single system, or organism, has only recently proceeded from poetic metaphor to actual scientific investigation, and on the whole Dr. Thomas's observation that "we do not really understand nature, at all" still holds. It is as much on the basis of this ignorance, whose scope we are only now in a position to grasp, as on the basis of the particular items of knowledge in our possession that I believe that the following judgment can be made: Bearing in mind that the possible consequences of the detonations of thousands of megatons of nuclear explosives include the blinding of insects, birds, and beasts all over the world; the extinction of many ocean species, among them some at the base of the food chain; the temporary or permanent alteration of the climate of the globe, with the outside chance of "dramatic" and "major" alterations in the structure of the atmosphere; the pollution of the whole ecosphere with oxides of nitrogen; the incapacitation in ten minutes of unprotected people who go out into the sunlight; the blinding of people who go out into the sunlight; a significant decrease in photosynthesis in plants around the world; the scalding and killing of many crops; the increase in rates of cancer and mutation around the world, but especially in the targeted zones, and the attendant risk of global epidemics; the possible poisoning of all vertebrates by sharply increased levels of Vitamin D in their skin as a result of increased ultraviolet light; and the outright slaughter on all targeted continents of most human beings and other living things by the initial nuclear radiation, the fireballs, the thermal pulses, the blast waves, the mass fires, and the fallout from the explosions; and, considering that these consequences will all interact with one another in unguessable ways and, furthermore, are in all likelihood an incomplete list, which will be added to as our knowledge of the earth increases, one must conclude that a full-scale nuclear holocaust could lead to the extinction of mankind.

To say that human extinction is a certainty would, of course, be a misrepresentation—just as it would be a misrepresentation to say that extinction can be ruled out. To begin with, we know that a holocaust may not occur at all. If one does occur, the adversaries may not use all their weapons. If they do use all their weapons, the global effects, in the ozone and elsewhere, may be moderate. And if the effects are not moderate but extreme, the ecosphere may prove resilient enough to withstand them without breaking down catastrophically. These are all substantial reasons for supposing that mankind will not be extinguished in a nuclear holocaust, or even that extinction in a holocaust is unlikely, and they tend to calm our fear and to reduce our sense of urgency. Yet at the same time we are compelled to admit that there *may* be a holocaust, that the adversaries *may* use all their weapons, that the global effects, including effects of which we are as yet unaware, *may* be severe, that the ecosphere *may* suffer catastrophic breakdown, and that our species *may* be extinguished. We are left with uncertainty, and are forced to make our decisions in a state of uncertainty. If we wish to act to save our species, we have to muster our resolve in spite of our awareness that the life of the species may not now in fact be jeopardized. On the other hand, if we wish to ignore the peril, we have to admit that we do so in the knowledge that the species may be in danger of imminent self-destruction. When the existence of nuclear weapons was made known, thoughtful people everywhere in the world realized that if the great powers entered into a nuclear-arms race the human species would sooner or later face the possibility of extinction. They also realized that in the absence of international agreements preventing it an arms race would probably occur. They knew that the path of nuclear armament was a dead end for mankind. The discovery of the energy in mass—of "the basic power of the universe"—and of a means by which man could release that energy altered the relationship between man and the source of his life, the earth. In the shadow of this power, the earth became small and the life of the human species doubtful. In that sense, the question of human extinction has been on the political agenda of the world ever since the first nuclear weapon was detonated, and there was no need for the world to build up its present tremendous arsenals before starting to worry about it. At just what point the species crossed, or will have crossed, the boundary between merely having the technical knowledge to destroy itself and actually having the arsenals at hand, ready to be used at any second, is not precisely knowable. But it is clear that at present, with some twenty thousand megatons of nuclear explosive power in existence, and with more being added every day, we have entered into the zone of uncertainty, which is to say the zone of risk of extinction. But the mere risk of extinction has a significance that is categorically different from, and immeasurably greater than, that of any other risk, and as we make our decisions we have to take that significance into account. Up to now, every risk has been contained within the frame of life; extinction would shatter the frame. It represents not the defeat of some purpose but an abyss in which all human purposes would be drowned for all time. We have no right to place the possibility of this limitless, eternal defeat on the same footing as risks that we run in the ordinary conduct of our affairs in our particular transient moment of human history. To employ a mathematical analogy, we can say that although the risk of extinction may be fractional, the stake is, humanly speaking, infinite, and a fraction of infinity is still infinity. In other words, once we learn that a holocaust *might* lead to extinction we have no right to gamble, because if we lose, the game will be over, and neither we nor anyone else will ever get another chance. Therefore, although, scientifically speaking, there is all the difference in the world between the mere possibility that a holocaust will bring about extinction and the certainty of it, morally they are the same, and we have no choice but to address the issue of nuclear weapons as though we knew for a certainty that their use would put an end to our species. In weighing the fate of the earth and, with it, our own fate, we stand before a mystery, and in tampering with the earth we tamper with a mystery. We are in deep ignorance. Our ignorance should dispose us to wonder, our wonder should make us humble, our humility should inspire us to reverence and caution, and our reverence and caution should lead us to act without delay to withdraw the threat we now pose to the earth and to ourselves.

In trying to describe possible consequences of a nuclear holocaust, I have mentioned the limitless complexity of its effects on human society and on the ecosphere—a complexity that sometimes seems to be as great as that of life itself. But if these effects should lead to human extinction, then all the complexity will give way to the utmost simplicity—the simplicity of nothingness. We—the human race—shall cease to be.

FOR FURTHER READING

Adelson, Joseph, and Chester E. Finn, Jr. "Terrorizing Children." *Commentary* 69:4 (April 1985), pp. 29–36. A response to the Congressional hearing which heard statements from psychiatrist John Mack and others. Adelson and Finn argue that data used to support the conclusion (that psychological trauma was real and serious) were methodologically flawed and that the "experts" were motivated by their political sympathies.

Davidson, Donald L. *Nuclear War and the American Churches: Ethical Positions on Modern Warfare.* Boulder, Colo.: Westview Press, 1984. A useful overview and analysis of ethical issues and perspectives.

Dwyer, Judith A., ed. *The Catholic Bishops and Nuclear War: A Critique and Analysis of the Pastoral Letter, The Challenge of Peace.* Washington, D.C.: Georgetown University Press, 1984 (paperback).

Escalona, Sibylle. "Growing Up with the Threat of Nuclear War: Effects on Personality Development." *American Journal of Orthopsychiatry* 52 (October 1982). An important article, written by a child development authority who has studied this issue for more than twenty years. (There are several other valuable and relevant articles in this special issue.)

Falk, Richard. "Nuclearism and the End of Democracy." *Harvard International Review* 5 (May/June 1983), pp. 21–24. Analyzes antidemocratic implications of nuclear weapons.

Ford, Harold P., and Francis X. Winters, eds. *Ethics and Nuclear Strategy?* Maryknoll, New York: Orbis Books, 1977. An indispensable collection of articles, critically analyzing the moral dimensions of nuclear weapons and exploring alternatives to present policies.

Gardiner, Robert. *The Cool Arm of Destruction: Modern Weapons and Moral Insensi-*

tivity. Philadelphia: Westminster Press, 1974. An excellent appraisal of moral, cultural, and psychological dimensions of nuclear weapons. Especially recommended are Chapters 3 and 5: "Deterrence: The Deadly Paradox," and "Horror Domesticated: The Semantics of Megadeath," respectively.

Glynn, Patrick. "Why an American Arms-Buildup is Morally Necessary." *Commentary* (Feb. 1984), pp. 17–28. Criticizes the peace movement and advocates more weapons to contain the Soviet menace.

Kattenburg, Paul M. "MAD is the Moral Position." In Charles W. Kegley, Jr., and Eugene R. Wittkopf, eds. *The Nuclear Reader: Strategy, Weapons, War.* New York: St. Martin's Press, 1985 (paperback). Argues that warfighting and winning strategies are immoral.

Kovel, Joel. *Against the State of Nuclear Terror.* Boston: South End Press, 1983 (paperback). Argues that Americans' awareness of the nuclear threat and capacity to respond effectively to it have been insidiously weakened by antidemocratic aspects of national security policy formation and implementation.

Miller, Richard. "Catholic Bishops on War." *Bulletin of the Atomic Scientists* 39 (May 1983), pp. 9–13. A concise and generally favorable analysis of the Catholic Bishops' Pastoral Letter on war and peace.

National Conference of Catholic Bishops. *The Challenge of Peace: God's Promise and Our Response.* Washington, D.C.: United States Catholic Conference, 1983. The controversial statement on moral aspects of nuclear weapons.

Novak, Michael. *Moral Clarity in the Nuclear Age.* Nelson, 1983 (paperback). A critical response to the Catholic bishops by a well-known conservative Catholic thinker.

Ostling, Richard. "Bishops and the Bomb." *Time* (Nov. 29, 1982), pp. 68–77. An excellent journalistic account of the evolution and provisions of the Bishops' Pastoral Letter.

Sivard, Ruth Leger. *World Military and Social Expenditures 1984.* Leesburg, Va.: World Priorities, 1984. Published each year, Sivard's invaluable compendium compares the escalating worldwide spending on conventional and nuclear weapons with the growing problem of unmet human needs.

Speath, Robert L. *No Easy Answers.* Winston Press, 1983 (paperback). A critique of the Bishops' Pastoral Letter by a noted Catholic theologian.

Stanmeyer, William. "Toward a Moral Nuclear Strategy." *Policy Review* 21 (Summer 1982), pp. 59–71. Warns about the pitfalls of pacificism in the face of Soviet imperialism and argues that mutually assured destruction is immoral and that counterforce capability and an ABM defensive strategy are moral.

Task Force on Psychosocial Aspects of Nuclear Developments. *Psychosocial Aspects of Nuclear Developments.* Washington, D.C.: American Psychiatric Association, 1982. Includes, among others, articles on "The Impact on Children and Adolescents of Nuclear Developments," "Soviet-American Relations Under the Nuclear Umbrella," and "Nuclear Weapons and Secrecy."

Thomas, Lewis. *Late Night Thoughts on Listening to Mahler's Ninth Symphony.* New York: Viking, 1983. In the title essay, noted physician Thomas questions how the omnipresent a.id inescapable danger of nuclear war will affect the mental health of young persons.

Wohlstetter, Albert. "Bishops, Statesmen, and Other Strategists on the Bombing of Innocents." *Commentary* (June 1983), pp. 15–33. An important critical response of the Pastoral Letter and analysis of ethical and political dimensions of nuclear weapons.

Yudkin, Marcia. "When Kids Think the Unthinkable." *Psychology Today* (April 1984), pp. 18–25. An overview of recent studies of psychological impacts of the nuclear threat on children and adolescents. Includes important data on interviews with Soviet youth.

12

Current Proposals to Reduce the Threat of Nuclear War

There are as many ways to prevent a nuclear war as there are to start one. This much is suggested by our first article, "Thinking About Preventing Nuclear War." The authors are Ground Zero, a public education organization, and they identify six "doomsday scenarios" only to respond by identifying five separate approaches to *preventing* nuclear war. All of the approaches merit attention. They are: (1) improved relations among countries (especially between the Soviet Union and the United States), (2) arms control, (3) nuclear nonproliferation (controlling the spread of nuclear weapons to other countries), (4) improved techniques for conflict resolution, and (5) better systems for crisis communications.

However, four of the five approaches will not be examined here—beyond the discussion they receive from the Ground Zero authors—so that this final chapter can focus on the future of U.S.-Soviet efforts to control nuclear arms. Included in this narrower focus will be President Reagan's proposal for a Strategic Defense Initiative (or what some have dubbed "Star Wars"). And despite the limited focus of this chapter, we will find the discussion more than once centering on the relationship between U.S. national security and global or planetary security.

The first half of the 1980s has seen popular concern about nuclear war and the future of arms control with the Soviet Union swell to remarkable and unprecedented proportions in the United States. For the first time, a broad-based public movement, with its demand for progress in reducing the threat of nuclear war, has become a prominent political force in discussions of national nuclear weapons policy.

In part, this upsurge represents an anxious popular reaction to the shift towards a nuclear war-fighting posture in U.S. strategic policy. As we have seen, this shift began with the revelation of Presidential Directive 59 in the last few months of the Carter Administration, and has continued into the next with loose talk by Reagan officials about "nuclear warning shots" (former Secretary of State Alexander Haig), "limited nuclear war" in Europe (President Reagan), and "prevailing" in strategic nuclear war (Secretary of Defense Weinberger). Public agitation is also rooted in a widespread perception that past efforts to curtail nuclear arms have been inadequate. The superpowers' arsenals, as we learned in Chapter 6, have grown enormously since the inception of the SALT process in 1969. SALT has failed as well to significantly arrest potentially destabilizing qualitative changes like MIRV and improved missile accuracy.

The United States' failure to ratify the SALT II treaty in 1979, and the Reagan administration's decision to pursue its ambitious "Strategic Modernization Program" have also contributed to popular dissatisfaction with previous arms control efforts, and have fed public anxieties about an increased risk of nuclear war. By the early 1980s, many people felt the time had come to break with the past and make a serious push for U.S.-Soviet arms limitations that would significantly reduce the risk of nuclear war and the costs of the arms race.

The Nuclear Weapons Freeze Campaign—the grass roots political organization which surged to national prominence during this period—became the most visible element of this popular movement against nuclear war. To growing numbers of Americans, "the freeze" represented a concrete proposal designed to directly address the dangers and costs of the nuclear arms race. Drafted in 1980 by Randall Forsberg, a former researcher at the Stockholm International Peace Research Institute, the original "Call to Halt the Nuclear Arms Race" proposed that the Soviet Union and the United States halt or "freeze" the production, testing, and deployment of all new nuclear weapons systems. As popular enthusiasm for the freeze spread nationally, Congressional interest in the proposal grew. In March 1982, Senators Edward Kennedy and Mark Hatfield introduced the freeze proposal as a formal resolution in Congress. Although the Kennedy-Hatfield resolution was defeated in August 1982 in the House of Representatives by the slim margin of 204–202, it later came up for another vote and passed. Just as importantly, local freeze referendums in the 1982 national election gathered the support of over 60 percent of those voting in them. By 1984, freeze supporters had succeeded in making nuclear war and the freeze a central issue in the Presidential race between Ronald Reagan and his unsuccessful challenger, Walter Mondale.

In the "Case for a Freeze," Kennedy and Hatfield explain the rationale for a comprehensive halt to further nuclear weapons production, testing, and deployment by the Soviet Union and the United States. At root, they argue that a freeze would do a much better job of achieving the traditional goals of arms control than has the U.S.-Soviet SALT process. In addressing the risk of nuclear war, for example, they point out that the freeze would inhibit or arrest many of the qualitative weapons improvements—like the development of highly accurate, "counterforce-capable" ballistic missiles—that SALT did not. In addition, a freeze would also reduce the burdens of maintaining security, by releasing some 18 billion dollars a year (as they estimated in 1982) that would otherwise be spent on nuclear weapons. That money could be put to use in addressing other national problems.

Kennedy and Hatfield also stress that a freeze would not weaken

U.S. security. By virtue of the large inventory of invulnerable nuclear warheads currently deployed by the United States—warheads which would survive even a "worst case" Soviet first strike—a freeze would preserve an adequate U.S. deterrent to Soviet nuclear attack. A freeze would also be verifiable, they argue, because the testing and deployment of weapons is readily discernible through "national technical means" (satellite and other forms of remote, nonintrusive reconnaissance). Moreover, the Soviets have indicated that they might accept some forms of "on-site inspection." Finally, the comprehensive character of the freeze would make significant violations easier to detect than in past SALT agreements.

Pressured by burgeoning popular and Congressional support for the freeze, the Reagan administration responded in 1981 and 1982 with negotiating proposals for reductions in strategic arms and the so-called Zero Option for intermediate nuclear forces in Europe. At the same time, the administration minced no words in criticizing the central assumptions of freeze supporters. Christopher Lehman, a Reagan State Department official, outlines the Administration's objections in "Arms Control Versus the Freeze."

A central weakness of the freeze, Lehman argues, is that contrary to the assertions of Senators Kennedy and Hatfield, it would not preserve an adequate U.S. deterrent capability. In addition, Lehman argues that a freeze would undermine the administration's efforts to obtain arms reductions in strategic arms and force the United States to unilaterally renounce the Pershing II and GLCM deployment "track" of NATO's 1979 "two-track" decision, without gaining corresponding reductions in Soviet SS-20 IRBMs facing Western Europe. Finally, Lehman contends that an across-the-board freeze would be unverifiable, which, because the Soviets could covertly develop new weapons while the U.S. could not, would undermine U.S. security all the more.

Out of the debate between the administration and its Congressional supporters on the one hand, and Congressional advocates of the freeze and their grass roots supporters on the other, a new proposal emerged, put forward by a group of self-styled "moderates" in Congress. That proposal—for a "guaranteed build-down" of nuclear forces—represented an effort to reconcile the Reagan administration's desire to completely overhaul and substantially enhance U.S. nuclear forces with the widespread and intense demands on Congress for tangible progress in arms control. Under the "build-down" concept, various forms of which were proposed in the Congress and considered by the administration, each side would be free to deploy new systems. The catch would be that for each new strategic nuclear warhead a country deployed, it would be obligated to eliminate two warheads from its existing arsenal. Modernization for both countries, in other words, would come at the price of reductions in its inventory of strategic warheads. In theory, each side would be encouraged to replace existing vulnerable, land-based multiple warhead missiles with newer, single warhead missiles. Supporters argued that this would discourage a first strike by reducing the number of warheads that could be destroyed in attacking an individual missile silo. More importantly, it would also reduce the number of warheads that would *be available* for carrying out an attack, eventually creating an "unfavorable exchange ratio," in which an attack would consume more missile warheads than it would succeed in destroying. In this way, build-down advocates claimed, each country would be free to modernize its forces in a way that contributes to crisis stability and reduces the risk of nuclear war.[1]

Critics were quick to point out, however, that the "build-down" concept had a fundamental weakness: namely, that reductions would only be achieved if each side deployed new weapons, and there would be no guarantee that these new weapons would have a stabilizing effect on the nuclear balance. Thus, build-down critics like Christopher Paine argued that a reduction in American strategic forces under a build-down, if it were achieved through the introduction of the MX and "Midgetman" ICBMs, and the Trident I and Trident II SLBMs, could include several thousand accurate missile warheads capable of destroying Soviet land-based missile silos. A similar evolution could take place in Soviet forces under a build-down, resulting in a substantial reduction in the survivability of retaliatory forces on both sides. Paine thus argued that a build-down could actually *undermine*—rather than *enhance*—strategic stability.[2]

In the aftermath of Ronald Reagan's successful bid for reelection, the freeze–reductions–build-down debate has subsided. Public attention has now come to focus on President Reagan's March 1983 proposal that the United States initiate a long-term anti-ballistic missile research program, looking toward future development and deployment of a defensive system designed to *shield* U.S. society from ballistic missile attack. According to administration spokespersons, the "Strategic Defense Initiative," or "Star Wars" as it is often referred to by its detractors, could allow the United States to adopt a more humane strategic policy. In "Strategic Defense and U.S. National Security," for example, Secretary of Defense Caspar Weinberger contends that adequate defenses against a Soviet nuclear attack would permit the U.S. to radically alter its basic deterrent policy. Threatening offensive retaliation in response to an attack, he argues, could be replaced by a policy in which deterrence would be based on the United States' capacity to destroy Soviet missiles after they are launched, and before they reach their targets in the United States. The President's hope, according to Weinberger, is that U.S. defenses would (eventually) so reduce the potency of Soviet missiles that the Soviets would be willing to drastically reduce their missile forces in arms reduction negotiations with the United States. Ultimately, contends Weinberger, if the Strategic Defense Initiative (SDI) bears fruit, it could produce a strategic environment in which neither superpower is vulnerable to attack, and the world is eventually free of the threat of nuclear arms.

In "Ballistic Missile Defense: A Strategic Issue," Robert Bowman presents a much more skeptical view of the SDI. Bowman, a retired Air Force officer who managed the Pentagon's ABM research programs in the mid 1970s, believes that a concerted push for a ballistic missile defense system by the United States, as envisioned in the SDI, would increase

---

[1] The evolution of the build-down concept and its strategic merits are described in the article by Alton Frye listed in the suggested readings for this chapter.
[2] Paine's arguments are presented in his article listed in the suggested readings for this chapter.

the risk of nuclear war. It would also fail to provide any greater protection for the U.S. population in the case of a Soviet nuclear attack.

Bowman argues that each of four foreseeable BMD postures would either undermine crisis stability or prove to be unnecessary. Take, for example, the goal originally stated by President Reagan in his March 1983 speech: to develop a "leakage-proof" system of defenses that would allow only one or two Soviet weapons to penetrate to their targets in the United States. This is impractical and could be dangerous, Bowman argues. Developing such a system would confront staggering technological obstacles. Even if these imposing goals are reached, he argues, the Soviets could easily nullify the effectiveness of such a system through the use of countermeasures. The second problem is that an effort by the United States to develop a leakage-proof defense would probably be interpreted by the Soviets as an attempt by the U.S. to develop a first-strike capability. Given the current emphasis in U.S. doctrine on counterforce, and the plans to deploy the Pershing II, MX, and Trident II ballistic missiles, the Soviets will have difficulty distinguishing between a BMD system designed to *replace* deterrence and one which is intended to *enhance* a U.S. first-strike posture. This, he argues, could increase the risk of a nuclear war, by leading the Soviets to adopt a launch on warning or preemptive attack policy in a crisis. An alternative would be to develop a ballistic missile defense system which could protect U.S. deterrent forces, as opposed to U.S. society. Yet, as Bowman points out, we probably don't *need* a BMD system to guarantee a survivable deterrent. Current U.S. retaliatory forces, he argues, are sufficient to pose a convincing threat of retaliation *without* the additional protection afforded by BMD. Given these prospects, Bowman concludes that the SDI should be scaled back to a basic research program, and the United States should continue to rely on deterrence to prevent nuclear war with the Soviet Union.

THINKING ABOUT PREVENTING NUCLEAR WAR
Ground Zero

Ground Zero is a nonpartisan public education organization based in Washington, D.C., that deals primarily with issues related to the dangers of nuclear war. Among its other publications are *Nuclear War: What's In It For You?* and *What About the Russians and Nuclear War?*

Imagine a bomb with a large number of separate fuses, each of them capable of independently detonating the bomb. That is the situation we face today in

Source: Excerpted from Ground Zero, *Thinking About Preventing Nuclear War* (Washington, D.C.: Ground Zero Fund, Inc, 1983).

confronting the threat which nuclear war poses to our lives and to our planet. There is not just *one* way that nuclear war might occur but instead *many* ways. And it is critically important that we recognize this fact as we attack the problem of preventing nuclear war.

There are *six* generic paths or sequences of events (nuclear strategists call these scenarios) that might culminate in an all-out nuclear war or "general" nuclear war, as it is sometimes called.

The six doomsday scenarios are:

1. **Bolt from the Blue:** A Pearl-Harbor-type surprise nuclear attack is launched by the Soviet Union against the U.S.—or vice versa.

2. **Escalation in a European Conflict:** A conventional war with the Soviets in Europe escalates to the point where nuclear weapons are used, and the conflict then continues to build to all-out nuclear war between the superpowers.

3. **Escalation in a Third World Conflict:** A future Third World conflict reaches the point where one of the Third World countries involved in the conflict uses nuclear weapons against another. As the "nuclear war" escalates, the U.S. and the Soviet Union are drawn in and ultimately turn upon one another with nuclear weapons. Alternately, the Third World conflict involves only conventional weapons, but the U.S. and the Soviet Union are drawn in and use nuclear weapons as escalation gets out of control.

4. **Escalation after a False Alarm:** A crisis and eventually nuclear war results from the mistaken belief that one side has launched nuclear weapons against the other.

5. **Escalation after Terrorist Use of Nuclear Weapons:** A terrorist attack with nuclear weapons leads to chaos and confusion. The crisis escalates and eventually nuclear weapons are exchanged by the superpowers.

6. **Escalation after Accidental or Unauthorized Use of Nuclear Weapons:** Nuclear weapons are launched either accidentally or by someone who does so without proper authority (that is, without the authorization of a head of government or military commander).

As suggested [on the cover of Ground Zero's original booklet], each of these scenarios corresponds to one fuse on the nuclear bomb. Not surprisingly, experts believe that some of the fuses are more easily ignited than others. For instance, most (but not all) experts currently believe that for the foreseeable future—the next decade or so—the most likely of the six generic routes to nuclear war would be a Third World crisis in which the superpowers are gradually drawn into the conflict. On the other hand, it wasn't long ago that there was much more concern about escalation in a European conflict. At the same time the public is often led by the rhetoric in debates over strategic weapons and strategic nuclear arms control to focus their concerns on the bolt-from-the-blue scenario.

Clearly it is important to try to identify which of the "fuses" is most dangerous so that we can allocate more time and energy to the greatest threat—and to this end both expert *and* public opinion on the most likely route to nuclear war is useful. Since we have no experience on how nuclear war might begin, however, we must view each of the six routes to nuclear war as a very real possibility. Furthermore, the stakes are so high that we cannot afford to relax our efforts until we are confident that nuclear war cannot occur through *any* of these scenarios.

Firebreaks—Snuffing out the Fuse

Having identified the six generic scenarios by which nuclear war might occur, we must now ask ourselves how we are going to insure that no one of them ever leads to nuclear war. What are the tools available to us—the policies, practices, weapons agreements, relationships, etc.—that might be employed to prevent the scenarios from starting in the first place or, once started, from escalating to higher and higher levels and eventually reaching general nuclear war?

Using our six-fused nuclear bomb analogy, the challenge we face is to prevent the fuses from being lit or, if any one of them is lit, to insure that it cannot burn all the way to the bomb. Thus what we seek can be compared to the "firebreaks" used to halt the spread of forest fires. By knocking down a wide area of trees and bulldozing away brush from the path of the forest fire, firefighters seek to prevent the fire from racing totally out of control. In the same manner, we might view nuclear war prevention efforts as attempts to cut effective "firebreaks" along the paths of our six fuses, lest one of these fuses burn all the way down and explode the bomb.

TYPES OF POTENTIAL FIREBREAKS

It would be nice if the United States could, by its own independent actions, insure that none of the nuclear war fuses would ever be lit or, if lit, could be quickly snuffed out. However, it has become abundantly clear that we do not live in a world in which this is possible. To insure that nuclear war never occurs we must look for effective firebreaks that involve cooperation with other countries.

With this in mind, what then are the resources available to us? Nuclear war firebreaks fall into the following categories:

- Improved Relations Between Countries
- Arms Control
  - Strategic nuclear arms control

- Nuclear arms control in Europe
- Conventional arms control
- Nuclear Nonproliferation
- Conflict Resolution
- Crisis Communications

1. **Improved Relations:** Perhaps the firebreak with the greatest potential to prevent nuclear war is the effort to reduce tensions between nations by seeking improved relations. In fact, a successful effort to improve relations between nations is tantamount to insuring that several of the nuclear war scenarios are not even credible—that the fuses cannot even be lit. If nations which are currently adversaries can be persuaded to settle their differences peacefully or simply put them aside—whether these differences stem from disputes over territory, religion, political ideology, economic systems, or whatever—then the likelihood of war, including nuclear war, would be greatly reduced.

Clearly this argument applies not only to improving relations between nations in the Third World, but to the industrialized nations as well, and especially to relations between the superpowers.

2. **Arms Control:** Strategic nuclear arms control efforts (such as SALT and START, which cover long-range nuclear weapons delivery systems including ICBMs, submarine-launched missiles, and intercontinental bombers) represent a potentially useful firebreak in that such agreements can help to make the outcome of an all-out nuclear exchange so certain (mutual assured destruction) that neither side would rationally be tempted to launch such an attack. Since virtually every scenario eventually comes to a point where superpower decision-makers—those with their fingers "on the button"—face the certainty of mutual destruction if that button is pushed, strategic arms control negotiations are a vital element in a comprehensive plan to prevent nuclear war.

But will cool heads always prevail in a crisis? We would like to think so, but the lessons of history and the impact of emotion on crisis behavior provide no assurance that this is the case. Nevertheless, the predictability achieved through strategic arms control, along with certain unilateral actions, offer an important tool for stopping conflicts short of all-out nuclear war.

Other arms control measures might also provide effective firebreaks for specific scenarios. These include, for example:

- Intermediate-range nuclear arms control measures in Europe to reduce tension and insure a balance of shorter-range nuclear forces.
- Regional arms control measures to reduce tension, insure a balance of conventional forces, and reduce the incentive to initiate conventional conflict.
- Controls on conventional arms sales to countries to lessen hostility and tension between adversaries and reduce the likelihood of Third World conventional conflict.

3. Nuclear Nonproliferation: Halting the spread of nuclear weapons to nations which do not yet have them (sometimes referred to as "restricting membership in the Nuclear Club") is an important firebreak for several of the nuclear war scenarios. The more countries that have nuclear weapons, the greater the danger that such weapons may actually be used in the midst of a conventional war—especially if one country is about to suffer a disastrous defeat.

A major part of the effort to halt the spread of nuclear weapons is the need to prevent the spread of certain technologies and weapons-grade "fissionable" (explosive) material—the uranium or plutonium used in first-generation nuclear weapons. Measures such as strict export controls on "sensitive" technologies and facilities can help prevent other countries from developing a nuclear weapons capability. Tight monitoring of all nuclear reactors which contain or produce fissionable material can also help insure that none of the material is diverted to military use.

4. Conflict Resolution: The term conflict resolution can be applied to those techniques or mechanisms which seek to prevent differences or disputes from reaching the stage of military conflict in the first place. Once ordinary bombs and bullets start flying, the possibility of escalation to the use of nuclear weapons obviously becomes much greater. However, it is clear that military conflicts will occur and that finding techniques or methods of controlling or deescalating these conflicts *short of a final military solution* presents an extraordinary challenge.

Within the last year, both the Falkland Islands and Lebanese crises vividly illustrated the ineffectiveness of current conflict resolution techniques. In the Falklands crisis, mediation efforts by (1) a superpower (the U.S.), (2) the U.N., (3) a Latin American U.N. Secretary General, (4) the Organization of American States, and (5) the Pope, all failed to keep the crisis from going all the way to a military solution. These failures led U.N. Secretary General Perez de Cuellar to remark, "We are perilously near to a new international anarchy."

It seems clear that nations must make a more committed effort to develop effective conflict resolution techniques. In the nuclear age, conflict that evolves to a military solution is extremely dangerous—especially in the future, when both sides to a dispute might possess nuclear weapons.

5. Crisis Communications: The term crisis communications refers to those efforts to maximize highly personal leadership-to-leadership communications in the midst of an escalating crisis. This is particularly relevant with respect to the superpowers—and the basic rationale for the current U.S.-Soviet Hot Line.

Crisis communications are particularly important in situations where there is the possibility of a tragic miscalculation or misunderstanding. This could be the case, for example, if there were a nuclear explosion of uncertain origin or purpose—as could be the case in at least two of the six scenarios for general nuclear war.

Crisis communications also constitute the "last ditch" firebreak—when almost all else has failed and there remains the possibility that personal communication between the leaders of the two superpowers might still avert a nuclear war. It seems unlikely that the current Hot Line, a slow teletype machine requiring translation at both ends, is adequate to such a task.

Conclusion

The first step in dealing constructively with the threat of nuclear war is recognizing that the threat will not go away. The sobering truth is that the prevention of nuclear war is not a short-term problem that will fade away in a few years or even a few generations. Even total nuclear disarmament—a goal that seems virtually impossible in today's world—would not permanently guarantee the prevention of nuclear war. Even with all of our current weapons dismantled, the knowledge of how to make them would still remain. Thus, even in a world free of nuclear weapons, we would be only weeks or months from making new ones and turning a conventional war into a nuclear one.

Since the threat of nuclear war is henceforth to be an abiding fact of human existence, we have no choice but to learn to manage the threat and find ways to keep it under control. The community of nations—and particularly the United States and the Soviet Union—must develop a variety of means to keep nuclear weapons from being used. The challenge of doing that is enormous. It is nothing less than the greatest challenge that the human community has ever faced.

The concept of "firebreaks" which has been discussed in this booklet is one way of viewing the long-term problem of preventing nuclear war. Wherever a fuse is ignited that could lead to nuclear war—and there is little doubt that many such fuses will be lit in future years—the leaders and citizens of the world will be faced with the challenge of stopping the burning fuse. Fully and effectively utilizing *all* of the various resources available to the burning fuses must be a national and international priority of the highest order.

In thinking about the prevention of nuclear war, it is important not to become too rigid about causes and means of prevention. Solutions that are appropriate today may not be tomorrow. The world's political environment is like a child's kaleidoscope, with patterns, shapes, and relationships constantly changing, constantly revealing new and different arrangements. For us, this means that the answers to the two questions that began our inquiry—How might nuclear war occur? and What must we do to prevent it?—are likely to change over time. New pathways to nuclear war might emerge and old ones disappear. Hopefully, new firebreaks will also be discovered. So, we must not only begin with these two simple questions, we must keep returning to them.

The task of preventing nuclear war is an awesome one. It requires utilizing a wide variety of resources effectively in countless different situations. It requires the institutionalization of a type of crisis management and international cooperation that is different from anything the world has ever seen. The very difficulty of the task may discourage many people from participating in the effort. At the same time, the horrible spectre of the threat may provide some hope for achieving the kind of breakthroughs in international problem-solving that are necessary to prevent nuclear war from ever occurring.

THE CASE FOR A FREEZE
Edward M. Kennedy and Mark O. Hatfield

Edward M. Kennedy is United States Senator from Massachusetts. Mark O. Hatfield is United States Senator from Oregon.

In 1963 when President Kennedy, in a commencement address at American University, proposed high-level negotiations with the Soviet Union on the issue of nuclear testing, he was trying in a single but sensible stroke to break a deadlock that had lasted for years. He had dismissed the counsel of some advisers that his offer would be perceived as American weakness. He had listened with disbelief to the argument that the rest of the details had to be worked out before we could ask the Soviet Union to agree to the general principle of an atmospheric test ban. After his address, in the remarkably short span of two months, the remaining details were disposed of and the Test-Ban Treaty of 1963 was signed.

Today there are some officials who, like their counterparts two decades ago, believe that a freeze followed by major reductions in nuclear arsenals is improbable and who argue, in effect, that peace is also impossible. Too many defense experts who have grown up with the arms race have become accustomed to guiding it. The agreements negotiated in SALT I and SALT II have not prevented steadily higher levels of weaponry. As Senators, we supported SALT II because we thought the country and the world would be better off with it than without it. It offered a number of limits on nuclear weaponry; without it, there would have been no limits at all on Soviet and American buildups. But in fact, the SALT II Treaty, which was never put before the

Senate for a ratification vote, was mostly a means of setting down rules for limiting the arms buildup, instead of stopping the arms race and then reversing it. . . .

The weakness of the SALT process in addressing technological breakthroughs has plagued efforts at arms control for the past decade. The first SALT agreement ignored the advance called MIRV, multiple independently targetable reentry vehicles, which meant that a single ballistic missile could carry several warheads, each aimed at a separate enemy city or military installation and each sufficient to obliterate it. Many experts felt that SALT did too little to stop the qualitative arms race and restrain ongoing scientific revolution in weaponry.

In the 1980s, technology has marched on. Guidance systems have become increasingly and exquisitely accurate; a missile may now be able to fly 5000 miles and land within a few hundred feet of the intended target. But exquisitely accurate land-based missiles may also be vulnerable to the other side's exquisitely accurate missiles. Even in a decade governed by SALT II both sides could pass beyond the "first-strike" threshold, where either side might assume that it had first-strike capability and first-strike vulnerability simultaneously. The inexorable development of nuclear technology is heading inevitably to a world bristling with hair-trigger nuclear missiles and governed by a "use them or lose them" nuclear psychology. Like sulfur coating a matchstick, the layering of nuclear technology on top of other disputes could erupt in nuclear war any time Americans and Soviets rub each other the wrong way.

Once this strategic Rubicon has been crossed, the possibility of accidental war will rise to an even more dangerous level. On 147 occasions within the past 20 months, U.S. computer malfunctions have signaled a Soviet strategic attack. Four of the incidents were severe enough so that orders were issued to move our strategic forces to a higher state of alert. Once, a mistake caused by a programming error flashed a warning of a Soviet submarine attack. According to the Pentagon, it took six minutes for U.S. command authorities to make a positive identification of the mistake; in a few minutes more, if there had been no mistake, a fusillade of Soviet submarine missiles would have struck our coastal cities. On another occasion, a false signal was flashed from satellites that mistook the rising of the moon for the launching of Soviet missiles.

Some defense analysts behave as if the purpose of arms control is, at most, permanent management of the arms race. But it is unlikely that it can be managed forever and more likely that it will finally manage to destroy much of civilization forever. A nuclear freeze, followed by reductions, is not the only avenue to arms control, but it is the only idea which can stop the spiral of

nuclear arms development without the self-defeating delays of endless negotiation over what constitutes equality. In a matter of months, the two superpowers, assuming their goodwill, could reasonably work out verification
procedures for a freeze. The former Chief of Naval Development, Admiral
Thomas Davies, says:

> Now the virtue of the freeze is to prevent the continued increase of
> weaponry and the worsening of the situation during a prolonged negoti-
> ation. In fact, the history of our negotiations [for arms reductions
> shows] that they are lengthy and difficult, and during that time there is
> always a great increase in the number of warheads deployed. So I would
> say that the freeze is the only practical way to go at that problem.

To freeze first and then negotiate reductions makes sense on many levels.
It recognizes the urgency of taking a step that is as simple as it is practical,
and that is more feasible now than it has ever been before, because both sides
are so nearly equivalent in their arsenals of annihilation.

The freeze agreement would be a firebreak, encircling and containing a
weapons race threatening to break out of control. Once armaments and technological advances are stopped at present levels, the two superpowers can negotiate phased and balanced reductions. The Kennedy-Hatfield resolution calls
for such reductions "through annual percentages or equally effective means."
George Kennan, our former Ambassador to the Soviet Union and our foremost
expert on that country, and Admiral Hyman G. Rickover, Director of Naval
Nuclear Propulsion under seven Presidents, have argued eloquently and com-
pellingly for deep cuts of at least 50 percent in the nuclear armories of both
sides. These cuts could be achieved by the end of this decade, if we mutually
agree to reasonable reductions of 7 percent a year. This is the appproach proposed in the Kennedy-Hatfield resolution, and suggested by the Senate Committee on Foreign Relations in 1979, which sought sustained major reductions
from SALT II ceilings on weaponry.

As the process of reductions moves along, it will be in the interests of
both the United States and the Soviet Union to direct their reductions to vulnerable land-based missiles that also provide particularly rapid and precise offensive capability: weapons that could seriously unbalance the basic retaliatory
equation which yields mutual deterrence. In short, a freeze on nuclear weapons followed by reductions from their current levels can strengthen deterrence
as the purpose of our defense, diminish the risk of accidental nuclear war, and
curtail the incentives for the hair-trigger use of nuclear weapons during an
escalating crisis.

A freeze will enhance, not reduce, our overall security, because it will
prevent the development of more powerful Soviet rockets and block their further deployment of existing weapons. A freeze will prevent one side from per-

fecting its capacity for a first strike against the other by prohibiting the testing and production of such weapons; the result will be a substantial reduction in the fear of a U.S. or Soviet preemptive attack.

A freeze will also help to strengthen our economy and other areas of our national defense, both of which have heavily suffered from neglect and from the cost of this nuclear buildup. The $90 billion that a freeze alone could save in the next five years could be spent on conventional defenses and domestic priorities. In fact, the strategic arms race is crippling our capacity to meet human needs. We are cutting immunization for children in order to finance the weapons that may someday kill them. Every new shelter for a missle means more spending, a bigger deficit, and higher interest rates, but fewer homes for families. Every new warhead guidance system that can read enemy defenses means there will be more schools where more students will never learn to read. Every new escalation that could mean death at an early age across the earth also darkens the golden years of senior citizens who rely on Social Security, Medicare, and Medicaid, all of which are in danger from cutbacks due to the budget crisis.

The nuclear buildup is an extremely important aspect of the current economic distress. The B-1 bomber alone will cost more than all the job training programs enacted by Congress in the past 20 years. In short, the two greatest issues of our time—the prosperity of the economy and the probability of survival in the nuclear age—are inextricably intertwined. Not only could a freeze save at least $18 billion annually; negotiated reductions could save billions more. A process of mutual nuclear restraint is a needed defense against the prospect of endless budget deficits.

As we have noted, some of the savings from a freeze can be reallocated to improve the readiness and the reliability of our conventional forces. But just as important, when the total burden of military expenditures on the budget is lessened, we will have the resources for the revitalization of our industries and the restoration of America's competitive position in the markets of the world. We will have the funds to develop, and share, alternative energy sources. These tasks are at the heart of the great national security challenges of the 1980s; they are the central arena of testing for the United States, which cannot endure as an insecure or failing economy amid international economic disarray and deprivation. . . .

. . . In 1982 the economic burden of the effort weighs heavier and heavier upon Americans and Soviets alike. President Reagan has observed of the Soviet Union: "Their great military build-up . . . at the expense of the denial of consumer goods . . . has now left them on a very narrow edge." But it is not the adversary alone that now suffers from major economic difficulty. There is no question that if we continue to run an expensive, escalating arms race, we run the risk of Sovietizing our own economy. Investment capital has been

drained by the crunching combination of massive increases in military spending, massive deficits, and the resulting scarcity of credit. When resources and
strategic materials shortages are factored into the equation, unprecedented
military spending may make it impossible for our society ever to return to its
previous peaks of prosperity.

We must start retooling now for the future economic character of states
from Oregon to Massachusetts, and Michigan to Louisiana. We cannot afford
to imitate our adversary by limiting economic progress so that strategic military spending can multiply, vacuuming up every kind of resource. Generally
our government has sought to budget federal dollars in ways that leverage private capital formation, jobs and thriving communities; but excessive defense
spending actually means more, not less, unemployment. The military has the
least multiplier effect of any dollar we spend, while the highest multiplier
comes from a dollar spent on preventive medicine and health. Strategic spending is capital intensive, not labor intensive. Every billion dollars that we spend
on the MX missile program will hire 17,000 people, while the same $1 billion
could hire 48,000 hospital workers or 65,000 people in the building trades,
or 77,000 teachers, police officers, and firefighters.

Few will deny the costs of the arms race in economic and human terms.
Instead, opposition to a nuclear freeze, followed by reductions, has focused on
military and technical issues. There are certain experts who claim, in effect,
that the freeze is a nice but impractical idea. They resist the notion that an
issue which was formerly the exclusive province of a professional elite has now
become a matter of public debate and intensifying citizen concern. Of course,
the management of the nuclear arms race since 1945 has not been a model of
success. One argument which freeze opponents are raising now—that the issue
is too complex and too important to be left to the people—echoes the argument of an earlier generation, that the popular effort to end the Vietnam war
was a mistake, or the parallel argument of 1982 that American policy in El
Salvador and Central America should be decided in secret.

A number of other analysts and former officials who decry the present
arms control stalemate regard the freeze as nothing more than a popular movement which may be beneficial in pressuring the administration, but which
does not make sense as national policy because, they say, our strategic forces
are not equal to those of the Soviet Union. In fact, there are many experts
who favor the Kennedy-Hatfield resolution, ranging from former Secretaries of
State and Defense to former CIA executives to America's most capable scientists. There is not a single sensible military or diplomatic official who would
trade our strategic forces for the Soviet arsenal. At the present time, the United
States is fully capable of defending itself by retaliating fully against any Soviet
nuclear attack. America is secure today, and a freeze will preserve that security
for the future. Despite all the talk of a "window of vulnerability," this nation

and the Soviet Union are at approximate equivalence in strategic nuclear power. In the event of an immediate freeze, we would have 9400 available strategic nuclear warheads and the Soviets would have 7500. Even if a Soviet first strike destroyed all American land-based missiles, we would still have a retaliatory capacity of at least 4000 warheads at sea and in the air. Even congressional testimony from military experts makes reference to the "rough parity" between the two countries. The Defense Department's military posture statement last year stated explicitly that a condition of parity continues to prevail. The current nuclear balance is relatively stable; deterrence still works. By freezing now, we would avoid an age of perceived first-strike threats in which the Soviets would face their own window of vulnerability and which could tempt either side to launch a preemptive strike. And it is that new arms race, not the present situation, which could irrevocably shatter the present balance.

We stand now at a unique moment in the history of the nuclear age where a freeze can work and must be tried. Rather than a window of vulnerability, we now have a window of opportunity for arms control. That window could be slammed shut in the coming years. It is no longer merely enough to call for reductions in nuclear weaponry without calling for a freeze as a first step, and as the only way to keep the window of opportunity open. Critics charge that the Soviets would have no incentive to reduce their arsenals after a freeze. They call for building new systems in order to pile up bargaining chips for negotiations with the Kremlin. But in the past, the arms race has been needlessly perpetuated by this bargaining-chip theory, because both sides feel forced to match new and threatening developments with their own. MIRVs, multiple independent warheads, were defended as a bargaining chip during the SALT I talks. So the United States continued to deploy them and then we were told that they were too important to bargain away.

In contrast, after a freeze both sides will have a vested interest in reductions, since they will still be saddled with weapons which do not add to their security or the effectiveness of their deterrent, which detract from the overall stability of the nuclear balance, and which they can no longer work to perfect. For those whose real aim is a new buildup, the rationale that we need reductions, but not a freeze, is merely a rationalization for amassing the B-1, the MX, and other new strategic weapons while engaging in protracted negotiations with the Soviets. Frankly, often during negotiations, the United States and the Soviet Union have behaved like fevered patients whose temperature rises from 103 to 104 degrees and who think they're getting better because they're getting sicker at a slower rate.

Past agreements have also been defective because they have not prevented impending leaps in the sophistication of weaponry. Thus the Vladivostok accord and the SALT II Treaty permitted the development of cruise missiles. The military planners saw the loophole and proceeded to rush through it with a weapons system in which they had previously shown only minimum interest. Where there is a loophole, it will almost certainly be exploited. Where a system is permitted, it will be pursued; otherwise, the thinking goes, the adversary will gain an advantage. A comprehensive freeze already in place during reduction talks would plug past loopholes and prevent future ones for the simple reason that it would impose a general moratorium on any and all additions to nuclear arsenals.

Critics of the freeze next suggest that it would leave the United States behind the Soviets in nuclear weaponry in Europe. Officials in the Reagan Administration have presented varying statistics to prove this proposition, citing an inferiority ranging between three-to-one and six-to-one. But such critics exaggerate the facts and distort the true situation in Europe, where the United States, according to the authoritative International Institute for Strategic Studies, has 1,168 available warheads and the Soviets have 2,004. With such numbers each nation has enough to blow up the continent many times over. In any event, the Kennedy-Hatfield resolution rejects a freeze in Europe alone. We are calling for a global freeze. In the case of a Soviet nuclear attack on NATO, the United States could call on its entire nuclear arsenal to respond. For the administration to suggest that it no longer relies on this option would signal a major and destabilizing change under which Europe would no longer enjoy the protection of America's nuclear umbrella.

The real and present danger to the NATO alliance, by the estimate of former Under Secretary of State George Ball, is the uncertain and unclear attitude of the United States with respect to the nuclear issue. The sense of apprehension in Europe has been amplified by American discussion of limited nuclear war and nuclear warning shots and by American insistence on the neutron bomb, a malignant scientific break-through designed to destroy people through, "enhanced radiation" while minimizing damage to buildings and equipment. Campaigns for unilateral European disarmament gain strength when Washington sounds casual about nuclear conflict and seems uninterested in arms control or unable to achieve progress. Given this record, it is "grotesque," in Secretary Ball's phrase, for the administration to suggest that the Kennedy-Hatfield freeze will undermine the American position in Europe. To the contrary, it can reassure the Europeans that this nation is finally being serious about reducing the risk of accelerating nuclear competition.

Other critics of the resolution have focused on the question of verification. The Kennedy-Hatfield resolution specifically calls for a verifiable freeze. What cannot be verified will not be frozen. But there are many experts who agree that a freeze is largely and sufficiently verifiable. We can have high confidence that one critical aspect of the freeze, deployment, can be verified through "national technical means"—that is, satellites and listening posts equipped with sensors—and through data exchange and restrictions on concealment. A second critical aspect of the freeze, testing, can also be verified by such means together with unmanned seismic stations and opportunities for on-site inspection—both of which the Soviets have already accepted in principle in the recent negotiations for a Comprehensive Test Ban Treaty. In the past, the United States has regarded such measures as fully adequate for verifying SALT restrictions on deployment and limits on nuclear weapons testing, and they would be fully adequate for verifying these aspects of a nuclear weapons freeze.

A freeze on production of nuclear weapons may be harder to verify, but our intelligence is so well developed, according to former Under Secretary of Defense William Perry, that we have been able to "monitor Soviet activity at the design bureaus and production plants well enough so that we have been able to predict every ICBM before it began its tests." It may be that some form of on-site inspection will be necessary to closely verify production and to check certain limited aspects of testing. To presume that the Soviets will not permit any such inspection overlooks the record of the Comprehensive Test-Ban Treaty negotiations, now postponed by the Reagan administration, where the Soviets have agreed to the principle of on-site verification.

Even areas where there may be verification problems, such as some areas of production, do not present serious difficulties, since verification in other areas would assure overall enforcement of the freeze. Indeed, Herbert Scoville, onetime Deputy Director of the CIA, contends that a freeze is *easier* to verify than a treaty like SALT I or SALT II. Such treaties contain complicated limits on numbers and modifications of missiles and planes; to detect a violation requires continuing and exact measurements of a vast array of possible and prohibited activity. With a freeze, however, a violation would be known if the adversary did anything new at all. And even the one-for-one replacement that would be permitted by a freeze could be verified with high confidence.

We are also told by critics that a freeze will interfere with arms control negotiations now planned or underway. But as we have seen, it could be years before any overall agreement is concluded. Meanwhile a comprehensive freeze can break the fever of the arms race and bring the thermonuclear temperature down. It can also contribute to progress on the formidable problem of nuclear proliferation, the spread of the bomb to other nations, including unstable regimes in the Third World. American and Soviet appeals against such proliferation tend to fall on cynical ears so long as our own nuclear production moves ahead. A freeze can draw a line not only across the arms race, but across the attitudes of the world. It would give the superpowers the moral authority to deal with the gathering disaster of proliferation. It would deprive aspiring nuclear powers of the too ready excuse that they have every right to acquire the bomb so long as we are striving to augment our own massive arsenals.

The Indian nuclear explosion in 1974 forcefully reminded the world of the deadly threat of proliferation. Pakistan has reacted predictably by trying to catch up with India. We now have an arms race in the subcontinent. Where one nation becomes a nuclear power, however modest, neighboring states feel driven to get bombs of their own; this process is globalizing the deadly logic of nuclear threat and counterthreat. And this, in turn, could set off a nuclear confrontation between the United States and the Soviet Union.

Expanding numbers of nuclear weapons around the world could encourage terrorism in the form of nuclear blackmail. The possible scenarios are chilling. Suppose that, Libya, long frustrated in the quest for a nuclear bomb of its own, receives a gift from Pakistan as an act of Islamic solidarity. Colonel Qadhafi then brandishes the bomb against the state of Israel, which he is sworn to destroy. The crisis escalates and engages Qadhafi's Soviet allies and Israel's American allies; there is a regional and then a global nuclear catastrophe.

A credible and effective strategy to prevent such nightmares depends on a number of mutually reinforcing steps. We must strengthen international nuclear safeguards against the diversion of nuclear materials from peaceful to military uses. We must restrain reckless commerce in nuclear energy, by prohibiting the transfer of plutonium reprocessing, and uranium enrichment equipment and technology, and by insisting on nuclear weapons-free zones such as the one in Latin America.

The key to all of these developments is greater adherence to the current Nuclear Nonproliferation Treaty. A freeze, followed by reductions, can promote that. It is exactly what the treaty itself calls for. By embarking on such a course, the United States and the Soviets can prove that at last, they are observing their pledge under Article VI of the treaty:

> Each of the parties . . . undertakes to pursue negotiations in good faith on effective measures relating to cessation of the nuclear arms race at an early date and to nuclear disarmament, and on a treaty on general and complete disarmament under strict and effective international control.

In effect, a freeze would also be a comprehensive test ban between the superpowers. They could then move to expand it into more formal sanctions against all nuclear tests or explosions.

Finally, some critics suggest that a freeze proposal will be dismissed outright by the Soviet Union. They point to the Soviet rejection of the so-called "deep cuts" suddenly proposed by the Carter administration in 1977. In fact, that experience argues for the more modulated, less complicated strategy of an initial freeze followed by negotiated reductions. The 1977 proposal was highly specific; it asked for agreement to detailed cuts before agreement to the principle of deep cuts. After analyzing the details, Soviet leaders almost certainly interpreted the proposal as locking them into a position of nuclear inferiority. A freeze today would mean a more nearly equivalent balance. In any event, the possibility of rejection by the Soviets is hardly an argument against the desirability of trying for a freeze. If there is any case in history where the imperative of bold initiative applies, it is the nuclear arms race. In the search for arms control, nothing ventured is truly nothing gained, and perhaps in the end, everything truly lost.

In reality, much of the attack on the freeze resolution is a disguise for a different and more unsettling position. The 1983 budget proposal asks for funds to "successfully fight either conventional or nuclear war." This is the first time that any budget proposal has ever said any such thing. We must continue to insist that the American purpose is to deter a nuclear exchange, not to fight one. We must reject the concept of a limited nuclear battle. Admiral Noel Gayler, former Director of the National Security Agency, has acidly dismissed the musings of the limited war theorists: "I have no confidence in the imaginary situations and chess games that a certain school of analysts dreams up. Real war is not like these complicated tit-for-tat imaginings. There is little knowledge of what's going on, and less communication. There is blood and terror and agony, and these theorists propose to deal with a war a thousand times more terrible than any we have ever seen, in some bloodless, analytic fashion. I say that's nonsense. We deceive ourselves, and we deceive our opponent into believing we have aggressive intentions that we do not have." Indeed that is the danger: someday the nuclear wargame theorists may actually find themselves playing the game for real.

The fascination of some experts and politicians with such games, or their attachment to traditional approaches to arms control, has spurred a constant effort to find some simple argument, any simple argument, to dismiss or deflect the freeze proposal. When the critics come to admit, as former Secretary of Defense Harold Brown recently did, that a complete freeze "if immediately and fully implemented and completely verified" might be in the American national interest, they often shift ground and begin charging that even the attempt to negotiate a freeze would be dangerous, because the U.S. might stop building but the Soviets would continue to build. But if the two sides can agree in principle to a freeze, they can also agree to an interim moratorium while the details of the plan are discussed. It would be plain common sense to begin freeze talks with a "negotiator's pause" to hold weaponry constant. A similar pause was put in place and it was effective prior to the 1963 test-ban negotiations.

And sometimes critics even suggest that a nuclear weapons freeze will not, by itself, eliminate the danger of nuclear war. The freeze which they first assailed as too ambitious is then attacked as insufficient to be meaningful. In reality, it is a first but essential step back from the nuclear precipice; it can stop the arms race from rushing over the edge of that precipice, and subsequent reductions can truly move us back to a safer place, farther from the brink. . . .

The Kennedy-Hatfield resolution, by combining a mutual freeze and major reductions, provides the most promising way to move back the hands of the Doomsday Clock. . . . The freeze concept has the inestimable political virtues of simplicity and practicality. Its benefits to humanity are readily apparent to ordinary human beings, rather than to only a select handful of scientists and strategic analysts. There would be no mistaking the moral implications of an agreement to stop the arms race now, and an intense national and international campaign for ratification could be effectively mounted. To a world increasingly apprehensive over the awesome dangers and technological complexities of the arms race, a freeze offers the symbol and the substance of hope.

ARMS CONTROL VS. THE FREEZE
Christopher M. Lehman

Christopher M. Lehman is Director of the Office of Strategic Nuclear Policy, Department of State, Washington, D.C.

Over the past year, the nuclear freeze movement has brought to the forefront of public discussion a deceptively attractive, simple solution to the arms race— freeze it! Calling for an absolute prohibition on the production, testing, and deployment of nuclear weapons and their delivery systems, advocates argue that a freeze can truly bring about a halt in the arms race and reduce the dangers of nuclear war.

The nuclear freeze has been as popular as it is simple. But is it really a plausible path to meaningful arms control, or is it a distraction that makes genuine arms control far more difficult to achieve?

There has been much debate on this question, and surely there is more to come. However, a serious review of the issue forces the conclusion that the nuclear freeze proposal has serious drawbacks as to make it unsuitable as the basis for meaningful arms control.

Source: Christopher M. Lehman, "Arms Control vs. the Freeze," in Steven Miller, ed., *The Nuclear Weapons Freeze and Arms Control* (Cambridge, Mass.: Ballinger, 1984), pp. 65–71. Reprinted with permission. Copyright 1984, Ballinger Publishing Company.

The Freeze as Sentiment

The rapid growth of the nuclear freeze movement is a phenomenon which cannot be fully explained. However, it is clear that a number of factors were instrumental in boosting the visibility and the political clout of the freeze movement, and they all have a common element—fear. The fear of nuclear war has once again spawned a movement of concerned men, women, and children who demand that we avoid Armageddon.

The roots of the freeze movement go as far back as we care to look, but its more recent impetus has come from the increased attention to defense issues and the undeniable growth in the Soviet threat. The 1980 election in large part turned on the question of defense, and the Reagan Administration has made the rebuilding of U.S. defenses a central element of its program.

The continuing public focus on threats to U.S. security and the huge defense expenditures necessary to meet those threats have helped to create a backlash or an aversion to matters related to defense. This aversion has been particularly strong with respect to our nuclear arsenal where a major modernization of our nuclear forces has served to rekindle strong anti-nuclear sentiment. Anxieties were boosted even further by several statements by Reagan Administration officials concerning nuclear weapons and nuclear war, and since then some politicians have sought to exploit anti-nuclear sentiment for ballot-box gains, and authors and publishers have cashed in as well.

The fear and anxiety that is so much a part of the nuclear freeze movement is, of course, understandable. There have been dangerous developments in the nuclear balance in recent years, and a nuclear war would most certainly be unimaginably horrible. But it takes more than fear to prevent nuclear war. It takes a dual strategy of deterrence and arms control.

The very foundation of peace in the nuclear age has been America's strategy of deterrence. Since the earliest days of our possession of nuclear weapons, the United States has sought to prevent war by discouraging aggression against the United States and its allies. By threatening any aggressor with the certainty of unacceptable levels of destruction, an uneasy peace has been maintained. The history of the twentieth century makes it sadly clear that peaceful intentions and good motives alone never stop aggressors. Military strength does, and the strategy of deterrence has been highly successful in protecting America's security since the end of World War II.

But America has pursued a dual policy since the end of World War II. In addition to maintaining strong military forces for deterrence, we have also vigorously pursued arms control as a complement to our policy of deterrence.

Thus while anxiety over the threat of nuclear war is well warranted, we cannot let fear dictate our response. The proven course of deterrence and arms control is the best means of preventing nuclear war and preserving the peace. A nuclear freeze would be harmful to deterrence and to meaningful arms control and thus a freeze should be rejected.

The Flaws of the Freeze

The arguments against the nuclear freeze proposal are many and would apply to most, if not all, of the various freeze formulae that have been proposed. The most popular freeze proposal, and the one which has earned *the* nuclear freeze label, is the Congressional Resolution introduced by Senators Kennedy and Hatfield and its companion measure introduced in the House of Representatives. This resolution calls for an immediate mutual and verifiable freeze on production, testing, and deployment of nuclear weapons and their delivery systems. This proposal is surely well intentioned, but it will not help accomplish effective arms control. In fact, if a freeze were to be implemented, it would endanger American security and the security of our allies.

The first, and probably the strongest, argument against the nuclear freeze proposal is that a freeze would preserve the current high level of nuclear forces, and would thus preserve an unequal and unstable strategic balance.

The experts have hotly debated the exact status of the strategic balance for years, but there is no debate that the balance has shifted dramatically in recent years in favor of the Soviet Union. There is debate over whether parity still exists, but there is little opposition to the view that present trends cannot continue without directly harming the security interests of the United States.

As a result of a massive 15-year military buildup, the Soviet Union has now surged ahead of the United States in every static measure of strategic power except one—total strategic warheads. In missile throwweight, missile warheads, ICBMs, SLBMs, and even strategic bombers, the Soviet Union has gained the advantage; and qualitatively the Soviet Union has caught up as well.

In addition to numerical advantages, the average age of Soviet strategic weapons and their delivery systems has come down considerably while the average age of U.S. systems has gone up. According to U.S. Department of Defense figures, 77 percent of Soviet systems are less than five years old, while 77 percent of U.S. systems are in excess of 15 years of age.

Thus, if a freeze were implemented, the United States would be frozen with aging systems with no opportunity to modernize those forces to ensure a strong and credible deterrent.

Our current strategic weapon systems will also become increasingly vulnerable over time, and a vulnerable deterrent is an invitation to catastrophe. The vulnerability of our land-based missile force is already a matter of major concern. While the freeze would lock us into these and other current systems, the freeze would not prevent advances in conventional air defenses or anti-submarine warfare that would threaten the remaining two elements of our strategic triad. But a freeze would prevent the production of the Stealth bomber and other advances that could counter steadily improving Soviet air defenses. Similarly, the freeze would prevent the production of new Trident submarines and other efforts to stay ahead of advances in anti-submarine warfare.

In short, a nuclear freeze would weaken deterrence over time and thus make nuclear war more rather than less likely.

The present nuclear balance in Europe is also one which should not be frozen in its present state. A freeze now would give the Soviet Union an overwhelming nuclear advantage in intermediate-range nuclear weapons in Europe to the detriment of our own and our allies' security.

A second important argument that flows from the first is that by freezing at today's high and unequal levels a nuclear freeze would undercut our START and INF negotiations and make the prospects for actual arms reductions less likely.

The United States is currently engaged in two separate negotiations with the Soviet Union seeking nuclear arms reductions. In those negotiations, the United States has put forward dramatic reductions proposals: in START, the U.S. is calling for one-third reductions in ballistic missile warheads, and a cut in the number of deployed missiles to about one-half the current U.S. levels. In the INF negotiations, the U.S. has proposed the elimination of a whole category of intermediate-range ballistic missiles. The Soviet Union has responded with counterproposals that also envisage arms reduction. While the Soviet proposals have not been acceptable to the United States, it is important to note that the principle of reductions has been accepted. This is quite significant, especially in view of the fact that the recent SALT II negotiations produced a draft treaty which would have allowed both sides to almost double their nuclear warhead inventory within the terms of the agreement.

Thus, in a very real sense we have already moved far beyond a freeze, and we should not waste the months and years it would take to negotiate the terms of a verifiable nuclear freeze if, in fact, that were possible. Supporters of a freeze may believe that a freeze agreement could be easily arrived at, but experience has shown that any meaningful agreement would require agreed definitions, counting rules, and other details which would unavoidably complicate the implementation of the conceptually simple nuclear freeze proposal.

Aside from the complexities of implementing a freeze, U.S. agreement to a freeze would destroy Soviet incentives for accepting an arms reduction agreement. A freeze at today's force levels would preserve the Soviet Union in a position of relative advantage. The Soviets thus would have every incentive to prolong a freeze and avoid coming to an agreement on arms reductions to lower but equal levels.

Unless the United States and its allies demonstrate their will to take the actions necessary to restore the nuclear balance, the Soviets will have little incentive to agree to reductions in their own forces. Indeed, the Soviet Union initially refused our offers to negotiate on INF systems while they deployed several hundred SS-20 missile systems. They agreed to come to the negotiating table only when it became clear that we and our NATO allies were determined to take steps to counter those SS-20 deployments unless an arms control agreement were reached. A unilateral U.S. withdrawal from the allied "dual track" decision of 1979, which has consistently been endorsed by all NATO governments, would also cause serious doubt on American leadership of NATO and our readiness to fulfill our commitments to the defense of Europe.

Similarly, the freeze would leave the U.S. with a vulnerable land-based missile system, an aging and less credible bomber force, and a submarine fleet which faces block obsolescence in the 1990s. The Soviet Union, on the other hand, would have an arsenal of newer, heavier ICBMs, newer ballistic missile-firing submarines, and over 250 modern Backfire bombers built during the 1970s. Under these circumstances, there would be little reason for the Soviet Union to agree to reductions.

A third important argument against the nuclear freeze is that it is just not verifiable in many important respects. Simply prefacing a freeze proposal with an incantation that it must be mutual and verifiable just doesn't make it so.

As proposed, a freeze would cover production, testing, and deployment of strategic nuclear weapons. However, of those three categories, only deployment is verifiable with high confidence, and there are exceptions to that. Verifying a ban on nuclear testing at lower-yield levels would be significant. With respect to production of nuclear weapons, however, the task of verifying a freeze becomes unmanageable. Even with on-site inspection, the possibility of detecting the production of nuclear weapons would be low.

Thus inadequate verification alone is sufficient argument against the nuclear freeze as proposed.

The Freeze Ignores Deterrence

There are other arguments against the nuclear freeze, but they are mostly subsidiary to those mentioned here. However, there is one additional criticism of the freeze that needs to be made. The freeze proposal ignores deterrence. It assumes that deterrence is stable and easily maintained no matter what the strategic nuclear balance sheet looks like. It assumes that the vulnerability and looming obsolescence of U.S. strategic systems will not affect the viability of deterrence. In short, it assumes that the concept of minimum deterrence is valid—that so long as the United States retains the capacity to destroy a few Soviet cities then deterrence will prevail.

This simple view of deterrence has been rejected by every administration since Eisenhower as being inadequate and incredible and therefore dangerous. Deterrence requires capable and survivable nuclear forces on both sides so that neither side can expect advantage under any circumstances by initiating the use of nuclear weapons. Allowing gross imbalances in the level or capabilities of nuclear forces would be destabilizing. Allowing our nuclear forces to be vulnerable to a pre-emptive disarming first strike would only invite attack and greatly increase the probability of war.

These are things we must not allow to happen, yet these are the very things which a nuclear freeze would mandate.

The Freeze Is Bad Arms Control

The arguments against the nuclear freeze are powerful and persuasive. It is a superficially attractive concept, but one which has hidden within it serious flaws that make it unsuitable as the basis for serious arms control. A substantial number of respected arms control experts have supported this view, and even some who support the freeze concept do so as a means of building political pressure in support of arms control while recognizing the internal flaws of the actual nuclear freeze proposal. Respected journals such as the *New York Times*, the *Washington Post*, and the *Wall Street Journal* have all editorialized against the freeze.

Those who support the concept of a nuclear freeze need to stop thinking with their heart and start thinking with their head. We all share the common goal of avoiding the catastrophe of nuclear war. We all share the desire for peace. But we all have a responsibility to work toward practical solutions to man's most serious problem.

The practical solution, in my view, is the proven course of deterrence and arms control. That has been the course adopted by every administration in the postwar era, and it is the course which the Reagan Administration is vigorously pursuing.

We are now engaged in two nuclear arms control negotiations with the Soviet Union—START and INF. The United States has put forward serious arms reduction proposals at the negotiations, and the Soviets have made serious counter-proposals.

It is time for all those who truly desire arms control to support the arms control efforts which the United States is now pursuing. These negotiations seek deep reductions in the levels of nuclear weapons. A freeze at today's high levels of nuclear weapons would be a step backward.

STRATEGIC DEFENSE AND U.S. NATIONAL SECURITY

Caspar W. Weinberger

Caspar W. Weinberger is U.S. Secretary of Defense.

Thank you for inviting me to join you today. This is a good time for us to meet together, as President Reagan prepares to begin his second term. Before his reelection, Ronald Reagan told the American people where he stood on the most important issue before us: how to prevent nuclear war and build a more secure world, so that this generation—and future generations—will live in peace with freedom.

President Reagan has made it clear that he wants to reduce the threat of all nuclear weapons, particularly the most dangerous ones—the nuclear-tipped ballistic missiles. By strengthening conventional forces—through both traditional and new technologies—he has begun with our allies to restore a balanced deterrent and to reduce reliance on nuclear arms in Europe. And now, by initiating a research and technology program on defenses against ballistic missiles, he has opened the door to a future in which nuclear missiles will become less and less capable of their awful mission, until we could hope for the day when the threat of nuclear weapons could be removed entirely.

The American people have overwhelmingly endorsed these objectives. In the second Reagan administration, the President is determined to meet his commitment to the American people . . . and to America's allies. For in presenting the challenge of strategic defense, he said of our global allies: "Their safety and ours are one; no change in technology can, or will, alter that reality."

This journey to a safer world will not be easy, . . . nor short. The strategic defense research program will have to bear fruit before we will be in a position to make any decisions on deployment options. I am confident, though, that we can master the technical task before us, as we have accomplished so many other technical miracles in the past.

For twenty years now, the Soviet nuclear missile forces that threaten our nation and our allies have grown relentlessly. I am afraid they will continue to do so, unless we can convince the Soviet leadership that we can mutually agree to reduce the nuclear ballistic arsenals through negotiations. We are also

Source: Caspar W. Weinberger, "Strategic Defense and U.S. National Security," remarks before the Foreign Press Center, December 19, 1984 (Washington, D.C.: Office of Defense, Public Affairs News Release No. 648–84).

embarked on a program that we, and I am sure all men and women of good will, hope will render these missiles impotent and obsolete. The President's strategic defense initiative can contribute to curbing strategic arms competition by devaluing nuclear missiles and thus imposing prohibitively high costs on the Soviets, if they continued in their quest for missile superiority.

In the 1960's and early 1970's, we had different expectations. For example, one of my predecessors even predicted the Soviets would be satisfied with a few hundred ballistic missiles. He said they had given up trying to match, much less surpass, our strategic force. We thought our self-restraint in offensive nuclear forces, combined with a ban on missile defenses, would lead the Soviets also to restrain *their* offensive arms, abandon defenses, and accept mutual nuclear deterrence between our countries for the indefinite future. The United States acted on this expectation.

Through the 1960's until the end of the 1970's, we cut the budget for nuclear forces every year. Today, the total megatonnage of the U.S. stockpile is only one-fourth the size of our 1959 stockpile. Seventeen years ago, we had one-third more nuclear warheads than we do today. We thought this would induce the Soviets to restrain the growth of their nuclear forces.

We also thought we could reinforce Soviet restraint and facilitate limits on offensive arms by guaranteeing our own total vulnerability to a Soviet ballistic missile attack. We unilaterally gave up all defense, not only of our cities, but of our Minuteman silos as well. We did so even though the ABM treaty permitted each side one ABM site. Advocates of this policy reasoned that if the Soviets could easily strike American cities, they would have no incentive to deploy more missiles.

In the mid-1970's, however, the scope and vigor of the Soviet build-up became apparent. Once more, we tried to restore stability by negotiating the SALT II treaty. Despite the lessons of SALT I, American negotiators again expected that the Soviets would curb their build-up if we continued to deny ourselves protection against Soviet missiles.

Again, we were wrong. Improvements and additions to the Soviet missile force continue at a frightening pace, even though we have added SALT II restraints on top of the SALT I agreements. The Soviet Union has now built more warheads capable of destroying our missile silos than we had initially predicted they would build, even without any SALT agreement. We now confront precisely the condition that the SALT process was intended to prevent. That is why the president and I have always criticized the SALT II agreement so vigorously. It will *not* reduce arsenals. And the so-called "limitation" of arms permitted, and indeed accepted, the Soviets build-up of nuclear arms.

Moreover, as the President reported to Congress, the Soviet Union has violated several important SALT provisions, including a ban on concealing telemetry of missile tests. Since that provision was designed to allow verification of the SALT agreement, even President Carter stressed that "a violation of this part of the agreement—which we would quickly detect—would be just as serious as a violation on strategic weapons themselves."

The vast majority of Americans are deeply concerned about this pattern of Soviet violations. Yet some people who pride themselves on their expertise and concern for arms control have taken an upside-down view. Instead of recognizing the problem of Soviet violations, they have criticized President Reagan for informing Congress about those violations. They argue that this showed he was "not sincere" about arms control; as if sincerity required that we ignore Soviet violations.

I do not wish to be captious about past mistakes. My point here is that we must learn from experience. Some people who refuse to learn from the past now assert that President Reagan must choose between having his initiative on strategic defense, or trying to obtain set arms reductions. Yes, a choice is necessary. But the choice is between a better defense policy that offers hope and safety and which could bring us genuine and significant reductions, or to continue with only disproven strategic dogmas that have put us in a far less secure position.

The real choice is between strategic defense which will facilitate genuine reductions in offensive arms with greater security for East and West; or a perpetuation of our total vulnerability to any attacking missiles—whether launched by accident or by design—in the hope, twice proven vain, that this would slow the Soviet arms build-up.

We are all agreed that nuclear war must be prevented. This is the overriding imperative for our defense policy today, and has been for decades. However, we need to recall the United States and the Soviet Union have experienced vast changes in their relative strength, in their basic strategies, and in the types and number of weapons each possesses.

During the first four years of the nuclear era, there was no *mutual* nuclear deterrence—we had a monopoly. Because the monopoly was ours, no one seriously feared nuclear war. Even Stalin—often described as defensive minded—violated the Yalta agreement on Poland, crushed democracy in Czechoslovakia, blockaded Berlin, and encouraged North Korea's attack on South Korea. He had no fear, paranoid or otherwise, that the U.S. would use its nuclear monopoly to maintain compliance with Yalta, much less to launch an unprovoked attack.

Later, when the Soviet Union also built nuclear weapons, there was still no mutual deterrence based on absolute vulnerability. For during the 1950's we spent some $100 billion (in current dollars) to defend against Soviet strategic bombers—then the only nuclear threat to the United States. At that time, some of today's loudest critics of strategic defense advocated a large expansion of defensive systems against the bomber threat, and urged development and deployment of a ballistic missile defense for both our cities and our critical military forces.

It was not until the Kennedy and Johnson administrations that we began to abandon our efforts to defend against nuclear attack, and instead base our entire security on the odd theory that you are safe only if you have no defense whatsoever. It came to be known as mutual-assured destruction, or MAD. It has played a central role in the U.S. approach to arms control for the past 20 years; even though for many years now, actual U.S. strategy has adjusted to the fact that the original MAD concept was flawed. Our strategy has moved well beyond this to the point that it now seeks to avoid the targeting of populations.

Today, supporters of the traditional simplistic MAD concept supply most of the criticisms of the President's strategic defense initiative. Sometimes they admit that if both sides could protect themselves perfectly the world would be better off, but they oppose any effort, including seeking major arms reductions, that could move the world in that direction.

True believers in the disproven MAD concept hold that the prime, if not the only, objective of the strategic nuclear forces of both the United States and the Soviet Union is the ability to destroy each other's cities. They believe that any U.S. defense against this threat is "destabilizing." It will, they say, inevitably provoke an overwhelming increase in Soviet forces and will increase Soviet incentives to strike preemptively in a crisis. They fail to appreciate the deterrent value of missile defenses, because they wrongly project upon the Soviet military their own irrational idea of the purpose of a Soviet attack. In fact, the Soviet military have designed their offensive forces to be capable of destroying allied and U.S. military forces, in particular our silo-based missiles and military targets in Europe. At the same time, the Soviet Union has never abandoned its objective of defending its homeland against nuclear attack.

The ABM treaty never blinded the Soviets to the need for effective defenses. They have continued to place great emphasis on air defense. They are now ready to deploy a defense system with capabilities against both aircraft and many ballistic missiles. They have a massive program of underground shelters. They have built five ABM radars, with another one under construction, that give them double coverage of all ICBM approaches to the Soviet Union; and they have exploited fully the provisions of the ABM treaty and—what is more—almost certainly violated it, as they advance their capacity for deployment of a widespread ballistic missile defense. Since the signing of the ABM treaty, the Soviet Union has spent more on strategic defensive forces than on strategic offensive forces. Clearly, the Soviets do not share the MAD philosophy that defenses are bad.

So, it is quite wrong to argue that the President's initiative on strategic defense would "upset 35 years of mutual deterrence," and spoil a successful approach to arms control and stability. On the contrary, the President's initiative will finally correct the conventional wisdom, which is so often wrong.

As we proceed, we will of course not give up our triad of deterrent offensive systems. Rather, we continue to maintain deterrence, and indeed strengthen and modernize all three elements of our triad, because we do not know when we will actually be in a position to put our strategic defense system in place. But reliance exclusively on these offensive systems, without pursuing effective defenses, condemns us to a future in which our safety is based only on the threat of avenging aggression. Our safety and that of our allies should be based on something more than the prospect of mutual terror.

Another mistake critics of strategic defense make is to contend that effective defense is technically unobtainable. History is filled with flat predictions about the impossibility of technical achievements that we have long since taken for granted. Albert Einstein predicted in 1932: "There is not the slightest indication that [nuclear] energy will ever be obtainable. It would mean that the atom would have to be shattered at will."

Based on our research so far, we cannot now say how soon we will be in a position to make decisions on defensive options; nor can we today describe all the specific forms of such defenses. But clearly, the Soviet military and their scientists at least are confident that strategic missile defenses will be effective. Their extensive effort to acquire such defenses gives ample evidence of their conviction, as does their major effort to stop us from proceeding with our defense initiative.

We all recognize from the outset that a complete system, or combination of systems, for strategic defenses could not be deployed overnight. There could be a transitional period when some defenses would be deployed and operating before others would be ready. Some have argued that this transition would be particularly dangerous, that it would upset the present deterrent system without putting an adequate substitute in its place.

The opposite is the case. If properly planned and phased, the transitional capabilities would strengthen our present deterrent capability, which is one of President Reagan's high priorities. In fact, they could make a major contribution to the prevention of nuclear war, even before a fully effective system is deployed.

If the Soviet leaders ever contemplated initiating a nuclear attack, their purpose would be to destroy U.S. or NATO military forces that would be able to oppose the aggression. Defenses that could deny the Soviet missiles the military objectives of their attack, or deny the Soviets confidence in the achievement of those objectives, would discourage them from even considering such an attack, and thus be a highly effective deterrent.

But we would not want to let efforts towards a transitional defense exhaust our energies, or dilute our efforts to secure a thoroughly reliable, layered defense that would destroy incoming Soviet missiles at *all* phases of their flight. Such a system would be designed to destroy weapons not people. With such a system we do not even raise the question of whether we are trying to defend missiles or cities. We would be trying to destroy Soviet missiles by non-nuclear means. And I emphasize again—by non-nuclear means—before the Soviet missiles get near any targets in this country or in the Alliance. The choice is not between defending people or weapons. Even the early phases in deployment of missile defenses can protect people. Our goal is to destroy *weapons* that kill people.

Thus, based on a realistic view of Soviet military planning, the transition to strategic defense would not be destabilizing. In fact, initial defense capabilities would offer a combination of benefits. They would contribute to deterrence by denying Soviet attack goals. And should deterrence ever fail, they would save lives by reducing the scope of destruction that would result from a Soviet military attack. The more effective the defenses, the more effective this protection would be. This objective is far more idealistic, moral, and practical than the position taken by those who still adhere to the mutual-assured destruction theory, namely that defenses must be totally abandoned.

I know that some Europeans fear that our pursuit of the defense initiative would tend to "decouple" America from Europe. This is quite wrong. The security of the United States is inseparable from the security of Western Europe. As we vigorously pursue our strategic defense research program, we work closely with all our allies to ensure the program benefits our security as a whole.

In addition to strengthening our nuclear deterrent, such defenses would also enhance NATO's ability to deter Soviet aggression in Western Europe by reducing the ability of Soviet ballistic missiles to put at risk those facilities essential to the conventional defense of Europe—airfields, ports, depots, and communications facilities, to name just a few examples. An effective strategic defense would create great uncertainties in the mind of the aggressor, reduce the likelihood of a successful conventional attack on Western Europe, and thereby reduce the chance the Soviet Union would contemplate such an attack in the first place.

Yet some of the discussions of the President's initiative, are based on the assumption that the United States can prevent indefinitely Soviet deployment of defenses merely by abstaining from *our* research and technology program.

Soviet history, the doctrines elaborated by their military leadership, and their current programs amply show that the Soviet leaders do not feel they are restrained by the ABM Treaty's prohibition against a widespread defense against ballistic missiles. If the Soviets develop such a system from their intensive research program, in all probability they will deploy it.

Recent political comment on the relationship of arms control and strategic defense fails to confront that reality. Our strategic defense initiative truly is a bold program to examine a broad range of advanced technologies to see if they can provide the United States and its allies with greater security and stability in the years ahead by rendering ballistic missiles obsolete. We have approached this program from the beginning according to the principle that SDI and arms control should work together . . . that each can make the other more effective. SDI is a research and development program that is being conducted completely within the ABM treaty.

In the near term, our initiative on strategic defense also provides a powerful deterrent to a Soviet breakout from the ABM treaty, a prospect made more worrisome by recent compliance questions—such as the new Soviet radar which is almost certainly in violation of the ABM treaty. Our strategic defense research program also makes clear that we take seriously the Soviet build-up in offensive arms. We have reminded the Soviet Union that both sides agreed to the ABM treaty in the first place, with the understanding that it would be followed by effective limitations on offensive arms. The strategic defense initiative is not only the strongest signal we can send that we mean what we agreed to, it is the only real hope for a future without nuclear weapons. So we cannot accept the refusal of the Soviet Union to agree to real reductions in offensive arms, as we pursue the strategic defense initiative.

In the long term, strategic defense may provide the means by which both the United States and the Soviet Union can safely agree to very deep reductions and, someday, even the elimination of nuclear arms. Many *talk* about such reductions, but we are *working* on the means by which they could actually come about without creating dangerous instabilities. We have sought to engage the Soviet Union in comprehensive discussions on how to make arms reductions more effective in the near term and on how to provide a safer future for all mankind.

This is not a process that will be aided by partisan or uniformed rhetoric aimed at forcing unilateral restraint upon the United States, as the history of the ABM treaty itself has shown us that.

Progress toward a more secure future will, instead, require both a determined strategic defense R&D effort, and persistent and patient dialogue with the Soviet Union in the months and years ahead.

Of course, we must negotiate with the Soviet Union—not for the purpose of freezing forever the vast numbers of existing warheads or permitting more and more of them—as SALT II did—with their hideous threat of total destruction and mutual vulnerability. No, we should negotiate with them to find a path to escape from that horror. That is why President Reagan holds before us the vision of a future world free from the threat of nuclear destruction. We must try to get the Soviet Union to join us in making such threats impotent, so that we can someday rid the world of the nuclear arms that underlie such threats. This goal may seem far away, but difficulties should never cloud an inspired vision, nor slow us in our constant striving to realize that vision for all humanity. Let us move on to the bright, sunny upland where there is hope for a better future for all, of which we all dream.

BALLISTIC MISSILE DEFENSE: A STRATEGIC ISSUE
Robert M. Bowman

Robert M. Bowman is a retired career Air Force officer who directed ballistic missile defense research in the Pentagon during the Carter Administration. He is now President of the Institute for Space and Security Studies in Potomac, Maryland.

Introduction

The President has challenged the scientific and engineering community with "the development of an intensive effort to define a long-term research and development program aimed at the ultimate goal of eliminating the threat posed by nuclear ballistic missiles." He also held out the hope of rendering nuclear weapons "impotent and obsolete" and asked if it wasn't better to "save lives, rather than avenge them." These statements, along with some of the clarifications issued later, indicate a desire to replace the policy of deterrence through the threat of retaliation with a new policy of pure defense. Indeed, in his "Star Wars" speech, he clearly acknowledged the fact that the systems he was talking about, if combined with offensive systems, would be threatening and destabilizing. Clearly, he was talking about the kind of defensive system that would allow us to (indeed, *require* us to) discard our offensive systems.

The systems requirements and technological demands of such a defensive system are staggering. The allowable leakage rate would be something like 0.01% or less. The system would have to be itself invulnerable, impervious to countermeasures, and absolutely reliable. Moreover, it would have to provide such a defense against not only ballistic missiles, but all other means of delivery (cruise missiles, light aircraft, sailboats, diplomatic pouches, . . .) as well.

So far, numerous study groups both in and out of government have de-

Source: Robert M. Bowman, "Ballistic Missile Defense: A Strategic Issue," in Committee on Appropriations, Subcommittee on the Department of Defense, Hearings on Department of Defense Appropriations for 1985, Part 5, May 9, 1984, pp. 869–80.

clared such a system an impossibility. Impossible or not, it is a worthy objective and worthy of serious consideration. It was perhaps imprudent to announce such a long shot objective so publicly and give the American people the idea that the technology was available. But it was perfectly proper for the President to ask for the idea to be studied. The problem is that all the groups studying it have quickly concluded that a perfect defense is impossible, but instead of telling the President so, they have waffled. They have spent 99% of their time investigating systems for a different objective (enhancing retaliatory deterrence) or no objective at all. Now there is nothing wrong with enhancing deterrence. But it is wrong to confuse the public about our objectives. It is wrong to ask the public to pay 25 billion dollars or so as the initial step in a program to protect missile silos and let them think they are buying protection for people. It is also wrong to mislead the President. We must insist that his original question be answered. The President deserves the truth—whether or not it's what we think he wants to hear.

As a first step in a rational discussion of BMD—before looking at system requirements and technology challenges—it is necessary to look at the various possible objectives of a BMD program, and the strategic issues associated with each. Then for each of the objectives, the consequent system requirements and technology issues can be analyzed.

BMD Objectives

There are four possible objectives for ballistic missile defense:

(1) to replace a policy of deterrence by the threat of retaliation with a policy of assured survival based on a near-perfect defense against all types of offensive weapons (as proposed by the President in his "Star Wars" speech of March 23, 1983.)

(2) to enhance deterrence by reducing the vulnerability of our retaliatory offensive forces,

(3) to complete a disarming first strike capability by providing a shield against the 5% of enemy missiles surviving our MX, Trident II, and Pershing II attack, and

(4) to limit the damage to our country should deterrence fail, by reducing the number of warheads getting through.

Each of these four objectives results in its own unique set of system requirements and associated technology challenges. Each also presents its own political and diplomatic challenge. The first, in particular, faces the diplomatic problem of managing the transition from the current offense-dominated to a defense-dominated strategy without passing through an unstable situation. Implementing it would have to be done so that at no time did the combination of offensive and defensive capabilities bring about the situation sought for in objective 3, the disarming first strike.

The fourth possible objective for a BMD system (limiting the damage should deterrence fail) is particularly troublesome. Such an objective is legitimate, provided the system implementing it doesn't increase the likelihood of deterrence failing. And since the system requirements are very similar to those for objective 3, the chances of it doing so are very good. Damage-limiting is essentially preparing to fight and win (or at least survive) a nuclear war. There is almost unanimous agreement now that a nuclear war cannot be won and must not be fought. Scientists are arguing over whether even people in the southern hemisphere, thousands of miles from the battle, can survive. Since it is not clear that damage-limiting will do any good, we should not allow it to increase the likelihood of war occurring in the first place.

Having now enumerated the possible objectives of BMD, let us turn to establishing the system requirements, technology requirements, and strategic implications of each.

BMD to Replace Deterrence

The following is quoted from the beginning of a typical position paper on Ballistic Missile Defense:

> There can be no perfect defense against nuclear ballistic missiles. Avoidance of nuclear conflict must therefore always be our nation's primary security objective, whether through arms control or deterrence. To deter war we must continue to convince any potential attacker that on balance his losses would be unacceptable.

Having thus disposed of the President's initiative, the rest of the paper was devoted to systems serving other objectives. Rather than take that easy way out, however, let us take an honest look at BMD to replace deterrence and the threat of retaliation with pure defense, and what such a system would require.

First, it would require that the country possessing it get rid of all its offensive strategic weapons. Otherwise, a nation protected behind such a shield could threaten its neighbors in the world community with impunity, even with a small number of nuclear weapons. If a nation attempted to complete such a system while retaining offensive weapons, the other nations would never allow it, but would attempt to destroy the shield before it was complete or even launch a preemptive nuclear attack.

Secondly, once the transition is made and a nation has entrusted its security to the defensive system instead of retaliation, it is then totally dependent on the defensive system. It must therefore be totally reliable, invulnerable to destruction by opposing forces, impervious to countermeasures employed by opposing offensive forces, and essentially perfect in its ability to protect against thousands of nuclear weapons deployed against it in any manner whatsoever. The Soviet Union now has about 8000 strategic warheads (we have 10,000). Thus if one or two warheads getting through is acceptable, we can get by with a leakage rate of 0.01% *(an order of magnitude better than the Fletcher commission was asked to consider)*. Of course, by the time a system is deployed, it may be facing 100,000 warheads and ten times as many decoys. (If we abrogate the limitations on defensive systems contained in the ABM portion of the SALT I Treaty, we can hardly expect the Soviet Union to continue to abide by the already-expired limits on offensive weapons in the same Treaty and watch their retaliatory deterrent made impotent.)

It is commonly accepted that to even approach these low leakage rates a layered system utilizing several different technologies would be required. Moreover, an extremely high percentage of attacking ballistic missiles would have to be destroyed in the boost phase, before they could release large numbers of RV's and decoys.

One of the obvious countermeasures which an attacker would employ would be to shorten the boost phase by using quick-burn rockets. Without much difficulty, the burn phase could be shortened to the point where it would terminate while the missile was still within the atmosphere. Since most of the proposed BMD kill mechanisms are unable to penetrate even the outer fringes of the atmosphere (this is true of particle beams, x-rays, and homing kinetic-energy kill vehicles, for example), this simple measure would make boost-phase interception using such systems impossible. This would leave lasers of relatively long wavelength as the only remaining boost-phase candidate. But such systems have enormous problems of their own, including a host of technical difficulties (such as making the enormous cooled mirrors required), special vulnerabilities (the mirrors, for example, can be rendered useless by a bucket of sand, a balloon full of water, or a thimbleful of oil), and unique susceptibilities to countermeasures (like spinning the ICBM to distribute the laser energy, using ablative coatings, or polishing the missile surface to reflect away the energy). It appears therefore that if a boost-phase interception system is to be found, it will use a kill mechanism not even thought of as yet.

But the kill mechanism (discussed above) is only one of many elements in a BMD system. The Department of Defense has identified at least eight other elements, including the sensors that detect and track the missiles, the battle-management computers that must automatically initiate hostilities and direct thousands of defensive systems against as many targets within seconds, and the pointing and tracking systems which must aim the kill mechanisms to within inches over distances of thousands of miles. UnderSecretary DeLauer has testified that each of these nine elements is individually as complex as the Manhattan Project. The advances in individual technical parameters (such as pointing accuracy, sensor sensitivity, and computation speed) needed to make the system even theoretically possible are typically factors of 10^6 to 10^8, that is, we need to be able to do things a million or so times faster and better than we can now.

Once all these technical problems are overcome, then the whole thing must be made to work together—and it must work flawlessly the very first time, for it can never be tested under realistic conditions. With the difficulty we have had making such relatively simple things as cruise missiles, air defense guns, and tanks work, the thought of such a complex system as this working perfectly boggles the mind—even without enemy countermeasures or attempts to destroy or disrupt the system.

With all this, there is an overwhelming temptation to dismiss such a system as an utter impossibility. Rather than doing so, however, let us merely point out that such defenses are the proper subject of basic research. An appropriate broadly-based research program need not cost a lot of money. One cannot obtain the kind of scientific breakthroughs needed for such a system by simply throwing money at the problem.

The worst mistake we could possibly make would be to let our fascination with the possibility of such a system cause us to neglect the means we have in hand for preventing nuclear war—survivable deterrent forces, arms control to ward off destabilizing changes, and quiet diplomacy.

BMD to Enhance Deterrence

Another legitimate objective of Ballistic Missile Defense is the enhancement of deterrence by reducing the vulnerability of retaliatory offensive forces. The ABM Treaty allows each side to deploy one such system with up to 100 ABM interceptors, providing the system is ground-based and within certain constraints. The constraints are designed to preclude either side being able to shield a broad area containing its populace and industrial base and thereby approach the capability for first strike to be discussed in the next section.

The United States chose to dismantle its one allowed system some time ago, believing the system was not worth its cost of upkeep. The Soviets have chosen to maintain their system, and now have 64 of the allowed 100 interceptors. (They had 100 interceptors at the time the treaty was being negotiated 15 years ago, but have replaced them with a smaller number of more capable systems. It is expected that they will deploy a second layer (also ground-based, but with longer-range interceptors) bringing them back up to the allowed limit. It is interesting to note that the 64 Soviet interceptors compares with 10,000 we expected them to have by 1980 in the absence of treaty constraints. Keep that in mind the next time someone suggests that treaties never do any good.)

With this background in mind, let us examine the system requirements for a BMD system to enhance deterrence. The basic requirement is that enough offensive missiles survive any enemy attempt at a disarming first strike to enable us to retaliate in sufficient strength to cause unacceptable damage to the attacking country.

The first task is thus to determine what constitutes unacceptable damage to the Soviet Union in the minds of their leaders. We can never know this exactly, of course, and the answer undoubtedly depends on the desperateness of their situation. But we should be able to bound the answer in a conservative way. Would they be willing to lose ten of their cities? Who knows? How about 50? Probably not. Certainly the prospect of losing 100 of their cities should be more than deterrence enough. Let us adopt that as the basic requirement.

The next question is: How good a BMD system would we need in order to assure the survival of enough offensive systems to destroy the heart of 100 Soviet cities? The answer for the foreseeable future is . . . none.

It is estimated that if the Soviet Union continues to modernize their ICBM fleet with missiles containing many warheads and ever greater accuracy, by the end of this decade they will be able to destroy about 95% of our land-based ICBMs in their silos. This would leave us with about 50 missiles, 45 of which would be Minutemen III with 3 warheads apiece and 5 of which would be MX with 10 warheads apiece. That would give us 185 remaining warheads to retaliate with, which should be more than enough. Even without the MX, we would have 150 warheads.

Of course, that isn't the whole story. We would also have our manned bombers, the second leg of the triad. Whether at the time they are B-52s, B-1s, or Stealth, they will carry a couple of thousand cruise missiles, any one of which can devastate a city. Of course, the Soviets have an air defense system. We saw it in action against the KAL airliner. And they are developing the capability to "look down, shoot down" against low-flying targets like cruise missiles. Perhaps by the 1990s, they will have the capability to shoot down most of our cruise missiles, but under the worst of circumstances we should expect a few hundred to get through. This second leg of the triad should thus provide sufficient deterrence by itself. It is possible, though, that unforeseen air defenses could change the picture and render the manned bomber totally obsolete. This would certainly seem to be an easier task than defending against ICBMs. We should therefore not count on this leg of the triad by itself, but should retain the capability within the other legs to attack at least 100 cities.

The third leg of the strategic triad is the nuclear-powered ballistic missile submarine. This leg is by far the most important leg of the triad because it contains the majority of our nuclear warheads and, more importantly, because it is completely invulnerable to a disarming first strike. Most analysts agree that it should remain invulnerable for the foreseeable future, certainly for the next twenty years. This means that well into the next century the sea leg will be able to deliver over 5000 nuclear warheads to their targets. But what if the Soviets pull off a miracle and find a way to overcome our enormous lead in anti-submarine warfare (ASW), so that they are able to locate our submarines in the ocean depths, track them, and destroy them? What if they get an ASW capability so good that they could count on being able to destroy almost all our submarines in a first strike (along with all our land-based missiles and all our bombers and cruise missiles)? What if they could figure that they might only have to face retaliation from a single submarine? What kind of retaliation could they expect? The answer is that they would face about 240 warheads, more than twice what we would need to gut their 100 largest cities.

The surprising answer from this analysis is that for the foreseeable future, even after absorbing everything the Soviets could throw at us, we would retain sufficient capability in each one of the three legs of the triad to retaliate with devastating results. Then why does deterrence need enhancing? How much deterrence is enough? The answer is that our survival is at stake (as is that of the Soviet Union). That's why neither of us seems to ever have "enough." Rationally, BMD to enhance deterrence is unnecessary. But our land-based leg does face a known and growing threat, and there is something that can be done about it—BMD point defense. It is natural to expect that military leaders, charged with ensuring our survival as they are, would wish to investigate this option.

There doesn't seem to be much that a BMD system could do to enhance the survivability of the other two legs of the triad. But it could do something for land-based ICBMs (assuming we don't decide just to scrap them all to eliminate targets in our homeland). What would it take then, in terms of BMD, to ensure the survival of twice as many ICBM warheads—at least 300, even if we didn't deploy the MX? The answer is that it could be done by redeploying the one ground-based ABM system we are allowed by treaty. There would still be technical problems associated with making the radar system survivable, but this problem is more amenable to solution than it was 15 years ago. While it could certainly be argued that it is unnecessary, such additional protection for our land-based ICBMs could be achieved at relatively low cost and without abrogating the ABM Treaty (and thereby touching off an unconstrained arms race in both offensive and defensive systems). Indeed, the Pentagon has been pursuing research toward such a system continuously since the late 1950s, and considerable progress has been made. One of the effects of the Strategic Defense Initiative (SDI) has been to constrain the funding for this work in favor of the more exotic space-based technologies.

The question arises: Wouldn't "Star Wars" space-based elements contribute to this effort to make our land-based ICBMs more survivable? The answer has to be an unqualified "NO!" As shown above, they are unnecessary. But in addition to that, an attempt to add space-based elements runs into all the problems discussed in connection with the first objective. Even if one is demanding only 10% effectiveness, instead of 99.99%, one has to deal with the enormous technical complexities, the many countermeasures, and the vulnerability of space-based systems. In addition, since such systems involve abrogation of the ABM Treaty and therefore the SALT limits on offensive weapons, one would wind up always losing ground. If we spent half a trillion dollars or so putting up a system capable of stopping 10% of attacking weapons, the Soviets would probably fear that it could stop 50%. They would therefore double the number of offensive weapons in their arsenal (at a fraction of the cost of our defenses). The result would be that in the event of an attack, many more weapons would get through than if we had done nothing.

The simple fact is that if the objective is enhancing deterrence, space-based BMD systems are both unnecessary and counterproductive.

BMD for First Strike

The vast majority of American citizens would say that a disarming first strike against the Soviet Union is unthinkable, and that seeking such a capability is not a legitimate objective of U.S. military preparations. Yet this is one of the military uses of Ballistic Missile Defense and must be analyzed, if only to understand the legitimate fears raised by the "Star Wars" speech in the Soviet Union.

Unfortunately, "Flexible Response" and the many variations of this strategy over the last few years have taken us closer and closer to a military posture which seems to be designed solely and purposefully for first strike.

The original purpose of the MX, for example, was to give us a mobile missile which would be more survivable than our existing Minuteman force. What we have wound up with is a missile no more survivable than its predecessors, but with awesome silo-busting accuracy, and which therefore poses a first-strike threat to Soviet forces. Worse than that, by concentrating ten warheads in each vulnerable silo, we present the Soviets with a very tempting target. Because this system does very little for our retaliatory capability, the obvious conclusion of cautious planners on the other side is that it is intended for exactly what it seems to be designed for—a first strike.

The Pershing II is an even better example. It is an extremely accurate system capable of destroying Soviet hardened command posts and communications nodes, targets which would have to be eliminated quickly in a first strike, with very little warning. Sited in Western Europe, only minutes from the Soviet Union, this system gives us the capability of dealing with these "time-urgent targets".

Finally, the backbone of our retaliatory forces, the Trident submarine, is being given first-strike accuracy in its upgrade to Trident II.

Faced with all this, the Soviets have to go through a similar analysis to what we went through in the last section. They must determine how much deterrence is enough. But their problem is a little different. Whereas only 35% of our warheads are potentially vulnerable (being on land-based ICBMs or submarines in port), 96% of Soviet warheads are potentially vulnerable!

In addition, we have an enormous lead in anti-submarine warfare (ASW), and therefore have the potential for even putting the other 4% of their retaliatory capability at risk. Soviet strategic planners must therefore face the prospect that the "modernization" program now underway could give the United States the capability to destroy up to 95% of their warheads in a first strike. This would leave them with perhaps 70 missiles containing some 400 warheads, clearly enough to wreak unacceptable damage to the United States and therefore enough to deter us from attacking them in the first place. But what if we also had a "Star Wars" system?

The proponents of systems like the "High Frontier", the laser battle stations, and the "Excalibur" nuclear-pumped X-ray laser claim that they could stop a very high percentage of attacking missiles—up to 99.9% with a layered defense. As shown in the discussion of BMD to replace deterrence, such claims are wildly optimistic, particularly if they were attempting to deal with 1000 or so missiles. But if they were faced with only 70, their task would be immensely simpler (though probably still impossible). From the point of view of Soviet reactions, however, it isn't the real capability of the system that counts, but the worst fears of Soviet planners faced with them. If *we* only had 70 missiles and were faced with the Soviet deployment of a "Star Wars" defense, would we still have confidence in the ability of our retaliatory capability to deter a Soviet first strike? Hardly.

Even if we believe that the United States would never initiate a nuclear war, we must acknowledge that Soviet *fears* are real. When faced with such a capability, those fears could cause the Soviets to launch a desperation preemptive attack.

For the sake of understanding, therefore, let us compute the kind of system we'd need if we really wanted to be able to disarm the Soviet Union and have a chance of escaping unscathed. Faced with about 400 warheads after a first strike by MX, Pershing II, and Trident II, we would want to give ourselves a decent chance to stop them all. To give ourselves an even chance (about 50/50) of stopping all 400 warheads, we'd need a leakage rate of about 1 in a thousand (0.1%)—exactly what was laid down as a requirement to the Fletcher Commission!

If we compare the system required for this objective (aiding first strike) to that for replacing deterrence with assured survival, we note the following differences:

- The allowable leakage rate is greater by a factor of 20.

- The total amount of energy required to accomplish the mission is reduced by a factor of 20.
- The speed of engagement (which dictates the speed of operation of battle management computers and the time available for repointing and retargeting, for example) is reduced by a factor of 20.
- The element of surprise is no longer with the attacker (retaliator), but is with the defender (first striker).

These factors make a big difference, of course. But they still leave enormous technological shortfalls, the inherent vulnerability of space systems, and the lack of a good kill mechanism for boost-phase interception. We should conclude that, in addition to being morally repugnant, a BMD system for first strike is probably unobtainable. Hopefully, the Soviets will come to the same conclusion and quit worrying—but I wouldn't bet on it.

The above analysis points up one fact quite clearly. Except for the factors listed above, a BMD system for replacing deterrence looks exactly like a BMD system for first strike. The only difference is in whether or not you discard your offensive weapons—*before you complete the defense.*

BMD for Damage Limiting

It must be reiterated here that *prevention* of nuclear war is and must be our overriding objective. Nothing should be done to compromise that objective. Having said that, let us consider what the system requirements would be on a BMD system for limiting damage to this country should deterrence fail.

If more than 50 warheads were to fall on the United States we would lose most of our people and probably cease to function as a society. It might not take even that many. I think we could agree that unless a BMD system could reduce the number of warheads impacting to this level, it's probably not worth having. So we would be looking for a system that would stop 199 out of every 200 missiles. This is a 99.5% system—not quite as high a requirement as the one to support first strike, but one which has to achieve this rate against 20 times as many attacking missiles. Except for the difference in the leakage rate, this system would have the same set of impossible technical requirements as the system to replace deterrence.

The strategic situation in which this system would operate, however, would be very different, for we would have retained our offensive deterrent forces. Potential adversaries would still fear us. They would see a system in place as capable as one which could shield us from retaliation after we conducted a first strike. They would therefore be under intense pressure to preempt. If they restrained, they would at least be on a hair trigger. Our space-based layered defense would, of necessity, be under computer-automated response. The chances of a software error, a computer malfuction, or a response to a natural event initiating war would be immense.

The net result of attempting to implement such a system would therefore be an enormous increase in the likelihood of war occurring and little if any improvement in our chances of surviving it.

We must conclude therefore that a BMD system for damage limiting makes no sense whatsoever.

Conclusions

We have examined the four possible objectives for BMD systems and have concluded that the last two should be rejected out of hand. To pursue an extremely effective defensive shield while retaining offensive weapons carries an enormous danger of provoking war or causing one by accident, while yielding very little hope of providing sufficient protection to enable the nation to survive.

The first two objectives, on the other hand, are worthy of closer scrutiny.

The first, BMD to replace deterrence, seems to be impossible, but is a legitimate objective of long-range basic research. It would demand a permanently invulnerable system with a leakage rate of better than 0.01% and could only be based on scientific phenomena as yet undiscovered. None of the technologies proposed to date have any chance of meeting these requirements.

The second, BMD to enhance deterrence, does not seem to be required by a rational look at the strategic situation, but could be implemented at a reasonable cost within the constraints of the ABM Treaty and without increasing the danger of war. It does not require any space-based elements beyond existing launch detection and early warning systems, which are required in any event. Such a system would not be impacted by a treaty banning space weapons.

If the United States is going to pursue BMD, it is absolutely essential that the objective of such a program be clearly defined and that the nature of the program is in keeping with its objectives. The American people will enthusiastically support any such clearly-defined program in the security interest of the United States.

FOR FURTHER READING

Beres, Louis René. "Steps Toward a New Planetary Identity." *Bulletin of the Atomic Scientists* (February 1981), pp. 43–47. Calls for more substantial progress in East-West arms control, and proposes an agenda for world order reforms that would contribute to a reduced likelihood of nuclear war.

Burrows, William E. "Ballistic Missile Defense: The Illusion of Security." *Foreign Affairs* (Spring 1984), pp. 843–56. Critique of the Strategic Defense Initiative which argues that "Star Wars" will only precipitate large increases in Soviet offensive nuclear capabilities, not protect American society.

Federation of American Scientists. *Seeds of Promise: The First Real Hearings on the Nuclear Arms Freeze.* Andover, Mass.: Brick House, 1983. Testimony from Randall Forsberg and other expert witnesses on strategic and technical questions posed by the freeze, in hearings organized by FAS and held September 1982 in Washington.

Fischer, Dietrich. *Preventing War in the Nuclear Age.* Totowa, New Jersey: Rowen and Allanheld, 1984. Comprehensive examination of the nuclear threat that combines a short- and a long-term focus in proposing changes in policies to reduce the risk of nuclear holocaust.

Frye, Alton D. "Strategic Build-Down: A Context for Restraint." *Foreign Affairs* (Winter 1983/1984), pp. 293–317. Describes the political background and strategic rationale for a "build-down" in U.S. and Soviet strategic forces.

Graham, Daniel O. *High Frontier: A Strategy for National Survival.* New York: TOR Books, 1983. Influential proposal for shift in U.S. deterrence policy from the current strategy—based on the threat of offensive retaliation—to one based on effective defense of American society. Proposes a major effort to develop defenses against nuclear attack based on "off-the-shelf" weapons technologies.

Jastrow, Robert. "The War Against Star Wars." *Commentary* (December 1984), pp. 19–25. Technical rebuttal of the assumptions and calculations of the Union of Concerned Scientists' *Fallacy of Star Wars* and other critiques of the Strategic Defense Initiative.

Kennedy, Edward M., and Mark O. Hatfield. *Freeze: How You Can Help Prevent Nuclear War.* New York: Bantam Books, 1982. The case for the freeze as put forward by the authors of the Congressional nuclear weapons freeze resolution. Includes chapters on the origins of the freeze movement, questions and answers on the freeze, and other important issues.

Miller, Steven, ed. *The Nuclear Weapons Freeze and Arms Control.* Cambridge, Mass: Ballinger, 1984. Proceedings of a conference on the freeze held in Boston in January 1983, containing articles from a variety of political perspectives on different nuclear freeze proposals, public opinion and the freeze movement, deterrence, verification, and other issues.

Paine, Christopher. "Breakdown on the Build-Down." *Bulletin of the Atomic Scientists* (December 1983), pp. 4–6. A thorough critique of the strategic build-down concept, which points out that this form of arms control would allow many new, potentially destabilizing strategic weapons to be deployed by the United States and the Soviet Union.

Payne, Keith B. and Colin S. Gray. "Nuclear Policy and the Defensive Transition." *Foreign Affairs* (Spring 1984), pp. 820–42. Strategic rationale for shifting to a defensive-based deterrence strategy in U.S. nuclear policy.

Talbott, Strobe. *Deadly Gambits: The Reagan Administration and the Stalemate in Nuclear Arms Control.* New York: Alfred A. Knopf, 1984. Critical look at the arms control proposals of the Reagan administration, including detailed discussions of the U.S.-Soviet INF and START talks.

Teller, Edward, et al. " 'Star Wars' and the Scientists." *Commentary* 79 (March 1985), pp. 4 *ff.* Supportive and critical replies to Robert Jastrow's December 1984 *Commentary* article, "The War Against Star Wars" (see above citation).

The Union of Concerned Scientists. *The Fallacy of Star Wars.* New York: Vintage Books, 1984. Comprehensive strategic, political, and technical critique of the Reagan administration's Strategic Defense Initiative and anti-satellite weapons programs.

United States Department of Defense. *The President's Strategic Defense Initiative.* Washington, D.C.: U.S. Government Printing Office, January 1985. Ten-page pamphlet that explains the Reagan administration's rationale for the SDI.

von Hippel, Frank. "Attacks on Star Wars Critics a Diversion." *Bulletin of the Atomic Scientists* (April 1985), pp. 8–10. Critical evaluation of SDI supporters' criticism of "Star Wars" critics. A direct response to Robert Jastrow's December 1984 *Commentary* article (see above citation).

Appendix

Global Nuclear Capabilities

Table I
U.S. and Soviet Strategic Nuclear Delivery Capability, March 1985

1. United States

Category and Type	First Deployed	Deployed Launchers 2/85	Warheads per Launcher	Yield per Warhead	CEP (m)	Total Warheads
ICBM						
Titan II	1962	33	1	9 мт	1300	33
MMII	1966	450	1	1 мт	370	450
MMIII/ Mk12	1970	250	3	170 кт	280	750
MMIII/ Mk12A	1970	300	3	350 кт	220	900
Total ICBM		1,033				2,133
SLBM						
Poseidon C-3 [a]	1971	256	10	40 кт	450	2,560
Poseidon C-4	1978	192	8	100 кт	450	1,536
Trident C-4 [b]	1980	144	8	100 кт	450	1,152
Total SLBM		640				5,248
Bomber [c]						
B-52G	1959	84	20	(note d)	45	1,680
B-52H	1962	90	8	(note e)	45	720

1. United States

Category and Type	First Deployed	Deployed Launchers 2/85	Warheads per Launcher	Yield per Warhead	CEP (m)	Total Warheads
ICBM						
FB-111	1969	56	6	(note f)	56	336
Total Bomber		230				2,736
Total Force		1,884				10,117

2. Soviet Union

Category and Type	First Deployed	Deployed Launchers 2/85	Warheads per Launcher	Yield per Warhead	CEP (m)	Total Warheads
ICBM						
SS-11	1966	520	1[g]	1 MT	1100	520
SS-13	1968	60	1	1 MT	2000	60
SS-17	1975	150	4	750 KT	450	600
SS-18	1975	20	1	20 MT	350	20
SS-18	1977	288	10	500 KT	300	2,880
SS-19	1975	360	6	550 KT	300	2,160
Total ICBM		1,398				6,240
SLBM						
SS-N-6	1968	368	1	1 MT	900	368
SS-N-8	1972	280	1	1 MT	900	280
SS-N-17	1977	12	1	1 MT	1500	12
SS-N-18	1978	224	7	200 KT	600	1,568
SS-N-20	1981	60[h]	10	200 KT	n.a.	600
Total SLBM[i]		924				2,828
Bomber						
Tu-95 Bear	1956	127	4	(note j)	40	508
Mya-4 Bison	1956	43	4	(note k)	20	172
Tu-26 Backfire	1969	130[l]	4	(note j)	17.5	520
Total Bomber		230				2,736
Total Force		2,622				10,268

Notes

[a] Excludes 480 Poseidon C-3 warheads assigned to Supreme Allied Commander Europe (SACEUR).

[b] Five Trident submarines, each carrying 24 C-4 missile launchers, were operational as of March 1985. A sixth had begun sea trials, with a seventh launched and to begin sea trials sometime in 1985.

[c] Excludes some 61 B-52G configured for conventional strike role, 15 additional B-52G and 1 B-52H configured as ALCM carriers, and 23 other B-52G/H training and support aircraft, all of which are "SALT countable."

[d]Operational weapons load: 12 ALCM (@ 200 KT), 4 SRAM (@ 200 KT), 4 gravity bomb (@ 1 MT).
[e]Operational weapons load: 4 SRAM, 4 bomb.
[f]Operational weapons load: 4 SRAM, 2 bomb.
[g]Some SS-11 have 3x200 KT Multiple Reentry Vehicle (MRV).
[h]Based on three Typhoon operational or in sea trials as of March 1985.
[i]Excludes 12 SS-N-8 and 6 SS-N-6 missiles carried on Hotel and Gulf class submarines not counted against strategic launcher limits in SALT.
[j]Assumes 2 air-to-surface missiles (AS-3/-4) and 2 gravity bombs per plane.
[k]Assumes 4 gravity bombs per plane.
[l]Soviet Long Range Aviation (LRA) Backfires only. An 105 additional deployed with Soviet Naval Aviation.

Sources: Caspar W. Weinberger, *The Annual Report of the Secretary of Defense to the Congress for Fiscal Year 1986* (Washington, D.D.: U.S. Government Printing Office, 1985), pp. 52–53; The U.S. Joint Chiefs of Staff, *United States Military Posture for Fiscal Year 1986* (Washington, D.C.: U.S. Government Printing Office, 1985), pp. 19, 23; International Institute for Strategic Studies, *The Military Balance 1984–1985* (London: International Institute for Strategic Studies, 1984), pp. 3–5, 13–17, 130–31, 133–35; U.S. Department of Defense, *Soviet Military Power 1984* (Washington, D.C.: U.S. Government Printing Office, 1984), pp. 19–31.

Table II
Long-Range Theater Nuclear Forces

1. NATO and Other Western Europe[a]

Category and Type	Country Deploying	Range (km)	Warheads per Launcher	Yield per Warhead	Deployed Launchers 7/84	Total Warheads
Land-based						
Tomahawk GLCM	U.S.A.	2,500	1	200 KT	64	64
Pershing II MRBM	U.S.A.	1,800	1	5–50 KT	48	48
SSBS S-3 IRBM	France	3,500	1	1 MT	18	18
Sea-based						
Poseidon C-3 SLBM[b]	U.S.A.	4,600	10	40 KT	48	480
Polaris A-3 SLBM	Britain	4,600	1	(3x200 KT MRV)	64	64
MSBS MS-20 SLBM	France	3,000	1	1 MT	80	80
TLAM-N SLCM	U.S.A.	2,500	1	200 KT	48	48
Totals					370	802

2. Soviet Union

Category and Type	Country Deploying	Range (km)	Warheads per Launcher	Yield per Warhead	Deployed Launchers 7/84	Total Warheads
Land-based						
SS-11/-17 /-19 ICBM[c]	—	—	—	—	—	—

2. Soviet Union

Category and Type	Country Deploying	Range (km)	Warheads per Launcher	Yield per Warhead	Deployed Launchers 7/84	Total Warheads
Land-based						
SS-4 MRBM	—	2,000	1	1 MT	224	224
SS-20 IRBM	—	5,000	3	150 KT	378[d]	1,134
Sea-based						
SS-N-5 SLBM	—	1,400	1	1 MT	45	45
SS-N-6[e] SLBM	—	3,000	1	1 MT	6	6
SS-N-8[e] SLBM	—	8,000	1	1 MT	12	12
Aircraft						
Tu-16 Badger	—	4,800	2	(note g)	410	820
Tu-22 Blinder	—	4,000	2	(note g)	160	320
Tu-26 Backfire[f]	—	8,000	4	(note g)	105	420
Totals					1,340	2,981

3. China[h]

Category and Type	Country Deploying	Range (km)	Warheads per Launcher	Yield per Warhead	Deployed Launchers 7/84	Total Warheads
Land-based						
DF-5 ICBM	—	13,000	1	5 MT	2	2
DF-4 ICBM	—	10,000	1	3 MT	4	4
DF-3 IRBM	—	5,500	1	2 MT	60	60
DF-2 MRBM	—	1,800	1	20 KT	50	50
Sea-based						
CSS-NX-3 SLBM	—	2,800	1	2 MT(?)	12	12
Aircraft						
H-6[i]	—	—	—	—	120	120
Totals					248	248

Notes

[a]French and British forces under national control, British forces integrated with U.S. Single Integrated Operations Plan (SIOP).

[b]480 "SALT-countable" Poseidon warheads assigned to Supreme Allied Commander Europe (SACEUR).

[c]Some SS-11/-17/-19 ICBMs assigned to targets in European theater.

[d]243 within range of targets in Western Europe, 135 Asian-based.
[e]Non-SALT.
[f]Soviet Naval Aviation only.
[g]Soviet theater bombers carry a combination of air-surface missiles (@ 200–800 KT) and gravity bombs (@ 5, 20, or 50 MT).
[h]No Chinese development or deployment of *tactical* nuclear weapons has been detected.
[i]Nuclear and non-nuclear dual-capable.

Source: The International Institute for Strategic Studies, *The Military Balance 1984–1985* (London: International Institute for Strategic Studies), pp. 132–37.

Table III
European Tactical Nuclear and Nuclear-Capable Forces

1. NATO and Other Western Europe[a]

Category and Type	Country Deploying	Max. Range (km)	Warhead Yield	Launchers Deployed 7/84	Warheads per Launcher
SRBM					
Pershing 1A	U.S.A., W. Ger.	720	60/400 KT	162	1
Lance	U.S.A., Allies[b]	110	1/10/50 KT	146	1
Honest John	Greece, Turkey	40	KT range	54	1
Pluton	France	120	15/25 KT	44	1
Artillery[c]					
M-109 155m	U.S.A., Allies[b]	30	.1 KT	3,386	1
M-110 203mm	U.S.A., Allies[b]	20	5–10 KT	1,482	1
M-198 155mm	U.S.A.	14	.1 KT	907	1
					–
Aircraft[c] **(land-based)**					
F-104	Allies[b]	2,400	variable, sub KT–1 MT	281	n.a.
F-4E/F	U.S.A., Allies[b]	2,200	"	571	1
F-111E/F	U.S.A.	4,700	"	230	3
F-16	U.S.A., Allies[b]	3,800	"	634	1–2
Buccaneer	Britain	3,700	n.a.	25	n.a.
Mirage IVA	France	3,200	60 KT	28	1
Mirage IIIE	France	2,400	15 KT	30	2
Jaguar	France	1,600	n.a.	45	n.a.
Tornado	Allies[b]	2,800	n.a.	223	n.a.
Aircraft[c] **(sea-based)**					
A-7/F-18	U.S.A.	2,800/ 1,000	variable, sub KT–1 MT	48[d]	2/4
Super Etendard	France	1,500	15 KT	36	2
					–

2. Warsaw Pact[e]

Category and Type	Country Deploying	Max. Range (km)	Warhead Yield	Launchers Deployed 7/84	Warheads per Launcher
SRBM					
SS-21/FROG	USSR/ USSR, Allies	120/70	KT range	628	1
SS-23/Scud	USSR/ USSR, Allies	500/ 150–300	200 KT	632	1
SS-12/SS-22	USSR	900	200 KT	90	1
Artillery[c]					
various howitzer types	USSR	10–30	sub KT–5 KT	3,500	1
Aircraft[c]					
Su-7 Fitter A	USSR, Czech, Poland	1,400	250, 350 KT	225	2
Su-17 Fitter D/H	USSR	1,800	"	850	2
Su-20 Fitter C	Poland	1,800	"	35	2
Su-24 Fencer	USSR	4,000	"	630	2
Mig-21 Fishbed L	USSR	1,100	"	160	2
Mig-23 Flogger F/H	Allies	1,400	"	60	2
Mig-27 Flogger D/J	USSR	1,400	"	730	2
Sea-launched Cruise Missiles					
SS-N-3/-7/ -9/-13	USSR	45–1000	200–800 KT	680	1

Notes

[a]Excludes nuclear and nuclear-capable ADM, SAM, and naval ASW weapons. Warheads for all NATO weapons except British held in U.S. custody. French weapons are non-NATO and are held under national control.

[b]For specifics on allied deployments of these weapons, see the International Institute for Strategic Studies, *The Military Balance 1984–1985* (Washington, D.C.: International Institute for Strategic Studies, 1984), pp. 131–32, 136–37.

[c]All nuclear/non-nuclear dual-capable.

[d]Assumes two U.S. carriers in European theater.

[e]All warheads held in Soviet custody. For allied missile and aircraft deployments see *The Military Balance 1984–1985*, pp. 135–37.

Source: The International Institute for Strategic Studies, *The Military Balance 1984–1985* (London: International Institute for Strategic Studies, 1984), pp. 130–32, 134–37.